A March of Liberty

A March of Liberty

A CONSTITUTIONAL HISTORY OF THE UNITED STATES

VOLUME II: FROM 1877 TO THE PRESENT

Second Edition

MELVIN I. UROFSKY
Virginia Commonwealth University

PAUL FINKELMAN
University of Tulsa College of Law

New York Oxford
OXFORD UNIVERSITY PRESS
2002

Oxford University Press

Oxford New York
Athens Auckland Bangkok Bogotá Buenos Aires Calcutta
Cape Town Chennai Dar es Salaam Delhi Florence Hong Kong Istanbul
Karachi Kuala Lumpur Madrid Melbourne Mexico City Mumbai
Nairobi Paris São Paulo Shanghai Singapore Taipei Tokyo Toronto Warsaw

and associated companies in
Berlin Ibadan

Published by Oxford University Press, Inc.
198 Madison Avenue, New York, New York, 10016
http://www.oup-usa.org

Library of Congress Cataloging-in-Publication Data

Urofsky, Melvin I.
A march of liberty : a constitutional history of the United States / Melvin I. Urofsky, Paul Finkelman.—2nd ed.
p. cm.
Includes bibliographical references and index.
Contents: v. 1. From the founding to 1890—v. 2. From 1877 to the present.
ISBN 0-19-512634-3 (v. 1 : cloth)—ISBN 0-19-512635-1 (v. 1 : pbk.)—ISBN 0-19-512636-X (v. 2 : cloth)—ISBN 0-19-512637-8 (v. 2 : pbk)
1. Constitutional history—United States. I. Finkelman, Paul, 1949–II. Title.

KF4541.U76 2002
342.73′029—dc21 2001037041

Printing number: 9 8 7 6 5 4 3 2 1

Printed in the United States of America
on acid-free paper

For Susan and Byrgen—yet again

Let me not to the marriage of true minds
Admit impediments. Love is not love
Which alters when it alteration finds,
Or bends with the remover to remove:
O no! it is an ever-fixed mark,
That looks on tempests and is never shaken;
It is the star to every wandering bark,
Whose worth's unknown, although his height be taken.
Love's not Time's fool, though rosy lips and cheeks
Within his bending sickle's compass come;
Love alters not with his brief hours and weeks,
But bears it out even to the edge of doom.
    If this be error, and upon me prov'd,
    I never writ, nor no man ever lov'd.

SHAKESPEARE, SONNET CXVI

Contents

Preface

The transformation of American constitutional and legal history over the past few decades has been remarkable. What was once little more than an examination of the "great cases" has now expanded to include the economic, social, and political as well as the legal circumstances surrounding those controversies. Although great constitutional scholars such as E. S. Corwin and J. Willard Hurst had always understood the interconnection between law and history, in far too many universities a wide and often uncrossed street separated history and government departments from law schools. Today, more and more law schools are offering courses in legal and constitutional history and hiring nonlawyers who can bring the insights of other disciplines to bear on the law. Historians, on the other hand, are demonstrating that they can explicate the legal rulings in a case and place them in a developmental context.

The first edition of *A March of Liberty* attempted to blend the so-called new legal history with the usual emphasis on great cases. Large sections were devoted to topics that did not appear in the traditional constitutional history texts: common law developments, the relationship of commercial growth to legal change, the rise of the legal profession, changes in legal education, and the handling of certain key issues at the state level. These section grew out of a belief that the Supreme Court does not act in a vacuum, and that the great powers of the federal government to regulate interstate commerce, for example, is closely related to commercial law and economic developments in the states. In some instances, the high court reflects trends already apparent at the state level; in other cases, its decisions determine what happens in state law.

The generous reception accorded to that first edition made it clear that many teachers who have been trained in the new legal and constitutional history found its premises welcome, and they reported that their classes found it "student friendly" as well. When it came time to revise the text, the large growth that had taken place in legal and constitutional studies pointed to the clear need of a coauthor. Both of us share the premises that underlay the first edition of *A March of Liberty*, and hope that this edition will carry on that view.

As in the first edition, no claims are made for total inclusion; even a work many times longer than this would be hard-pressed to cover everything. It is, as are all books, reflective of the authors' priorities-namely, what we teach in our own courses. But we have had the good fortune to have consulted with many colleagues who teach constitutional history, and to learn what they consider important; the feedback we have received from the first edition led us to leave certain things alone, revise others in the light of new scholarship, and to add some issues that had not been treated. As with the first edition, we wish to point out to readers that this is a survey of a large and growing field, and the bibliographic notes at the end of each chapter are but a small indication of the wealth of materials awaiting their perusal.

We have also benefited from having the manuscript read by people who are not only our colleagues, but who have a discerning eye. This edition is better for having been read by Richard Polenberg of Cornell University, Judith Schafer of Tulane University, Rebecca Shoemaker of Indiana State University, and William M. Wiecek of Syracuse University Law School. We are grateful to them but, needless to say, any errors or defects in the book remain our responsibility.

We would also like to thank everyone at Oxford University Press who worked on this project: Peter Coveney, Linda Jarkesy, Robert Tempio, Christine D'Antonio, and Natalie Goldstein.

Finally, the book is dedicated to our wives, who when they promised to take us "for better or for worse," were not told that they would also have to take our books and the writing of them as well. To them this edition is but a small token of love and expiation.

Melvin I. Urofsky
Paul Finkelman

A March of Liberty

22

The Court and Civil Rights

FREEDOM HAD BEEN the driving force of American law in the first half of the nineteenth century, leading up to the fight to end slavery and the Civil War. However, the meaning of that freedom was often contested. For Southern whites, for example, "freedom" implied the right to own slaves; for African Americans and their white allies, freedom meant an end to bondage. After that great outpouring of energy and creativity to end slavery, the latter decades of the century marked a withdrawal, a time of consolidation rather than advance, and in some areas retreat. The Republican Congresses of the war and Reconstruction era had attempted to write some statutory as well as constitutional safeguards to protect the former slaves, but the Supreme Court nullified nearly all this work. The greatest impact of the Civil Rights Acts and the Fourteenth and Fifteenth Amendments would come nearly a century later in the civil rights struggles of the 1960s.

The Court also seemingly had little interest in expanding the protection of constitutional safeguards over other minorities as well, and in general acquiesced in congressional and presidential initiatives as well as state laws discriminating against Native Americans, Asians, and peoples living in the territories won in the Spanish-American War, as well as against Mormons. After some mid-century reforms, women found little that could be considered hopeful after the war. The suffrage drive had been shunted aside to focus all available energy on abolition and the drive for racial equality, and the effort to secure the vote would not be successfully revivified until the early twentieth century. Both at the state level and in the Supreme Court, judges interpreted the law to reflect the dominant social view that women had few rights and ought to be kept confined in their proper domestic sphere.

The few hopeful signs could be found only when bigotry pushed too far, but even then, the Court reacted slowly and cautiously. In terms of legal and constitutional agendas, the protection of minority rights did not place high on the list. The great drive to end slavery seemed to have consumed all the available energy in that area, and the nation wanted to move on to other things. The Court, which had always protected slavery before the war, helped lead the nation away from civil rights afterward.

The Abandonment of the Freedmen

Most lawyers, teachers, and law writers of the latter nineteenth century gave little thought to rights other than property. They believed firmly in a federal system with state governments as the chief protectors of individual liberties. The Civil War and Reconstruction had given the national government enormous power vis-à-vis the states, but Republicans as well as Democrats saw that as a temporary aberration from the normal constitutional structure. While the Southern states would no longer be able to use the cry of "internal improvements" to block federal support of industrial expansion, for the most part the end of Reconstruction meant a return to the old relationship between states and national governments. This fit in perfectly with classic legal thought, but it carried a high price—the abandonment of the freed slaves to the prejudices of their former owners.

Prior to the Civil War, the inferior status of slaves and Southern free blacks had obviated the need for any formal laws segregating them from white people. Both races could work side by side, so long as the slave recognized that his or her place remained subordinate. In the cities, where most free blacks lived, rudimentary forms of segregation existed before the war, but no uniform pattern of separation; segregation rarely had the force of law, and enforcement varied. Moreover, every city had a demimonde in which the two races mixed freely. Free blacks in some parts of the North labored under harsher restrictions and often found a more formal and unyielding segregation than in the South. But, segregated facilities and opportunities were better than none at all. Thus, most Southern states prohibited blacks, free or slave, from attending schools, while in the North many towns and cities provided public education for blacks, but only in segregated schools.

One might have expected the Southern states to create immediately some system to segregate the races, but this did not happen. Instead, the confusion of Reconstruction led to a number of patterns, any one of which might have emerged as dominant in the end. In some states, the new Black Codes established fairly rigid separation in certain areas; Texas, for example, required that passenger trains carry one car in which all freedmen had to sit. Segregation in Southern schools seemed fairly widespread, although New Orleans had fully integrated public schools until 1877. In North Carolina, blacks sat on juries with little protest from whites, and shortly after the Civil War, the *Raleigh Standard* complained that "the two races now eat together, work together, visit and hold debating societies together." The Reconstruction Act of March 1867 encouraged freedmen in all parts of the South to protest, often successfully, against the incipient Jim Crow rules, and following the Civil Rights Act of 1875, blacks could be found riding railroad and steamer lines beside whites.

Inconsistent segregation practices dominated the North and South well into the 1880s. One white proponent of civil rights noted that in Virginia in 1885, blacks "may ride exactly as white people do and in the same cars." That same year, a black man took trains from Boston to South Carolina with the intent of discovering if any restrictions existed; although he was ready to find the worst, he admitted at the end of his journey that he had been treated far better in the South than in the North. Yet one must also note evidence of racial violence in the South, especially lynching, which reached an all-time high in the 1880s and early 1890s.

But if legally established and enforced segregation did not emerge immediately after the war, the evidence points to a widespread de facto separation of the races. There is a great deal of scholarly debate both over the extent of this de facto segregation, and also as to whether blacks as well as whites wanted separation. Howard Rabinowitz has suggested that the real option for blacks vis-à-vis public institutions such as schools and transportation in the 1870s and 1880s was not between segregation and integration (which occurred rarely), but between segregated facilities and total exclusion. Having a black school or a black railroad car would be preferable to having no school or no means of public transportation.

The proponents of overt segregation began to get the upper hand in the 1880s and early 1890s, when one Southern state after another adopted Jim Crow regulations that eventually reached into all aspects of life. Initially, segregation laws applied only to schools, passenger trains, steamboats, and other forms of transportation, though some states did not enact these restrictions until the turn of the century. By then, however, not only had Northern liberals abandoned Southern blacks, but the Supreme Court had given the segregation process a green light through its rulings in several civil rights cases.

The Civil Rights Cases

In the last of the great Reconstruction statutes, the Civil Rights Act of 1875, the Republican majority in Congress tried to secure by law some semblance of racial equality that could be protected by the government and the courts. It is doubtful that the country as a whole endorsed this idea, for most white Americans, Northern and Southern, believed in white supremacy. Secretary of the Navy Gideon Welles captured the prevailing sentiment when he wrote: "Thank God slavery is abolished, but the Negro is not, and never can be the equal of the White. He is of an inferior race and must always remain so." No one, therefore, expected that civil rights legislation would change white attitudes or compensate for what many took as the natural inferiority of blacks; rather, the law aimed to protect the freedmen from deprivation of the minimal rights of citizenship.

A crucial feature of the law was a prohibition of racial discrimination in public places, what would later be called "public accommodations," which rested on Section 5 of the Fourteenth Amendment. Five cases testing the application of this section arose in both the North and the South, and the Court combined them for a single hearing in *The Civil Rights Cases* (1883). The government argued that the Thirteenth Amendment had not only abolished slavery, but had conferred all the rights of free citizens on the former slaves, while the Fourteenth Amendment had given Congress the power to legislate in order to protect those rights.

In his opinion for the Court, Justice Joseph Bradley denied both of the government's contentions and in doing so, robbed the amendments of much of their meaning. Bradley stood on fairly firm ground when he claimed that not every example of discrimination against blacks could be interpreted as a renewal of slavery, and therefore that the Thirteenth Amendment could not be invoked as a ban on all forms of racial prejudice.

Although the Fourteenth Amendment, on the other hand, had been drafted specifically to ensure freedmen's rights, Bradley decided to deny that Congress had any affirmative powers under the amendment. According to him, Congress could act only in a remedial manner; that is, if a state enacted a law that restricted black rights, Congress could act to correct the injustice. In the absence of positive state action, Congress could not initiate legislation in this area. Bradley also indicated that if a state failed to act itself, but by inaction tolerated private discrimination—such as exclusion from hotels, restaurants, and clubs—Congress could still not legislate. This essentially put so-called private discrimination beyond the reach of legislation. By this decision, the Court in one stroke severely restricted congressional power under the Fourteenth Amendment to protect the freedmen and left their fate to the states and the courts.

Justice John Marshall Harlan entered a lone dissent, pointing out correctly that the Court had deprived the Fourteenth Amendment of most of its meaning. He also noted the inherent bias in the Court's judgment, since before the war the Court had accorded Congress comparable powers in upholding the various fugitive slave laws. But although he wrote in dissent, Harlan sketched out a theory of "state action" that would become the basis of civil rights jurisprudence six decades later. He utilized the idea of "affected with a public interest," which the Court had expressed in *Munn v. Illinois* (1877), and argued that facilities such as railroads, hotels, restaurants, and theaters filled a public function, which is why they had long been regulated. If such businesses discriminated, then they did so with the consent of the state; this constituted state action, and could be reached under the Fourteenth Amendment, even using Bradley's limited view of Section 5 power.

The Civil Rights Cases effectively barred Congress both from taking affirmative steps against racial discrimination and legislating against private discrimination. But what if the states took positive steps to impose racial segregation? Theoretically, Congress still had the power to reach this type of state action; but if Congress did not choose to act, would the courts find a violation of the Fourteenth Amendment?

Jim Crow Enthroned

In *Hall v. DeCuir* (1878), the Court ruled that states could not prohibit voluntary segregation by interstate common carriers, such as railroads, streetcars, or riverboats. A dozen years later, it approved a Mississippi statute requiring segregation on intrastate carriers in *Louisville, New Orleans & Texas Railway v. Mississippi* (1890); in doing so it acquiesced in the South's solution to the problems of race relations. Only Justices Harlan and Bradley dissented, on the grounds that such laws, even if confined to intrastate railway lines, interfered with interstate commerce.

In the best known of the early segregation cases, *Plessy v. Ferguson* (1896), Justice Henry Billings Brown asserted that distinctions based on race ran afoul of neither the Thirteenth nor Fourteenth amendments. Although the Fourteenth had been intended to establish an absolute equality of the races before the law, Brown noted that "in the nature of things it could not have been intended to abolish distinctions based upon color, or to enforce social, as distinguished from political, equality, or a commingling of the two races unsatisfactory to either." Although nowhere in the opinion can the phrase "separate but equal" be found, the Court's ruling approved legally enforced segregation, so long as the law did not make facilities for blacks inferior to those for whites.

In a famous and eloquent dissent, Justice Harlan protested that states could now impose criminal penalties on a citizen simply because he or she wished to use public highways and common carriers. Such legislation is "inconsistent not only with equality of rights which pertains to citizenship, National and State, but with the personal liberty enjoyed by everyone within the United States." As for the majority's disingenuous contention that segregation did not in itself constitute discrimination, the Kentucky-born justice condemned segregation statutes as "conceived in hostility to, and enacted for the purpose of humiliating citizens of the United States of a particular race." Such laws defeated the entire purpose of the Civil War amendments and made any real peace between the races impossible. "The destinies of the two races . . . are indissolubly linked together, and the interests of both require that the common government of all shall not permit the seeds of race hate to be planted under the sanction of law." Harlan's plea that the "Constitution is color-blind" fell on deaf ears, not only within the Court, but in the country as well. The surest sign of the changing temper of the nation was that where there had been a vociferous protest in the North over the Civil Rights Cases thirteen years earlier, the Plessy decision caused hardly a ripple.

The Court seemed only too willing to wash its hands of responsibility for minority protection and to leave the fate of minorities to state and local governments. The justices no doubt shared the general sentiment that enough had been done for blacks,

> Why may [the State] not require all red-headed people to ride in a separate car? Why not require all colored people to walk on one side of the street and the whites on the other? Why may it not require every white man s house to be painted white and every colored man's black? Why may it not require every white man's vehicle to be of one color and compel the colored citizen to use one of a different color on the highway? Why not require every white business man to use a white sign and every colored man who solicits custom a black one? One side of the street may be just as good as the other and the dark horses, coaches, clothes and signs may be as good or better than the white ones. The question is not as to the *equality* of the privileges enjoyed, but *the right of the State to label one citizen as white and another as colored* in the common enjoyment of a public highway as this court has often decided a railway to be.
>
> Brief of Albion Tourgée and James C. Walker, submitted to the Supreme Court in *Plessy v. Ferguson* (1896).

and the country ought to get on with its other business. If a regulation appeared to apply equally to all citizens, the Court would not look beneath the surface to see how it affected particular groups. It made this clear in upholding the conviction of a black man for murder in *Williams v. Mississippi* (1898). The case involved more than a federal court's unwillingness to interfere with the state criminal process, for Williams had claimed that his indictment by an all-white jury had been unconstitutional. Mississippi restricted jury duty to eligible voters; a literacy test and poll taxes effectively barred blacks from the franchise and thus from serving on juries.

A unanimous Court, speaking through the newly appointed Joseph McKenna of California, ignored the practical application and, in a marvel of formalistic logic, looked only at the letter of the law. Nothing in the Constitution prohibited either a literacy test or a poll tax, provided the law did not single out any specific group for discrimination. The fact that local officials *might* apply the law in a biased manner could not be used to attack the law's legitimacy.

Within a few decades after *Williams,* the Southern states had taken several steps to disenfranchise blacks. Poll taxes and literacy tests effectively deprived the vast majority of blacks of the right to vote, while loopholes such as grandfather clauses or good character vouchers allowed poor, illiterate whites to vote. And even if some black men learned to read and had the money to pay the poll tax, their vote had virtually no effect on an election. The primary, which Progressives hoped would curb the power of the urban machines, became in the South a useful tool of racism. Well before the turn of the century, all Southern states had become overwhelmingly Democratic. With the institution of the primary, whoever won the Democratic primary had for all practical purposes won the general election. When political parties became defined as private organizations in the 1920s, the states could exclude blacks from voting in the primary, the only election that really counted.

Between 1900 and 1920, Jim Crow—the legal and systematic segregation of the races—triumphed throughout the former slave states. Signs marked "Whites Only" and "Colored" showed up everywhere—in theaters, restaurants, railroad cars, boarding houses, and even water fountains. South Carolina prohibited blacks and whites from working together in the same room in textile plants, and from using the same entry ways, exits, or lavatories, as well. Mississippi statutes required segregation in hospitals, a practice soon adopted by other states. The state even forbade white nurses from attending black patients. Hundreds of Jim Crow laws existed on the books, but the laws by themselves did not provide an adequate gauge of the extent of segregation and its accompanying discrimination in Southern life at the turn of the century. The laws established minimal requirements; in practice, segregation normally went well beyond what the statutes required. Institutionalized segregation bred hatred and distrust among both whites and blacks, attitudes that would not be easily broken down even after the Supreme Court reversed itself and declared segregation unconstitutional in 1954.

But in sustaining racial segregation in the early 1900s, the Court certainly reflected popular opinion, not only in the South but in the North as well. When the Court in 1908, again over a strenuous objection from Justice Harlan, upheld a state statute requiring segregation in private schools (*Berea College v. Kentucky*), editorial opinion proved as favorable above the Mason–Dixon line as below it. President Theodore Roosevelt looked down on blacks "as a race and as a man . . . altogether inferior to the whites," despite making a few token black appointments and inviting educator Booker T. Washington to the White House. President Taft had no better opinion, and Wilson's was even worse. As the first Southerner elected president since the Civil War, Wilson and his lieutenants approved the segregation of all federal facilities. Indeed, racist thought permeated much of the Progressive movement.

The Treatment of Native Americans

Given the nation's and the Court's acquiescence in the subjugation of the freedmen, it is little wonder that other minorities fared just as badly. Native Americans had been pushed constantly off their lands ever since European settlers had landed in Virginia in 1607. By the time of *Cherokee Nation v. Georgia* in 1831, the notion that the tribes could exercise any sovereignty comparable to that of the United States no longer made any sense. In that case, John Marshall redefined the status of Indian tribes from that of independent sovereigns to "domestic dependent nations." The chief justice described the Indians as "in a state of pupilage," with a relation to the federal government of "a ward to his guardian." For all practical purposes, the tribes and their members would henceforth be under the dominion of the United States.

Prior to the Civil War, federal policy had been to resettle most of the eastern tribes in the Great Plains, which most people thought unsuitable to cultivation. The years after Appomattox saw an enormous surge of white settlers to the West, and by the 1890s, official policy had destroyed tribal sovereignty among the Indians. Starting in 1871, Congress began weakening what little tribal authority remained by declaring that the government would no longer negotiate treaties (which implied some parity on both sides), but would instead enter into agreements. In the so-called *Cherokee Tobacco* case (1871), the Supreme Court handed down a new ruling regarding the relationship of Indians to the federal government: that general congressional acts would apply to the tribes unless Congress explicitly excluded them. In essence, congressional policy to disregard treaties with the tribes now received a judicial imprimatur.

In the next two decades, Congress exercised direct control over the tribes, and in the words of one scholar, it did so in a way "which, if asserted against State citizens, would not have survived constitutional challenge." In many ways, the legal status of Indians, members of "domestic dependent nations," resembled that of slaves before the war, in that they were neither citizens nor aliens, but simply subjects. The Fourteenth Amendment's definition of a citizen as anyone born within the United States did not apply to Native Americans born on reservations. The resulting breakdown in tribal society led to growing crime and disorder, and to demands for reform, which culminated in the Dawes Act of 1887.

To some extent, the Court made congressional action necessary after it ruled in *Ex parte Crow Dog* (1883) that the United States had no jurisdiction under existing law over crimes committed by Indians against each other, and in *Elk v. Wilkins* the following year that Indians who voluntarily left their tribes did not become citizens of the United States. Congress responded by establishing specific courts for Indian offenses, and in 1885, extended federal criminal jurisdiction over the reservations for major crimes such as murder, arson, and rape. Two years later, Congress passed the Dawes

Act, which supposedly looked toward assimilating the Indians into the larger society. It allotted tribal land within the reservations on an individual basis, although tribal law had never recognized the European notion of individual ownership of the land. By making individuals into property owners, Congress hoped to make Indian society more like that of the white man. To encourage assimilation, the act also subjected those Indians who accepted the allotments to the laws of the state or territory in which they resided. In addition, Indians who took the allotments or who voluntarily left their tribes became citizens of the United States; those who refused the allotment or stayed in the tribes remained excluded from citizenship.

In 1890, the government abrogated its last major treaty with the tribes by opening up the Oklahoma territory to white settlement, and resettled the so-called Five Civilized Tribes in what became known as the Indian Territory, comprising about twenty million acres within the current boundaries of the state. But good grazing land as well large mineral deposits proved too strong a lure, and the Curtis Act of 1898 unilaterally abrogated the treaties with the Five Tribes and gave over the land and its wealth to federal control. The government also continued the effort to make Indians into whites. In 1901, Congress conferred citizenship on tribal members living in the Indian territory. In 1919, all Indians who had served in the armed forces during World War I became citizens; in 1924, all other Indians finally became citizens of the United States. For all these efforts, the policy of assimilation proved a dismal failure. Most Native Americans fought against losing their cultural heritage. Those who left the reservations found themselves objects of racism, treated just as badly as other people of color. Life for those who stayed on the reservations proved just as dismal, subject on the one hand to poverty and sickness and on the other to the arbitrary and often corrupt rule of the Bureau of Indian Affairs. Not until the New Deal would the federal government finally abandon the policy of the Dawes Act and encourage Native Americans to reassert both tribal authority and traditional culture.

The Supreme Court gave its blessings to all of these measures. In *United States v. Kagama* (1886), the Court completely denied the existence of tribal sovereignty, and upheld the Major Crimes Act of the previous year. Four years later, in *Cherokee Nation v. Southern Kansas Railway Company*, the Court upheld a congressional grant of a right-of-way through acknowledged Indian lands without the consent of the tribes. Congress took this decision as a signal, and in the Omnibus Railroad Act of 1899, gave railroads, upon a simple application to the Interior Department, a general right-of-way to construct lines through reservations, across Indian lands, and even through individual allotments.

In *Ward v. Race Horse* (1896), the high court reversed a federal district court ruling that treaty rights granting Shoshone-Bannock certain hunting rights could not be

> As with the American Indian, the only way to prevent his extermination is to civilize him, so the only way to preserve the remaining buffalo is to domesticate them.
>
> —U.S. House of Representatives,
> *Protection of American Bison and Other Animals* (1890)

overridden by Wyoming state laws. Speaking through Justice Edward D. White, a near unanimous Court ruled that for all practical purposes, treaties with the Indians no longer had any force, and any hunting rights provided for by treaty had to give way to the laws of the state. A few years later, the Court took the power of determining who is a member of a tribe out of the hands of tribal authorities and gave it over to a congressional commission charged with land allotments. (*Stephens v. Cherokee Nation* [1899]).

The rape of Indian lands and the judicial approval of it reached its apogee in *Cherokee Nation v. Hitchcock* in 1902 and *Lone Wolf v. Hitchcock* the following year. In the former case, the Court upheld the power of the secretary of the interior to grant mineral leases on Cherokee land with the approval of tribal elders, and in the latter it upheld the cession of tribal land to the United States, even though the transfer had been surrounded by fraud and had not complied with treaty requirements. According to Justice White, a treaty did not give rise to any property rights that fell under the protection of the Fifth Amendment. Whatever intent Congress may have had in assimilating Native Americans, the Court's decisions firmly established that Indians stood outside the constitutional community, even less protected than the former slaves.

The Chinese Cases

The railroads that drove through western Indian lands often had been built by people of color, for tens of thousands of Chinese had been imported to the United States to work on the railroads. While for some Chinese life in the United States may have been better than what they had left behind, most found themselves subject to dangerous working condition, low pay, racial discrimination, and a law that offered little protection.

Chinese had begun coming to the United States in the middle of the nineteenth century, and were welcomed as a relief to the severe shortage of unskilled labor on the West Coast. Eventually, racial prejudice as well as fear that lower-paid Chinese would "steal" jobs from whites led to a demand for legislative action. In 1882, Congress suspended Chinese immigration for ten years, and in 1888, passed a law refusing readmission to Chinese workers who had left the United States even if they had identity cards entitling them to reenter the country. This second act directly contravened treaty provisions between China and the United States.

A Chinese national with an identity card, upon being denied readmission to the United States, sought a writ of habeas corpus, claiming the 1888 act not only violated exisiting treaty and statutory obligations, but also his vested right to return. The justices unanimously rejected this argument in *Chae Chan Ping v. United States,* commonly known as the *Chinese Exclusion Case* (1889). Just as the Court had found that Congress had the power to abrogate treaties with the Indian tribes, it now ruled that Congress could abrogate treaty provisions with foreign countries simply by passing legislation inconsistent with the treaty. Justice Stephen Field, who wrote for the Court, found sufficient justification for limiting Chinese immigration, and held that such an act based "on the experience of years," might well be essential not only to preserving the peace of communities on the West Coast, but also to the national civilization.

Congress tightened the restrictions in 1892 by requiring that Chinese laborers in the United States register and obtain certificates, and gave the administering officials in the Treasury Department broad and arbitrary discretion to determine who should receive the certificates. Those who could not get a certificate could be summarily deported by a federal judge. By a 5–3 vote in *Fong Yue Ting v. United States* (1893), the Court upheld the law, and ruled that aliens resided in the United States were under the absolute authority of Congress, which could expel them whenever it thought it appropriate. Justices Fuller, Brewer, and Field entered vigorous dissents, and argued that even aliens enjoyed some protection under the Constitution.

The *Chinese Exclusion* and *Fong Yue Ting* cases appeared to say that Asians, like Native Americans, stood outside the constitutional community. But other cases led to the opposite conclusion, that in some areas the Chinese did enjoy basic constitutional protection.

In *Yick Wo v. Hopkins* (1886), the Court struck down a San Francisco ordinance that required a permit to operate a laundry in a wooden building. On its face the ordinance seemed like a legitimate fire protection measure, but in practice it proved quite discriminatory. The city granted permits to all but one of the non-Chinese applicants and denied licenses to all 200 Chinese who applied, even though some of them had been operating laundries for more than twenty years. Anticipating the equal protection argument used by the Warren Court eight decades later, the Supreme Court concluded that the ordinance as applied discriminated against a particular group. The Chinese were not outsiders, Justice Matthews declared. "The Fourteenth Amendment . . . is not confined to the protection of citizens," but applies "to all persons within the territorial jurisdiction."

And what about the children of the Chinese workers, children born in the United States? Did they automatically become citizens under the Fourteenth Amendment, even though their parents could never be citizens? Undoubtedly anti-Chinese sentiment on the West Coast would have preferred to deny citizenship to the children, so that they too could be deported. But in *United States v. Wong Kim Ark* (1898), a majority of the Court ruled that all persons born in the United States of Chinese parents became citizens at birth under the Fourteenth Amendment, and no act of Congress could deny them this constitutional birthright. Chief Justice Fuller dissented, arguing that the Fourteenth Amendment did not apply when parents had been legitimately barred from citizenship, but although he apparently lobbied his colleagues for nearly two years, he could not get them to adopt his position.

Despite *Yick Wo* and *Wong Kim*, the Court for the most part deferred to the legislative branches in dealing with Asians. Congress had full control over immigration,

> No euphemism can disguise the character of the act in this regard. It directs the performance of a judicial function in a particular way, and inflicts punishment without a judicial trial. It is, in effect, a legislative sentence of banishment, and, as such, absolutely void. Moreover, it contains within it the germs of the assertion of an unlimited and arbitrary power, in general, incompatible with the immutable principles of justice, inconsistent with the nature of our government, and in conflict with the written Constitution by which that government was created and those principles secured.
>
> —Justice Fuller, dissenting in *Fong Yue Ting v. United States* (1893)

and if it wished to exclude certain groups, the Constitution posed no objections. But the times in general provided little tolerance for groups of color, be they from Africa, Asia, or the Americas, and the Court reflected these sentiments in its opinions.

The Insular Cases

In the same era that the Court confirmed Jim Crow laws in the South and approved congressional dismemberment of the Indian treaties, it heard a number of cases, commonly called the Insular Cases, dealing with the reach of constitutional protection to the native inhabitants of America's newly acquired overseas territories—those gained in the settlement following the Spanish–American War of 1898.

Unlike previous acquisitions of territory, these new possessions did not strike contemporaries as likely to become future states. With the exception of the purchase of Alaska in 1867 (primarily to remove Russian colonial influence from the New World), lands acquired in the nineteenth century by purchase, annexation, or conquest had been contiguous to already existing states or territories, and it had been assumed that they would ultimately enter the Union as states. The march across the continent, even during the fever pitch of Manifest Destiny, had never been imperialistic; Americans sought new territory to permit growth, not to acquire subordinate colonies.

Puerto Rico, Guam, the Philippines, and Hawaii were already populated—and not by white races with "developed" cultures. If the United States retained them, it appeared that they would be nothing more than colonies, a proposal viewed with alarm by a highly vocal minority but with satisfaction by men like Theodore Roosevelt and Senator Henry Cabot Lodge. They believed that the time had come for the nation to join European countries in the race for empire and, in Rudyard Kipling's words, to "take up the white man's burden" of bringing Western civilization to Asia, Africa, Latin America, and the Pacific rim.

No one questioned the right of the nation to acquire new lands under its sovereign powers; that issue had been resolved years earlier in *American Insurance Co. v. Cantor* (1828). But if the new lands were to be colonies, then did the Constitution follow the flag, providing the residents of the new territories with the full range of constitutionally guaranteed rights? The imperialists claimed that the Constitution did not follow the flag and that Congress could govern colonies as it saw fit, its inhabitants enjoying only those rights that Congress specifically extended to them. The anti-imperialists argued that all persons under American jurisdiction had to be treated alike, the traditional policy of the Union toward residents of the continental territories.

The political branch resolved the question of whether or not the United States would keep these new possessions when the Senate ratified the Treaty of Paris with Spain in April 1899, and secured American possession of the former Spanish holdings. Defining the legal status of the new territories proved to be the chief business of the Supreme Court at the 1900 term. In the first of the Insular Cases, *Neely v. Henkel* (1901), the justices had little trouble agreeing that Cuba, although occupied by American forces, remained a foreign country, since at the outset of the war Congress had passed a resolution that Cuba could not be annexed to the United States. But the treaty also conveyed Puerto Rico and the Philippines as direct possessions, and their status had to be determined. In cases triggered by the tariff laws, a badly divided Court gradually worked out a doctrine to govern the future status of the new colonies.

In *DeLima v. Bidwell,* decided in May 1901, the Court had to decide whether, after the cession by treaty of Puerto Rico, but before any specific congressional action, customs duties could be collected on goods imported into the United States from the island. The collector of the Port of New York had imposed duties on sugar, as if that product still came from a foreign country, and the purchaser then sued to recover, claiming that the Constitution prohibited taxes on goods exported from one part of the country to another. By a 5–4 vote, the Court held that as a consequence of the Treaty of Paris, Puerto Rico did not constitute a foreign country and that the tariffs had therefore been unlawfully collected. Four justices—Joseph McKenna, Edward Douglass White, George Shiras, and Horace Gray—dissented strongly in separate opinions. McKenna claimed that Puerto Rico "occupied a relation to the United States between that of being a foreign country absolutely and of being domestic territory absolutely, and because of that relation its products were subject to the duties imposed by the Dingley act." The majority claimed that this vague halfway status could not exist; Justice Henry Billings Brown, who delivered the majority opinion, argued that the island had to be one thing or the other, and to hold otherwise would place Puerto Rico in a disastrous position of "practical isolation."

The Incorporation Theory

The most important of the Insular Cases proved to be *Downes v. Bidwell* (1901), which tested the constitutionality of the Foraker Act of 1900, which established a civil government for Puerto Rico and established import duties from the island. Challengers claimed that the tariff provisions violated the constitutional requirement that duties be "uniform throughout the United States." A majority of five justices sustained the statute, but they could not agree on a common rationale. Justice Henry Billings Brown, speaking for the majority, reflected the imperialistic spirit of the day, and spoke of "alien races" and "Anglo-Saxon principles." While acknowledging that constitutional protections of rights applied to some extent in the territories, he stopped just short of granting Congress unfettered power over the nation's new possessions.

Justice White's concurring opinion in the *Downes* case proved to be the key in the Court's development of a viable constitutional doctrine, one he termed "incorporation." White emphasized the power of Congress to provide for new territories and its discretion in defining their status. As for the application of the Constitution to these new lands, since mere acquisition did not bring them into the Union, neither did it entitle them to any of the rights and privileges guaranteed by the Constitution. So long as they remained in a subordinate condition, these territories would enjoy only those rights specifically granted by Congress; the full benefits of the Constitution would only apply if and when Congress acted to incorporate the territory into the Union. In this case, the Constitution did not follow the flag.

White's theory did not gain immediate adherence from a majority of his brethren. Justice Harlan especially objected to the racist implications of White's argument, and he noted that the natives of these new lands did not enjoy any rights, but relied on the whims of the legislature, without any judicial review to protect them. In his *Downes* dissent, Harlan claimed that Congress could act only under the Constitution, and "the idea that this country may acquire territories anywhere upon the earth, by conquest or treaty, and hold them as mere colonies or provinces—the people inhabiting them to enjoy only such rights as Congress chooses to accord to them—is wholly inconsistent with the spirit and genius as well as with the words of the Constitution."

Over the next few years, White's incorporation theory moved from dicta in a concurrence to full acceptance as doctrine in *Dorr v. United States* (1904). Fred Dorr had been convicted for libel under an act passed, not by Congress, but by the Philippine Commission, and had been tried without a jury in Manila. Justice William R. Day, who had joined the Court in 1903, delivered the majority opinion. "Until Congress shall see fit to incorporate territory," he ruled, that territory "is to be governed under the power existing in Congress." In a patronizing dictum that fully reflected the racist views of the time, he denied that the Constitution followed the flag, since the natives of the new territories might be totally unfit to enjoy the advanced rights of Western civilization.

Finally, in *Dowdell v. United States* (1911), the entire Court, save Harlan, who consistently opposed the theory, joined in Justice Day's opinion that the Philippines had never been incorporated into the Union and thus that criminal trials there did not require a twelve-person jury. White's longevity on the bench assured him of success. By 1920, none of the original dissenters remained when he ruled in *Board of Public Utility Commissioners v. Ynchausti & Co.* that the Philippines had never been incorporated and that therefore constitutional limitations did not restrain Congress in its governance of the islands.

The Court, however, never imposed an absolute application of the doctrine that the Constitution did not follow the flag, which literally would have denied any rights except those granted by Congress. The early commercial cases had not involved personal rights, while the later criminal cases, although the procedures followed departed from nominal American standards, nonetheless still provided the basic requirements for a fair trial. But if local law imposed unacceptable results, the Court could find a way around it. In *Weems v. United States* (1910), for example, a Coast Guard officer had been convicted under an old Spanish law still in effect in the Philippines. He had falsified public documents, and for this he had been sentenced to fifteen years in prison at hard labor in chains and the perpetual loss of his civil liberties. Justice McKenna wrote that "such penalties for such offenses amaze those who have formed their concepts of [justice] . . . from the practice of the American commonwealths, and believe it is a precept of justice that punishment for crime should be graduated and proportioned to the offense." Although the question had not been raised in the lower court, McKenna cited the Eighth Amendment's ban on cruel and unusual punishment, of which a variant could be found in the Philippine law, and set aside both the conviction and sentence—the first time the Eighth Amendment had been invoked by the Supreme Court on behalf of a convicted defendant.

If a common thread ran from the *Civil Rights Cases* through the Insular decisions, it was the racism that permeated the nation—and Western Europe—in this age of imperialist expansion. Pseudolearned volumes appeared extolling the Anglo-Saxon or Teutonic "race" as superior to the colored peoples of the world. For evidence, commentators pointed to the allegedly primitive cultures of nonwhite groups and their inability to resist white expansion. Most Americans shared this view, and even if they believed that inferior peoples should not be enslaved, they did not consider brown and black people to be their equals. The Supreme Court merely reflected this sentiment; its decisions did not create a new prejudice so much as place an imprimatur of respectability on existing racism. But the Court did draw a line on how far this racism could go.

Women and the Law

Although comprising half the population, and technically not a "minority," women had long been disfavored by the law. Earlier in the century, legislation had established judicial procedures for divorce and had given married women some control over their property, but women still had few real rights in the latter part of the nineteenth century. Despite the revolutionary era battle cry of "No taxation without representation!" women property owners had to pay taxes without the suffrage. The campaign for the vote begun at Seneca Falls, New York, in 1848 had stalled; women would not achieve success at the national level until 1920, with the passage of the Nineteenth Amendment.

After the Fourteenth and Fifteenth Amendments had been passed, however, one group of suffrage militants, known as the New Departure, attempted to use the Reconstruction provisions to secure the vote. In October 1869, a husband and wife team of Missouri suffragists, Francis and Virginia Minor, began offering an interpretation of the Constitution to prove that women already had the right to vote. They argued that popular sovereignty preceded and supported constitutional authority, and that the federal government had been created to protect individual rights. The Reconstruction amendments, they claimed, merely nationalized all rights, including the right to vote, and applied them to all persons, including the former slaves and women.

Virginia Minor attempted to vote, and when refused, she took her case to court, as had been her plan all along. Before the Supreme Court, she claimed the right to vote as one of the privileges and immunities enjoyed by all citizens under the Fourteenth Amendment. Chief Justice Morrison R. Waite, speaking for a unanimous court in *Minor v. Happersett* (1875), declared that women had always been citizens, but he denied that the right to vote constituted an essential privilege of citizenship. The power to award the suffrage belonged to the states, and the only restraint placed on that power had been that states could not use race to deny the vote. But all sorts of groups lacked the vote, Waite concluded, and if women were to get the ballot it would have to come through the states. The Constitution stood silent on the issue.

Some opportunities for women did open up in the latter part of the nineteenth century, as more colleges accepted women students, although formal training for the professions remained almost exclusively a male prerogative. A few women, however, began to study the law, since in those days, most lawyers prepared for the bar by reading in a law office rather than attending law school. At the same time that Virginia Minor was attempting to secure the franchise, Myra Bradwell tried to get the courts to permit her to practice law.

Bradwell had studied law, and then had petitioned the Illinois Bar for admission. Had she been a man, there is no question Bradwell would have been admitted, and the bar examiners made it quite clear that they had no intention of allowing a woman to practice. Bradwell brought the case up to the U.S. Supreme Court, where Matthew Carpenter, the Republican senator from Wisconsin represented her. Carpenter's argument for Bradwell's right to practice law ran parallel to Minor's claim for the vote, namely that the Fourteenth Amendment gave all citizens equal rights, and that a woman, as a citizen, could not be denied the right to be a lawyer.

Decided on the same day as the *Slaughterhouse* cases, *Bradwell v. Illinois* (1873) reinforced the judicial evisceration of the Fourteenth Amendment's key provisions aimed at regulating state conduct. Justice Miller, writing for the majority, denied any constitutional right to practice law, and declared that such privileges could be granted or withheld by the states. In a concurring opinion, Justice Bradley noted that "the natural and proper timidity and delicacy which belongs to the female sex" unfitted it for many of the occupations of civil life, including the practice of law. Women should stay at home, in "the domestic sphere . . . which properly belongs to the domain and functions of womanhood."

Despite these and other setbacks, women persevered. They gained the right to practice in some states and in the District of Columbia, and they also won the right to appear before the Supreme Court, thanks to the efforts of Belva Lockwood. Lockwood had studied at the National University Law School, where she suffered not only discrimination in classes but the authorities' refusal to grant her a diploma. Nonetheless, she applied to the D.C. bar, and after a long struggle won admission in 1873, shortly after the pioneering African American woman lawyer, Charlotte E. Ray, had also secured a license.

Lockwood established a busy practice, arguing cases in all the various divisions of the D.C. courts, as well as handling veteran pension claims. In 1874, Lockwood asked a Washington attorney, A.A. Hosmer, to sponsor her admission to the Claims Court bar, and given the *Bradwell* ruling the year before, it proved no surprise when the court turned her down, claiming that it had no power to authorize the admission of women into practice. Two years later, the Supreme Court also denied her request, and Lockwood then turned to Congress, where she lobbied successfully for a bill to remove such hindrances. A reluctant Congress in 1879 approved an "act to relieve certain legal disabilities of women," and ordered that any woman who met the qualifica-

> [This court finds] no authority for the admission of females to the bar of any court of this state. . . . We cannot but think the common law wise in excluding women from the profession of the law. . . . The law of nature destines and qualifies the female sex for the bearing and nurture of the children of our race and for the custody of the homes of the world and their maintenance in love and honor. . . . [Admitting women as lawyers] would emasculate the constitution itself and include females in the constitutional right of male suffrage and male qualification. Such a rule would be one of judicial revolution, not of judicial construction.
>
> —Chief Justice Edward G. Ryan, Motion to admit Lavinia Goodell to the bar of the Wisconsin Supreme Court (1875)

tions of practice and good standing should be admitted to practice before the Supreme Court. A few weeks later, Belva Lockwood became the first woman admitted to the Supreme Court bar, and the year after she argued her first case before the high court, *Kaiser v. Stickney* (1880).

But the success of Lockwood and a few other women should not mask the fact that the law, even if it considered women citizens with certain rights, still treated them as second-class persons. If a man and wife mingled their monies, then courts considered it all as belonging to the husband. As the Industrial Revolution expanded, women began to work in large numbers outside the home, yet courts still held that a woman's labor belonged to her husband. Only if she could keep her work and wages completely separate from that of her husband could a woman make claim to her property under the recently passed "earnings" laws, an option not available to most working-class women. As her husband's property, a wife's earnings, even if not commingled, could be claimed for his debts. As the former Abolitionist, Rev. Thomas Wentworth Higginson aptly put it, the wife was only "half way out" of the "feudal shell," and courts seemed little interested in moving her any farther.

The Court Draws Limits

Despite the Court's acquiescence in Jim Crow and its disregard for the claimed rights of other minorities, the era is not without some redemption. American occupation of the lands won from Spain eventually led to an administration that included nearly all the guaranties of the Constitution. Women began moving out of the confines of the domestic sphere, into college and, in limited ways, into the professions. Even the freedmen could look on this period with some hope and sense of accomplishment. In 1900, only half of all black adults could read; by 1913, the ratio had risen to seven out of ten. The number of blacks who owned businesses, houses, and farms rose steadily. Dedicated whites like Moorfield Storey joined black activists like W. E. B. Du Bois to organize the National Association for the Advancement of Colored People, which began the long, slow fight for justice. And much to everyone's surprise, during Edward Douglass White's tenure as chief justice, the Supreme Court began to interpret the Civil War amendments to reflect their original intent—to safeguard the rights of black persons.

The Louisiana-born White had been appointed to the Court by President Grover Cleveland in 1894, and for the next sixteen years, the former Confederate soldier voted with the majority in every case to uphold segregation or restrict blacks' rights. Yet after taking the center chair in 1910, he helped shape majorities for important civil rights decisions. Moreover, the White Court reached out to ensure racial justice in several cases in which it could easily have avoided the issue.

The first Jim Crow case to come before the White Court is *McCabe v. Atchinson, Topeka & Santa Fe Railway* (1914); the case marked the arrival on the Court of Charles Evans Hughes of New York, who took White's place as associate justice. Hughes refused to "wink" at the facts and applied the same legal logic to race cases as he did to other subjects coming before the Court. *McCabe* involved an Oklahoma law that required separate but equal railroad coaches but exempted luxury units, such as parlor, dining, and sleeping cars, which could be used by either race, but not jointly. Since few blacks had the funds for these services, railroads used the law to avoid providing separate black facilities. Black plaintiffs challenged the rule as discriminatory, although they did not attack the broader principle of segregation. In effect, they said they could accept "separate but equal," but objected to the inequality of "exclusive but not joint."

By a 5 to 4 vote, the Court sustained their argument. Hughes reiterated the *Plessy* rule and said that if railroads attached luxury cars for white passengers, equal facilities had to be available for blacks, regardless of the anticipated demand or lack of it. But after this refusal to accommodate to expediency, Hughes found a dodge to deny the petitioners relief—they had brought suit before the law went into effect and therefore lacked standing. The lower courts had erred in reaching the merits before determining if the question was ripe for adjudication. Hughes decided the merits anyway, in order to put Oklahoma and other states on notice that while the Court would accept racial segregation, it would insist that separate facilities be available and equal. But with the exception of one case, the Court would not deal with Jim Crow on the railroads again until 1941, when Hughes, then chief justice, had by this time begun to reverse the Court's position.

Residential segregation came before the Court in *Buchanan v. Warley* (1917), a case contrived by the NAACP to test segregation ordinances in Louisville, Kentucky. Warley, a black, arranged to buy a lot from Buchanan, a white who was friendly to the NAACP, and the contract was drawn to invite litigation. Warley refused to pay for the land, on grounds that residential segregation laws prevented him from building a house there, which the sales contract specifically identified as his reason for buying the property. Buchanan sued for payment, but the local court upheld the ordinance and declared it a full defense for Warley. Buchanan then appealed to the Supreme Court, where both parties had hoped to go anyway. Other Southern cities then considering similar ordinances all stopped to await the Court's decision. Moorfield Storey, a white lawyer from Boston, representing the NAACP, sought to distinguish residential segregation from other Jim Crow laws because it demeaned property rights, one of the bases of free government. Louisville's attorneys responded with the full rhetoric of racism: Law and Divine Writ demanded the full separation of the races.

The unanimous opinion Justice Day delivered masked internal disagreement in the Court over how far it should or should not go in such essentially local matters. The Fourteenth Amendment protected property, Day noted, but the state could certainly exercise some controls under its police powers to maintain health and safety. But could it regulate property solely on the basis of the skin color of the owner or would-be buyer? After an impassioned review of how the Civil War had been fought to protect civil rights, Day dismissed *Plessy* as controlling; in that case there had been no effort to deprive blacks of transportation, whereas in this case Louisville would neither allow blacks to buy certain property nor permit whites to sell it to them. He then held residential segregation laws unconstitutional—the first time the Supreme Court ever restricted the reach of Jim Crow.

The Peonage Cases

The White Court also showed itself willing to defend black rights in the so-called *Peonage Cases, Bailey v. Alabama* (1911) and *United States v. Reynolds* (1914). Forced labor statutes had been passed in all Southern states, permitting arrests for vagrancy, breach of labor contract, and other crimes. Once convicted, the defendant could be bound to a term of labor on a chain gang to work off fines and court costs. Although some whites, especially new immigrants, became ensnared in the peonage system, for the most part it operated to control blacks; a number of reformers, including white Southerners, attacked peonage as a violation of the Thirteenth Amendment's ban on involuntary servitude. In fact, the two leading cases both came before the Court as a result of Southern reform efforts.

Bailey v. Alabama involved a state statute that made breach of a labor contract prima facie evidence of intent to injure or defraud the employer. As Booker T. Washington charged, this "simply means that any white man, who cares to charge that a Colored man has promised to work for him and has not done so, or who has gotten money from him and not paid it back, can have the Colored man set to the chain gang." Washington found a test case, one Alonzo Bailey, who had left his job without repaying a wage advance. Even before the state court had ruled, defense lawyers sought a direct appeal to the Supreme Court in 1908. Justice Oliver Wendell Holmes ruled that the case had come prematurely, since there had been no final decision from the lower court, and over objections from John Marshall Harlan, the Court sent the case back to Alabama for final adjudication.

After Bailey had been duly convicted in state court, his second appeal came before the White Court in 1911. He had been ordered to pay his employer $15 and assessed a fine of $30 and costs; since he had no money, the local court sentenced him to four and a half months at hard labor. Justice Hughes attacked the statute as a restriction of personal rights, and noted that the Alabama Supreme Court had previously struck down legislation abridging employees' contractual rights as a violation of the Fourteenth Amendment. The state was now trying to accomplish a similarly impermissible objective by criminal sanctions, and in doing so violated the Thirteenth Amendment. Hughes's decision relied on relatively narrow grounds and did not invalidate all forced labor statutes. Not until 1944, in *Pollock v. Williams,* did the Court finally strike a death blow to the peonage system.

Bailey dealt with peonage for the state. In *United States v. Reynolds* the following year, the Court dealt with another Alabama forced labor statute, one that assigned a person's labor to private parties. A person convicted of an offense could have his fine and costs paid by another person (a surety), who then executed a labor contract under which the defendant would work a set amount of time to pay off the debt. If the laborer defaulted, he could be convicted of breaching the contract and another surety would appear, pay off the debt and new fines, and bind the defendant to a still longer term of service. In May 1910, for example, Ed Rivers pleaded guilty to petit larceny in county court in Monroeville, Alabama. The judge fined him $15 and assessed $43.75 in costs. Since Rivers had no money, the judge sentenced him to ten days hard labor for the fine, and another forty-eight days to pay the court costs. One J. A. Reynolds paid the fine and costs, and Rivers agreed to work for him for ten months, at $6 a month, plus room, board, and clothing. After a month, Rivers left, but the police soon rearrested him and charged him with failing to perform his contractual duties. The same judge fined him only one penny, but assessed court costs of $87.05. A new surety came forward to pay, but now Rivers faced a contract for fourteen months, seven times what he would have had to work to pay his original sentence.

The Justice Department, under Attorney General Wickersham, had been looking for test cases to challenge the labor surety system, which it termed an "engine of oppression" against blacks. After fastening on the Rivers incident, it took the department more than two years to work out the details of how to proceed. Both the federal and state governments wanted a case that would go to the Supreme Court, so as to resolve the issue, since planters and others who stood the surety needed to know if the system would continue. The government promised that if the Court found against the sureties, it would ask for a minimal fine, since it did not want to punish individuals, but test the system.

In the end, a unanimous Court, speaking through Justice Day, struck down the surety contract, but it did so in a formalistic and defensive manner—as if the justices knew that it was wrong to permit blacks to be so mistreated, but could not quite figure out why. Day, like Hughes in *Bailey,* did not want to point out the racial nature of the system. Most prisoners condemned to the chain gang for breach of contract, or bound to a surety, were black; peonage constituted one of the South's means of controlling blacks in a way that assured a reliable labor force. Holmes, who dissented in *Bailey,* grudgingly concurred in *Reynolds,* and his brief opinion bespoke volumes about the innate racism that afflicted many Northern Progressives. But, even if for the wrong reason, the Court at least put an end to one of the worst aspects of Southern racism.

A Few Small Steps

The White Court also took hesitant steps to address the widespread disenfranchisement of blacks by Southern states. It will be recalled that in *Williams v. Mississippi* (1898), the Court had indirectly given its approval to restrictions such as the poll tax and literacy test. Five years later, in *Giles v. Harris* (1903), Holmes admitted that the Court did not have the capacity to remedy discrimination in voter registration. The question of the grandfather clauses, however, came before the bench in a strange case. Oklahoma, where blacks comprised less than 10 percent of the population, and which, unlike other Southern states, had a vigorous two-party political system, had adopted a grandfather clause shortly after it became a state. As the head of the Oklahoma Republican party complained, the clause had been adopted to stop blacks from voting not because of their race, but because they voted Republican.

In *Guinn v. United States* (1915), the Justice Department attacked the Oklahoma grandfather clause as violating the Fifteenth Amendment. At the same time, the Court heard a challenge to a similar Maryland statute in *Myers v. Anderson.* The clauses waived the literacy test for voting for anyone entitled to vote under any form of government, for those living in a foreign country as of January 1, 1866, and for their lineal descendants. Since neither clause specified race, both states denied any constitutional violation; both also claimed that voting requirements remained primarily a matter of state and local jurisdiction. Chief Justice White disagreed. Although neither law mentioned race, their application worked specifically to keep blacks from voting, while allowing whites to bypass the literacy test and poll tax. In a companion case, *United States v. Mosely,* the Court upheld the conviction of Oklahoma officials for depriving blacks of their right to vote, in violation of Section 19 of the Ku Klux Klan Enforcement Act of 1870.

Conclusion

The promise of freedom made during the Civil War era remained unfulfilled for many Americans at the turn of the century. African Americans may not have been formally enslaved as they had been before the war, but they lived and worked in a demeaning system of apartheid that clearly marked them as second-class citizens. Native Americans, Asians, and people living in the nation's new colonies also failed to share in the promise of equality made in the Fourteenth Amendment, while women remained disfavored by the law. There were some bright spots, and a few glimmerings in the Court that racism embedded in law could go only so far. But the bright spots were few, and the glimmerings would take more than six decades before they would flower into the Warren Court's attack on segregation.

For Further Reading

A good general work looking at the South after the Civil War is Edward L. Ayers, *The Promise of the New South: Life After Reconstruction* (1992). In terms of segregation, the key work is C. Vann Woodward's classic, *The Strange Career of Jim Crow* (3rd ed., 1989), which argues that segregation need not have become the dominant pattern in Southern racial relations. A case study testing and supporting this thesis is Joseph H. Cartwright, *The Triumph of Jim Crow: Tennessee Race Relations in the 1880s* (1976). A variation on the Woodward thesis is Howard Rabinowitz, *Race Relations in the Urban South, 1865–1890* (1978), while questions of black interest in separation as well as the timing of segregation laws are explored in two books by Joel Williamson, *After Slavery: The Negro in South Carolina during Reconstruction, 1861–1877* (1965) and *The Crucible of Race: Black-White Relations in the American South since Emancipation* (1984). Specifics on various states are found in Pauli Murray, *State Laws on Race and Color* (1952), which documents the adoption of Jim Crow laws. Other works dealing with the treatment of blacks after the Civil War include William Gillette, *Retreat from Reconstruction, 1869–1879* (1979), and Daniel A. Novak, *The Wheel of Servitude: Black Forced Labor After Slavery* (1978). Also important is William Cohen, *At Freedom's Edge: Black Mobility and the Southern White Quest for Racial Control, 1861–1915* (1991).

Some specialized studies include J. David Hoeveler, Jr., "Reconstruction and the Federal Courts: The Civil Rights Act of 1875," 31 *History* 604 (1969); John A. Scott, "Justice Bradley's Evolving Concept of the Fourteenth Amendment from the Slaughterhouse Cases to the Civil Rights Cases," 25 *Rutgers Law Review* 552 (1971); and Roger L. Rice, "Residential Segregation by Law, 1910–1917," 34 *Journal of Southern History* 179 (1968). The standard work on *Plessy* is Charles A. Lofgren, *The Plessy Case: A Legal-Historical Interpretation* (1987). The worsening position of blacks in Southern agriculture is detailed in William Cohen, "Negro Involuntary Servitude in the South, 1865–1940: A Preliminary Inventory," 42 *Journal of Southern History* 31 (1976), and Harold D. Woodman, "Post-War Southern Agriculture and the Law," 53 *Agricultural History* 319 (1979). For peonage, see Peter Daniel, *The Shadow of Slavery: Peonage in the South, 1901–1969* (1972), and David E. Bernstein, *Only On Place of Redress: African-Americans, Labor Regulations and the Courts from Reconstruction to the New Deal* (2001). For the Insular cases, see José A. Cabranes, *Citizenship and the American Empire* (1979), and Julius W. Pratt, *America's Colonial Experiment* (1950). On blacks and the legal profession in this period, see J. Clay Smith, *Emancipation: The Making of the Black Lawyer, 1844–1944* (1993).

For Indian policy, the basic collection of documents is Francis P. Prucha, *The Great Father: The United States Government and the American Indian* 2 vols. (1984), while a good overview of federal policy during this period is Frederick E. Hoxie, *A Final Promise: The Campaign to Assimilate the Indians, 1880–1920* (1984). For the Court's role, see David E. Wilkins, *American Indian Sovereignty and the U.S. Supreme Court* (1997). For materials on specific cases, see Blue Clark, *Lone Wolf v. Hitchcock: Treaty Rights and Indian Law at the End of the Nineteenth Century* (1994); Brian Czech, "*Ward v. Race Horse*—Supreme Court as Obviator?" 35 *Journal of the West* 61 (July 1996); and Robert K. Heimann, "The Cherokee Tobacco Case," 41 *Chronicles of Oklahoma* 299 (1967).

For the Chinese cases, see Hyung-Chan Kim, *A Legal History of Asian Americans, 1790–1990* (1994); Stuart Creighton Miller, *The Unwelcome Immigrant: The American Image of the Chinese, 1785–1882* (1969); Lucy E. Salyer, *Laws Harsh as Tigers: Chinese Immigrants and the Shaping of Modern Immigration Law* (1995); and chapter 10 of Owen M. Fiss, *Troubled Beginnings of the Modern State, 1888–1910* (1993). For the Insular Cases, see James Edward Kerr, *The Insular Cases: The Role of the Judiciary in American Expansionism* (1982). The development of the incorporation doctrine is explicated in Robert B. Highsaw, *Edward Douglass White: Defender of the Conservative Faith* (1981).

The literature on women and the law is growing rapidly, but for this era, see Sandra F. VanBurkleo, *"Belonging to the World": Women's Rights and American Constitutional Culture* (2001); Joan Hoff, *Law, Gender and Injustice: A Legal History of U.S. Women* (1991); Virginia G. Drachman, *Women Lawyers and the Origins of Professional Identity in America* (1993); and *Sisters in Law: Women Lawyers in Modern American History* (1998). The issue of taxation without representation is discussed in chapter 3 of Linda K. Kerber, *No Constitutional Right to Be Ladies: Women and the Obligations of Citizenship* (1998). Legal burdens faced by average women after the Civil War is detailed in Amy Dru Stanley, *From Bondage to Contract: Wage Labor, Marriage, and the Market in the Age of Slave Emancipation* (1998). For two unusual women lawyers, see Jane M. Friedman, *America's First Woman Lawyer: The Biography of Myra Bradwell* (1993); and Jill Norgren, "Before It Was Merely Difficult: Belva Lockwood's Life in Law and Politics," 1999 *Journal of Supreme Court History* 16 (April 1999), the first installment of a forthcoming biography.

23

The Constitutional World of the Late Nineteenth Century

Classical Legal Thought • The Emergence of Substantive Due Process • Due Process Enthroned • Freedom of Contract • The Law Writers • The Importance of Oliver Wendell Holmes, Jr. • The Emergence of the Modern Legal Profession • Conclusion • For Further Reading

IN THE DECADES after Reconstruction, American jurists built a constitutional structure that closely reflected the predilections of the Gilded Age—protective of property rights, distrustful of governmental intervention in the market, and disdainful of the rights of labor and minority groups. It rested on two pillars, freedom of contract and substantive due process, and even though the realities of a changing economy as well as political developments would outdate many of its assumptions even as they were articulated, it remained the dominant legal paradigm until finally crumbling in the 1930s. But for more than a half-century, what legal historian William Wiecek has called "classical legal thought" dominated the thinking of the American bench and bar.

Classical Legal Thought

Legal classicism derived from common beliefs about the character of liberty and power, human nature and rights, and the limits of republican government. It did not emerge fully formed, but grew out of ideas as old as the Republic, as well as the free labor ideology associated with the birth of the Republican party in the 1850s. It provided what might be termed a "unified field theory" in that it explained not only a general rationale of limited government, but also the role of courts in a free society. It had its own methods of reasoning, and clearly articulated social values, both undergirded by sources of law.

Its mode of thinking has been described as formalistic and abstract, methods that are no longer stylish but which dominated both jurisprudence as well as philosophy in much of the nineteenth century. The innovations introduced by Christopher Columbus Langdell at the Harvard Law School in the 1870s are illustrative of the nature of classical legal thought. In place of learning legal rules by rote, Langdell broke the curriculum into particular courses in which instructors taught the case method.

In place of treatises, Langdell substituted casebooks, collections of edited cases grouped to illustrate a particular rule of law. Instead of student recitation from memory, teachers used the Socratic dialogue in which, through a series of questions, they led their classes to understand basic principles. Langdell himself wrote the first casebook on contracts in 1871, consisting primarily of English decisions, with a few cases from Massachusetts and New York.

Langdell hoped to establish law as a science, and wrote that: "The number of fundamental legal doctrines is much less than is commonly supposed; the many different guises in which the same doctrine is constantly making its appearance, and the great extent to which legal treatises are a repetition of each other, being the cause of much misapprehension. If these doctrines could be so classified and arranged that each should be found in their proper place, and nowhere else, they would cease to be formidable from their number."

The case method's goal of making law into a science also required that lawyers think of legal matters in a scientific manner—detached, objectively, and abstractly. The facts of the case meant little, the rule everything. Books and cases stopped using names and referred to litigants as "A" and "B," or "seller" and "purchaser." Facts meant little because legal thinkers wanted to articulate general rules applicable to all cases. Just as the rules of physics or chemistry applied with equal impartiality in all situations, so should the law. If the facts in some cases could not be made to fit into the rule, then they could and should be ignored as anomalies. To quote the famous parody of this reasoning by Harvard law professor Thomas Reed Powell, "If you think that you can think about a thing, inextricably attached to something else, without thinking of the thing it is attached to, then you have a legal mind."

Formalism, as legal historian Herbert Hovenkamp has argued, is "law without policy—except perhaps for the policy that the law must be internally consistent and self-contained, and must not draw its wisdom from outside." This type of formalism

> Law schools are splendid institutions. Aside from the instruction there received, being able continually to associate with young-men who have the same interest and ambition, who are determined to make as great progress as possible in their studies and devote all their time to the same—must alone be of inestimable advantages. Add to this the instruction of consummate lawyers, who devote their whole time to *you*, and a complete law-library of over fifteen thousand volumes and then compare the opportunities for learning which a student of the law has at Harvard Law School and in a law-office. After one has grasped the principles which underlie the structure of the Common Law, I doubt not, that one can learn very much in an office. That first year at law is, however, surely ill-spent in an office.
>
> —Louis D. Brandeis to Otto A. Wehle, 12 March 1876

is indeed sterile, and had the Langdellian revolution fully succeeded, it would have been as well. Lawyers and judges, even as they eagerly grasped this new way of thinking about the law, also embraced certain values, although no ideological clarity paralleled the rigor accompanying legal reasoning. For the most part, bench and bar believed strongly in laissez-faire, the notion that government should not play an active role in the market. In fact, the state had never been absent from the market, and American history from its founding is rife with state and, later, federal laws and programs that affected the market. The same businessmen who railed against efforts to regulate railroad rates had no qualms about accepting enormous subsidies in the form of land grants or overly protective tariffs.

Individualism constituted the most pervasive value of classical thought, and related closely not only to a free market but also to social Darwinism's belief in the survival of the most fit. A free market, uninhibited by government rules, would allow each person the greatest opportunity to succeed. The market provided an arena in which the caliber (morality) of a man could be tested; if he had courage and ability he would succeed, and this would not only benefit him but the greater society as well. If he failed, then he would fall into the great pool of unskilled workers, doing the pick and shovel work necessary for the talented entrepreneurs to succeed. A free market had moral as well as economic attributes, and any effort to help the weak (the immoral) could only hurt the strong (the moral), on whose shoulders rested the prosperity of the nation.

Classical thinkers had little notion of equality, other than the equality of the market, and when they thought of rights they tended to focus on contract and property. Legal writers argued that these rights predated the nation; the Constitution did not create them, but recognized their existence and articulated their protection. John Locke had argued that the state existed to protect rights; any effort to undermine property rights had to be single-mindedly opposed, especially by bench and bar. William Ramsey told his fellow lawyers that "the right to contract and to be contracted with . . . is sacred, and lies at the very foundation of the social state." William Guthrie warned his colleagues of "the despotism of the majority." "We lawyers," he intoned, "are delegated not merely to defend constitutional guaranties before the courts for individual clients, but to teach the people in season and out to value and respect individual liberty and the rights of property."

This conservative mindset obviously looked askance at the rise of positive government in the late nineteenth century, and above all feared a majoritarian tyranny that would strip the well-to-do of their accomplishments, taking their wealth and redistributing it to the less "fit." Private law existed to protect that wealth, to ensure that those who had earned their money in the arena of the market would keep the fruits of their labor. Public law, especially the Constitution, had the primary purpose of limiting governmental authority.

According to Morton Horwitz, the distinction between public and private law constituted an important element of classical legal theory. Law writers and judges wanted to create a sharp distinction between the supposedly coercive public law, primarily criminal and regulatory law, and the noncoercive private law of tort, contract, property, and commerce. Ideally, private law stood immune from politics, and conservative thinkers in the nineteenth century wanted to separate the public and private realms of life as much as possible. In law, the public-private distinction had been articulated in the *Dartmouth College* case (1819), which dovetailed nicely into the vested rights doctrine. The private sphere, and the rights attached to it, should be untouched by political coercion. Beginning in the 1840s, the public-private distinction played a major role in state constitutional cases, in which judges differentiated between legitimate exercises of the state's power, especially in eminent domain, and the illegitimate use of that power either to further or hinder an essentially private undertaking.

Classical legal thought relied heavily on law to sustain this worldview. In particular it looked to "natural law," what Thomas Jefferson had referred to in the Declaration of Independence as "the Laws of Nature and Nature's God." To men of the revolutionary generation, natural law, property rights, and "vested rights" all meant essentially the same thing. Property constituted the foundation of the social contract; take away the protection of property and anarchy would ensue. The people of the United States, asserted Justice Samuel Chase in *Calder v. Bull* (1798), created government to establish justice, promote the general welfare, secure the blessings of liberty, and "protect their *persons* and *property* from violence." Any legislative act that failed to further these goals, that detracted from one's vested rights in property, had no force, for it violated natural law.

While today we tend to view law as a social development that reflects the changing needs of a changing society, the post–Civil War generation believed, as had Blackstone a century earlier, that law rested on universal principles of justice and morality. As such, law did not change with the flux of the times, but stood as an unyielding arbiter of right and wrong. Contemporary jurisprudence sees law as a balance of competing values, in which moral concerns are absent from large areas of the law. Believers in natural law find a natural harmony between law and morality, and in particular, with the basic elements of Christian morality.

Because law embodied morality, then judges had to administer the law impartially. The "rule of law" guaranteed the greatest good for all people because it allegedly favored none. Law existed to protect society, the family, the individual, and rights, especially property rights. The law writers of this period saw law as embodying the values of society, which antedated the state; therefore law served as a protection of the society and of the individual from the state. The courts had a key role to play in the rule of law. Judges had the sole responsibility of discovering the right rule, and then applying it impartially. The courts, especially the Supreme Court, had been given the authority to interpret the Constitution and to ensure that the state did not overstep the bounds imposed upon it.

All of these elements—abstract reasoning, the emphasis on individualism and the limited role of the state, and the belief in an immutable law—combined to make up classical legal thought.

But to defend property, bench and bar needed newer and more powerful concepts. The Contract Clause had only limited value, since state legislatures, following Story's clue in *Dartmouth College*, routinely reserved the power to amend or even repeal corporate charters. The vested rights doctrine, especially after the Jacksonian era, aroused too much popular suspicion and also lacked clarity; it did not offer precise guidelines on how and when it could be invoked. Moreover, the transition from a mercantile to an industrial society raised questions about the validity of older doctrines. Property, for example, had been fairly well defined before the Civil War as consisting largely of tangibles, such as land and chattels, and to a lesser extent, business; only a few courts occasionally spoke of property rights inherent in a trade or profession. The new industrial age extended property far beyond its traditional physical limits. Thus, in *National Telegraphic News Co. v. Western Union Telegraph Co.* (1902), Circuit Court Judge Peter Grosscup noted:

> [Property] is not, in its modern sense, confined to that which may be touched by the hand, or seen by the eye. What is called tangible property has come to be, in most great enterprises, but the embodiment, physically, of an underlying life, a life that, in its contribution to success, is immeasurably more effective than the mere physical embodiment.

This underlying life extended to all aspects of business, including the policies that entrepreneurs adopted to achieve their goals, and it had to be protected.

The Emergence of Substantive Due Process

The new principle to protect property, substantive due process, evolved slowly in the latter part of the nineteenth century and finally received the imprimatur of the Supreme Court in 1897, in *Allgeyer v. Louisiana.* The phrase "due process of law" derived from the older "law of the land," which referred to general legal rules and customs accepted as the normative base of the legal system. From the beginning, due process has meant a bundle of procedural rights, some of which are spelled out in constitutions, statutes, and regulations, and some of which are of common law derivation. The right to a jury trial is a substantive right, but how the jurors are chosen, how evidence may be presented, how witnesses may be procured, and how the trial is conducted in a fair and impartial manner are all procedural in nature. Procedural due process, it has been said, regulates the courts and constitutes the rules of the game; substantive due process regulates the legislature and *is* the game.

The idea that due process of law could also include substantive rights to protect property appeared in a few cases before the Civil War. In the best known state decision, *Wynehamer v. People* (1856), the New York high court read due process to prohibit certain types of legislative interference with business, regardless of the method used. The following year in *Dred Scott*, Chief Justice Roger Taney commented without elaboration that an "Act of Congress which deprives a citizen of the United States of his liberty or property, merely because he came himself or brought his property into a particular Territory of the United States, and who had committed no offense against the law, could hardly be dignified with the name of due process of law." In other words, various rights in property might well exist within the scope of the Due Process Clause.

In 1873, the Supreme Court almost adopted substantive due process in the *Slaughterhouse Cases.* A Louisiana law of 1869 had chartered the Crescent City Live-Stock Landing and Slaughterhouse Company and granted it a twenty-five-year monopoly to maintain landings for cattle, slaughterhouses, and stockyards in the three parishes comprising greater New Orleans. The growth of cities led many legislatures to enact measures of this sort for health reasons. By concentrating and regulating animal slaughter for a city of 200,000 people, the city could more easily control rats, limit the stench, and inspect the butchering. But butchers not included in the monopoly challenged the law, claiming that it deprived them of their right "to exercise their trade," a right protected by the Thirteenth and Fourteenth amendments as well as the 1866 Civil Rights Act.

Justice Samuel Miller, speaking for a five-man majority, rejected this argument. Since the regulation of abattoirs historically lay within the police powers of the state, the real question was the grant of a monopoly and whether the Thirteenth and Fourteenth amendments related to that issue. Miller noted that "the one pervading purpose" of the Reconstruction amendments had been the liberation of the slaves and the establishment of their rights as citizens, not the enhancement of white persons' rights. He went over the various provisions of Section 1 of the Fourteenth Amendment in detail, explaining how they applied to the freedmen. But the amendments made no significant change in the federal system, he claimed; to adopt the butchers' thesis would shift the protection of individual rights, traditionally the responsibility of the states, to the national government. It would "fetter and degrade the State governments by subjecting them to the control of Congress," and would "constitute this court a perpetual censor upon all legislation of the States."

Four justices dissented, and three of them, Joseph Bradley, Stephen J. Field, and Noah Swayne, filed opinions; Chief Justice Salmon Chase concurred in Field's dissent. Field and Bradley pointed the way to the future.

Bradley had heard a predecessor case on circuit (*Live Stock Association v. Crescent City Company* [1870]), and his decision then presaged the later due process argument. "There is no more sacred right of citizenship," he had written, "than the right to pursue unmolested a lawful employment in a lawful manner. It is nothing more nor less than the sacred right of labor." Every American had the right to follow such pursuits "as he may see fit, without unreasonable regulations or molestation, and without being restrained by any of those unjust, oppressive, and odious monopolies or exclusive privileges which have been condemned by all free governments; it is also his privilege to be protected in the possession and enjoyment of his property." In his slaughterhouse dissent, Bradley now went further, talking of "valuable rights . . . which the legislature of a State cannot invade," and he invoked, by name, "substantive due process" as a protection against the legislature. While admitting the need for some governmental regulation in order to protect the community, he ascribed extremely narrow limits to the state police power.

Field's dissent, like Bradley's, reached back to the vested rights/natural rights tradition of *Calder v. Bull* (1798), and he also seemed to lump the various guarantees of the Fourteenth Amendment together. Only later would the Due Process Clause emerge as the clear repository of "the fundamental rights, privileges and immunities which belong to [a person] as a free man and a free citizen," rights, as Field here asserted, that "do not derive their existence from [state] legislation, and cannot be destroyed by its power." Field, even more than Bradley, recognized the need for state police powers to protect the health and safety of the people; in fact, he seemed willing to allow the states a wider latitude in striking a balance between individual freedom and the need to preserve social order and promote the general welfare. Some of the later and more extreme interpretations of due process ignored this aspect of Field's opinion and emphasized only the protection of individual and property rights.

Because of the narrowness of the vote, lawyers kept coming back to ask the Supreme Court to intervene against state regulation of business. A somewhat vexed Justice Miller remarked in *Davidson v. New Orleans* (1877), that

> the docket of this court is crowded with cases in which we are asked to hold that state courts and state legislatures have deprived their own citizens of life, liberty, or property without due process of law. There is here abundant evidence that there exists some strange misconception of the scope of this provision as found in the Fourteenth Amendment.

The misconception arose from several factors, including the growing effort by state legislatures to place some controls over the rapidly expanding power of large industries. For example, the Granger movement had caused several Midwestern states to pass laws regulating grain elevator charges. The elevators provided storage facilities for farmers shipping their produce to urban markets, and in many rural areas with only one elevator, the company took advantage of its monopoly to exact what farmers considered exorbitant rates.

In 1877, the Court gave its approval to some state regulation of grain elevators and similar businesses in *Munn v. Illinois*. Chief Justice Morrison R. Waite, whom Grant had appointed to replace Chase in 1873, wrote the majority opinion upholding the law; he confirmed that the state police power included the regulation of private property when "such regulation becomes necessary for the public good." He referred back to earlier English works to the effect that private property "affected with a public interest" could be controlled by the government and that property becomes "clothed with a public interest when used in a manner to make it of public consequence, and affect the community at large." The owners of property could do with it what they chose, but once they elected to use it in a manner that brought it within the scope of "public interest," they had to accept state regulation as one of the conditions for doing that type of business. The Court majority refused even to consider the rate schedule; if the power to regulate existed, then the legislature had the discretion to set maximum rates. Acknowledging that this power could be abused, Waite ruled that "for protection against abuses the people must revert to the polls."

Waite upheld state railroad regulation nearly a decade later in the *Railroad Commission Cases* (1886), yet both there and in *Munn* he appended statements that would be invoked to justify judicial review of the rates themselves. In *Munn* he noted that in some instances the courts could determine the reasonableness of rates; in the latter case, he warned that the

> power of regulation [is not] without limit. The power to regulate is not a power to destroy. Under pretense of regulating fares and freight, the State cannot require a railroad corporation to carry persons or property without reward; neither can it do that which in law amounts to a taking of private property for public use without just compensation, or without due process of law.

By then, the idea of substantive due process had gained considerable ground, especially in the state courts. In the leading case of *In re Jacobs* (1885), Judge Robert Earl, speaking for a unanimous New York court, struck down a statute prohibiting cigar making in tenements. The law bore no relation to health or safety, he declared, but interfered "with the profitable and free use of his property by the owner . . . and arbitrarily deprives him of his property and some portion of his personal liberty." The following year, in *Santa Clara County v. Southern Pacific Railroad*, the Supreme Court ruled that corporations were "persons" within the meaning of the Fourteenth Amendment and that therefore they could enjoy the same rights, privileges, and judicial protection as did natural persons.

By 1887, only Miller remained from the *Slaughterhouse* majority, while Bradley and Field had been joined by men who shared their concern over the increasing role of government in the economy. Although the Court upheld a state prohibition law in *Mugler v. Kansas*, Justice John Marshall Harlan announced that the Court would no longer accept every statute "ostensibly" enacted for the public welfare as a legitimate exercise of the police power. The courts would not be "misled by mere presence," but would "look at the substance of things." If the legislation "had no real or substantive relation to those objects, or is a palpable invasion of rights secured by fundamental law, it is the duty of the courts to so adjudge."

Judicial deference to the legislature in the area of rate regulation went next. In 1890, the Court invalidated a state law providing for administrative rate-making because it did not provide for judicial review. Reasonableness of rates, which Waite had considered outside the province of courts in *Munn*, became "eminently a question for judicial investigation." Denying a railroad the right to charge reasonable rates would be, "in substance and effect," a deprivation of property without due process of law (*Chicago, Milwaukee & St. Paul Railroad Co. v. Minnesota*). By the end of the decade, the Court had fully immersed itself in scrutinizing rates; under *Smyth v. Ames* (1898), it set rules that would entangle the judiciary in rate-making for decades to come.

Due Process Enthroned

The triumph of substantive due process came in *Allgeyer v. Louisiana* (1897), a case involving a state law that banned the sale of insurance covering property within Louisiana by a company not licensed to do business there. The E. Allgeyer Company had been convicted for mailing a letter to a New York marine insurance company (not licensed by Louisiana), advising it of shipment of goods, in accordance with its policy. Justice Rufus Peckham (appointed in 1895) struck down the law as a deprivation of property without due process. What made the *Allgeyer* opinion so forceful is that Peckham merged the due process idea with another theory, freedom of contract, which had also been developing in the state courts and in the works of the leading law writers. The liberty of the Fourteenth Amendment, declared Peckham,

> means not only the right of the citizen to be free from the mere physical restraint of his person, as by incarceration, but the term is deemed to embrace the right of the citizen to be free in the enjoyment of all his faculties; to be free to use them in all lawful ways; to live and work where he will; to earn his livelihood by any lawful calling; to pursue any livelihood or avocation, and for that purpose to enter into all contracts which may be proper, necessary and essential to his carrying out to a successful conclusion the purposes above mentioned. [In] the privilege of pursuing an ordinary calling or trade and of acquiring, holding and selling property must be embraced the right

> to make all proper contracts in relation thereto, and although it may be conceded that this right to contract in relation to persons or property or to do business within the jurisdiction of the State may be regulated and sometimes prohibited when the contract or business conflict with the policy of the State as contained in its statutes, yet the power does not and cannot extend to prohibiting a citizen from making contracts of the nature involved in this case.

Peckham and other advocates of vested rights philosophy thus wrote these ideas into the Constitution, clothing them with the highest legal protection. The right to contract, to conduct a business, or to follow a particular profession may or may not have been among the unenumerated rights referred to in the Ninth Amendment, though there is evidence that these "natural" rights were what the Framers had in mind. But, as we shall see, it is questionable if the Founders had meant to elevate commercial relations to such a point and then sanctify them with constitutional protection.

The substantive due process/freedom of contract theory reached its apogee in 1905 in *Lochner v. New York* (see Chapter 25), and for the next thirty years, it provided the rationale for the Court to strike down nearly 200 regulations. Among legal reformers, *Lochner* became the code word for unwarranted judicial interference in matters properly belonging to legislative judgment. By the early 1940s, the theory had been largely discredited, and the modern Court no longer applies due process to economic issues. Thus in *Williamson v. Lee Optical Co.* (1955), the Court announced that henceforth it would defer to legislative discretion in business regulation; if the state had any "rational basis" to warrant the controls, and if they did not violate a specific constitutional prohibition, the Court would not intervene. Substantive due process had gained such a bad name that when the Warren Court began its expansion of personal autonomy and political rights, the justices bent over backward to avoid labeling their rationale for what it was—substantive due process.

The strength of due process theory derived, first of all, from its lodging in specific written portions of the Constitution: the Fifth and Fourteenth amendments. By appealing to the Constitution, defenders of liberty and property could claim that they wanted nothing more than to carry out the intentions of the Framers. Adding to this, the "law of the land" tradition had a venerable history, dating back to the Magna Carta, and had been sanctified by generations of scholars and jurists. The vagueness of the phrase also made it a powerful tool, because at any time due process meant whatever the judges said it did, in either substantive or procedural terms. It could absorb the vested rights/natural rights arguments, it could draw on common law doctrines, and it proved compatible with the dominant social and legal theories of the day.

Recently, scholars have suggested that the problem of substantive due process was not the theory itself, but its application. Although its expansive views of liberty and property went beyond the limited references of the Constitution, that by itself should not have created such consternation. Rather, the Court selected the wrong values for judicial protection; it failed to articulate specific standards in decision making, it did not appear neutral in adjudication, it ignored real-world data, and it failed to show proper judicial restraint or deference to legislative wisdom.

All these criticisms are, of course, true, but they apply with equal force to other areas of judicial activism: The Supreme Court has expanded constitutional references to produce vigorous new fundamental rights, especially in the areas of civil liberties and personal autonomy. Yet attacks on the modern Court's activism do not compare to the sustained criticism against its defense of property after *Lochner*. Government control of business constituted *the* major political issue of the late nineteenth and early twentieth centuries, and Court decisions overturning protective legislation and other regulations had a direct impact on a large part of the population.

One should also note that the justices who manned the Court at this time had come to maturity in a nonindustrial world, and they clung to political and legal ideas which, at the very least, needed modification in the light of new realities. They seemed like intellectual prisoners, held captive by the doctrines of laissez-faire and the inverted logic of legal formalism. When Holmes, in his famous *Lochner* dissent, shouted that "The Fourteenth Amendment does not enact Mr. Herbert Spencer's Social Statics," reformers cheered; but many conservatives believed that it did. For them, substantive due process meant maximum individual liberty and minimal governmental interference. Property had to be protected, for it supported and held society together; the race of life produced social and economic inequality, and government had no business trying to change it.

Freedom of Contract

Freedom of contract constituted an essential part of conservative legal thought in the latter nineteenth century and, together with substantive due process, provided the main legal bulwark against legislative efforts to interfere in private business. The contract argument did not derive from the Contract Clause of the Constitution (the Article I, Section 10 prohibition against states' altering the terms of an agreement after it had been executed). Freedom of contract exercised such a potent influence because it developed out of the pre–Civil War "free labor" ideology. The North had considered itself a morally superior region because its people labored by their own will and for their own gain, whereas in the South slaves worked involuntarily for the benefit of their owners. This economic individualism distinguished the free person from the slave and had to be cherished and protected against any encroachments. After the war, although the Republican party split on any number of issues, its devotion to free labor never wavered, and this idea soon captured the allegiance of other important segments of the society, too.

Whereas substantive due process applied to nearly all areas of legislation concerning property, freedom of contract related primarily to agreements between employer and employee on the conditions of work, such as hours, wages, and liability. Legislative interference with other types of contracts rarely attracted judicial notice, much less hostility. In fact, the common law recognized a variety of reasons to justify the state's intervention, such as fraud, duress, and even public policy. But the labor contract somehow seemed special. In *Western & Electric Railroad Co. v. Bishop* (1873), a Georgia judge wrote he knew "of no right more precious . . . than the right to fix by contract the terms upon which [one's] labor shall be engaged."

In the preindustrial age, the ideal of the labor contract and its reality merged fairly well. An employer would bargain at arm's length on terms of relative equality with a laborer; taking into account the customs of the local market, they would strike a bargain.

If the agreement did not prove satisfactory, it could be terminated, and the two parties would either renegotiate or seek new partners. With the rise of factories, the legal notion that both employer and employee enjoyed parity in bargaining power diverged from the reality that the thousands of workers in any particular mill, factory, or mine did not bargain, but had to accept whatever the employer offered. Their only freedom consisted of walking away and seeking other employment—where inevitably they would face the same circumstances. Manufacturers controlled the market, since the millions of immigrants pouring into the country provided a vast labor pool eager to find work under almost any conditions and at any wage. As early as 1762, Lord Northington had argued in *Vernon v. Bethel* that "necessitous men are not, truly speaking, free men, but, to answer a present exigency, will submit to any terms that the crafty may impose on them."

Labor unions offered one way to redress the imbalance of bargaining power. By acting together, the workers would wield a combined strength comparable to that of the owners and would have true leverage in negotiating. Workers tried this route beginning in the 1870s, with the Knights of Labor, and the following decade with the American Federation of Labor, but they immediately ran into overwhelming opposition from mine and factory operators. Blacklists, scabs, and armed strikebreakers proved but a few of the weapons used against the unions in a war that burst into violence on more than one occasion.

Reformers concerned about the plight of labor suggested another route—legislative control of working conditions exercised under the state's police power. The resulting protective legislation took many forms, including regulation of child labor, maximum hours, and minimum wages; initially all ran up against the stone wall of judicial opposition. The earliest efforts at worker protection were restrictions on payment in scrip rather than money (the paper coupons could be redeemed for merchandise and food, but only at company-owned stores that charged premium prices). The Pennsylvania high court, in its often quoted decision in *Godcharles & Co. v. Wigeman* (1880), set the tone in striking down the law, which it described as

> an insulting attempt to put the laborer under a legislative tutelage which is not only degrading to his manhood, but subversive of his rights as a citizen of the United States. He may sell his labor for what he thinks best, whether money or goods, just as his employer may sell his iron or coal, and any and every law that proposes to prevent him from so doing is an infringement of his constitutional privilege and consequently vicious and void.

That the worker really had no choice in the matter, that all the mines paid in scrip, and that refusal to accept scrip meant not working at all made no difference. Legal formalism clung to the fiction of both employer and employee as *sui juris*, fully competent to negotiate with each other on an equal basis. So long as the courts promulgated this idea, legislative interference with how businessmen ran their operations could be minimized. As we shall see later (Chapter 25), not all state or federal courts fully accepted this view, and many proved amenable to the use of the police power to ameliorate both working conditions and inequality in bargaining. But well into the twentieth century, the freedom of contract doctrine served conservative interests well. As late as 1923, Justice George Sutherland, in *Adkins v. Children's Hospital*, could proclaim "liberty of contract is the rule, restraint the exception."

The defenders of freedom of contract insisted that labor as well as management had to be let alone; legislative interference damaged the freedom of workers, in addition to the property rights of capital. The fact that bargaining equality no longer prevailed in the marketplace made no difference; markets operated under natural laws of their own, and men had to exercise their rights in the conditions they found. The reality of the market, however, stirred other defenders of free labor to just the opposite conclusion.

Prior to the Civil War, Southerners had argued that workers in the new Northern textile mills were not free, and were in fact worse off than slaves, who enjoyed the continued support of their owners even when they became sick, disabled, or too old to work. This argument never made sense to slaves or free blacks, and it is clear that most free workers were markedly better off than slaves. Nonetheless, at least part of the Southern argument gained new force during industrialization; factory workers could hardly be considered "free" in the old sense, and reformers proposed legislation to assist labor to make fair terms. Yet even those who took this view recognized that any interference with the labor contract, even to remedy inequities, undermined individual rights and went against the prevailing ideas of laissez-faire. The right to be free outweighed any other considerations, and not until conditions got much worse at the end of the century did reformers begin to develop the police power argument against the alleged constitutional guarantee of freedom to contract. By then, however, the freedom of contract philosophy, if not universally accepted, had secure strongholds in both the state and federal courts.

The Law Writers

Classical legal thought expressed itself in more than court decisions. The development of substantive due process and freedom of contract received great support from a handful of influential writers who provided the intellectual scaffolding upon which lawyers and judges could flesh out the doctrines. Two men in particular, Thomas M. Cooley and Christopher G. Tiedeman, popularized these ideas, both within the profession and for the public, with enormous skill and force. Cooley's *Constitutional Limitations* may have been the most cited legal treatise of the nineteenth century; in some state courts, major decisions relied on little more than a reference to this volume.

As a young man, Cooley settled in Michigan, where he read for the bar and entered practice. In 1864, voters elected him to the Michigan Supreme Court on a Republican ticket, and he served until he was defeated in the Democratic landslide of 1884. In an age of relatively mediocre state judges, Cooley soon won renown for his ability and extensive knowledge of the law; in fact, he taught at the University of Michigan law school from its inception in 1859 until 1885. In 1887, President Cleveland named him to the newly created Interstate Commerce Commission; he soon became chairman, but had to retire because of ill health in 1891.

Cooley's reputation rested in part on *A Treatise on Constitutional Limitations*, first published in 1868, which went through five more editions during his lifetime. Revised twice after his death, it retained its authority well into the 1920s. The book provided the first systematic analysis and compendium of state constitutional law and allowed state judges—with whom it immediately became the authority—to see the law of other jurisdictions, as well as that of their own state. Perhaps more important, Cooley not only argued for limits on government activities, as the title implied, but in a cogent manner, he justified such restrictions.

In the 1883 edition, Cooley listed the liberty to make contracts as one of the five natural rights. In a passage often quoted in state court decisions, he wrote:

> If the legislature should undertake to provide that persons following some specified lawful trade or employment should not have capacity to make contracts, or to receive conveyances, or to build such houses as others were allowed to erect, or in any other way to make such use of their property as was permissible to others, it can scarcely be doubted that the act would transcend the due bounds of legislative power. The man . . . would be deprived of liberty in particulars of primary importance to his "pursuit of happiness."

In the minds of later reformers, Cooley's work epitomized conservative, laissez-faire legal dogmatism, a view that is both unfair and fails to credit him for solid research and inventive thought. He did not create the law, but took nascent trends and developed them into a coherent and forceful pattern. Hardly a reactionary, both his decisions on the Michigan bench and his writings showed sensitivity to the social and economic events of his day. He agreed, for instance, that certain kinds of protective legislation fell within the police power of the state. His influence appeared greatest in the state courts (the leading labor contract decisions of the Supreme Court did not mention him), but even there judges tended to select the most conservative ideas from his work.

A few years before Cooley died, Christopher Tiedeman published *A Treatise on the Limitations of Police Power in the United States* (1886). A professor of law at the University of Missouri, Tiedeman wrote treatises on a variety of subjects, many of which became standard texts in the newly emerging law schools, but his fame rested primarily on this book. Far more conservative than Cooley, he believed that the proper role of government consisted of no more "than to provide for the public order and personal security by the prevention and punishment of crimes and trespasses." By the time he wrote, Tiedeman not only could benefit from a growing number of court cases supporting his position, but could also raise the alarm against the demands of reformers for protective legislation. As he candidly admitted, he set out explicitly to prove that the police powers of the state could not be employed to interfere in the marketplace. In fact, he wanted to limit the police power to enforcing the ancient legal maxim, *sic utere tuo ut alienum non laedas*—use your own property in such a way as not to injure another's property. Far more than Cooley, Tiedeman denounced any type of government regulation: He even opposed usury laws (which limited the interest rates lenders could charge), declaring that "free trade in money is as much a right as free trade in merchandise." While he admitted that usury laws had long been accepted, he urged a fresh inquiry into their constitutionality.

Treatises such as Cooley's and Tiedeman's were, of course, nothing new; English and American writers had been producing learned summaries of particular fields of substantive law and procedure for centuries. Practicing lawyers needed such compendiums if for no other reason than to get a handle on the main currents of law. In

1810, there had been only a handful of American reports; the number grew geometrically, so that by 1848, more than 100 had appeared, and by 1885, nearly 4,000. Attorneys relied on such works as John Dillon's pioneering *Law of Municipal Corporations* (1872), Emory Washhurns's two volumes on *Real Property* (1860–1862), and Theophilus Parson's enormously popular *Contracts* (1853). As new areas of litigation opened, law writers quickly entered the field, as Edward Keasbey did with his *Law of Electric Wires in Streets and Highways* (1892).

Aside from treatises, lawyers also relied on law magazines, such as the *Albany Law Journal* and the *American Law Register*, which summarized leading cases in different jurisdictions and offered scholarly essays on legal issues. But the sheer volume of cases made it impossible for a practicing attorney to know more than the small area of his own local law. Beginning in 1879, however, the National Reporter System and the digests published by the West Publishing Company not only imposed some order on reporting the nation's cases, but grouped them under a topical key system; now one could find cases from all jurisdictions, state and federal, relating to a particular subject.

Reliance on precedent made the treatises, reports, and digests indispensable. Lawyers and judges would find references to all the major cases on a particular subject and, by stringing together a list of such citations, bolster their pleadings or reinforce their opinions. Nevertheless, the sheer volume of cases was threatening to overwhelm the profession; something would have to be done to make the law more manageable, by changing either the way lawyers learned the law or the way they practiced it.

The Importance of Oliver Wendell Holmes, Jr.

While the law writers played a major role in helping judges develop public law regarding the state's use of its powers (public law), no one exercised greater influence on the development of private law than Oliver Wendell Holmes, Jr. Holmes published his first piece on legal theory in 1870, and for the next quarter-century wrote countless articles, book reviews, and case notes, edited a new and influential edition of *Kent's Commentaries*, and published *The Common Law* (1881), by general agreement the most important work in American legal thought. From 1881 to 1902, he sat on the Supreme Judicial Court of Massachusetts, and then for the next thirty years on the U.S. Supreme Court.

Blackstone had posited divine authority as the source of the law, and assumed that law reflected morality. As such, it had to be somewhat subjective, so that judges could apply the correct moral rule in order to find the proper legal solution. Holmes above all wanted to do away with subjectivity in the law and replace it with objectivity, rules that ignored the mental or moral conditions of the actors. He dismissed natural rights theories, and asserted that law served the general good as defined by the state. He used the example of the doctrine that ignorance of the law is never an excuse for wrongful action. Thus he wrote in *The Common Law*: "The true explanation of the rule is the same as that which accounts for the law's indifference to a man's particular temperament, faculties and so forth. Public policy sacrifices the individual to the general good."

> The life of the law has not been logic: it has been experience. The felt necessities of the times, the prevalent moral and political theories, intuitions of public policy, avowed or unconscious, even the prejudices which judges share with their fellow-men, have a good deal more to do than the syllogism in determining the rules by which men should be governed.
>
> —Oliver Wendell Holmes, Jr., *The Common Law* (1881)

Holmes's obsession with objective standards can be seen in several ways. From a theoretical point of view it is part of American pragmatism's rejection of German idealism and its philosophy of natural rights, and Holmes attacked Hegel, Kant, and especially the English legal writer John Austin. But Holmes also responded to the changing economic and social conditions in the United States in the late nineteenth century. Classical legal thought assumed—indeed demanded—that judges not be policy-makers but merely find and impose the proper legal rule. But with rapidly changing conditions, judges had to make decisions, and in doing so they made policy. In the early nineteenth century, judges had adopted an instrumentalist approach to law, utilizing it to advance what they saw as necessary economic developments. Holmes's arguments in private law attempted to free judges from this policy-making obligation, by establishing objective criteria. Although Holmes always opposed formalism in legal thinking, he did share with other nineteenth century jurisprudents the desire to create objective criteria for judging. The law, he once said, is nothing more than what a judge decides; to keep the law from becoming totally idiosyncratic, judges had to be able to impose objective standards, and these had to be free from the moralism implicit in natural rights theory.

Public law could and should reflect the policy decisions of the government, decisions in which moral considerations could be taken into account. Criminal law is the best example of this, in which society sets forth a moral code that brings heavy penalties for its violation. In the private sphere, rules had to be neutral. In tort law, for example, Holmes opposed strict liability, since it imposed damages upon people who had not willfully acted in a bad manner, and substituted for it the notion of negligence, the objective criterion of what a reasonable person would have done in the circumstances to avoid the accident. If a person had acted prudently and taken reasonable precautions (all of which could be determined through objective standards), then there should be no liability.

Similarly, contract law had long carried a burden of moralism, with breach viewed as an immoral act. Holmes tried to set contract law free by arguing that in some circumstances breach made good sense. As such, the aggrieved party should not be rewarded, but merely put in the position that he would have been had the contract been fulfilled; there would be no punitive damages assessed against the breacher.

In these areas, Holmes in many ways buttressed the world of classical legal thought. He supported the differentiation between public and private law, and tried to make private law as noncoercive as possible. People entered into agreements voluntarily, and the penalities for failing to live up to that agreement should be limited. Negligence, not the morality of strict liability, should govern tort law, and people who acted prudently should not be subject to damages. But Holmes also saw law as a social creation, one which, as he put it in *The Common Law*, "embodies the story of a nation's development through many centuries, and it cannot be dealt with as if it contained only the axioms and corollaries of a book of mathematics." Law grew, it was organic, and in this he rejected the formalism of classical legal thought.

The Emergence of the Modern Legal Profession

The very way in which men (and a very few women) learned and practiced the law reinforced the intellectual and social values of legal classicism. The Langdellian method changed law schools from vocational training institutes to scientific laboratories. They became true professional schools, and the better ones prided themselves on being national schools, drawing students from all over the country and teaching enduring principles rather than local rules of practice. Before long, the familiar modern law school had emerged, including stringent entrance requirements, the case method, course organization, large libraries that kept up to date with state and national reporters, and law journals, run by students, featuring articles on important points of law. This type of preparation fit in perfectly with the law profession's own desire to upgrade its stature and public image. To ensure quality education, the leading schools joined together in the Association of American Law Schools, which, along with the American Bar Association, controlled accreditation. After students took their LL.B., they then had to pass another examination given by the state bar, a device used primarily to regulate the number of new practitioners entering the field each year.

The professionalization of law education accompanied and complemented significant changes in the organization of law practice. Prior to the Civil War, the legal profession had fairly accurately reflected the social fabric of the times. Law offices had been small, staffed by an attorney and one or two clerks, or, in some cases, by two or three lawyers who, if not in actual partnership, at least shared office space and books. The problems they dealt with had been fairly simple and had concerned not so much conflicting interpretations of law as questions of fact. Compared to the economic and legal intricacies of the later nineteenth century, the facts had been simpler and more easily understandable; the intelligent layperson could understand the facts with as much clarity as the lawyer.

People came to attorneys only when all other recourse had failed, and they had to fight. The lawyer's duty, then, had been to play advocate for his client and to make the best legal representation possible. Given these demands, the successful lawyers had been the generalists; actually, there had been few specialists of any kind. A lawyer who hoped to earn a living in an expanding frontier society had to be competent in such diverse fields as land and criminal law, water rights, and equity.

By 1870, all this began to change; as society became more complex, it required a more complex law. One-to-one relationships gave way to multifaceted operations, and simple business yielded to large undertakings. Now it could be too expensive to go wrong, too costly to call the lawyer at the last minute, too wearing to fight a battle that would be taxing even if won. More and more lawyers found themselves consulted by clients on future actions, on what to do to avoid going to court. "A lawyer's chief business," said attorney Elihu Root, "is to keep his clients out of litigation."

This shift from advocate to counselor and the adjustment to the new requirements proved painful. It had been one thing to enter a case with all the facts available, and then sort out those that would be most helpful to the client's case. New modes of business operation, however, required the lawyer to pay close attention to economic trends and to evaluate developments in which he often lacked expertise. The creation of trusts and estates and corporate organizations called for planning and analysis of a large number of variables, including questions of economics, psychology, and labor, as well as business. The lawyer of the future, Holmes predicted in his famous essay, "The Path of the Law" (1897), would not be the lawbook scholar, but "the man of statistics and the master of economics."

The old-style generalist could normally handle almost any type of case. The post-Civil War era saw the emergence of the specialist, first in commercial law as a whole and then in particular aspects of it. Soon lawyers devoted their entire careers to trusts and estates or receiverships or stock issues. Big business needed all these skills, and, in some instances, they created their own in-house law offices, staffed with specialists in different areas. At the same time, large private firms developed, also staffed by specialists and subordinates, most of whom worked entirely on corporate problems.

To man these offices, law firms looked increasingly to the law schools, and especially to the more prestigious ones such as Harvard, Yale, and Columbia. The establishment of the student law reviews provided a fairly simple device to determine the brightest graduates, and "making" law review became a ticket to the large corporate law firms on Wall Street or their equivalents in Boston, Philadelphia, Chicago, and elsewhere. Although they had spent three years learning the principles of law, graduates still had to prove that they could apply what they had been taught to real situations; if not, they would be of no use to the firm or its clients. The large firms soon adopted a practice of taking on law school graduates for a period of years as "associates," during which time they would be taught the practical aspects of lawyering. For those who proved capable, a lucrative partnership awaited at the end of the apprenticeship; those who did not measure up would be let go.

Many law school graduates assumed that to prove their worth, they should master a particular specialty that was needed by the firm's clients. They soon became like all the other attorneys in the office—narrow specialists. This no doubt allowed them to provide better legal advice on particular problems, but they paid a price; very few lawyers could see beyond their particular niche. The earlier generalists had been admired as men of affairs; no one expected the specialists to know anything outside their narrow enclaves. Businessmen soon stopped asking their advice on what to do, and instead started demanding that attorneys find ways for them to do what they wanted. Lawyers thus abdicated their responsibility as moral instructors and confined their activity to devising the best way for corporate clients to effect certain ends, some of them of questionable legality. "Instead of being advisers" wrote Felix Frankfurter, "lawyers were collaborators in their clients' short-sightedness." The independent practitioner gave way to what many reviled as a "hired hand" working in a "law factory." "The practice of law," charged reform lawyer Louis D. Brandeis, "has become commercialized. It has been transformed from a profession to a business, and a hustling business at that."

Stung by criticisms such as these, lawyers took several steps to refurbish their image. In February 1870, a group of mainly old-line, well-to-do business lawyers established the Association of the Bar of the City of New York. At the organizational meeting, James Emott complained that lawyers had lost their reputation for independence. "We have become something of a multitude of individuals, engaged in the same business . . . [who] are and do simply what their employers desire." By banding together, they hoped to create and enforce standards of integrity that would win back the public's confidence. The association movement soon spread, with state and local bars organizing around the country, although how successfully it achieved its goals is open to question. For many years, the annual meetings of state and national bar associations heard speakers bemoan the condition of the profession.

One of the first steps taken to improve the profession's image was the reform of admission procedures. In many states, especially in the Midwest, an individual could become a lawyer without any formal training or examination. Even in Massachusetts, where the courts did maintain a regular procedure, the requirements were minimal: two examiners had each asked young Oliver Wendell Holmes a few questions; he answered them, paid his $5 fee, and was admitted to practice law in the Bay State. This laxity enabled many incompetent persons to open law offices, where they preyed on a gullible public. The bar associations took the lead in petitioning legislatures to tighten up admission requirements. By 1890, one-half the states required some minimal, formal training; the other states soon followed suit.

The higher qualifications undoubtedly benefited both bar and public by weeding out incompetents, but it proved a useful tool to keep out women, blacks, and ethnic minorities as well. Moreover, most lawyers still remained firmly attached to corporate work and interests, including the passionate defense of property. The establishment of bar associations did little to erase the public image of the lawyer as the robber baron's hired gun, a fact many lawyers recognized. At the 1906 meeting of the American Bar Association, James D. Andrews told his colleagues that "instead of client and lawyer the relation of employer and employee has been substituted. . . . A great many of our lawyers, those who are now exercising great weight and influence in the country, are employees."

There is also little evidence that the bar associations had as great an impact as their founders had hoped or their leaders claimed. The American Bar Association enlisted only a minority of the nation's lawyers; state and local bar groups attracted a

> If we examine ourselves closely, we shall find that, associated with much thankfulness there is yet a feeling of discontent, a feeling that we are not individually, nor collectively as a profession, all that we ought to be, a consciousness of unsatisfied desires, . . . a dream if you please, that there is for us lawyers a higher condition and a higher life that we nowhere see realized; in short, we find ourselves moved by the everlasting contrast, everywhere exhibited, between the ideal and the actual; and by that longing—the noblest which inhabits the human breast—of lifting up the actual to a nearer approach to the ideal.
>
> —James C. Carter, address to American Bar Association, 1890.

larger percentage, but hardly proved representative even at these levels. One examination of the proceedings of the bar associations from 1870 to 1930 found "a distinct aura of triviality and ineffectualness," and the few accomplishments limited to narrowly professional concerns. The larger issues remained unresolved, and as Willard Hurst noted, they "busied themselves with matters which they took up in isolation from the social context, and matters which were generally of secondary social importance." The important and effective work of the organized bar would not take place until after the First World War.

Conclusion

The mindset created by classical legal thought would dominate the constitutional, legal, and in some measure political environment until the mid-1930s. It had an internal cohesion that supported stability in a time of rapid change. The legal principles it enunciated, and the values it embraced, appealed to both past and future, the great principles of freedom, equality and vested rights developed before and during the Civil War, as well as the notion of individual opportunity, which seemed to be at the heart of the new economic order. But classical legal thought, while formalistic in many ways, was not sterile. Especially on the constitutional level it proved highly creative in developing the doctrines of substantive due process and freedom of contract.

It failed, however, to take into account individual rights other than that of property, and as a result had little to say about how the nation treated labor, women, and especially the former slaves. In that failing, it to a large extent echoed the national mindset as well. In the latter nineteenth century, the business of America, as one American president would later say, was business, and classical legal thought set up the parameters in which the constitutional and legal battles over how to deal with business would be fought.

For Further Reading

The best place to start is William M. Wiecek, *The Lost World of Classical Legal Thought: Law and Ideology in America, 1886–1937* (1998). How this ideology played out in the Supreme Court can be seen in Owen M. Fiss, *Troubled Beginnings of the Modern State, 1888–1910* (1993), volume 8 of the Holmes Devise, and in James W. Ely, Jr., *The Chief Justiceship of Melville W. Fuller, 1888–1910* (1995), a comparable volume in the University of South Carolina series edited by Herbert Johnson. Good overviews of American law include James Willard Hurst, *The Growth of American Law: The Law Makers* (1950); Lawrence M. Friedman, *A History of American Law* (1973), Part III; and Kermit Hall, *The Magic Mirror: Law in American History* (1989). The ideology in daily practice can be examined in Morton Horwitz, *The Transformation of American Law, 1870–1960: The Crisis of Legal Orthodoxy* (1992); and Herbert Hovenkamp, *Enterprise and American Law, 1836–1937* (1991). Among older works, students will find Grant Gilmore's *The Ages of American Law* (1977), both witty and stimulating. Morton White, *Social Thought in America: The Revolt Against Formalism* (1957); and Robert G. McCloskey, *American Conservatism in the Age of Enterprise, 1865–1910* (1964), both have useful sections on the law.

Substantive due process is treated in a number of works. See among others, Robert E. Riggs,

"Substantive Due Process in 1791," 1990 *Wisconsin Law Review* 941; Edward Keynes, *Liberty, Property, and Privacy: Toward a Jurisprudence of Substantive Due Process* (1996); Loren P. Beth, *The Development of the American Constitution, 1877–1917* (1971); William E. Swindler, *Court and Constitution in the Twentieth Century: The Old Legality, 1889–1932* (1969); and E. S. Corwin, *Liberty Against Government* (1948). See also, Corwin's pioneering article, "The Supreme Court and the Fourteenth Amendment," 7 *Michigan Law Review* 643 (1909), and Walton H. Hamilton, "The Path of Due Process of Law," in C. Read, ed., *The Constitution Reconsidered* (1938). The subject is also treated in the biographies of late nineteenth-century justices; see particularly, Michael J. Brodhead, *David J. Brewer: The Life of a Supreme Court Justice, 1837–1910* (1996); and Paul Kens, *Justice Stephen J. Field: Shaping Liberty from the Gold Rush to the Gilded Age* (1997). The property aspect of legal thought at this time is explicated in James W. Ely, Jr., *The Guardian of Every Other Right: A Constitutional History of Property Rights* (2nd ed., 1998).

Freedom of contract and its abuses were attacked in a famous article by Roscoe Pound, "Liberty of Contract," 18 *Yale Law Journal* 454 (1909). The free labor ideology and its relation to contractual freedom is brilliantly explored in Charles W. McCurdy, "The Roots of Liberty of Contract Reconsidered: Major Premises in the Law of Employment, 1867–1937," 1984 *Yearbook of the Supreme Court Historical Society 20* (1984). McCurdy has written a number of articles that take a fresh look at Supreme Court doctrines during this period; of special interest is "Justice Field and the Jurisprudence of Government-Business Relations: Some Parameters of Laissez-Faire Constitutionalism, 1863–1897," 61 *Journal of American History* 970 (1975). See also the works on the regulation of labor in the next chapter.

For the law writers, see Clyde E. Jacobs, *Law Writers and the Courts: The Influence of Thomas M. Cooley, Christopher M. Tiedeman, and John C. Dillon on American Constitutional Law* (1954). Alan Jones, *The Constitutional Conservatism of Thomas McIntyre Cooley: A Study in the History of Ideas* (1987) suggests that Cooley was never as reactionary as his admirers—and detractors—claimed.

The literature on Oliver Wendell Holmes, Jr., is enormous, and continues to grow apace. The best single biography is that by G. Edward White, *Justice Oliver Wendell Holmes: Law and the Inner Self* (1993). See also the two volumes of Mark DeWolf Howe's unfinished authorized biography, *Justice Oliver Wendell Holmes: The Shaping Years* (1957) and *Justice Oliver Wendell Holmes: The Proving Years* (1963). Robert W. Gordon, ed., *The Legacy of Oliver Wendell Holmes, Jr.* (1992) has some good recent essays on various aspects of his work.

Changes in legal education can be examined in two influential studies of the early twentieth century, Josef Redlich, *The Common Law and the Case Method in American University Law Schools* (1914); and Alfred Z. Reed, *Training for the Public Profession of the Law* (1921). See also Albert J. Harno, *Legal Education in the United States* (1953); and William C. Chase, *The American Law School and the Rise of Administrative Government* (1982), which highlights a particular weakness in the Langdellian method. Institutional histories, unfortunately, tend to be self-congratulatory, and this is true of Julius Goebel, Jr., ed., *A History of the School of Law, Columbia University* (1953); and Arthur E. Sutherland, *The Law at Harvard: A History of Men and Ideas, 1817–1967* (1967). For a realistic look at the Langdell reforms and their continuing impact, see William P. LaPiana, *Logic and Experience: The Origin of Modern American Legal Education* (1994).

Changes in legal practice are to be found in numerous places, not the least of which are firm and individual memoirs. See, among others, Robert T. Swaine, *The Cravath Firm* (1946); Walter K. Earle, *Mr. Shearman and Mr. Sterling and How They Grew* (1963); and Edward F. McClennan, "Louis D. Brandeis as a Lawyer," 33 *Massachusetts Law Quarterly 1* (1948). See also, Hurst, *The Law Makers*; and Gerard W. Gawalt, ed., *The New High Priests: Lawyers in Post-Civil War America* (1984). For the organization of the bar, see George Martin, *Causes and Con-*

flicts: The Centennial History of the Association of the Bar of the City of New York, 1870–1970 (1970); Edson R. Sutherland, *History of the American Bar Association* (1953); and Wayne K. Hobson, *The American Legal Profession and the Organizational Society, 1890–1930* (1986). The growing conservatism of lawyers and judges is well detailed in Arnold M. Paul, *Conservative Crisis and the Rule of Law: Attitudes of Bar and Bench, 1887–1895* (1960); and in a far more polemical fashion, in Benjamin R. Twiss, *Lawyers and the Constitution: How Laissez Faire Came to the Supreme Court* (1942).

For assessments of justices who contributed to legal classicism, see Jonathan Lurie, "Mr. Justice Bradley: A Reassessment," 16 *Seton Hall Law Review* 343 (1986); C. Peter Magrath, *Morrison R. Waite: The Triumph of Character* (1963); Loren Beth, *John Marshall Harlan: The Last Whig Justice* (1992); Linda C. A. Przybyszewski, *The Republic According to John Marshall Harlan* (1999); James W. Ely, Jr., "Melville W. Fuller Reconsidered," 1998 *Journal of the Supreme Court Historical Society* (#1) 35; and especially Paul Kens, *Justice Stephen Field* (1997).

24
The Regulation of Commerce, 1877–1914

THE PRACTICAL EFFECT of the new legal culture can best be seen in how courts responded to laws attempting to regulate commerce and labor (see next chapter). The new dispensation, with its emphasis on individualism and laissez-faire, looked askance at governmental interference in the new marketplace, despite the fact that from time immemorial, governments had established a variety of laws regulating how people did business with one another and under what conditions certain businesses could operate. But now the market had taken on a near sacred status, a place where liberty and opportunity could flourish, and where the state, at least in the eyes of social Darwinists and others, had no business.

Legal regulation of commerce dates back to ancient times; the ancient Israelites, Babylonians, and Romans all imposed some limits on how one could conduct business. Colonial and early national governments adopted numerous rules regulating public conveyances, the quality of products, and at times even the prices that could be charged for certain merchandise. In the latter part of the nineteenth century, however, industrial leaders called for laissez-faire, for the government to keep out of business and to leave the regulation of commerce to the "natural" laws of the marketplace. At the same time, the enormous power of large industries and utilities to affect the economy and people's lives led to demands for public control. The battles took place both in the legislatures and in the courts. During this period, the U.S. Supreme Court appeared to reverse a century of precedent, in which the Court had taken a broad view of commerce and of the government's power to regulate it. The opinions left many in the country with a sense that the nation's highest tribunal did not speak for all Americans, but only for the monied classes.

Farmers, Railroads, and Elevators

As they pushed across the continent in the nineteenth century, railroads totally transformed local markets. In the Great Lakes region, large boats combined with railroads to give Midwestern grain producers access to urban markets. Mechanical grain elevators, first introduced in the 1840s, facilitated the loading of river and canal barges, lake boats, and railroad cars. The elevators often belonged to the railroads, whose managers cared less for the well-being of the farmer than for the profitability of the rail systems. Before long, Midwestern farmers began to see themselves as victimized by Eastern financiers, who exacted exorbitant charges for storing and shipping produce, and they demanded that state legislatures control the rates.

Many farm problems resulted from conditions beyond the control of farmers, the railroads, or even the government; a crop failure in Europe, for example, could push up American grain rates, while a bumper crop there could just as easily send them plummeting. Farmers tended to ignore these impersonal global conditions and blamed their woes on financiers, who allegedly manipulated markets in order to keep profits high and farm income low.

Nevertheless, farmers and local shippers did have some legitimate complaints. The railroads would never have come into existence without the help and largesse of the state. In the early part of the century, the new industry had depended upon state charters to protect them from liability suits and to gain control of privately held lands through eminent domain. During the Civil War, Congress had provided charters for the transcontinental railroads, and in addition to significant monetary support also provided hundreds of thousands of acres of free land as an additional subsidy. Now, with government apparently doing nothing, railroads charged whatever the market would bear, and if competition along some lines required lower rates, profits could be boosted by setting higher tariffs on other routes. Local railroad agents used preferential rates, rebates to larger shippers, underweighing, underclassification, and other devices to get business; while these helped a few of the larger farmers and shippers, the smaller ones paid compensatingly higher rates as a result. The tariff schedule published by each line was no more than a base from which to bargain.

Common law had long held that common carriers had to serve all persons on reasonable terms and without undue favor, and that their methods of business, as well as their rates, could be governed by the state's police power and reviewed by the courts. Many of the early charters and statutes affecting railroads included provisions for regulating rates; although courts rarely interfered in this matter, the few cases all upheld the state's power. In *Beekman v. Saratoga and Schenectady Railroad Company* (1831), Chancellor James Wentworth of New York declared that

> the legislature may also from time to time, regulate the use of the franchise [corporate charter], and limit the amount of the toll which it shall be lawful to take, in the same

> manner as it may regulate the amount of tolls to be taken at a ferry, or for grinding at a mill, unless they have deprived themselves of that power by a legislative contract with the owners of a road.

Other state courts, as well as the U.S. Supreme Court, upheld this power of the states to regulate utilities and carriers, and in 1850, most of the railroad mileage of the country came under some form of statutory rate restriction. These, however, normally set maximum tolls and did not forbid a line from charging lower rates to any or all of its customers. Common law did not proscribe all discrimination, so long as the highest rate did not go beyond either the statutory level or the customary and usual amount. Price cutting, or favors to particular shippers, did not constitute a violation.

Munn v. Illinois

Farmers wanted the states to use their powers to regulate rates, and the Granger movement quickly embraced the cause. Originally a social and educational organization founded in 1867 by Oliver H. Kelly, the Patrons of Husbandry, or Grange, mushroomed to 1.5 million members by 1874. It promoted farmer-owned cooperatives and soon became involved in Midwestern politics as well. Blaming the railroads for their economic problems (which in fact resulted from the postwar collapse of foreign and domestic markets), the Grangers secured legislation in five states regulating charges for grain warehouses and railroads. The major case testing the Granger laws, *Munn v. Illinois* (1877), resulted from an Illinois statute fixing rates for grain warehouses in cities of 100,000 or more people. The only city in the state that size was Chicago, and the law really aimed at the monopoly that the nine elevator companies had established in the region's major terminus.

Chief Justice Morrison Waite's opinion noted that "from time immemorial" property "affected with a public interest" had been subject to public regulation, and that owners who entered such a field implicitly accepted regulation as one of the conditions under which they did business. On the face of it, Waite's opinion clearly upheld the state's power to regulate railroads and other public utilities, and his copious references to English and American legal history confirmed that such regulation had long been acknowledged as legitimate. Yet his opinion gave away much of the state's power that he intended to save.

Instead of restricting himself to precedent, which clearly supported the Granger laws, Waite attempted to answer all the various claims made by counsel for the elevator owners. The most creative of these arguments involved the Due Process Clause of the recently adopted Fourteenth Amendment. While the clause clearly indicated that procedures in court had to follow the accepted norms of the law, lawyers argued that an implicit "substantive due process" placed limits on the legislature insofar as it could pass laws that affected private property. While denying the Fourteenth Amendment due process argument, Waite admitted that "under some circumstances" the states might violate the clause; he thus conceded that a substantive due process right existed. His emphasis on property affected with a public interest implied that purely private business, which remained undefined, would be exempt. Furthermore, although the commerce involved could be classified as intrastate, and therefore subject to Illinois control, "We do not say that a case may not arise in which it will be found that a State, under the form of regulating its own affairs, has encroached upon the exclusive domain of Congress in respect to interstate commerce."

The chief justice thus laid out three paths by which businessmen and their lawyers could seek to avoid state regulation. First, the implication that a right to substantive due process existed led lawyers to flood the courts with suits seeking to declare it, until the Court finally confirmed due process as a substantive right in *Allgeyer v. Louisiana* (1897). Second, businesses sought to define themselves as wholly private and thus immune from control. Finally, business in general and railroads in particular claimed to be engaged in interstate commerce, which only Congress could regulate. Taken together, these arguments would be marshaled to practically strip the states of effective regulatory power over business.

Removal to Federal Courts

Although the decisions of the Supreme Court set the constitutional rules that lower federal and state courts must follow, one should keep in mind that throughout this period state courts handed down hundreds of decisions on local regulations. The trends toward consolidation and growth, however, led companies that did business in more than one state to try to escape both the difference in laws from state to state, as well as the varying degrees of regulation. Federal court judges, appointed for life tenure by a succession of conservative presidents, tended to be more favorable to business claims than state court judges, who often had to stand for election and thus tended to be more sympathetic to legislative efforts at regulation. As a result, businesses whenever possible tried to fight their battles against state regulation in federal courts.

The ability of the federal courts to intervene in state regulation derived in part from the Reconstruction era's removal laws. The 1875 law, in particular, is crucial to understanding the enormous power that federal courts wielded in economic matters for the next half-century. Although originally directed toward enforcement of Reconstruction legislation and civil rights, removal soon took on a different and not unintended purpose—the nationalization of the law. In the debate over the bill, Senator Matthew Hale Carpenter made it clear that the Republicans had this larger purpose in mind. The 1789 Judiciary Act, he noted, had been appropriate for a small nation of thirteen states. But now thirty-seven states comprised the Union, and the American people had "become totally changed in their methods of doing business. . . . The whole circumstances of the people, the necessities of our business, our situation, have totally and entirely changed."

At the time of the bill's passage, a number of states, especially in the Midwest, had already begun to enact regulatory measures to control big corporations and railroads. To avoid state courts, where these laws might be rigorously enforced, an attorney merely had to devise one claim among many that could be construed, no matter how tenuously, as involving a federal right or law, and the case could be removed to the more sympathetic environs of a federal court. There, operating under the permissive mandate of *Swift v. Tyson* (1842), judges could ignore state regulations or interpret them in such a way as to render them harmless to commercial interests. Justice Bradley, in the *Pacific Railroad Removal Cases* (1885), urged just such a broad reading of the law. "No cases are more appropriate to [federal] jurisdiction or more urgently call for its exercise than those which relate to . . . railroads extending into two or more states." As for the increased burden of cases on the federal system, Bradley had a simple answer: Let Congress create more courts and provide more judges. Within a short time, Congress did just that.

Business and financial interests welcomed the removal laws, and in general considered federal courts far more sympathetic to their views than state courts. This lesson had been learned during and after the Civil War in connection with suits involving bond repudiation. A number of frontier states and municipalities had competed for railroad lines by offering tax advantages and financial assistance through the issuance of bonds to underwrite construction. Population change and economic fluctuation, however, often thwarted the hopes of many small cities that dreamed of growing into prosperous railroad termini. Instead, they found themselves saddled with unneeded tracks and insufficient revenue to pay their debt obligations. Default on these bonds plagued banks and investment houses for years and cluttered state courts with countless lawsuits.

In 1862, the scene shifted to federal court, where the holders of bonds issued by the city of Dubuque, Iowa, sued for payment on their securities. Federal judges supposedly followed rules of decision that bound them to accept state court interpretations of state law. But in this matter there were conflicting state court decisions, some upholding bond repudiation and some condemning it. The district judge chose the former and in effect permitted a default on the Dubuque bonds. Holders of the now worthless paper appealed to the Supreme Court, which accepted the case in 1864.

In *Gelpcke v. Dubuque*, the Court not only overruled a state court on a matter of state law, but it construed the state law to require payment of the bonds. Moreover, in entering the judicial wilderness of municipal bond finance, the Supreme Court arrogated to itself the power to make uniform rules in an area previously considered the sole domain of the states. *Gelpcke* is as dramatic an assumption of power by the Court over state affairs as *Marbury* and *Dred Scott* had been for federal legislation.

Gelpcke assumed its full significance, however, when it was tied to Justice Story's 1842 opinion in *Swift v. Tyson*. There, Story had posited a "general commercial law" for federal judges to invoke in lieu of Section 34 of the 1789 Judiciary Act, which required federal courts to follow local law in diversity suits. With federal judges often proving far more conservative and sympathetic to business interests than their state counterparts, businesses flooded the federal courts with suits. The system always tended to favor the large corporations, whether cases involved tort suits arising out of accidents involving employees between 1870 and the adoption of workmen's compensation laws, or the insurance suits that followed. In nearly all of these thousands of cases, the corporations either won the cases outright, secured a dismissal, or forced a settlement on favorable terms. As Edward Purcell has shown, the legal system in effect conferred "a kind of de facto subsidy on business enterprise," not in the form of outright grants, but from "a variety of social, procedural and institutional factors that allowed corporations to impose steep discounts on the amounts they had to pay individual claimants to induce them to settle out of court." The situation also added to the general belief that courts favored the rich and powerful at the expense of the common people.

The Interstate Commerce Commission

The Granger laws proved ineffective in restoring farm prosperity, since, despite agrarian complaints, the railroads had never been the real culprit in depressing farm prices. Moreover, the simplistic views of early railroad critics such as the Grangers failed to take into account the complex economic issues of railroad regulation. Simply put, a railroad connecting two points is a natural monopoly; a single line can usually handle all of the freight and passenger traffic between those two points. But the largest costs of establishing that line are not the rolling stock or even the rails, but the acquisition of land, and then the construction and maintenance of the track. Theoretically, once these costs are covered, the rates charged to shippers ought to decrease as the volume of traffic increases. In railroading, size should mean economies of scale and cheaper rates. But since privately owned railroads also sought to maximize their profits, the public rarely saw the benefits of increased growth.

Instead, by the early 1880s, the catalog of discriminatory practices included pools, rate-fixing agreements, rebates, basing point systems (in which shippers had to pay freight to a specified terminal—even if their goods did not go that far—and additional freight if they went farther), and long haul-short haul differentials, in which per mile charges for shorter trips greatly exceeded those for longer runs. State commissions, even those granted investigatory and rate-fixing powers, proved unable to control the railroads.

Senate committee hearings in 1874 made clear the extent of state failure to regulate the nation's railroads and led to demands for some form of federal control. In 1878, the House of Representatives passed a bill establishing federal regulation, but a potent business lobby killed it in the Senate. Congress considered several other bills to the same effect, but despite a growing public outcry against the railroads, none of them came close to passage. Then in 1886, the Supreme Court, in *Wabash, St. Louis, and Pacific Railway Co. v. Illinois*, seriously retarded the states' ability to control rates.

Under a statute prohibiting long haul–short haul discrimination, Illinois had enjoined the railroad from charging more for freight shipped to New York City from Gilman, Illinois, than from Peoria, a distance 86 miles greater. Since most of the journey lay outside the Illinois borders, the state had obviously impinged on the federal interstate commerce power. Although the Court previously had ruled that states might act under concurrent authority when Congress had failed to legislate, those cases had

> Such businesses [railroads] are by nature monopolies. We certainly deceive ourselves in believing that competition can secure for the public fair treatment in such cases, or that laws compelling competition can ever be enforced. If it is for the interest of men to combine no law can make them compete. For all industries, therefore, which conform to the principle of increasing returns, the only question at issue is, whether society shall support an irresponsible, extra-legal monopoly, or a monopoly established by law and managed in the interest of the public.
>
> —Henry C. Adams, "The Relation of the State to Industrial Action" (1887)

all dealt with relatively local matters, such as pilot licenses for a harbor that handled some interstate traffic. Justice Samuel Miller conceded that a state, in regulating commerce within its borders, might legitimately affect some interstate commerce indirectly, but he pointed out that here the state had attempted to do directly what the Constitution expressly forbid. Since nearly all state regulations affected interstate commerce to some extent, the decision, as the Court recognized, seriously impaired all state control.

Spurred on by the *Wabash* decision, a Senate committee under Shelby Cullom of Illinois recommended a federal statute to regulate railroads. With public opinion now inflamed, Congress responded and, on February 4, 1887, passed the Interstate Commerce Act. The law prohibited rebates, rate-fixing agreements, pools, and long haul–short haul discrimination, and provided that all railroad charges should be reasonable and just. The bill did not define what "reasonable and just" meant, but left it to the new Interstate Commerce Commission (ICC), whose five members would be appointed by the president and confirmed by the Senate. Modeled on existing state regulatory bodies, the commission had the power to hear complaints, examine railroad records, hold hearings, and issue cease-and-desist orders against any line it found violating the law. The act did not give the ICC direct power to set rates, but implied that it could fix maximum tariffs through its power to issue orders against unreasonable tolls.

The creation of the ICC and its early relationship with the railroads has generated a great deal of conflicting scholarship. Business leaders in large part opposed any governmental efforts to regulate their operations. The chaotic conditions in the railroad industry resulting from overbuilding and cut-throat competition led at least some operators to see the ICC as a means of imposing order, and perhaps even proving itself friendly to railroad interests. But from a constitutional point of view, the Interstate Commerce Act undoubtedly ranks as the most important legislative enactment of the latter nineteenth century, for it introduced a new organ of government unforeseen by the Framers—the administrative agency. In the next hundred years, Congress would create dozens of administrative bodies, until they constituted what some argue is literally a fourth branch of government. Yet in the debate over the bill, scarcely a word was said about the constitutional legitimacy of a body that combined legislative, executive, and judicial functions.

Technically officials of the executive branch, ICC members were appointed by the president, but unlike other executive appointees, once confirmed by the Senate they held office for a fixed term, which often extended beyond that of the president who named them. They thus enjoyed an independence in office unknown to other government officers, with the exception of judges, who held tenure during "good behavior." The commission administered the law, an executive function, but through its powers to issue orders, which had the force of law, it also exercised legislative responsibility. And in holding hearings, taking evidence, and adjudicating conflict, the commission served as a court. Although it would be two decades before Congress created another administrative agency, the ICC became the model; its operations provided the initial building blocks of the entirely new subject of administrative law, with its own unique rules and procedures.

The commission obviously marked a departure from the strict separation of powers embodied in the Constitution, and the reason is not difficult to discern. The federal government could regulate railroads under its Commerce Clause powers, but to do so required a knowledge beyond the normal range of political experience. Determining rate structures and evaluating schedules and other rail operations required special expertise and ongoing familiarity with the industry; only experts could untangle the mysteries of railroad economics and make rules to carry out legislative policy effectively. Neither the Congress nor the president has ever given up control of areas in which they felt competent to act, but, recognizing the growing complexity of modern society, they have willingly delegated not only the execution of policy but even some aspects of policymaking to technical experts.

The Courts and the ICC

The judiciary opposed this trend, however, and for the next half-century it fought against and questioned the necessity for administrative agencies. At first, the justices seemed uncertain about just how much power the commission could legitimately exercise, but soon they embarked on a campaign to limit its authority. In *Cincinnati, New Orleans and Texas Pacific Railway Co. v. Interstate Commerce Commission* (1896), the Court, speaking through Justice George Shiras, announced that nothing in the Interstate Commerce Act "expressly or by necessary implication" gave the commission power to fix rates. As for the commission's arguments that it had the power to determine reasonable and just rates, the Court interpreted that to mean that the commission could gather facts on the issue, but fact-finding and rate-making constituted separate functions.

A year later, the Court took an even narrower view in *Interstate Commerce Commission v. Cincinnati, New Orleans and Texas Pacific Railway Co* (1897). The ICC had held hearings on the railroad's rates, determined them to be unreasonable, and ordered the line to put a new schedule into effect. When the railway appealed, Justice David Brewer denied that the commission had any power over rates. He cited one statute after another to show that when legislatures intended to give agencies authority to set rates, they granted such powers in clear and unequivocal terms. The Interstate Commerce Act included no such language, and one could not infer important powers from imprecise terms. Brewer went on to note that fixing rates constituted a legislative function, and for Congress to assign it to an executive agency violated separation of powers.

Following this case, the ICC could do little more than investigate rates and declare them unreasonable. It could then issue a cease-and-desist order against the existing rates and apply to the courts if the carrier refused to obey the order. But with railroads more than willing to go to court (where they faced sympathetic judges) and with far greater legal resources than the commission could muster, the agency recognized that this approach would only tie it up in perpetual legal battles. For the while, the ICC essentially abandoned any effort at rate-making.

Shortly afterward, in *Interstate Commerce Commission v. Alabama Midland Railway Co.* (1897), the Court also restricted the commission's investigatory powers. Congress had given the commission extensive fact-finding authority, and, to prevent railroads from appealing questions of fact to the courts, it had provided that judges had to accept the ICC's findings of fact as conclusive. Congress had hoped to prevent ju-

> My impression would be that, in looking at the matter from a railroad point of view exclusively, it would not be a wise thing to undertake to abolish the Commission. The attempt would not be likely to succeed—if it did not succeed and were made on the ground of the inefficiency and uselessness of the Commission, the result would very probably be giving it the powers it now lacks. The Commission, as its functions have now been limited by the Courts, is, or can be made of great use to the railroads. It satisfies the popular clamor for a government supervision of railroads, at the same time that the supervision is almost entirely nominal. Further, the older such a commission gets to be, the more inclined it will be to take the business and railroad view of things. It thus becomes a sort of barrier between the railroad corporations and the people and a sort of protection against hasty and crude legislation hostile to railroad interests. The Commission costs something, of course. But so long as its powers are advisory merely, for the reasons just stated, it strikes me it is well worth the money. The part of wisdom is not to destroy the Commission, but to utilize it.
>
> —Richard S. Olney to Charles C. Perkins, December 2, 1892

dicial reinvestigation, but the Supreme Court ignored this provision. Since the act had designated the federal circuit courts as courts of equity to hear appeals from commission orders—and a court of equity always has the right to look anew at the facts—the decision gave the carriers an effective weapon against the commission. By withholding data at the initial hearings, a line could introduce "new" evidence before the circuit court to "prove" that the ICC had not taken all the facts into account.

Justice Harlan's dissent in this case accurately summed up what the Court had done. The various decisions, he declared, go "far to make that Commission a useless body for all practical purposes, and to defeat many of the important objects designed to be accomplished by the various enactments of Congress, relating to interstate commerce." In fact, the ICC had been reduced to little more than an information bureau, its powers stripped away by a hostile Court. Between 1897 and 1906, the agency won only one major case out of sixteen before the high bench.

Courts and Rate-Making

While the Court crippled the ICC, it also limited state regulatory agencies as well. The *Munn* case had held that rate-making was a legitimate legislative function and beyond judicial scrutiny; if the legislature abused this power, Chief Justice Waite had said, "the people must resort to the polls" and not to the courts. State statutes explicitly establishing rate-making authority could not be construed away, nor had the carriers been able to have the Court reverse *Munn*. In 1890, however, railroad lawyers hit upon an indirect approach to bring the judiciary into the state rate-making process in *Chicago, Milwaukee and St. Paul Railway Co. v. Minnesota*.

The Minnesota statute made its railroad commission the final judge of the reasonableness of rates. But counsel for the carrier argued that "it is always a judicial question as to whether a statute is repugnant to provisions of the constitution." Did the courts wish to abdicate their constitutionally prescribed role of review in the legislative process? The Court, already leery of the mixed nature of administrative agencies, took the bait, and by a 6 to 3 vote, struck down the state scheme. Justice Samuel Blatchford practically echoed the railroad counsel's brief when he declared:

> The question of the reasonableness of a rate . . . is eminently a question for judicial investigation, requiring due process of law for its determination. If the company is deprived of the power of charging rates for the use of its property, and such deprivation takes place in the absence of an investigation by judicial machinery, it is deprived of the lawful use of its property, and thus, in substance and effect, of the property itself, without due process of law.

The Court's attitude toward rate-making cannot be characterized as completely hostile from the start. In *Budd v. New York* (1892) the justices, by a 6–3 majority, upheld a New York statute establishing maximum rates for grain storage. The majority distinguished this case from the Minnesota case because in New York the legislature, and not a commission, had fixed the rates. In addition, reaffirming the earlier *Munn* ruling, the majority held that rates set by a legislature would not be subject to judicial review. This evoked a strong dissent from Justice David Brewer, who attacked both the rationale of *Munn* as well as the notion that confiscation of property by a legislature in the form of rate-making differed at all from confiscation by a commission. The logic of this argument soon won over the Court. In *Reagan v. Farmer's Loan & Trust Co.* (1894), Brewer, for a unanimous bench, declared that courts could inquire into the reasonableness of rates set by either a legislature or a commission, a position reaffirmed two years later in *Covington and Lexington Turnpike Road Company v. Sandford* (1896).

Blatchford, in referring to due process in the Minnesota case, did not in this case mean substantive due process, but rather the traditional procedural safeguards that attached to public takings of private property. Once the Court adopted substantive due process in 1897, it wasted no time in applying the concept to rate regulation in the important case of *Smyth v. Ames* in 1898. Nebraska had passed a law setting intrastate rail rates, and the Court held the rates unconstitutional because they did not allow a "fair return on a fair valuation of the investment." The Court found that the unreasonable state-mandated rates deprived the owners of a substantive right in their property, the right to a fair return.

Smyth v. Ames may be one of the worst mistakes the Court ever made, for it plunged the judiciary into the business of second-guessing both legislatures and administrative agencies on the complex issue of rate structures. The concept of a "fair return on a fair value" is a cost-plus formula, subject to all the difficulties associated with determining the original costs and the various other items to be added. In practice, as business historian Thomas McCraw noted, "these problems promoted the rise of ingenious accounting methods by corporations, all calculated to maximize revenues in the face of regulatory limits on percentage rates of return. At worst, they made the process of rate regulation a ritualistic charade." Beyond that, the concept of a "fair return" is strictly neither a legal nor an economic term. Rather, it is an ethical question: how much should investors be allowed to earn on property devoted to public use, such as railroads or other utilities? What factors should be taken into account, and how should they be weighted? Should the state, which passed special legislation that made the creation of the railroad possible, be able to help determine how much this new public utility could charge for its services?

Neither John Marshall Harlan, who wrote the opinion, nor his brethren had more than a smattering of economic expertise. Harlan listed several matters to be evaluated, including the original cost of construction, permanent improvements, market value of stocks and bonds, cost of replacement, projected earnings capacity, and operating expenses—and then added that "we do not say that there may not be other matters to be regarded in estimating the value of the property." This formula, no matter how interpreted, was full of ambiguity. The Court offered no guidance as to how much weight, if any, should be assigned to each item. Legislatures, recognizing the complexity of the issue, had delegated this evaluation to experts, but the justices now said that the courts would review the work of either legislature or administrative agency, even though few judges had even a modicum of the required knowledge to make an educated judgment. For the next forty years, courts floundered in this morass before finally abandoning the effort. In that time, they severely hampered the effectiveness of the rate-making agencies and gave railroads one more weapon to fight regulation. If carriers did not get the rates they wanted from the legislatures or commissions, they appealed to the courts, claiming that unreasonable rates deprived them of their property without due process of law. In most cases, the courts rewarded the railroads for their perseverance by granting them rate increases.

Congress Strengthens the ICC

The Court's decisions of the 1890s left the ICC, as Harlan had noted, practically useless as an instrument of effective regulation. The evils that the commission had been created to combat not only continued but grew worse, as overbuilt rail systems struggled to secure sufficient operating revenue. In a situation of intense competition, the railroads themselves began to find laissez faire less than a blessing, and they gradually came to favor giving up some of their competitive prerogatives in return for stable rates. They assumed that if they stopped fighting the ICC and began to cooperate with it, the agency would become less adversarial and more of an ally in securing a stable market. Many business leaders, in fact, began to advocate order in the market, and this energy supported the burst of reform during Theodore Roosevelt's administration. Pushed from one side by reformers clamoring against railroad abuses and from the other side by operators seeking stability, Congress moved to revive the ICC and give it effective powers.

The Elkins Act of 1903 struck at rebates by making any deviation from published schedules unlawful and permitted prosecution of both the carrier and the shipper. In December 1905, President Roosevelt called on Congress to enact effective railroad regulation, and the House of Representatives quickly responded in February 1906 by passing a measure introduced by William P. Hepburn of Iowa. The Hepburn bill gave the ICC power to review and, if necessary, revise railroad rates, and then to enforce these rates by its own orders. It also allowed only limited judicial review of commission findings of fact. Although courts could not be denied the power to declare rates confiscatory or unreasonable, they could not review facts, determine questions of policy, or try the issues anew.

The Hepburn bill ran into stiff opposition in the Senate, where conservatives lined up against it. Joseph Foraker of Ohio claimed that only courts could fix rates; the legislature did not have this power and therefore could not delegate it to an agency that Congress created. Other senators complained that the agency's responsibilities violated separation of powers, and that it had failed to do anything useful in nearly twenty years. At first Roosevelt backed the so-called Long amendment, which narrowed judicial review of commission findings, but then, evidently at the request of the Senate's Republican leaders, he withdrew his support in favor of a vaguely worded proposal that in effect left the courts to determine the extent of their power. The measure thus passed the Senate, and after the House acquiesced in the changes, the bill became law at the end of June 1906. The Hepburn Act gave the ICC definite rate-setting authority and shifted the burden of appeal to the courts onto the carriers. Nevertheless, if the courts continued to insist on broad review, the commission would remain as moribund as ever.

The Court Acquiesces

In a series of cases beginning in 1907, the Supreme Court did a complete turnabout in its treatment of the ICC. In *Illinois Central Railroad Co. v. Interstate Commerce Commission* (1907), the Court acquiesced to the intent of the original 1887 law, as well as to the earliest version of the Hepburn bill, by declaring that it would not reinvestigate all the facts of a case on appeal. Three years later, in *Interstate Commerce Commission v. Illinois Central Railroad Co.* (1910), the Court fully confirmed the basic ideas of administrative regulation. Justice Edward White ruled that in reviewing commission orders, it would look only at whether the agency had the necessary constitutional authority, whether Congress had delegated the appropriate powers, and whether the action constituted a reasonable exercise of its power. The Court would not second-guess policy decisions. Judicial review did not permit the Court to "usurp merely administrative functions by setting aside a lawful administrative order upon our conception as to whether the administrative power has been wisely exercised." If the agency had the power, the Court would not question the wisdom of its policies. Now the commission's orders had to be taken seriously, without the escape route of constant appeals to courts over issues of fact and jurisdiction, and the commission could effectively carry out its mandate of regulation. The final triumph of the ICC came with the Court's validation of the agency's power to regulate intrastate rates when they directly affected interstate commerce (*Shreveport Rate Cases* [1914]).

Why the Supreme Court reversed itself so dramatically in so short a time is difficult to say. Perhaps it recognized the folly of *Smyth v. Ames* once the justices tried to sort through the intricacies of rate-setting. Changes in Court personnel certainly made a difference. Between 1902 and 1912, seven new appointees came on the bench, including Oliver Wendell Holmes, Jr., and Charles Evans Hughes. Only Joseph McKenna, who had joined the Court in 1898, and Edward D. White remained from the Court of the late 1890s, and White, more sympathetic to the exercise of national power, replaced the conservative Melville Fuller as Chief Justice in 1910. Moreover, these later opinions meshed perfectly with other decisions of this time strengthening the power of the federal government over the states in a variety of areas.

The Growth of Monopolies

The second great effort by the government to regulate the national economy came in response to the growing problem of trusts and monopoly. The decades following the Civil War witnessed a marked trend toward the consolidation of firms in particular industries, as well as an expansion of factory production. John D. Rockefeller's Standard Oil empire controlled between 90 and 95 percent of the oil refining capacity of the country by 1879, and in other major industries as well, one or two large firms frequently dominated the market. Often these giants grew out of the merger of dozens of smaller companies. Between 1898 and the end of 1901, 2,274 firms disappeared as a result of mergers, and merger capitalization totaled over $5.4 billion. U.S. Steel, created in 1901 by J. P. Morgan and capitalized at over $1 billion, was only the biggest and most striking example of consolidation.

Well into the 1880s, the prevailing economic thought had denied the inevitability or the naturalness of large concentrations of capital. Much of the debate over monopoly in the 1870s and early 1880s had focused on railroads, which economists treated as a special case. But with the emergence of Standard Oil and other large companies, the question changed from what to do about so-called natural monopolies such as railroads (which critics hoped could be regulated through state agencies or the ICC) and large manufacturing corporations, for which no tradition of regulation existed. In the 1880s, in addition to Standard Oil, five other nationwide trusts came into being—the American Cotton Oil Trust (1884), the National Linseed Oil Trust (1885), the National Lead Trust (1887), and the Whiskey and Sugar Trusts (1889).

The emergence of monopolies and trusts sparked a national debate on the economy early in the 1880s, which intensified in volume until World War I. Opponents charged big business with destroying individual opportunity, enslaving labor, engaging in immoral practices, and bilking the consumer. Many thoughtful people who did not consider themselves enemies of business worried about the danger monopolies posed to a democratic society, especially the unduly concentrated wealth and power of the large firms, because of the influence they could exert on government. But the legal defenders of the corporations found strong support among economists, many of whom now justified the emergence of large-scale enterprise as inevitable.

Champions of the new giants maintained they had resulted from natural causes. S. C. T. Dodd, one of Standard Oil's lawyers, praised the technical superiority of consolidated operations and described them as the catalytic agents in "the march of civilization." Using the current Social Darwinist philosophy, business apologists dismissed smaller firms elbowed out of the way as "weaklings": monopolies represented the survival of the fittest in the economic jungle. When reformers called for government action, business leaders called for laissez-faire. Although business had accepted government subsidies in the form of road-building, protective tariffs, and land grants for railroads, the business community agreed almost unanimously that governmental re-

> All our education and habit of mind make us believe in competition. We have been taught to regard it as a natural if not a necessary condition of a healthful business life. We look with satisfaction on whatever favors it, and with distrust on whatever hinders it. We accept almost without reserve the theory of Ricardo, that, under open competition in a free market, the value of different goods will tend to be proportional to their cost of production.
>
> —Arthur T. Hadley, *Railroad Transportation* (1885)

straints would constitute interference in the natural economic laws and would lead to disaster. Lawmakers, business advocates argued, should defer to constitutional guaranties of property rights, while their opponents claimed the interdependence of private rights and the public interest, in which private property had to give way to the public needs of the citizenry.

The common law, however, had long opposed monopoly. As early as 1602, English judges in the *Monopolies Case* had accepted the economic arguments that monopolies led to higher costs and poorer quality for the consumer and cut off entrepreneurial opportunity. English courts recognized that the Crown or Parliament could grant certain monopolies, but without governmental approval, "the sole exercise of any known trade throughout England is a complete monopoly, and against the policy of law" (*Mitchel v. Reynolds* [1711]). As a result, contracts whereby one party agreed not to compete constituted restraint of trade and could not be enforced. Agreements to fix prices and wages were similarly illegal; concerted action by workers to better their lot also fell under the common law bans against conspiracies.

In response to public outcry against the trusts, several states codified the common law in statutory form in the 1880s. But no one state could hope to control the problem, for by then the large companies operated in national markets. Standard Oil of Ohio, the foundation stone of the Rockefeller empire, could not under state law own property outside Ohio. So it acquired companies elsewhere and placed them under a trustee. Since the death of the trustee would endanger this scheme, Rockefeller created a new trust in 1882; all the stockholders of the various Standard Oil interests conveyed their shares to nine trustees, receiving trust certificates in return. The nine trustees operated the different companies in near-total insulation from state rules on corporations. When the Ohio Supreme Court ordered the Standard Oil Trust dissolved in 1892, Rockefeller merely created a holding company, Standard Oil of New Jersey, under that state's exceedingly liberal corporation law. Only a national law, reformers claimed, would be able to rein in such abuses.

The Sherman Act

Congress had two models from which it could choose in attempting to regulate large corporations. It could have chosen, under its commerce powers, to require federal incorporation of firms doing interstate business. By defining strict standards for behavior and limits on what corporations could legally do, this would have established a uniform national policy and eliminated the problem of corporations seeking liberal charters in Delaware or New Jersey that allowed them to do almost anything they wanted. If corporations acted in violation of charter provisions, or went beyond the limits imposed by them, the government could then have brought *quo warranto* actions against them. This would have been a fairly strict and effective means of controlling corporations, and for this reason reformers continued to seek a federal incorporation law for the next twenty years.

Instead, Congress chose what many termed a weaker model for dealing with the trusts, perhaps betraying a lack of enthusiasm for the whole enterprise, or perhaps indicating a reluctance to create a huge federal agency to issue corporate charters to interstate companies and then to supervise the behavior of those firms. The Sherman Antitrust Act of 1890, which remains the basis for nearly all federal antitrust prosecutions to this day, outlawed every "contract, combination in the form of trust or otherwise, or conspiracy in restraint of trade or commerce." The act nowhere defined what any of these terms meant, nor did it set up any specialized agency to interpret or enforce the statute. Enforcement of this law, like that of other federal laws, would be the responsibility of the executive, in this case the Justice Department, and interpretation would be left to the courts. There is evidence that Congress, which passed the bill almost unanimously, acted more to assuage public feeling than in hopes of securing effective legislation.

The wording of the statute is so vague perhaps because Congress did not really know what it wanted to do. The bill specifically embodied the traditional common law prescriptions against restraint of trade, yet the legislators knew that in the highly competitive atmosphere of the late nineteenth century, all successful businesses restricted trade to some extent. The statute nominally outlawed combinations, which reformers claimed had done the most to limit commerce, yet the relatively short clauses did not indicate if *all* combinations and monopolies, or only *some*, would be prohibited. Did the law apply only to future companies, or did it refer to already existing monopolies as well? As Lawrence Friedman has noted, the act "hardly reflected any coherent economic theory at all." Certainly the legislators did not intend to retard economic growth, yet the fastest growing parts of the economy in 1890 appeared to be those areas with the greatest merger activity. It appears as if the Congress, having made the legislative gesture to quiet public concerns, preferred that the courts now decide what, if anything, the Sherman Act really meant.

The *Knight* Case

In constitutional terms, some questions existed as to the extent of congressional power over manufacturing. Congress certainly had authority over commerce, and decisions reaching back to the Marshall Court supported a broad interpretation of what commerce included. But a more recent line of decisions had differentiated between manufacturing and commerce. Senator James George of Mississippi, in the debate over the Sherman bill, claimed that Congress could not regulate manufacturing, an essentially local enterprise. Several other senators agreed, and many probusiness congressmen evidently voted for the bill, expecting the Supreme Court to nullify it. Given the fact that the Court had already crippled the ICC, they saw little to fear from the Sherman Act.

Nor did the Court disappoint them in its first pronouncement on the law in *United States v. E. C. Knight Co.* (1895). The government sought dissolution of the American Sugar Refining Company, through which a handful of firms controlled over 90 percent of the nation's sugar refining capacity. The Justice Department argued that the agreements used to secure this monopoly substantially restrained trade and caused higher prices for the consumer. The Court, led by Chief Justice Melville Fuller, found against the government, and drew a severe line between commerce and manufacturing. "Commerce succeeds to manufacturing," he declared, "and is not a part of it." The Sherman Act applied only to firms in interstate commerce, and while the defendants had conspired to monopolize the production of sugar, under the terms of the law that by itself could not be held illegal. While Congress might be able to reach manufacturing that had a *direct* impact on interstate commerce, such an influence had not been demonstrated in this case. Fuller denied that the federal power could be invoked to control indirect effects, for then "comparatively little of business operations would be left for state control."

The *Knight* decision has been criticized for the Court's apparent blindness to the realities of modern industrial economics, for turning its back on Marshall's broad interpretation of commerce as an organic whole, and for its nitpicking reading of the Sherman Act and the government's brief. Yet there is a more positive way to interpret Fuller's opinion. He sought not to lessen the federal commerce power—in fact, he hinted that if the government had focused on its effects in restraining trade rather than on the manufacturing monopoly, the decision might have gone in its favor—but to strengthen the states and encourage them to carry out their responsibilities. States, and not the federal government, issued corporate charters, and states, therefore, had the authority to revoke these licenses if the companies acted ultra vires, beyond the powers granted to them. Fuller believed in the federal system and wanted the states to regulate the firms they chartered; if they did not, as he noted, the federal government would soon control everything.

This was laudable, but unrealistic, logic. Technically, one can separate not only manufacturing from commerce, but also production of raw resources from fabrication and transportation from retail trade. But when integrated companies like Standard Oil and U.S. Steel controlled all aspects of production and distribution, from mining raw materials to final sale, technical distinctions made no sense. As for the states policing their creations, pressure for the Sherman Act had arisen because it had become quite plain that the states could not do the job. So long as a company could get a charter from Delaware or New Jersey, which placed practically no restrictions on what a firm could do, other states had only limited authority to control what these firms did within their borders, and no power beyond. The Court eventually realized this, and before long took a different tack. But Fuller's dichotomy between manufacturing and commerce remained a powerful tool for later justices, who would use it to thwart legislative programs with which they disagreed.

The Court Changes Its Mind

The Court began its retreat from the implications of *Knight* in *Addystone Pipe & Steel Co. v. United States* in 1899. A group of manufacturers had formed the Southern Associated Pipe Works and agreed to divide the market into territories, fix the price of pipes, and charge a bonus of $2 per ton, to be divided among the members. Circuit Court judge William Howard Taft, in a well-reasoned opinion, recognized what the high court had refused to see: the intimate connection between manufacturing and commerce. The pipe manufacturers had joined together to control prices of goods that, no matter where produced, were sold in an interstate market. Taft dismissed the companies' contention that the association could not be deemed a monopoly because its members between them accounted for less than a third of the nation's pipe-making capacity. Within the area they served they controlled the market, and the Sherman Act applied not only to national monopolies, but also to "every combination" that restrained trade. The Supreme Court affirmed Taft's decision, emphasizing the effect of the pool on interstate commerce, the element the government had failed to show in the sugar case.

The government successfully exploited this approach a few years later in a meatpacking case, *Swift & Co. v. United States* (1905). In his majority opinion, Justice Holmes got around the manufacturing/commerce distinction by inventing the "stream of commerce" theory in order to show the effect of monopolies on interstate commerce. The stockyard constituted a "throat" through which commerce passed, and therefore came within the reach of Congress. The refusal of the Court simply to abandon Fuller's dichotomy led to the awkward reasoning that a stockyard was part of commerce, while the slaughterhouse next door, to which it sent the livestock, remained manufacturing, and therefore outside commerce. *Swift* marked a broadened view of commerce, which, Holmes declared, must be looked at "not as a technical legal conception but a practical one, drawn from the course of business." But the Court still remained ambivalent, aware of the realities of the situation, yet unwilling to recognize the implications for the exercise of federal power.

The *Northern Securities* Case

By the time of *Swift*, the executive branch had adopted a far different view of the antitrust law. The McKinley administration had accepted *Knight* as essentially nullifying the Sherman Act, and did not initiate a single case against industrial combinations. When Theodore Roosevelt entered office after the assassination of McKinley in September 1901, he and Attorney General Philander C. Knox decided that the law still retained vitality, and they launched several suits. Looking for a test case that they felt confident they could win, Roosevelt and Knox went after the Northern Securities Company, a railroad combination recently created by James J. Hill, J. P. Morgan, and E. H. Harriman, and capitalized at $400 million.

The Harriman interests controlled the Union Pacific Railroad; the Hill-Morgan group owned the Northern Pacific and Great Northern lines and had just bought the Burlington line to secure a terminal in Chicago. Harriman had been rebuffed in his request to join in the Burlington, so he tried to buy a controlling interest in the Northern Pacific, sending the railroad securities market into a panic. To stabilize the situation, the principal figures agreed to a compromise: they established the Northern Securities Company to hold Great Northern, Northern Pacific, and Burlington stock and to operate the three lines as an integrated system, with both Hill and Harriman interests represented on the board of directors. The Justice Department successfully brought a suit in equity in circuit court to dissolve Northern Securities, and the case went on appeal to the Supreme Court. In 1904, by a 5 to 4 vote, the Court ruled in *Northern Securities Co. v. United States* that the firm constituted an unlawful combination under the terms of the Sherman Act.

The company, relying on *Knight*, claimed first that the merger represented nothing more than a stock transfer, which did not constitute commerce. Second, the corporation had done nothing illegal under the terms of its New Jersey charter and, since state law controlled the incorporation of businesses, application of the Sherman Act would violate the Tenth Amendment by unconstitutionally intruding federal power into a domain reserved to the states.

Justice Harlan rejected both propositions. Whatever the technical aspects of the stock arrangement, the purpose had been to restrain competition in the railroad industry; the Sherman Act outlawed all contracts, combinations, or conspiracies that directly or indirectly affected commerce. As for the states' rights argument, Harlan dismissed it as a false assertion that a state could grant immunity from federal law. The idea that a state could prevent the national government from exercising its constitutional powers could not "be entertained for a moment."

Although the government won the case—launching Roosevelt's reputation as a "trustbuster"—the narrowness of the vote indicated that the Court had not yet found a comfortable means of evaluating the Sherman Act. Moreover, the dissenting opinion by Oliver Wendell Holmes not only called attention to this problem, but questioned the intent of Congress in passing the law. Privately, Holmes considered the Sherman Act "a humbug, based on economic ignorance and incompetence." Congress wanted to preserve competition from overweening power, but it also wanted to preserve the benefits of consolidation. As he noted in his dissent, although the statute said "every" combination, Congress could not possibly have meant that, since that would "disintegrate society so far as it could into individual atoms." All business, he noted, to some extent "monopolizes whatever business it does," whether within one state or between states. In attempting to discern congressional intent, Holmes hinted that perhaps the law should apply only to those contracts, combinations, or conspiracies that *unreasonably* restrained trade, and not to those in which restraint proved ancillary to the major purpose of securing greater efficiency. As for Northern Securities, Holmes thought the consolidation of the lines made sense and did not restrain trade.

The Rule of Reason

The so-called rule of reason hinted at by Holmes gave the Court the key it had been seeking, and seven years later a unanimous bench adopted it in *Standard Oil Co. v. United States* (1911). The justices needed some decisional rule that would avoid the Charybdis of the *Knight* decision and the Scylla of a literal construction, in which every combination would be outlawed. Certainly the interpretation meshed well with Theodore Roosevelt's distinction between good and bad trusts, and it satisfied large segments of both the business community and reform groups.

Chief Justice Edward White ruled that Standard Oil had violated the Sherman Act and should be dissolved, but he gave over the bulk of his opinion to an explanation of how the Court had reached its decision and the meaning of the rule of reason. The Sherman Act would now be interpreted to mean that only unreasonable restraint of trade would be outlawed. The general words of the statute left their particular application open to interpretation, and judges had traditionally been called upon to interpret the meaning of the law. Judicial discretion had, of course, long been part of the judging process, and White insisted that it would not become an excuse for an activism in which the courts substituted their own judgment for that of the legislature. Rather, the rule of reason would allow courts to carry out the legislative intent without falling into the trap of literalism that Holmes had warned against in his *Northern Securities* dissent, whereby they either had to rule all or none of the combinations illegal.

Two weeks later, in *United States v. American Tobacco Co.*, the Court (again speaking through White) reiterated the rule of reason in holding the company guilty of restraint of trade. But it refused to order the complete dissolution of the trust, finding combination in this field not totally unreasonable. Justice Harlan, who concurred in the result in both cases, dissented from the adoption of the rule; Congress had not been obscure, he said, but had in fact been quite clear in its intent, namely, to break up *every* contract, combination, or conspiracy restraining trade. Looking to the future, he warned that the rule of reason would throw businesses into confusion, for without a clear rule, they would never know whether they had acted reasonably or not. Even worse, the Court had departed from its traditional and proper role of strictly construing the law, by substituting its own views for those of Congress in determining which combinations could be dissolved and which allowed to continue.

Harlan's fears proved well grounded. The rule of reason, while certainly a more flexible approach than the Court's earlier either/or interpretation, did generate confusion over what exactly the Sherman law meant. Within a few years, Congress would pass the Clayton Act and create the Federal Trade Commission to clarify its intent and give business some guidance. The Court itself has never been able to define the rule of reason with great precision. It came closest in *National Society of Professional Engineers v. United States* (1978), when it claimed that it has always "adhered to the position that the inquiry mandated by the Rule of Reason is whether the challenged agreement is one that promotes competition or one that suppresses competition." But even with all the modern tools of economic and market analysis to aid them, courts in the end must still make a subjective judgment as to what constitutes promotion or suppression of competition. The inherent ambivalence in antitrust policy between a desire for competition and a fear of the results of that competition has never been resolved.

The Income Tax

The Interstate Commerce and Sherman acts represented two efforts by the federal government to respond to the new realities of the industrial age. In 1894, Congress took another step by imposing an income tax. With the exception of the Civil War years, for the first century of its existence, the government had relied primarily on tariffs and excise taxes to meet its needs. The Constitution, while granting Congress the power to lay and collect taxes (Article I, Section 8), had prohibited any "Capitation, or other direct, Tax . . . unless in Proportion to the Census" (Article I, Section 9). That provision had been inserted at the insistence of Southern states, which feared that the government would tax their lands and slaves while allowing Northern commercial interests to go untaxed. "Direct taxes" generally meant poll taxes and levies on real property. Since the Constitution required that direct taxes be apportioned by population, a tax on realty raised seemingly insurmountable problems of fairness, since states with high numbers of working people without property holdings would have to pay a disproportionate share of the tax. Fortunately, revenues from customs, excises, and the sale of public lands more than met the needs of government until the Civil War.

The war spawned a variety of taxes to finance the Union effort. In 1861, Congress imposed an apportioned tax on land, as well as the first income tax. The following year, it enacted an inheritance tax, revised the income tax schedule, and repealed the land tax. The 1862 law taxed income on a progressive scale of 3 percent on incomes up to $10,000 and 5 percent on incomes above $10,000, with a $600 exemption. In 1864, the tax rates were increased to 5 percent on incomes to $5,000, 7.5 percent to $10,000, and 20 percent above that level. The income tax provided between 15 and 20 percent of the federal government's revenue. At the end of the war, Congress bowed to pressure from financial interests and first reduced and then repealed the income and inheritance taxes. From 1868 to 1913, excise taxes on liquor and tobacco constituted the major source of federal revenue.

The demand for an income tax, however, remained alive as part of labor and agrarian programs. The Populist party platform of 1892 urged an income tax, while the Democrats, who swept into office with Grover Cleveland that year, called for significant reductions in the tariff. The depression of 1893 and the accompanying decline in tariff receipts led to a series of government deficits, and Congress had to find some new source of income. The agrarian bloc, led by the young William Jennings Bryan, pushed vigorously for an income tax against the protests of business spokesmen, who decried the tax as "socialism, communism and devilism." Farm and labor interests won out, and the Wilson–Gorman Tariff of 1894 provided for a 2 percent tax on all individual and corporate incomes, with a $4,000 exemption for the former. Personal property received by gift or inheritance also counted as income.

From an economic standpoint, the income tax represented a logical response to significant shifts in the nature of the country's wealth. At the time of the Constitutional Convention, land and personal property had been the chief form of wealth, and the requirement of apportioning direct taxes had effectively put realty beyond the reach of federal taxation. After 1865, however, new forms of wealth such as stocks, bonds, and other nontangible assets expanded enormously and provided an opportunity for revenue through a manageable tax plan. Business and financial interests viewed the new tax with an alarm bordering on panic. In the midst of a severe depression, with labor troubles often breaking into violence and the unemployed of Coxey's "army" marching on Washington, the tax seemed one more example of the dangers of radicalism, socialism, populism—the upper classes did not bother to differentiate among them.

The income tax came before the Supreme Court within a few months in *Pollock v. Farmers' Loan & Trust Co.* (1895), a collusive suit by a stockholder to prevent payment of the tax, which cleverly got around an 1867 prohibition against suits to restrain the assessment or collection of taxes. Joseph Choate of New York and former Senator George Edmunds of Vermont headed the impressive battery of lawyers who importuned the Court to save the country from communism. In his oral argument, with copious references to the Philadelphia Convention, American and English history, and economics, Choate and his colleagues attacked the income tax on three major points. First, it violated the constitutional ban on direct taxes, since a tax on income from property was the same thing as taxing the property itself. Second, the $4,000 exemption violated Article I, Section 8, which required that all taxes be uniform. Finally the law violated states' rights by taxing the income from state and municipal bonds.

Judicial precedent, however, lay with proponents of the tax. All previous cases dealing with the question of direct taxes indicated that only capitation (poll) taxes and specific duties on land met the constitutional definition of a direct tax. *Hylton v. United States* (1796) had sustained a 1794 tax on carriages, and Justice Paterson, who had been at the Philadelphia Convention, noted that the Framers had intended a narrow definition of direct taxes. In *Pacific Insurance Co. v. Soule* (1868), the Court had upheld as an excise tax the 1864 tax on the business of insurance companies, and in *Veazie Bank v. Fenno* (1869), it had approved the tax on nonfederal bank notes. In *Scholey v. Rew* (1874), the Court had confirmed a succession tax as an excise and had specified that direct taxes did not include levies on income. In the most important precedent, *Springer v. United States*, decided in 1880, the Court had sustained the constitutionality of the 1864 income tax; direct taxes, it had ruled, consisted only of capitation and real estate taxes. To many observers, the debate over an income tax had centered on whether it constituted good public policy; its constitutionality had been assumed.

The precedents, however, proved of no avail. Chief Justice Fuller dismissed them as "a century of error," and by a vote of 6 to 2, the Court invalidated the main tax as a direct but unapportioned tax on land. A tax on income from land, the Chief Justice declared, was the same as taxing the land itself. The Court also struck down, this time by a unanimous vote of the eight participating justices, the tax on income from state and municipal bonds as invading the power of a state to borrow money. The Court divided 4 to 4 on three other questions: whether a tax on income from personal property constituted a direct tax; whether the invalidity of the section on income from property voided all of the tax provisions; and whether, if any part of the tax could be considered indirect, it still failed for want of uniformity.

> The [income tax] is communistic in its purposes and tendencies, and is defended here upon principles as communistic, socialistic—what shall I call them—populistic as ever have been addressed to any political assembly in the world. . . . No member of this court will live long enough to hear a case which will involve a question of more importance than this, the preservation of the fundamental rights of private property and equality before the law, and the ability of the people of these United States to rely upon the guaranties of the Constitution.
>
> —Joseph Choate in oral argument to the Court in the *Income Tax Cases*

Normally, when the Court splits evenly, it leaves the lower court decision in place, but these questions had to be fully resolved, so the Court quickly granted the application for a rehearing. Justice Howell Jackson, who had been ill during the first case (he would die within a few months), returned to participate in the second *Pollock* case. Although he voted to sustain the tax, one of the earlier dissenting justices now joined with Fuller and the antitax group to invalidate the entire plan as violating the constitutional ban on direct taxes. Fuller's opinion again distorted history and precedent. The rights of property, and not a strict construction of the Constitution, obviously informed both the majority and minority opinions.

All four members of the minority entered dissents, but only that of Justice Henry Brown—who could hardly be considered a radical—openly expressed the political rather than the judicial concerns that had motivated the Court. "The decision involves nothing less than a surrender of the taxing power to the moneyed class," he asserted. "Even the spectre of socialism is conjured up to frighten Congress from laying taxes upon the people in proportion to their ability to pay them."

The Court had obviously overreached itself, and the extent of the Court's action astonished even conservative opinion. Although major eastern and midwestern papers applauded the decision, the majority of the country reacted in disbelief and anger. Newspapers throughout the Midwest, South, and West portrayed the ruling as an unjust and selfish class decision. The *Augusta Chronicle* claimed it "robs the masses . . . for the few who own the wealth of the country." The *New York World* charged that "Great and rich corporations, by hiring the ablest lawyers in the land and fighting against a petty tax upon superfluity as other men have fought for their liberties and their lives, have secured the exemption of wealth from paying its just share toward the support of the government that protects it."

Before the end of 1895, a constitutional amendment to overturn *Pollock* and legitimize income taxes had been introduced into Congress. But even beyond the issue of the tax, the Court, in declaring an act of Congress unconstitutional—and by the narrowest possible margin—had raised a number of troubling questions. What limits, if any, existed on the Court's power? The traditional justification for judicial review, that the Court did no more than clarify the terms of the Constitution, fell to pieces by the Court's arrogant disregard of a century of precedents and its distortions of history. The Court had frustrated the legislative and popular will, and between 1895 and 1912, every session of Congress saw proposals designed to reduce the power of the courts, limit the terms of judges, and give Congress the power to override Court decisions.

These proposals all failed, and for more than a decade, the proposed income tax amendment languished in Congress, blocked by a powerful conservative bloc. Then in 1909, a combination of Democrats and Insurgent Republicans threatened to reenact the income tax as part of a new tariff bill. Senate Republican leader Nelson Aldrich (father-in-law of John D. Rockefeller, Jr.) secured a deal with President Taft, whereby Taft would veto any such measure in return for which Aldrich would secure passage of an income tax amendment in the Congress. Aldrich counted on the difficulty of the amendment process to ensure the proposal's defeat, but he badly misjudged the temper of the country. By early 1913, forty-two states had ratified the Sixteenth Amendment, six more than the required thirty-six.

The Wilson administration wrote an income tax into the Underwood Tariff, and would rely heavily on the levy to finance World War I. Even before the Amendment's passage, however, the Court backed off from the extreme position of *Pollock* and upheld taxes barely distinguishable from income taxes. Few cases epitomized the Court's allegiance to vested rights as did *Pollock*, and few cases gave as much fuel to critics of the judiciary who derided judges as interested only in the protection of property and not in human rights.

Conclusion

Given the pervasive sentiment among federal judges in favor of property rights and opposition to governmental interference with those rights, it is hardly surprising that initial efforts to regulate the new economic order ran into judicial opposition. The key characteristics of classical legal thought had developed out of an earlier economic model, but came into power as that economy disappeared, to be replaced by one marked by large-scale, multistate corporations. The courts grudgingly accepted the need for some restraints on big business and some regulation of rates charged by railroads and other public utilities, and they especially disliked the new administrative commission.

Eventually, the courts met the legislatures at least half-way, agreeing that in some instances monopolies could be restrained or broken up and that commissions could set rates, subject to judicial oversight. But as the country entered the twentieth century, the popular mind saw courts as bastions of reaction and protectors of vested interest, a portrait not fully accurate but not totally wrong either.

For Further Reading

All studies of the Gilded Age deal extensively with the rise of big business. One of the best studies is the classic by Robert H. Wiebe, *The Search for Order, 1877–1920* (1966); but see also John H. Garraty, *The New Commonwealth, 1877–1890* (1968); and Glen Porter, *The Rise of Big Business, 1860–1910* (1973). Morton Keller, *Affairs of State: Public Life in Late Nineteenth Century America* (1977) provides a fascinating analysis of the interaction of law, politics, and government.

For constitutional overviews of the efforts to regulate the economy, see the relevant sections in Owen M. Fiss, *Troubled Beginnings of the Modern State, 1888–1910* (1993); and James W. Ely, Jr., *The Chief Justiceship of Melville W. Fuller, 1888–1910* (1995); as well as Loren P. Beth, *The Development of the American Constitution, 1877–1917* (1971). Books that look particularly at the interaction of law and economics are Herbert Hovenkamp, *Enterprise and American Law, 1836–1937* (1991); Morton Keller, *Regulating a New Economy: Public Policy and Economic Change in America, 1900–1933* (1990); and Morton J. Horwitz, *The Transformation of American Law, 1870–1960* (1992).

For railroad regulation, see the chapter on Charles Francis Adams in Thomas K. McCraw, *Prophets of Regulation* (1984); as well as Jordan Jay Hellman, *Competition and Railroad Price Discrimination: Legal Precedent and Economic Policy* (1968), which explores the contradictory goals of regulation. See also, George H. Miller, *Railroads and the Granger Laws* (1973); and the relevant chapters in Stephen Skowronek, ed., *Building a New American State: the Expan-*

sion of National Administrative Capacity, 1877–1920 (1982). Gabriel Kolko, *Railroad and Regulation, 1877–1916* (1965), first set forth the thesis that railroads themselves sought regulation in order to secure stability, an idea further explored in Edward A. Purcell, Jr., "Ideas and Interests: Businessmen and the Interstate Commerce Commission," 54 *Journal of American History* 561 (1967). Albro Martin, *Enterprise Denied: Origins of the Decline of American Railroads, 1897–1917* (1971) stands alone as a polemic against regulation. The ICC's problems are analyzed in Ari and Olive Hoogenboom, *A History of the Interstate Commerce Commission: From Panacea to Palliative* (1976). The impact railroads had on constitutional development is explored in Richard C. Cortner, *The Iron Horse and the Constitution: The Railroads and the Transformation of the Fourteenth Amendment* (1993). In this regard see also James W. Ely, Jr., "The Railroad Question Revisited: *Chicago, Milwaukee & St. Paul Railway v. Minnesota* and Constitutional Limits on State Regulations," 12 *Great Plains Quarterly* 121 (1992).

Federal diversity jurisdiction and questions of removal are covered in Tony A. Freyer, *Forums of Order: The Federal Courts and Business in American History* (1979); and Edward A. Purcell, Jr., *Litigation and Inequality: Federal Diversity Jurisdiction in Industrial America, 1870–1958* (1992).

Antitrust law and its development are discussed in Hans Thorelli, *The Federal Anti-Trust Policy: Origination of an American Tradition* (1955); Robert H. Bork, *The Antitrust Paradox: A Policy at War with Itself* (1978); and William Letwin, *Law and Economic Policy in America: The Evolution of the Sherman Antitrust Act* (1965). A comparative study is Tony A. Freyer, *Regulating Big Business: Antitrust in Great Britain and America, 1880–1990* (1992). The same author looks at the connection between antitrust and constitutional thought in "Economic Liberty, Antitrust, and the Constitution, 1880–1925," in Ellen Frankel Paul and Howard Dickman, eds., *Liberty, Property, and Government* (1989). See also, James May, "Antitrust in the Formative Era: Political and Economic Theory in Constitutional and Antitrust Analysis, 1880–1918," 50 *Ohio State Law Journal* 257 (1989).

Bruce Bringhurst, *Antitrust and the Oil Monopoly: The Standard Oil Cases, 1890–1911* (1979), traces the tangled skein of the nation's most notorious monopoly. Charles L. McCurdy, "The Knight Sugar Decision of 1895 and the Modernization of American Corporate Law, 1869–1903," 53 *Business History Review* 304 (1979), argues that the case represents an effort by the Court to compel states to enforce their corporate laws. Barry Cushman examines a key element in Commerce Clause cases in "A Stream of Legal Consciousness: The Current of Commerce Doctrine from *Swift* to *Jones & Laughlin*," 61 *Fordham Law Review* 105 (1992).

For the income tax, see Robert Stanley, *Dimensions of Law in the Service of Order: Origins of the Federal Income Tax, 1861–1913* (1993); and Jerold L. Waltman, *Political Origins of the U.S. Income Tax* (1985). For the income tax cases, see Gerald E. Eggert, "Richard Olney and the Income Tax Cases," 48 *Mississippi Valley Historical Review* 24 (1961), and David G. Farrelly, "Justice Harlan's Dissent in the Pollock Case," 24 *Southern California Law Review* 175 (1951).

25

Protective Legislation and the Police Power

The Progressive Agenda • Conservative Opposition • The Police Power • Child Labor and State Courts • Child Labor in the Supreme Court • Hours for Women Workers • A Feminist Critique of Muller *• Separating Factory from Home • Hours on Public Works • Hours for Men • The* Lochner *Decision • Wage Regulation • Employers' Liability • Workmen's Compensation • Federal Employers' Liability • The* Debs *Case • The Courts and Labor Unions • For Further Reading*

THE INDUSTRIAL REVOLUTION in the United States brought enormous material prosperity, but with great cost in human misery. At the turn of the century, reformers pushed through various remedies to protect workers, especially women and children, from the harmful effects of factory life. This protective legislation called for extensive state intrusion into business affairs and the alteration of traditional assumptions about the relations between employer and employee. The reform program directly challenged one of the core elements of classical legal thought—freedom of contract. Progressives had no desire to overturn the capitalist system; they sought merely to eliminate its malignant excesses, while preserving the benefits they acknowledged that free enterprises had brought to the nation. Progressives differed greatly in their methods and goals, however, and it is more accurate to talk of a plenitude of Progressive reforms than of a unified ideology. Yet some common themes undergirded their efforts; they all sought to use the power of government in promoting their programs, and in some areas it is possible to talk of a Progressive agenda.

Given the probusiness, laissez-faire attitude of the courts at this time, reformers expected difficulties from the judiciary, and in some well-publicized cases, conservative judges indeed struck down some of the new laws. Yet despite the lingering perception that courts opposed and frustrated protective legislation, the facts are just the opposite. Moreover, in this area one can trace the interaction between state and federal courts in dealing with legislative responses to industrial problems. In only one area—recognition of union rights—did reformers fail to achieve their program.

The Progressive Agenda

The Progressive litany began with the basic assumption that industrialization had so altered traditional economic and social relationships as to endanger not only the health and safety of workers, but the moral and political bases of democratic society as well. One study after another detailed the long hours, poor health, and lack of recreational and educational opportunities for workers—men, women, and children—who often toiled twelve or more hours a day. How, they asked, could democracy survive without an educated citizenry able and interested in taking part in public life?

The general legislative outline of the reform program emerged fairly early: minimum standards to reduce the incidence of child labor; maximum hours for women and children and for men employed in dangerous occupations; payment of wages in cash, to eliminate the abuse of the scrip system and the company store; establishment of a minimum wage, first for women and children, and then for men; elimination of employers' common law defenses against liability for job-related accidents; creation of workmen's compensation plans to insure against death and disability in the factory; and laws supporting labor's right to organize and bargain collectively. As historian Richard Hofstadter concluded, "it was expected that the [neutral] state, dealing out even-handed justice, would meet the gravest complaints. Industrial society was to be humanized through the law."

The reformers, operating primarily in the state legislatures, succeeded in securing much of this program, and in the first two decades of the twentieth century, they significantly transformed the environment of industrial workers. How Progressives secured their victories, however, concerns us less than the opposition they faced within the legal community, where conservatives appealed to freedom of contract and due process in an effort to defeat the reformers.

Conservative Opposition

Conservatives opposed to governmental interference to protect workers used the Fourteenth Amendment's Due Process Clause to erect a barrier that legislation could not breach. Thomas Cooley left no doubt that he relied on the courts to protect the nation against kind-hearted but ill-advised attempts by legislatures to meddle with the social or economic order. Similarly, Christopher Tiedeman invoked "the power of constitutional limitations to protect private rights against the radical experimentation of social reformers."

Courts seemed to take this advice seriously. One judge noted disapprovingly the "sentiment favorable to paternalism in matters of legislation," while Judge Robert Earl, speaking for a unanimous New York Court of Appeals in *In re Jacobs* (1885), attacked a state law prohibiting the manufacture of cigars in tenements as trammeling "the application of [the worker's] industry and the disposition of his labor, and thus, . . . it deprives him of his property and some portion of his personal liberty." A Georgia judge declared that he knew "of no right more precious, and one which laboring men ought to guard with more vigilance, than the right to fix by contract the terms upon which their labor shall be engaged." Statements such as these led to a general view in the popular press of a judiciary that was unalterably opposed to reform.

Recently, scholars have begun to revise the view of a reactionary bench resolutely blocking progress. Although one can certainly find cases in which judges struck down protective legislation and invoked sacred doctrines to defend property, a closer look discloses that famous cases like *Lochner v. New York* (1905) and *Adair v. United States* (1908) were a minority. Common law typically operates after the fact, responding to rather than anticipating new situations and new institutions. As society underwent significant changes in the latter nineteenth century, all agencies of government had to deal with these new facts. Even if judges had been prescient, it is unlikely they would have rushed to approve a wide spectrum of innovative laws, especially since many proposals ran counter to long-established common law principles. Fortunately for reformers, however, the law did provide a rationale for protective legislation under the states' police powers.

The Police Power

Progressives and conservatives alike recognized that as part of its sovereign powers, a state could override both individual and property rights in order to preserve the health, safety, and welfare of the people. Conservatives conceded the existence of this authority, but argued for severe limits on its use. Progressives, on the other hand, saw the power as far more extensive, allowing the state to intervene actively on behalf of the oppressed. The police power, declared Oliver Wendell Holmes in *Noble State Bank v. Haskell* (1911), "may be put forth in aid of what is sanctioned by usage, or held by the prevailing morality, or strong and preponderant opinion to be greatly and immediately necessary to the public welfare." By that reading, the police power could reach almost anything the legislature wished to regulate.

While it is generally assumed that the state exercised relatively little police power in the nineteenth century, in fact quite the opposite is true. While the state took only a few small steps into regulating labor, state and local governments exercised a vast amount of oversight in areas such as fire restrictions, public safety, local market conditions, regulation of public space, as well as the traditional areas of public health and morality. The common law, even while it zealously guarded property rights, also contained a vision of a well-regulated society, with the state, and not the market, serving as the regulator.

In the police power lay the key to constitutional approval or denial of protective legislation. If courts took a narrow view of the power, reform measures faced tough sledding; when judges adopted a more expansive interpretation, Progressives could expect a sympathetic hearing. Merely declaring that certain policies promoted the public good did not by itself bring a statute within the sanction of the police power. The law had to relate specifically to a clearly recognized health or safety objective; some courts demanded that the law be "reasonable" as well. Not only did there have to be a threat to the public welfare, but the response by the legislature had to appear appropriate in the eyes of the court.

Two things remained clear to reformers. First, freedom of contract was not absolute. Courts had long put restrictions not only on contract but on other liberties as well. Not even the most ardent advocates of laissez-faire denied that the state had, in the police power, the tool and the obligation to prevent individuals from exercising their own liberty in a way that abused the rights of others or harmed the health, safety, and welfare of society. Second, in looking at the conditions spawned by industrialization, Progressives found exactly those dangers that they believed justified police regulation to mitigate social evils.

To see how the Progressive reforms fared in court, we shall find it easier to examine them topically. We should bear in mind that the first efforts to secure protective legislation began in the 1880s, and that the Progressive impulse played itself out by the end of World War I. The judicial response in most of these areas displayed a general pattern of initial hostility to protective legislation, followed by acceptance through common law adaptation of the meaning of the police power.

Child Labor and State Courts

Suits challenging laws restricting child labor were among the earliest cases to come before the courts, and judges had to choose between two legal traditions. On the one hand, English common law gave parents an almost unlimited right to the custody, services, and earnings of their minor children. As late as 1936, twenty-five states still had laws on their books specifically declaring the right of parents to the earnings of their offspring. Because minors could not contract by themselves, fathers (and, later, mothers) could contract out their children's labor; in doing so, the parents enjoyed nearly all the protection of freedom to contract. On the other hand, the common law also recognized that children came under the power of the state as *parens patriae*, that is, as the sovereign and guardian of persons under a legal disability. This originally narrow power expanded over the years to cover such areas as the obligations of parents to support their children, to furnish them with a means of earning a living, and, in some states, to provide a basic education. But well into the nineteenth century, few people questioned the morality or, for the poor, the necessity of children working.

The view of child labor as a preventable evil had begun to attract support in the mid-nineteenth century, and the drive first to restrict and then to abolish child labor picked up momentum in the 1880s. While the nascent labor unions consistently opposed child workers because they undercut the wage structure, reformers generated support among the general public for regulation by publicizing the dangerous conditions in mines and factories, as well as the long hours young children labored. By 1900, thirty-eight states had adopted some protective legislation, although nearly all the laws suffered from inadequate enforcement. Reformers had difficulty establishing appropriate regulatory agencies or getting assemblies to vote money for sufficient inspectors, but they did not have any trouble in securing approval from the courts on the constitutionality of the laws themselves.

By 1896, the authoritative *Handbook of the Labor Law of the United States* by Frederic J. Stimson noted the proliferation of child labor statutes and almost in passing commented that "these laws are, of course, constitutional." Rulings from the very conservative New York high court upholding such legislation bore out legal scholar Ernst Freund's judgment that even conservative judges who "are inclined to condemn paternal legislation would concede that such paternal control may be exercised over children." In fact, not a single state court invalidated child labor regulations; arguments about freedom of contract, parental rights, and class legislation found no sympathy from state judges. As the Oregon high court ruled in *State v. Shorey* (1906): "It is competent for the state to forbid the employment of children in certain callings merely because it believes such prohibition to be for their best interest. . . . Such legislation is not an unlawful interference with the parents' control over the child or right to its labor, nor with the liberty of the child."

Child Labor in the Supreme Court

Child labor legislation enjoyed such wide support that only one case testing a state law ever reached the U.S. Supreme Court. Justice Charles Evans Hughes set forth an expansive interpretation of the police power as it related to child labor in a two-page unanimous opinion in *Sturges & Burns Manufacturing Co. v. Beauchamp* (1913). He dismissed the employer's argument that strict liability for determining the child's age denied due process: if the child looked older than sixteen and claimed to be so, it unfairly penalized the employer for believing the statement. Hughes responded that the imposition of absolute requirements of that sort had long been a familiar exercise of the protective power of government. When it came to shielding children from harm, the legislative judgment carried very far.

However, even though the courts sustained *state* child labor legislation, part of the judiciary's reputation for conservatism rested on two later child labor cases in which the Supreme Court struck down *federal* statutes. Both cases came at the end of the Progressive era, and by then the general attitude of the Court as well as its personnel had changed. (Ironically, the judges named by three Progressive presidents—Roosevelt, Taft and Wilson—proved with few exceptions to be as conservative on issues of economic regulation as their predecessors. In some ways this points up the fact that for all of the reforms proposed by and even enacted during the period of 1901–1917, progressivism was at heart a conservative movement, and its adherents opposed much of what would later be the liberal state.)

Because not all states adopted child labor statutes—and large discrepancies existed among those that had—reformers called for a federal statute to ensure minimal standards nationwide. The Wilson administration responded with the Child Labor Act of 1916. Congress relied on its interstate commerce power, which had been given fairly broad meaning by the Court in efforts to police lottery tickets, impure food and drugs, and even sexual immorality (see Chapter 26). The Child Labor Act prohibited the transportation and sale in interstate commerce of goods from factories where children under sixteen worked more than eight hours a day or six days a week.

So widespread was support for banning child labor that it came as a shock to the country when the Court, by a 5 to 4 vote, struck down the act in *Hammer v. Dagenhart* on June 3, 1918. Justice William Day, speaking for the majority, based his decision on the old distinction between commerce and manufacturing. He conceded that Congress, by its control over commerce, could reach manufacturing on occasions when the commerce furthered harmful results: Congress could use the commerce power to prevent the manufacturing of impure food and drugs, for example. But here the products themselves were not intrinsically harmful; Congress had intended to regulate child labor, which Day categorized as totally local in nature and therefore beyond the reach of the Commerce Clause. As to the government's argument that Congress wanted to close interstate commerce to prevent unfair competition from states having less protective legislation, Day denied that the Constitution gave the federal government the power to coerce the states in the exercise of their police powers over local trade and manufacture. Such power had always been reserved to the states by the Tenth Amendment, which the conservative majority now erected as a substantive barrier to federal control over commerce.

In his dissent, Justice Holmes agreed that Congress could not directly regulate factories, but he argued that since the Constitution granted Congress the power over interstate commerce, its use of that power could not be fettered by any indirect effects it had on production. Precedent, he claimed, clearly supported a broad reading of the Commerce Clause. As for Day's contention that the goods produced by child labor were not intrinsically harmful, Holmes noted that all civilized countries agreed that "premature and excessive child labor" constituted an evil. The majority's reasoning struck him as saying that prohibition "is permissible as against strong drink but not as against the product of ruined lives." Holmes also denied Day's contention that only the states could exercise police power over manufacturing, asserting that "the national welfare as understood by Congress may require a different attitude within its sphere from that of some self-seeking State. It seems to me entirely constitutional for Congress to enforce its understanding by all the means at its command."

Reaction to the decision proved so overwhelmingly unfavorable that Congress responded with a second Child Labor Act less than nine months later. This time the legislature relied on the taxing power and imposed heavy duties on goods introduced into interstate commerce by firms employing child labor. Congress felt itself on sure constitutional footing, since the Court had consistently held, in such cases as *Veazie Bank v. Fenno* (1869), and more recently in *McCray v. United States* (1904), that the broad reach of the taxing power precluded the judiciary from looking behind the tax to evaluate the motive.

Nevertheless, in *Bailey v. Drexel Furniture Co.* (1922), the Court struck down the statute as an invasion of an exclusive state function, this time by an 8 to 1 vote. Chief Justice William Howard Taft denied that the Court had gone behind the tax to judge intent; the justices had found the law unconstitutional because Congress had tried to use the tax not as a revenue measure but as a criminal penalty, a power beyond its authority. Extolling the dual nature of the federal system, Taft's opinion repeated and enlarged on the traditional arguments of laissez-faire, declaring that if the Court permitted the law to stand, it would break down the traditional limits on congressional authority imposed by the Tenth Amendment. Even Holmes and Brandeis joined the majority, not out of sympathy for Taft's conservatism, but because they too believed that Congress had abused its taxing power. Not until 1941, in *United States v. Darby*, did the Court grant Congress the power to control labor conditions, when it overruled *Hammer v. Dagenhart* and adopted a broad reading of the Commerce Clause. But at no time did the Supreme Court, or the state courts, deny to the *states* the authority to control child labor under their police powers.

Hours for Women Workers

The special consideration given to children opened the door to a second area of protective legislation—the regulation of hours for another legally disadvantaged group, women. By emphasizing the special restraints on women as well as their unique status as "mothers of the race," Progressives sought to establish a beachhead, as it were, before striking out in pursuit of their larger goal, an eight-hour day for all workers.

By the 1890s, the call for an eight-hour day had become a standard demand of organized labor. In 1899, American workers averaged more than fifty-seven hours per week on the job; a decade later, the figure had declined by only two and a half hours. It is little wonder that by 1918, forty-three states, Puerto Rico, and the District of Columbia had enacted statutory limits on working hours. For analytical purposes, these laws can be grouped into three major categories: hours of women; hours of laborers on public works; and hours of men in special occupations. (Hours for children workers were often tied to compulsory school attendance laws and other restrictions on child labor.)

The earliest case dealing with hours for women arose in Massachusetts. In 1874, the Supreme Judicial Court upheld a law prohibiting employment of women for more than sixty hours a week (*Commonwealth v. Hamilton Manufacturing Company*). In a short opinion, the court brushed aside employers' arguments that the statute violated freedom of contract and impinged on the rights granted to the corporation in its charter. The court found the law a valid exercise of the police power. "The principle has been so frequently recognized in the Commonwealth," the court concluded, "that reference to decisions is unnecessary." Although *Hamilton Manufacturing* would be cited in nearly every case involving women's hours, one wishes that the learned judges had spelled out their reasoning in more detail or at least had cited the "unnecessary" precedents. A suspicion lingers that the court decided the case more on an intuitive rather than on an analytical basis, a situation not unknown in the common law.

Ritchie v. People (1895) at least did not evade the issue. In one of the most condemned state court decisions of the period, the Illinois Supreme Court struck down an 1893 statute limiting women's hours in factories or workshops to no more than eight per day and forty-eight per week. Judge Benjamin Magruder conceded the extensive reach of the police power, but denied that this particular law had any relation to the comfort, health, or safety of society. It merely discriminated against women and denied them the equal rights to contract that men enjoyed. A distinction based merely on sex could not be deemed reasonable, according to the court, and therefore could not stand. Before one lauds this opinion as a forerunner of modern feminism, one should recall that this same Illinois court found that women could be denied the right to practice law simply because of their gender (*Bradwell v. Illinois* [1873]). Conservative courts used equal protection when it suited their purpose, and ignored it otherwise.

Ritchie became a model for courts opposed to protective legislation: they subjected the police power to tests of directness and reasonability and then found the laws lacking in those areas. In opposition to the police power, they set up a constitutional right, sometimes substantive due process but more often freedom of contract, which they held as controlling in the particular instance.

The public in general condemned *Ritchie*, as well as *People v. Williams* (1907), a similar ruling by New York's high court, which denied the legislature the power to make special laws for women. In other states, every women's hours statute received state court approval (except in Colorado, where the Court did not deny the legislative power, but invalidated a particular law on technical grounds). A typical decision came in *State v. Muller* (1906), an Oregon case that upheld a law limiting women working in factories and laundries to no more than ten hours a day. Oregon Chief Justice Robert Bean noted that any labor contract is "subject to such reasonable limitations as are essential to the peace, health, welfare and good order of the community." The legislature had made a policy decision to protect women workers by limiting their hours. He found nothing unreasonable in that belief, nor could the court find any violation of the constitutional rights of either employer or employee.

Unlike employers in earlier decisions, Curt Muller, the defendant laundry owner, decided to appeal to the U.S. Supreme Court, believing that its 1905 decision in *Lochner v. New York*, which had struck down a state law limiting hours for bakery workers, would lead the justices to overturn the Oregon statute. (The *Lochner* decision, which will be discussed below, had not invalidated all work hours legislation, but had found the New York law unrelated to health and safety.) The National Consumers' League arranged for Louis D. Brandeis of Boston, the "people's attorney," to represent Oregon; he defended the law by showing how the legislature could have determined that health and safety required a limitation of hours. In the famed "Brandeis brief," he devoted only a few pages to legal precedent and over a hundred to facts gleaned from

THE DANGERS OF LONG HOURS

Physical differences between men and women. The dangers of long hours for women arise from their special physical organization taken in connection with the strain incident to factory and similar work.

Long hours of labor are dangerous for women primarily because of their special physical organization. In structure and function women are differentiated from men. Besides these anatomical and physiological differences, physicians are agreed that women are fundamentally weaker than men in all that makes for endurance; in muscular strength, in nervous energy, in the powers of persistent attention and application. Overwork, therefore, which strains endurance to the utmost, is more disastrous to the health of women than of men, and entails upon them more lasting injury.

—Louis D. Brandeis and Josephine Goldmark, *Women in Industry* (1908)

both American and foreign sources detailing the impact long hours had on women's physical and mental well-being. The brief became the model of how lawyers could effectively introduce sociological and economic evidence into a case, and ever since, the legal arguments on major social issues, such as civil rights, have elicited extensive "Brandeis briefs" in support of the cause.

The Supreme Court, in *Muller v. Oregon* (1908), unanimously upheld the Oregon law (without, however, overruling *Lochner*). Justice David Brewer's "discovery" of women's unique physical structure and maternal functions struck many as disingenuous, but his opinion left no doubt that when the state could provide a reasonable justification for its policy, the police powers had extensive reach. He found legitimate reasons for classifying female workers as requiring the state's protection, and therefore that the exercise of the police power did not violate either due process or contract strictures. Following *Muller*, state courts consistently upheld similar legislation whenever challenged. In the second *Ritchie* case, for example, *Ritchie v. Wayman* (1910), Illinois reversed its previous ruling and held a ten-hour law for women constitutional. Why, then, had the court struck down the earlier statute? Because, as Judge John Hand explained, the previous act had made no reference to the health of women workers. In New York, the high court also reversed itself and judicially took notice of the "vital importance to the state that the health of thousands of women working in factories should be protected" (*People v. Charles Schweiner Press* [1915]).

A Feminist Critique of *Muller*

For years the *Muller* decision, and especially the Brandeis brief, enjoyed enormous popularity in the academy and among reformers, for whom it became a model of securing change through law. The Brandeis brief served as a template for numerous efforts by reformers to change the law, including the NAACP argument in the landmark civil rights case of *Brown v. Board of Education* (1954). With the rise of the new feminist movement in the 1960s, however, *Muller*'s reputation has fallen. Some critics charged that the decision embedded the notion of female difference in constitutional

> The argument based on sex ought not to prevail, because women's rights are as sacred under the Fourteenth Amendment as are men's. The Supreme Court of Illinois in *Ritchie v. People*, in speaking of this point, very forcefully says: "It is not the nature of the things done, but the sex of the persons doing them, which is made the basis of the claim that the act is a measure for the promotion of the public health. . . ."
>
> Is there any difference between the case of the healthy, adult woman, contracting for service for more than ten hours in a laundry, and that of a man employed as a baker for more than ten hours a day? Certainly conditions are as favorable in a laundry as in a bakery. The character of labor is not such in the case of a laundry to justify the assumption that it is more dangerous than that of the work of a baker.
>
> —William D. Fenton and Henry M. Gilfry, *Brief for Curt Muller* (1907)

law, and thereby, legitimized treating women differently from men. Protective legislation that considered women as a separate class remained in force well into the 1960s and 1970s. The principle of sex as a legitimate basis for differentiation provided a rationale for gender discrimination in other areas as well, such as family law. For some feminist critics, *Muller* was not a high point of progressive reform and sociological jurisprudence, but an enormous error that in the long run harmed women far more than it did them any good and retarded the arrival of a true sexual equality in American law. "Beyond any doubt *Muller* opened the door to gender bias in protective legislation," declared Joan Hoff. In retrospect "it is possible to question the long-term wisdom of the Brandeis approach in *Muller*." Other scholars have been far more militant in their attack, starting with Judith Baer's The *Chains of Protection* (1978), which, among other things, debunked the so-called expert medical testimony used by Brandeis.

One cannot deny that both the arguments put forward by Brandeis and Goldmark, as well as the Court's opinion, viewed women as different from men, and in some respects inferior to them. But to claim that this case embedded sexual discrimination in constitutional law for three generations is to misread both history and the law, and to demonstrate that the marriage of politics and scholarship is not always fruitful.

As a number of scholars have pointed out, discrimination based on gender had been firmly grounded in Anglo-American law for centuries before *Muller*. Married women had been forbidden to own or convey property, to sit on juries, or to vote long before 1908. Liberty of contract, that core ingredient of classical legal thought, belonged solely to adult males. The idea that women, especially married women, needed special protection had long been a staple of common law. As for viewing women as inferior, the law had frequently classified women along with children and mental incompetents as "persons under a disability" and unable to care for themselves legally.

Even had there been no Brandeis brief, according to Nancy Erickson, the Court could easily have gone from *Lochner* to *Muller*. Liberty of contract had been sex based since its beginning, and a long string of state court decisions existed to support women-only hours laws. One need look no further than the bible of conservative jurists, Cooley's *Constitutional Limitations*, to find ample precedent as well as reason for treating women as a separate category of legal being. Laws, wrote Cooley, "may extend to all the citizens or be confined to particular classes, as minors, or married women, bankers, or traders, and the like."

One should also note that securing hours laws first for women and children represented a conscious decision on the part of reformers, who hoped to use victories in this area to support broader laws. Brandeis and Goldmark favored shorter hours for all workers, men and women alike, and had accumulated a significant amount of data showing that long hours adversely affected men as well as women. They made the tactical decision to focus on women, knowing that precedent would give them a better chance to win this battle, and thus position them for a future campaign in favor of general hours laws. To ensure that the data collected about men would not go to waste, they encouraged the Russell Sage Foundation to publish it as a separate study.

Finally, the feminist argument not only reads the mentality of the 1960s backward to the Progressive era, but assumes that women opposed protective legislation. While some of the early feminists may have thought through the entire issue of women's inequality with men, the women's movement of the Progressive era focused on securing the suffrage. Even here, women could hardly be said to be united, and just as women proved to be among the bitterest foes of the Equal Rights Amendment in the 1970s, so too many of them opposed the suffrage prior to the First World War. Nor can protective legislation be characterized as a male device, since the Oregon law and others similar to it had been championed by two of the premier women's organizations of the time, the National Consumers' League and the Women's Trade Union League. Most women—including most female social activists—wanted the special protection offered by the law.

That the *Muller* decision reaffirmed already existing gender biases in the law may be true; that it placed them there is not, and that it raised them to a new high is questionable. The true significance of the case may be less for what it said about women than for its legitimization of economic regulation of the labor market by the government.

Separating Factory from Home

Women workers benefited from protective legislation, but the legal status of all women as inferior to men did not change. Upper- and middle-class women began to come out of the home and took the lead in the settlement house and other social service movements. But these same women insisted upon imposing, often through law, a particular, class-based view of how women should live, work, and behave.

Many of the leading women reformers of the time, even if they themselves had eschewed the typical path of home and hearth, believed that family obligations stood at the top of a woman's priorities. They attempted to use the police power of the state to shield the home from the factory, often in laws that prohibited piecework production in tenements. Mary Simkhovich testified at hearings in New York State in 1915, calling for the prohibition of manufacturing in the home and insisting that society required a sharp distinction between home and workplace. The state legislature had passed a limited law in 1913, prohibiting tenemant-made infant clothing, dolls, and food items, and that law would be sustained in *People v. Balofsky* (1916), which finally turned its back on the *Jacobs* decision.

Behind this and similar laws regulating child labor and compulsory school attendance stood the same notion as that which animated the Supreme Court in *Muller*, that

> Do the mothers of children force their babies to work at night because they wish to see them suffer? Do they like to whip their children to keep them at toil when they should be asleep? No. It is simply not to be believed. The mother heart is still the resting place of love and tenderness, in the ghetto as well as everywhere else. It is the mother's instinct to guard well the slumber of her child. These mothers of the slum are not by nature less kind than others. They are themselves the victims of the system of toil which they force upon their children.
>
> —"The Cry of Children for Protection," *New York Evening Mail*, December 7, 1912

women had an obligation to nurture their children and to oversee a proper family home. These beliefs, which went hand in hand with the conviction of a man's obligation to support his wife and children, reflected the dominant gender view of the Progressive era. But the loudest voices in this crusade to separate home and factory often belonged to women, and as a number of recent studies have shown, a wide chasm of class often separated the reformers from the women and children they wanted to help.

Hours on Public Works

A second area in which states acted to regulate hours involved workers on public projects and employees of public agencies. Here again the pattern of initial rejection and then acceptance can be seen. In *Ex parte Kuback* (1890), the California Supreme Court struck down a Los Angeles ordinance establishing eight hours as a day's work when performed under a contract with the city. The court claimed that this went beyond the limits of the police power and interfered with the right of employer and employee to make valid contracts. Interestingly, the court cited only one authority for its decision—Thomas Cooley's *Constitutional Limitations*. Over the next several years, other state courts also invalidated hours regulations for public works. "We cannot see," wrote Judge Irving Vann of New York, "that [such a law] bears any reasonable relation to public health, safety or morals" (*People ex rel. Williams v. Metz* [1908]). Vann nonetheless had to sustain the statute, because by then the U. S. Supreme Court had ruled the limitation of hours on public works constitutionally permissible, in *Atkin v. Kansas* (1903).

The Kansas high court had approved an eight-hour limit for those employed on public works projects. In the opinion, the judges had compared the state to a corporation, which had the power to tell its agents—in this case the contractors—what they could or could not do. The Supreme Court accepted this reasoning; only three justices supported the employer's argument that the law violated freedom of contract. Speaking for the majority, Justice Harlan gave the state almost carte blanche in establishing rules for work done under its sponsorship. "It cannot be deemed part of the liberty of any contractor that *he* be allowed to do public work in any mode he may choose to adopt, without regard to the wishes of the State. . . . Regulations on this subject suggest only considerations of public policy. And with such considerations the courts have no concern." *Atkins* set the rule for state public works laws, and in two 1911 cases the Court confirmed the power of the federal government in this area as well. In *United States v. Garbish*, the Court upheld an 1892 statute establishing eight hours as the norm on federal government projects; in *Baltimore & Ohio R.R. Co. v. ICC*, it affirmed a 1907 act of Congress regulating the hours of certain railroad employees on trains moving in interstate commerce.

Hours for Men

Even as the courts were accepting women and children as protected classes who fell within the ambit of the police power and for whom the state could set terms for their labor contracts, reformers began their efforts to cut down excessive hours for all workers—men as well as women and children. The early efforts in this direction immediately ran into trouble. In Nebraska, the legislature set eight hours as a day's work in private industry, except for those in domestic or farm work. Shortly thereafter, the state supreme court, in *Low v. Rees Printing Company* (1894), relying on Cooley's argument against so-called class legislation (that is, legislation that benefited only a particular group), struck the law down because it violated freedom of contract by "a classification which is purely arbitrary . . . [with] no relation to the natural capacity of persons to contract." Several other state courts employed similar reasoning to invalidate eight- and ten-hour laws, finding no justification under the police power.

In Utah, however, the state constitution required the legislature to "pass laws to provide for the health and safety of the employees in factories, smelters and mines." The state court found that working conditions in mines and smelters constituted a health hazard to the workers, and thus that the legislature had a legitimate reason to limit working hours. The assembly, according to the court, could find that certain classes of people needed special protection, because different business activities introduced different problems. The legislature had the right, therefore, to fine tune its police regulations almost on a business-to-business basis, and neither freedom of contract nor Cooley's proscription against class legislation could withstand the larger interests of health and safety.

In *Holden v. Hardy* (1898), the Supreme Court affirmed the Utah court's decision by a 7 to 2 vote. Speaking through Justice Henry Brown, the Court set forth a liberal interpretation of how states might use their police powers, which closely followed the state court's reasoning. But the Court went even further. It dismissed the right to contract argument altogether, because employer and employee did not stand in a position of bargaining equality. When such a disparity existed, the state could intervene to protect the welfare of the worker, who had significantly lesser bargaining power. That discretion resided in the legislature, and although the Court did not hold the police power limitless, within its rather broad parameters courts should not second-guess the wisdom of elected representatives.

Just as *Ritchie* had been the model for conservative courts in striking down protective legislation, *Holden v. Hardy* became the model for approval, with its rationale that special or dangerous conditions justified the intervention of the state. In the next few years, several state courts followed that reasoning to uphold a variety of laws reg-

> Proprietors of these [mines] and their operatives do not stand upon an equality, and their interests are, to a certain extent, conflicting. The proprietors lay down the rules and the laborers are practically constrained to obey them. . . . [The employer's] defense is not so much that his right to contract has been infringed upon, but that the act works a peculiar hardship to his employees, whose right to labor as long as they please is alleged to be thereby violated. The argument would certainly come with better grace and greater cogency from the latter class.
>
> —Justice Henry Brown, *Holden v. Hardy* (1898)

ulating men's working hours. It came as a great shock, therefore, when the Supreme Court in 1905 invalidated a New York law establishing a ten-hour day and sixty-hour week for bakery workers in *Lochner v. New York.*

The *Lochner* Decision

There is some dispute over the exact grounds on which New York State enacted this law. On its face it appeared to be a simple health measure, since working too many hours could lead to illness, and one surely did not want sick men (who could not afford to take a day off) baking one's bread. But there may have been some other considerations, including the desire of unionized bakeries to force nonunion shops into working shorter hours and the desire of housing reformers to eliminate bakeries from operating in tenement basements. There is also some suggestion that the law was aimed, at least in part, at driving small-scale immigrant bakers out of business. However true these allegations may be, one could still make a strong case for the measure as a health and safety law.

The long string of decisions supporting protective legislation masked the fact that a majority of the Fuller Court still saw liberty of contract as the constitutional norm, and that in order to restrict this right, states had to present solid justification. The right to sell one's labor through contract could be limited only to promote the health, safety, or morals of the larger community. In *Lochner,* freedom of contract ran head-on into a claimed exercise of the police power, and a bare majority of the bench came down in favor of contract rights.

Justice Rufus Peckham, who had dissented in both *Holden v. Hardy* and *Atkin v. Kansas*, ignored any claims regarding health and safety and condemned the New York law as nothing more than an effort "to regulate the hours of labor between the master and his employees (all being men, *sui juris*), in a private business, not dangerous in any degree to morals or in any real and substantive degree, to the health of the employees." Peckham agreed that a state could enact legislation to protect the health of bakers, but no evidence had been presented to show that the baking trade posed any health problem to workers, nor had the state put forth any rationale tying the number of hours worked to health.

Peckham, undoubtedly the most conservative member of the Court and a disciple of Justice Stephen Field, posed the issue in terms of due process: "Is this a fair, reasonable and appropriate exercise of the police power of the State, or is it an unreasonable, unnecessary and arbitrary interference with the rights of the individual?" The very phrasing of the question left no doubt that Peckham believed that courts should examine not only the limits of the police power, but the policy decisions behind state laws, and he said so bluntly: "the Court looks beyond the mere letter of the law in such cases" to determine the *purpose* of the statute. Here the purpose had been labor regulation, which Peckham viewed as beyond the reach of the state. *Lochner* became the classic statement of substantive due process, and apparently spun the Court completely around from its previously expansive interpretations of the police power. In the turmoil, few people noted that three state courts had earlier heard the case, and that the law had thrice been upheld. The matter first arose in the Oneida County Court, where the sitting judge ruled in favor of the law. In the Appellate Division the court split, 3 to 2, to uphold the statute, and the Court of Appeals (New York's highest bench), also voted to sustain it, 4 to 3. Of the twenty-two judges who participated in the four decisions, only ten thought the law unconstitutional, but five of those men also sat on the Supreme Court.

Both Justices John Marshall Harlan and Oliver Wendell Holmes entered powerful dissents. Apparently the justices had first decided to sustain the law by a 5–4 vote, and Harlan's opinion had been written as the decision of the Court. Then one justice had changed his mind, and Harlan now dissented. In many ways his opinion differs little from that of Peckham in accepting the basic premises of freedom of contract and substantive due process. But Harlan denied that the Court had any business inquiring into the legislative motive. "I find it impossible," he wrote, "in view of common experience, to say that there is here no real or substantial relation between the means employed by the State and the end sought by its legislation." He found in the briefs submitted by New York the evidence that Peckham had denied existed—a link between shorter hours and the health of the bakery workers. The Court might not like the policy, but that was not its business; he cited several other cases, including *Atkins* (which he had written) to show that the Court had sustained broad legislative discretion in a state's utilization of the police power.

Holmes dissented alone in a brief statement that soon achieved classic status, to be quoted time and again by those attacking the judiciary for exceeding its authority. "This case," he declared, "is decided upon an economic theory which a large part of the country does not entertain." The Constitution exists "for people of fundamentally differing views, and the accident of our finding certain opinions natural and familiar or novel and even shocking ought not to conclude our judgment upon the question of whether statutes embodying them conflict with the Constitution of the United States." The Brahmin Holmes had little personal sympathy with these laws, yet he believed firmly in judicial restraint. The determination of policy had been delegated to the elected political branches, not to appointed judges, and he struck a popular chord in his deference to democratic rule. By his detached tone, he showed up Peckham and the majority for doing just what they claimed not to be doing—writing their personal preferences into law.

There has been an odium about the case and its alleged abuse of judicial power ever since, and it took the Court more than three decades before it finally buried the

> This case is decided upon an economic theory which a large part of the country does not entertain. If it were a question whether I agree with that theory, I should desire to study it further and long before making up my mind. But . . . my agreement or disagreement has nothing to do with the right of a majority to embody their opinions into law. . . . The Fourteenth Amendment does not enact Mr. Herbert Spencer's Social Statics. . . . A constitution is not intended to embody a particular economic theory, whether of paternalism and the organic relation of the citizen to the State or of laissez-faire. It is made for people of fundamentally differing views.
>
> —Justice Holmes, dissenting in *Lochner v. New York* (1905)

concept of substantive due process in economic legislation. Liberals have presented the case as the leading example of improper judicial activism, in particular a reflection of the justices' antilabor biases, and gave the entire period of conservative domination of the Court the title of "the *Lochner* era." In the past few years, a number of scholars have attempted to rehabilitate the decision, spurred on in part by the Court's rediscovery of property rights, as well as the revival of substantive due process in noneconomic cases. Critics have argued that Peckham in fact got it right and that the New York bakery act covered up special interest legislation. They picture the measure as an anticompetitive façade designed to drive small-scale immigrant bakers out of business. Whether these revisionist theories are completely accurate or not, they nonetheless invite a reexamination of the case.

In terms of judicial response to protective legislation, however, *Lochner* should not be seen as the rule but as an aberration. Few state courts accepted it as binding, and indeed, within a few months, the Supreme Court reaffirmed its ruling in *Holden* with a *per curiam* decision upholding a similar Missouri statute (*Cantwell v. Missouri* [1905]). Two years later, it extended *Atkin* by validating a federal eight-hour law for government employees (*Ellis v. United States* [1907]). In this latter case, Holmes specifically denied any power of the Court to speculate as to legislative motive. In *Muller v. Oregon* (1908), the entire Court seemed to abandon *Lochner* and conceded the relationship between health and hours to warrant the legislation.

So far as future hours legislation went, most state courts and even the Supreme Court ignored *Lochner*. Within a few years, in fact, state legislatures started enacting hours regulations for all workers. Reformers had initially felt it necessary to justify hours laws as applicable only to groups recognized as legally entitled to some protection, such as women, children, and men in dangerous occupations. But by the end of the Progressive era, they claimed that regulating the number of hours for all workers fell within the states' police powers. Most state legislatures and many courts agreed.

Wage Regulation

By the time of the later hours cases, courts and reformers had begun to move beyond the question of maximum hours to the closely related issue of wage regulation. Even more than in the dispute over hours, the question of state control of wages hinged on freedom of contract. The rationale for maximum hours was the commonsense understanding that certain occupations were inherently dangerous, long hours unhealthy, and that disadvantaged classes needed some protection. A minimum wage, however, meant that all of the lowest-paid workers had to be paid according to arbitrary, fixed standards that bore no relation to the work involved and that, according to many critics, could not be determined by objective criteria. In the view of conservatives, such interference in the natural workings of the economy could lead only to social disruption. When reformers complained that the prevailing "iron law of wages" ground the "marrow out of the bones, the virtue out of the souls, and the souls out of the body," conservatives responded that people earned what they deserved. "Any wages are fair," declared W. A. Croffut, "which are as high as that sort of work commands in the open market. . . . One might as well say that a farmer 'ought' to get more than the market price for his wool or his potatoes. . . . Charity and business are and ought to be perpetually divorced."

Both medieval England and colonial America had regulated wages (although to set maximum rather than minimum scales), but the modern minimum wage movement originated in Australia and New Zealand in the 1890s. While some nineteenth-century visionaries such as Matthew Carey, Edward Bellamy, and Frank Parsons argued for a floor under wages, as late as 1900, few reformers included the idea in their programs. As Progressives began to explore more deeply the interrelationship of wages, hours, and the quality of life, they developed the theory of a "living wage"—the amount necessary for a person to live decently according to minimal middle-class standards. In 1905, one estimate placed this figure at $8 a week, yet the Census of Manufactures of that year reported that of one million factory women sixteen years of age or over, 77.6 percent earned less than that even during the busiest week of the year. Progressives recognized that the hours laws they promoted would also affect wages; a reduction in hours without some adjustment of pay scale would work immense hardships on working men and women. Many of the eight-hour laws directly affected wages, for until the 1880s, most laborers were paid not by the hour but by the day. Thus, a worker earning $1 a day would earn more *per hour* if the working day were reduced from ten or twelve to eight hours a day—unless employers cut wages correspondingly.

The first wage regulations to come before the courts dealt not with minimal levels, but with the manner of payment. Many mines and factories paid their workers in scrip, redeemable only in company-owned stores that charged premium prices. When Pennsylvania attempted to outlaw scrip payment, the state's highest court struck down the statute as an infringement on the rights of both employer and employee (*Godcharles & Co. v. Wigeman* [1886]).

Most of the cases challenging scrip law came in the 1880s and early 1890s; despite their devotion to freedom of contract, the courts held almost all of the new laws constitutional. Even Tiedeman, no friend to "paternalistic" legislation, considered the scrip laws legitimate because they reduced the coercive power of the employer and thus allowed a fairer bargaining process. The trend proved irreversible after the U.S. Supreme Court validated legislative power over methods of payment in *Knoxville Iron Co. v. Harbison* (1901) and of computing wages in *McLean v. Arkansas* (1909).

> The act is an infringement alike of the right of the employer and employee; more than this, it is an insulting attempt to put the laborer under a legislative tutelage which is not only degrading to his manhood, but subversive of his rights as a citizen of the United States. He may sell his labor for what he thinks best, whether money or goods, just as his employer may sell his iron or coal, and any and every law that proposes to prevent him from doing so is an infringement of his constitutional privilege and consequently vicious and void.
>
> —*Godcharles & Co. v. Wigeman* (Pennsylvania, 1886)

The scrip law cases proved a warm-up for the real battle—the effort to establish a legally enforceable minimum wage. Again, one finds a pattern of initial hostility from the courts, followed by acceptance. The first laws applied only to workers on state projects, as was the case with the hours laws, and the first court decisions, in New York, Indiana, and Nebraska, all went against the laws. Then, in 1904, New York partially reversed its decision, reasoning that if the state could fix hours for its workers, then it could also establish wages. A similar argument led the state of Washington's high court to support a Spokane ordinance setting rates on city projects.

In 1912, Oregon established an Industrial Welfare Commission to fix minimum wages and maximum hours for women and minors. In *Stettler v. O'Hara* (1914), the state court upheld the wage section, and Judge Robert Eakin declared that all the arguments that had been put forth to sustain hours applied "equally in favor of the constitutionality of the minimum wage law as also within the police power of the state." As for the differing classifications established by the state, sufficient evidence supported the legislative choice, and the court would not interpose its judgment. The Oregon court, interestingly enough, did not even bother with the argument that the statute interfered with freedom of contract.

Stettler v. O'Hara went on appeal to the Supreme Court, amid high expectations that the act would be sustained, thus doing for wage legislation what *Muller* had done for hours laws. By this time, ten states had adopted some legislation either fixing wages or creating a commission to investigate and then to set rates. The National Consumers' League again secured Brandeis to represent Oregon, and he began preparation of another massive, data-laden brief to show the necessity for the law. But in January 1916, President Woodrow Wilson named Brandeis to the Court, and when the case came up for argument, Brandeis recused himself. The remaining justices split 4 to 4, which left the Oregon decision in place but did not establish any clear constitutional rule. The Court would not hear another minimum wage case until 1923, when it struck down a federal statute for the District of Columbia in *Adkins v. Children's Hospital.*

In state courts, however, minimum wage laws met with approval wherever challenged. Nearly all the decisions took judicial notice of the inferior physical capacity of women and the need for the state to protect them. The contract argument seems to have worn thin by then, for it rarely appeared in the opinions, and if mentioned, received scant consideration before being dismissed. Had the Supreme Court not struck down the federal statute in 1923, it is likely that state courts would have extended their approval to general wage legislation, as they had already done for regulation of child labor and hours.

> As the wage is fixed irrespective of the earning capacity of the employee and is theoretically based upon the individual cost of living, then why has one worker a right to a living wage greater than that of another? . . . Moreover, each wage, when fixed, is only a stepping-stone to a higher wage. Each class of employees is constantly seeking an increase . . . regardless of the worth of the employee to the employer.
>
> —Rome Brown, "Oregon Minimum Wage Cases," *Minnesota Law Review* (1917)

Employers' Liability

The courts also responded to reforms in the way employers handled industrial accidents. Reform-minded legislatures first enacted changes in the common law doctrines governing relations between masters and servants and then established workmen's compensation plans. The two measures went together, for workmen's compensation required the abolition of the old law of employers' liability, under which—short of gross negligence in limited areas—employers had practically no responsibility for what happened to those working for them.

The common law had developed three major defenses against employer liability that made sense in a preindustrial society. The *fellow servant* rule allowed employers to evade responsibility by claiming that an accident resulted from the negligence of an injured worker's fellow employee, for which the master had no liability. The rule of *contributory negligence* absolved employers if they could show even a trace of evidence that the injured person had been partially at fault. This led to the third doctrine, *assumption of risk*: if a laborer knew of dangers in the workplace, the law assumed that the servant had bargained for higher wages to compensate for the additional risk.

Since all three defenses had been created by judges as part of the common law, they could be revised through legislation. As early as 1855, Georgia had modified the fellow servant rule, and by 1906, a sporadic but definite trend could be discerned. Seven states had abolished the rule completely, and eighteen others had modified it significantly, especially as it applied to railroads. Nearly twenty states limited assumption of risk, often allowing recovery under a theory of "proportional negligence."

Reformers argued that because workers in modern industrial factories or mines had little control over either the workplace or the actions of their fellow employees, the risk ought to be placed on the employer, who could more easily absorb the costs either by buying liability insurance or by passing them on to consumers in the form of marginally higher prices. Some business leaders, especially those in the National Civic Federation, recognized the force of the argument and supported it as a means of rationalizing business costs. It would be far cheaper to set up an objective and predictable insurance scheme than to pay litigation fees for hundreds of personal injury suits. Some Progressives framed the issue in terms of social costs. If breadwinners suffered injury or disability, they and their families would be thrown on the public dole; but since business profited by ignoring worker safety, ran the argument, industry and not the public ought to bear the cost.

Although courts followed a general rule that legislation annulling common law would be subject to close scrutiny, judges recognized that legislatures had the right, in the absence of constitutional prohibitions, to amend or abrogate common law doctrines. Thus, although employers constantly claimed that employer liability legislation violated due process or freedom of contract, state courts almost invariably upheld the new laws. Moreover, as a sign of how courts often limited the freedom of contract argument, they even upheld statutory prohibitions against "contracting out" of the statutory scheme.

As the states shifted liability to the employer, thousands of personal injury suits flooded the courts, and a number reached the Supreme Court on appeal. As early as 1880, the Court had held constitutional two statutes abolishing the fellow servant rule as applied to railroads. Justice Field, in *Missouri Pacific Railway Co. v. Mackey* (1888), ruled that legislatures always had discretion to change common law liability. The fact that it applied only to certain groups did not make it class legislation, but only reflected appropriate legislative judgment. Over the next few decades, the Court sustained in principle nearly all such state laws, although employees did not win all their suits. In many cases, technicalities or the failure to prove a claim led to dismissing the suit or returning it to the lower courts. In some cases, the Court upheld the common law policies because a state had failed to statutorily repeal the doctrine. The fellow servant rule, Holmes declared in *Beulter v. Grand Trunk Junction Ry. Co.* (1912), may be a "bad exception to a bad rule, but it is established, and it is not open to the courts to do away with it upon their personal notions of what is expedient."

Workmen's Compensation

Shifting liability constituted but one prong—and the easier one—of the Progressive plan; reformers also wanted to provide an orderly, rational scheme to compensate employees for injuries and deaths resulting from job-related accidents. Private employer liability insurance had been introduced in the United States in the 1880s, and the total premiums paid rose from about $200,000 in 1887 to more than $35 million by 1912. No one objected to private workmen's compensation programs, but what if companies did not secure insurance in the belief that they could bear litigation costs better than individual workers? The benefits of shifting liability would be lost if it proved too costly for injured unemployed workers to pursue a lengthy court battle.

To meet this problem, reformers called on the states to establish government-operated workmen's compensation insurance pools, and then to require all employers either to subscribe to the public plan or to secure comparable private coverage. In return, employers would be immune from liability for those accidents covered under the plan—although they would still, as under the common law, be subject to suits in cases of gross negligence. By the end of 1910, six states had enacted some form of compulsory workmen's compensation, eliciting a variety of responses from state courts.

In perhaps the most famous of these cases, *Ives v. South Buffalo Railway Co.* (1911), the New York Court of Appeals termed the law "plainly revolutionary" and struck it down as a taking of private property without due process of law. To alter the old common law rule so radically, Judge William Werner declared, by imposing "upon an employer who had omitted no legal duty and has committed no wrong, a liability based solely on legislative fiat . . . is taking the property of A and giving it to B, and that cannot be done under our Constitutions." In terms reminiscent of its earlier decisions on hours, the court denied that workmen's compensation had anything to do with health and safety, and concluded that the law therefore fell beyond the police power's acceptable parameters.

The case predictably aroused the ire of reformers. Former President Theodore Roosevelt claimed that such a decision served "to absolutely bar the path of social reform," an opinion shared even by many business leaders. Nevertheless, in the other five states with workmen's compensation laws, the courts upheld the statutes. In the state of Washington, for example, the court easily found the plan within the limits of the police power. The test is not whether the law did objectionable things, noted the court, but "rather in the inquiry, Is there reasonable ground to believe that the public safety, health, or general welfare is promoted thereby?" Since the legislature had believed it did, the judiciary would not question its wisdom (*State ex rel. Smith-Davis v. Clausen* [1911]). Within a short time, even the New York court had to reverse itself, after an angry electorate passed a constitutional amendment specifically permitting workmen's compensation. In two 1915 cases, the court agreed that the new plan, almost identical to the one invalidated in *Ives*, now met the test of both state and federal constitutionality.

Federal Employers' Liability

Because some states acted more quickly than others to limit liability or establish compensation plans, and others acted not at all, reformers agitated for Congress to set a national example. Congress passed an employers' liability act in 1906, but the Supreme Court struck it down two years later in the *First Employers' Liability Cases*. Justice White delivered the opinion of the Court, which held that while Congress had the power to modify or even abolish the common law in its regulation of interstate commerce, in this instance it had reached too far, because the law affected employees not engaged in interstate activities. Only three of the brethren, however (the conservative bloc of Peckham, Brewer, and Fuller), actually denied Congress any power in this area. The other six indicated that if Congress cured the act of its overreach, it would meet Court approval.

Congress did just that in the Federal Employers' Liability Act of April 1908. The railroads, the direct object of the law, challenged it in nearly six hundred federal court cases over the next seven years, but the Supreme Court upheld it unanimously in *Mondou v. New York, New Haven & Hartford Railroad Co.*, commonly called the *Second Employers' Liability Cases* (1912). By then Peckham, Brewer, and Fuller had left the Court; a new appointee, Willis Van Devanter of Wyoming (who would later be considered one of the archconservatives on the Taft and Hughes courts), delivered an opinion that took an expansive view of congressional power.

Congress also addressed the related problem of compensation. In 1908, Congress provided that certain of its employees could receive compensation for injuries sustained on their jobs, which replaced the older system by which a special act of Congress had been the only way a federal employee could recover. In 1910, Congress authorized a commission to make a thorough study of employers' liability and workmen's compensation. After the commission recommended a federal plan in 1912, Senator George Sutherland, later to be vilified as an enemy of labor, led the floor fight, finally winning approval in 1916.

In 1917, several cases involving workmen's compensation reached the Supreme Court, and on March 6, opinions came down upholding the three prevailing types of compensation laws. In a 5 to 4 decision, the Court sustained a Washington state law requiring employer participation in an exclusive state fund (*Mountain Timber Co. v. Washington*). It then unanimously upheld the Iowa elective statute. "The Fourteenth Amendment," declared Justice Mahlon Pitney, "does not prevent a state from establishing a system of workmen's compensation without the consent of the employer, incidentally abolishing his [common law] defenses" (*Hawkins v. Bleakley*). The most extensive case dealt with New York's compulsory law; in *New York Central Railroad Co. v. White*, Pitney dismissed the plaintiff's traditional arguments against the program—property taken without due process, interference with liberty of contract, and restriction of employer and employee rights—as largely outdated. Modern industrial life, he declared, required that law fit reality; the legislature had the discretion to abolish common law doctrines and use its police power to create a new system responsive to social needs. Although conservatives continued to attack the compensation plans, the imprimatur of the Supreme Court led to a steady expansion of state schemes.

The *Debs* Case

The one area in which courts did not receive protective legislation favorably involved labor unions. During this period, most judges viewed the labor contract as somehow special, involving not only the property rights of employers, but workers' rights to dispose of their labor freely. Arguments of inequity, health, safety, or general welfare failed to secure workers the right to organize and bargain collectively. Judges, in fact, went far beyond merely striking down prounion legislation; they actively sided with management in labor disputes. In Wisconsin, for example, Judge James G. Jenkins went so far as to prohibit workers not only from striking but even from quitting their jobs, since that would infringe on the property rights of the employer!

One week after disposing of the second Income Tax case, the justices delayed their summer recess to hear the third great case of the 1894 term, *In re Debs* (1895). Late in June 1894, members of the American Railway Union, protesting an arbitrary 20 percent wage cut ordered by the Pullman Palace Car Company, refused to handle Pullman cars; the strike paralyzed rail transportation east and west of Chicago. Attorney General Richard Olney directed the local U. S. attorney to seek an injunction against the union leaders for obstructing passage of the mails. The district court issued an overly broad order against the strikers, which union president Eugene V. Debs and three other union leaders refused to obey. Over the objections of Illinois Governor John Peter Altgeld, President Cleveland then sent in federal troops to break the strike, after which the government sought contempt convictions against the strike leaders. When their attorneys claimed that the original injunction had exceeded judicial authority, the trial court judge declared that the defendants had engaged in a combination in restraint of trade, in violation of the Sherman Antitrust law. He imposed a six-month contempt sentence on Debs and three-month sentences on each of the codefendants. Represented by attorneys Clarence Darrow and former Senator Lyman Trumbull, Debs appealed to the Supreme Court for a writ of habeas corpus.

Two years earlier, in *Pettibone v. United States*, the Court had unanimously reversed a federal conviction for conspiracy to obstruct justice in a labor dispute, ruling that federal courts did not have jurisdiction, directly or indirectly, over a state's criminal law process. Since Debs had been imprisoned by a federal court for an offense committed solely within Illinois, the *Pettibone* decision should have led to his release. But Justice David Brewer ignored the precedent and instead developed the idea that the injunction was a special form of relief that could be used to prevent irreparable damage to property that could not be adequately compensated in later actions at law. This use of the injunction had long been available through equity to private parties, but Brewer expanded its use to protect public rights and punish public wrongs. In doing so, he significantly enlarged the federal courts' equity jurisdiction and gave the federal and state governments a powerful tool to use against labor.

In stark contrast to the *Knight* and *Pollock* decisions, *Debs* proclaimed a broad interpretation of national sovereignty and the supremacy of the federal government over the states. President Cleveland praised the Court for establishing "in an absolutely authoritative manner and for all time, the power of the national government to protect itself in the exercise of its functions." But while the strike had little public support, the specter of "government by injunction" caused serious concern among legal scholars, as well as great resentment by labor.

The Courts and Labor Unions

The *Debs* decision did not surprise labor activists, since courts had never shown much friendliness to unions. Philadelphia shoemakers had run afoul of the courts as early as 1806; there and in other cases, judges found that striking workers could be charged with the common law crime of conspiracy. Although Chief Justice Lemuel Shaw of Massachusetts, in *Commonwealth v. Hunt* (1842), had ruled to the contrary, no other court picked up the potential solution to labor strife that he offered. Prosecutions for conspiracy did slow in the 1850s and 1860s; strikes in themselves remained technically legal, and establishing conspiracy to a jury, which often included workingmen, proved beyond the competence and patience of many prosecutors.

Beginning with the railroad strikes of the 1870s, however, judges handed employers a far more potent weapon—the injunction—which did not require proof of conspiracy or trial by jury. The injunction could be granted quickly, and if labor leaders refused to obey, they could be summarily jailed for contempt of court. Following the *Debs* case, state and lower federal courts issued hundreds of injunctions against labor activities. In 1896, the Democratic platform denounced "government by injunction," and friends of labor tried to pass legislation forbidding its use. But the business community had no intention of losing this wonderful weapon, and it used its influence to prevent any restriction on judicial discretion in this area.

Anticipating what economists would later term *countervailing* power, Progressives supported labor unions and collective bargaining as a means of giving workers parity with their employers in the bargaining process. Each side could then negotiate for the best arrangement it could get, but it would do so fairly. Reformers believed that the state's police power justified intervention to eliminate unfairness, and the Supreme Court had suggested in *Holden v. Hardy* that the state could protect labor from overreaching by management. Although effective legislative support of unions and collective bargaining would not come until the New Deal in the 1930s, reformers began chipping away at some of management's advantages. Protective legislation sought to redress part of the imbalance. In addition, some states prohibited the use of blacklists and "yellow-dog" contracts, which made workers promise not to join a union as a condition of employment.

Only a few courts sustained this legislation; for the most part judges would have none of it. Mere inequality in bargaining, without specific evidence of health and safety considerations, did not justify state intervention in the bargaining process. In the area of union cases, above all others, freedom of contract truly reigned supreme. No doubt, as some scholars have suggested, the potential power of the new, large labor unions scared conservative jurists, much as the power of big corporations alarmed reformers. The American Federation of Labor, with its militant leadership, struck judges as a threat to individual rights, to the personal independence of workers, and to what they believed to be the essential element of liberty, a marketplace in which employer and employee could freely negotiate the terms of their labor relationship. The fact that such a market had long since disappeared did not matter to the courts, any more than that the economic model of Adam Smith no longer resembled American business in the Gilded Age.

The courts attacked labor on several fronts. The Sherman Antitrust Act, designed by Congress to halt the depredations of big business, proved an effective weapon in the hands of judges, who found that strikes constituted combinations and conspiracies in restraint of trade. District Judge Edward C. Billings of New Orleans appears to have been the first to grant an injunction in a labor dispute under the Sherman Act (*United States v. Workingmen's Amalgamated Council of New Orleans* [1893]). Although the statute did not mention labor, Billings inferred, probably correctly, that the drafters had intended to include labor. Congress wanted to deal with any burden on commerce, Billings reasoned, and "the source of the evil was not regarded as material, and the evil in its entirety was dealt with. They made the interdiction include combinations of labor, as well as of capital."

In the *Debs* case two years later, even though the lower court invoked the Sherman Act, the Supreme Court avoided ruling on its applicability, preferring to rest on the federal government's mail and commerce powers. The Court finally faced the issue squarely in the Danbury Hatters case, *Loewe v. Lawler* in 1908. When their employer had resisted their efforts to unionize his hat factory, the United Hatters sought a boycott of Loewe's products by members of the American Federation of Labor. Loewe argued that this secondary boycott threatened the interstate nature of his business; for its part, the union reminded the Court of the narrow definition of commerce it had adopted in the *Knight* case. If sugar manufacturing had not been commerce, then neither could the manufacture of hats.

For a unanimous Court, Fuller ruled the boycott a combination in restraint of trade. As for the meaning of commerce, the Chief Justice showed that he could manipulate definitions when it suited him.

> Although some of the means whereby the interstate traffic was to be destroyed were acts within a State, and some of them were beyond the scope of Federal authority, still, as we have seen, the acts must be considered as a whole, and the plan is open to condemnation, not withstanding a negligible amount of intrastate business might be affected in carrying it out.

Even more disturbing, the Court showed no hesitation in approving treble damages against the union, although businesses rarely had to pay the fines established by the law.

The Court bolstered its antilabor reputation in several other cases. In *Adair v. United States* (1908), it invalidated a federal statute passed a decade earlier in the wake of the great railroad strike of 1894. A commission appointed by President Grover Cleveland had determined that antiunion practices, including use of yellow-dog contracts, had fomented much of the worker dissatisfaction. Congress picked up the commission's suggestions and prohibited yellow-dog contracts on railroads, claiming that they led to labor disputes that burdened interstate commerce. In a 6 to 2 decision, Justice Harlan condemned the law as repugnant to the Fifth Amendment. Although the government could limit personal rights in the public interest, he found no evidence of such an interest in this case. Moreover, "there is a liberty of contract which cannot be unreasonably interfered with by legislation." The employee could quit whenever he wanted, and in turn the employer retained an equal freedom to dismiss workers. "Any legislation which disturbs that equality," declared Harlan, "is an arbitrary interference with the liberty of contract which no government can legally justify in a free land."

In separate dissents, McKenna and Holmes attacked the majority reasoning. McKenna called the ruling too narrow and detached from reality; strikes did interfere with commerce, and Congress had made a reasonable judgment on one way to deal with the matter. Neither the Fifth Amendment nor liberty of contract were absolute, but had to bow before the public interest. Holmes, whom many considered the most prolabor member of the Court, had a more positive view of unions than did his brethren. Congress had recognized a disparity in bargaining power between labor and management and had acted within its powers to ameliorate that discrepancy. Holmes attacked Harlan's opinion for stretching the meaning of liberty and freedom of contract "to its extreme." As for the purpose of the bill, that did not concern the judiciary. "I could not pronounce it unwarranted," he concluded, "if Congress should decide that to foster a strong union was for the best interest, not only of the men, but of the railroads and the country at large."

The issue came back to the Court a few years later in *Coppage v. Kansas* (1915). With the federal government barred by *Adair* from prohibiting yellow-dog contracts, several states had passed proscriptions under their police powers. The Kansas high court had sustained the law, but by a 6 to 3 vote, the Supreme Court invalidated it. Justice Pitney conceded that the state could, under appropriate circumstances, redress some inequality in bargaining, but he argued that in doing so it could not violate the Fourteenth Amendment, which protected both property rights and freedom of contract. Holmes, joined by Day and Hughes in dissent, insisted that *Adair* should not be controlling, since it had been wrongly decided. Moreover, the police power gave the states greater discretion than the federal government had under the Commerce Clause to deal with labor matters. The antiunion bias of the Court would be a constant until the end of the 1930s and, if anything, would get worse. In *Hitchman Coal & Coke Co. v. Mitchell* (1917), the majority reaffirmed the right of an employer to insist on a yellow-dog contract; this elicited one of Brandeis's early and powerful dissents, which meticulously exposed the antiunion attitudes of the six-man majority. And even though the Clayton Antitrust Act of 1914 had explicitly exempted labor unions from the antitrust laws, the Court held in *Duplex Printing Press Co. v. Deering* (1921), that certain union activities could be considered illegal interference in interstate commerce and therefore subject to injunction under the antitrust laws.

Decisions such as these have left a lasting impression of the courts as antireform. It is true that judges seemingly went out of their way to strike down prounion statutes, but in other areas of protective legislation, the Progressives could hardly have asked for more from the courts.

For Further Reading

There are many fine works that provide a good introduction to progressivism, including Robert H. Wiebe, *The Search for Order, 1877–1920* (1966); Samuel P. Hayes, *The Response to Industrialism, 1885–1914* (1957); Richard Hoftsadter's classic *The Age of Reform: From Bryan to F.D.R.* (1955); and Nell Irvin Painter, *Standing at Armageddon: The United States, 1877–1919* (1987).

The full extent of police power legislation in the nineteenth century is reviewed in William J. Novak, *The People's Welfare: Law and Regulation in Nineteenth-Century America* (1996). The best general overview of the Supreme Court and protective legislation is John E. Semonche, *Charting the Future: The Supreme Court Responds to a Changing Society, 1890–1920* (1978); see also William F. Swindler, *Court and Constitution in the Twentieth Century; The Old Legality, 1889–1932* (1969). The reaction of state courts is surveyed in Melvin I. Urofsky, "State Courts and Protective Legislation During the Progressive Era: A Reevaluation," 72 *Journal of American History* 63 (1985).

The bases of classical legal thought are listed earlier, but see also Arnold M. Paul, *Conservative Crisis and the Rule of Law: Attitudes of Bar and Bench, 1887–1895* (1960); and E. S. Corwin, *Liberty Against Government: The Rise, Flowering and Decline of a Famous Judicial Concept* (1948). See also E. S. Corwin, "The Supreme Court and the Fourteenth Amendment," 7 *Michigan Law Review* 643 (1909); Roscoe Pound, "Liberty of Contract," 18 *Yale Law Journal* 454 (1909); and Felix Frankfurter and Nathan V. Greene, *The Labor Injunction* (1930). Ernst Freund's *The Police Power* (1904) remains an important work on the nature and extent of the state's authority.

Walter I. Trattner, *Crusade for the Children: A History of the National Child Labor Committee and Child Labor Reform in America* (1970), is the standard account; more of a legal emphasis can be found in Stephen B. Wood, *Constitutional Politics in the Progressive Era: Child Labor and the Law* (1958). Lee R. Altman, *A History of Regulatory Taxation* (1973) has a good section on the second federal child labor law.

For women and labor, see Leslie Woodcock Tentler, *Wage Earning Women: Industrial Work and Family Life in the United States, 1900–1930* (1979). Older sources that are still valuable for women's protective legislation are Elizabeth Faulkner Baker, *Protective Labor Legislation* (1925); Marion C. Cahill, *Shorter Hours: A Study of the Movement Since the Civil War* (1932); and Elizabeth Brandeis, "Labor Legislation," in John R. Commons, ed., *History of Labor in the United States*, vol. 3 (1935). More recent studies include Susan Lehrer, *Origins of Protective Labor Legislation for Women, 1905–1925* (1987); and Theda Skocpol, *Protecting Soldiers and Mothers: The Political Origins of Social Policy in the United States* (1992). How the Brandeis brief came into being, along with other fascinating material on Progressive reform, can be found in Josephine Goldmark, *Impatient Crusader: Florence Kelley's Life Story* (1953). A perceptive look at the struggle for a minimum wage is James T. Patterson, "Mary Dewson and the American Minimum Wage Movement," *5 Labor History* 134 (1964).

The feminist critique of the Brandeis brief and the *Muller* decision began with Judith A. Baer, *The Chains of Protection: The Judicial Response to Women's Labor Legislation* (1978), which strains to unite scholarship and feminism. See also Ann Corinne Hill, "Protection of

Women Workers and the Courts: A Legal Case History," 5 *Feminist Studies* 247 (1979); Vivien Hart, *Bound by Our Constitution: Women, Workers, and the Minimum Wage* (1994); and Nancy Erickson, "*Muller v. Oregon* Reconsidered: The Origins of a Sex-Based Doctrine of Liberty of Contract," 30 *Labor History* 228 (1989). A very useful combination of interpretive essay and original documents is Nancy Woloch, *Muller v. Oregon: A Brief History with Documents* (1996). The relation of class and gender in protective legislation is Eileen Boris, "Reconstructing the 'Family': Women, Progressive Reform, and the Problem of Social Control," in Noralee Frankel and Nancy S. Dye, eds., *Gender, Class, Race and Reform in the Progressive Era* (1991): 73–86.

The literature on *Lochner* is growing by leaps and bounds, but the suggestion that it should be viewed as a labor union case is made by Sidney G. Tarrow, "Lochner Versus New York: A Political Analysis," 5 *Labor History* 277 (1964). An early effort at revision is Bernard H. Siegan, "Rehabilitating *Lochner*," 22 *San Diego Law Review* 453 (1985). The best single study of the case is Paul Kens, *Judicial Power and Reform Politics: The Anatomy of Lochner v. New York* (1990). A somewhat broader perspective is Howard Gillman, *The Constitution Besieged: The Rise and Demise of Lochner Era Police Powers Jurisprudence* (1993).

One has to go to a variety of sources to piece together the story on employers' liability and workmen's compensation. See, among others, James Weinstein, "Big Business and the Origins of Workmen's Compensation," 8 *Labor History* 156 (1967); Roy Lubove, "Workmen's Compensation and the Prerogatives of Voluntarism," ibid. at 254; and Robert F. Wesser, "Conflict and Compromise: The Workmen's Compensation Movement in New York, 1890s–1913," 12 *Labor History* 345 (1971). The changing views of liability are discussed in Bernard Schwartz, *The Law in America: A History* (1974).

A good general introduction to labor and labor problems is David Montgomery, *The Fall of the House of Labor: The Workplace, the State, an American Labor Activism, 1865–1925* (1987). For examinations of labor unions and the law, see Christopher L. Tomlins, *The State and the Unions: Labor Relations, Law, and the Organized Labor Movement in America, 1880–1960* (1985); William E. Forbath, *Law and the Shaping of the American Labor Movement* (1991); and Daniel R. Ernst, *Lawyers Against Labor: From Individual Rights to Corporate Liberalism* (1995).

26

Progressivism Triumphant, 1901–1917

THE PROGRESSIVE RESPONSE to industrialism started in the cities, and then spread upward through the states to the federal level, as reformers realized that some of the problems they faced involved more than one city or even state. Progressives did not always agree on philosophy or method, but they all shared a strong belief in the democratic process, in the use of the latest techniques of efficiency in management, and in the desirability of government intervention at all levels to promote the welfare of citizens.

Democracy and Efficiency

Belief in democracy exemplified a major aspect of progressivism. Reformers proposed a variety of measures to make government more responsive to the popular will. Nearly twenty states adopted the *initiative,* by which a petition signed by a designated number of voters would put a proposal on the ballot. The proposal would then be voted on in a *referendum,* and if approved, would become law. Another dozen states instituted the *recall,* which gave the public an opportunity to remove both elected and some appointed officials by petition and vote. The adoption of preferential *primaries* in a number of states allowed voters to indicate their choice for U.S. senators, then still named by state legislatures. The popular election of senators required a constitutional amendment, and although the House of Representatives passed such an amendment in 1894,

1898, 1900, and 1902, the Senate, increasingly under attack as a "millionaires' club," turned it down. By 1912, thirty states had preferential primaries, and that year, the Senate finally bowed to the inevitable. It passed the Seventeenth Amendment, authorizing the popular election of senators, which the states ratified within a year.

Efficiency constituted a second watchword of Progressive programs. To some extent, efficiency ran counter to democracy, for it called for government to be run, not by elected officials, but by nonpartisan experts. Progressives advocated the commission and city-manager plans for municipal government. The commission system gained national attention after a hurricane and tidal wave nearly destroyed Galveston, Texas, in 1900. The local government collapsed, and business leaders led the way in entrusting authority to a board composed of elected administrative heads and the commissioners of police, sanitation, utilities, and so on. The city-manager plan won wider approval, however, since it kept policy-making in the hands of an elected council, while turning implementation over to a professional administrator. Staunton, Virginia, adopted the city-manager scheme in 1908, and within a half-dozen years, the idea spread to dozens of other cities.

Reformers also wanted to make the daily operation of government more efficient. Local groups worked to rationalize tax assessment and collection systems and to institute modern budgeting methods. They won a major victory when the federal government finally adopted a central budget system in the Budget and Accounting Act of 1921. In Wisconsin, Governor Robert M. La Follette established a Legislative Reference Bureau to provide research and technical advice in drafting legislation, an idea soon copied by other states. Modern government had grown so complex, reformers explained, that only experts could handle the people's business efficiently and effectively. The implications of such ideas would not be apparent immediately, but they pointed toward a shift of power away from the legislative toward the executive and administrative agencies of government, a trend that took place most dramatically at the national level.

The Roosevelt Presidency

Theodore Roosevelt's Progressivism reflected the conservative view of reform, a Burkean belief that some change is necessary and desirable to keep society in balance. Roosevelt viewed politics as the art of the possible and would always accept half a loaf rather than nothing. He talked a good game, however, and if his rhetoric often outpaced his deeds, he nonetheless helped to win acceptance of the idea of a positive government that took an active role in everyday affairs.

Following Lincoln's death there had been no first-rate politicians in the White House, men who knew how to use the leverage of the political machinery to effect particular programs. Following the impeachment of Andrew Johnson, there had been no strong leaders in the office, men who by force of their personality could dominate the government as Andrew Jackson and Lincoln had done. The balance of power in government had therefore resided in the legislative branch since 1866. While some presidents, such as Hayes and McKinley, had been able to put through particular measures or make the executive bureaucracy more efficient, for the most part the presidency had been seen as a weak leg in the governmental tripod. Some observers of American government, such as Woodrow Wilson, bemoaned the absence of an effective leadership and called for the adoption of the British governmental system.

All that would change with Theodore Roosevelt. For the first time since the Civil War, the nation had a chief executive willing and able to use the powers of the office and also attuned to the public aspects—some would say public relations aspect—of the modern presidency. From the time he took office, Roosevelt made himself accessible to the press and used it both to get across a positive public image of himself as an active, vigorous leader, as well as to publicize his political program. Roosevelt and his family became good copy, and as a result the American people began to see the White House (a name Roosevelt gave it; it had formerly been called the Executive Mansion) and its occupant in a different light. The president and vice president are the only officeholders in the national government for whom all of the people vote, and Roosevelt fostered the idea that the president and the people therefore had a link that was more powerful and important even than the connections to the local representative.

Roosevelt, however, never dominated the Congress. Even though Republicans controlled both houses, congressional leadership stood solidly in the conservative camp, and Roosevelt was careful not to challenge the established order. His dealings with old guard leaders such as Senators Marcus Hanna of Ohio and Nelson Aldrich of Rhode Island, and Speaker of the House Joseph Cannon, bordered at times on the obsequious. But after the chaos and corruption following the Civil War, these men had restored discipline within Congress, and with it respectability and power. Roosevelt bided his time and even in his second term could get a reluctant Congress to pass only a few of his measures.

As a result, Roosevelt accomplished much more through strong executive action than by legislation. The president took an expansive view of his authority, arguing that he could do anything that was not expressly forbidden by the Constitution. That document, he explained, "must be interpreted not as a straight jacket, not as laying the hand of death upon our development, but as an instrument designed for the life and healthy growth of the Nation."

His actions during the 1902 coal strike exemplified this view. On May 12, the United Mine Workers went on strike, demanding a 20 percent wage increase, a reduction in daily hours from ten to nine, and union recognition. The operators, who had granted a 10 percent increase two years earlier, refused to negotiate, shut down the mines, and prepared to starve out the workers. The owners' spokesman, George F. Baer, gave the miners their greatest publicity weapon when he arrogantly declared that "the rights and interests of the laboring man will be protected and cared for, not by the labor agitators, but by the Christian men to whom God in His infinite wisdom has given control of the property interests of the country."

Roosevelt could have sat by and done nothing; except for Hayes's use of federal troops in the 1877 railroad conflict and Cleveland's interference in the 1894 Pullman strike, presidents had never involved themselves in labor disputes. But the prospect of a national coal shortage the following winter led Roosevelt to call both sides to a conference at the White House on October 3. The owners came, but they refused to talk to the union leaders; an angry president then threatened to take over the mines and run them using the army. Although he had absolutely no authority to do this, the owners feared that Roosevelt might try anyway—and that the public would back him.

While he threatened in public, in private Roosevelt quietly secured the aid of J. P. Morgan, who used his great financial power to force the owners to agree to arbitration. The president named the panel, and when the operators objected to a union man, Roosevelt blithely reclassified E. E. Clark, the head of the railway conductors' union, as an "eminent sociologist." The commission gave the workers a 10 percent pay increase and a nine-hour day, but not union recognition. The big winner proved to be Roosevelt, whose use of the White House as a "bully pulpit" showed how effective a president could be by merely invoking the authority of his office. Roosevelt viewed the president as being responsible for the general welfare of the people, a steward, as he put it, of their interests. As such, he not only faithfully executed statutory law, but when he felt it necessary, could act under the broad implicit powers of the chief executive.

Roosevelt did not rely solely on this theory of implied power; he often asked Congress to grant statutory authority as well. Despite the Supreme Court's cramped reading of the commerce power at this time, he worked with Congress to strengthen both the Interstate Commerce Commission and the Sherman Act. For example, the Expedition Act of 1903 directed circuit courts to give priority to antitrust suits, while the new Bureau of Corporations, although lacking direct regulatory powers, received a broad mandate to study and report on the business activities of interstate corporations. Although its findings could be used in antitrust suits, Roosevelt saw it more as a tool to help the big companies avoid both illegal activities and lawsuits. Several of the Morgan firms, such as International Harvester and U.S. Steel, agreed to work with Commissioner James R. Garfield. Standard Oil and American Tobacco refused, however, and Attorney General Philander C. Knox brought Sherman Act suits that led to their breakup in 1911.

Roosevelt had succeeded to the presidency after McKinley's assassination in 1901. After winning election in his own right in 1904, the popular Roosevelt moved to enact the "Square Deal" he had promised the American people. In 1903, he had secured passage of the Elkins Act, outlawing railroad rebates, and now, over the resistance of conservative Senate Republicans, he brilliantly guided the Hepburn Act through Congress, finally giving the ICC effective rate-making power. Muckraking exposés, such as *The Jungle* by Upton Sinclair, that detailed the filthy conditions in slaughterhouses, the harmful ingredients added as food preservatives, and the actual poisons used in drugs helped the president win approval of other regulatory measures, including the Meat Inspection and Pure Food and Drug Acts, both passed in June 1906. The former required federal inspection of meat shipped in interstate commerce and gave officials of the Agriculture Department power to impose sanitary standards in meat-processing facilities. The Food and Drug law restricted the manufacture, sale, or transportation of adulterated, misbranded, or harmful food and drugs. Although such laws appear modest by today's standards, at the time they marked a significant step away from the laissez faire of the latter nineteenth century.

The Federal Police Power

Roosevelt's bold steps in regulating commerce inevitably came before the courts for approval. We have seen how in the areas of the federal commerce power and the state police power, the courts, after their initial opposition, confirmed fairly broad governmental activity. One might have expected that the conservative justices would have opposed a strong federal police power. Yet the Court, with a few significant exceptions, proved remarkably receptive to reading broad authority into the Commerce Clause, and to a lesser degree, the taxing power.

The first major case, *Champion v. Ames* (1903), dealt with a seemingly innocuous 1895 federal statute prohibiting interstate traffic in lottery tickets. Charles F. Champion and his codefendant, Charles B. Park, had hired the Wells Fargo Company to transport Paraguayan lottery tickets from Texas to California, but they claimed that this did not constitute interstate commerce. The government responded that express companies such as Wells Fargo were instruments of commerce; that the carrying of any article from one state to another could be regulated by Congress; and that such regulations could take the form of absolute prohibitions or even criminal sanctions. The case involved new and difficult questions for the justices and had to be argued three times before a bare 5 to 4 vote upheld the government.

Justice Harlan, who personally disliked lotteries, spoke for the majority, and termed the federal commerce power near absolute; he defined commerce as embracing "navigation, intercourse, communication, traffic, the transit of persons and the transmission of messages by telegraph." Only those limits spelled out by the Constitution restricted congressional discretion; if the legislature viewed an article as inherently evil, it could completely ban the entry of that article into the stream of commerce. Harlan recognized that such an interpretation would allow Congress to prohibit whatever it chose, and he warned that the legislative power had limits. Although "the possible abuse of power is not an argument against its existence," further adjudication would determine just how far Congress could go.

For the minority, led by Chief Justice Melville Fuller, Congress had already gone too far. The real target of the law had not been the tickets but the lottery itself, and gambling had always been a subject for local control. Fuller objected to the very idea of a federal police power, which he feared would be used to circumvent constitutional limitations and to undermine state powers. As for Harlan's argument that only the federal power could suppress evils in interstate commerce, Fuller noted that under the Constitution there might be areas beyond the reach of *either* the state or federal governments. Regrettable as this might be, the Court had to uphold the larger objective of maintaining a federal system under constitutional restraints.

Reflecting Fuller's alarm, the majority continued to find a constitutional basis for federal police authority. The next term, in *McCray v. United States* (1904), the Court by a 6–3 vote sustained a tax on manufacturers and dealers in oleomargarine that had the obvious purpose not of raising revenue but of destroying the competition from butter. Uncolored oleo bore a tax of only one-quarter cent a pound; the duty on colored margarine stood at ten cents a pound. Justice White acknowledged that the tax might have other purposes than simply raising revenue, but he maintained that this question did not fall within judicial scrutiny. "The taxing power conferred by the Constitution knows no limits except those expressly stated in that instrument." Because the taxing power extended beyond interstate commerce, *McCray* could conceivably open the door for Congress to regulate indirectly by taxation what it could not reach directly through the Commerce Clause.

In *Buttfield v. Stranahan* (1904) that same term, the Court confirmed congressional power to exclude articles from entry into the country, and more importantly, approved the delegation of discretionary power to federal tea inspectors. The legislative branch had determined the policy, Justice White noted, and it would be unrealistic to expect that Congress could anticipate all the questions that might arise. The delegation of limited policy determination by executive officers did not violate the separation of powers.

The "noxious articles" doctrine propounded by Harlan in the lottery opinion led a unanimous Court to uphold the 1906 Pure Food and Drug Law in *Hipolite Egg Company v. United States* (1911). Justice McKenna ruled that the seizure of adulterated eggs—which he termed "outlaws of commerce"—carried out the intention of Congress to ban them from commerce and to protect the consumer. McKenna gave a broad reading to the Commerce Clause, declaring it "subject to no limitations except those found in the Constitution."

Two years later, in a series of cases, the Court affirmed another of the Progressives' regulatory measures. In response to lurid stories of national vice rings, Congress had passed the Mann Act, or White Slave Act, in 1910. The statute provided criminal penalties for the transportation of women across state lines "for the purpose of prostitution or debauchery, or for any other immoral purpose." In *Hoke v. United States* (1913), the defendants appealed a federal conviction under the law for enticing two young women to go from New Orleans to Beaumont, Texas, for purposes of prostitution. McKenna, for a unanimous Court, dismissed the argument that the law invaded a matter reserved exclusively for state control. "We are one people," he declared, "and the powers reserved to the States and those conferred on the Nation are adapted to be exercised, whether independently or concurrently, to promote the general welfare, material and moral." The fact that the two young women were already established New Orleans prostitutes and not innocent young maidens made no difference. Congress had the power to regulate commerce, and could use whatever means it found "convenient," even though it "may have the quality of police regulation."

The full reach of the Mann Act had not yet been explored. *Hoke* dealt with two prostitutes. What about unmarried lovers? Although Congress had not discussed the matter in its deliberation, the Mann Act wording seemingly left federal prosecutors wide discretion in how far they could pursue allegedly immoral people. Drew Caminetti and Maury Diggs, two young men from prominent and wealthy San Francisco families, were both married, close friends, and involved with two unmarried women, Marsha Warrington and Lola Norris, both of whom also came from respectable families. Because of the men's family connections, word of their relationships eventually became known, and after the four took a trip from San Francisco to Reno in March 1913, federal marshals arrested Caminetti and Diggs for violation of the Mann Act.

John McNab, the U.S. District Attorney, informed Attorney General James C. McReynolds that it was "being openly charged that political influence would stop the cases and that the prosecution would be 'fixed.'" The fact that Wilson had just appointed Anthony Caminetti as Commissioner of Immigration also supported rumors that the young men would be discharged without a trial. When McReynolds agreed to a postponement of the trial, a not unusual event, McNab, a Republican holdover from the Taft administration, resigned and charged that the case had indeed been fixed. Although Republicans tried to make the postponement into a scandal, in fact McReynolds ordered the case to go forward, and juries in separate trials found the two men guilty. Judge William C. Van Fleet, in sentencing the two men, insisted that the language of the Mann Act covered noncommercial cases, that the incidents involved were not as grave as sex committed for monetary gain, and went so far as to declare that "the act originally did not contemplate cases of this character."

Given this encouragement from the trial judge, Caminetti and Diggs appealed to the U.S. Supreme Court. On June 14, 1915, the Court denied the petition for a writ of certiorari, but a week later, changed its mind. In a 5–3 vote (McReynolds recusing from the case), the Court upheld the trial verdict. Justice Day, in writing for the majority, declared as irrelevant the facts that the interstate travel had not been for gain or for the furnishing of women for prostitution. The Court needed to follow the plain meaning rule of statutory construction. Whatever Congress may have said about its intent in a law, the Court must follow what Congress had written in the statute. In this case, the wording had been "any other immoral purposes," and while commercial immorality may have been the prime target of the law, the wording left no doubt that it reached noncommercial immorality as well. (Day also dismissed the title of the law, the "White-Slave Traffic Act," since statutory construction relied on the body of the law, not the title.)

Day had a second argument—precedent. The immigration acts of 1875 and 1903 had forbidden the importation of women for the purpose of prostitution. In 1907, Congress had amended these laws to include the phrase, "or any other immoral purpose." The following year, in *United States v. Bitty*, the Court had reasoned that the phrase must mean something other than prostitution, or Congress would not have added it. Similarly, the phrase in the Mann Act must mean something or Congress would not have added it. Seemingly, the federal police power could be very broadly implemented.

In *Hoke* and *Caminetti*, the Court moved beyond the noxious articles doctrine, for the women themselves were not the issue, but the purposes for which they would be used. The expansive language of this and other cases masked the fact that the Court had arrogated to itself the power to determine when articles were noxious or their uses so evil as to warrant federal control.

The first glimmering of this came in *United States v. Johnson* (1911), decided shortly after *Hipolite Egg*, which also dealt with the Pure Food and Drug Law. A patent medicine that claimed it could cure cancer had been banned under the act for mislabeling. Holmes, for the 6 to 3 majority, conceded the claim was a misrepresentation, but ruled that it did not constitute the misbranding that Congress had outlawed. Taking an excessively narrow statutory construction, he held that misbranding occurred only when the label did not accurately convey the chemical analysis of the contents. Holmes personally thought the law a farce to begin with; he believed that laws should not try to save gullible people from their own foolishness. For all his preaching on judicial restraint, Holmes could inject his prejudices into law with the best of them; but he did so through strict or even tortured readings of the statute rather than with sweeping interpretations of due process. Congress responded to the decision by quickly amending the law to include fraudulent claims of curative or therapeutic effect within false labeling. The *Johnson* case pointed the way toward the Court's infamous invalidation of the Federal Child Labor Law of 1916 in *Hammer v. Dagenhart* (1918), discussed in the previous chapter.

The Attack on the Courts

In his last years in office, Theodore Roosevelt began to show signs of moving toward the insurgent wing of the Republican party. In August 1907, he spoke of "certain malefactors of great wealth" who had, he claimed, exacerbated the recent stock market and banking panic in order to discredit the government. In his annual message to Congress that December, he proposed inheritance and income taxes, national incorporation of business, regulation of railroad securities, establishment of postal savings banks, limiting labor injunctions, and extension of the eight-hour day and workmen's compensation. When Congress seemed disinclined to consider these proposals, the president at the end of January 1908 sent it the most radical message of his entire term in office. In addition to repeating the proposals of the previous December, Roosevelt now called for federal regulation of the stock market and lashed out at the courts for obstructing badly needed reforms.

The president's attack on the judiciary is somewhat puzzling, although it certainly was part of the general Progressive campaign against a bench that allegedly stifled reform. The immediate cause for Roosevelt's pique, the Supreme Court's invalidation of the first Employers' Liability Act, had been widely denounced not only by radicals but by many moderates as well. "No servant of the people," declared Roosevelt, "has the right to be free from just and honest criticism." To Justice Day, the president wrote that if the same spirit behind the *Liability* decision persisted in the future, "we should not only have a revolution, but it would be absolutely necessary to have a revolution, because the condition of the worker would become intolerable." In his final message to Congress that winter, he took another swipe at the courts, ironically designating them "the chief lawmakers of our country," and terming some of the judges "incompetent."

Despite the generally favorable attitude of both state and federal courts toward reform legislation, the few major cases that went the other way captured the headlines and made it appear as if all courts stood opposed to the Progressive agenda. As we have seen, the doctrines of substantive due process and freedom of contract sometimes had been employed at both the state and federal levels to block reform. The Supreme Court had eviscerated the Sherman Antitrust Act and crippled the ICC; it had struck down prolabor statutes in *Adair v. United States* and had invalidated a ten-hour law in the infamous *Lochner* decision. The fact that conservative justices often read their biases into law could hardly be denied, and reformers lashed out at the courts for imposing their views against the wishes of the people and their elected representatives.

The temper of criticism ran the gamut from studied to vitriolic. The less restrained publicists condemned the courts as tools of the trusts and the judges as enemies of the common people. More learned critics attacked the whole idea of judicial review, arguing that the Framers had never intended the courts to have power over the legislature and that the doctrine had been invented by John Marshall in *Marbury v. Madison.* Judicial usurpation, according to writer and critic Louis Boudin, had gone on long enough, and the judicial hammerlock on reform had to be broken. Other writers found historical and legal justification for judicial review but claimed that it had been misused by the courts. Too often, they charged, judges invalidated laws not because of specific constitutional prohibitions, but because the statutes ran counter to accepted social or economic philosophies. This criticism received an enormous boost in 1913, when Charles A. Beard published *An Economic Interpretation of the Constitution*, in which he claimed that the entire frame of government had been set up for the benefit of the monied classes, and not by disinterested patriots for the benefit of the people. Although later scholars would dispute the Beardian thesis and some of the evidence on which it relied, the fact remained that economic interests had played a significant role in the creation of the Constitution. Opponents of the courts now had even more fuel for their attacks.

Most critics of the courts believed judicial review necessary to sustain a system of balanced powers. Instead of abolishing the power, they proposed other remedies. George Norris of Nebraska and Hiram Johnson of California, two of the leading Progressives in Congress, objected specifically to the Supreme Court's voiding laws by a 5 to 4 vote, and suggested prohibiting the Court from declaring any act of Congress unconstitutional by less than a 6 to 3 majority. Louis Brandeis took another approach; judges, he maintained, relied too much on precedent because they did not know or understand the realities of modern life. In his famous address on "The Living Law," delivered only a few weeks before his nomination to the Supreme Court, Brandeis detailed many of the changes that industrialization had caused in the country. "Political as well as economic and social science noted these revolutionary changes," he declared, but legal science—the unwritten or judge-made laws as distinguished from legislation—was largely deaf and blind to them.

Brandeis spoke for the new theory of sociological jurisprudence advocated by many legal reformers, most notably Roscoe Pound of the Harvard Law School. By sociological jurisprudence, Pound and others did not refer to the formal theories of the new academic discipline of sociology. Rather, they wanted judges to take into account nonlegal considerations, such as social and economic data. Brandeis had used this approach in his famous *Muller* brief, in which more than 100 pages of data on the effect of long working hours on women completely overshadowed the bare three pages on legal precedent. Reformers like Brandeis, Pound, Ernst Freund, and others did not oppose judicial review *per se*; they objected to judges invalidating laws on the basis of a sterile formalism that ignored real-world conditions. As Oliver Wendell Holmes, Jr., had de-

> In periods of rapid transformation, challenge of existing law, instead of being sporadic, becomes general. Such was the case in Athens, twenty-four centuries ago, when Euripedes burst out inflaming words against "the trammelings of law which are not of the right." . . . Has not the recent dissatisfaction with our law as administered been due, in large measure, to the fact that it had not kept pace with the rapid development of our political, economic and social ideals? In other words, is not the challenge of legal justice due to its failure to conform to contemporary conceptions of social justice?
>
> —Louis D. Brandeis, "The Living Law" (1916)

clared in *The Common Law* (1881), "The life of the law has not been logic, it has been experience." Lawyers, according to Brandeis, must educate judges so they could understand and act on that experience.

Judicial Recall

Education takes time, however, and popular dissatisfaction with the courts led to a demand for more immediate relief. By 1910, some Progressives, including ex-President Roosevelt, began talking about judicial recall, both of judges and their decisions. Judges, declared Roscoe Pound, the dean of the Harvard Law School, "do nothing and obstruct everything." Congressman William Kent urged that the time had come "to dispense with the fallacy that by the accident of appointment or election to office [judges] become an order of superior beings, infallible and answerable to nobody." Recall of judges gained national attention in the summer of 1911, when Congress debated the admission of Arizona and New Mexico into the Union. The proposed Arizona constitution, which allowed for recall of judges by popular vote, touched off a strenuous debate, with Progressives defending the measure and conservatives attacking it. Congress finally passed the enabling legislation, but with a proviso that the state legislature submit a constitutional amendment to the voters that, if approved, would exempt judges from recall.

Whether Congress has the power to impose what is known as a "condition subsequent" is debatable. Nothing in the Constitution gives the federal government the power to force a state, once in the Union, to carry out conditions imposed on it earlier and against its will. However, before the public had a chance to digest this unusual procedure, President William Howard Taft vetoed the entire measure. He did not bother to note any constitutional problem with the condition subsequent, but attacked the very

> This provision [judicial recall] of the Arizona constitution, in its application to county and State judges, seems to me so pernicious in its effect, so destructive of independence in the judiciary, so likely to subject the rights of the individual to the possible tyranny of a popular majority, and, therefore, to be so injurious to the cause of free government, that I must disapprove a constitution containing it. . . . We can not be blind to the fact that often an intelligent and respectable electorate may be so roused upon an issue that it will visit with condemnation the decision of a just judge, though exactly in accord with the law governing the case, merely because it affects unfavorably their contest. Controversies over elections, labor troubles, racial or religious issues as to the construction or constitutionality of liquor laws, criminal trials of popular or unpopular defendants, the removal of county seats, suits by individuals to maintain their constitutional rights in obstruction of some popular improvement—these and many other cases could be cited in which a majority of a district electorate would be tempted by hasty anger to recall a conscientious judge if the opportunity were open all the time.
>
> —William Howard Taft, Veto of Arizona Enabling Act (1911)

idea of recall of judges in blistering language. Recall would destroy the independence of the judiciary and lead to popular tyranny, he averred; a handful of truly reactionary decisions did not warrant such "radical action."

Arizona had no choice but to remove the offending provision, after which it easily gained admission to the Union. But then, exercising its full rights as a sovereign and equal state, Arizona immediately amended its constitution to include an even stronger procedure for recall of judges. Taft fumed in the White House, as did the conservatives in Congress, although both should have foreseen that once admitted, Arizona, like any state, could (within the limits of the federal Constitution) do as it pleased. Within the next three years, five other states adopted some device for the recall of judges. Progressives never used these laws, however. Most state courts, as we have seen, proved sympathetic to reform legislation and had moved away from their earlier opposition even before recall had been suggested.

State Courts and the Constitution

In 1912, Roosevelt again helped to focus on the judiciary by backing a Colorado plan allowing the people, through a referendum, to pass upon any state law held unconstitutional by a state court. The former president agreed that when the U.S. Supreme Court had adjudicated an issue, its decision should stand, but he thought that otherwise the will of the people should be the law of the land. Conservatives naturally damned the idea of a referendum on decisions as dangerous and radical, and even moderates who studied the matter found it questionable.

State judges not only interpreted local law in the light of their state constitutions, but also had to look to federal law and the Constitution. The Supremacy Clause bound them to do so: how could a state allow the people to determine the validity of a statute if it ran counter to the Constitution? The advocates of the Colorado plan had simplistically assumed that only state matters would be involved; the difficulty of squaring the proposal with the Constitution led to its quick and silent demise.

The use of the Fourteenth Amendment's Due Process Clause by state courts to invalidate state laws did result in one reform that significantly affected the ability of state judges to kill reform legislation. Under the 1789 Judiciary Act, appeals could be taken from state to federal courts only when the state bench had *denied* a federal claim, that is, one arising under the Constitution or federal laws and treaties. The purpose of this section had been to ensure the supremacy of federal law over state law. But if the state courts *upheld* a federal claim, no appeal could be taken, since there had been no challenge to federal supremacy.

When Fourteenth Amendment challenges to reform legislation became common around the turn of the century, reformers found themselves in a trap. If a state court denied the Fourteenth Amendment claim and upheld the law, the decision could be appealed to the Supreme Court; but if state judges invalidated the law on Fourteenth Amendment grounds, there could be no appeal. In states with conservative judiciaries like New York and Illinois, reactionary judges literally had the power of life and death over reform measures, with no recourse from their decisions.

No one worried too much if one state's law system differed somewhat from another's in terms of procedure or even substantive law; but problems arose because different state courts reached varying interpretations of what the Constitution did or did not allow, and the Supreme Court had no power to impose uniformity. Thoughtful conservatives as well as Progressives found this situation disturbing, for it invited contradiction and unreliability in the nation's legal system.

The issue came into sharp focus after the New York Court of Appeals struck down the state's employers' liability act in 1911, in the widely condemned *Ives* decision. Because the court had upheld a federal claim, the case could not be appealed to the Supreme Court, although many commentators believed that the law would have been approved by the high court. Soon afterward, the New Jersey Supreme Court ruled that state's employers' liability statute valid. The House Judiciary Committee considered the situation ludicrous, and noted that "the Fourteenth Amendment means one thing on the east bank of the Hudson and the opposite thing on the west bank."

The obvious remedy was to allow appeal to the Supreme Court whenever a federal claim was raised. The House adopted a measure giving the Court power to accept writs of error from the highest state courts whenever they had upheld or denied a federal claim. The Senate, in light of the Court's already crowded docket, modified the bill to allow appeal only upon a writ of certiorari. Certiorari still gave the Court review authority, but allowed it discretion as to whether review would be necessary in particular cases; the writ of error implied an appeal as of right and would have limited the Court's discretionary power. Although the bill had few opponents and was sponsored by the respected and conservative New York senator, Elihu Root, it took nearly three years to get through Congress, finally becoming law on December 23, 1914. The delay resulted not from opposition, but because Congress had its hands full with other matters in those tumultuous years.

The Taft Record

In the election of 1912, Republican William Howard Taft campaigned as the candidate of standpat conservatism. Although certainly the most conservative of the four candidates, Taft was never the reactionary he has often been painted as, and, in fact, his record as a progressive in the White House stands up pretty well in some areas. In his four years in office, he withdrew more public lands for conservation than Theodore Roosevelt had in eight. The Appalachian Forest Reserve Act had extended the concept of national forests to the East, and Taft had begun the purchase of eastern forest lands, which today comprise some of the country's most beautiful parks. At his urging, Congress passed the Mann–Elkins Act in 1910, which gave the ICC the power to initiate rate changes, and extended regulation to telephone and telegraph companies. The passage of postal savings in 1910 and the establishment of the Bureau of Mines and the Federal Children's Bureau in 1912 owed much to him. He supported the Sixteenth Amendment, authorizing a federal income tax (ratified in 1913, just before he left office) and the Seventeenth Amendment, providing for the direct election of senators. Even Roosevelt's record as a trustbuster pales next to Taft's; in his four years, Taft initiated eighty antitrust suits, including attacks on U.S. Steel, International Harvester, and other Morgan firms, as compared with twenty-five for Roosevelt.

But Taft, although no reactionary, did not agree with many of the reform demands, and his political ineptitude often made him seem far more conservative than he actually was. His veto of the Arizona enabling bill because of his sincere opposition to any inhibition on judicial independence could be admired as an act of principle, but anyone with a modicum of political sense would have recognized that once Arizona became a state, it would do whatever it wanted. Taft's veto only delayed the adoption of the recall and made him appear as a protector of property over human values, of business over democracy.

Reforming the House

Taft's political maladroitness can be clearly seen in one of the major Progressive battles of his administration, the insurgent effort to restrict the powers of the Speaker of the House of Representatives. The Speaker had always been an important figure in Congress; his power to recognize members during debate and name committees dated back to the first Congress under the Constitution. The strengthened congressional machinery of the Civil War period gave him even more authority; together with the chairmen of key committees, the Speaker had a stranglehold on the House. Only those bills he approved would reach the floor of Congress; the rest would die in committee.

The House needed some organizational leadership, for it had grown enormously. On the eve of the Civil War, it had had 243 members; a half-century later it had 443. Thomas Reed of Maine, who became Speaker in 1889, forged the administrative apparatus that allowed the House to function effectively, but at the cost of vesting enormous powers in the Speaker and the five-man Rules Committee. Reed also arbitrarily did away with some of the obstructionist devices that those in the minority had previously used to delay legislation, such as not voting on a roll call and then demanding a quorum count. Even within the majority, representatives who earned the Speaker's displeasure could be banished to insignificant committees and could forget any hopes that the bills they sponsored would ever come to the floor for a vote.

Joseph G. Cannon, who succeeded Reed in 1903, ruled with the same iron hand until 1910, when a coalition of Democrats and insurgent Republicans overrode one of his rulings and adopted a new set of rules for the House. The old five-man Rules Committee appointed by the Speaker gave way to a ten-member Committee on Rules elected by the House, with the Speaker explicitly excluded from serving on it. In the next session, Cannon lost the power to make appointments to the other standing committees. The chairman of the Ways and Means Committee, elected by the House, would now have that authority, as well as the responsibility for the organization of the House. Although the Speaker retained a great deal of influence, he could no longer be the dictator Reed or Cannon had been.

During the fight, the insurgents had looked to Taft for support, and the president had given them hints that he backed them. During the 1908 election, Taft had complained that the greatest burden he had to carry was "Cannonism," which people equated with "reactionaryism." He had never liked the Speaker, and when Cannon opposed the party platform's pledges of reduced tariffs and restrictions on labor injunctions, Taft had written Roosevelt that the Speaker "would have to go." In fact, between his election and the special session of Congress, Taft called a meeting on tariff reform in March 1909 and informed a number of party elders of his desire to clip Cannon's wings. But Roosevelt and the conservative leaders of the party warned Taft of the Speaker's strength and urged the new president not to get into a fight he could not win. So when the insurgents launched their first effort to limit the Speaker in 1909, Taft did nothing to help them; instead, he "deprecated" the revolt and actually helped get Cannon reelected. When the reformers finally overthrew Cannon, they felt no obligation to Taft, whom they considered as reactionary as Cannon. Instead, many of them looked for reform leadership to the governor of New Jersey, whose successes there had thrust him into the national spotlight.

Woodrow Wilson's Views on the Presidency

Although a relative newcomer to practical politics, Woodrow Wilson, the Democratic candidate for the presidency in 1912, had long thought about the problems of government in general and the presidency in particular. In his doctoral dissertation, *Congressional Government* (1885), he had criticized Congress for failing to provide leadership or to bear responsibility for dealing with the complexities of modern industrial life. For this, Wilson partially blamed the separation of powers imposed by the Constitution; he considered the British system, in which the legislative leadership served as the executive, as far superior to our own. Under the British cabinet system there could never be a governmental paralysis resulting from different parties controlling the executive and legislative branches, of the type Wilson had seen as a youth during Andrew Johnson's tenure. In Great Britain, the failure of a party to maintain its parliamentary majority automatically led to its loss of the executive branch as well.

The administration of Theodore Roosevelt had led Wilson to revise his views on the alleged weaknesses of the presidency; a strong person, he now realized, could provide leadership and get results from the Congress. Although an American president obviously did not have the same relation to Congress as a British prime minister did to Parliament, the right man could overcome the inherent deficiencies of congressional government and give the nation a coherent legislative program. The president is the political leader of the nation, he wrote in 1908: "Let him once win the admiration and confidence of the country, and no other single force can withstand him, no combina-

> This is not a day of triumph; it is a day of dedication. Here muster, not the forces of party, but the forces of humanity. Men's hearts wait upon us; men's lives hang in the balance; men's hopes call upon us to say what we will do. Who shall live up to the great trust? Who dares fail to try? I summon all honest men, all patriotic, all forward-looking men, to my side. God helping me, I will not fail them, if they will but counsel and sustain me.
>
> —Woodrow Wilson, "Inaugural Address" (1913)

tion of forces will easily overpower him." After his victory in the 1912 election, Wilson had the opportunity to test his theories, not only in making the presidency a position of effective political and moral leadership, but in giving Congress a specific program to enact his campaign promises. He proved to be a bold and forceful president, who more than either Taft or Roosevelt, concentrated the powers of the executive branch in the Oval Office. He viewed the cabinet as men responsible to him, and he delegated authority only to those he believed completely loyal to him.

Tariffs and Taxes

Wilson took the oath of office on March 4, 1913. In his inaugural, he set out at least part of the legislative agenda of the New Freedom—the tariff would be lowered and the banking system overhauled to make it the servant and not the master of business. Strangely, he said not a word about amending the antitrust law, although the monopoly issue had been the focal point of his campaign. The election had given the Democrats solid majorities in both houses of Congress, and they looked to Wilson for the leadership he had promised. He immediately called for a special session of Congress, and on April 8, he personally delivered a short message to Congress on the need to revise the tariff. Not since John Adams had a president appeared in person before Congress; the dramatic gesture reflected Wilson's perception of the president as the head of government and not just as chief of one branch.

The House, led by Oscar W. Underwood, chairman of the Ways and Means Committee, quickly produced a bill that was described as "the most honest tariff measure" since 1861; it cut the rate from a little over 40 percent to 29 percent. Unlike Taft, who had refused to interfere with the legislative process, Wilson worked closely with Underwood, personally helping to negotiate some of the more politically sensitive schedules. Still, when the bill reached the Senate, protectionists threatened to repeat their victory of four years earlier in the Payne-Aldrich tariff; lobbyists swarmed over the Capitol, buttonholing senators with pleas for special consideration and protection of their industries.

Wilson struck back in another daring move that again reflected his belief in the president as leader of the country. On May 26, 1913, he issued a public statement denouncing the special interest groups. "It is of serious interest to the country," he declared, "that the people at large should have no lobby and be voiceless in these matters, while great bodies of astute men seek to create an artificial opinion and to overcome the interests of the public for their private profit." Although some senators resented Wilson's charges, Progressives secured the appointment of a special congressional committee to look into the matter. The investigation exposed not only the extent of special interest lobbying, but also the economic interests of every senator. Under the spotlight of this public scrutiny, the lobbyists scuttled for cover; when the Senate finished its work, the nation could hardly believe that it had cut another 4 percent from the Underwood rates. The House quickly accepted most of the Senate amendments, and Wilson signed the tariff into law on October 2. The country rightly saw it as a brilliant political victory for the Democratic party and for the new president.

Since the Underwood tariff reduction would cost the government an estimated $100 million annually in customs receipts, the House Ways and Means Committee had added a provision, drafted by Cordell Hull of Tennessee, for an income tax, the first such tax proposed under the newly ratified Sixteenth Amendment. The Hull amendment called for a flat 1 percent tax on all corporate and individual incomes over $4,000 a year, with graduated surtaxes up to 3 percent on annual incomes in excess of $100,000. This relatively modest proposal, with its low rates and high exemptions, satisfied the House of Representatives but not the insurgents in the Senate, who wanted a maximum rate of 10 percent, as well as an inheritance tax of up to 75 percent. Wilson stepped in and helped work out a compromise that raised the maximum rate to 7 percent on incomes over $500,000 a year.

Predictably, opponents challenged the tax in the courts. The Sixteenth Amendment merely provided that "The Congress shall have power to lay and collect taxes on income, from whatever source derived, without apportionment among the several States, and without regard to any census or enumeration." Could such a tax be graduated, so that those with greater incomes paid a higher rate of tax? Could Congress provide for specific exemptions and deductions that favored one group over another?

After the protest over the *Pollock* cases, the Supreme Court had retreated from its highly controversial position and, given the changes on the bench, might well have sustained an income tax even without the Sixteenth Amendment. In 1911, for example, a unanimous Court had upheld a 1909 federal corporation tax of 1 percent on net incomes over $5,000. Although obviously an income tax, Justice Day in *Flint v. Stone Tracy Company* (1911), had characterized it as an excise tax to avoid having to overrule *Pollock.*

The Underwood tax could hardly be passed off as an excise, and the Court heard and decided a half dozen cases challenging the tax in 1916. In *Brushaber v. Union Pacific Railroad Company*, Chief Justice White ruled that the purpose of the Sixteenth Amendment had been to relieve Congress of all limitations of apportionment or source of income on the taxing power. Congress could provide for graduated rates, provided they applied uniformly throughout the country; similarly, it could establish exemptions and deductions. White dismissed contentions that the Due Process Clause of the Fifth Amendment prohibited a graduated scale; the Fifth Amendment, he declared, did not apply to the taxing power. If people found injustice in the rates, the proper recourse was to the polls, not to the courts. Although there would be future challenges to particular aspects of subsequent income tax laws, *Brushaber* and its companion cases established once and for all the almost unlimited taxing power that Congress had under the Constitution as augmented by the Sixteenth Amendment.

The Underwood tariff and its accompanying taxes provided sufficient revenue for the government until the Wilson administration began a military buildup in 1916. The Revenue Act of that year marked a major step in the income tax's becoming the chief source of the federal revenue. The basic tax rate doubled to 2 percent, and the individual surtax ran as high as 13 percent. Congress also imposed a special tax of 12.5 percent on the income of munitions makers and a specific tax on stock dividends. An estate tax appeared for the first time, with a $50,000 exemption, and the highest rate of 10 percent on estates that exceeded the exemption by $5 million or more.

Later that year, the Supreme Court held the inheritance tax constitutional in *New York Trust Co. v. Eisner*. The taxpayer, represented by future Justice George Sutherland, argued that an inheritance tax did not come within the Sixteenth Amendment and was therefore void as a direct and unapportioned tax. Holmes dismissed all these complaints for a unanimous Court, "on the practical and historical ground that this kind of tax always has been regarded as the antithesis of a direct tax. . . . Upon this point a page of history is worth a volume of logic." Over the next five years, the Court regularly upheld the constitutionality of the other special provisions of the 1916 Revenue Act. As the laws grew more complex, the Court had to decide literally hundreds of cases on what constituted income; in doing so, it helped work out the basic rules of the modern tax structure.

Banking Reform

After the passage of the Underwood tariff, Wilson turned to what many Americans—reformers as well as business people—considered the most urgent economic need of the time, reorganization of the nation's banking and currency system. The nation had lacked a central bank since the demise of the Bank of the United States in 1837, and no one considered the makeshift national banking system created during the Civil War as adequate to meet the needs of a modern industrial society. The 1907 Panic had demonstrated the government's inability to mobilize the country's reserves in an emergency, as the money supply fluctuated in total disregard of the needs of business.

Following the Panic, Congress had created the National Monetary Commission, headed by Senator Nelson W. Aldrich, which submitted its findings and recommendations in 1911 and 1912. Everyone agreed on the need for reform, just not on how to achieve it. The Aldrich plan, backed by the American Bankers' Association, called for the establishment of a central bank—the National Reserve Association—capitalized at not less than $100 million, with fifteen branches in different parts of the country. The branches and the central bank would be under private control, but they would issue currency, carry members' reserves, discount commercial paper, and hold government deposits.

There was no consensus within the Democratic party on just what should be done. Shortly after his election, Wilson gave tentative approval to a variation on the Aldrich Commission proposal drafted by Carter Glass of the House Banking Committee and economist H. Parker Willis. It called for a decentralized, privately controlled reserve system of not more than twenty independent reserve banks. Wilson added an "altruistic Federal Reserve Board in Washington" to provide general supervision of the system. But when the president submitted the revised Glass-Willis plan to his advisers in the late spring of 1913, secretary of state and three-time Democratic presidential candidate William Jennings Bryan, Secretary of the Treasury William Gibbs McAdoo, and others expressed strong opposition. They proposed instead that the reserve system and currency issue become strictly governmental functions. Once convinced of the need for greater government involvement, Wilson managed to reconcile the various elements within the Democratic party, fight off banker attacks that summer and fall, and get Congress to pass the Federal Reserve Act by the end of the year.

Imperfect in many ways, the new plan did give the country a central bank again, which it had sorely missed for more than three-quarters of a century. It took currency issue out of private hands and made it the sole responsibility of the government. Through their ability to discount commercial paper, the reserve banks could manipulate the money supply in response to the changing needs of the economy. The basic structure of the twelve reserve banks, regulated in the public interest by a Federal Reserve Board appointed by the president, moved the government significantly into the regulation of the banking system, although the full expression of this would not come until the New Deal. That the banking system remained essentially private disappointed some of the more radical reformers, but Wilson had met his own criteria for reform—the government would now prescribe and enforce minimum rules to keep business operating honestly.

Practically no one questioned congressional authority to *create* the Federal Reserve system. Ignoring Andrew Jackson's century-old claim that the Bank of the United States was unconstitutional, Wilson and all the Democratic leaders relied on Marshall's expansive interpretation of Article I powers in *McCulloch v. Maryland* (1819). But the question did arise as to what powers Congress could invest in its creation. One of the various provisions of the Federal Reserve Act allowed private federally chartered banks to act as trustees, executors, administrators, and registrars of stocks and bonds. A state bank in Michigan, fearing that it would lose some of its business to national banks, sought an injunction to prevent them from exercising these powers. In *First National Bank v. Union Trust Company* (1917), Chief Justice White extended Marshall's reasoning in McCulloch to validate extensive federal control over banking. Marshall had inferred the power of Congress to charter a bank from the implied powers that he found attached to the Constitution's specific grant of fiscal functions. Now White argued that if Congress had the power to establish a bank, it could authorize it to do things that banks normally do. These functions need not have any direct connection to federal power; managing an estate obviously did not relate to any of Congress's Article I powers, but it did relate to banking, and therefore came within congressional reach. Ultimately the "Fed" developed into one of the most powerful of all government regulatory agencies, with enormous discretion as to how it carried out its mandate. It is doubtful if Wilson and his advisers, who in principle opposed big government, anticipated that the relatively innocuous "capstone" he had suggested would eventually become so powerful. Yet the Progressive idealization of experts and the gospel of efficiency led the administration, time and again, to set up boards and commissions when confronted by complex issues. For example, although Wilson and Brandeis had both derided Theodore Roosevelt's suggestion of a federal commission to guide business and help industry avoid illegal activities, when it came time to revise the antitrust laws, such an agency seemed the only way to resolve several difficult problems.

Antitrust Legislation

In late January 1914, Wilson delivered a special message on trusts to Congress. He proposed outlawing interlocking directorates in large corporations; allowing the ICC to supervise capital financing and stock issues by railroads; imposing penalties for individuals guilty of malpractices; requiring that all facts proven in government suits be accepted as binding in private suits to collect damages; and setting up a federal commission to provide businessmen with "the advice, the definite guidance, and information" they needed. Reformist critics saw the proposed trade commission as little more than a bureau of information; that, of course, was exactly what Wilson wanted.

But as Wilson's advisers wrestled with the problems of amending the Sherman Act, they realized that even though they could outlaw some specific practices, such as interlocking directorates, they could not anticipate everything that ingenious businessmen might concoct to restrain trade. It might thus be better for Congress to set out general policies on the type of practices it wished to outlaw and leave determination of specifics to the commission. This, however, would mean a complete reversal of Wilson's original idea. In order to enforce the antitrust laws, the new agency would require powers similar to those of the ICC, including the authority to issue cease-and-desist orders.

The Federal Trade Commission Act passed Congress in the summer of 1914; but at least in its early years, it failed to become the active force for regulating competition that its authors had envisioned. Wilson's choice of personnel nearly ruined the agency; the first chairman, Joseph E. Davies, proved so incompetent that the other members deposed him. Edward N. Hurley, a Chicago industrialist, took his place, but while far abler than Davies, Hurley used the commission primarily as a vehicle to preach cooperation between government and business. Well before the Republicans took over the commission in the 1920s, the agency had abandoned its role as a watchdog of business practices; it would not begin to fulfill that duty until revivified by Franklin Roosevelt in the late 1930s.

Critics also charged that the Clayton Act of 1914, which embodied Wilson's specific antitrust proposals, did nothing to rein in monopoly. Senator James Reed of Missouri described it as a "tabby cat with soft gums, a plaintive mew, and an anaemic appearance. It is a sort of legislative apology to the trusts, delivered hat in hand, and accompanied by assurances that no discourtesy is intended." Even Wilson considered the final version weaker than he had wanted, but by then he had pinned his faith on the Federal Trade Commission putting real teeth into the law.

Although the Clayton Act may not have been as tough or precise as some reformers wanted, it and the Sherman Act have remained the basic components of American antitrust law ever since. They have proven sufficient for prosecution whenever an administration has decided to use them. Whereas the earlier Sherman law proscribed existing restraints of trade, the Clayton Act also forbade a *tendency* to monopolize. In the future, this would give the Justice Department and the Federal Trade Commission (FTC) the power to head off a monopoly before it had restricted a market rather than having to wait until after the damage had been done.

The Supreme Court, which had adopted the rule of reason in 1911, saw the Clayton Act as confirming this policy. Although it sustained the power of the government to pursue an antitrust policy under the Commerce Clause, the Court has never developed a clear line of antitrust jurisprudence. Part of the problem is that all markets include some practices that tend to limit competition. In a civil world, competitors do talk with one another; they often trade information that allows them to understand the market better; they make informal agreements that do not necessarily restrain competition, but may eliminate some types of competitive activities. All this theoretically restrains competition, yet it may also foster it. Interestingly, the great trade association movement of the 1920s had its roots in the Progressive era, as some business people and reformers advocated cooperation as a necessary ingredient of true competition.

Although on occasion the Court has taken a literalist view of the antitrust laws, for the most part it has followed not one but several rules of reason. This has allowed the Court not only to interpret the law, but, critics claim, to create policy as well. This is true, but neither the Congress nor successive presidents have ever devised clear statements of just what specific results they expect from the antitrust laws. This has left the courts, and eventually the revivified FTC, to become the chief architects of antitrust law by default.

Completing the Reform Agenda

Tariff revision, banking reform, and antimonopoly legislation marked the original limits of the New Freedom, and if Wilson had had his way, he would have stopped there. But the forces of reform that had been building for well over a decade could not be halted. Although Wilson had promised that the New Freedom meant that there would be "special privilege to none," he had already begun to accommodate the reform impulse. In the Sundry Civil bill of 1913, he had allowed a rider prohibiting the Justice Department from using funds to prosecute labor unions or farm organizations. The president had also been forced to accept the creation of short-term agricultural credits in the Federal Reserve Act and the exemption of labor unions from antitrust prosecution under the Clayton law.

By the time America entered World War I, Wilson had for the most part abandoned his nineteenth-century, laissez-faire liberalism and had signed into law much of the more advanced Progressive program. Pressure from American farmers led Wilson to change his mind and approve the passage of the Federal Farm Loan Act in 1916, which provided for federal subsidization of rural credits. The government established twelve farm loan banks and provided each of them with an initial capital of $500,000; a Federal Farm Loan Board, similar to the Fed, supervised their operations.

Wilson also changed his mind on other aspects of the social justice agenda. Although he had once argued that a federal child labor law would be unconstitutional, he forced the passage of the Keating–Owen child labor bill through a Senate roadblock and signed it into law on September 1, 1916. That same year, Wilson endorsed the Kerr–McGillicuddy bill, a model workers compensation measure for federal employees. The longtime demand by businessmen for a "scientific" tariff finally found favor, and although the Tariff Commission, established in 1916, had little more than advisory functions, it marked a major step forward in the effort to depoliticize the tariff.

Wilson did not have to change his mind on the La Follette Seamen's bill, which had passed Congress earlier, only to be pocket-vetoed by Taft in the closing days of his term. The bill strengthened maritime safety standards and freed American sailors from labor conditions little better than peonage. Wilson favored the bill, but once in office, he learned that it would have international ramifications. The measure in effect canceled the contractual obligations of alien sailors on foreign-owned ships in American ports and thus violated treaties the United States had with most other maritime nations. In 1915, despite the worries of the State Department and the failure to resolve all these problems, Wilson approved the bill, "because it seemed the only chance to get something like justice done to a class of workmen who have been too much neglected by our laws."

In the spring of 1916, the four major railroad brotherhoods announced their demands for an eight-hour day with no reduction in wages, and time-and-a-half pay for overtime.

The operators refused, but before the workers could go out on strike, Wilson intervened. After listening to both sides, he proposed that the workers should get the eight-hour day and regular pay, but not the overtime. In addition, he would appoint a commission to investigate the entire problem of railway labor. The union chiefs accepted the compromise, but the owners, who apparently thought they could break a strike, refused. With the country beefing up its defenses and a presidential campaign in full heat, the administration could hardly countenance a paralyzing rail strike. At Wilson's urging, Congress passed the Adamson Act, which established an eight-hour day for railroad workers effective January 1, 1917, and created a commission to study the railroad problem.

A general rail strike would certainly have imposed a burden on interstate commerce, but did Congress have the power to relieve that burden by imposing hours and wages regulations on a private sector of the economy? Before the act even went into effect, the railroads filed numerous suits, claiming that they could not adopt their operating procedures to the law. The unions grew restless and finally threatened to strike on March 17, 1917. But the railroads, confident that the Supreme Court would invalidate the Adamson Act, refused to budge. With war imminent and merchant ships already arming, both sides gave into a presidential demand for mediation; they settled their differences on March 19, according to the Adamson provisions. A few hours later, Chief Justice White delivered the Court's opinion in *Wilson v. New*, which both upheld the law and ratified the settlement.

In his opinion, the chief justice noted that the law fixed both hours and wages, and although Congress had power over the former, it could not establish wages. In essence, while upholding congressional authority to prevent or settle a strike, he denied the legislature any power over wages, except as they might be incidentally related to a settlement. White implied that the Court felt constrained to ratify the agreement, but he and the four dissenters obviously did not want to allow Congress any wage powers at all. The narrowness of the decision and the reservations of several of the justices over the extent of the federal police powers boded ill for the social justice legislation soon to come before the high court.

Race and the Progressive Era

Despite the accomplishments of reformers in addressing the worst abuses of industrialization, significant areas of social unrest remained unresolved, especially race. Shortly after taking the oath of office, Theodore Roosevelt invited Booker T. Washington to the White House to discuss patronage and how to forge a coalition between blacks and conservative whites in an effort to rebuild the Republican party in the South. A few weeks later, when Washington returned to the District of Columbia, he received an invitation to dine with the president, his family and a few other guests. Washington's visit appeared as a routine item in the New York and District newspapers, the normal reporting of the president's schedule. The Southern press, however, reacted angrily, with a typical editorial calling it "the most damnable outrage that has ever been perpetrated by any citizen of the United States." The *Richmond Times* charged that the invitation showed Roosevelt's willingness "that negroes shall mingle freely with whites in the social circle—that white women may receive attentions from negro men."

Despite his invitation to Washington—a gesture never repeated—and a few token black appointments, Roosevelt looked down on blacks "as a race and as a man . . . altogether inferior to whites." Presidents Taft and Wilson had no better opinion, and Wilson had far the worst record. During his administration, Southerners rode high for the first time since before the Civil War, and they demanded segregation in government agencies and the dismissal or downgrading of black civil servants. Wilson and his cabinet believed in segregation, and the issue first arose one month after Wilson took the oath of office. Postmaster General Albert Sidney Burleson proposed the segregation of all blacks in federal service. Apparently no one objected, and soon the Bureau of the Census, the Post Office, the Bureau of Engraving and Printing, and other federal agencies quietly began to segregate workers in offices, workshops, building restaurants, and restrooms. Any employee who objected was discharged. Post office and treasury officials in the South received free rein to discharge and downgrade black employees. "There are no Government positions for Negroes in the South," the Georgia Collector of Internal Revenue announced. "A Negro's place is in the cornfield."

While some black organizations and their white supporters opposed this development, once again the protest proved remarkably limited. It would appear that Northern and Southern racial views had converged by the 1890s, due to several factors. The great migration beginning in 1880 had brought to the United States millions of people, mainly Catholics and Jews from southern and eastern Europe and Lutherans from Scandinavia. Northerners concerned about the dilution of Anglo-Saxon racial stock began to agitate for limits on immigration, and also began to find Southern views on race attractive. The imperial ventures of the 1890s brought a host of nonwhite peoples under American rule, and neither North nor South wanted to treat them as potential citizens of the United States. The Republican party, which had been the freedmens' champion after the war, had given up on this venture. Congress easily defeated the Lodge Elections Bill in 1890–1891, a bill designed to retain voting rights for blacks, and which has been characterized as the last effort of the old Republican party on behalf of equal political rights for the American Negro. There would be no further attempts until the failed efforts to enact antilynching legislation in the 1920s.

The Court Draws Limits

Despite the Court's earlier acquiescence in Jim Crow and its disregard for the claimed rights of other minorities, it appears that the justices found some constitutional limits on segregation beyond which they were not willing to go. In this endeavor they were aided—and pushed—by dedicated whites like Moorfield Storey, who helped to organize the National Association for the Advancement of Colored People (NAACP), which began the long, slow fight for justice in the courts. Much to everyone's surprise, this turnaround came during the tenure of a Southerner, Edward Douglass White, as chief justice of the United States.

The Louisiana-born White had been appointed to the Court by President Grover Cleveland in 1894, and for the next sixteen years, the former Confederate soldier voted with the majority in every case to uphold segregation or restrict black rights. Yet after taking the center chair in 1910, he helped shape majorities for important civil rights decisions. Moreover, the White Court reached out to ensure racial justice in several cases where it could easily have avoided the issue.

The first Jim Crow case to come before the White Court also marked the arrival of Charles Evans Hughes of New York, who took White's place as associate justice. Hughes refused to "wink" at the facts and applied the same legal logic to race cases as he did to other subjects coming before the Court. The case involved an Oklahoma law that required separate but equal railroad coaches, but exempted luxury units, such as parlor, dining, and sleeping cars, which could be used by either race, but not jointly. Since few blacks had the funds for these services, railroads used the law to avoid providing separate black facilities. Black plaintiffs challenged the rule as discriminatory, although they did not attack the broader principle of segregation. In effect, they said they could accept "separate but equal," but objected to the inequality of "exclusive but not joint."

By a 5 to 4 vote, the Court sustained their argument in *McCabe v. Atchison, Topeka & Santa Fe Railway* (1914). Hughes reiterated the *Plessy* rule and said that if railroads attached luxury cars for white passengers, equal facilities had to be available for blacks, regardless of the anticipated demand or lack of it. But after this refusal to accommodate to expediency, Hughes found a dodge to deny the petitioners relief—they had brought suit before the law went into effect and therefore lacked standing. The lower courts had erred in reaching the merits before determining if the question was ripe for adjudication. Hughes decided the merits anyway, in order to put Oklahoma and other states on notice that while the Court would accept racial segregation, it would insist that separate facilities be available and equal. But with the exception of one case, the Court would not deal with Jim Crow on the railroads again until 1941, when Hughes, then Chief Justice, began to reverse the Court's position.

Another form of Jim Crow came before the Court in *Buchanan v. Warley* (1917), a case contrived by the NAACP to test residential segregation ordinances in Louisville, Kentucky. Warley, a black, arranged to buy a lot from Buchanan, a white friendly to the NAACP, and the contract was drawn to invite litigation. Warley refused to pay for the land, on grounds that residential segregation laws prevented him from building a house there, which the sales contract specifically identified as his reason for buying the property. Buchanan sued for payment, but the local court upheld the ordinance and declared it a full defense for Warley. Buchanan then appealed to the Supreme Court, where both parties had hoped to go anyway. Other Southern cities then considering similar ordinances all stopped to await the Court's decision. Moorfield Storey, representing the NAACP, sought to distinguish residential segregation from other Jim Crow laws because it demeaned property rights, one of the bases of free government. Louisville's attorneys responded with the full rhetoric of racism: Law and Divine Writ demanded the full separation of the races.

The unanimous opinion Justice Day delivered masked internal disagreement in the Court over how far it should or should not go in such essentially local matters. The Fourteenth Amendment protected property, Day noted, but the state could certainly exercise some controls under its police powers to maintain health and safety. But could it regulate property solely on the basis of the skin color of the owner or would-be buyer? After an impassioned review of how the Civil War had been fought to protect civil rights, Day dismissed *Plessy* as controlling; in that case, there had been no effort to deprive blacks of transportation, whereas in this case, Louisville would neither allow blacks to buy certain property nor permit whites to sell it to them. He then held residential segregation laws unconstitutional—the first time the Supreme Court had so severely restricted the reach of Jim Crow.

A Few Small Steps

The White Court also took hesitant steps to address the widespread disenfranchisement of blacks by Southern states. It will be recalled that in *Williams v. Mississippi* (1898), the Court had indirectly given its approval to restrictions such as the poll tax and literacy test. Five years later, in *Giles v. Harris,* Holmes admitted that the Court did not have the capacity to remedy discrimination in voter registration. One form of voter discrimination involved "grandfather" clauses, by which men who would have been eligible to vote in 1867 and their legal progeny were exempt from the literacy or property requirements established to keep blacks from voting. The question of the grandfather clauses came before the bench in a strange case. Oklahoma, where blacks comprised less than 10 percent of the population, and which, unlike other Southern states, had a vigorous two-party political system, had adopted a grandfather clause shortly after it became a state. As the head of the Oklahoma Republican party complained, the clause had been adopted to stop blacks from voting not because of their race, but because they voted Republican.

In *Guinn v. United States* (1915), the Justice Department attacked the Oklahoma grandfather clause as violating the Fifteenth Amendment. At the same time, the Court heard a challenge to a similar Maryland statute in *Myers v. Anderson.* The clauses waived the literacy test for voting for anyone entitled to vote under any form of government, for those living in a foreign country as of January 1, 1866, and for their lineal descendants. Since neither clause specified race, both states denied any constitutional violation; both also claimed that voting requirements remained primarily a matter of state and local jurisdiction. Chief Justice White disagreed. Although neither law mentioned race, their application worked specifically to keep blacks from voting, while allowing whites to bypass the literacy test and poll tax. In a companion case, *United States v. Mosely,* the Court upheld the conviction of Oklahoma officials for depriving blacks of their right to vote, in violation of Section 19 of the Ku Klux Klan Enforcement Act of 1870.

Conclusion

The great burst of reform activity between 1897 and American entry into the First World War marked not only an expansion of governmental activity at all levels, but an expansion of the constitutional limits on governmental power, especially in the fields of commerce and taxation. The opposition of classical legal thought seems to have been subdued, although it could still burst forth in such cases as *Lochner* and the federal child labor cases. And despite the general racism in the country during the era, the Court finally stopped its retreat from the promises made in the Reconstruction era amendments. The battles had not been won, and during the rest of the twentieth century one would see a battle between reform and its opponents in the political field and a parallel struggle between an expansive and a restrictive jurisprudence in the courts.

For Further Reading

Good overviews of the Progressive period and especially of presidential leadership can be found in George E. Mowry, *The Era of Theodore Roosevelt* (1958); and Arthur S. Link, *Woodrow Wilson and the Progressive Era* (1954). The efficiency movement is well treated in Samuel Haber, *Efficiency and Uplift: Scientific Management in the Progressive Era* (1964). The application of expertise to governmental problems is also the focus of Lewis L. Gould, *Reform and Regulation: American Politics, 1900–1916* (1978). Local reform is explored in the early chapters of Jon C. Teaford, *City and Suburb: The Political Fragmentation of Metropolitan America, 1850–1970* (1979); see also Clifford W. Patton, *The Battle for Municipal Reform: Mobilization and Attack, 1870–1900* (1940); and Samuel P. Hays, "The Politics of Reform in Municipal Government in the Progressive Era," 55 *Pacific Northwest Quarterly* 157 (1964). A contemporary view of several popular proposals is William B. Munro, ed., *Initiative, Referendum and Recall* (1912).

For banking reform, see Eugene Nelson White, *The Regulation and Reform of the American Banking System, 1900–1929* (1983), which provides a good analysis of the legal and political factors involved, as well as the economic factors. The ideological basis of the New Freedom antitrust policy is explored in Melvin I. Urofsky, "Wilson, Brandeis, and the Trust Issue, 1912–1914," 49 *Mid-America* 3 (1967). For taxation under the new Sixteenth Amendment, see Sidney Ratner, *American Taxation* (1942); and R. Alton Lee, *A History of Regulatory Taxation* (1973).

The emerging regulatory state is explored in Thomas K. McCraw, ed., *Regulation in Perspective* (1982); Marver H. Bernstein, *Regulating Business by Independent Commission* (1955); and Arthur M. Johnson, *Government-Business Relations: A Pragmatic Approach to the American Experience* (1965). The failure of the FTC to live up to the expectations of its founders is explored in G. Cullom Davis, "The Transformation of the Federal Trade Commission, 1914–1929," 49 *Mississippi Valley Historical Review* 437 (1962). Judicial response to regulation is in John Dickinson, *Administrative Justice and the Supremacy of Law in the United States* (1927).

The first two decades of this century mark an important transformation in the nature of the presidency, and all three incumbents played important roles in that change. For Roosevelt, see John Morton Blum, *The Republican Roosevelt* (1954); William Harbaugh, *Power and Responsibility: The Life and Times of Theodore Roosevelt* (1961); and Lewis L. Gould, *The Presidency of Theodore Roosevelt* (1991). Donald F. Anderson, *William Howard Taft: A Conservative's Conception of the Presidency* (1973), is far more critical than Paolo E. Colletta, *The Presidency of William Howard Taft* (1973). Wilson is the only one of the three to have written extensively on the nature of government, in *Congressional Government* (1885), and *Constitutional Government in the United States* (1908). His presidency up to April 1917 is detailed in Arthur S. Link, *Wilson*, 5 vols. (1947–1965).

For the Supreme Court, John E. Semonche, *Charting the Future: The Supreme Court Responds to a Changing Society, 1890–1920* (1978), provides a broad overview of the Court in the setting of political and social change. Alexander M. Bickel and Benno C. Schmidt, Jr., *The Judiciary and Responsible Government, 1910–1921* (1984), is Volume IX of the Holmes Device *History of the Supreme Court*, and is far better than the earlier volumes in the series in its sensitivity to nonjudicial affairs and influences.

A good case study of the Mann Act and the Court's responses is David J. Langum, *Crossing Over the Line: Legislating Morality and the Mann Act* (1994). For the attack on the judiciary, see Gilbert E. Roe, *Our Judicial Oligarchy* (1912); and Louis B. Boudin, *Government by Judiciary* (1932); as well as Stephen Stagner, "The Recall of Judicial Decisions and the Due Process Debate," 24 *American Journal of Legal History* 257 (1980). For peonage, see Peter Daniel, *The Shadow of Slavery: Peonage in the South, 1901–1969* (1972). The activity of the NAACP in its early years is detailed in Barbara Joyce Ross, *J.E. Spingarn and the Rise of the NAACP, 1911–1939* (1972); and Carolyn Wedin, *Inheritor of the Spirit: Mary White Covington and the Founding of the NAACP* (1998). A longer view, connecting the organization to earlier pro-black efforts, is James M. McPherson, *The Abolitionist Legacy: From Reconstruction to the NAACP* (2nd ed., 1995).

27

Constitutional Problems During World War I

Preparedness • Control of the Railroads • The Draft Cases • The Lever Act • Rent Control • The Overman Act • Prohibition • Women's Suffrage • Wilson and Foreign Policy • The Treaty of Versailles • An Incapacitated President • Free Speech in Wartime • The Speech Tradition Before Schenck • *Clear and Present Danger • The Beginnings of the Free Speech Tradition • The American Civil Liberties Union • The Red Scare • For Further Reading*

WOODROW WILSON, LIKE Thomas Jefferson over a century earlier, had hoped to ignore foreign affairs and concentrate on domestic reform. But Europe went to war in August 1914, and although the United States tried to avoid involvement, the country finally declared war on Germany in April 1917. The president therefore had to deal with war-related problems of enormous magnitude. Some of the constitutional problems raised during the Civil War appeared again during World War I, but in a far more extensive and worrisome manner.

The major issue facing the Wilson administration was the organization of governmental and private resources to prosecute the war. Congress of necessity had to delegate authority to the executive branch, but how far could the legislators go and what constraints could they impose? At the end of hostilities someone had to negotiate a peace, and while historically the president had "spoken for the nation," did that mean that he had sole responsibility for and control over the nation's foreign policy? Wilson certainly believed that the president as commander-in-chief had near unlimited powers during an emergency and that Congress should follow his lead and accept his proposals, a view that alarmed as well as antagonized many members of the legislature. A third area of constitutional activity related to reforms that the war accelerated and brought to fulfillment. Finally, as in any crisis, some personal liberties had to be restricted, but the federal government under Wilson went much further in restricting basic First Amendment rights than any administration in American history.

Preparedness

The United States was hardly prepared to go to war in early 1917. With the president intent on serving as a peacemaker, the government had taken only a few steps to ready the country for war. Although the federal bureaucracy had grown considerably in the previous half-century, it remained fairly small and could not begin to compare with the private sector in those areas of expertise necessary to put the nation and its economy on a war footing. Wilson further complicated matters by his insistence that under the Constitution the president, in his role as commander-in-chief, had the prime responsibility for preparing the nation for a possible war and for developing the necessary plans. The man who had worked so effectively with Congress in getting the New Freedom enacted now demanded that Congress follow his lead unquestioningly. Members of Congress, as well as liberals and conservatives outside government, saw this as little more than a ultimatum that Congress abdicate its constitutional responsibilities.

Wilson announced a preparedness program on November 4, 1915, calling for significant expansion of the army and navy. In addition to criticism from pacifist groups that such a buildup would inevitably involve us in the conflict, Wilson also had to deal with opposition in Congress. No one questioned the president's responsibility as commander-in-chief to recommend measures that he believed necessary for the country's defense, but the large increases in military spending he proposed required hundreds of millions of dollars, which only Congress could appropriate. During the long debate over preparedness in 1916, a deadlock developed between the president, who appealed directly to the people to support his plan, and congressional leaders apathetic or hostile to it. In the struggle for preparedness, one can see the same scenario that will be played out during the war and after, a president insistent that he has the full constitutional prerogative to determine what should be done, and a Congress equally insistent that the Constitution grants it an important role to play. Only after one of the chief architects of the preparedness scheme, Secretary of War Lindley M. Garrison, resigned did Wilson finally win approval for some of his army requests and nearly everything he had asked for to expand the navy.

Administration leaders recognized that modern warfare required mobilization of industrial resources as well, so Section 120 of the 1916 National Defense Act provided for a Council of National Defense, which would, among other things, assemble a national industrial inventory. The council included the secretaries of war, navy, commerce, labor, and agriculture, as well as an advisory committee of several experts from the private sector. The government had, of course, frequently called in private persons for advice on particular matters, but during the war, the Council for National Defense and its successor, the War Industries Board, relied on private individuals to shape and then execute government policy to an unprecedented extent. Although Congress had established these bodies, for the most part the businessmen who staffed these agencies and their advisory committees paid little attention to the vague statutory limits on their authority. Instead, they adopted the prevalent industrial attitude of doing whatever seemed necessary to get the job done. The national government, previously a relatively insignificant actor in the daily economic and social affairs of the country, became a pervasive and influential presence. The government at war, its extensive ties—both formal and informal—to the private sector, and the near total eclipse of state authority became the model later on for the New Deal and presaged the transformation of government-societal relations in the twentieth century.

The people who served on the council committees recognized that if the nation went to war, the government would have to mobilize private industry and allocate vital resources. But this implied a measure of federal control over local affairs never before seen in this country, not even in the Civil War. The adequacy-of-the-Constitution argument could—and did—justify the expansion of national power, but especially in the early part of the war, it did not sit well with many congressmen, particularly those who had opposed American entry into the fray.

Control of the Railroads

The earliest expansion of federal power had been sanctioned by Congress in the summer of 1916, when it authorized the president to take over the nation's railroads in the event of war. Within a few months of America's entry into the conflict in April 1917, a paralyzing traffic jam on East Coast lines nearly choked off movement of troops and goods. In a proclamation on December 26, 1917, Wilson assumed control of the railroads and named Secretary of the Treasury William Gibbs McAdoo as director general. In March 1918, Congress passed supplemental legislation ratifying the takeover and providing additional guidelines for the operation of the roads.

The owners would be compensated for the temporary loss of their property, but all earnings during the time the government retained possession would belong to the United States. The president could set rates, which the Interstate Commerce Commission could review; but unlike rates set by the railroads, the ICC could not suspend presidentially established schedules during adjudication and by statute had to give these rates great consideration. The act specifically preserved the state police powers, including the power of the states to tax the lines. McAdoo, acting for the president, promulgated rates for all classes of service, intrastate as well as interstate, which ran somewhat higher than those that had prevailed before the war.

Although the ICC could review, and by adjudication force changes in these rates, McAdoo denied that state regulatory commissions had any power over government-operated lines. The North Dakota rate commission disagreed and sued the Northern Pacific Railway and the director general to prevent interference with state-established intrastate rates. When the case reached the Supreme Court on appeal, thirty-seven states and the National Association of Railway and Utility Commissions filed an amicus curiae brief challenging the government's power to regulate intrastate rates.

Speaking through Chief Justice Edward White, the Supreme Court upheld the government in *Northern Pacific Railway Co. v. North Dakota* (1919). The president had not acted under the Commerce Clause, but under the government's war powers, which, according to White, reached as far as necessary to meet the emergency. Since the federal government had obligated itself to pay a just compensation to the owners, it could set whatever rates proved necessary for that purpose. Moreover, since the government had chosen to run all the lines as a unified system, the peacetime distinction between intra- and interstate lines had been obliterated. The Court also approved the government's takeover of telephone and telegraph lines in a series of cases argued with the railroad suit, notably *Dakota Central Telephone Co. v. South Dakota* (1919.)

The Draft Cases

Wilson had implicitly assumed that the decision to go to war belonged to the chief executive as commander-in-chief; once the nation entered the war, however, he explicitly assumed that he would receive an unusual degree of deference from Congress, not only in managing the war but also in the proposals he would send to the legislature for enactment. In his war message, he told Congress that he would send them bills for the raising of and support of a larger army and navy and for the mobilization of the country's economic resources. Wilson hoped "that it will be your pleasure to deal with them as having been framed after very careful thought by the branch of Government upon which the responsibility of conducting the war and safeguarding the nation will most directly fall." The administration then began sending one sweeping bill after another to Congress, including an espionage measure allowing for large-scale government censorship of the press, the creation of a food administration, and a draft of young men for the army.

The proposals triggered intense reaction, not so much for their content but for the manner in which Congress, ostensibly charged by the Constitution to make the laws, had been asked to simply endorse without qualification some of the most sweeping legislation the country had ever seen. During the debate over the conscription bill, the chair of the House Military Committee, Hubert Dent of Alabama, declared that he would resign his seat before he would accept the argument "that in time of war the executive department shall draft its legislation and send it to Congress, and Congress shall not exercise the right to cross a 't' nor dot an 'i'" The anger did not stem from partisanship; Dent was a Democrat, and members of both parties resented what they saw as Wilson's high-handed, even dictatorial attitude.

Despite their resentment, members of Congress recognized that conscription would be necessary, and on May 17, 1917, Congress enacted Wilson's draft law, which opponents of the war immediately challenged. Lower courts expedited the various draft cases; men could not be allowed to die should the law be unconstitutional, nor could the government's mobilization be derailed if it were valid. Six suits, grouped together as the *Selective Draft Law Cases* came before the Court for argument in December 1917. All involved convictions for obstructing or resisting conscription.

Harris F. Taylor, the chief counsel for the defendants, berated Congress for expanding the executive power. Wilson had already become a political dictator, Taylor charged, and his decision to commit American troops abroad—a power nowhere found in the Constitution—had plunged the country into a military dictatorship as well. Taylor claimed that the Militia Clause (Article I, Section 8) limited their use "to execute the Laws of the Union, suppress Insurrections and repel Invasions." Militia troops could not be used, therefore, to prosecute foreign conflicts.

The Court handed down its decision the first week of January 1918; in almost summary fashion, it unanimously dismissed all the arguments raised against the law. Chief Justice White noted Congress's explicit powers in Article I to "provide for the common Defence," "to raise and support Armies," "to provide and maintain a Navy," and "to declare War." "As the mind cannot conceive an army without the men to compose it," White asserted, "on the face of the Constitution the objection that it does not give power to provide for such men would seem too frivolous for further notice." The Court also made short shrift of the argument that the Constitution allowed only a volunteer army and did not authorize conscription. The chief justice noted that just as the government owed certain obligations to its citizens, so the people had reciprocal duties to the state, including rendering military service, which the government could compel. Beyond that, Congress could deploy the army anywhere it deemed necessary, even overseas.

Most Americans had expected the Court to sustain the draft law. It would have been difficult, declared one journal, "to conceive how any other view could ever have been seriously argued by anyone familiar with constitutional law or the Anglo-Saxon principles of free institutions." A writer in a respected legal journal, anticipating the impatience later shown toward free speech, charged that those who had challenged the laws belonged to "that treacherous hostile propaganda with which we now know our country has been menacingly infiltrated." Yet even if the antidraft arguments failed to persuade a single member of the Court, they did raise at least two issues that would eventually receive more serious attention.

First, the act allowed the president to delegate nearly all the tasks involved in selecting and processing the conscripts to local draft boards. The Court had held laws involving delegation of powers constitutional ever since the question first came before it in *Field v. Clark* (1892), but none of the previous statutes had been as vague in prescribing guidance or oversight. In the various war statutes, Congress merely set out general goals and gave the president carte blanche to carry them out. At some point, the Court would have to determine how much power Congress could delegate and how much discretion the president could exercise.

A second issue involved the generous exemption from the draft that Congress allowed ordained ministers and theology students, as well as exemption from combat granted to members of some sects that opposed war on religious grounds. The Court shrugged off a challenge that this provision violated the First Amendment because it amounted to an establishment of religion. White casually derided the unsoundness of the claim as well as a collateral argument that the limited exemptions violated the Free Exercise Clause. In the future, the Court would wrestle with the problem of conscientious objectors in a number of cases.

The Lever Act

The need to coordinate transportation and commerce, as well as to secure sufficient men for an army, seemed obvious to both the government and the public. Once again, Wilson sent down a measure to Congress with an expectation that it would immediately approve it without change. But some members of Congress rebelled at the administration's request for extensive powers to regulate the distribution of foodstuffs, control mines and factories, and fix prices. The Lever, or Food Control, bill of 1917 proposed giving the president extraordinary powers over the agricultural sector of the economy. He would be able to establish an agency to buy and sell food, offer guarantees to farmers, prevent hoarding and speculation, fix trading margins on the grain exchanges, and in general organize the food industry to eliminate waste. The bill provided no standards for judging his actions except the general welfare and the successful prosecution of the war. Not even Lincoln had exercised this much power, and certainly it had not been delegated to him by the Congress. George Young, a representative from North Dakota, warned that the bill would establish a presidential dictatorship.

In the Senate, both Democrats and Republicans argued that Congress could not give so much discretion to the executive without some sort of oversight. Senator Robert Owen, an Oklahoma Democrat, proposed a Joint Committee on Expenditures in the Conduct of the War as an amendment to the food bill in July 1917. Owen urged the president to accept the measure, terming it consistent with Wilson's often stated belief in "common counsel," the give-and-take that Owen and Wilson had engaged in during the shaping of the Federal Reserve Act. Wilson responded harshly, declaring that the Owen proposal would "render my task of conducting the war practically impossible."

Republican John Weeks of Massachusetts proposed creating a ten-man committee—three Democrats and two Republicans from each house—to confer and cooperate with the president and executive agency heads on the prosecution of the war. In addition, the committee could investigate any and all aspects of war-related activities. Weeks modeled his proposal on a Civil War committee, and even if one conceded some partisanship here, the proposal won the support of a number of Democrats, who joined Senate Republicans to tack on a modification of the Weeks proposal to the Lever bill. In the House, however, Wilson condemned the measure as "nothing less than an assumption on the part of the legislative body of the executive work of the administration." He made the defeat of the committee proposal a vote of confidence in him; the House deleted the amendment and passed the Lever Act into law on August 10, 1917.

Following passage of the Lever Act, Wilson quickly created a Food Administration and named Herbert Hoover to head it. The purpose was not merely to ensure an adequate supply of food; Section 4 made it unlawful to charge or conspire "to exact excessive prices for any necessaries." Persons convicted faced fines of up to $5,000 and/or jail sentences of up to two years. Probably no other war measure resulted in so many prosecutions, but the vagueness of the statute led to conflicting interpretations of its validity. Federal courts in Missouri, Colorado, and Michigan found indictments under Section 4 faulty; courts in Mississippi, New York, Ohio, and Georgia upheld them. Although the hostilities ended in November 1918, the Lever Act remained in force until Congress approved a peace treaty. So the Supreme Court agreed to hear a group of cases testing the law's constitutionality.

In the major case, *United States v. Cohen Grocery Store* (1921), the government had charged the owner with selling a 50-pound bag of sugar for $10.07, and a 100-pound bag for $19.50, both allegedly above a fair price. The defendants attacked the Lever Act for its vagueness in Section 4, claiming that it violated their rights under the Fifth and Sixth amendments. The Court, speaking through Chief Justice White, agreed. The act had failed to provide "an ascertainable standard of guilt . . . adequate to inform persons . . . of the nature and cause of the accusation against them." The mere existence of a state of war, White explained, did not suspend or alter the guarantees and limitations of the Constitution in terms of assuring a fair trial. The decision, coming well after the armistice, had no effect on wartime food prices. Hoover used the threat of criminal prosecution during the war to secure consensual price agreements, and while a number of profiteers escaped jail sentences or fines, the Lever Act, at least in 1917 and 1918, had the desired effect.

Rent Control

The Lever Act proved to be the only wartime statute to run afoul of the courts, and it might have been saved had Congress or the administration provided consistent standards by which to judge prices. When Congress did so, as in the October 1919 law imposing rent controls in the District of Columbia, the Court sustained the act. The severe shortage of housing in the capital, which continued well after the armistice, led Congress to freeze rental rates at the current level. The statute did, however, assure landlords a reasonable return on their investment and the ability to regain possession of the premises if they chose to occupy it themselves. In *Block v. Hirsch* (1921), Holmes, for a narrow majority, upheld the law as a legitimate exercise of the police power. The law had been carefully drafted, its criteria clear, and its tenure limited to two years. In a companion case, *Marcus Brown Co. v. Feldman*, the Court sustained a similar New York statute.

One line in Holmes's opinion in the District rent case deserves special notice. The question, he declared, was "whether Congress was incompetent to meet [the emergency] in the way in which it has been met by most of the civilized countries of the world." Holmes took a broad view of the police power, which he claimed extended "to all the great public needs," and could be exerted in aid of what "the prevailing morality or strong and preponderant opinion [believes] to be greatly and immediately necessary to the public welfare." Compare this to White's warning in *Cohen Grocery* that an emergency did not create new powers or wipe away constitutional limits. In *Block*, White joined Van Devanter and McReynolds in McKenna's dissent, which took just this line: war admittedly constituted an emergency, but it neither created new powers nor abolished the Constitution. The debate had not been settled when a new emergency rose a decade later that would invoke this same question.

The Overman Act

Following the Lever Act, Congress continued to assign, albeit reluctantly, additional responsibilities to the president. Nevertheless, by the winter of 1917–1918, the domestic war program seemed stalled in a confusing welter of bureaus, commissions, informal arrangements, and overlapping jurisdictions. Things came to a head in January 1918, when the administration unilaterally imposed a "coal holiday"—a period in which people would not use coal—in an effort to ease a chronic shortage of fuel on the East Coast. Republican Senators on the Military Affairs Committee cited this as one more example of the administration's inability to prosecute the war effectively, and they called for the creation of a war cabinet. Composed of "three distinguished citizens of demonstrated ability," appointed by the president with the advice and consent of the Senate, it would have control of all aspects of domestic administration that pertained to the war. Wilson immediately responded and told the legislators that if there were to be a war cabinet, it would happen not over his veto pen but over his dead body. Wilson's charge of partisanship rang true in this instance, but he could not deny that there had to be some better way to bring together and manage the various efforts related to the war.

On February 6, 1918, Democratic Senator Lee Overman of North Carolina introduced an administration-sponsored bill to impose order on this chaos. In essence, it gave the president a blank check to reorganize the executive agencies "as he may deem necessary," for the duration of the war and one year afterward. By its terms, the president could reassign any function, no matter where it had been lodged previously, even if Congress had specifically given that responsibility to a particular agency, such as the monetary duties of the Federal Reserve Board. The bill imposed no checks on presidential discretion and provided no standards for evaluating the executive's conduct.

The debate in Congress on the Overman bill rang some of the same changes as had been heard the previous summer regarding the Lever Act. Senator Frank Brandegee of Connecticut claimed that Congress would be abdicating its constitutional responsibilities and handing over the legislative power to the executive. Yet even those who opposed powerful central government in principle could not ignore the obvious need to impose order on a nation involved in modern warfare. Senator Henry Cabot Lodge, certainly no friend of Wilson, thought the Overman bill unnecessary, since the president already had the authority under his war powers and did not need an act of Congress to spell it out. Nonetheless, both houses of Congress passed the bill, and by large majorities.

Wilson recognized, of course, that no one man could carry out all the responsibilities or use all that power effectively. So even before the passage of the Overman Act he had created, through either statutory authority or executive ordinance, a series of administrative bodies, each responsible for a particular aspect of mobilization. The Lever Act had authorized the U.S. Food Administration, the Sugar Equalization Board, and the Office of Fuel Administration. In 1916, Congress had also provided for a U.S. Shipping Board and had allowed for the central control of railways under a director general. The Trading with the Enemy Act established an Export Trade Board. But two of the most important executive agencies—the War Industries Board, which coordinated all industrial activity, and the Committee on Public Information, which managed the country's propaganda—Wilson created completely on his own authority as president.

Thus did the man elected on a platform of limited government bring Leviathan to the nation. One can hardly blame Wilson, for he had not caused World War I and had done all he could to keep the United States out of the conflict. Short of totally isolating itself from the rest of the world, the United States could not have avoided a war that threatened too many of the country's interests. Given the autocracy that has characterized so many modern nations at war, Americans did not fare badly. Civil liberties suffered, as we shall see, but they were not eradicated. Democratic political institutions remained intact: the courts operated, legislatures debated, and the populace elected. The American people learned how to live under a modern government, and they recalled this experience in a positive manner when faced with other emergencies during the Depression and in the next world war. If nothing else, they did not fear the government, and for that Wilson deserves at least some of the credit.

Prohibition

According to some historians, war has always been the nemesis of reform. The need to pour all energies into one effort, the desire not to introduce divisiveness, and the usefulness of established interests to the war program all supposedly protect the status quo. Yet war can also extend reform. Labor advocates saw the government accept and impose many of their demands through the War Labor Board and the War Labor Policies Board. Social welfare groups played a prominent role in training American troops and in supplying them with what Secretary of War Newton D. Baker called "moral armor." And the war provided victory for one of the most insistent reform demands—Prohibition.

Crusaders against drink had won their first victory in Congress with the passage of the Webb–Kenyon Act in 1913. That measure reinforced state prohibition laws by closing off the channels of interstate commerce to liquor destined for a state where its use or sale had been prohibited. The law did not stop all shipments, and if a state allowed importation for personal use, such shipments remained legal. The law lacked any provisions for federal enforcement, since the prohibitionists always intended that states should enforce dry laws. The Webb–Kenyon Act embodied the prohibitionist idea of concurrent exercise of state and national power against liquor. In 1917, a divided Supreme Court upheld the law in *Clark Distilling Co. v. Western Maryland Railway*. Since many states refused to adopt Prohibition, reformers saw the Webb–Kenyon Act not only as a blueprint but also a milestone in the drive toward their ultimate goal, a constitutional amendment to secure the desired national dryness. The war gave them a great boost. In the draft law passed in the spring of 1917, Congress forbade the sale of liquor to servicemen. The Lever Act, under the mandate of preserving scarce food resources, authorized the president to limit or forbid the use of foodstuffs for the production of alcoholic beverages. In December 1917, Congress passed a constitutional amendment and sent it on to the states for ratification. Wilson issued a series of war proclamations from December 1917 through September 1918 that in effect established near total prohibition.

When the fighting ended, Wilson seemed ready to relax some of these regulations, but on November 21, 1918, Congress passed the Wartime Prohibition Act. (Even though the armistice had been signed, the peace treaty had not, and technically the United States remained in a state of war.) For the alleged purposes of conserving manpower and increasing efficiency in war production, the statute prohibited the manufacture or distribution of alcoholic beverages until the war came to a formal end and demobilization had been completed. Then in January 1919, the thirty-sixth state ratified the Eighteenth Amendment, which prohibited the "manufacture, sale, or transportation of intoxicating liquors within, the importation thereof into, or the exportation thereof from the United States," and gave Congress and the states concurrent powers of enforcement. The amendment was to go into effect on January 29, 1920, one year after ratification. In October 1919, Congress, over Wilson's veto, passed the Volstead Act, which defined an intoxicating beverage as one with 0.5 percent or more alcohol by volume.

Although all but two states ratified the Eighteenth Amendment, anti-Prohibition sentiment ran strongly, and "wets" went into the courts to challenge not only the implementing legislation, but the amendment itself. In the *National Prohibition Cases* (1920), a distinguished battery of lawyers, including William D. Guthrie and the venerable Elihu Root, attacked the amendment on two grounds. First, the Constitution had not created an unlimited amending power, and the Eighteenth Amendment had passed those limits. Second, the unique enforcement provision of Section 2, giving both Congress and the states concurrent powers, undermined the federal system. The Court brushed aside these arguments. The Eighteenth Amendment had to be treated the same as any other amendment, and Section 2 did not alter any of the traditional lines of authority. Congress had plenary power that could reach both inter- and intrastate commerce; the states' concurrent powers did nothing more than supplement federal power. In essence, the Court said, Section 2 meant nothing.

In the fall of 1919, the Supreme Court heard several cases on the validity of the wartime prohibition and Volstead acts. In *Hamilton v. Kentucky Distilleries*, the Court sustained the former statute over the distilleries' claim that when the fighting ended, the government's war powers lapsed. The state of war depended on more than actual fighting, the Court declared; Congress had the discretion to determine if the emergency still existed, and if so, it could continue the wartime controls. In *Jacob Ruppert v. Coffey*, decided the first week in 1920, the Court by only a 5 to 4 vote upheld the Volstead Act's 0.5 percent definition of intoxicating beverages. Brandeis, speaking for the Court, explained the need of Congress to establish some definitive standard. Whether or not 0.5 percent did, in fact, constitute an intoxicating level did not concern the Court; that determination had been made by Congress, and the judiciary would not venture to second-guess the legislature.

Prohibition reflected the Progressive faith that law could be used to transform public morality, and it failed miserably. Although law can certainly be an instrument of reform, as in the struggle for civil rights in the 1960s, it can rarely be successful against enormous hostile public opinion. A number of people supported Prohibition, and because many of them came from the articulate middle classes, they generated an impression of approval far greater than that which actually existed. Prohibition more than many issues reflected some of the social divisions in the country—such as immigrants versus native-born Americans, and Catholics and Jews versus Protestants. Many or perhaps more people either opposed Prohibition from the start or came to oppose it within a short period of time. To them, the law seemed perverse, and so they ignored it. It is hard to think of any law of this century that has been so ridiculed, so violated, and so despised, or that has led to so much lawlessness.

Women's Suffrage

The Nineteenth Amendment, on the other hand, reflected the Progressive faith that greater participation in the political process would ensure better government, and its passage was also a result of the war. The drive to give women the right to vote had begun much earlier, of course, and had been articulated in the manifesto of the 1848 Seneca Falls Convention. Women activists, such as Susan B. Anthony, Lucretia Mott, Elizabeth Cady Stanton, and Lucy Stone, had labored diligently in the cause, but although they had effected some improvements in the legal status of women, the right to vote remained beyond their grasp.

Because suffrage had always been considered a matter of state power (even the Fourteenth and Fifteenth amendments had left the primary control of voting to the states), women began by lobbying state legislatures for the ballot. The Wyoming Territory gave women the vote in 1869, but by 1900, only four states had granted women full political equality. The movement picked up steam during the Progressive era, especially after 1912, when Alice Paul, a Quaker and social worker, returned from an apprenticeship with the militant suffragists of England. Adopting the techniques she had learned in the mother country, she led a march in Washington on the day before Wilson's inauguration to promote the new goal of the movement—a constitutional amendment. When unruly opponents broke up the parade, the suffragists suddenly had the publicity they needed. By 1916, the Republican party had endorsed the amendment, and eleven states had given women the franchise.

Wilson, who had extremely traditional views about women, opposed giving them the vote. He refused to endorse the proposed amendment, insisting that states should control the suffrage. But the president found himself in a rapidly shrinking minority. Under Alice Paul's leadership, the new Women's party regularly picketed the White House, provoked arrests, and went on well-publicized hunger strikes in prison. When the United States entered the war, allegedly to save democracy, political wisdom dictated that one could not send Americans to fight and die for an ideal overseas while denying it to half the population at home. Wilson finally capitulated, and he went before Congress on September 30, 1918, to recommend a constitutional amendment. Congress had turned down similar proposals ever since Reconstruction, and the Senate now rejected the amendment again, once in 1918 and twice in 1919. With Wilson's backing, however, Congress finally approved the Nineteenth Amendment on June 4, 1919, and Tennessee became the thirty-sixth state to ratify on August 18, 1920, in time for women to vote in that fall's presidential election.

The Nineteenth Amendment doubled the number of eligible voters, but whether it had any qualitative effect on American politics is doubtful. Some reformers believed that the moral purity of women would lead to some sort of cleansing process, but nearly all studies show that women voted just about the same as men of comparable class and

> If women suffrage meant only the enfranchisement of the women of high character and good education, there would be little opposition among the men, provided such women actually desired the ballot. But the introduction of women suffrage also means the enfranchisement of those classes of women who correspond in character and education to the plantation negro and the ignorant immigrant.
>
> —Carl Schurz, *Women Suffrage* (1894)

section. In all, the presence of women at the polls neither destroyed family life nor purified the political process, but it did make American government more representative and took women one large step down the road to the elusive goal of equality.

Wilson and Foreign Policy

The great powers granted to Wilson by Congress, or assumed by him through ordinance, paralleled in many ways the Civil War experience. Given the social, economic, and technical changes of the half-century between the two wars, the expansion of executive power under Wilson probably corresponded to that under Lincoln. But a significant difference existed. In Lincoln's presidency foreign affairs was not a major concern except to the extent that his policy aimed at preventing any European recognition of the Confederacy or interference in the Union war effort.

Important foreign policy issues marked Wilson's entire administration, and the man who viewed the presidency as a premiership showed no hesitation in assuming full responsibility for foreign as well as domestic decisions. It is true that since Washington's time the presidency had been viewed as the embodiment of the nation vis-à-vis other countries. But with only a few major exceptions, foreign affairs had not previously intruded into American life. Washington had abrogated the French treaty of alliance, and Monroe had sealed the New World to further European colonization. Our contacts with Great Britain, after the War of 1812, had been cordial, and the two countries had managed to resolve the Canadian border disputes peacefully.

With the Spanish–American War, however, the United States had entered world affairs. Theodore Roosevelt had expanded American influence, both by show of force in sending the great white fleet around the world and by his personal diplomacy in negotiating the end of the Russo–Japanese War, for which he won the Nobel Peace Prize in 1906. Roosevelt had also, as he liked to put it, "taken" the Panama Canal Zone, and he, Taft, and Wilson had all followed domineering policies toward Latin America. Wilson, in fact, had almost gone to war with Mexico in 1914 because he disapproved of the revolutionary government of Victoriano Huerta, and in 1916, he sent General John Pershing with 15,000 troops back and forth across the Texas–Mexico border in a wild-goose chase after the bandit, Pancho Villa. Although Wilson disapproved of Taft's "dollar diplomacy," he kept American marines in Nicaragua, where they had been sent in 1912 to prevent civil war, and in 1915 he dispatched marines to Haiti to calm matters there.

But all this paled before the problems of the Great War and Wilson's dream—or delusion—that he could be a peacemaker to the world. Ignoring the State Department, he carried on a personal diplomacy through his friend and confidant, the enigmatic Colonel Edward M. House. After his reelection in 1916 on a platform of peace and preparedness—with the slogan "He kept us out of war!"—Wilson went before the Senate on January 22, 1917, to call for "peace without victory," suggesting that he was speaking "for the silent mass of mankind everywhere." Once America was in the war, Wilson continued to try to define the goals of the conflict, most notably in the Fourteen Points, which he enunciated to Congress on January 8, 1918, "as the only possible program" for peace. In one way, at least, Wilson's plan had an impact; Germany surrendered on the basis of the Fourteen Points. In a war of wolves, Wilson often seemed a lamb, the only one of the Allies truly concerned with making a better and more just world after the fighting had ended.

Although Wilson had gone to Congress in April 1917 to ask for the declaration of war as the Constitution required, he had never really consulted the legislature. Foreign policy matters, he believed, rested in his hands, and he assigned no role in foreign affairs to the Congress. Then, in the fall of 1918, Wilson made two fateful decisions. He announced that he would personally attend the peace conference in Versailles in January 1919, the first time a president would be out of the country for so long a time. And, in the midterm election of 1918, he made a partisan appeal for a Democratic Congress that would ensure support of his foreign policy, implying that Republicans had not wholeheartedly supported the war. An angry electorate returned Republican majorities in both the House and Senate, and Wilson sailed for Europe repudiated, at least in part, by the people.

The Treaty of Versailles

Wilson spent more than six months in Europe, making two separate trips, during which time he gave up any effort at domestic leadership. Demobilization turned into chaos, as war agencies folded overnight and the army rushed to return soldiers to civilian life. Because of his view that he alone stood constitutionally responsible for making foreign policy, he failed to take a single senator with him, even though the upper house would have to ratify any treaty he might negotiate in Paris. Although he acknowledged that any treaty he negotiated would have to be approved by the Senate, Wilson contended that a president "may guide every step of diplomacy, and to guide diplomacy is to determine what treaties must be made, if the faith and prestige of the government are to be sustained. He need disclose no step of negotiation until it is complete, and when in any critical matter it is completed the government is virtually committed. Whatever its disinclination, the Senate may feel itself committed as well." To his sorrow, Wilson would learn that the Senate did not agree.

> [When faced by a recalcitrant Senate, a President might well follow a more conciliatory course] which one or two Presidents of unusual political sagacity have followed, with the satisfactory results that were to have been expected. He may himself be less stiff and offish, may himself act in the true spirit of the Constitution, and establish intimate relations of confidence with the Senate on his own initiative, not carrying his plans to completion and then laying them in final form before the Senate, to be accepted or rejected, but keeping himself in a confidential communication with the leaders of the Senate while his plans are in course, when their advice will be of service to him and his information of the greatest service to them, in order that there may be veritable counsel and a real accommodation of views instead of a final challenge and contest.
>
> —Woodrow Wilson, *Constitutional Government* (1908)

The details of the Treaty of Versailles, including the Covenant of the League of Nations, are well known. What is of concern here is the conflict between the president and the Senate over ratification of the treaty. Wilson could not avoid submitting the document for the upper chamber's approval, for although the Constitution (Article II, Section 2) gave the president the power to make treaties, it required the concurrence by a two-thirds vote of the Senate. Wilson reported the draft of the treaty at the peace conference on February 14, 1919; two weeks later, Republican Henry Cabot Lodge, chairman of the Senate Foreign Relations Committee, issued a statement that the treaty "in the form now proposed" would be unacceptable. Thirty-nine senators or senators-elect signed the Lodge statement, more than enough to block ratification

Over the next several months, the terrible tragedy played itself out. Wilson's idealism, especially as expressed in the League of Nations, struck a resonant chord among Americans, who saw the treaty as progressivism writ large in foreign affairs. A third of the state legislatures endorsed the League, as did thirty-three governors, but they had no say in approval. In the Senate, a group of "irreconcilables"—fourteen Republicans and two Democrats—vowed to do anything they could to block American entry to the League on any terms. Another group, far larger, wanted to join the League, but many of them had reservations about particular points. Lodge, who detested Wilson, forged an alliance between the irreconcilables and the reservationists strong enough to defeat the treaty, and in this endeavor his greatest ally proved to be Woodrow Wilson. Partisanship played a major role in the struggle, but one should not overlook the fact that many of Wilson's opponents in the League fight also worried about the Constitution. Lodge and others—both Democrats and Republicans— had grown increasingly alarmed as the war progressed and the president arrogated more and more power to himself and the executive branch. These objections had surfaced before and during the war in debates over the administration's preparedness and war measures. During the war, opponents had been somewhat bound by charges that they were obstructing the prosecution of the war; with the war over, they could now try to restore what they considered the proper separation of powers between Congress and the president.

The reservationists had some legitimate questions, both as to the policy implications of the treaty as well constitutional provisions. Among the latter, none stood out more clearly than Article X of the League Covenant, which called for collective action against aggression. Did this mean that if the United States ratified the treaty and

> The power of the Senate in making treaties has always been held, as the Constitution intended, to be equal and co-ordinate with that of the President, except in the initiation of a negotiation. . . . The Senate has the right to amend, and this right it has always exercised largely and freely. It is also clear that any action taken by the Senate is part of the negotiation, just as much so as the action of the President through the Secretary of State. In other words, the action of the Senate upon a treaty is not merely to give sanction to the treaty, but is an integral part of the treaty making, and may be taken at any stage of a negotiation.
>
> —Henry Cabot Lodge, "The Treaty-Making Powers of the Senate" (1902)

joined the League, it automatically had to go to war if aggression occurred? What did this imply for the constitutional requirement that only Congress could commit the country to war? The reservationists wanted a clarification, to which the Allied powers willingly agreed, that Article X could not commit a nation to war without first going through its normal constitutional processes.

But Wilson would have no changes, and by refusing to meet his opponents even part way, he doomed ratification of the Treaty of Versailles to defeat. Under orders from the president, enough Democrats voted against the treaty with the clarification to give the irreconcilables the victory. A stubborn president and a small group of equally stubborn senators thus crippled American foreign policy for a generation. Wilson's rigid interpretation of presidential powers would not allow him to compromise, and together with the Senate's insistence on doing its constitutional duty of reviewing treaties, he played into the hands of Lodge.

An Incapacitated President

In a last-ditch effort to save the treaty, Wilson went to the people in a strenuous speaking tour in September 1919. He traveled over 8,000 miles in twenty-two days and gave some forty speeches, before collapsing in Pueblo, Colorado, on September 25.[1] A week later, he suffered a stroke and subsequent paralysis on his left side, which left him incapacitated for weeks. For seven months, he did not meet with the cabinet, and messages from department heads had to be routed to him through his wife and physician.

Until the adoption of the Twenty-fifth Amendment in 1967, the Constitution had no provision for such a situation. In case of a president's "Death, Resignation, or Inability to discharge the Powers and Duties of the said Office, the Same shall devolve on the Vice President" (Article II, Section 1). But it gave no guidance as to what constituted "inability" or how serious an illness had to be before a vice president took over. Vice President Thomas Marshall, best remembered for his declaration that what the country most needed was a good five-cent cigar, made it clear that he did not want to be president; since no one else wanted him in the White House either, the country had no real head of government for several months.

While on his sickbed, Wilson mulled over the impasse on the treaty and bemoaned the fact that a president lacked the power of a prime minister to dissolve the legislature. He came up with a scheme that the fifty-three senators who opposed the treaty should resign and run again for their seats in a special election. He believed the American people supported the League, and if they voted to replace these senators, then the deadlock would be broken. If, however, they returned a majority of them to the Senate, then he would appoint a Republican secretary of state, and he and Vice president Marshall would resign. The result would be a new government in the parliamentary sense of the term. This far-fetched plan, which had absolutely no constitutional sup-

1. Wilson's health appears to have been deteriorating before October 1919. He had suffered a viral infection in Paris in April, and apparently had had a minor stroke in July, both of which, according to some scholars, diminished his emotional and mental capacities to deal with the Senate.

port, never made it out of the sickroom. Perhaps it would have been better had another idea, a Jackson Day letter to Democrats, also remained stillborn. But Wilson did send a letter in which he declared that "We cannot rewrite this treaty. We must take it without changes which alter its meaning, or leave it." For many Democrats and nearly all Republicans, this was the final nail in the treaty's coffin.

During the time of Wilson's incapacitation, the cabinet heads ran their departments, and Secretary of State Robert Lansing settled certain questions by calling together the cabinet. It was probably the best way to make a policy decision, but Wilson never forgave Lansing for this supposed affront, and forced him to resign. Congress also took the lead in some areas, such as returning the railroads to private hands in the Transportation Act of 1920. But the once proud president, who had epitomized the Progressive movement and led the nation successfully through a world war, ended his term embittered and impotent.

Free Speech in Wartime

Ironically, the war to make the world safe for democracy triggered the worst invasion of civil liberties at home in the nation's history. The government obviously had to protect itself from subversion, but many of the laws seemed aimed as much at suppressing radical criticism of administration policy as at ferreting out spies. In the Selective Service Act, Congress authorized the jailing of people who obstructed the draft. The Espionage Act of 1917, aimed primarily against treason, also punished anyone making or conveying false reports for the benefit of the enemy, seeking to cause disobedience in the armed services, or obstructing recruitment or enlistment in the armed forces. The postmaster general received power in the Trading with the Enemy Act of 1917 to ban foreign language and other publications from the mails. The 1918 Sedition Act, passed at the behest of Western senators and modeled after Montana's statute to curb the Industrial Workers of the World, struck out at a variety of "undesirable" activities, and forbade "uttering, printing, writing, or publishing any disloyal, profane, scurrilous, or abusive language." Finally, the Immigration Act of 1918 permitted the deportation of alien anarchists or those who believed in the use of force to overthrow the government; in fact, the deportation of alien anarchists had been possible since 1903, and that power had been expanded in the Immigration Act of 1917.

It is certainly understandable that a government should wish to protect itself from active subversion, especially during wartime. But the evidence indicates that Wilson, preoccupied first with mobilization and then with peace-making, gave little thought to the problem and deferred to some of his conservative advisers, especially Postmaster General Albert Burleson, a reactionary who considered any criticism of the government unpatriotic. There is a suspicion that in coming down so hard on Socialist newspapers, such as the *Milwaukee Leader,* Burleson intended to send a message to the larger, more middle-class journals that they should not get too far out of line.

The federal laws and similar state statutes caught radicals, pacifists, and other dissenters in an extensive web. The total number of indictments ran into the thousands; the attorney general reported 877 convictions out of 1,956 cases commenced in 1919 and 1920. Although the laws had been challenged early, the government had shown no desire to push for a quick decision on their constitutionality. As a result, some half-dozen cases did not reach the Supreme Court until the spring of 1919, after the end of hostilities.

These cases marked the beginning of a civil liberties tradition in American constitutional law. There had been no such tradition prior to the war, because neither the states nor the federal government had seriously restricted First Amendment rights. These cases also began the process of developing criteria for permissible limitations on speech; the dissents of Holmes and Brandeis initiated the counterprocess by which the courts ultimately became the defenders of civil liberties against the executive and legislative branches.

The Speech Tradition Before *Schenck*

Although modern speech jurisprudence begins with the Holmes opinions in *Schenck* and *Abrams*, a jurispurdence of free speech did exist prior to 1919. Different writers and groups tried to put forward theories that would be speech protective, but they had little success. One reason may have been their identity. The International Workers of the World, the feared and radical "Wobblies," put forward an extensive rationale for speech completely free from any governmental regulation. Today we would find that rationale not very different from that put forward by contemporary jurists; before the First World War, only fellow radicals took the IWW seriously.

The scholar David Rabban has also identified what he terms a "lost tradition of libertarian radicalism," which defended as a primary value individual autonomy against the power of church and state. This tradition reaches back before the Civil War in various movements, including abolitionism, labor reform, and women's rights. With the arrival of the Comstock Acts in 1873 and 1876 to censor materials moving through the mails, the libertarian radicals organized in such groups as the National Defense Association (1878) and the Free Speech League (1902), the latter actively involved in defending those whose speech had been restricted, usually radicals such as Emma Goldman and Margaret Sanger. The leader of the Free Speech League, Theodore Schroeder, worked out a philosophy of free speech premised on the belief that everyone had a right to say whatever they wished and that government had no business acting as a censor. Schroeder rejected earlier theories of speech and press that would allow governmental interference should the speech have a "bad tendency," or which would allow publication but then provide punishment.

Despite the best efforts of the Free Speech League, as well as of writers like Schroeder and Ernst Freund, the overwhelming weight of judicial opinion before the war, in both federal and state jurisdictions, did little to recognize the notion that the First Amendment meant speech should not be curtailed. Speech, or at least the expression of unpopular or strange views, received little sympathy from the public at large or the men who sat on the bench.

Most judges relied on Sir William Blackstone, who in his *Commentaries* argued that the right of free speech precluded prior restraint (that is, the government could not stop a person from speaking or publishing ideas), but the law could punish speakers and writers if their expressions tended to harm the public welfare. In the leading

> For the legislature absolutely or conditionally to forbid public speaking in a highway or public park is no more an infringement of the rights of a member of the public than for the owner of a private house to forbid it in his house.
>
> —Oliver Wendell Holmes, Jr., *Commonwealth v. Davis* (Mass. 1895)

Supreme Court opinion of this time, *Patterson v. Colorado* (1907), Justice Holmes closely followed Blackstone's analysis. Thomas Patterson could hardly be described as a radical. A U.S. senator from Colorado and a newspaper publisher, he had actively supported a referendum that provided home rule for Denver. He became outraged when the Republican legislature enlarged the state supreme court and packed it with judges who overturned the results of the referendum. His newspapers carried editorials, cartoons, and letters ridiculing the court. The state attorney general brought criminal contempt proceedings against Patterson on behalf of the supreme court, which in turn fined him and his publishing company $1,000, without allowing him to prove truth as a defense.

Patterson appealed to the U.S. Supreme Court, but Holmes rejected all of his arguments about the nature of free speech. The First Amendment, Holmes declared, "prevents all previous restraints upon publications," but allows "the subsequent punishment of such as may be deemed contrary to the public welfare." Interestingly, Holmes dismissed the notion of truth as a defense. "The preliminary freedom extends to the false as to the true; the subsequent punishment may extend as well to the true as to the false." The Court heard only a few other First Amendment cases before the wartime convictions reached it on appeal in 1919, and all of them essentially followed Blackstone as explained by Holmes in *Patterson.*

Clear and Present Danger

In the first case, *Schenck v. United States* (1919), the secretary of the Philadelphia Socialist Party had been indicted for urging resistance to the draft. He had sent out circulars condemning conscription as despotic and unconstitutional and calling on draftees to assert their rights and refuse induction. Under the terms of the Espionage Act, Schenck had urged unlawful behavior; but did the Constitution's guarantee of free speech protect him? Holmes attempted to develop a standard based on the common law rule of proximate causation, and he took a fairly traditional view of speech as a limited right. One could not, he pointed out, falsely shout "Fire!" in a theater. In a famous passage, Holmes attempted to define the limits of speech:

> The question in every case is whether the words used are used in such circumstances and are of such a nature to create a clear and present danger that they will bring about the substantive evils that Congress has a right to prevent. It is a question of proximity and degree. When a nation is at war, many things that might be said in time of peace are such a hindrance to its effort that their utterance will not be endured so long as men fight and no Court could regard them as protected by any constitutional right.

The "clear and present danger" test became the starting point for all subsequent free speech cases, and within a week, the Court sustained two other convictions under this rule. In *Frohwerk v. United States*, a German-language newspaper had run articles attacking the draft and challenging the constitutionality of the war, whereas in *Debs v. United States*, Holmes accepted a jury finding that in a militant antiwar speech, Debs had intended interference with mobilization.

The three decisions, as well as the clear and present danger test, upset defenders of free speech, especially because they had come from a man they believed to be an ardent libertarian. Legal scholars such as Zechariah Chafee, Jr., Ernst Freund, and others attacked Holmes for his insensitivity to the larger implications of free speech. "Tolerance of adverse opinion is not a matter of generosity," Freund declared, "but of political prudence." In an influential article (later expanded into a book) on "Free Speech in the United States," Chafee insisted that the Framers of the First Amendment had more in mind than simple censorship. They intended to do away with the common law of sedition and make it impossible to prosecute criticism of the government in the absence of any incitement to law-breaking. In none of these three cases could one argue that the defendants had been attempting to incite active law-breaking; for Chafee, Learned Hand's test in *Masses Publishing Company v. Patten* (1917) made far more sense. Hand, then a district judge, displayed considerable solicitude for free speech in his opinion and would allow all but speech that directly incited unlawful action.

Holmes, stung by this criticism, agreed to meet with Chafee. The Harvard professor convinced Holmes that free speech served broad social purposes and that the national interest would suffer more from restrictions on speech than from some alleged and vague dangers posed by unpopular thought. Moreover, through a clever, if somewhat inaccurate reading of history, Chafee convinced Holmes that his phrase "clear and present danger" had not only historial roots, but actually was very speech protective. Chafee's missionary work bore fruit at the next term, when Holmes, along with Brandeis, began reformulating the clear and present danger test.

> Political agitation, by the passions it arouses or the convictions it engenders, may in fact stimulate men to the violation of the law. Detestation of existing policies is easily transformed into forcible resistance of the authority which puts them in execution, and it would be folly to disregard the causal relation between the two. Yet to assimilate agitation, legitimate as such, with direct incitement to violent resistance, is to disregard the tolerance of all methods of political agitation which in normal times is a safeguard of free government. The distinction is not a scholastic subterfuge, but a hard-bought acquisition in the fight for freedom, and the purpose to disregard it must be evident when the power exists. If one stops short of urging upon others that it is their duty or their interest to resist the law, it seems to me one should not be held to have attempted to cause its violation. If that not be the test, I can see no escape from the conclusion that under [§3 of the 1917 Espionage Act] every political agitation which can be shown to be apt to create a seditious temper is illegal. I am confident that by such language Congress had no such revolutionary purpose in view.
>
> —Learned Hand, *Masses Publishing Co. v. Patten* (1917)

The Beginnings of the Free Speech Tradition

In *Abrams v. United States* (1919), the defendants had distributed pamphlets in Yiddish and English criticizing the Wilson administration for sending troops to Russia in the summer of 1918. The government had no way to prove that such leaflets actually hindered the war with Germany, but a lower court judge found that they *might* have caused revolts and strikes and thereby diminished the number of troops available to fight the Germans. Seven members of the Court, led by Justice John H. Clarke, agreed that the government had provided sufficient proof to support this charge and that the conviction could be sustained under the *Schenck* test of clear and present danger.

Both Holmes and Brandeis disagreed, and in an eloquent dissent, Holmes limned one of the great defenses of free speech. The "silly leaflets" hardly posed a danger to society, and the fact that the ideas expressed were unpopular or even considered dangerous made no difference:

> When men have realized that time has come to upset many fighting faiths, they may come to believe even more than they believe the very foundations of their own conduct that the ultimate good desired is better reached by free trade in ideas—that the best test of truth is the power of the thought to get itself accepted in the competition of the market and that truth is the only ground upon which their wishes safely can be carried out. That at any rate is the theory of our Constitution. It is an experiment, as all life is an experiment.

Holmes's dissent in the *Abrams* case is often seen as the beginning of the Court's concern with free speech as a key right in democratic society, and it put forward the notion of democracy as resting upon a free marketplace of ideas. Some ideas might be unpopular, some might be unsettling, and some might be false. But in a democracy, one had to give all ideas an equal chance to be heard, in the belief that the false, the ignoble, and the useless would be crowded out by the right ideas, the ones that would facilitate progress in a democratic manner. Only if society took the guaranty of the First Amendment seriously could that happen.

> Workers, Russian emigrants, you who had the least belief in the honesty of our Government must now throw away all confidence, must spit in the face of the false, hypocritical military propaganda which had fooled you so relentlessly, calling forth your sympathy, your help, to the prosecution of the war.
>
> With the money which you have loaned, or are going to loan them, they will make bullets not only for the Germans, but also for the Workers Soviets of Russia. Workers in the ammunition factories, you are producing bullets, bayonets, cannon, to murder not only the Germans, but also your dearest, best, who are in Russia and are fighting for freedom. . . .
>
> Workers, our reply to the barbaric intervention has to be a general strike! An open challenge only will let the Government know that not only the Russian Worker fights for freedom, but also here in America lives the spirit of revolution.
>
> "Workers—Wake UP!!
>
> —Pamphlet (original in Yiddish) that led to arrest of Jacob Abrams

Four months later, the Court announced its decision in *Schaeffer v. United States*. All five defendants had been connected with a German-language newspaper in Philadelphia accused of publishing unpatriotic articles critical of the Allies and favorable to the Central Powers. McKenna, for the majority, did not mention clear and present danger, but used a more permissive standard, the "bad tendency" test. Did the words *intend* a proscribed action? If so, that would be enough to sustain the conviction.

Now Brandeis led the dissent. Although he had been uncomfortable with Holmes's earlier arguments, he had not been sure what other options the Court had. Chafee's article gave him his clue, and he had gladly joined Holmes in *Abrams*. With *Schaeffer* he entered the debate and helped refine clear and present danger so that it would serve more as a protection for free speech than as a license for government repression. He set forth the utility of free speech in a democratic society: even though it could be abused, the benefits of untrammeled discourse far outweighed any inconvenience. Above all, basic rights should not be crippled because of wartime hysteria. An intolerant majority, he declared, "swayed by passion or fear, may be prone in the future, as it has often been in the past, to stamp as disloyal opinions with which it disagrees. Convictions such as these, besides abridging freedom of speech, threaten freedom of thought and of belief."

The last of the major Espionage Act cases came down soon after; *Pierce v. United States* involved prosecution of three Socialists for distributing a strongly antiwar pamphlet. Justice Mahlon Pitney quickly disposed of the constitutional arguments, merely citing the string of cases from *Schenck* through *Schaeffer* to sustain the conviction; but he then went to great length to disprove the allegations made in the pamphlet, especially that the war had economic causes. Such a false view, he claimed, could not help but have an adverse, even if indirect, effect on the successful prosecution of the war. (Interestingly, six months earlier, Woodrow Wilson had stated: "Who does not know that the seed of war in the modern world is industrial and commercial rivalry. This was a commercial and industrial war." By the *Pierce* opinion, the president could have been prosecuted under the Espionage Act!)

Brandeis, again joined by Holmes, entered a long and thorough dissent, claiming the government had failed to prove that the publication had posed any danger to the war effort. To urge men to better their lot by creating new laws and institutions could not be labeled a criminal act "merely because the argument presented seems to those exercising judicial power to be unfair in its portrayal of existing evils, mistaken in its assumptions, unsound in reasoning, or intemperate in language." The "falsity" of one's view, according to the interpretation of free speech Brandeis and Holmes advocated, had nothing to do with one's right to promote that view.

One other excess of the Espionage Act came before the Court later that term in the *Milwaukee Leader* case. Congress had given the postmaster general the authority to close the mails to any newspaper violating the act, and Albert Burleson had revoked the second-class mailing privileges of the Socialist *Milwaukee Leader*. The government charged the paper with publishing false reports with the intent to hinder American military operations, obstruct recruiting, and aid the enemy. Speaking for the majority, Justice Clarke upheld the government's action and rejected the defense claim that the First Amendment's protection of a free press had been violated. The First

Amendment, Clarke declared, is not intended "to serve as a protecting screen for those who while claiming its privileges seek to destroy it."

For Brandeis, whose dissent Holmes joined, the question did not involve distinctions between war and peace, but the basic right of a free press. Even where Congress had previously declared certain materials unmailable, only issues containing that type of material had been excluded. Here the postmaster had banned all issues, becoming in effect "the universal censor." Freedom of the press could not be limited either directly or, as in this case, indirectly by denying the mailing privilege. "In every extension of governmental function," he warned, "lurks a new danger to civil liberty."

Despite the justifiable applause with which civil libertarians had greeted Holmes's *Abrams* dissent in 1919, by the end of the 1920 term, Brandeis had emerged as the Court's most powerful defender of free expression. Holmes had the gift of generalization, of the quotable phrase, but the more stolid Brandeis built the foundation of future constitutional protection of free speech with facts, logic, and, on occasion, impassioned and eloquent language as well. Such an occasion arose in *Gilbert v. Minnesota* (1920), when Holmes went along with the majority in sustaining a conviction under a state sedition law that prohibited the teaching or advocacy of certain ideas. Gilbert had made a speech questioning American democracy, declaring that "if they conscripted wealth like they have conscripted men, this war would not last over forty-eight hours." His appeal claimed that the federal sedition law had preempted the field and that his conviction under state law violated his right to free speech. Justice McKenna, for the majority, denied that the state had no power, and said it "would be a travesty" to allow Gilbert to find protection within the Constitution.

Brandeis dissented along with White, although the chief justice's only objection was his belief that the federal law preempted the field. To Brandeis, the Minnesota law posed a far greater danger to speech than did the federal law, because it applied in peacetime as well as in war; it banned pacifism, among other ideas, for all time. Only the federal government had the power to curtail free discussion in the national interest; moreover, he believed that the personal protections assured in the Bill of Rights should apply to the states, as well as to the federal government. "I cannot believe that the liberty guaranteed by the Fourteenth Amendment," he told his colleagues, "includes only liberty to acquire and to enjoy property." Brandeis's dissent pointed the way to the future, in which the Bill of Rights would in fact be "incorporated" through the Fourteenth Amendment so as to limit state action. The majority had not foreclosed that possibility; it had just not reached the issue. Five years later, in *Gitlow v. New York* (1925), the Court began coming around to the Brandeisian point of view.

The American Civil Liberties Union

The restrictions on speech and press worried many people even during the war. Newspaper publishers and editors naturally worried about any restrictions on their right to print news or to editorialize, but they did not want to be seen as in any way unpatriotic. After all, nearly all of the major English-language papers and periodicals supported the war. But who would stand up for those who opposed war, whose opinions ran against the grain? The American Union Against Militarism, one of the nation's leading prewar pacifist organizations, established a National Civil Liberties Bureau in October 1917, and its members included social workers (many of them pacifists), Protestant clergy (also mainly pacifist), and conservative lawyers, most of whom supported the war but also venerated the Constitution and were outraged by what they saw as the administration's violations of free speech and due process. Albert DeSilver, an outspoken, prowar patriot, declared that "my law-abiding neck gets very warm under its law-abiding collar these days at the extraordinary violations of fundamental laws which are being put over." Independently wealthy, DeSilver quit his law practice and devoted full-time help to the Bureau to defend radicals, often putting up the war bonds he had purchased for their bail.

During the war, the bureau had plenty to keep it occupied, as the Wilson administration attempted to muzzle the foreign-language press, close off the mails to dissidents, and punish antiwar speech. When the bureau printed a pamphlet explaining why it defended what it called "war's heretics," the postal service seized that as well, and it took nearly a year in court to force the release of the material.

The bureau represented the defendants in nearly all of the major cases that eventually made their way to the Supreme Court. The bureau and its head, Roger Baldwin, attacked the administration policies as a violation of old-fashioned American liberties, but the fact of the matter is that defense of the First Amendment, at least as we know it today, did not exist at the time. The tradition did not permit prior restraint of speech, but did allow the full strength of the government to come down on those whose views offended the majority. Unwittingly, perhaps, the bureau helped to convince Holmes and Brandeis, and later a majority of the Court, that a free society must allow even unpopular speech. After the war, Baldwin transformed the bureau into the American Civil Liberties Union and would head it for more than two decades. In time, the ACLU became the chief defender of freedom of speech and eventually expanded its activities into other areas of civil liberties and civil rights. In the conservative years of the 1980s, it would be attacked repeatedly, but also would be imitated by many other groups working in the public interest on both liberal and conservative sides.

The Red Scare

The speech and press cases of 1919–1920 provide a transition from the war to the decade that followed. On the one hand, the Court upheld the powers of the government, as it had on the draft and economic regulations; on the other, the decisions foreshadowed the indifference to civil liberties that marked so much of the 1920s. With the peace, for example, thirty-two states enacted new sedition and criminal syndicalism laws to control supposedly dangerous ideas, and many of the more notorious speech cases of the decade involved prosecution of people who held ideas different from those of the majority. In New York, the infamous Lusk Committee directed raids on the headquarters of allegedly radical groups, whose only "crime" had been to expound unpopular doctrines. But the worst outrage came with the Palmer raids, which triggered the great "Red Scare."

The awkward transition from war to peace unsettled the American people. The Wilson administration, obsessed with foreign affairs after the 1918 armistice, made no effort to effect a smooth demobilization. The War Industries Board, for example, closed shop on January 1, 1919, and its chairman, Bernard Baruch, had to lay out his own money so his aides could travel home. The War Department canceled hundreds of contracts, throwing thousands of men out of work at the same time that the armed forces were discharging some 4,000 men a day from uniform. Industry used the end of the war as an excuse to cut wages or negate union recognition. As a result, some four million workers went out on strike in 1919, and by the end of the year, the public began to hear—and believe—rumors that radicals had instigated the strikes.

Seattle Mayor Ole Hansen denounced the general strike of 60,000 workers in his city as a Bolshevik plot. The great four-month strike in the steel mills certainly had its share of radicals among the strike leaders. On September 9, 1919, most of Boston's police force went on strike. Governor Calvin Coolidge called up the National Guard to maintain order and break the strike, and then refused to take the men back on the force. He gained national approval when he declared, "There is no right to strike against the public safety by anybody, anywhere, any time."

Aside from economic strife, the summer of 1919 witnessed bloody racial riots in both the North and South. In July, whites invaded the black section of Longview, Texas, looking for a man who had been accused of a liaison with a white woman. A week later, reports of black attacks on white women in the nation's capital brought out white mobs who rampaged for four days. But the worst were the Chicago riots of late July, which left 38 people dead and 537 injured. Racial tensions continued over the next few years, and in 1921, another major race riot broke out in Tulsa, Oklahoma.

In addition to this turmoil, in April 1919, the post office intercepted several dozen packages addressed to leading businessmen and politicians that in fact contained bombs, triggered to explode when opened; some actually reached their destinations and seriously wounded several people. Two months later, eight bombs exploded in eight cities within minutes of each other, suggesting a nationwide conspiracy. Attorney General A. Mitchell Palmer, a Pennsylvania Quaker and formerly a Progressive congressman, saw radical plots everywhere. He urged Congress to enact peacetime sedition laws, and he decided to deport radical aliens. In June 1919, Palmer installed the young J. Edgar Hoover as head of the new General Intelligence Division of the Bureau of Investigation, with orders to collect files on radicals. On November 7, 1919, agents began raiding the headquarters of suspected subversive groups, arresting people without warrants and paying little attention to basic procedural rights. In the largest raid, on January 2, 1920, agents arrested between 4,000 and 6,000 people, detaining half of them in crowded jails for long periods of time. Later that month, the New York Assembly ousted five duly elected members because they were Socialists.

Fortunately for the country, the Red Scare receded almost as quickly as it had come. Palmer overplayed his hand, and after the widespread disruptions he had predicted for May Day 1920 failed to materialize, his credibility—and his hopes for the Democratic presidential nomination—vanished. Acting Secretary of Labor Louis F. Post managed to slow down the deportations, while prominent conservatives such as Charles Evans Hughes, as well as church and civic leaders, spoke out against the high-handed abuse of civil liberties. It had been in this milieu of the "scare" that the Supreme

Court had decided the Espionage Act cases, but by the end of January 1920, the justices signaled their displeasure at federal abuse of constitutionally protected rights in the case of *Silverthorne Lumber Company v. United States.*

Two men had been arrested after indictment by a grand jury. The Justice Department, without a warrant, then ransacked their office, removing books, papers, and other documents. Holmes, writing for the Court, branded the government's action an "outrage" and blocked any use of the illegally seized material by the government in legal proceedings. Holmes's insistence that the documents "shall not be used at all" helped expand the "exclusionary rule" that the Court had first propounded in *Weeks v. United States* (1914). In *Weeks*, *Silverthorne*, and other cases, the Court stressed two themes: the exclusionary rule provided the only effective means of protecting Fourth Amendment rights and judicial integrity required that the courts not sanction illegal search by admitting the fruits of this illegality into evidence.

Within a short time, liberal lower court judges picked up on the Holmes statement to block deportations based on illegally seized materials and to overturn arrests carried out without proper warrants. In *Colyer v. Skeffington* (1920), federal judge George W. Anderson chastised the Justice Department for its "hang-first-and-try-afterward" techniques. "A mob is a mob," he declared, "whether made up of government officials acting under instructions from the Department of Justice or of criminals, loafers, and the vicious classes." Unfortunately, such common sense came too late to save hundreds of aliens from being illegally deported from the United States.

For Further Reading

For a good overview of America in wartime, see Robert H. Ferrell, *Woodrow Wilson and World War I, 1917–1921* (1985). See also Daniel M. Smith, *The Great Departure: The United States in World War I, 1914–1920* (1965); and the older but still useful Frederic L. Paxton, *American Democracy and the World War* 3 vols. (1936–1948). Wilson's views on the wartime powers of the presidency and the problems they caused are well detailed in Daniel D. Stid, *The President as Statesman: Woodrow Wilson and the Constitution* (1998).

The problems of organizing for war are best explained in Robert D. Cuff, *The War Industries Board: Government-Business Relations During World War I* (1973). Other useful works include Valerie Jean Connor, *The National War Relations Board: Stability, Social Justice, and the Voluntary State During World War I* (1983); William F. Willoughby, *Government Organization in War Time and After* (1919); Maxcy R. Dickson, *The Food Front in World War I* (1944); essays on this war in Benjamin F. Cooling, ed., *War, Business, and American Society: Historical Perspectives on the Military-Industrial Complex* (1977); and Jerry Israel, ed., *Building the Organizational Society* (1972).

For problems of securing the peace, see Lawrence E. Gelfand, *The Inquiry: American Preparation for Peace, 1917–1919* (1963); Charles L. Lee, Jr., *The End of Order: Versailles, 1919* (1980); and Arthur S. Link, *Woodrow Wilson: War, Revolution, and Peace* (1979). Highly critical is Thomas A. Bailey, *Woodrow Wilson and the Great Betrayal* (1945). See also J. Chalmers Vinson, *Referendum for Isolation: Defeat of Article Ten of the League of Nations Covenant* (1961); Ralph Stone, *The Irreconcilables: The Fight Against the League of Nations* (1970); and William C. Widenor, *Henry Cabot Lodge and the Search for an American Foreign Policy* (1980).

Reform in wartime is treated generally in Otis L. Graham, Jr., *The Great Campaigns: Reform and War in America, 1900–1928* (1971); and Ellis Wayne Hawley, *The Great War and the*

Search for a Modern Order, 1917–1933 (1979), which ties the war experience to broader trends. For women's rights, see Jane Jerome Camhi, *Women Against Women: American Anti-Suffragism, 1880–1920* (1994); and Susan E. Marshall, *Splintered Sisterhood: Gender and Class in the Campaign against Woman Suffrage* (1997). Richard F. Hamm, *Shaping the Eighteenth Amendment: Temperance Reform, Legal Culture, and the Polity, 1880–1920* (1995) is the best work on the prohibitionists and their successful effort to amend the Constitution.

William Preston, Jr., *Aliens and Dissenters: Federal Suppression of Radicals, 1903–1933* (1963), fits the war and postwar repression of civil liberties into a broader context. Paul Murphy, *World War I and the Origin of Civil Liberties in the United States* (1979), argues the case that no civil liberties tradition existed before the war, while David M. Rabban, *Free Speech in its Forgotten Years* (1997), claims that a vigorous speech protective tradition existed. The beginning and subsequent history of the ACLU is told in Samuel Walker, *In Defense of American Liberties* (1990). A fine study of a landmark case is Richard Polenberg, *Fighting Faiths: The Abrams Case, the Supreme Court, and Free Speech* (1987). The classic exposition of the problem remains Zechariah Chafee, Jr., *Free Speech in the United States* (1920, rev. ed., 1941).

For Holmes and Brandeis, see the relevant sections of G. Edward White, *Justice Oliver Wendell Holmes: Law and the Inner Self* (1993); and Philippa Strum, *Brandeis: Beyond Progressivism* (1993). Holmes's search for an appropriate standard is well told in Fred D. Ragan, "Justice Oliver Wendell Holmes, Jr., Zechariah Chafee, Jr., and the Clear and Present Danger Test for Free Speech: The First Year, 1919," 58 *Journal of American History* 24 (1971). The long-term development of the test is examined in Frank E. Strong, "Fifty Years of Clear and Present Danger: From Schenck to Brandenberg-and Beyond," 1969 *Supreme Court Review.* 41 (1969). For the contribution of Learned Hand, see Gerald Gunther, "Learned Hand and the Origins of Modern First Amendment Doctrine: Some Fragments of History," 27 *Stanford Law Review* 719 (1975). The standard treatment of the postwar trauma remains Robert K. Murray, *Red Scare: A Study of National Hysteria* (1955).

28

"The Business of America Is Business!"

The Taft Court Forms • William Howard Taft as Chief Justice • Crippling the Regulatory Agencies • Maintaining the National Power • Federal Grants-in-Aid • Utilities Regulation • Labor and the Taft Court • The Adkins *Case • The Fate of Reform Legislation •* Euclid v. Ambler Realty *• Conclusion • For Further Reading*

WOODROW WILSON ONCE commented that the American people can be raised to greatness once in a generation. For the better part of two decades, Americans had worked hard at reforming their society, improving the condition of workers, protecting natural resources, making government at all levels more responsive to the citizenry, and regulating monopoly; then, in the apotheosis of Progressivism, they had tried to "make the world safe for democracy." The failure of the Versailles Treaty left many people disillusioned, not only with foreign affairs, but with reform in general. They wanted, in Warren Harding's words, "not heroics but healing, not nostrums but normalcy."

The law, which had justified the growth of governmental powers in peace and in wartime, had been viewed by Progressives as a positive instrument for social betterment. The Palmer raids showed how the law could also be perverted to destroy basic freedoms. The majority of Americans in the 1920s wanted to be left alone to enjoy the nation's rampant prosperity; they wanted law and courts that would not disturb the status quo. The broadly conservative policies of all three branches of the national government perfectly suited the mood of the times. Those reformers who had not abandoned the faith could do little more than protest and bide their time.

Despite the perception that the twenties represented the triumph of judicial conservatism, closer examination reveals that the old legal classicism had begun to disintegrate. A majority of the high court justices could still strike down prolabor laws and find only narrow grounds for classifying a business as affected with public interest, and in the *Adkins* case they erected a monument to the old thought, resurrecting *Lochner* for at least another decade. But the distinction between public and private, critical to classical thought, had begun to break down, and the recognition that modern business had to be conducted and regulated differently from the way it had fifty years earlier led to a reluctant but necessary expansion of the commerce powers. In the early 1920s, many leaders of the bar bemoaned what they termed the widespread confusion in the law, even as they applauded the Taft Court for its probusiness decisions.

The Taft Court Forms

Prosperity constituted the dominant characteristic of America in the 1920s. After a brief postwar recession, the United States surged ahead to achieve the highest standard of living any people had ever known. After two decades of stagnation, real wages—what income could buy in goods at the store—shot upward; at the same time, working hours decreased. U.S. Steel finally abandoned the twelve-hour day in 1923, Henry Ford instituted a five-day work week, and International Harvester stunned the nation and the world with its plan for a two-week annual vacation with pay for its employees. The increase in benefits matched the rise in productivity, as the widespread adoption of the assembly line and the electric motor revolutionized manufacturing. Perhaps the single most impressive demonstration of the new era came in October 1925, when Ford began rolling a finished car off his assembly line every ten seconds. No matter where one looked—construction, chemicals, or textiles—one found a similar story. Little wonder that Calvin Coolidge, who succeeded Warren Harding as president, could say that "the business of America is business!"

In the courts, the prevailing mood also endorsed industrial civilization, and at the highest level, the Supreme Court displayed a probusiness stance that had not been seen since the 1890s. The bench that had approved nearly all protective legislation and confirmed widespread governmental powers gave way to new personnel. Of Wilson's three appointees, only Louis Brandeis fulfilled the president's hopes for a strong liberal voice on the Court. John H. Clarke of Ohio, who shared many of Brandeis's views, caught the vision of Wilson's new world order, and in 1922, he resigned from the bench to work for international cooperation, much to Wilson's distress. The ex-president had been counting on Clarke along with Brandeis to, as he put it, "restrain the Court in some measure from the extreme reactionary course which it seems inclined to follow." One of the strongest proponents of that "reactionary course" proved to be Wilson's other appointee, James C. McReynolds of Tennessee. As attorney general, he had earned plaudits from reformers for his tough antitrust policy, but he had little sympathy with any other items on the Progressive agenda. Wilson had reportedly kicked McReynolds upstairs to get him out of the cabinet; in doing so, he saddled the country for almost three decades with the most reactionary jurist of the century. McReynolds's anti-Semitism was overt and embarrassing to the Court; he pointedly read a newspaper while Brandeis took the oath of office because he did not want to watch a Jew sworn into the Court.

When Edward White died in 1921, President Harding gave former President William Howard Taft the prize he had sought for so long, the chief justiceship. A true advocate of property rights, Taft believed that the Court had a particular role to play in sustaining the constitutional system. To do so, it had to be unified and powerful, and Taft accomplished both of these ends during his tenure; he proved, in fact, a far more effective chief justice than chief executive. To secure a unified outlook on the Court, Taft used his influence with Warren Harding, who, in his scant twenty-nine months in the White House, named four men to the Court. Taft had a hand in the selection of George Sutherland to replace Clarke and Pierce Butler to take Day's seat, both in 1922, and Edward Sanford to replace Pitney the following year.

Sutherland, a former senator and, like Taft, a former president of the American Bar Association, opposed change in general, and he forcefully articulated his views. He enjoys the singular reputation of having more of his decisions subsequently overruled than any other justice who ever served on the nation's highest court. Butler had been a railroad lawyer, and in the complicated utility rate cases that came before the Court in the 1920s, it often seemed that only he and Brandeis understood the issues, although they rarely agreed. One study shows that only three justices in the history of the Court were more reluctant to overrule precedent than Butler. Of the older justices, Willis Van Devanter (appointed by Taft in 1910) could always be counted on to vote with the conservatives; although he suffered from a writing block, he had the talents, according to Brandeis, of a renaissance cardinal in maintaining voting coalitions behind the scenes.

Van Devanter, McReynolds, Sutherland, and Butler made up the "Four Horsemen," who opposed any and all social legislation, and who would eventually precipitate the constitutional crisis of the New Deal era. They subscribed to essentially the same laissez-faire legal and economic values as Thomas M. Cooley. They had matured when America was still a relatively wide-open society, where self-reliance and individual initiative marked out a man for success. In opposing any regulation of business, however, they appeared blind to the fact that large corporations, not governmental interference, had foreclosed the type of opportunity that they had known in their youth.

The four archconservatives, along with justices Sanford and McKenna, gave Taft the unity he sought. In fact, in order to preserve that unity, Taft often found himself voting for positions far more reactionary than he would otherwise have adopted. In the early part of his tenure, only Holmes and Brandeis opposed the general trend of the Court—Brandeis because of his belief in the need to restrain business and to allow the states to use their powers to protect the less fortunate members of society, and Holmes because of his skepticism and his advocacy of judicial restraint. In 1925, Coolidge named Harlan Fiske Stone of New York to the Court to replace McKenna. Except for civil liberties, Stone had never shown any liberal tendencies; nevertheless, he immediately joined with the two dissenters.

The Taft Court majority soon settled on the broad outlines of the policies it would follow. Just as Harding and Coolidge called for a return to traditional values, so the conservative majority intended to reaffirm the natural law/vested interests interpretation of the Constitution. Its tools would be liberty of contract, substantive due process, and dual federalism, a device that the majority could manipulate to create a limbo in which neither federal nor state governments could act. Instead of a "mere truism," the Tenth Amendment would emerge as an active barrier to federal intervention in matters reserved to the states; even powers specifically granted to the national government did not necessarily take precedence over state autonomy. But when it suited their predilections, the justices could rein in state action as contravening national supremacy.

Overall, the Taft Court preferred as little governmental interference with economic liberty or property rights as possible; it showed no similar desire to rein in state restrictions on labor, radicals, or other groups that criticized the status quo. In his desire to "mass the Court," the chief justice did not care for dissent from the brethren either. The bench would be well rid of Holmes, Taft told Henry Stimson, for Holmes "is so completely under the control of Brother Brandeis that it gives to Brandeis two votes instead of one." But there are inconsistencies in a portrait that paints only the reactionary side of the Court, for, as we shall see, the Court in the 1920s did not completely abandon the Progressive legacy.

William Howard Taft as Chief Justice

The man who had been so politically inept as president soon proved himself one of the most politically astute men ever to occupy the center chair. As scholars have noted, William Howard Taft completely refashioned the role of chief justice and at the same time modernized the structure of the federal court system. All chief justices before him, of course, had to deal with the daily management of the high court's business. Taft saw the judicial system as a coequal and coherent branch of the federal government that had to be managed, and he saw the chief justice as the chief administrator of the judiciary. For the first time the country had a man willing and able to carry out both constitutionally assigned roles—the chief justice of the United States as well as the chief justice of the Supreme Court.

Taft utilized his extensive contacts in Congress as well as his good relations with the executive to secure a reorganization of the federal judiciary in the Act of September 14, 1922, which marked a new chapter in the administration of the federal courts. The chief justice now had the power to reassign district court judges on a temporary basis, and Taft immediately began transferring judges from courts that had a low caseload to those where they were most needed to relieve clogged dockets. In addition to the various administrative portions of the law, for the first time Congress recognized the entire judiciary as a single branch of government. Up until then, federal district judges acted as barons in their own fiefdoms, responsible to no authority and subject to impeachment only for egregiously bad behavior.

Not all judges liked this new authority, but a majority of them responded positively, especially after it became clear that they now had an advocate in the highest reaches of government lobbying for their needs, such as up-to-date libraries and sufficient support staff. Taft also established the Judicial Conference, a meeting of the senior circuit judges, as a device to determine where problems existed and how they could be resolved. In time, the conference became the chief means through which judges could articulate their ongoing needs to the Congress. By 1925, Taft could tell the judges that "the recommendations of this Conference have a good deal of influence. I mean that they are accepted as matters for serious consideration."

No item seemed to small for Taft's notice, and he said on numerous occasions that he believed it part of his job to bring deficiencies in the judicial system to the notice of those who could remedy them. When a small-town lawyer complained to the chief justice that the government did not provide a copy of the indictment to a defendant,

> On the personal side the present C.J. has admirable qualities, a great improvement on the late C.J.; he smoothes out difficulties instead of making them. It's astonishing he should have been such a horribly bad President, for he has considerable executive ability. The fact, probably, is that he cared about law all the time and nothing else. He has an excellent memory, makes quick decisions on questions of administration that arise and if a large output were the chief desideratum, he would be very good.
>
> —Louis Brandeis to Felix Frankfurter, 28 June 1923

Taft took the matter up first with William Mitchell, the solicitor general. Mitchell responded that supplying the information would place a financial and bureaucratic burden on the government. Unsatisfied with the answer, Taft went to Albert B. Cummins, chair of the Senate Judiciary Committee, who immediately prepared a bill to fix the problem.

Taft took a major step in strengthening the Court itself when he secured congressional approval of the Judiciary Act of 1925. The workload of the Court had increased to the point where it took nearly two years for a case to be heard after its initial filing. Taft named a committee from the Court to prepare a bill that not only streamlined the Court's operations, but gave it greater discretionary power over which cases it would hear. The Court in the future would only take cases it could process within a reasonable period and that raised significant constitutional issues. As a result, the cases it did hear assumed more importance, and the Court's pronouncements received greater attention.

Taft also lobbied against bills that he believed would harm the judiciary. Southern champions of states rights as well as some midwestern insurgents opposed federal diversity jurisdiction, and in 1928, George Norris of Nebraska and Thomas Walsh of Montana sponsored S.3151 to strip federal district courts of both federal question and diversity jurisdiction. Norris, who then headed the Senate Judiciary Committee, managed to get the bill reported favorably to the floor. Although Taft could not openly oppose the bill, he displayed a deft political touch as he rounded up influential lawyers and bar association heads to speak against the measure, which ultimately failed.

Finally, Taft took it upon himself to find the Court more dignified quarters. In the 1920s, the Court still met in the Old Senate Chamber in the Capitol, where they lacked privacy (after robing in one room they had to parade down a corridor to the courtroom), had no private offices, and had only a cramped room in the basement for the library. In 1925, Taft began lobbying vigorously for a separate building that would be totally under the Court's control. Congress responded favorably, and approved the site he recommended, on East Capitol Street next to the Library of Congress and facing the Capitol. Taft involved himself in all aspects of the building's architecture and decoration, although he did not live to see its completion in 1935.

Crippling the Regulatory Agencies

Even before Taft took over the center chair, the shift in the Court's attitude was clear. On March 1, 1920, nearly ten years after the government had first instituted antitrust proceedings against the U.S. Steel Corporation, the Supreme Court dismissed the suit. The Wilson administration had asked the Court to suspend action on the case during the war, lest a guilty finding require breakup of the giant firm and thus impede war production. Brandeis, who had long been a critic of the company, and McReynolds, who as attorney general had participated in the prosecution, recused, and four of the justices—McKenna, joined by White, Holmes, and Van Devanter—reaffirmed the rule of reason. Bigness in and of itself did not automatically constitute unlawfulness; it was only the deliberate abuses that might result from size. Justice Day entered a vigorous dissent; the firm had been founded for illegal purposes, and by condoning the company, the majority was in effect nullifying the Sherman Antitrust Act by judicial decree.

A few months later, the Court began its attack on the Federal Trade Commission. In *Federal Trade Commission v. Gratz* (1920), Justice McReynolds denied the commission the power to determine "unfair methods of competition," because the statute had not defined what this phrase meant. Just as the Court had earlier crippled the Interstate Commerce Commission by reserving to the judiciary the ultimate authority to determine the fairness of rates, so now the courts would decide, as a matter of law, what constituted unfair competition. The act had been designed to allow the commission flexibility in meeting new modes of unfair practices, and factual findings by it were supposed to be conclusive. By turning factual findings into questions of law, the Court robbed the FTC of any finality in its actions.

In other cases involving the commission, the Court expanded on the *Gratz* holding. In *Federal Trade Commission v. Curtis Publishing Company* (1923), McReynolds overturned a cease-and-desist order that the commission had issued after investigating an exclusive sales contract and finding it an unfair trade practice. He dismissed the FTC's extensive investigation and declared that the courts had the power to look at the evidence *de novo*. If it agreed with the findings, then it would consider them as conclusive. If not, the court would make its own determination. In effect, the FTC now found itself in the same position as the ICC before 1906. Hostile courts would give its investigations little credence and dismiss its factual findings if they did not care for the results. Companies could appeal to the courts for review not only of the legal issues but of the facts as well.

The resulting impotence of the FTC and other regulatory agencies can only partially be blamed on the Court; the Harding and Coolidge administrations did their best to pack the commissions with men sympathetic to the very business interests that the agencies supposedly supervised. One of Harding's first appointments put John J. Esch, the prorailroad author of the Transportation Act of 1920, on the ICC, replacing Robert W. Wooley, whom the railroads had found most annoying because of his concern for the public interest. As other openings occurred, conservatives and political hacks who opposed any government regulation of the railroads filled the commission. In 1925, Coolidge named Thomas F. Woodlock, a well-known publicist for Wall Street; putting him on the ICC, lamented *The Nation*, meant turning the agency over to those it had been meant to curb.

Similarly, the Republicans put bankers on the Federal Reserve Board and businessmen on the FTC. William E. Humphrey, the lumber attorney Coolidge nominated to head the Trade Commission in 1925, denounced the agency as "an instrument of oppression and disturbance and injury instead of help to business." The Tariff Commission suffered a similar fate, as business interests made sure protectionists replaced low-tariff advocates. The only requirement for appointees, exclaimed Senator George W. Norris of Nebraska, was that their "whole lives disclose the fact that they have always advocated an exorbitantly high tariff." The Harding-Coolidge appointees to the regulatory boards and commissions, Norris claimed, had done indirectly what the administrations could never have done openly—repeal a quarter-century's work to impose some control over business for the benefit of the public.

Although the Court's decisions usually sided with business interests, much to the satisfaction of the Republican administrations, in several cases the Court obviously had other considerations in mind.

Maintaining the National Power

The Transportation Act of 1920, which restored the railroads to private control, also expanded the authority of the ICC not only over interstate rates, but over intrastate fares as well. The commission had set new and higher rates in 1921, which in many areas overrode the schedules established by the state regulatory agency. In Wisconsin, for example, the commission set the minimum passenger rate at 3.6 cents per mile, even though a state regulation imposed a maximum fare of 2 cents per mile. Wisconsin and twenty other states attacked the law and the commission's actions as exceeding the federal government's powers. But in *Railroad Commission of Wisconsin v. Chicago, Burlington & Quincy Railroad* (1922), the Court unanimously upheld the ICC. The law "imposed an affirmative duty," explained Chief Justice Taft, to "fix rates and to take other important steps to maintain an adequate railway service for the people of the United States." The commission had also been charged with assuring a fair rate of return for the roads. If intrastate rates were too low, then excessive fares would have to be charged on interstate traffic to secure a fair total return. For all practical purposes, the decision wiped out any real distinction between intra- and interstate rates for the roads. By sustaining the commission, the Court might be said to have acted in the interests of higher rates for the railroads, but the decision also recognized the country's need to have a functioning national transportation system.

That reasoning reappeared when the Court upheld the recapture provisions of the 1920 law in *Dayton-Goose Creek Railway Company v. United States* (1924). The act required setting aside a reserve fund from railroad earnings over a fair return, with these recaptured funds distributed to keep less productive lines in business. The measure in effect treated all the lines as the unified system that they had been during the war. While some sections might be more profitable than others, the public interest required that something be done to keep the less profitable roads in operation. Again, for a unanimous Court, Taft denied that a public service industry had any constitutional right to more than a fair return on its property. To the argument that the recaptured profits constituted a taking without due process, Taft replied that since the roads had never been entitled to income above the fair return, they had never *owned* that revenue, and therefore it had not been taken from them. The need to see the railroads as a system also informed the Court's decision in *Colorado v. United States* (1926), sustaining an order to abandon an intrastate branch of a railroad because the deficit incurred in operating it burdened the railroad's interstate activities.

These cases illustrated not only the Court's somewhat inconsistent attitude toward the regulatory commissions, but also indicated more general trends of the tribunal in the 1920s. The *Wisconsin* decision constituted one of a number of cases in which the Court upheld an expanded power of the federal government over the states. In the landmark decision of *Missouri v. Holland* (1920), the Court had earlier sustained the supremacy of a federal treaty over state law. A 1916 treaty between Great Britain and the United States for the protection of migratory birds called for closed hunting seasons on several species, and Congress had enacted these provisions into law in the Migratory Bird Act of 1918. Missouri attacked both the law and the treaty, claiming that the subject matter—local hunting—lay beyond the powers of Congress because of the Tenth Amendment. A treaty, the state claimed, could not convey to the federal government powers that were not provided in the Constitution.

Holmes, speaking for a 7 to 2 majority, rejected Missouri's argument and put forward an interpretation of the treaty power breathtaking in scope. Unlike acts of Congress, which relied on the Constitution for their authority, the treaty-making power derived from the basic sovereignty of the nation. As a result, almost anything that the government conceived to be in the national interest could be the subject of a treaty; and under the Supremacy Clause, treaties took precedence over any state powers. Although Holmes conceded that there might be some limits to the power, such parameters would not be determined by the same criteria used to judge acts of Congress.

Similarly, the recapture provision cases, which one would have thought a conservative court would nullify, point out that at least in some areas, the justices understood the nature of interstate commerce in the twentieth century. In *Stafford v. Wallace* (1922), Taft expanded on the earlier idea of a "stream of commerce" to uphold the Packers and Stockyards Act of 1921, which gave the secretary of agriculture broad powers to proscribe unfair, discriminatory, and deceptive practices in the meat-packing industry. "The stockyards are not a place of rest or final destination," Taft wrote, "but a throat through which the current [of commerce] flows." The ruling hinted that the commerce power could reach certain private manufacturers if they did not live up to the standards imposed on broadly defined public service industries.

Congress had written the Packers and Stockyards Act with Holmes's *Swift* decision clearly in front of them. Even while they humorously debated whether the Chicago

> The application of the commerce clause of the Constitution in the *Swift* Case was the natural development of interstate commerce conditions. It was the inevitable recognition of the great central fact that such streams of commerce from one part of the country to another which are ever flowing are in their very essence the commerce among the States and with foreign nations which historically it was one of the chief purposes of the Constitution to bring under national protection and control. This court declined to defeat this purpose in respect of such a stream and take it out of complete national regulation by a nice and technical inquiry into the non-interstate character of some of its necessary incidents and facilities when considered alone and without reference to their association with the movement of which they were an essential but subordinate part.
>
> —William Howard Taft, *Stafford v. Wallace* (1922)

stockyards were more like a railroad bridge or a hotel for pigs, they understood that only businesses somehow affected with a public interest (*Munn*) could be part of a stream of interstate commerce amenable to federal regulation. Nonetheless, Taft's opinion, even while acknowledging the changing nature of modern commerce, still clung to certain verities of classical legal thought. As long as the essential categories of substantive due process jurisprudence as well as the critical differentiation between public and private remained intact, the stream of commerce doctrine posed no threat to the dual federalism established by the Court.

The Packers Act came under attack again toward the end of Taft's tenure in *Tagg Bros. & Moorhead v. United States* (1930). A group of commission agencies in the Omaha Union Stockyards sought to stop the government from regulating their fees. The decision in *Stafford* forced them to acknowledge that they operated at a public stockyard engaged in interstate commerce and were therefore subject to some federal regulation. They argued, however, that only capital-intensive businesses could be affected with a public interest; since their work was labor-intensive, fixing rates equaled wage regulation, which the Court had condemned as unconstitutional. Their commissions, in essence, constituted their wages.

The Court, speaking through Brandeis, unanimously rejected the claim. "Plaintiffs perform an indispensable service in the interstate commerce in livestock," he wrote. They also enjoy a monopoly of those services in the Omaha yards. "The purpose of the regulation attacked is to prevent their service from thus becoming an undue burden upon, and obstruction of, that commerce." *Tagg Bros.* represented another step in the Court's acceptance of the mechanics of modern commerce, and in some respects the Court seemed to say that to be in the stream of interstate commerce by definition meant that one's business was affected with a public interest. The Court seems to have abandoned the old direct/indirect distinction of *E.C. Knight*, and with it—at least within acknowledged interstate commerce—the public/private distinction as well.

A few years earlier, the Court had sustained the National Motor Vehicle Theft Act of 1919 in *Brooks v. United States* (1925). The statute forbade the movement of stolen goods in interstate commerce; it bore a striking resemblance to the Child Labor Law, which had also prohibited the movement of things that were not in themselves harmful. Did the transportation of stolen goods, however, constitute commerce in any traditional sense of the word? Taft ignored these issues for a unanimous Court by approving the moral intent of the law. Federal authority could thus be extended without regard to legal fine points to achieve a socially desirable end, provided the courts approved of the goal; if they did not, then legal fine points could become significant limits on state and federal power.

Federal Grants-in-Aid

The Court also sustained federal power in the first case involving the new device of a federal grant-in-aid, grants of money from the national government to the states, with conditions attached to the use of the funds. State legislatures did not have to accept these grants, but if they did, they had to agree to some federal supervision of how they spent the money and also provide some state funds, usually on a matching basis, for the program. State violation of the agreement would result in the cancellation of the grant.

The modern grant-in-aid traces to the Weeks Act of 1911, designed to stimulate and aid states in forest fire prevention. Additional programs soon followed. The Smith-Lever Act of 1914 set up agricultural extension programs, and the Smith-Hughes Act of 1917 fostered vocational education. The Federal Road Act of 1916 initiated the partnership between state and federal governments that led first to the national road network and later to the interstate highway system. In 1920, the Fess–Kenyon Act provided funds for state programs to rehabilitate disabled veterans, and the following year Congress passed the Sheppard–Towner Act to promote state infant and maternity care programs. Where the Weeks Act had authorized $200,000, by 1925, the total sum appropriated for federal grant-in-aid programs had reached $93 million, the lion's share of which went to highway construction.

These various programs reflected the positive view of the state expounded by the Progressives and constituted a creative federal endeavor in which the national government could aid and encourage—but not compel—states to support certain socially beneficial activities. But the reactionary mood of the 1920s had little sympathy for social "frills" like vocational education or maternity care, and critics claimed that the grant programs would destroy local self-government. The programs, they charged, extended federal power into areas specifically reserved to the states. In 1923, the Supreme Court had the opportunity to rule on this question in *Massachusetts v. Mellon*, when the state attacked the constitutionality of the Sheppard—Towner Act.

The decision, by Justice Sutherland, sustained the act indirectly by denying that the Court had jurisdiction, because Massachusetts had presented "no justiciable controversy either in its own behalf or as the representative of its citizens." A state could not act for its citizens against the United States, because they were American citizens as well. As to the issue of Congress invading the realm of state power, the Court ruled that a political question and therefore not amenable to judicial resolution. In his comments, however, Sutherland clearly implied the constitutionality of noncoercive grants. If the state did not wish to engage in the program or accept federal regulations, it could simply refuse to participate and thus would retain all its prerogatives. But it had no power to question the use of legitimately collected tax monies.

A little earlier, the Court had upheld a state's discretion in expending its tax funds in *Green v. Frazier* (1920). The progressive Non-Partisan League had gained control of North Dakota, and had used public money to build grain elevators, warehouses and mills, and even to set up a bank. Critics had denounced these measures as socialistic or not true public purposes, and had sued on the ground that this deprived them of their property (tax dollars) without due process of law. For a unanimous Court, Justice Day had upheld the state. If one relied on these two decisions, it appeared that the Court would not inquire into how a state or the federal government wished to spend its tax revenues.

Utilities Regulation

A rash of rate cases plagued the Court during the 1920s, resulting directly from the Court's insistence in *Smyth v. Ames* that the judiciary had to be the final arbiter of the fairness of administratively set rates. Unfortunately, few of the Court's members really understood either the complex economic issues involved or the facts required to establish rates. Holmes absolutely detested rate cases. He disliked facts to begin with, and much preferred to play with ideas and theories. Butler, a former railroad lawyer, certainly understood the problems, since he had argued on the carriers' behalf many times. But, according to Harold Laski writing in 1934, "no man of his generation so fully understood the inner workings of the economic system" as did Louis Brandeis, and he fought an apparently losing battle in the 1920s to get the courts to leave the business of setting rates to the regulatory commissions.

When the Court upheld public regulation of utilities during the first decade of the century, it had also decreed that a company had a constitutionally protected right to a fair return on its property. Although few economists agreed on what constituted the best way to determine the value of property, the Court insisted that the rate-making commissions use a formula based on current or replacement value of the property. Current value, however, often proved difficult to determine as compared to original costs, which could be accurately ascertained. In 1922, in *Southwestern Bell Telephone Company v. Public Service Commission of Missouri*, Justice McReynolds charged that the commission had not allowed for a fair return on invested capital because it had been negligent in assessing the current value of the property. The case showed how a determined company could eviscerate state rate-making agencies by constant appeals to sympathetic courts, claiming that valuations had been incorrectly determined.

Although he agreed that in this case the rates had been too low, Brandeis entered a separate opinion that attacked the whole basis of current valuation as the criteria for return. He noted that prices fluctuated from year to year, so that it would be impossible to establish any fixed amount on which to predicate a reliable rate schedule. As soon as a commission had completed the lengthy process of determining replacement costs, the companies could appeal on the basis that prices had changed. While the current value system might make some sense legally, it made no sense economically. Characteristically, Brandeis did not just attack the current system, but proposed an alternative, the so-called prudent investment principle, which defined a fair return as equivalent to the rate that a prudent investor could secure on conservative investments. Although the system had its own initial complexities, it had the benefit that once value had been ascertained and the methods and standards approved, the courts could withdraw from the regulatory procedure, leaving the administrative agencies free to do their work. At least in the 1920s, Brandeis's proposal received little encouragement from his brethren or from business interests, which believed that courts would give them a more sympathetic hearing than regulatory agencies. Eventually, however, even if not all states and courts adopted the prudent investment scheme, Brandeis's arguments against courts regulating public utilities bore fruit, and in the 1930s, the judiciary withdrew from the rate-making business.

Labor and the Taft Court

The Court's probusiness posture involved not only striking down federal and state laws that attempted to regulate commercial activities; it included a definite antilabor prejudice.

Labor leaders thought that they had won a major victory in the Clayton Act of 1914. Section 6 had explicitly declared that labor did not constitute a commodity or an article of commerce and that consequently the antitrust laws should not be interpreted to forbid unions from seeking their legitimate objectives. Section 20, a direct response to the government by injunction of the 1890s, had prohibited federal courts from issuing injunctions or restraining orders in labor disputes "unless necessary to prevent irreparable injury to property, or to a property right." The same section also forbade injunctions against peaceful picketing or primary boycotts. Labor leaders claimed that these two sections made perfectly clear that courts should no longer interfere in labor conflicts; however, time would show that the wording could be interpreted in several ways.

The Supreme Court did not rule on these sections of the Clayton Act until 1921, in *Duplex Printing Press Company v. Deering*. The case had arisen when unions boycotted a manufacturer's products in New York to enforce a strike in Michigan. Justice Mahlon Pitney ruled that the law had not legitimized such secondary boycotts, nor had Section 6 provided a blanket exemption from the antitrust laws. Its wording only protected unions in lawfully carrying out their legitimate objectives; and since secondary boycotts were unlawful, neither Section 6 nor 20 applied. Moreover, Pitney interpreted Section 20 to mean that injunctions could be issued not only against the immediate parties—the employer and his striking workers—but to restrain another union from supporting the strikers. Upon hearing of the decision, AFL president Samuel Gompers, who had declared the Clayton Act to be labor's Magna Carta, now wailed "O Liberty, Liberty! How many crimes are committed in thy name." The American Anti-Boycott Association, on the other hand, rejoiced, and saw the decisions as a rebuke to organized labor's efforts "to become a class apart, exempt from the legal restraints to which other citizens are subject."

The *Duplex* case came down immediately after *Truax v. Corrigan*, in which the Court struck down a state anti-injunction statute. In this case, an Arizona restaurant owner had sought an injunction in state court against peaceful pickets, claiming that the state law that denied him that injunction had deprived him of his property rights without due process of law. Taft agreed and declared the law unconstitutional as an arbitrary and capricious exercise of power and as a highly injurious invasion of property rights. Even Pitney found this too much, and in his dissent he argued that states had considerable latitude to determine, "each for itself, their respective conditions of law and order, and what kind of civilization they shall have as a result." Holmes's separate dissent decried the probusiness activism of Taft's opinion. Business activity in and of itself did not invoke any "sacred" nature of a property right; the state had the power to respond to abuses of property as well as to attacks upon it. Here, Arizona had perceived an evil in the misuse of injunctions and had legitimately responded to it; the courts had no business second-guessing the legislature in determining social policy.

Brandeis also dissented in both cases. In *Truax*, he differed from Holmes, as the two differed on so many issues, even when, as here, they reached the same result. For Holmes, judicial restraint required the courts to defer to legislative policy decisions in the absence of a specific constitutional prohibition. The skeptical Holmes had little faith in reform legislation and thought much of it misguided and useless, but such judgments did not concern the courts. If the elected branches wanted to do something foolish, and the Constitution did not forbid it, then let them do it. Brandeis, on the other hand, saw the anti-injunction statute as a positive good; whenever he could, especially in his powerful dissents (which bore a striking resemblance to the "Brandeis briefs"), he explored the social needs that had called forth the legislative response. In *Duplex*, he explained how Congress, in the Clayton Act, had determined that abuses of the injunction had gone too far in limiting labor's legitimate activities and had set up a standard that it considered fair to both parties. Judges did not have the prerogative to undo congressional policy because they disagreed with it or because their own economic and social views ran counter to those of the legislative branch. As with so many of his dissents in the 1920s, Brandeis's reasoning here would eventually be adopted by a later Court as constitutionally correct.

The two decisions created the gray area typical of dual federalism arguments and precluded both state and federal restrictions on the injunction. Whenever unions threatened to strike, employers could go into court and get an injunction, a court order barring workers from going out on strike. As a result, the rest of the decade saw government by injunction as extensive as before the Clayton Act. More than 200 injunctions were issued during the 1920s Railway Shopmen's strike alone, and by the end of the decade, one commentator after another had joined in the general condemnation of the use of injunctions. The American Civil Liberties Union's annual report for 1928–1929 declared that "the most extreme restrictions on free speech and assemblage are caused by injunctions in industrial conflicts. It is the weapon of repression most difficult to combat." But not until the Depression undermined the dominance of business interests did reformers finally get the Norris–LaGuardia Anti-injunction Act through Congress in March 1932; a number of states then followed with similar measures of their own.

Meanwhile, labor's supposed protection under the Clayton Act suffered further erosion in the two Coronado Coal cases in 1925. The United Mine Workers had been trying to unionize southern coal fields to prevent the ruination of northern mines by the cheaper southern coal. Following the *Knight* standard, Chief Justice Taft ruled that coal mining itself did not constitute interstate commerce. A strike, as the simple withholding of labor, could thus not be enjoined under the Clayton Act. But a strike that aimed at stopping the interstate shipment of nonunion coal certainly fell within the proscriptions of the Sherman Act. Therefore, any labor activity that had the intent, and not just an incidental result, of interfering with interstate commerce violated the antitrust laws.

Two years later, in *Bedford Cut Stone Company v. Journeymen Stone Cutters Association*, the Court again showed how it would manipulate definitions to restrict labor. In conformity with their union's constitution, a handful of peaceful stonecutters refused to work on limestone cut by nonunion workers in the unorganized Bedford Cut Stone Company. The firm sought an injunction, but in order to enjoin the strikers, the lower court had to rely on the Sherman Act's restriction on secondary boycotts. The Supreme Court agreed with this approach and then justified it by turning a very local and limited strike into a burden on the stream of interstate commerce. The difference between the Court's decision in the child labor cases—where it had taken a narrow, *Knight* view of commerce—and *Bedford*—where it had all but obliterated any distinction between local and national commerce—could hardly be missed. Reasonable restrictions on trade caused by industry would be tolerated by the Court under the rule of reason; but the bench would disregard its own rule when asked to apply it to the clearly reasonable activities of a labor union. What is striking here is not necessarily the Court's reasoning. As we shall see, in the 1940s, the Court would take a similar view of commerce to *justify* state intervention. But the Court under *Stone* was at least consistent, applying the same definition of commerce to industry, agriculture, and labor.

Until the high court handed down these decisions, lower federal courts had shown a marked diversity in how they interpreted the labor provisions of the Clayton Act and the validity of injunctions in labor disputes. The Taft Court rulings in effect told federal judges to issue as many injunctions as they wanted, that for all practical purposes the Clayton Act labor exemptions meant nothing. Moreover, even when antilabor judges went too far, the high court could offer organized labor little relief. By the time the Supreme Court heard an appeal against an overly broad injunction, so much time had passed that the restraining order had already served its purpose. In one instance, four years passed between the time a federal judge issued an injunction and the Supreme Court overturned it (*United Leather Workers v. Herkert & Meisal et al.* [1924]).

The *Adkins* Case

Protective legislation also fell on judicial hard times. The two federal child labor acts failed to be approved, the first because the Court held that control of child labor exceeded the commerce power (*Hammer v. Dagenhart*), and the second because it went beyond the taxing power (*Bailey v. Drexel Furniture*). But even some conservatives protested when the majority resurrected the *Lochner* doctrine in *Adkins v. Children's Hospital* (1923). In striking down a federal statute establishing minimum wages for women in the District of Columbia, Justice Sutherland reaffirmed the paramount position of freedom of contract in economic affairs. Freedom, he declared, "is the general rule and restraint the exception; and the exercise of legislative authority to abridge it can be justified only by the existence of exceptional circumstances." Emancipated by the Nineteenth Amendment, women no longer had need for protective laws, but could work for whatever amount they freely chose to contract for, just like men.

> The feature of this statute which, perhaps more than any other, puts upon it the stamp of invalidity is that it exacts from the employer an arbitrary payment for a purpose and upon a basis having no causal connection with his business. . . . If one goes to the butcher, the baker or grocer to buy food, he is morally entitled to obtain the worth of his money but he is not entitled to more. If what he gets is worth what he pays he is not justified in demanding more simply because he needs more; and the shopkeeper, having dealt fairly and honestly in that transaction, is not concerned in any particular sense with the question of his customer's necessities.
>
> —George Sutherland, *Adkins v. Children's Hospital* (1923)

The decision shocked the nation for the holding as well as for the reasoning behind it. Most people had assumed that after *Muller* and *Bunting*, the Court had accepted the need to protect certain classes of society through the state's police power. Sutherland ignored a decade of cases and went back to *Lochner*; even in the conservative 1920s, his opinion seemed overly reactionary. The Consumers Union had asked the eminent Harvard law professor Felix Frankfurter to defend the statute, but Sutherland dismissed Frankfurter's elaborate "Brandeis brief" as irrelevant. He launched into a vigorous attack on minimum wage legislation of any sort. Wages constituted the "heart of the contract," and could never be fixed by legislative fiat. Human necessities could never take precedence over economic rights, for "the good of society as a whole cannot be better served than by the preservation of the liberties of its constituent members." In his denunciation of wage legislation, Sutherland went far beyond constitutional arguments and launched into an attack better suited to a legislative assembly than a judicial chamber, as he denied that such laws helped anyone or that more highly paid women "safeguard their morals more carefully than those who are poorly paid." Although a few scholars have lauded Sutherland's seeming acknowledgment of women's equality, in fact Sutherland opposed any and all wage regulation. His references to women's legal position following the suffrage is no more than another nail driven into the coffin of wage laws.

Even Chief Justice Taft, who could hardly be described as liberal, could not swallow this, and registered one of only twenty dissents he filed during his decade on the Court. He conceded that people differed over the efficacy of minimum wage legislation, but in as strong a statement of judicial restraint as Holmes or Brandeis ever delivered, Taft argued that "it is not the function of the Court to hold congressional acts invalid simply because they are passed to carry out economic views which the Court believes to be unwise or unsound." Holmes agreed with Taft, and added a few pithy comments in a dissent of his own. He deplored the fact that liberty of contract, which had started out as an "innocuous generality," had now become dogma. As for Sutherland's fatuous claim that women's suffrage had ended the need for special legislation, Holmes simply observed that "it will need more than the Nineteenth Amendment to convince me that there is no difference between women and men." (Brandeis took no part in the 5 to 3 decision because his daughter Elizabeth served on the District of Columbia Minimum Wage Board.)

The year after *Adkins,* the Court, again speaking through Sutherland, upheld a state statute prohibiting the employment of women between the hours of 10 p.m. and 6 a.m.

> Will the learned justices of the majority be pardoned for overlooking the cardinal fact that minimum-wage legislation is not and never was predicated upon political, contractual or civil inequalities of women? It is predicated rather upon evils to society, resulting from the exploitation of women in industry, who as a class labor under a tremendous economic hardship. The problem is one of economic fact, not of political, contractual or civil status.
>
> —Barbara Grimes, *California Law Review* (1923)

in restaurants in large cities. In *Radice v. New York* (1924), Sutherland declared that facts existed to justify such regulation (even though he had dismissed the extensive facts supplied in *Adkins*), and sounding more like Holmes and Brandeis, indicated that courts should defer to factual findings reached by a legislature. Apparently Sutherland believed that a significant difference existed between the very limited police powers of the federal government and the more extensive authority enjoyed by the states. Working conditions could be subject to state regulation, but the courts would determine the reasonableness of the regulations.

The Fate of Reform Legislation

Adkins influenced the later protective legislation cases that came before the high court in the rest of the decade. Between 1920 and 1930, the Court found approximately 140 state laws unconstitutional, a large majority on the grounds that they violated the liberties of property and contract guaranteed by the Fourteenth Amendment's Due Process Clause. Among some of the more striking decisions were these:

- A coal company, seeking access to potentially rich deposits, challenged a Pennsylvania statute prohibiting mining in a way that would damage streets and residences. The Court struck the law down as arbitrary and a deprivation of property without due process. *Pennsylvania Coal Company v. Mahon* (1922).
- Nebraska had set minimum sizes for bread loaves sold in retail stores to prevent shortchanging; the Court found the regulation an "intolerable burden." *Jay Burns Baking Co. v. Bryan* (1924).
- Iowa contractors penalized because they had paid workers on state projects less than the prevailing daily wages complained that their due process had been violated; the Court agreed. *Connally v. General Construction Company* (1926).
- A Pennsylvania health statute prohibited the use of shoddy (reclaimed wool) in bedding materials; the Court ruled the measure so arbitrary and unreasonable as to violate due process. *Weaver v. Palmer Brothers Company* (1926).

Looking at these and a whole string of similar cases, legal historian Paul Murphy argued that liberty meant "judicially enforced freedom for private homes to fall in coal mines, for bakers to sell underweight breads, . . . for contractors to chisel on their workers' wages, and for manufacturers to stuff mattresses with floor sweepings."

In *Adkins*, Sutherland had conceded four well-delineated areas in which courts would accept restraints on contractual freedom: (1) work on public projects; (2) the character, time, and method of wage payments; (3) fixing the hours of labor; and (4) rates charged by businesses affected with the public interest. Reformers saw very little flexibility in the first three categories, but hoped that an expansive view of the fourth would permit some experimentation by the states. They soon learned differently.

In late 1923, the conservative majority, in *Wolff Packing Company v. Court of Industrial Relations*, adopted a narrow view of business affected with a public interest. After the war, Kansas had embarked on a major experiment in molding law to meet current needs. In 1920, it passed an Industrial Relations Act, requiring arbitration of all disputes in key industries such as food, clothing, and shelter, and it created a special Industrial Court to handle the arbitration. The act also gave the court powers to enforce its decisions, including the authority to set wages and control working conditions. In the *Wolff* case, Taft destroyed the Industrial Court by ruling the act unconstitutional. Merely because a state declared a business affected with a public interest did not make it so, and the state could not use that rationalization to interfere with property rights.

Taft listed the only businesses that could be so characterized: public utilities, carried on by a public license; traditional businesses long recognized as subject to regulation, such as inns and grist-mills; and businesses in which natural economic laws did not operate, such as monopolies, or when the nature of the business had changed so as to warrant some governmental regulation. For all practical purposes, Taft had apparently negated a half-century of legal development since *Munn* and put nearly all businesses outside the reach of state regulation. The distinction between public and private, a key element of classical thought, might have faded in stream of commerce cases, but Taft and the conservatives here reminded the nation that they intended to view that as an exception rather than as the rule.

The results of this new doctrine appeared quickly. For example, New York had declared theater ticket prices to be a matter of public concern and enacted legislation regulating the resale price of tickets from agencies. In *Tyson v. Banton* (1927), Sutherland simply pointed out that a ticket agency did not fall into any of the three categories that Taft had listed in *Wolff*, and he invalidated the law. Holmes, Brandeis, and Stone all dissented, and pleaded for judicial restraint; state legislatures should have the right to determine what affected public interest, not the courts.

But the majority could not be stopped. In *Ribnik v. McBride* (1928), the Court struck down a New Jersey statute regulating the fees of employment agencies. Sutherland insisted that an employment agency "is essentially a private business," and he declared that "it is no longer fairly open to question that the fixing of prices for food, clothing, house rental, wages to be paid, whether minimum or maximum, is beyond the legislative power." The following year, the Court reemphasized this point when it struck down a Tennessee law that authorized a state official to fix gas prices within the state (*Williams v. Standard Oil Company*).

> It has never been supposed, since the adoption of the Constitution, that the business of the butcher, or the baker, the tailor, the wood chopper, the mining operator or the miner was clothed with such a public interest that the price of his product or his wages could be fixed by state regulation . . . nowadays one does not devote one's property or business to the public use or clothe it with a public interest merely because one makes commodities for, and sells to, the public in the common callings of which those above mentioned are instances.
>
> —William Howard Taft, *Wolff Packing Co. v. Court of Industrial Relations* (1923)

Euclid v. Ambler Realty

Perhaps no case better illustrates the conflicted rulings of the Taft Court than one involving zoning for land use. Among conservatives, property had always held a near sacred status, and the core of substantive due process had been the almost unlimited right of an owner to use and dispose of property. In 1917, the Court had struck down a local ordinance prohibiting blacks from living in certain areas but had done so not on equal protection grounds, but because the rule deprived people of their right to buy and sell property (*Buchanan v. Warley*).

During the first quarter of the twentieth century, many municipalities enacted comprehensive land use or zoning plans in an effort to manage growth and sustain the aesthetic nature of the community. The codes varied, but nearly all of them included some limits on land use in certain areas, and placed limits on the type and size of buildings that could be erected. A commercial establishment, for example, could not be built in an area designated for residential use. Land owners and developers challenged these codes on a variety of constitutional grounds, but state courts disagreed on their legitimacy. Eventually the challenge to the zoning ordinance of Euclid, Ohio, reached the high court in 1926.

Ambler Realty owned a parcel of 68 acres in Euclid, a suburb of Cleveland, and intended to develop it for industrial purposes. Most of the land had a U-6 designation, which allowed for commercial development, but some parts had different ratings that restricted use and thus made the property less valuable for Ambler's purposes. Ambler sued in district court on due process, equal protection, and taking grounds, and won. The village appealed to the high court, which by a 6–3 vote reversed and held the zoning ordinance constitutional.

The author of the majority opinion was George Sutherland, the same justice who had written *Adkins*. Sutherland had been absent for the first oral argument and apparently doubted the ordinance's constitutionality, when Stone convinced him to rethink the case. The Court ordered the case reargued, Sutherland was present at the second hearing, and abandoned the conservative block to uphold the law. In an effort to explain this vote, Sutherland's biographer suggests that Thomas Cooley's ideas strongly influenced the outcome. Sutherland's opinion describes the zoning act not as a deprivation of property but as an enhancement. Common law had long allowed for the abatement of nuisances even if doing so restricted property rights, since the end result would be the enhancement of value in all adjoining property. The fact that Euclid was undergoing rapid expansion could not be denied, and overcrowding as well as chaotic development would be harmful to all property owners. Sutherland may also have been influenced by the fact that when Ambler had bought the property, the zoning ordinance had already been in effect, and this undermined the company's claim that its property had been taken without due process; he might have thought differently had the ordinance been passed *after* Ambler had purchased the land.

But if the state could regulate private property to ensure rational growth, then what remained of the old distinction between public and private? If one's land could be said to be affected with a public interest, then what limits, if any, could be imposed on state regulation?

Conclusion

It was no wonder that the National Association of Manufacturers passed resolutions throughout the decade praising the Taft Court for its rulings and calling it the "indispensable interpreter of our written Constitution," the "safest repository of power," and the protector of property from the "babel voices of the mob." So long as the country appeared prosperous, business continued to have its way, and the Court, like the Congress and the president, did all it could to placate industry. Ideas of judicial restraint, of private property balanced by public good, of the police power as an instrument of social justice, as well as a willingness to allow states to experiment—all of which had flourished in the Progressive era—gave way to a rigid laissez-faire interpretation of the Constitution by an activist Court which emphasized property rights and freedom of contract above all else.

And yet even while the Court struck down some police regulations, it supported others. It conflated the public/private distinction that lay at the core of classical legal thought, and in its interstate commerce decisions, seemed to indicate that all aspects of such commerce could be regulated. The justices continued to oppose any efforts to help labor unions, and found much but not all protective legislation unconstitutional. It is little wonder that some observers of the legal scene in the 1920s found the situation quite confusing.

For Further Reading

Good introductions to America in the 1920s are William E. Leuchtenburg, *The Perils of Prosperity, 1914–1932* (1958); Frederick Lewis Allen's classic and still charming *Only Yesterday* (1931); and Lynn Dumenil, *Modern Temper: American Culture and Society in the 1920s* (1995). For the Supreme Court, see Paul L. Murphy's excellent overview, *The Constitution in Crisis Times, 1919–1969* (1972). The inconsistencies in the Taft Court's jurisprudence are explored in William M. Wiecek, *The Lost World of Classical Legal Thought: Law and Ideology in America, 1886–1937* (1998); and Barry Cushman, *Rethinking the New Deal Court: The Structure of a Constitutional Revolution* (1998).

The great skills of Taft as chief justice are well described in Alpheus T. Mason, *William Howard Taft: Chief Justice* (1965); Peter Graham Fisk, *The Politics of Federal Judicial Administration* (1973); and Robert Post, "Judicial Management and Judicial Disinterest: The Achievements and Perils of Chief Justice William Howard Taft," 1998 *Journal of Supreme Court History* 50 (1998). Many of the works cited in the previous chapter on Holmes and Brandeis are relevant here as well. Joel F. Paschal, *Mr. Justice Sutherland: A Man Against the State* (1951), captures the conservative mindset of the Four Horsemen; a more recent book by Hadley Arkes, *The Return of George Sutherland: Restoring a Jurisprudence of Natural Rights* (1994), is an extended polemic.

For relations between business and government, including the Court, see Carroll H. Wooddy, *The Growth of the Federal Government, 1915–1932* (1934); Carl McFarland, *Judicial Control of the Federal Trade Commission and the Interstate Commerce Commission, 1920–1930* (1932); and Bernard C. Gavit, *The Commerce Clause of the United States Constitution* (1932). See also Robert E. Cushman, *Independent Regulatory Commissions* (1932).

Labor problems are examined in Felix Frankfurter and Nathan V. Greene, *The Labor Injunction* (1930); Edward Berman, *Labor and the Sherman Act* (1930); and Stanley I. Kutler,

"Labor, the Clayton Act, and the Supreme Court," 3 *Labor History* 19 (1962). See also Daniel R. Ernst, *Lawyers Against Labor* (1995); and Christopher L. Tomlins, *The State and the Unions: Labor Relations, Law and the Organized Labor Movement in America, 1880–1960* (1985).

Critiques of the Court's antireform biases are exemplified by Thomas Reed Powell, "The Supreme Court and State Police Power, 1922–1930," 17 and 18 *Virginia Law Review* (1931–1932) 529 et seq.; Maurice Finkelstein, "From *Munn v. Illinois* to *Tyson v. Banton*: A study in the Judicial Process," 27 *Columbia Law Review* 769 (1927); and Walton Hamilton, "Affectation with a Public Interest," 39 *Yale Law Journal* 1089 (1930). A more sympathetic view of the Court is Ray A. Brown, "Police Power—Legislation for Health and Personal Safety," 42 *Harvard Law Review* 866 (1929). For Euclid, see Michael Allan Wolf, "'Compelled by Conscientious Duty': *Village of Euclid v. Ambler Realty Co.* as Romance," 1997 *Journal of Supreme Court History* 2 (1997) 88. A good overview of the Court's jurisprudence is Robert C. Post, "Defending the Lifeworld: Substantive Due Process in the Taft Court Era," 78 *Boston University Law Review* 1489 (1998).

29

A Tangled Skein of Liberties

The Reform Remnant • Legal Realism • Realism and Reform on the Bench • Political Fundamentalism • The Nationalization of Standards • The "Incorporation" of Free Speech • Whitney v. California *• Criminal Justice • Wire Tapping and Privacy • Lynch Law • Race and Alienage • Incorporating Freedom of the Press • For Further Reading*

THE TRADITIONAL INTERPRETATION of the 1920s has emphasized not only the probusiness, antilabor attitudes of the courts, but also a corresponding indifference—if not outright hostility—to civil rights and civil liberties. The same Court that struck down a state's efforts to ensure the cleanliness of mattress stuffing casually approved the forced sterilization of mental patients. The Court that began the decade by affirming the persecution of wartime dissenters ended by approving government snooping through wiretaps. Yet the story is far from simple and must be seen against the larger background of the clash between tradition and modernism in American life. There is no question that some decisions of the Taft Court displayed an almost cavalier disregard of civil liberties; at the same time, however, the Court took the first steps in formulating the modern view of the Bill of Rights.

The Reform Remnant

For many liberals, the economic conservatism of the Supreme Court spelled an end to progressivism. Decisions such as *Adkins* not only reinforced conservative state courts in their attitudes but also precluded legislatures from pursuing reform programs, since they anticipated that any protective measures would be voided by the courts. Although a few governors achieved some success as moderate reformers, for the most part the states and the federal government worshiped together at Mammon's altar.

Business dominance did not go totally unchallenged. In Congress, a small group of Progressives including George W. Norris, Robert M. La Follette, Thomas J. Walsh, and Burton K. Wheeler fought a rearguard campaign to preserve some of their earlier gains. Norris, for example, managed to prevent the sale of the government power plant at Muscle Shoals, Alabama; only presidential vetoes sidetracked his efforts to set up the plant as a yardstick against which to measure the efficiency of private companies (an idea that he later sold to Franklin Roosevelt as a centerpiece of the Tennessee Valley Authority). In his run for president on the Progressive party ticket in 1924, La Follette attacked a judiciary that, he charged, had usurped the powers of the legislature to make public policy. Senator Henrik Shipstead of Minnesota and others kept up a constant critique of the use of labor injunctions throughout the decade.

Outside of government, agencies such as the American Civil Liberties Union, backed by liberal journals such as *Survey*, *The Nation*, and *The New Republic*, articulated the concerns of a variety of groups, including social workers, labor, intellectuals, and the clergy. Gradually the ACLU, led by Roger N. Baldwin and Arthur Garfield Hays, organized campaigns against state sedition laws, antilabor statutes, and the highhandedness of law enforcement officials, such as the notorious detective, William Burns, Jr., the head of the Bureau of Investigation (precursor to the FBI) during the Harding administration.

Legal Realism

In the law schools, men like Felix Frankfurter, Karl N. Llewellyn, Thomas Reed Powell, Robert Hutchins, Jerome Frank, and others kept up a constant barrage of criticism of the courts and the law. They developed what came to be know as "legal realism," a tough-minded analysis of the nonlegal as well as legal considerations that affected judicial decision making. Llewellyn, perhaps the person most closely identified as a Realist, often commented that the Realist movement lacked an ascertainable ideology. Instead, many people with differing ideas shared some basic tenets, chief among them the conviction that law derived from facts. They preferred to base their legal arguments on empirical research rather than on traditional legal rules and institutions.

Legal realism came to flower during the early years of the Depression, but its antecedents reached back to the late nineteenth century. One could start with Oliver Wendell Holmes, for Llewellyn claimed that from Holmes "we all derive." In his 1881 book, *The Common Law*, Holmes had noted that experience determined the law, not logic. Holmes argued that one had to be aware of all sorts of nonlegal matters, including sociology, political science, economics, and psychology to understand how a particular law had developed. A clear line runs from those opening lines of *The Common Law* through sociological jurisprudence, the Brandeis brief, and the infatuation of reformers in the 1920s with the social sciences.

Holmes had also anticipated the functional aspect of realism in an 1897 speech entitled "The Path of the Law." "What constituted law?" he asked. "The prophecies of what the courts will do in fact, and nothing more pretentious, are what I mean by the law." Holmes then asked lawyers to try to gauge what factors a judge would take into account, such as precedent and mitigating circumstances, in reaching a decision. He rejected the Blackstonian idea that human law reflected divine justice and eschewed notions of moral absolutism or even natural law; instead, he suggested, many differ-

> I was much troubled in spirit, in my first years on the bench, to find how trackless was the ocean on which I had embarked. I sought for certainty. I was oppressed and disheartened when I found that the quest for it was futile. I was trying to reach land, the solid land of fixed and settled rules. . . . As the years have gone by, and as I have reflected more and more upon the nature of the judicial process, I have become reconciled to the uncertainty, because I have grown to see it as inevitable. I have grown to see that the process in its highest reaches is not discovery, but creation.
>
> —Benjamin N. Cardozo, *The Nature of the Judicial Process* (1921)

ent reasons lay behind the discrete decisions of particular judges. Sentiments such as these led Jerome Frank to call Holmes the "complete adult jurist."

Holmes's "The Path of the Law" is a forebear to one of the most influential legal essays of the decade, Benjamin N. Cardozo's 1921 Storrs Lectures at Yale, published the following year as *The Nature of the Judicial Process*. Cardozo, the most creative state court judge of the twentieth century, shocked many conservatives by confirming that judging was at best uncertain and that one rarely could find a simple answer in precedents. The process of judging "in its highest reaches is not discovery, but creation," he declared, and out of the turmoil of creation "principles that have served their day expire, and new principles are born." In that act of creation, judges relied not only on case law, but on all branches of knowledge, experience, information, and not least, their own intuition.

The Realists saw law not as fixed but in constant flux, responding to changing social conditions. Since law always lagged behind social change, modern lawyers, judges, and legal scholars should pay less attention to what earlier cases said and more to current conditions that would determine future law. Realists wanted people to recognize that the law was not necessarily what moralists thought it *ought* to be. Realists emphasized that law, like other human institutions, is imperfect. Karl Llewellyn of the Columbia Law School and one of the leading Realists urged his colleagues to distrust traditional legal rules and maxims about how law supposedly worked and to look at the specific behavior of particular agencies and courts to see what really happened. To do this, they had to draw not only on empirical research, but also on the understandings of human behavior provided by the social sciences and the new teachings of psychology.

Realism and Reform on the Bench

The Realists found some allies on the bench—Learned and Augustus Hand, Julian W. Mack, and Arthur C. Denison on the lower federal bench; the brilliant Benjamin N. Cardozo, who made the New York Court of Appeals the second most important tribunal in the country, and who showed how law could be creatively fashioned to meet new needs; and, of course, Oliver Wendell Holmes and Louis D. Brandeis on the high court. Holmes had been a hero to two generations of legal reformers. His essays on the common law had energized Roscoe Pound and other advocates of sociological jurisprudence who had attacked legal formalism at the end of the nineteenth century.

Now his skepticism and his bluntness in identifying the economic and social biases that informed the opinions of his conservative colleagues made him the darling of the Realists—although they occasionally despaired at some of his lapses, such as the opinion striking down the Pennsylvania law designed to prevent mine cave-ins. Above all, they looked to Brandeis, who had pioneered the practice of introducing nonlegal data into the judicial process.

Brandeis's 1908 *Muller* brief had epitomized the arguments advocates of sociological jurisprudence had been making for years—that the law had to look to facts for guidance. Once on the bench, Brandeis continued to press for judicial cognizance of relevant information from any reliable source. In *Adams v. Tanner* (1917), he dissented from the majority opinion that a state may not prohibit employment agencies from charging fees. To show that the legislature had legitimate reasons for the prohibition, Brandeis drew on varied sources such as the federal Bureau of Labor *Bulletin*, congressional hearings, reports of the Washington State Bureau of Labor, the *Political Science Quarterly*, *American Labor Legislation Review*, and *Survey* magazine. He also cited a law review article, the first Supreme Court justice to do so.

His constant stream of dissents against the conservatives utilized massive amounts of information explaining why the legislature had chosen this particular policy, as well as criticizing the majority's legal reasoning. Political scientist Harold Laski once complained to Holmes that Brandeis's judicial opinions read too much like advocates' briefs, but Laski missed the point about what Brandeis was trying to do. Holmes's brilliant epigrams would be cheered by the liberals, but they gave no clues as to how to attack the conservative dogma. Brandeis used his opinions and dissents to educate, not only his brethren, but also the legal community at large. After painstakingly building up his case, he would often turn to his law clerk and say, "Now I think the opinion is persuasive. What can we do to make it more instructive?" He fired off constant memoranda to Felix Frankfurter as to how the legal journals could highlight the inconsistencies of some opinions, or how they should praise the soundness of others. He once wrote, "My faith in time is great," and he believed that in the end, the efforts of the legal reformers would be triumphant. Today there are few, if any, of the economic and social decisions of the Taft Court still accepted as law; Brandeis lived to see many of his dissents turned into law and cited as the proper enunciation of legal principle.

Brandeis and Holmes provided the core of the civil liberties faction on the Court. They gained a potent ally in 1925, when Harlan Fiske Stone came to the bench. As dean of the Columbia Law School, Stone had been considered almost rigidly conservative, but his disgust at the excesses of the Red Scare and the illegal practices of the Justice Department under attorney generals Palmer and Daugherty led him to rethink his values. When Coolidge named Stone attorney general, he immediately called for the resignation of William Burns as director of the Bureau of Investigation. Stone publicly announced that he had taken federal agents out of politics; they would no longer be sent out to chase radicals. Civil libertarians and many conservatives applauded this move, the former because they feared that Daugherty and Burns intended to set up a secret police, and the latter because they opposed any government intrusion into the private affairs of the citizenry.

Once on the bench, Stone not only adopted the Holmes–Brandeis position on judicial restraint, but he wasted little time in charging his conservative colleagues with reading their own biases into law. Taft wrote in disgust to his brother that "Stone had become subservient to Holmes and Brandeis. . . . He hungers for the applause of the law-school professors." In fact, Stone did want the approval of his former colleagues, and he had already imbibed more of their views than either he or they realized.

Finally, civil liberties often picked up advocates from among the conservatives, both on and off the bench, who deplored the excesses of overly zealous patriots as much as did a Brandeis or a Baldwin, although for different reasons. Charles Evans Hughes, for example, defended the five Socialists who had been expelled from the New York Assembly because he believed that the people had a right to elect whomever they wanted as their representatives, and the expulsion had violated that basic right. Justice Pierce Butler advocated a broad reading of the Fourth Amendment in his protest against wire tapping. Justice McReynolds defended the right to teach in a language other than English, as well as the right of parents to send their children to parochial schools. In both cases, he argued that both parents and teachers had a property interest in how children would be educated, and by thus expanding the meaning of property, he opened the door to later Court decisions on civil liberties. Justice Edward T. Sanford, although economically conservative, joined with Holmes and Brandeis in several cases, including the defense of Rosika Schwimmer, who was denied naturalization because of her pacifist views.

Thus, a rather strange assortment of radicals and conservatives, socialists and social workers, professors and judges, lawyers and ministers, set out to preserve and protect American civil liberties in the 1920s.

Political Fundamentalism

Threats to civil liberties were anything but imaginary, but the decade that began with the Palmer raids cannot be characterized as totally repressive. The hedonism of the times and the desire of Americans to have fun and make money defined the era far more than did Palmer's scare tactics. In many parts of the nation, efforts to smoke out radicals and ban their writings ran into responses such as that of New York's Mayor Jimmy Walker, who, during a debate over a censorship bill, commented that he had never yet heard of a girl being ruined by a book. Nonetheless, the dark side of the Roaring Twenties included the Ku Klux Klan, persecution of aliens and radicals, hostility to organized labor, the Sacco and Vanzetti case, and the Scopes trial.

In the political fundamentalism of the decade, middle America condemned any and all efforts at social change as unpatriotic. "Individualism?" snorted an American Legion leader. "Down with all Isms!" Protestant fundamentalists called for a "Bible-Christ-and-Constitution" campaign, while the Klan and many "respectable" people denounced Jews, blacks, Catholics, Asians, and all foreigners. Opponents of everything "foreign" finally got their way in the National Origins Act of 1924, which not only severely restricted the number of immigrants who could enter the country, but stipulated that most of them had to come from the Northern European, Protestant countries of the "Old Immigration."

The Ku Klux Klan preyed on many of the fears that racked the country. Distinct from the Klan that had flourished during Reconstruction, the second Klan had been founded on Stone Mountain near Atlanta in 1915. The Klan admitted only "native born, white, gentile Americans" who believed in white supremacy. Although remembered primarily for its antiblack outrages, the new Klan of the 1920s had great strength not only in the Old South, but in the midwestern and western states as well, where people feared the "foreigner" more than the occasional black person they met. With its secret rituals, the Klan provided a vicious outlet for many nativist fears and hatreds. Wherever the Klan gained power, terror followed with kidnappings, floggings, mutilations, cross burnings, and even murders. Blacks who attempted to exercise their rights, "immoral" persons, Catholics, and foreigners provided the main targets. More than most groups of the 1920s, the Klan emphasized social conformity. The new world did not appeal to its members, who found the city, with its sexual freedom and modern ideas, alien and frightening.

Another aspect of the conservative campaign to preserve the older and supposedly "purer" America involved fundamentalist opposition to the theory of evolution. Charles Darwin's ideas seemed perfectly reasonable to most people, but in 1922, the Kentucky legislature came within a vote of barring the teaching of evolution in the schools. Soon afterward, William Jennings Bryan, Wilson's former secretary of state and an ardent Prohibitionist, joined the antievolutionary forces, and the battle took on national proportions. In many states, the fundamentalists got nowhere; in Delaware, for example, a bill prohibiting teaching that man evolved from lower animals died in the committee on Fish, Game and Oysters. But the antievolutionary forces, who believed in the literal interpretation of the biblical tale of creation, won partial victories in several states. In Tennessee, where the legislature had prohibited teaching evolution, young biology teacher, John T. Scopes, deliberately taught a lesson on Darwin's theory to challenge the law, and the trial of the decade began.

The so called monkey trial, which pitted the eminent lawyer Clarence Darrow against Bryan, involved more than academic freedom or even the struggle between science and religion. It epitomized the gulf between the city and the countryside, the former advocating a newer, more tolerant and ethnically diverse America, the latter clinging to the familiar world it had always known, with its social cohesion and intellectual conformity. The local jury convicted Scopes, but the Tennessee Supreme Court threw out the conviction on technical grounds, thwarting Darrow's plans to appeal to the U.S. Supreme Court. The law remained on the books for many years, but no one else was ever prosecuted for violating the statute.

One case, more than any other, polarized the country, setting liberal against con-

> Darrow: "You claim that everything in the Bible should be literally interpreted?"
>
> Bryan: "I believe everything in the Bible should be accepted as it is given there; some of the Bible is given illustratively. . . ."
>
> Darrow: "But when you read that . . . the whale swallowed Jonah . . . how do you literally interpret that?"
>
> Bryan: "I believe in a God who can make a whale and can make a man and make both of them do what he pleases. . . ."
>
> Darrow: "But do you believe he made them—that he made such a fish and it was big enough to swallow Jonah?"
>
> Bryan: "Yes sir. Let me add: One miracle is just as easy to believe as another."
>
> —Clarence Darrow cross-examining William Jennings Bryan, Scopes Trial (1925)

servative, urban dweller against rural, modernist against traditionalist. In May 1920, police arrested two Italian aliens, Nicola Sacco and Bartolomeo Vanzetti, for a payroll robbery at a shoe company in South Braintree, Massachusetts, in which two men were killed. Self-confessed anarchists, Sacco and Vanzetti were convicted and sentenced to death at a trial in which the judge and jury paid more attention to the defendants' radical ideas than to the circumstantial evidence tying them to the crime. Although the original trial had attracted little attention, a variety of legal experts now rallied to the cause, trying to get either a new trial or a pardon because of the gross irregularities and open prejudice that they claimed had marked the proceedings. The Sacco–Vanzetti case filled the nation's press with charges and countercharges, with all the defenders of conservative, middle-class values seemingly arrayed against the proponents of liberalism and tolerance. Appeals to the governor and the Supreme Court failed, and on August 23, 1927, the two men died in the electric chair at Charlestown prison.

The attack on civil liberties represented by the Klan, the Scopes trial, and the Sacco–Vanzetti case reflected the tension in the country between the forces of modernism and tradition. Not surprisingly, these same forces operated on the Supreme Court, and some of the majority opinions displayed an almost casual indifference to those liberties of ideas and expression that we now believe guaranteed by the First Amendment. But the cases hardly form a cohesive pattern of repression. A conservative majority of the Court, like the conservative majority of the country, found comfort in tradition and conformity, but the justices also had a keener perception of constitutional liberties. In the 1920s, therefore, the Court slowly began to establish the modern interpretation of the Bill of Rights.

The Nationalization of Standards

Ever since *Barron v. Baltimore* (1833), the Bill of Rights had been held to apply only to the federal government; although some people argued that the Fourteenth Amendment had extended those guarantees to the states, that view had not yet gained Court approval. This left the protection of civil liberties to the states, where conservative businessmen successfully lobbied legislatures to enact measures stifling their critics. They claimed that labor unrest, pickets, strikes, and all other symptoms of a less than perfect system had been caused by Communists, anarchists, and other radicals. Dean John Wigmore of the University of Chicago Law School derided people who complained about these laws as being "parlor bolsheviks and pink radicals." Conservatives claimed that while the Constitution guaranteed individual liberties, it did not protect license. People who abused their liberties had to face the consequences, and legislatures could make whatever arrangements they believed necessary to control dissidence. Correspondingly, local law enforcement officers could not be shackled by too careful a concern for procedural fairness; the radicals who wanted to overthrow the system had no right to the legal protections of that system.

In 1922, in *Prudential Insurance Company v. Cheek*, the Court reaffirmed that state infringement of civil liberties remained beyond the control of the federal government or its courts. The Fourteenth Amendment, according to Justice Pitney, had not extended the Bill of Rights to the states. He thus denied Brandeis's argument, made two years earlier in his dissent in *Gilbert v. Minnesota*, that the liberty guaranteed by the Fourteenth Amendment went beyond property rights to include personal freedoms as well.

The first fruits of that dissent finally appeared the same year as *Prudential*, when the Court struck down a state statute that forbade the teaching of foreign languages in elementary schools. In *Meyer v. Nebraska*, Justice McReynolds applied the *Lochner* doctrine, declaring that liberty denotes:

> not merely freedom from bodily restraint but also the right of the individual to contract, to engage in any of the common occupations of life, to acquire useful knowledge, to marry, to establish a home and bring up children, to worship God according to the dictates of his own conscience, and generally to enjoy those privileges long recognized at common law as essential to the orderly pursuit of happiness by free men.

To be sure, McReynolds found property rights involved in the case, since the Nebraska law "materially" interfered "with the calling of modern language teachers." But he also found the measure a violation of free speech. The goal of the legislature to foster "a homogeneous people with American ideals" was understandable in light of the recent war, but now "peace and domestic tranquility" reigned, and he could find no adequate justification for the restraints on liberty. Without using the exact words, McReynolds in effect applied the clear and present danger test and found the statute lacking. Interestingly enough, the *Meyer* decision came over the dissent of Justice Holmes, who found no threat to freedom nor cause for the Court to question legislative decisions.

Two years later, McReynolds spoke for a unanimous Court in *Pierce v. Society of Sisters* (1925). The Ku Klux Klan had pushed through a law in Oregon requiring children to attend public schools, with the clear intent of driving the Catholic schools out of existence. Again, McReynolds found "no peculiar circumstances or present emergencies" to justify such an extraordinary measure. The law interfered with both personal and property rights. "The child is not the mere creature of the State," he wrote; "those who nurture him and direct his destiny have the right, coupled with the high duty, to prepare him for additional obligations." Moreover, the law directly attacked the vested property rights of private and parochial schools (a military school was the codefendant along with the Catholic school appealing in this case). McReynolds had only hinted at the constitutional foundation for parochial education in *Meyer*; he firmly established it in *Pierce*.

McReynolds found the justification for both *Meyer* and *Pierce* totally within the Due Process Clause of the Fourteenth Amendment; he applied the *Lochner* doctrine but intimated that other than property rights might be protected as well. Civil Liberties Union attorneys, especially Walter H. Pollak, picked up on McReynolds's two school opinions and Brandeis's *Gilbert* dissent and decided to challenge directly the traditional doctrine that the Bill of Rights did not apply to the states. Their opportunity came in *Gitlow v. New York* (1925).

The "Incorporation" of Free Speech

The *Gitlow* case posed a challenge to New York's 1902 Criminal Anarchy Act. Benjamin Gitlow, a leading figure in the American Communist party, had been convicted for publishing a radical newspaper, a "Left-Wing Manifesto," and other allegedly subversive materials. If Fourteenth Amendment liberty reached as far as McReynolds had suggested, Pollak argued, then surely it would include the protection of the press and speech. Although the Court affirmed the conviction by a 7 to 2 vote (Holmes and Brandeis dissenting), Justice Sanford agreed with Pollak's argument. "For present purposes we may and do assume that freedom of speech and of the press—which are protected by the First Amendment from abridgement by Congress—are among the fundamental personal rights protected by the due process clause of the Fourteenth Amendment from impairment by the States." So for the first time, the Supreme Court put forward what came to be known as the doctrine of incorporation, by which the Fourteenth Amendment "incorporated" the liberties protected in the Bill of Rights and applied them to the states.

There has been a continuing debate ever since over whether the framers of the Fourteenth Amendment intended to extend the Bill of Rights to the states, with historical evidence marshaled on both sides of the argument. The weight of the evidence supports the claim that the drafters wanted to extend and protect the rights of the new freedmen and apply the Bill of Rights to the states as well as to the federal government. But the "original intent" argument is somewhat sterile, given the subsequent perversion of the Civil War amendments in the retreat from Reconstruction. Brandeis was certainly right in his claim that due process had to include more than just protection of property, and he could refer to the older English idea of the "law of the land," which went way beyond the rights of property.

If there are certain minimal procedural and substantive guarantees that the constitutional system provides, they must be derived from either explicit or implicit clauses of the Constitution. The Court from the 1920s on has ruled that the Fourteenth Amendment's Due Process Clause means that the states cannot infringe on fundamental rights. Defining those fundamental rights has been a continuing task of the Court, one that has engendered much controversy, as we shall see. The process is still not complete, because a developing society is constantly reexamining and redefining its values. For the Constitution to remain a viable organic law, it too must grow; any other policy, such as a rigid reliance on original intent, would lead to what some scholars have termed a "clause-bound literalism" that would make the Constitution a strait jacket rather than a loose-fitting "suit of clothes" with room for growth and change.

Justice Sanford, of course, did not explore the full extent of this theoretical argument in his *Gitlow* opinion; in fact, he concluded that the state could limit Gitlow's speech in this instance:

> It is a fundamental principle, long established, that the freedom of speech and of the press which is secured by the Constitution, does not confer an absolute right to speak or publish. . . . A State may punish utterances endangering the foundations of organized government and threatening its overthrow by unlawful means.

The New York statute was a legitimate response to a perceived threat, and although he accepted the clear and present danger test, Sanford interpreted it in such a manner as to make it more rather than less restrictive of speech. As Holmes had refined the test in the *Abrams* case, the rule applied to speech that directly caused bad acts; the New York law, however, aimed not at the deed but at the evil words themselves, which might, or might not, incite action. Sanford's ruling meant that words could now be punished for their bad nature regardless of whether or not they caused particular acts. The legislature could brand certain ideas and sentiments dangerous to society and outlaw their dissemination.

Holmes entered a brief opinion, joined by Brandeis, agreeing with the Court's application of the First Amendment to the states, but dissenting from the majority's ruling that words separated from action could be punished. "It is said," he wrote, "that this manifesto was more than a theory, that it was an incitement. Every idea is an incitement . . . Eloquence may set fire to reason. But . . . the only meaning of free speech is that [beliefs] should be given their chance and have their way." Holmes implied that a mere statement of an idea, no matter how objectionable the sentiment, should never be punished, but he did not directly confront the question of whether a legislature could judge some ideas so dangerous as to warrant criminal sanctions for their mere utterance, a position that his advocacy of deference to legislative discretion might have commanded.

Whitney v. California

Brandeis did deal directly with the issue of legislative discretion in speech cases in his concurring opinion in *Whitney v. California* (1927). Charlotte Anita Whitney, a niece of Justice Stephen J. Field and "a woman nearing sixty, a Wellesley graduate long distinguished in philanthropic work," had been convicted under the California Criminal Syndicalism Act of 1919 for helping to organize the Communist Labor party there. Originally aimed at the Industrial Workers of the World, the law made it a felony to organize or knowingly become a member of an organization founded to advocate the commission of crimes, sabotage, or acts of violence as a means of bringing about political or industrial change. Miss Whitney denied that it had ever been intended for the Communist Labor party to become an instrument of crime or violence; nor was there any proof that it had ever engaged in violent acts. She retained two prominent corporate attorneys, J.E. Pemberton and Nathan Coghlan, to appeal her conviction, and they brought in Walter Pollak of the ACLU and his associate, Walter Nelles. Nevertheless, the conservative majority, again led by Justice Sanford, upheld the act as a legitimate decision by the California legislature to prevent the violent overthrow of society. The Due Process Clause did not protect one's liberty to destroy the social and political order.

Because of technical issues, Brandeis chose not to dissent, but his concurring opinion, joined by Holmes, provided an eloquent defense of intellectual freedom unmatched for its powerful reasoning in the annals of the Court. The majority, Brandeis claimed, not only here but in other speech cases, was operating on a totally inappropriate set of assumptions. They had measured the limits of free speech against potential danger to property, thus ignoring the benefits that free exchange of ideas conferred on society as a whole. He agreed that under certain circumstances a legislature could limit speech, but the proper test for exercising that power would be if the words posed a clear and imminent danger to *society*, not just to property interests. Suppression of ideas worked a great hardship on society, and before that could be allowed, the Court had the responsibility of developing objective standards, a responsibility that it had thus far failed to meet. Brandeis made it quite clear that, like Holmes, he did not fear ideas, and Americans need not do so either. Moreover, Brandeis set out what would become the basis for First American jurisprudence.

Holmes rested his First Amendment views on what has been termed the marketplace of ideas. Since we cannot know immediately which ideas are good and true and useful and which are not, we must let them vie against one another in the faith that after full exposure and discussion, the truth will win out. This is to some extent a "negative" view of the First Amendment and reflects Holmes's famed skepticism. He saw nothing particularly good or bad in free speech other than the forum it allowed for intellectual competititon.

Brandeis, on the other hand, saw free speech as an essential aspect of citizenship. Men and women had the duty in a democracy to be good citizens, which meant being informed on the issues confronting them. How could they make intelligent decisions about these matters if they lacked basic information about them? How could they judge if one side or the other had the better argument unless they could hear both sides and then join in the debate? The fact that some viewpoints ran against the grain or disturbed popular sensibilities made no difference; history was replete with examples of unpopular ideas that had eventually gained public acceptance. Brandeis thus provided a positive justification for protection of speech, the necessity for the citizenry to be fully informed about issues and to be aware of all viewpoints. But Brandeis would not limit First Amendment protection to political speech alone; his opinion in *Whitney* clearly values speech as a cultural, social and educational, as well as a political value in a free society.

The same day as *Whitney*, the Court reversed a conviction under the Kansas criminal syndicalism law in *Fiske v. Kansas*. Justice Sanford did not rule the law invalid, but stated that in applying the statute to penalize a person for seeking new members for the International Workers of the World, the legislature had infringed on the defendant's liberty. Sanford made no mention of free speech, apparently relying on McReynold's Lochnerian views.

> Those who won our independence believed liberty to be the secret of happiness and courage to be the secret of liberty. They believed that freedom to speak as you will and to speak as you think are means indispensable to the discovery and spread of political truth; that without free speech and assembly discussion would be futile; that with them, discussion affords ordinarily protection against the dissemination of noxious doctrine; that the greatest menace to freedom is an inert people. . . . To courageous, self-reliant men, with confidence in the power of free and fearless reasoning applied through the processes of popular government, no danger flowing from speech can be deemed clear and present, unless the incidence of the evil apprehended is so imminent that it may befall before there is opportunity for full discussion. If there be time to expose through discussion the falsehood and fallacies, to avert the evil by the processes of education, the remedy to be applied is more speech, not enforced silence. Only an emergency can justify repression. Such must be the rule if authority is to be reconciled with freedom. Such, in my opinion, is the command of the Constitution.
>
> —Louis D. Brandeis, concurring in *Whitney v. California* (1927)

Criminal Justice

The criminal law provisions of the Bill of Rights, found in the Fourth through Eighth amendments, had also never been applied to the states, although many states had written some of these guarantees into their own constitutions. In the 1920s, the Court for the most part preferred to leave the control of criminal justice in the hands of the states, although in the face of outright abuse of fair procedures, it showed itself willing to extend federal standards and authority.

The decade had started with the *Silverthorne Lumber* decision, in which an outraged Holmes had chastised the Department of Justice for seizing books and papers from the suspects' office "without a shadow of authority." Six other members of the Court had joined in his expansion of the exclusionary rule, ensuring that the government could not benefit from illegally secured evidence. But the flood of cases in state and federal courts growing out of efforts to enforce the Nineteenth (Prohibition) Amendment led to some retreat from this position. In *Byars v. United States* and *Gambino v. United States*, both in 1927, the Court developed what came to be known as the "silver platter" doctrine: evidence obtained in an illegal state search would be admissible in a federal court so long as there had been no federal participation. The doctrine invited the abuses that followed; state law enforcement officials blatantly violated fair procedures (often in violation of their own state laws) and then turned the evidence over to federal officers, who secretly knew about, and had often instigated, the illegal search. Not until 1960 did the Court abolish the silver platter doctrine in *Elkins v. United States*.

Prohibition became a law enforcement nightmare. Aside from the fact that many Americans deliberately violated the law, the bootleggers applied the latest technology to their efforts to give a thirsty citizenry what it wanted. They used a relatively new invention, the automobile, to run illegal liquor into the country from Canada or from country stills into the cities. In December 1921, federal agents stopped a car outside Detroit, which because of its proximity to Ontario, Canada, had become a major entrepot for imported liquor. The agents searched the car without a warrant and found sixty-eight quarts of whiskey and gin behind the upholstery. After conviction for violation of the Volstead Act, the defendants appealed to the Supreme Court, claiming that their Fourth Amendment rights had been violated.

By a 7 to 2 vote, the Court upheld the conviction in *Carroll v. United States* (1925). Chief Justice Taft found the search reasonable because the agents had had probable cause; the defendants, all suspected of previous bootlegging operations, had been traveling on a road frequently used by smugglers. Because of time constraints, the officers had been unable to get a warrant; if they had applied for one, the car would have been gone by the time it arrived. So the Court carved the automobile exception out of the Fourth Amendment's requirement that no search or seizure take place without a warrant. Where a warrant could be reasonably secured, Taft urged, it should be; but otherwise, police did not need warrants to stop and search automobiles. The decision generated a strong, albeit confusing, dissent from McReynolds and Sutherland, as well as much criticism from legal scholars. The car exception and variants upon it would come back before the Court for further exegesis over the next half-century, but the *Carroll* doctrine is still the law.

Wire Tapping and Privacy

Technology also gave the government new means to prosecute its fight against crime, including the ability to pry into the private affairs of a suspect without actually entering the premises. By a bare majority, the Court gave its blessing to such wire tapping in *Olmstead v. United States* (1928). Chief Justice Taft took a formalistic view of wire tapping, which completely ignored the Fourth Amendment's intent. There had been no actual entry, but only the use of an enhanced sense of hearing, he claimed, and to pay too much attention to "nice ethical conduct by government officials would make society suffer and give criminals greater immunity than has been known heretofore."

The Taft opinion elicited dissents from Butler, Holmes, and Brandeis. In a well-reasoned historical analysis, the generally conservative Butler repudiated Taft's sterile interpretation of what the Fourth Amendment meant. Holmes, in a comment that soon caught the liberal imagination, condemned wire tapping as "a dirty business." But the most impressive opinion came from Brandeis, who forthrightly declared that he considered it "less evil that some criminals should escape than that the government should play an ignoble part. . . . If government becomes a lawbreaker, it breeds contempt for law."

The most noted and influential part of Brandeis's dissent dealt with the question of privacy. As a practicing attorney, he and his partner, Samuel D. Warren, had written a pioneering article "The Right to Privacy" (*Harvard Law Review* [1891]) on the common law right of privacy, an article that Roscoe Pound later credited with creating an entire new area of law. The Framers of the Constitution, Brandeis wrote in *Olmstead*, "sought to protect Americans in their beliefs, their thoughts, their emotions and their sensations. They conferred, as against the Government, the right to be let alone—the most comprehensive of rights, and the right most valued by civilized man." That passage would be picked up and elaborated on until finally, in *Griswold v. Connecticut* (1965), the Court recognized privacy as a constitutionally guaranteed liberty.

Wire tapping itself remained legally permissible for many years, although Congress in 1934 prohibited admitting wire tapping evidence in federal courts. Not until 1967, in *Berger v. New York*, did the Court finally bring wire tapping within the reach of the Fourth Amendment; now wiretap evidence may be introduced, but only if it has been secured after the issuance of a proper warrant. In another 1967 case, Justice Potter Stewart explained the Court's new philosophy when he declared that "the Fourth Amendment protects people, not places" (*Katz v. United States*).

Lynch Law

Although the Taft Court preferred to leave criminal matters to the states, occasionally it interfered. Two cases are particularly notable because they affected race relations, another area that the Court considered wholly within state authority. The racial tensions following World War I had led to a series of urban riots in the North and triggered a wave of lynchings in Southern states. The House of Representatives had approved a bill in 1921, making lynching a federal crime, but it had been defeated by a Southern filibuster in the Senate. Lynching offended the Court as nonviolent forms of discrimination did not. In *Moore v. Dempsey* (1923), Justice Holmes ruled that a federal court should hear the appeal of five black men, convicted of first degree murder by an Arkansas state court, where the constant threat of mob violence had dominated the proceedings. Such an atmosphere, he held, amounted to little more than judicially sanctioned lynching, and when state courts could not provide minimal procedural fairness, then the federal courts had a clear duty to "secure to the petitioners their constitutional rights."

The *Moore* ruling (joined by all except McReynolds and Sutherland) to a large extent vindicated Holmes's dissent nearly a decade earlier in *Frank v. Mangum* (1915). In that notorious case, Leo Frank, a Jew accused of killing a young white woman, had appealed his state court conviction for murder because the trial had been tainted by the threat of mob violence, and his lawyer, out of fear, had waived some of Frank's rights. For the majority, Justice Pitney had ruled that while federal courts could note the threat or the actual existence of violence, they had to examine the entire record to see if it had had any significant effect on the final outcome. Holmes, joined by Hughes, had dissented, claiming that if any one part of the proceedings had been tainted, then the federal courts could intervene to protect the rights of the defendant. (Following this decision, Georgia governor John Slayton, recognizing the gross irregularities in the trial, commuted Frank's death sentence to life imprisonment. An inmate attacked Frank in prison and almost killed him, and soon after a mob plucked Frank out of the hospital where he was recuperating and lynched him. Although most of the mob leaders were known, a local jury brought in a verdict of "death at the hands of persons unknown.")

Justice Sutherland, who dissented in *Moore*, wrote one of the Court's most important opinions expanding the reach of the Fifth Amendment in another case involving black defendants, the infamous Scottsboro affair. Nine black teenagers had been accused of raping two white girls, and Alabama officials raced through the legal motions, holding the trials in one day and sentencing all nine to the electric chair. As required under Alabama law, the trial court had appointed counsel, but the evidence showed that the lawyers had not consulted with their clients and had done little more than put in a *pro forma* appearance. The blatant perversion of due process became a national *cause célèbre*, and the Court agreed to review the case in *Powell v. Alabama* (1932).

Sutherland carefully detailed how unfair the trial had been and concluded that the lack of effective counsel had violated the defendants' rights to due process as required in the Fourteenth Amendment and to counsel as guaranteed in the Fifth Amendment. The Court thus overruled its earlier decision in *Hurtado v. California* (1884), in which, in sweeping language, it had specifically excluded Fifth Amendment rights from the due process protected by the Fourteenth. *Powell* represented a significant step in extending the Bill of Rights to the states, and the opinion came from a justice noted for his great concern that the federal government should not trespass on states' rights. (The youths were retried, found guilty, and sentenced to prison terms. Powell, the lead plaintiff, escaped to Michigan, where the governor refused to extradite him; the others were eventually paroled.)

Race and Alienage

The Court's expansion of constitutional protection in criminal procedure happened to have come in cases involving black defendants, but the Court generally showed very little concern over issues of racial prejudice. A typical case was *Corrigan v. Buckley* (1926), in which a unanimous Court refused to declare restrictive covenants—which prevented the sale or lease of property to blacks—as violative of due process. The following year, in *Nixon v. Herndon* (1927), the Court struck down a Texas law excluding blacks from voting in the Democratic primary as violating the Equal Protection Clause of the Fourteenth Amendment. But the decision had little lasting impact, for party leaders soon developed informal but effective ways to exclude blacks.

The Taft Court, including its liberal faction, showed no great concern for other racial minorities either, or for aliens. Asian immigrants had been considered eligible for citizenship under the first naturalization law of 1790, only because the statute had not explicitly excluded them. In 1870, however, Congress had formally limited naturalization to whites, and in *Ozawa v. United States* (1923), the Court, through Justice Sutherland, unanimously interpreted the act as excluding Japanese. The Court interpreted the 1870 statute, which had made blacks eligible for citizenship, as limiting other eligible immigrants to those of the Caucasian race. The Court then extended the ban to East Indians in *United States v. Bhagat Singh Thind* (1923), even though the defendant claimed that Asian Indians had pure Aryan blood. A year later, Filipinos also came under the ban in dictum in a case denying citizenship to a Japanese member of the armed services, although Congress in 1918 and 1919 had provided that "any alien" serving in the nation's military could file for naturalization. According to the Court, Congress had not meant to expand the idea beyond the limits of the 1790 and 1870 statues (*Toyota v. United States*).

In addition, the Court had no problem upholding various western state laws prohibiting land ownership by aliens who had not declared their intention to become citizens, laws specifically aimed at Asians ineligible for naturalization. In *Terrace v. Thompson* (1923), Justice Butler sustained a Washington State law on the grounds that although Congress had exclusive control over immigration and naturalization, in the absence of legislation or a treaty, a state retained full power to deny aliens economic rights within its borders.

Aliens also did not enjoy procedural rights akin to those of citizens. A 1920 statute expedited deportation of aliens convicted under the Espionage and Sedition Acts or the Selective Service Act of 1917. Many of these people had been charged under those laws for acts committed before their passage, but Chief Justice Taft rejected the contention that this constituted ex post facto legislation. The sovereign had complete powers to deport, limited only by treaty. An alien, therefore, could be deported for an act that might have been legal at the time it was committed. Deportation, although severe, did not constitute a criminal sanction and therefore did not come under the ban on ex post facto laws (*Mahler v. Eby* [1924]).

The idea of deportation as a civil rather than a criminal proceeding also figured in *United States ex rel. Bilokomsky v. Tod* (1923). The Court, through Justice Brandeis, granted the government great leeway in how it handled deportations. It did not have to provide aliens counsel, the right to confront witnesses, or immunity from self-incrimination, and it could secure and use evidence that would be impermissible in a criminal trial. In fact, the only procedural right that the Court seemed willing to grant relied on the claim that the person whom the government sought to deport was actually a citizen. In *Ng Fung Ho v. White* (1921), the Court ruled that if a person claimed to be a citizen, he or she could secure a judicial trial on that claim, though not on any other issue.

The superpatriotism of the decade manifested itself in the Court's denial of citizenship to aliens who, despite many exemplary qualities, happened to be pacifists. In the first case, *United States v. Schwimmer* (1929), an older Quaker woman of unblemished character had refused to promise to bear arms in defense of the country and had been denied naturalization as a result. The Court upheld the ruling and drew from Holmes one of his most eloquent dissents. "If there is any principle of the Constitution," he declared, "that more imperatively calls for attachment than any other it is the principle of free thought—not free thought for those who agree with us but freedom for the thought we hate." He failed to see how the country would suffer by taking as citizens those people "who believe more than some of us do in the teachings of the Sermon on the Mount."

Two years later, Charles Evans Hughes—who had resigned from the Court in 1916 to run for president—came back as chief justice, and the issue again came before the Court. Two Canadian-born pacifists, one a professor of divinity at Yale, the other a nurse who had spent nine months tending American soldiers in France, applied for U.S. citizenship. But Professor Macintosh sought to qualify the oath of allegiance by declaring that he would only bear arms if he believed it would serve the greater needs of humanity, whereas Miss Bland wanted to add the phrase "so far as my conscience as a Christian will allow." A bare majority of the Court again upheld the Immigration Service, with both rulings relying on the nation's right to survive. Hughes, joined by Holmes, Brandeis, and Stone, entered an eloquent dissent. Not until 1946, in *Girouard v. United States*, did the Court finally adopt their point of view.

The indifference to the lack of fair procedure for aliens reflected in part the Taft Court's general attitude toward civil liberties and in part the growing public animus toward aliens and all things foreign. Few voices protested the Court decisions, for even the liberals of the time recognized a distinction between the *rights* of an American citizen and the *privileges* accorded to an alien. Civil liberties jurisprudence, as well as popular ideas on this subject, had not yet fully developed. It is not so surprising, then, that the Supreme Court showed a minimal concern in this area.

One case from this time that shocks the modern conscience and displays in full the Taft Court's indifference to individual liberties dealt not with people of color or aliens or pacifists, but with a white Southern girl, Carrie Buck. The eugenics movement that spread across the United States in the early twentieth century led a number of states to enact involuntary sterilization laws in efforts to "improve" the race. Virginia enacted such a law, but it remained unclear whether it would pass constitutional muster. The superintendent of the State Colony for Epileptics and the Feeble-Minded at Lynchburg, Albert Priddy, decided to test the validity of the law, and the person he chose for his test case was eighteen-year-old Carrie Buck.

A victim of rape, Carrie had become pregnant, and the family with which she was living had her committed to the Lynchburg institution. There a relatively primitive I.Q. test showed her to have the intelligence of a nine year old. Carrie's mother, Emma, also confined to the colony, tested out at eight years old. After Carrie gave birth to her daughter, Vivien, Priddy recommended that she be sterilized, and he began the administrative process, hiring lawyers to test the law in the courts. At the trial, the state presented witnesses to prove Carrie's feeble-mindedness, and one described the Buck family as part of the "shiftless, ignorant, and worthless class of anti-social whites." Young Vivien was described as "not quite normal."

> We have seen more than once that the public welfare may call upon the best citizens for their lives. It would be strange indeed if it could not call upon those who already sap the strength of the State for these lesser sacrifices, often not felt to be such by those concerned, in order to prevent our being swamped with incompetence. It is better for all the world, if instead of waiting to execute degenerate offspring for crime, or to let them starve for their imbecility, society can prevent those who are manifestly unfit from continuing their kind. . . . Three generations of imbeciles are enough.
>
> —Oliver Wendell Holmes, *Buck v. Bell* (1927)

Carrie Buck's attorney, paid for by the institution, put on a weak defense, since he admittedly agreed with the sterilization policy. Nonetheless, he carried an appeal to the Supreme Court and there offered an equal protection argument; the law, he claimed, discriminated against people confined to institutions and denied them their "full bodily integrity." Holmes, speaking for an 8–1 Court in *Buck v. Bell* (1927), dismissed all of these arguments in a short, five-paragraph opinion, three paragraphs of which described the facts of the case. He dismissed the equal protection claim as "the usual last resort of constitutional arguments," and cited only one case in support of the judgment, a ruling upholding compulsory vaccination in Massachusetts (*Jacobson v. Massachusetts* [1905]). Paying his usual deference to the legislature, Holmes affirmed the judgment. Only Pierce Butler dissented without opinion.

Although Holmes became the darling of the eugenics movement, that movement faded with the rise of Nazism in the 1930s, and the case has had a bad odor about it ever since. Critics of Holmes constantly point to this opinion as a "true" indicator of his so-called liberalism, and Catholic scholars in particular have attacked him for falling into the error of abandoning natural law for positivism. But the worst aspect of the case is that years later, it turned out that Carrie Buck had not been feeble-minded. She had advanced with her class grade by grade in public school until taken out to work in her foster home. Her final report card rated her as "very good—deportment and lessons." In her later years, she had been active in reading groups and dramatics, and despite a very hard life, a social worker described her as an "alert and pleasant lady." There were no imbeciles at all among the three generations of Buck women.

Incorporating Freedom of the Press

On the other hand, as we have seen, the Taft Court took the first faltering steps toward incorporating the Bill of Rights into the Fourteenth Amendment's guarantees of liberty. In *Gitlow*, it extended the First Amendment protection of speech, and in *Powell*, the Fifth Amendment right of counsel. Then in the landmark case of *Near v. Minnesota* (1931), begun in the last year of Taft's tenure, the Hughes Court significantly expanded freedom of the press.

The Minnesota legislature had authorized suppression, as a public nuisance, of any "malicious, scandalous and defamatory newspaper, or other periodical." The law had been enacted with the specific intent of silencing the *Saturday Press*, a tabloid that had exposed corruption in the Minneapolis government, but in a lurid and at times irresponsible manner. The suit challenging the law, by the publisher, Jay Near, came before the Court with Taft still the chief justice, but the justices did not decide the case until after his death; it is possible that had he been alive, the 5 to 4 vote might have gone the other way. But the new chief justice voided the law as a form of prior restraint, which Hughes condemned as "of the essence of censorship"; thus began the Court's long and consistent opposition to any prior restraint of the press. Perhaps more important, Hughes declared that "it is no longer open to doubt that the liberty of the press and of speech is within the liberties safeguarded by the due process clause of the Fourteenth Amendment from invasion by state action."

Shortly before the *Near* opinion came down, the Court had decided a complex insurance regulation case. Brandeis, joined by Hughes, Holmes, Stone, and Owen J. Roberts, upheld a New Jersey statute regulating the fees of insurance agents. His short opinion summarized the policy of judicial restraint that he and Holmes had been preaching for years. The state legislature had made a reasonable determination that an evil existed and that it should take steps to correct that evil, and the Court should not examine policy, but should "presume" constitutionality unless a specific prohibition existed. Yet this same majority struck down the Minnesota press law in *Near*; it did inquire into policy, and it denied the presumption of constitutionality.

As Brandeis and Hughes argued on several occasions, an important difference existed between laws regulating economic conduct and those affecting basic rights such as freedom of speech and press. In the latter instances, freedom must be the rule and restraint the exception; the Court had a special obligation to protect individual liberties, and in cases in which the legislature had attempted to limit freedom, the Court could examine policy and require the state to show why it had needed to be repressive. The idea of the Court as the special guardian of liberties would underline the enormous expansion of the Bill of Rights in the post-World War II decades.

In the meantime, this view did not command the support of a majority on the Court. In fact, the four conservative members still completely opposed any and all forms of economic regulation and clung to the *Adkins* doctrine that "freedom of contract is the general rule, restraint the exception," and at least two others, Hughes and Roberts, had not completely rejected it. As the nation plunged into the Great Depression and both state and federal governments initiated new and radical efforts to deal with the economic distress, it seemed likely that a majority of the Court would question the legitimacy of experimentation. But no one expected that conservative adherence to an undiluted freedom of contract would create one of the most serious constitutional crises in American history.

For Further Reading

Overall studies of the 1920s are listed in the last chapter. The best general work on civil liberties in this decade is Paul L. Murphy, *The Meaning of Freedom of Speech: First Amendment Freedoms from Wilson to FDR* (1972); but see also the relevant chapters of Charles L. Markmann, *The Noblest Cry: A History of the American Civil Liberties Union* (1965); and Samuel Walker, *In Defense of American Liberties: A History of the ACLU* (1990).

Legal realism is discussed in Laura Kalman, *Legal Realism at Yale* (1986); John Henry Schlegel, *American Legal Realism and Empirical Social Science* (1995); and the relevant chapters of Neil Duxbury, *Patterns of American Jurisprudence* (1995). John W. Johnson, *American Legal Culture, 1908–1940* (1981), discusses some of the new ways in which judges sought and used information. See also Maxwell Bloomfield, *Peaceful Revolution: Constitutional Change and American Culture from Progressivism to the New Deal* (2000).

For the incorporation debate that began almost immediately after the *Gitlow* decision, see Charles Warren, "The New 'Liberty' Under the Fourteenth Amendment," 39 *Harvard Law Review* 431 (1926), which found the argument constitutionally indefensible. For extended discussions, see Richard C. Cortner, *The Supreme Court and the Second Bill of Rights* (1981); as well as the excellent essay by John Hart Ely, *Democracy and Distrust: A Theory of Judicial Review* (1980). See also Charles Fairman, "Does the Fourteenth Amendment Incorporate the Bill of Rights? The Original Understanding," 2 *Stanford Law Review* 5 (1949), and the answering critique by William W. Crosskey, "Charles Fairman, 'Legislative History,' and the Constitutional Limitations on State Authority," 22 *University of Chicago Law Review* 1 (1954). The best overall treatment is William Nelson, *The Fourteenth Amendment: From Political Principle to Judicial Doctrine* (1988); while a strong case that the Framers of the Amendment did intend to apply it to the states is Akhil Reed Amar, *The Bill of Rights: Creation and Reconstruction* (1998). Michael Kent Curtis, *No State Shall Abridge: The Fourteenth Amendment and the Bill of Rights* (1986) also argues for complete incorporation.

For material on some specific cases, see Edward J. Larson, *Summer of the Gods: The Scopes Trial and America's Continuing Debate over Science and Religion* (1997); David B. Tyack, "The Perils of Pluralism: The Background of the Pierce Case," 74 *American Historical Review* 74 (1968); Kenneth B. O'Brien, Jr., "Education, Americanization, and the Supreme Court in the 1920s," 13 *American Quarterly 161* (1961); Lloyd P. Jorgenson, "The Oregon School Law of 1922; Passage and Sequel," 54 *Catholic Historical Review* 455 (1968); Orville H. Zabell, *God and Caesar in Nebraska* (1955), and William G. Ross, *Forging New Freedoms: Nativism, Education and the Constitution, 1917–1927* (1994).

Forrest R. Black lacerated the majority opinion in "A Critique of the Carroll Case," 29 *Columbia Law Review* 1068 (1929). For the *Olmstead* case, see Walter F. Murphy, *Wiretapping on Trial* (1965); and Norman H. Clark, *The Dry Years: Prohibition and Social Change in Washington* (1965). Criminal law in general is well explicated in David J. Bodenhamer, *Fair Trial: Rights of the Accused in American History* (1992). Fred W. Friendly, *Minnesota Rag: The Dramatic Story of the Landmark Supreme Court Case That Gave New Meaning to Freedom of the Press* (1981), is certainly dramatic and well written, but it lacks a broad analysis of the legal issues. A beautifully written analysis is Vincent Blasi, "The First Amendment and the Ideal of Civil Courage: The Brandeis Opinion in *Whitney v. California*," 29 *William & Mary Law Review* 653 (1988).

Eldridge F. Dowell, *History of Criminal Syndicalism Legislation in the United States* (1939), explores the state measures of the period; Lawrence H. Chamberlain, *Loyalty and Legislative Action: A Survey of Activity by the New York Legislature, 1919–1949* (1951), is a fine case study that puts the activity of the 1920s into a long-term context. Black rights and the courts during this era are detailed in Charles S. Mangum, Jr., *The Legal Status of the Negro* (1940); and Bernard H. Nelson, *The Fourteenth Amendment and the Negro Since 1920* (2nd ed., 1967). For aliens, see Milton R. Konvitz, *The Alien and the Asiatic in American Law* (1946). The conflict between the "old" and "new" liberty, and the potential for ensuing crisis, is presciently explored in Harry Shulman, "The Supreme Court's Attitude on Liberty of Contract and Freedom of Speech," 41 *Yale Law Journal* 262 (1931). For the sterilization case, see William E. Leuchtenburg, "Mr. Justice Holmes and Three Generations of Imbeciles," in *The Supreme Court Reborn: The Constitutional Revolution in the Age of Roosevelt* (1995).

30

The Depression, the New Deal, and the Court

AFTER THE COMPLACENCY of "Republican Prosperity," the Depression that began in 1929 dealt the American people a psychological as well as an economic blow. Many of the earlier assumptions no longer seemed so credible, while the messages of radicals and reformers, who had been the chief victims of repressive laws, now demanded serious attention. As the state and national governments attempted to grapple with the economic distress, courts also faced some serious rethinking. Unfortunately, the judicial mind often lagged far behind the temper of the times. As a result, Roosevelt's administration—the most innovative in American history—faced by overwhelming economic problems, ran into a Court apparently oblivious to the world outside its doors.

The Depression and the Need for Action

The extent of the Depression can only partially be told by facts. Between 1929 and 1932, industrial production dropped more than half, while industrial construction fell from $949 million to a scant $74 million. Steel plants, the backbone of an industrial economy, operated at 12 percent of capacity, and the stock market average, which had stood at 452 on September 3, 1929, bottomed out at 52 in July 1932. But vast human suffering marked the real tragedy of the Depression: thirteen million people unemployed, two million homeless and riding the country in boxcars, people living in tarpapered shacks dubbed "Hoovervilles," and families fighting outside the backdoors of restaurants for scraps of garbage. "The country needs," declared the Democratic presidential candidate in 1932, "and, unless I mistake its temper, the country demands bold, persistent experimentation."

Experimentation would be the hallmark of Franklin Delano Roosevelt's New Deal. No other president had ever entered the White House committed to the idea of just trying something—anything—and if that did not work, trying something else. Some of the New Deal had been anticipated in Roosevelt's campaign speeches and in earlier strains of Progressivism: a reforestation program to employ youth, public power development, regulation of utilities and the stock market, economic planning and cooperation with business, and the repeal of Prohibition. Yet some of the most striking activities of the Roosevelt administration came on the public as out of the blue: deficit spending, federal works, agricultural relief programs, massive expenditures for housing and slum clearance, the Tennessee Valley Authority, heavily progressive tax schemes, a labor relations board, and Social Security. All these resulted from Roosevelt's fertile mind and his willingness not only to listen to new ideas, but to act on them.

In the states, people demanded action as well. In fact, Roosevelt had come to national attention in part for his innovative use of state resources in New York to alleviate suffering. Governors such as C. Ben Ross in Idaho and Floyd Olson in Minnesota personally intervened to prevent auctions of property when banks had foreclosed on mortgages. In a nation where farmers destroyed their unsalable crops while people went hungry, the sanctity of the marketplace no longer made sense, and state after state adopted measures that they hoped would do some good. The judicial response to state legislation proved far from consistent and thus anticipated the confused reaction of the courts to national New Deal legislation.

The Hughes Court

The Court that would decide on the legislation of the Depression era had a core of archconservatives, nicknamed the Four Horsemen: Willis Van Devanter, James C. McReynolds, George Sutherland, and Pierce Butler. All had matured in the late nineteenth century, believed that an unfettered economy had made America great, and resisted any encroachments on freedom of contract. Although they occasionally differed on noneconomic matters, when it came to regulation of the market they could be counted on to stand resolutely against any government interference.

> I do not know how it may have been in other places, but in Chicago, as we saw it, the city seemed to have died. There was something awful—abnormal—in the very stillness of the streets. I recall being startled by the clatter of a horse's hooves on the pavement as a mounted policeman rode past.
>
> —Louise Armstrong, *We Too Are the People* (1938)

The liberal bloc consisted of Louis D. Brandeis, Harlan Fiske Stone, and Benjamin N. Cardozo, whom Hoover had named to replace Holmes in 1932. Of these, Brandeis had the clearest vision of the type of society he wanted—a small unit economy governed primarily at the state and local rather than at the national level. Yet he had been anything but doctrinaire while on the bench; he had recognized that while state governments could sometimes be corrupt, inefficient, and ineffective, they nonetheless represented democracy at its closest level to the people. In the absence of any specific constitutional prohibition, he stood ready to let the states experiment and be the laboratories of democracy, and his fact-filled opinions and dissents tried to explain to the bench and bar why legislatures had adopted particular policies.

The appointment of Cardozo, generally considered the greatest state judge of his time, had been warmly applauded not only by liberals but by legal scholars as well. More than any of his colleagues, Cardozo reflected the new school of legal realism. His lectures on *The Nature of the Judicial Process* (1921) had eloquently argued that legal rules should be measured by their social utility and contribution to the overall good of society. His decisions in New York had carried out this view, and he had led the way in adapting the common law to the needs of industrial society. One of his most famous decisions, *Macpherson v. Buick Motor Company* (1916), totally revolutionized the law of products liability. Immediately after *Macpherson*, one jurisdiction after another abandoned the older requirement of privity in cases involving defective goods to adopt the Cardozo rule of strict liability.

Despite his earlier conservatism, Stone had proven his devotion to civil liberties; but he had also imbibed Holmes's skepticism. He had little faith in any legislative panaceas, but like the Realists, Stone believed that the facts of the situation had to be taken into account; especially in economic matters, the old rules had to give way to new realities. Although he lacked Brandeis's gift for factual analysis or Cardozo's facility for elegant analysis, Stone joined with them in trying to square legal cliches such as due process, equal protection, and federalism with the needs of a society in which one-third of the nation lacked decent housing, clothing, and food. He neither subscribed to the judicial activism of the conservatives nor completely agreed with Holmes's notion of restraint, but instead sought a pragmatic middle ground. More than most persons who came to the bench, Stone matured and grew intellectually. Brandeis, for example, had had few good things to say about Stone during the latter's first few terms on the Court; by the 1930s, he spoke of him in highly complimentary terms and rejoiced when Roosevelt elevated Stone to be chief justice in 1941.

In the middle stood Chief Justice Charles Evans Hughes and Owen J. Roberts, both appointed by Hoover in 1930. Ultimately to become one of the most controversial members of the Court, Roberts had no clear judicial philosophy. Although he tended to side with the liberals in civil liberties cases, he wavered on economic questions. Scholars have been unable to ascertain any consistent legal philosophy informing Roberts's decisions. He seems to have totally ignored the dynamic aspects of law and assumed that both law and society remained static.

The chief justice had been considered open-minded and progressive in his earlier tenure on the Court (1910–1916), but when Hoover named him to succeed Taft in 1930, liberals in Congress attacked Hughes as a tool of big business. Much of this criticism appears to have been hortatory, aimed less at Hughes himself than as a warning that

Congress expected the Court to pay more attention to the needs of the common people and less to the vested interests of business. Hughes needed few such reminders, and he started his tenure as chief justice by being far more sensitive than Taft had ever been to the risks of a Court blindly defending property rights and ignoring the general welfare. His career as governor of New York and then as secretary of state had sensitized him to the needs of providing the political branches greater flexibility in meeting economic and social crises. Although he had many lucrative corporate clients in his private practice, he had also taken on *pro bono* defenses of unpopular causes such as the Socialists ejected from the New York Assembly in 1920. He had been a strong supporter of the Legal Aid Society and, with Stone, had founded the American Arbitration Association in 1926.

Hughes recognized that the Depression, which had so discredited business, would lead the people to look to government for new programs to alleviate their distress. Courts could not, of course, write a blank check to the legislatures, but they could take a creative role in guiding the legislative response. The old-fashioned attitude of Taft—that the law consisted primarily of "thou shalt nots"—would destroy the Court's influence if the judges did nothing but negate legislative efforts to deal with the crisis. There is little doubt that philosophically, Hughes sided with the other Progressives on the Court, but as chief justice, he felt it necessary to vote with the conservatives in some cases to avoid too many 5 to 4 decisions. Unlike Taft, who stood solidly with the conservatives during a conservative era, Hughes was more of a centrist, in a time when the country called for liberal, indeed radical, solutions to economic problems, and expected the Court to acquiesce. In the end, however, Hughes proved an effective guardian of the bench.

These were the "Nine Old Men" who would review the reform legislation of the states and the Roosevelt administration. A Court divided into definite liberal and conservative factions with the two men in the middle swinging from one group to the other inevitably created public confusion over just what the Court considered constitutional.

State Legislation Before the Court

One of the earliest Depression cases to come before the Court involved an Oklahoma statute that treated the manufacture of ice as a public utility and required a certificate of convenience and necessity for entering the business. Chief Justice Hughes, who had voted earlier in the term to sustain a New Jersey law regulating commission rates for insurance agents, now joined with the conservative block to invalidate the Oklahoma law (*New State Ice Company v. Liebmann* [1932]). Speaking through Justice Sutherland, the majority denied that ice manufacture could be considered affected with the public interest and concluded that it could not be legitimately regulated by the state. Furthermore, the law tended to foster monopoly.

With his well-known antipathy toward monopoly, Brandeis might have been expected to vote against the regulation as well, but instead, he entered a powerful dissent. He criticized the majority for failing to take account of the Depression conditions that had led the Oklahoma legislature to view icemaking as affected with the public interest. "The true principle," he wrote, "is that the State's power extends to every regulation of any business reasonably required and appropriate for the public protection." In a depression, it might be necessary to limit certain types of business, and the state legislature had decided to try this approach. Whether or not it would work he did not know; nor did it matter. "It is one of the happy incidents of the federal system that a single courageous State may, if its citizens choose, serve as a laboratory, and try novel social and economic experiments without risk to the rest of the country."

Brandeis ended with an eloquent plea for judicial restraint. The Court, he said, had the power to prevent experiments, because the Due Process Clause had been interpreted to include substantive as well as procedural rights. "But in the exercise of this high power," he warned, "we must be ever on our guard, lest we erect our prejudices into legal principles. If we would guide by the light of reason, we must let our minds be bold."

The Court seemed to respond to Brandeis's plea when it reviewed the 1933 Minnesota Mortgage Moratorium Law in *Home Building & Loan Association v. Blaisdell* (1934). The state legislature had responded to the plight of farmers who were losing their property through foreclosure. The statute, clearly an emergency measure, permitted local courts to extend the period of redemption between foreclosure and sale to give farmers additional time to raise money. The law did not permit an indefinite extension, nor did it cancel the debt; it did no more than adjust the remedy available to the creditor. Five members of the Court, led by the chief justice, approved the law. While an "emergency does not create power," Hughes noted, it could be the occasion for the exercise of latent powers. He recited a lengthy list of devices that states had previously used to protect the health and safety of their citizens that also affected contract. Aware that the minority upheld the inviolability of contract in all circumstances, Hughes reminded them of Marshall's famous dictum in *McCulloch v. Maryland* (1819): "We must never forget, that it is a *constitution* we are expounding, a constitution intended for ages to come, and, consequently, to be adapted to the various *crises* of human affairs." The Court, therefore, had to look at the Contract Clause anew, in the light of the current emergency and recognize that the states' higher need to protect the welfare of their citizenry justified a departure from traditional interpretations.

Joined by his conservative colleagues, Justice Sutherland dissented, making an appeal to maintain the Contract Clause inviolate. He refused to acknowledge that emergencies could justify impairment of obligations. In fact, he claimed, the clause had been designed specifically to prevent states from granting relief to debtors in emergencies. While conceding that the Minnesota law made relatively minor changes, he warned that if the Court allowed it to stand, it would be the harbinger of greater invasions of the sanctity of contract—and if contract went, then all constitutional restrictions would inevitably collapse.

The majority had approved the Minnesota law because it had not prevented foreclosures, had been specific in how it adjusted the remedy, and had put a time limit on the extensions. When states attempted more than this, the Court proved less receptive. The same year as *Blaisdell*, for example, the justices struck down an Arkansas law exempting payments for life insurance policies from garnishment in *W.B. Worthen Co. v. Thomas* (1934). As Chief Justice Hughes explained, the relief was "neither temporary nor conditional," and the law contained "no limitations as to time, amount, circumstances, or need."

Nonetheless, the Four Horsemen recognized and feared that the Hughes approach in *Blaisdell* would allow greater legislative regulation of the market under the guise of protecting the people from the vicissitudes of the Depression. Hughes had come close to endorsing the broad, almost open-ended view of "affected with a public interest" that the liberals had propounded for more than a decade, most recently by Brandeis in his *New State Ice* dissent. Their worries seemed more than justified a few months later when, again by a 5 to 4 vote, the Court sustained the New York State Milk Control Act of 1933.

In response to the declining prices the state's dairy farmers received for milk, New York had created a control board to regulate the entire milk industry, with power to set minimum wholesale and retail prices. The law paralleled the Roosevelt administration's efforts to stabilize markets and eliminate cutthroat competition, and it elicited the same challenges in court. Leo Nebbia, a Rochester grocer, had been convicted of selling milk below the price set by the board, and he challenged the statute as violating his rights under the Fourteenth Amendment. The law unduly restricted the use of his property, he argued; moreover, the milk industry could not be considered as affected with a public interest, so any state control interfered unconstitutionally with the market.

The majority opinion in *Nebbia v. New York* (1934) came not from one of the liberals, but from Justice Roberts, who apparently adopted *in toto* the argument that the public need overrode traditional property rights. The state had recognized a problem and had taken reasonable steps in trying to mitigate the difficulties; the wisdom of those steps did not concern the Court. Did there exist any constitutional prohibition, he asked, to prevent the state from attempting to alleviate problems caused by an aberrant market? In words that chilled the conservatives, Roberts declared, "We think there is no such principle." The relation of any business to the public interest depended on current conditions, and thus any business might legitimately be deemed affected with the public interest and subject to regulation. Only a showing that the regulations had been unreasonable, arbitrary, or discriminatory would justify judicial intercession.

McReynolds in his dissent for the four conservatives openly admitted what Sutherland had sought to hide in his *Blaisdell* dissent, namely that the Court would look at the prudence of the act as well as its constitutionality. "This Court must have regard to the wisdom of the enactment," he wrote, conceding that he believed the Court should act as a superlegislature. Thus justices could, through the Due Process Clause, uphold the laws they liked and strike down as unwise those they did not care for. The conservatives also objected strenuously to Roberts's definition of the public interest as nearly anything the legislature declared it to be, for it took away one of their main weapons against economic regulation—the ability to declare a business as not affected with a public interest and therefore immune from state control. Following this decision, McReynolds wrote to former solicitor general James Beck that *Nebbia*, taken in tandem with *Blaisdell*, marked "the end of the constitution as you and I regarded it. An alien influence has prevailed."

If liberals thought the Court had eliminated the last vestiges of substantive due process or abandoned freedom of contract, they learned differently in June 1936. Roberts, the author of *Nebbia*, now joined the conservatives to invalidate a 1933 New York minimum wage law for women and children in *Morehead v. New York ex rel.*

Tipaldo. Justice Sutherland's majority decision rested entirely on the *Adkins* reasoning. Even normally conservative newspapers termed the ruling "regrettable," and the Republican candidate for president, Alfred M. Landon, carefully distanced himself from the Court's conservative bloc. The Republican party platform, in fact, specifically approved of state regulation of hours and wages for women and children.

Stone's dissent called for the Court to be consistent; it should follow the ruling in *Nebbia* and leave the wisdom of solving economic problems to the legislative branch. Chief Justice Hughes also found the majority ruling incomprehensible, declaring that he found nothing in the Constitution "which denies to the State the power to protect women from being exploited." Roberts, subjected to bitter criticism for his change in position from *Nebbia* to *Morehead* and then back again in such a short time, later explained that he had been willing to overrule *Adkins* from the start, but the counsel for New York had not asked the Court to do so. Rather, he had tried to distinguish the New York situation from that in *Adkins*, and Roberts had been unable to see any difference. So long as New York had not asked the Court to overrule *Adkins*, then Roberts believed it had to govern the case. When, in the next state minimum wage case, the attorney called on the Court to abandon *Adkins*, Roberts willingly did so.

So the Court upheld by bare majorities several important state laws designed to combat the Depression, but it drew a fairly tight rein around how far it would be willing to go. When it came to judging federal measures, however, the two swing votes, Roberts and Hughes, seemed less sure of where they stood. Unalterably opposed to any legislation regulating the market or affecting contract, the conservative bloc needed only one of their two votes to have its way.

A Change in Philosophy

Herbert Hoover did more than any president before him in trying to utilize federal powers to fight a depression. He proposed and Congress enacted an Agricultural Marketing Act to relieve pressures on agriculture. Hoover also secured a moratorium on international debt payments, encouraged Congress to erect tariff barriers to protect domestic industries, and created the Reconstruction Finance Corporation to lend money to banks and business. He established a public works program, one that spent more money than any previous works program in American history. More than his predecessors, he went out of his way to support the civil liberties of persons involved in labor disputes or accused of political subversion. Toward the end of his term, he reluctantly agreed to federal grants to localities for relief. But despite his earlier advocacy of contracyclical government programs while secretary of commerce, Hoover could never really shake his belief that government should never interfere in the economy, or provide relief—a "dole"—to individuals. As a result, instead of leading government policy, he often found himself forced into taking action as a result of strong congressional pressure and public demand that the government do *something*. Hoover's policies all suffered from being too little and too late.

Franklin Roosevelt, on the other hand, promised action, and he entered office in March 1933 with large Democratic majorities in both houses of Congress eager to follow his lead. The severity of the Depression left the new administration with no time

> We should use the powers of government to cushion the situation. . . . The prime needs were to prevent bank panics such as had marked the earlier slumps, to mitigate the privation among the unemployed, and the farmers which would certainly ensue. . . . We determined that the Federal government should use all of its powers.
>
> —Herbert Hoover, *Memoirs: The Great Depression* (1952)

to develop a coherent program; rather, different groups tackled separate issues, and occasionally their proposals worked at cross-purposes. Although Roosevelt lacked any clear ideological program, he did have a model of governmental action that influenced his administration, namely, the nation's experience in the Great War. People had recognized the emergency at that time and had buried petty and partisan differences in order to pull together. President Wilson had asserted emergency powers and then had delegated specific authority to commissions with the order to get things done. This "analogue" of war would inform the New Deal throughout the famous hundred days.

The New Deal Begins

Roosevelt first had to deal with the banking crisis. On February 14, 1933, Governor William Comstock of Michigan had declared an eight-day bank "holiday," which froze $1.5 billion in funds and prevented more than 900,000 depositors from getting at their money. Ten days later, the governor of Maryland had to close that state's banks, and by the end of the month banks in every part of the country were in trouble. All over the nation, people stood on lines hoping to get their life savings out before the financial system collapsed completely. By March 4, Roosevelt's inaugural day, thirty-eight states had closed their banks, and night, indeed, seemed to have fallen when governors Herbert Lehman and Henry Homer suspended banking operations in New York and Illinois, the two financial centers of the country. On that same day, Richard Whitney announced that the New York Stock Exchange would not open; the regional commodity and stock exchanges immediately followed suit. When Roosevelt took the oath of office, he exclaimed with as much literal as figurative truth that "the money changers have fled from their high seats in the temple of our civilization."

Although the new president made no specific proposals, he promised in his inaugural that if Congress could not solve the problems, he would ask it for "broad Executive power to wage a war against the emergency, as great as the power that would be given to me if we were in fact invaded by a foreign foe." That night, Roosevelt ordered the secretary of the treasury to prepare emergency banking legislation and gave him less than five days to have it ready. The following morning, the president called Congress into special session, to start March 9, and, under the rather doubtful legal authority of the old 1917 Trading with the Enemy Act, he issued a proclamation halting transactions in gold and declaring a national bank holiday.

The country responded to these drastic measures with relief; at last the national government had done something. The move—combined with assurances from the White House that only sound banks would reopen and that people could then be confident that their money would be safe—lifted the nation's spirits. Most of the banks were in fact sound, but few had the liquidity to survive a sustained run on deposits. The government lacked the personnel to do any extensive examination of bank books, but it could at least determine whether or not a bank had enough financial health to warrant reopening. The president gave depositors the psychological assurances that they needed; as banks began to reopen, they found people queuing up to put money *into* their accounts. Roosevelt's bold gamble had paid off, and despite the flimsy constitutional basis of his actions, it led both him and the American people to expect that a president could and should act decisively. Franklin D. Roosevelt did not invent the "imperial presidency," but he played a key role in developing the modern idea of strong executive leadership.

Unlike Abraham Lincoln and Andrew Johnson, Roosevelt did not perceive any need to keep Congress even temporarily on the sidelines; the large Democratic majorities only wanted to have the president give them their marching orders. On March 9, the special session of Congress met, and while newly elected representatives tried to find their seats, the clerk read Roosevelt's first banking message. The House had only one copy of the bill, and the Speaker recited the text to the members. It validated the banking holiday, gave the president complete power over gold transfers, and allowed Federal Reserve banks to issue additional paper currency. The House shouted its approval. In the Senate, some members grumbled that the only beneficiaries would be the bankers, but the upper chamber passed the measure at 7:30 that night, and the president signed it into law an hour later.

In another move designed to raise the nation's morale and to carry out a Democratic campaign promise, Roosevelt asked for a revision of the Volstead Act to legalize beer with a 3.2 percent alcoholic content by weight. A few months earlier, the lame-duck Congress had voted to end Prohibition, and the states had rapidly begun ratifying the Twenty-first Amendment, which repealed the Eighteenth. But the Democrats did not want to wait, and Congress legislatively put the breweries, pretzel makers, and bartenders back to work. But while having a legal drink might make the nation feel good, it would not solve the Depression, and Roosevelt, more than anyone, knew this.

Agricultural Reform

In his next step, Roosevelt presented Congress with a bill on March 16 to help the farmers with a domestic allotment plan. The agricultural depression dated all the way back to the collapse of high wartime prices in 1921, and throughout the decade, farm problems had contrasted grimly to the general prosperity. In 1927, Congress had yielded to the demands of southern and western farmers and had passed the McNary–Haugen bill. The plan called for growers of certain staple crops to pay an "equalization" fee to a Federal Farm Board, which would then regulate the market by buying up surplus crops and dumping them on the overseas market. Coolidge had vetoed the bill as economically and constitutionally unsound; the federal government had no powers, he declared, to buy and sell agricultural products. He had also condemned the fees as unconstitutional, since, like the Second Child Labor Act, the taxes were only a device by Congress to do indirectly what it had been forbidden to do directly. Congress passed the same bill the following year, only to meet with another veto. But the debate had at least focused attention on the farm problem. Finally, in the Agricultural Marketing Act of 1929, Congress created a federal Farm Board, with a $500 million budget, to assist in marketing farm products and to stabilize prices by buying up surpluses. The measure proved a dismal failure, for the Board had no power to regulate production (a power Hoover believed unconstitutional), and without crop limits, the half-billion dollars soon disappeared without any noticeable effect.

The Agricultural Adjustment Act Roosevelt submitted in 1933 was based on the notion of "parity"; the market would be regulated so as to assure farmers the same purchasing power for their crops as they had in the base period of 1909–1914. If farmers accepted voluntary restrictions on acreage, they could then participate in government price supports. The scheme would be financed by a tax on food processors, such as the millers who converted wheat to flour. But radical senators wanted more for the farmers, and to head off a threatened farm strike in May, the administration also accepted an inflationary measure in which the government would issue millions of dollars in unsecured paper money (greenbacks), as well as a supplemental Farm Credit Act, which provided temporary aid to farmers to stave off foreclosures.

Additional aid to farmers came in the Frazier–Lemke Farm Mortgage Act of 1935, which provided mortgage relief to bankrupt farmers. Under terms of the act, the property of the bankrupt would be appraised, and then the farmer would have the option of purchasing it at its appraised value with the mortgage holder's consent, or retain possession of the property for five years and pay a rental fixed by the bankruptcy court. In effect, it made it extremely difficult for banks to foreclose on farm mortgages at a time when many farmers could not meet their debt payments.

Inflation and Relief Measures

As part of the inflation program, the president announced that the country would go off the gold standard. A short time later, Congress, by joint resolution, canceled clauses in both private and governmental bonds that called for repayment in gold. The administration and many economists believed that these measures would halt the severe deflation afflicting the country and would trigger the rise in prices that they thought was necessary for recovery. Even the House of Morgan agreed with the policy, and its head, Russell Leffingwell, praised Roosevelt for saving the country from "complete collapse."

As the farm bill made its way through Congress, Roosevelt also demanded government aid for the millions of unemployed. The resources of private charities, such as the Red Cross, as well as of state and municipal governments had long since been exhausted, and local officials were pleading with the federal government for help. Roosevelt proposed, and Congress quickly approved, a half-billion dollars in direct grants to the states for relief. In addition, a Civilian Conservation Corps would hire unemployed young men to work in the national forests and elsewhere on conservation projects.

For Americans who owned their own homes, be they factory workers or executives, unemployment raised the specter of foreclosure. In 1932, 250,000 families lost their homes, and by the time Roosevelt took office, banks were foreclosing on 1,000 houses a day. To save these homes, and also to help hard-pressed real estate financial institutions, Congress created the Home Owners Loan Corporation, which refinanced four million homes during the Depression, and continued to have an important influence on home owning in the country afterwards.

Progressives suddenly realized that they no longer had an enemy in the White House, and they began to reexamine proposals that had been gathering dust for over a decade. George W. Norris went to see Roosevelt about his idea of using the power plant that had been built at Muscle Shoals, Alabama, during the World War as a yardstick for power regulation. The president, who had long been interested in land conservation, took up Norris's basic idea, but then carried it much further in the Tennessee Valley Authority. Flood control, hydroelectric power generation, fertilizer production, reforestation, and recreation all figured in a multistate experiment to raise the living standards of one of the poorest and most backward areas of the country.

Reviving the Economy

How to revive the moribund economy constituted the most important problem, and Roosevelt not only received conflicting advice from his inner circle, but had to deal with congressional panaceas as well. Senator Hugo Black of Alabama, for example, reintroduced his plan to bar products from interstate commerce that had been made in plants in which employees worked more than six hours a day, five days a week; much to the president's surprise, the Senate passed it, 53 to 30. Senators Wagner and La Follette stepped up their campaign for a public works bill. Industry leaders called for the suspension of the antitrust laws to allow trade associations to stabilize markets; labor champions threatened to block any bill that benefited industry unless workers also received concessions.

Roosevelt thought the Black bill unconstitutional and the other measures too narrow to have much effect. Totally eschewing ideology—and consistency—the president named a drafting committee representing nearly all these viewpoints and told the members to lock themselves in a room and to stay there until they had a bill. One week later, Roosevelt presented their efforts to Congress in what became the National Industrial Recovery Act (NRA).

The preamble to the act read like a lawyer's brief, justifying the measure as a legitimate response by Congress in trying to remove the burdens on interstate commerce caused by the Depression. There is some evidence that even the NRA's drafters and supporters believed the law could not survive a constitutional challenge and that it was

> Many good men voted this new charter with misgivings. I do not share these doubts. I had part in the great cooperation of 1917 and 1918 and it is my faith that we can count on our industry once more to join in our general purpose to lift this new threat.
>
> —Franklin D. Roosevelt, on signing the National Industrial Recovery Act (1933)

passed with the implicit understanding among the New Deal's senior legal advisors that since it would only be in effect for two years, it could probably evade judicial review by the Supreme Court.

Everybody got something. Business received permission to draft code agreements that would have the force of law and would be exempt from the antitrust laws (although a later section declared that nothing in the bill should be construed as suspending the Sherman and Clayton acts); the planners, intellectual heirs to Theodore Roosevelt's New Nationalism, won their demand for government licensing of business through federal oversight of the codes; to placate labor, Section 7(a), patterned after the War Labor Board's policies, guaranteed the right to bargain collectively and required the codes to set minimum wages and maximum hours; and the $3.3 billion appropriated for public works gave hope that many people would be able to leave the unemployment rolls. The bill established a National Recovery Administration to oversee all except the public works and to facilitate code drafting, which the bill's backers saw as the heart of the plan. If business could agree on what had to be done, and then, just as had been done during the Great War, agree on a fair way to cooperate, the economic recovery would soon occur. If businesses proved obstinate, the NRA had the power, in the name of the president, to draft and impose codes on recalcitrant industries. All codes, once approved by the president, had the force of law.

If the New Deal represented a struggle between the ideas of the New Nationalism and the New Freedom, the measures of the first hundred days all reflected Roosevelt's cousin Teddy. Planning during the New Deal seemed to reach its zenith in the Tennessee Valley, Agricultural Adjustment, and National Industrial Recovery Acts. Franklin Roosevelt sought a partnership with business, a joint mobilization to fight the Depression, just as government and industry had cooperated to "conquer the Hun" during the war. But even in the so-called First New Deal, one could find strong traces of the Wilsonian creed. Louis Brandeis, the architect of the New Freedom, sent word to the White House through Harvard law professor, Roosevelt confidante, and future Supreme Court justice, Felix Frankfurter, that the president should beware of big business—especially the big banks. Although he appeared to ignore, at least temporarily, the first part of this advice, Roosevelt needed little encouragement in his distrust of bankers. The Senate Banking and Finance Committee, headed by Ferdinand Pecora, was then exposing on a daily basis scandalous admissions of favoritism, malfeasance, tax avoidance, and outright corruption by the banking community during the heyday of Republican prosperity.

> The real truth . . . is, as you and I know, that a financial element in the larger centers has owned the Government ever since the days of Andrew Jackson—and I am not wholly excepting the administration of W[oodrow]. W[ilson]. The country is going through a repetition of Jackson's fight with the Bank of the United States—only on a far bigger and broader basis.
>
> —Franklin D. Roosevelt to Edward M. House, 21 November 1933

In late March, the president urged Congress to enact federal regulation of securities, thus adding, as he declared, "to the ancient rule of *caveat emptor*, the further doctrine 'let the seller also beware.'" The Securities Act gave the Federal Trade Commission power to supervise the issuance of new securities, required companies to provide full financial disclosures when offering stock, and imposed civil *and* criminal liability on company directors for misrepresentation. The Glass-Steagall Act then mandated the separation of investment from commercial banking, finally carrying out Brandeis's demand that bankers not be allowed to speculate with other people's money. The Glass-Steagall Act also created the Federal Deposit Insurance Corporation, one of the most brilliant achievements of the New Deal. By guaranteeing deposits and imposing higher standards of bank conduct, the act strengthened public confidence in the banks. Fewer banks suspended operations during the rest of the Depression than in even the most prosperous single year of the 1920s.

The special session of Congress ended on June 16. Roosevelt had sent an unprecedented fifteen messages to Capitol Hill, each of which had led to a major piece of reform legislation. But now came the true tests: Would these measures succeed in bringing economic recovery to the nation? And would they pass constitutional muster?

Constitutional Considerations and Problems

Although trained as a lawyer, Roosevelt had a politician's pragmatic view of the Constitution. In his inaugural, he explained that "our Constitution is so simple and practical that it is possible always to meet extraordinary needs by changes in emphasis and arrangements without loss of essential forms." Although he recognized that the Constitution forbade some things no matter what the circumstances, he had seen how flexible it had proven during the war, and he believed that the Depression posed just as great a danger to the country. Committed to experimentation because the old economic formulas no longer worked, Roosevelt saw no reason why the Constitution should not allow the government to try new and different remedies in attempting to cure the nation's economic ailments.

The enormous mass of legislation churned out in the first hundred days rested on constitutional bases as questionable as some of the economic theories that animated those statutes. Moreover, they had been drafted for the most part by enthusiastic but inexperienced young lawyers under impossible time constraints—Roosevelt had given the committee that drew up the National Industrial Recovery Act just one week to over-

> No actual dilemma between logic and expediency faces the Supreme Court if it supports the government. The fact is that the logic of the cases is in favor of the recent legislation, that new doctrine and new terminology are necessary only if the acts are held unconstitutional, and that resort to economics and sociology is required only of those who oppose the legislation.
>
> —Thurman W. Arnold, "The New Deal Is Constitutional," *The New Republic* (1933)

haul the nation's business structure, for example. In general, the drafters relied for constitutional authorization on the relatively permissive mandates of the Commerce Clause and the taxing power, with the emergency powers thrown in to bolster their case. When they did not quite know how to specify what they wanted, they indicated a general goal and delegated authority to the president to work out the particulars. The New Deal planners apparently ignored both traditional constitutional limits as well as the division of powers between state and national government in a federal system. The states, in their view, had already shown their inability to deal with a nationwide crisis, so the federal government should assume full powers.

Even if there had been no conservative bloc on the Supreme Court, the sloppy legislative draftsmanship would inevitably have caused the administration trouble with the judiciary. The cavalier attitude of many New Dealers toward constitutional considerations bothered all the members of the Court; Brandeis, although sympathetic to much of the Roosevelt program, commented caustically on what he termed the president's *kunstücke*, his "clever tricks," by which he tried to sneak things through. The administration's seeming indifference to basic constitutional doctrine appalled Hughes. After slapping down states for irresponsibly overbroad and vague statutes, he could hardly look kindly on national laws affecting nearly the entire nation that suffered from the same defects. Ideologically, even as they adhered to their stance for judicial restraint and were willing to give the administration the benefit of the doubt, even the liberal bloc of Brandeis, Stone, and Cardozo found some New Deal measures personally distasteful.

Finally, regardless of the hundreds of lawyers who had descended on Washington, Roosevelt had pitifully inadequate legal talent to defend his programs. Attorney General Homer Cummings spent most of his time aggrandizing and protecting his "territory," demanding that the Justice Department handle all cases involving any federal agency. Even those agencies with their own legal staffs had to use Justice Department lawyers unfamiliar and sometimes unsympathetic to their programs to defend them in court. Cummings seemed more interested in one's political than legal credentials; the solicitor general, J. Crawford Biggs, lost ten of the first seventeen cases he handled. A good part of the New Deal's troubles in court resulted from the political infighting that crippled efforts to defend the laws; only those agencies with enough political clout to stand up to the Justice Department and managed to secure control over their legal battles had adequate counsel to defend their interests. But even outstanding lawyers could not have saved many of the Roosevelt laws.

New Dealers had hoped that before the courts heard challenges, their programs would be so well entrenched as to withstand judicial hostility. The two decisions upholding state Depression laws, *Blaisdell* and *Nebbia*, gave the administration little comfort, for both had been reached by bare 5 to 4 majorities. When the Court began to hear cases involving federal legislation in December 1934, the New Deal quickly paid the costs of sloppy procedures, poor draftsmanship, and inadequate counsel.

The New Deal in Court

The first case involving federal legislation, *Panama Refining Company v. Ryan*, highlighted many of the problems the administration would face. Several of the oil-producing states, in an effort to raise oil prices, had imposed maximum production limits on wells within their borders, though they had no power to control excess illegal production, so-called hot oil, from being sold in interstate commerce. Section g(c) of the National Industrial Recovery Act gave the president authority to bar interstate shipment of oil produced in excess of state limits, a policy akin to the earlier Webb–Kenyon Act of 1913, in which federal power had been used to enforce state prohibition laws.

An astounded Court heard counsel for the oil producers tell how they had been unable to secure copies of the regulations and of the careless and casual way in which these regulations, which had the force of law, had been promulgated. At one point, Justice Brandeis asked Assistant Attorney General Harold Stephens, "Is there any way by which to find out what is in these executive orders when they are issued?" An embarrassed Stephens had to confess it would be difficult, but, he claimed, "it is possible to get certified copies of the executive orders and codes from the National Recovery Administration."

By a vote of 8 to 1, with only Cardozo dissenting, the Court invalidated Section g(c). Chief Justice Hughes noted that while the Court recognized the legitimacy and utility of delegating power, Congress had here given the president great authority over interstate commerce without any policy or standards to guide him. Although the decision did not touch the rest of the Recovery Act, the administration realized that the delegation there and in other programs could not measure up any better. The ruling returned the oil industry to a condition of unregulated, cutthroat competition, which need not have happened. The Court did not deny that Congress had the power to regulate hot oil, but it could not overlook the slipshod way it had gone about the job. One positive result of *Panama Oil* emerged soon after, when the government began publishing the *Federal Register*, which made government regulations available in an orderly and easily ascertainable manner.

Two months later, the administration had a close call in the gold clause cases. The first set of decisions dealt with the cancellation of the clause in private obligations, and the second set with repudiation in government bonds. First in *Norman v. Baltimore & Ohio Railroad Company*, by a 5 to 4 vote, the Court sustained the government's power to define the country's money. Chief Justice Hughes explained that the contracts merely defined gold as a method of payment. Relying on the *Second Legal Tender Cases,* he affirmed that Congress could declare what would pass as legal tender and that it could, under this broad authority, abrogate private contracts if they ran counter to a legitimate exercise of the national power.

Second, in *Perry v. United States*, the government emerged with a technical victory but sustained a moral loss not seen since John Marshall had tongue-lashed Jefferson and Madison in the *Marbury* case. Hughes distinguished between private obligations, which always had to bend to the public good, and government bonds, which represented the pledged word of the government of the United States. Congress could not break its promises, even in carrying out legitimate powers, and the Court held unconstitutional the Joint Resolution of June 1933, insofar as it abrogated the gold clauses in government bonds. Recognizing that enforcement of the decision might wreak havoc with the nation's finances and that the administration might very likely ignore it, Hughes then denied the plaintiff relief. He said in effect that the government had done a terrible thing, but since the plaintiff had suffered no real damages, he had no standing to sue. McReynolds dissented in such vitriolic terms that parts of his comments did not appear in the formal record. At one point he bitterly commented that "This is Nero at his worst. The Constitution as we know it is gone!"

Whatever relief the administration felt at its escape in the gold cases turned almost immediately to shock when the Court struck down the Railroad Retirement Act of 1934. In *Retirement Board v. Alton Railroad Company* (1935), Justice Roberts joined the conservatives in taking a highly restrictive view of the Commerce Clause, a view that seemed especially reactionary, since even the Taft Court had agreed that the interstate nature of railroads made them subject to federal control. Since Roberts could find no relationship between a pension plan and safety on the lines, he ruled that Congress had no power to institute a pension plan for railroad workers. Hughes, who as an associate justice two decades earlier had written the Court's expansive interpretation of the Commerce Clause in the *Shreveport Rate Cases*, protested that the majority opinion departed from sound principles and unjustifiably restricted the federal commerce power.

Black Monday

A few days before the Court handed down the Retirement Board decision, it began hearing oral argument on the most controversial of all New Deal measures—the National Industrial Recovery Act. Roberts's narrow view of the commerce power boded ill for a statute that depended on the broadest possible interpretation of that clause. The internecine battle between the Justice Department and National Recovery Administration lawyers had led to a test case involving one of the weakest of all the NRA codes. The government had originally wanted to use the lumber code and had initially proceeded with that case, since the interstate implications could be clearly shown. But the lumber code had a number of anomalies that in the end would have prevented a resolution of the major constitutional questions, and the high court dismissed the suit in *United States v. Belcher* (1935).

The government's lawyers turned next to the poultry code case, which seemed a better test, because in 1934, the Court had sustained an antitrust suit against the live poultry industry and had thus confirmed its interstate nature. The Schechter brothers operated a kosher poultry business in Brooklyn, and the government charged them with violating the live poultry code provisions on wages, hours, and fair trade requirements, including counts of selling unfit chickens. The government prepared an elaborate exhibit to show the interstate implications of the Schechter plant, but as one of the Justice Department officials later conceded, "no amount of economic research to unearth judicially noticeable matter could . . . show in a convincing manner that these practices in New York substantially affected the interstate poultry market."

On "Black Monday," May 27, 1935, the Supreme Court dealt the New Deal three blows. It unanimously struck down the Recovery Act in *Schechter v. United States*; it invalidated the Frazier–Lemke mortgage act in *Louisville Joint Stock Land Bank v. Radford*; and it ruled that the president could not remove members of independent regulatory commissions in *Humphrey's Executor v. United States.*

Although the Court as a matter of jurisprudential practice normally tries to decide cases on as narrow a basis as possible, Chief Justice Hughes posed three major questions in *Schechter* and proceeded to answer them all: Did the economic crisis create extraordinary governmental powers? Had the Congress lawfully delegated power to the president? Did the act exceed the government's authority under the Commerce Clause? This radical departure from the conservative procedures of the Court convinced many observers that not only Hughes, but the entire bench, wanted to make sure that after the Court had killed the National Industrial Recovery Act, the act would stay dead.

In his opinion in *Blaisdell* upholding the Minnesota mortgage moratorium, Hughes had clearly indicated that emergencies could call forth latent powers; however, he now reversed himself and declared that "extraordinary conditions do not create or enlarge constitutional power." The elaborate rationale in the Recovery Act's preamble tying the remedy to the Depression made not the slightest impression on the Court. As for the delegation of power, Hughes reiterated the Court's objections in *Panama Oil*. Congress certainly had the power to delegate power to the president, but it had to establish clear guidelines and standards. Here it had given the president a blank check to create and enforce codes or, worse yet, to enforce as the law of the land codes that were drafted by private parties. Justice Cardozo, who had entered the lone dissent in the hot oil case, added a concurring opinion here in which he described the problem as "delegation running riot."

The delegation problem, if that had been the only difficulty with the statute, could easily have been remedied. The ruling that emergencies did not create new powers might have cramped the administration somewhat but would still have been acceptable if the Court had at least conceded the government's power to regulate these industries. But Hughes—joined by all his colleagues—in answering the third question took an extremely restrictive a view of commerce. Hughes revived the old distinction between the direct and indirect effects of local activity on interstate commerce; he declared that only those intrastate activities that directly affected interstate commerce fell within the reach of the federal government's powers. The Schechter brothers' business had no direct effect—and in fact very little indirect effect—on interstate commerce and therefore could not be regulated by Congress. Cardozo's concurrence differed with the chief justice's assertion that clear principles determined the distinction between direct and indirect effects. He thought it more a matter of degree, but in this case, he too could not find any relation between selling sick chickens in Brooklyn and interstate commerce.

The second casualty of the day, the Frazier–Lemke Emergency Farm Mortgage Act of 1933, was struck down by a unanimous Court on the grounds that it gave the debtor rights in property that had belonged to the creditor prior to the statute's enact-

> This is the end of this business of centralization. I want you to go back and tell the President that we're not going to let this government centralize everything. It's come to an end. As for your young men, you call them together and tell them to get out of Washington—tell them to go home, back to the states. That is where they must do their work.
>
> —Louis Brandeis to Thomas Corcoran on Black Monday (1935)

ment. The act allowed the debtor to keep the property for up to five years after having been adjudged a bankrupt and denied the mortgage holder the power to foreclose immediately. Brandeis, who spoke for the Court, showed that like Holmes he could be quite disapproving when he thought a state had gone too far in restricting property rights. "The Fifth Amendment commands," he declared, "that however great the Nation's need, private property shall not be taken even for a wholly public use without just compensation." The federal government, unlike the states, could impair the obligation of contract, but it could not take property outright without paying for it.

Finally, in *Humphrey's Executor v. United States*, the Court restricted the president's power to remove members of independent regulatory commissions. Less than a decade earlier, in *Myers v. United States* (1926), Chief Justice Taft had ruled that the president had extensive power to remove executive officers without senatorial approval, thus, after sixty years, implicitly overturning the Reconstruction era Tenure of Office Act. Taft's broad interpretation of executive power had drawn dissents from Holmes, McReynolds, and Brandeis, the latter noting that separation of powers had been adopted "not to promote efficiency but to preclude the exercise of arbitrary power." Relying on this decision, Roosevelt had forced William Humphreys, a conservative advocate of big business, to resign from the Federal Trade Commission. The Court now said that, at least regarding the regulatory commissions, it had been the intent of Congress to make them independent of the executive and subject only to the legislature and the judiciary.

Roosevelt received the news of Black Monday in astonishment; he could hardly believe that even the liberals had gone against him. "Where was Ben Cardozo?" he asked. "And what about old Isaiah [Brandeis]?" To reporters he complained that the *Schechter* decision had relegated the nation "to the horse-and-buggy definition of interstate commerce." The president failed to understand that even many of his liberal supporters thought the Recovery Act unconstitutional and in fact detested the entire emphasis of early New Deal legislation on large-scale planning. They saw the National Recovery Administration as the worst possible manifestation of government-business entanglement.

The *Schechter* decision did not, as some wags claimed, turn the blue eagle (the NRA symbol) into a dead duck; the agency had been beset by trouble almost from its inception. Hugh Johnson, the bombastic administrator, had been so concerned with signing up industries that he paid little attention to the details of the codes under which business would be regulated. By early 1934, housewives were complaining about high prices, businesspeople were denouncing government rules, and labor leaders were lamenting that the government had not lived up to the promise of Section 7(a) (they called the NRA the National Run-Around). Many older Progressives, such as Carter Glass, Gerald Nye, and William Borah, charged the program with fostering monopoly.

In response to this criticism, Roosevelt appointed a review board in March, headed by the noted attorney, Clarence Darrow, to examine the codes. Darrow, who disliked the program, issued a biased report condemning it up and down; but the more balanced Brookings Institution study also found major problems. A far too ambitious program had gotten bogged down in detail. The NRA often promoted contradictory programs, and instead of concentrating on regulating big industries such as steel and textiles, it had tried to control peripheral industries such as Dog Food (Code #450) and Shoulder

Pad Manufacturers (Code #262). Under Code #348, the government "stabilized" the Burlesque Theatrical Industry by ruling that no show could have more than four strips. In sum, the National Industrial Recovery Act generated a lot of excitement and did much to raise the nation's morale, but while it may have prevented things from getting worse, it did not achieve the recovery that its backers had anticipated.

The Court and the Agricultural Adjustment Act

In contrast to the National Industrial Recovery Act, the Agricultural Adjustment Act, (AAA) did seem to work. Although it often suffered from the excessive enthusiasms of some administrators, the AAA began the necessary task of limiting production in order to raise the prices farmers received for their crops. During Roosevelt's first term, farmers' gross income rose more than 50 percent, and rural debts fell sharply—although the drought of 1934 to 1935 may deserve as much credit as the government for limiting production. Congress also acted after the *Schechter* decision to relieve the farm program of those problems of delegation that had plagued the industrial program. But New Dealers still worried that a restrictive view of interstate commerce, such as Hughes had explicated, would invalidate agricultural legislation, and their fears came true in January 1936, when, by a 6 to 3 vote in *United States v. Butler*, the Court struck down the New Deal farm program.

The AAA processing tax provided the funds to underwrite crop subsidies and soil restrictions, and the drafters had felt confident that in the taxing power at least they had a recognized federal power. But officials of the Hoosac Mills Corporation attacked the levy, which they characterized as an integral part of an unconstitutional plan to control agricultural production. The government challenged their right to sue, since several cases, especially *Frothingham v. Mellon* (1923), had held that taxpayers had no standing to question in court how the federal government spent its tax revenues. But the conservatives on the bench brushed this defense aside. The plaintiffs had not challenged just the tax and its uses, but the whole plan of which the tax, according to Justice Roberts, "is a mere incident of such regulation."

Roberts's majority opinion is the most tortured and confusing of all the Court's New Deal decisions. The tax, Roberts held, like the one in the Child Labor Act, could not be considered a true tax, for none of the proceeds went into the general coffers; instead, the tax purchased compliance with a program that went beyond the legitimate bounds of congressional power. Because of its local nature, agriculture could be regulated only by the state, and even if the sum of many local conditions had created a national problem, this still did not permit Congress to "ignore constitutional limitations" imposed by the Tenth Amendment.

Roberts then turned to the government's reliance on Article I, Section 8, which authorizes Congress to "lay and collect Taxes . . . and provide for the common Defence and general Welfare of the United States." The federal government had the unquestioned right to tax, and Congress had the discretion to determine how those revenues could best be used to provide for the general welfare. Roberts then reviewed the debate between Madison and Hamilton on the meaning of this clause. The Virginian had claimed that it served merely as an introduction to the enumerated powers and conferred no additional authority. Hamilton, on the other hand, had believed that the words had a separate meaning and allowed Congress a general power to tax and spend for what it believed to be in the best interests of the country. Roberts agreed with Hamilton but then declared that crop payments could not be justified under the General Welfare Clause, because they were no more than a subterfuge to get around the Tenth Amendment.

As for the government's claim that the voluntary nature of the plan distinguished it from an impermissible regulatory scheme, Roberts asserted that the power to confer or withhold government benefits "is the power to coerce or destroy. . . . The asserted power of choice is illusory." Roberts, however, made no mention of the Court's earlier decision in *Massachusetts v. Mellon* (1923), in which Justice Sutherland had upheld a plan in which states could freely choose or not choose to participate in a maternal health care program, with federal grants reserved for those who did join. Nor did he mention that the federal government had purchased compliance by holding out rewards ever since 1802, when it initiated a land grant program.

Lest he be accused of substituting his own judgment of what constituted the general welfare in place of congressional discretion, Roberts explained how the Court operated. It did no more than lay the challenged statute next to the Constitution, and see if the former squares with the latter. This so-called T-square rule, if true, would represent judicial decision making at its most mechanistic; but as the Realists and common sense indicate, judges rarely hear cases amenable to such a simplistic determination. Judges do read their biases into law; they do invade the legislative realm of policy-making; and no better example can be found than in Roberts's *Butler* opinion.

The ruling brought forth strong protests from within and outside the Court. Justice Stone, considered the most knowledgeable person on the high bench regarding taxation, dissented sharply from what he considered Roberts's myopic view of the taxing power. Joined by Brandeis and Cardozo, Stone pointed out that unlike the child labor tax, which admittedly had been regulatory, the processing tax did no more than raise revenue; the regulatory part of the farm program came through appropriations. He also attacked Roberts's "tortured construction of the Constitution," and the majority's resort to *argumentum ad horrendum*, its claim that if this terrible program were approved, then Congress would attempt to regulate all areas of the nation's economic life. Finally, he cut through the hypocrisy of Roberts's denial that judges interposed their own views and attacked the notion that courts should sit in judgment of the legislative wisdom.

> When an act of Congress is appropriately challenged in the courts as not conforming to the constitutional mandate, the judicial branch of the Government has only one duty—to lay the article of the Constitution which is invoked beside the statute which is challenged and to decide whether the latter squares with the former. All the court does, or can do, is to announce its considered judgment upon the question. The only power it has, if such it may be called, is the power of judgment. This court neither approves nor condemns any legislative policy.
>
> —Owen J. Roberts, *United States v. Butler* (1935)

The administration took some comfort from Stone's dissent. Unlike *Schechter*, in which Stone, Brandeis, and Cardozo had joined in the general condemnation of the National Recovery Administration, here they gave their approval to the most radical of the early New Deal measures. Moreover, rumor had it that Chief Justice Hughes had originally favored the law, but had voted with the conservatives to avoid another 5 to 4 decision. Within a few weeks, Congress responded to the decision by passing a Soil Conservation Act, which contained no tax and tried to avoid any semblance of coercion. It offered farmers bounties for planting grasses and legumes rather than commercial crops, a device that still aimed at limiting crop production. This response ought to have alerted the conservative bloc that Congress had grown impatient with the Court's obstruction of relief programs, since despite Roberts's declaration that agriculture lay outside federal authority, it had passed another federal farm bill.

The *Carter Coal* Case

Congress had earlier tried to salvage part of the National Recovery Administration with the Guffy–Snyder Coal Conservation Act of 1935. Coal mining had been hard hit by the Depression, and the NRA coal code had brought a desperately needed stability to the industry. The new law established a National Bituminous Coal Commission, with representatives of management, labor, and the public empowered to control production and prices. Mines producing two-thirds of the nation's tonnage signed agreements with the commission, and these included provisions for wages, hours, and collective bargaining. To enforce the code, the act imposed a 15 percent tax at the mine head, nearly all of which would be remitted to operators abiding by the agreement. To avoid *Schechter* problems, Congress declared coal production "affected with a national public interest" and so much a part of interstate commerce as to require federal regulation. Since nearly the entire industry, labor as well as management, supported the act, it seemed unlikely there would be an opportunity for judicial overturn. But in *Butler,* the conservative bloc had opened the door to allow stockholders to sue company officials for obeying allegedly unconstitutional federal laws, and such a stockholder's suit brought the Guffy Act to the Court early in 1936.

Justice Sutherland delivered the majority opinion in *Carter v. Carter Coal Company*, declaring the entire bill unconstitutional. He relied on *Schechter* for a highly restrictive view of interstate commerce and bolstered his opinion with citations to nineteenth-century cases such as *Kidd v. Pearson* (1888) and *United States v. E. C. Knight* (1895), which most scholars thought had been repudiated years earlier. Sutherland's determination to thwart the Roosevelt program could not be hidden behind neutral-sounding formulas. He ignored over two decades of congressional studies that supported the argument for treatment of coal as a national rather than a local energy resource; he dismissed the *amici* briefs of seven states that claimed that only federal regulation would save the industry. And despite the clear intention of Congress that the different sections of the act be considered separately, he invalidated the labor provisions, even though they had not been implemented at the time of the case. He declared that all the provisions were intertwined, all were terrible, and all were unconstitutional.

Even Chief Justice Hughes could not stomach this. In a separate opinion, he agreed that the labor provisions were invalid, but charged that the majority had no right to ignore the separability clause. In his view, the price control provision met the test of constitutionality and should have been approved. Cardozo, speaking for Brandeis and Stone as well, said he could hardly believe that the majority could turn its back on the realities outside the courtroom. If an industry so disrupted as coal, and so central to the nation's economic well-being, could not be federally regulated, then little hope remained for solving the country's economic woes.

The *Carter* decision fueled the growing public protest against the Court's war on the administration's recovery program, and in the next few weeks, the conservative bloc—determined to kill off what it considered radical governmental interference in business matters—only fanned the flames. First, it voided the Municipal Bankruptcy Act of 1934 in a 5 to 4 decision. The act allowed local governments and agencies, with the permission of the states, to file for voluntary bankruptcy (bankruptcy being governed by national law). Justice McReynolds condemned the law as interference with state sovereignty; Cardozo's dissent, joined by Hughes, Brandeis, and Stone, pointed out that since the states had to approve before a municipality could act, they lost nothing. A week later came Roberts's ruling in the *Morehead* case, striking down New York's minimum wage statute as a violation of freedom of contract.

In fact, the New Deal's only victory in the Court in 1935 and 1936 came in Chief Justice Hughes's narrow ruling supporting the Tennessee Valley Authority in early 1936. In *Ashwander v. Tennessee Valley Authority*, the Court approved the sale of power generated by the Wilson Dam to the Alabama Power Company, on the grounds that the federal government had undisputed power to sell off not only the lands it owned, but also any byproducts from those lands, such as minerals or power. For the time being, the Court completely ignored the extensive planning aspects of the program.

Conclusion: The Court Versus the New Deal

By 1936, the Court stood at the head of conservative protest against the New Deal. Nearly all the major parts of the so-called First New Deal, such as the National Industrial Recovery Act and the Agricultural Adjustment Act, had been struck down. The core bloc of McReynolds, Sutherland, Butler, and Van Devanter, often joined by Roberts, had made clear their objections to the extension of federal authority into areas they considered either the exclusive domain of the states or beyond the reach of either federal or state government. Even some conservative politicians felt the Court had gone too far; after the *Morehead* decision, for example, Herbert Hoover complained that the Court had taken away powers from the states that they legitimately had. Members of both parties now supported a constitutional amendment to affirm the states' ability to regulate working conditions.

The New Deal, without doubt, pushed national authority into new areas, and whether or not one believed these laws were necessary, they did represent a new vision of the federal system, involving a different sharing of power between the states and the government in Washington. This in turn required at the very least a rethinking of the Constitution, the exact thing the Four Horsemen would not do. For them, the Constitution remained fixed and immutable, a given that did not adjust to temporary political moods or economic dislocations. To expand the authority of Congress so that it could respond to the economic emergency meant that an enhanced federal power would remain when prosperity returned. To preserve constitutional liberties, the nation would have to endure some temporary suffering rather than abandon those limitations on government that made liberty possible in the first place.

Only Brandeis, Stone, and Cardozo seemed agreeable to the extension of federal authority. It is true they had voted with the majority in *Schechter*, but their objections, unlike those of the Four Horsemen, had not been based on a restrictive reading of the Commerce Clause but on the sloppiness of the legislative delegation of power and what Cardozo had termed delegation run riot. They also advocated a far different view of the judicial function than did the conservatives, a view Holmes had characterized much earlier as "judicial restraint." Whatever their personal views on New Deal legislation (and Brandeis objected to many of the early measures), they believed that the Court had no business reviewing the wisdom of Congress or state legislatures. If the authority existed, then so too did the discretion on how to use it. Finally, they viewed constitutional growth and change not as a tragedy, but as a necessity. Fundamentals remained the same, but as conditions changed, different responses might be required; in charting those responses, the legislature and the executive had as great a role to play as did the judiciary.

The New Deal had, of course, done far more than merely indicate a new division of authority between states and the federal government. It had challenged the prevailing orthodoxy of a self-regulating economy; it had attacked the supremacy of the business community and given a larger voice to labor interests. Roosevelt seemed to care far more for the "little man" than for his own class. But in 1936, despite the Court and vociferous conservative attacks on the New Deal, he determined to push on. The so-called Second New Deal definitely committed the government to programs of social justice and economic redistribution, and the American people signaled their full approval of this course in the 1936 elections. All but two states, Maine and Vermont, went Democratic, the most sweeping margin of victory since James Monroe more than a century earlier. The president enjoyed strong Democratic majorities in both houses of Congress; in the Senate, there were so many Democrats (seventy-five out of ninety-six), that twelve of the newcomers had to sit with the Republicans. With such a mandate to go forward, Franklin Roosevelt could hardly allow five old men, even five justices of the U.S. Supreme Court, to stop the New Deal.

For Further Reading

The best overall view of the Depression years is the first half of David M. Kennedy, *Freedom from Fear: The American People in Depression and War, 1929–1945* (1999). The bankruptcy of traditional ideas is the focus of Arthur M. Schlesinger, Jr., *The Crisis of the Old Order, 1919–1933* (1957); and Jordan A. Schwarz, *The Interregnum of Despair: Hoover, Congress, and the Depression* (1970). The Hoover administration is examined in Alfred U. Romascu, *The Poverty of Abundance: Hoover, the Nation and the Depression* (1965); and Craig Lloyd, *Aggressive Introvert: A Study of Herbert Hoover and Public Relations Management* (1972). William

E. Leuchtenburg, *Franklin D. Roosevelt and the New Deal, 1932–1940* (1963), remains a most useful classic.

Leuchtenburg's article, "The New Deal and the Analogue of War," in John Braemen, Robert Bremner, and David Brody, eds., *Change and Continuity in Twentieth Century America* (1965), provides a useful context in which to examine New Deal measures. See also Alan Brinkley, *The End of Reform: New Deal Liberalism in Recession and War* (1995); Joseph P. Lash, *Dealers and Dreamers* (1988); and Jordan A. Schwarz, *The New Dealers: Power Politics in the Age of Roosevelt* (1993). The very important idea of the "constitutional moment" and how it applies to the New Deal is expressed in Bruce A. Ackerman, *We the People* (1991) and *We the People: Transformation* (1998).

Fortunately for students of history, the period has generated a multitude of studies, and there is no end in sight. The following suggestions are only the tip of the iceberg. For state programs and the relationship between the federal and state anti-Depression measures, see James T. Patterson, *The New Deal and the States: Federalism in Transition* (1969); and Braemen et al., eds., *The New Deal: State and Local Levels* (1975). Banking problems are detailed in Susan Estabrook Kennedy, *The Banking Crisis of 1933* (1973); whereas farming reform is examined in Van L. Perkins, *Crisis in Agriculture* (1969). For stock market and securities regulation, see Michael Parrish, *Securities Regulation and the New Deal* (1970); see also Donald A. Ritchie, *James M. Landis: Dean of the Regulators* (1980), for a look at both the Federal Trade Commission and the Securities and Exchange Commission.

The NRA constituted the centerpiece of the First New Deal, and it has been the subject of a number of studies. See especially, Ellis Wayne Hawley, *The New Deal and the Problem of Monopoly: A Study in Economic Ambivalence* (1966); Robert F. Himmelberg, *The Origins of the National Recovery Act* (1976); and Bernard Bellush, *The Failure of the NRA* (1977).

Much, but certainly not all, of the administration's problems in the courts can be blamed on poor legal staffing, a problem that is brilliantly explored in Peter H. Irons, *The New Deal Lawyers* (1982); and from a different perspective in Ronen Shamir, *Managing Legal Uncertainty: Elite Lawyers in the New Deal* (1995). For the actual hostility of the courts, see Paul L. Murphy, *The Constitution in Crisis Times, 1919–1969* (1972); Alpheus T. Mason, *The Supreme Court: Vehicle of Revealed Truth or Power Group, 1930–1937* (1953); and Robert H. Jackson, *The Struggle for Judicial Supremacy* (1941). Edward S. Corwin wrote several books and articles at the time that are still relevant; see especially, *The Commerce Power Versus States Rights* (1936)

For explication of constitutional issues in particular cases, see William Prosser, "The Minnesota Mortgage Moratorium," 7 *Southern California Law Review* 353 (1934); John A. C. Hetherington, "State Economic Regulation and Substantive Due Process of Law," 53 *Northwestern University Law Review* 13, 222 (1958); Paul L. Murphy, "The New Deal Agricultural Program and the Constitution," 29 *Agricultural History* 160 (1955); Robert L. Stern, "The Commerce Clause and the National Economy, 1933–1946," 59 *Harvard Law Review* 656 (1946); Louis L. Jaffe, "An Essay on Delegation of Legislative Power," 47 *Columbia Law Review*. 359, 561 (1947); John P. Dawson, "The Gold-Clause Decisions," 33 *Michigan Law Review* 647 (1935); William E. Leuchtenburg, "The Case of the Contentious Commissioner: *Humphrey's Executor v. United States*," in Harold M. Hyman and Leonard W. Levy, eds., *Freedom and Reform* (1967).

31

Crisis and Resolution

The Second Hundred Days • The Roosevelt Court Plan • The "Switch in Time" • An Alternate View • Roosevelt Reshapes the Court • The Failure of Reorganization • A National Labor Policy • The Commerce Power and Agriculture • The Reach of the Commerce Power • The Demise of "Old Swifty" • The Court and State Powers • Conclusion: The Crisis Survived • For Further Reading

BY EARLY 1937, the stage had been set for the most serious constitutional crisis since the Civil War. The Supreme Court had opposed presidents before, as in Marshall's confrontation with Jefferson, and had in turn been challenged, as in Jackson's day. But never had the Court apparently set out to destroy an entire legislative program agreed on by both the executive and legislative branches. And, if the election results meant anything, never had the Court set itself up so completely against the will of the people. With the Depression still raging and Franklin Roosevelt promising action, Americans did not ask whether the president would challenge the Court, but when and how he would do so. At the same time, the Court's highly confusing pattern of decisions held out some promise that a confrontation might be unnecessary.

The Second Hundred Days

Even before the Court had passed final judgment on many early administration measures, Roosevelt had shifted political gears. If the first New Deal seemed to favor the planners and the intellectual successors to Cousin Teddy's New Nationalism, the second New Deal had much more of a social justice flavor, reflecting the neo-Brandeisians' hostility to big business and their emphasis on a small unit, competitive society. In part, this shift resulted from the pressure of demagogues such as Senator Huey Long of Louisiana and his "Share Our Wealth" plan, and Dr. Francis Townsend, whose program called for a $200-a-month pension to everyone over sixty. It also answered the demands of a newly militant organized labor, which insisted that the administration carry out the promises it had made in Section 7(a) of the National Industrial Recovery Act. Roosevelt had lost faith in business, and despite his public protests, he might well have welcomed the Court's invalidation of the National Recovery Administration. Instead of entering an honest partnership with government and labor, business had too often used the NRA codes to benefit itself at the expense of the public and had not kept its word to treat labor fairly. The message from the neo-Brandeisians—that business could not be trusted and that government had to tame it—gradually came to dominate in New Deal circles. The midterm elections of 1934 had returned a Congress eager to push for reform, and Roosevelt aides like Harry Hopkins declared that "We've got to get everything we want—a works program, social security, wages and hours, everything—now or never."

Roosevelt had said that if his first efforts at recovery failed, he would try something else, and he now proposed to the new Seventy-fourth Congress the most ambitious reform program in American history. First came a massive public employment plan, the Works Progress Administration. This not only built hospitals, schools, and playgrounds, but also provided work for actors, writers, historians, musicians, and other professionals, in such creative endeavors as the Federal Theater Project. Then, just as in the first hundred days, one proposal followed another, and Congress responded favorably to all of them.

The Wagner Labor Relations Act expanded the old Section 7(a) and guaranteed labor the right to organize and bargain collectively. The Social Security Act provided unemployment insurance through a unique collaboration between the states and the federal government, as well as old-age benefits and a public welfare program. The 1935 Banking Act strengthened the Federal Reserve System. The Wheeler–Rayburn Act attacked the pyramiding of public utilities companies, and its famous "death sentence" clause forbade holding companies more than twice removed from the actual operating firms. That same session, the "Soak the Rich" Revenue Act raised tax rates on large incomes. Finally, the Guffey–Snyder Act attempted to restore stability to the coal industry through a "little NRA."

Although the last act passed, the Guffey law came up first before the Court, which invalidated it by a 5 to 4 vote (*Carter v. Carter Coal Co.*). A month later, the Court struck down New York's model wage law (*Morehead v. New York ex rel. Tipaldo*). These two decisions created, Roosevelt claimed, a "no-man's land" in labor relations, where neither the federal government nor the states could act; the rulings certainly boded ill for the Wagner Act. A few commentators, such as Thomas Reed Powell of Harvard, found nothing wrong with a no-man's land, since some things lay totally out-

> We hold this truth to be self-evident, . . . that the test of representative government is its ability to promote the safety and happiness of the people. . . . On the foundation of the Social Security Act we are determined to erect a structure of economic security for all our people, making sure that this benefit shall keep step with the ever increasing capacity of America to provide a high standard of living for all its citizens.
>
> —Democratic National Platform (1936)

side the sphere of public power. But few people endorsed Powell's view. The private sector, so heralded in the 1920s as the savior of civilization, had failed; only government remained to alleviate the misery of the people.

Even in areas in which the Court had previously sanctioned certain types of governmental activity, it now reversed itself. Although it refrained from declaring the statute creating the SEC unconstitutional in *Jones v. Securities and Exchange Commission* (1936), the Court severely criticized the agency's investigative activities and administrative methods. The commission's efforts to prevent the issue of fraudulent stock led Chief Justice Hughes (who had once again joined with the conservatives) to condemn it for overstepping its bounds and to compare its hearings to a "star chamber." Stone, again joined by Brandeis and Cardozo, issued a biting dissent. Modern government demanded that complicated issues be delegated to qualified experts and not be a matter for constant attention by the courts. It now appeared that every measure, with the possible exception of the Revenue Act, would likely fall before the constitutional scythes of the Four Horsemen and their fellow riders, Hughes and Roberts.

Despite having seen the Court gut practically the entire first New Deal, Roosevelt said little about the judiciary during the 1936 campaign, other than to express his conviction that the Constitution had not been meant to be a dead hand "blocking humanity's advance," but rather "a living force for the expression of the national will with respect to national needs." He emphasized how much progress had been made since 1932; but much remained to be done, and the people gave him a mandate to do it. In his second inaugural on January 20, 1937, he indicated that he intended to move ahead to bring relief to a nation in which one-third of its citizens remained ill-housed, ill-clad, and ill-nourished. He could hardly sit back and wait for the Court to kill off the work of the second hundred days.

The Roosevelt Court Plan

Two weeks after his inaugural, the president dropped a bombshell on the country in a message to Congress calling for the reform of the federal judiciary. Roosevelt and his advisers had been mulling over different proposals for nearly two years in an effort to free New Deal legislation from the constant danger of judicial veto. The surest way would have been through a constitutional amendment, and one plan had called for differentiating between procedural and substantive issues. For the Court to invalidate a procedural item, it would have to do so by at least a 6 to 3 or 7 to 2 vote. On substantive matters, Congress would be able to repass legislation after an adverse court decision in a manner similar to the way it could override a presidential veto.

But the strategic obstacles seemed too high. Roosevelt could look at the speed with which the states had ratified the Twenty-first Amendment repealing Prohibition; but he could also note the long travail of the proposed Child Labor Amendment. (Passed by Congress as part of the reaction to the Court's voiding of federal child labor legislation, the amendment had been ratified by twenty-eight states and then bogged down.) Conservatives would have to win antiratification campaigns in only thirteen states to forestall any chance at judicial reform. In addition, the proposal for a 6 to 3 or 7 to 2 vote could alienate some liberal members of the Court, who might join with the conservatives in retaliation against what they would no doubt perceive as an attack on judicial independence. Rumor already had it that Chief Justice Hughes had switched his vote in some cases to avoid 5 to 4 decisions.

The frequent split decisions, however, had convinced Roosevelt that the real problem lay not with the Constitution or with the Court as an institution, but with the justices. The switch of just one vote would have handed the New Deal victory in several cases. Eventually mortality would have solved the problem, for the Court was then one of the oldest in history. Six members were over seventy, and Brandeis had passed his eightieth birthday. But Roosevelt could not wait for the actuarial tables to catch up with the bench; he had been denied any appointments to the high court in his first term, and the Four Horsemen, despite an average age of seventy-four, seemed in remarkably good health.

Roosevelt vividly remembered that when the House of Lords had blocked a bill to provide Irish home rule in 1913, Prime Minister Asquith had threatened to create several hundred new peers. He needed, the president concluded, enough new justices friendly to New Deal measures to ensure a permanent proreform majority. Since a straightforward proposal to pack the Court would offend many Americans, Roosevelt crowed with delight when Attorney General Homer Cummings brought him a plan that James C. McReynolds, now one of the conservative stalwarts, had suggested during his tenure as Wilson's attorney general.

In his February 5, 1937, message to Congress, Roosevelt claimed that a shortage of personnel had led to congested dockets in the federal courts, with the judges being unable to handle the caseload expeditiously. The Supreme Court, for example, had denied 87 percent of petitions for writs of certiorari in a single year, without citing its reasons. The problem could be attributed in part to "the capacity of the judges themselves," and the delicate question of aged or infirm judges could not be ignored. To remedy the situation and revitalize the courts, Roosevelt proposed that when a federal judge who had at least ten years' service on the bench waited more than six months past his seventieth birthday to resign or retire, the president could add a new judge to that particular court. In total, he could appoint no more than six justices to the Supreme

> The American form of government [is] a three-horse team provided by the Constitution to the American people so that their field might be plowed. The three horses are, of course, the three branches of government—the Congress, the executive, and the courts. Two of the horses, the Congress and the executive, are pulling in unison today; the third is not. Those who have intimated that the president of the United States is trying to drive the team, overlook the simple fact that the president, as chief executive, is himself one of the three horses.
>
> It is the American people themselves who are in the driver's seat.
>
> It is the American people themselves who want the furrow plowed.
>
> It is the American people themselves who expect the third horse to pull in unison with the other two.
>
> —Franklin D. Roosevelt, "Fireside Chat to the American People," 9 March 1937

Court, and forty-four to the lower benches. The whole plan, according to Roosevelt, would serve the higher principle of efficient and effective administration of justice. Only a few days later, in a "fireside chat" over the radio, did Roosevelt admit that "we cannot yield our constitutional destiny to the personal judgment of a few men who, fearful of the future, would deny us the necessary means of dealing with the present."

For once, Roosevelt's famed political sagacity had deserted him, and he now appeared too clever for his own good. Opponents had little difficulty showing that what the president really wanted was to pack the courts—especially the high court—so as to get majorities friendly to New Deal measures. The sophistic allusion to 87 percent of petitions denied fooled no one; the president, and certainly his legal advisers, knew that the Court routinely dismissed such a large proportion because the petitions either were frivolous, had no merit, or raised no federal question. The age argument made no sense either; the oldest member of the Court, Louis Brandeis, had been consistently sympathetic to the New Deal, and although one might argue with the logic of the Four Horsemen, no one could deny that they carried their share of the Court's work. The age issue, in fact, offended many older senators. Carter Glass, then seventy-nine years old, pointed out that Littleton had been seventy-eight when he wrote his great treatise on property, while Coke had been eighty-one when he produced his most enduring commentaries on the laws of England. Roosevelt's secrecy also disturbed many of his supporters. He had neither mentioned court reform during the campaign nor consulted key members of Congress ahead of time; even within the cabinet, only Homer Cummings had known about it. A mediocre attorney general, Cummings still thought in the political terms of the Democratic national chairman he had once been.

The patent desire of the president to pack the courts with new judges who would vote for New Deal legislation could not be hidden, nor could the fact that expediency would, at best, provide only a temporary solution, and maybe not even that. Senator Joseph O'Mahoney of Wyoming, normally a strong supporter of the administration, pointed out that nothing in the bill limited the Court's power of judicial review or remedied the problems of old age or divided opinions. Old judges could still vote, and instead of 5 to 4 decisions, there might now be 7 to 6 or 8 to 7 votes. New judges, as O'Mahoney correctly discerned, also had a habit of disappointing the presidents who appointed them.

Conservatives, of course, protested vociferously against any plan to tamper with the Court, and the Republican party, moribund after its crushing electoral defeat a few months earlier, now had an issue it could rally around. As one constituent wrote to her senator, "*Don't,* don't let that wild man in the White House do this dreadful thing to our country." But liberals also objected, fearful of what political meddling with the judiciary would do to the balance of powers. While the Court had opposed economic reforms, it had also begun to speak up for the protection of civil rights and liberties. If a liberal president could pack the Court now to get his legislation approved, the famed Kansas editor William Allen White asked, what would stop a future reactionary president, "as charming, as eloquent and as irresistible as Roosevelt," from packing it to abridge the Bill of Rights?

The political fight over the measure turned into the bitterest domestic battle of Roosevelt's twelve years in office and provided a rallying point for all the different factions opposed to the New Deal. But it also served a useful purpose in triggering

> [Brandeis] would have no hands laid upon the institution from the outside. It mattered not that the outside hands would in the main uphold his views and would rebuke those with whom he had long and often disagreed. Brandeis valued [the Court's] independence of decision even more than rightness of decision.
>
> —Robert H. Jackson, "Address to Brandeis Memorial Colony Dinner" (1943)

public debate over the role of the judiciary in the governmental system, its relationship to the public, and its responsibilities in the light of a national emergency. As had happened earlier during the Progressive era, critics loosed a barrage of books and articles claiming that the Founding Fathers had never intended the Supreme Court to have the power of judicial review. Although that argument still reappears occasionally, it had already become a sterile debate by the time of the court fight. For over a century and a half, the Court had gained power and respect as an institution to enforce constitutional limitations. By 1935, the majority of the American people expected the Court to act as a brake on social experimentation.

Brakes, however, can slow a vehicle down or make it stop completely. Unpopular decisions, such as *Adkins* or *Morehead* can be tolerated if the public views the Court as moving along in the same general direction as the other branches of government. However, the four conservatives on the Court in the mid-1930s did not want just to slow down the New Deal and deflect it from excesses (as liberals did in the *Schechter* decision), but to stop it altogether. McReynolds, Butler, Sutherland, and Van Devanter considered the New Deal completely wrong, its legislative program outside the narrow limits of federal power that they believed the Constitution allowed. They risked the considerable reserve of authority and legitimacy that the Court had built up over a century and a half and assumed that the public would applaud their efforts to turn back government from the positive steps Roosevelt had proposed toward the essentially negative government that Calvin Coolidge and Herbert Hoover had advocated.

Not only the Supreme Court but much of the lower federal judiciary, staffed primarily by Republican appointees, opposed the Roosevelt program. In 1935 and 1936, lower federal courts issued over 1,600 injunctions against New Deal measures. Typical of the comments that often accompanied these rulings was the remark of Kentucky judge Charles Dawson, who damned the NRA coal code as "the boldest kind

> The world is passing through an uncomfortable experience and in many respects will have to retrace its steps with painful effort. The tendency of many governments is in the direction of destroying individual initiative, self-reliance, and other cardinal virtues which I was always taught were necessary to develop a real democracy. The notion that the individual is not to have the full reward of what he does well, and is not to bear the responsibility for what he does badly, apparently, is becoming part of our present philosophy of government.
>
> —George Sutherland to Dean Henry Bates of the Michigan Law School, 21 April 1937

of usurpation—dared by the authorities and tolerated by the public only because of the bewilderment of the people in the present emergency."

The Depression, however, had led many Americans to rethink what they expected of government. With private resources depleted and the states unable to deal with anything other than local matters, only the federal government could develop and implement relief on a nationwide scale. Roosevelt promised, and the public demanded, positive action to mitigate the worst economic crisis in the nation's history. The negative government so cherished by the conservatives had no relevance to what everyone else perceived as the needs of the day. Except to a small coterie of anti–New Deal conservatives, obstruction in the courts appeared not as principled decision making but as judicial irresponsibility. Between 1934 and 1936, the Court voided more pieces of federal legislation than in any other comparable period in our history; to do so, it had to ignore one precedent after another that supported positive government. Even some conservative voices complained that the Four Horsemen had not acted on principle, but out of their own biases.

Fortunately for the Court, however, the reservoir of respect it had built up protected it not only from irresponsibility from within, but also from political frustration from without. The court measure bogged down in the Senate; Majority Leader Joe Robinson of Arkansas, to whom Roosevelt had promised the next seat on the Court, thought he could get the president an immediate expansion of the bench to eleven if Roosevelt abandoned the rest of the plan, but the president refused to budge. Chief Justice Hughes, with the concurrence of justices Van Devanter and Brandeis, publicly rebutted Roosevelt's charges of inefficiency. In a letter to Senator Burton K. Wheeler of Montana, a leading opponent of the president's plan, Hughes pointed out that the Court had just heard arguments on cases it had accepted for review barely a month earlier. An increase in justices, he asserted, instead of making the Court more efficient, would only cause delays because of "more judges to hear, more judges to confer, more judges to discuss, more judges to be convinced and to decide."

The "Switch in Time"

The death blow to the court-packing plan came in a series of decisions the Court handed down beginning in March 1937. Both Hughes and Roberts, each of whom had frequently given the conservative bloc its majority, now joined with Brandeis, Stone, and Cardozo to validate a string of state and federal measures.

On March 29, by a 5 to 4 vote, the Court sustained a Washington State minimum wage law in *West Coast Hotel Company v. Parrish*. Roberts, who had written the decision invalidating a similar New York law a year earlier, now joined the liberals in Chief Justice Hughes's opinion that *Adkins v. Children's Hospital* had been wrong and should be overruled. Hughes dismissed the relevance of the *Morehead* case by asserting that the Court had not reexamined the constitutionality of minimum wage legislation at that time because it had not been asked to do so. Sutherland, perhaps aware that the tide had turned against the conservatives, used his dissent to lash out against what he saw as the theory that the Constitution's meaning changed depending on current economic conditions.

Roberts's change of heart led to much speculation that the court-packing plan had scared the brethren, and they had reversed themselves to avoid drastic reorganization and loss of power. "A switch in time," contemporary wits claimed, "saves nine." But it is now fairly certain that Roosevelt's plan had nothing to do with the result in this case. Roberts had been dissatisfied with the *Adkins* ruling when the New York case had come before the Court, but since the state had not been willing to challenge *Adkins*, Roberts, one of the less creative members of the bench, believed that he had no choice but to go along.

Thus when *Parrish* was argued in December 1936 and counsel did ask for a reversal of *Adkins*, Roberts informed his colleagues that he would vote to sustain the Washington statute. But now Justice Stone's serious illness left the brethren divided evenly; had he been well, the Court would have issued a decision upholding state minimum wage legislation before Roosevelt delivered his court-packing speech—and might even have deterred the president from doing so. Roberts's decision can be criticized as resulting from mechanistic decision making (he had not been asked to decide a question and so had ignored it) or praised as adhering to principle (his views had not changed, but merely needed a proper vehicle for expression), but in neither case can it be seen as a response to political pressure.

West Coast Hotel v. Parrish helped pull the Court back to the path it had followed prior to 1935, in sustaining state economic regulations under the broad rubric of the police power. That same day, the Court approved three federal statutes, each similar to one struck down a few years earlier. *Wright v. Vinton Branch* sanctioned a federal plan for farm debtor relief. Collective bargaining, the same issue that the Court had condemned in the *Carter Coal* case, now won the stamp of constitutionality in *Virginia Railway v. Brotherhood*. Finally, the Court approved a penalty tax on firearms, designed to help law enforcement officials, in *Sonzinsky v. United States*. This last case greatly encouraged reformers, for the majority had in essence validated the use of the taxing power for regulatory purposes in direct opposition to the Roberts decision in *Butler*.

Two weeks later, a series of opinions, all by a 5 to 4 vote, sustained the National Labor Relations Act. Chief Justice Hughes dismissed both the *Schechter* and *Carter Coal* decisions to revive a broad interpretation of the commerce power. In *N.L.R.B. v. Jones & Laughlin Steel Company*, the chief justice used the "stream of commerce" theory to justify government regulation of labor relations in particular plants. "When industries organize themselves on a national scale, making their relation to interstate commerce the dominant factor in their activities," he noted, "how can it be maintained that their industrial labor relations constitute a forbidden field into which Congress may not enter when it is necessary to protect interstate commerce from the paralyzing consequences of industrial war?" The federal commerce power gave Congress the authority to protect interstate commerce "no matter what the source of the dangers which threaten it." In *N.L.R.B. v. Friedman–Harry Marks Clothing Co.*, the majority extended this ruling to a small manufacturer whose business had a negligible effect on interstate commerce; Hughes did not look at the single firm, however, but at the interstate nature of industry.

The labor relations rulings had important and immediate consequences in several areas. The Wagner Act had been the most controversial of the second New Deal measures, for it had not only injected the federal government into a new field, but had substantially changed the rules of the marketplace to give more power to workers and their unions. Freedom of contract, one of the main conservative weapons against reform legislation, gave way before the seemingly unlimited expanse of the commerce power, which could apparently now be utilized to justify a large spectrum of regulatory legislation. Although there would be many more N.L.R.B. cases before the Supreme Court, they would not deal with the agency's legitimacy, but with the reach of its enabling legislation. For the most part, the Court found that reach quite extensive.

On May 24, the Court sustained major provisions of the Social Security Act. In *Stewart Machine Company v. Davis*, the five-man majority approved the scheme that financed unemployment compensation benefits. Justice Cardozo's opinion, with its emphasis on the nearly unfettered extent of the taxing power, implicitly repudiated Roberts's narrow interpretation in *Butler*. Congress had not coerced the states to join the plan, but had proposed an attractive partnership between the states and the federal government in order to meet a national problem. Requirements that state plans should meet certain conditions did not violate states' rights; Congress had to ensure that state plans conformed to the agreement, and states had entered the compact aware that they had to live up to their side of the bargain.

In a companion case, *Helvering v. Davis*, Cardozo ironically cited Roberts's contention in *Butler* that Congress could spend money for the general welfare and used this argument to uphold the old-age tax and benefits provisions. The problems caused by the Depression, he noted, are "plainly national in area and dimensions. . . . Moreover, laws of the separate states cannot deal with [them] effectively. Only a power that is national can serve the interests of all."

A few days before the Court handed down the two Social Security decisions, Justice Willis Van Devanter announced his retirement from the bench after twenty-seven years of service. With Hughes and Roberts seemingly ensconced in the liberal camp, Roosevelt's new appointee could presumably ensure a 6 to 3 vote in cases involving New Deal legislation. Van Devanter's departure, the Hughes letter, and the string of favorable decisions depleted what little support still remained for the court-packing plan. Senator James Byrnes of South Carolina asked: "Why run for a train after you've caught it?" Vice President John Nance Garner went home to Texas in mid-June, making it plain that the administration could not count on his help; the following month, Joe Robinson, worn out from his efforts to pass the president's bill, collapsed and died. Finally, Roosevelt surrendered, and on July 22, 168 days after the president had stunned the nation with his proposal, the Senate voted to bury it. Congress enacted a more modest bill, embodying some procedural reforms, but it did not give Roosevelt any of the added judges he had sought.

An Alternate View

Recently scholars have begun to challenge what they term the "conventional view" of the 1937 crisis, a view that they describe as far too simplistic, that is, the conservative Court blocked New Deal measures, Roosevelt threatened to pack the bench, and Hughes and Roberts switched their votes. Instead they argue that Roosevelt's plan never had a chance at passage, and most people saw it as dead in the water from the day it arrived at the Capitol. Beyond that, they claim that the Court had already begun its abandonment of the old legal classicism and had given strong indications of this in several cases, especially *Nebbia v. New York*. Had New Deal measures been better crafted, they could easily have secured the approval of a majority of the Court. In short, Roosevelt never had to fight the battle because he had already won, and only legislative sloppiness in drafting the New Deal prevented an earlier announcement of the victory.

It is certainly true that the president's plan immediately triggered a massive protest. Not only business, which could be expected to oppose, but also normally pro–New Deal groups like organized labor and the farm bloc came down against it. Senators received an average of 10,000 letters each in the first two weeks of the campaign, and nine out of ten opposed the plan. Polls taken between February and May 1937 indicate that a majority of the American people—the same people who had just given him the largest electoral landslide in American history—did not approve of the first major initiative of his second term.

The justices also understood that the American people opposed the plan, since thousands of letters and telegrams arrived at the Court condemning the president's plan and urging the members of the Court to stand firm. Polls showed Roosevelt's popularity declining, and a number of Democrats, including many who had blindly followed the president in his first term, let it be known that they could not support him now. Every Republican came out against the plan, and powerful Democrats like Harry Byrd and Carter Glass of Virginia, Edward Burke of Nebraska, Walter George of Georgia, and David Walsh of Massachusetts soon joined the opposition. Hatton Sumners of Texas, the Democratic chair of the House Judiciary Committee, told his colleagues "Boys, here's where I cash in my chips."

The problem with this analysis is that despite the opposition, most contemporaries did not see the bill as stillborn on arrival. Franklin Roosevelt had just won the most lopsided victory in American presidential history, and the New Deal had been embraced by a large majority of the American people. No one underestimated Roosevelt's political skills, and it is only in hindsight that one can see how far he misgauged the situation. The Congress discussed the bill for almost three months, a strange activity if everyone believed it to be already dead. Similarly, debates in the press and in the law schools remained spirited and contentious during that spring.

Moreover, the justices themselves engaged in what can only be described as political activity, and rather strenuous activity at that for men who normally avoided overt politicking.

- Louis Brandeis, who carefully avoided the press, privately told reporters what he thought of the president's plan.
- Harlan Fiske Stone harangued Irving Brandt and other reporters about the evils of the plan, fully aware that these comments would get back to the White House.
- Alice Brandeis, no doubt at her husband's suggestion, arranged for Senator Burton K. Wheeler to visit the justice, and old Isaiah literally took Wheeler over to the telephone to have him call the chief justice.
- In response to the call, Charles Evans Hughes drafted the famous letter and then contacted only Brandeis and Willis Van Devanter about it, knowing full well that some of the other justices would oppose this maneuver.

- James Clark McReynolds, at his annual class reunion, with reporters present, accused Roosevelt of being a poor sport and damned the plan.
- George Sutherland wrote congratulatory letters to members of the Senate who spoke out against the bill.

One should keep in mind that unlike the present Court, where few of the justices have hands-on political experience, the Hughes Court (with the exception of Cardozo) consisted of men who had won their appointments through their political service. One former secretary of state (and former governor), two former attorneys general, and a former senator sat on that bench, and while Van Devanter, Pierce Butler, and Brandeis had held no elected office, they had been intimately involved with party politics throughout their careers.

The claim that the Court had already moved to support the type of measures proposed by Roosevelt is more complex and is based on two series of cases decided by the Court prior to 1937. In one, the argument goes, the Court had steadily expanded the stream of commerce theory it had first announced in the 1905 *Swift* case, and which even the Taft Court had embraced and enlarged. As a result, the New Deal's efforts to regulate the economy would have succeeded on jurisprudential grounds had it only taken the pains to craft its legislation more carefully. The other stream of cases involved the abandonment of the public/private distinction at the core of classical legal thought. Here the key case is *Nebbia v. New York*, in which a majority of the bench practically dismissed the old cleavage and indicated that almost everything could now be considered public. Once the administration started drafting its measures carefully, as it did in the second New Deal, the Court had no trouble sustaining them.

It is true that if one looks at the long run of cases from 1905 to the early 1940s, there is a definite shift both to expand the stream of commerce idea as well as to negate the distinction between public and private, which had been the basis for striking down so much regulatory legislation. But there are also too many cases in which the justices either ignored these developments, or went directly against them.

In *United States v. Butler*, for example, Roberts ignored two decades of precedent to declare farming an essentially local function and therefore beyond the reach of the commerce power. He also ignored a far longer tradition of upholding a wide reach for the taxing power, and Stone's dissent witheringly pointed out how Roberts had ignored precedent. Moreover, one might well ask why the Court even accepted this case when

> To those who regarded the Court as the protectors of the privileged, the Chief Justice was the very symbol of all they detested. But what those who calculated the probable outcome of the struggle often missed was that under that heavy disguise there operated one of the shrewdest of political intelligences. And these underestimators included Franklin [Roosevelt]. Hughes was a match even for the experienced tactician in the White House—and not only in experience but in wiliness as well. The combination of Hughes and Wheeler would prove too much for Franklin.
>
> —Rexford Guy Tugwell, *The Democratic Roosevelt* (1957)

everyone recognized it as a collusive suit, just the sort of case the Court supposedly never takes—except, of course, when it suits its purpose.

Even if the consensus on the National Industrial Recovery Act is that it stands as one of the most poorly drawn pieces of legislation in history, that does not explain why the Court went after it so rabidly. Normally, when striking down a piece of legislation as unconstitutional, the Court will use just one reason, and the most narrow possible, so that it does not have to rule on other matters. The NRA could easily have been voided simply on the grounds of inadequate guidelines for the delegation of power. But in *Schechter,* Chief Justice Hughes found three reasons for nullifying the law, and one of them relied on a narrow definition of commerce that derived straight from *E. C. Knight.* And after that, in *Carter Coal,* he again put forth a narrow view of commerce.

Finally, the Court had voted in *West Coast Hotel v. Parrish* before Roosevelt announced his plan, and so, the argument goes, the jurisprudential change had already occurred. In addition, the Court had already approved other New Deal measures, such as the conversion from the gold standard as well as the Tennessee Valley Authority, so that it is questionable if the Roosevelt proposal affected the Court at all.

The problem here is that the Court remained split, with at least four members thoroughly opposed to any and all reform measures. Roberts appears to have had no clear jurisprudence at all, but seems to have been more comfortable with the conservatives. Hughes may have personally stood closer to the liberal bloc of Brandeis, Stone, and Cardozo, but would vote with Roberts and the Four Horsemen to avoid 5–4 decisions. Whatever one might say about long-term trends, in 1937, neither Franklin Roosevelt nor anyone else could be certain how the Court would vote in any particular case. If the Court had already reached a point of support for New Deal measures, no one at the time saw it that way, and even after the Court started approving second New Deal measures, the conservative bloc remained steadfastly opposed.

One must, of course, look at long-range developments, but one should not forget that the judiciary is not an isolated ivory tower. It is a coequal branch of government, and while the Constitution attempts to shield judges from the effects of daily partisanship, the Court is involved in governing, and governing means politics. The constitutional crisis of 1937 can and should be seen as a struggle involving both jurisprudence and politics.

Roosevelt Reshapes the Court

Roosevelt later claimed he had lost the battle but won the war, and to some degree this was true. The same month he lost the battle, he made his first appointment to the Supreme Court, after Willis Van Devanter took advantage of the new law allowing judges to retire at full pay. The president named to the Court Senator Hugo L. Black of Alabama, a man despised by Southern conservatives for his populist liberalism. When Herbert Hoover heard of the appointment, he protested that the Court was now "one ninth packed." Black's nomination generated an ugly controversy when the press learned that he had once been a member of the Ku Klux Klan, but his later championing of civil liberties and civil rights more than confirmed the fact that he was neither a racist nor a bigot. Other changes soon followed. In January 1938, Justice Sutherland resigned, and Solicitor General Stanley F. Reed ascended the bench. When Benjamin Cardozo died toward the end of the year, the president nominated his friend, informal adviser, and the leader of the neo-Brandeisians, Harvard law professor Felix Frankfurter to the "scholar's seat." Within a week after Frankfurter took the oath of office in February 1939, Louis Brandeis finally acknowledged the toll of years and retired after twenty-three terms on the Court. He was succeeded by William O. Douglas, chairman of the Securities and Exchange Commission and former professor at the Yale Law School. Pierce Butler died in November, and Frank Murphy, the former governor of Michigan and then attorney general, took his place. Then, in February 1941, James C. McReynolds, the last of the Four Horsemen, resigned, and Roosevelt named Attorney General Robert H. Jackson, whose economic views diametrically opposed those of McReynolds.

Finally, in June, Chief Justice Charles Evans Hughes stepped down, and Roosevelt elevated Harlan Fiske Stone, a Republican, to the center chair. To replace him, the president chose Senator James Byrnes, but a little over a year later, Byrnes resigned to become Roosevelt's special assistant in the prosecution of the war. To take Byrnes's place, Roosevelt made his last appointment, Wiley Rutledge of Iowa, in February 1943. Thus the only justice whom Roosevelt did not replace was Owen J. Roberts, who did not resign until after Roosevelt's death in 1945.

The "Roosevelt Court," as many have called it, agreed on the extensive reach of the federal commerce power and the necessity to protect civil liberties. Over the next decade, it would abandon substantive due process and freedom of contract and completely revise accepted beliefs on the relationships among the government, the private sector, and the individual. Administration officials could at least breathe easier that any New Deal legislation that had not yet faced a court test would probably not be voided.

But those who claimed that Roosevelt had replaced an independent judiciary with a rubber stamp misunderstood the character of the men he had appointed, as well as the institutional integrity of the Court itself. Frankfurter, Douglas, Jackson, and Black did not fit the same cookie-cutter mold; they differed, sometimes bitterly, among themselves on a number of issues. They all agreed, however, on the need to preserve the independence and integrity of the Court from political interference. Roosevelt had appointed men whom he believed shared his own expansive view of what powers the Constitution allocated to government, as he had every right to do. But once they took their seats, he could no more dictate how they would decide cases than Cousin Teddy had been able to influence Oliver Wendell Holmes, Jr.

Conservatives had seen the exercise of judicial authority primarily in negative terms; they believed that the Constitution placed strict limits on governmental activities. The new Court saw its role as shaping how the government exercised its extensive powers. In the tradition of Holmes and Brandeis, Frankfurter preached judicial restraint not as an abdication of responsibility, but as the proper deference the judiciary paid to the policy-making powers of the elective branches. The courts, of course, could still influence that policy by the way they interpreted and applied the laws. The full implications of the change in view would not be apparent immediately, but the short-term shift in the Court's philosophy could not be missed. The decisions reached in that springtime of crisis led directly to an enormous expansion of judicially approved governmental activity.

The Failure of Reorganization

Three weeks before Roosevelt sent his Court proposal to Congress, he submitted an ambitious executive reorganization scheme. While the president may have won the war with the judiciary, the reorganization plan appears to have been a major casualty of the battle. Roosevelt recognized that the administrative structure of American government was ill suited not only to the problems created by the economic crisis, but to the demands upon government in the twentieth century. The modern bureaucratic state had already begun to develop in European countries, which had no antipathy to a strong central government. Americans, however, had long been suspicious of strong government, and while Lincoln and Wilson had used their emergency powers to create a strong government, the end of war had seen the quick evaporation of their efforts and a return to limited central authority.

Roosevelt, having gotten Congress to pass nearly all of the measures he had requested in his first term, wanted to devote his second term (which he assumed would be his last) to a major reorganization of the presidency, to fill, as one historian has described it, the "hollow core" in the state's bureaucratic apparatus. The Executive Reorganization bill proposed to create a number of new administrative tools and support staff not just for Roosevelt, but for the office of the president as an institution. Contrary to popular mythology, Roosevelt had thought long and hard about administration, and while assistant secretary of the navy under Wilson had testified before Congress on the inability of the president to carry out a coordinated public policy. He put much of the blame on the chaotic organization of the executive branch and the lack of administrative personnel to assist the chief executive. In particular he called attention to the lack of presidential authority to hold the various departments and agencies to a comprehensive budget plan.

The Budget Act of 1921 had created a Budget Bureau, but had placed it in the Treasury Department rather than under the direct supervision of the president, thus reinforcing the semi-autonomy of the major departments. During the 1920s, of course, American public opinion did not favor a strong government, but that changed with the Depression. Moreover, the many New Deal programs designed to help the common people weather the vicissitudes of economic crisis led to fundamental change in how Americans viewed their government. Instead of being a potential tyrant, as generations of Americans had been taught, the government now appeared to be the people's friend, the only institution that could, in fact, help them.

By 1937, due at least in part to its own legislative successes, the Roosevelt administration faced a confusing array of autonomous and semi-autonomous agencies. The president named a special committee, consisting of three of the country's leading scholars of public administration—Louis Brownlow, Charles E. Merriam, and Luther Gulick—which proposed that an Executive Office of the President be established to include not just the Bureau of the Budget, but a new White House Office, which would provide administrative and coordinating support for the chief executive.

When presented to Congress, the Brownlow Commission report provoked a firestorm of criticism, in part because if one tied it to the president's proposed court reform, it appeared that Roosevelt sought to aggrandize his power as none of his predecessors had ever done. In addition, even while Congress at this time remained fiercely isolationist, no American could miss the fact that Mussolini, Hitler, and Stalin had all created dictatorships, and many critics of the reorganization scheme quickly and loudly raised the cry of "Dictator!" The head of the Democratic National Committee, James Farley, lamented that "Apparently because of the situation that exists in Europe, the people have become fearful of such a possibility in this country." Although the bill passed the Senate in a watered-down form, it died in the House, despite a two-year campaign by the president for its passage.

In 1939, Congress, aware of the brewing war in Europe, passed an Executive Reorganization Act. It restricted Roosevelt's authority to overhaul the bureaucracy to two years and exempted twenty-one of the more important executive agencies from reorganization. By Executive Order 8248, Roosevelt managed to implement a number of the proposals of the Brownlow Commission. He created the Executive Office of the President and moved several agencies into it, including the Budget Bureau and the National Resources Planning Board. Eventually the Budget Bureau managed to gain control over, and bring some rationality into, the federal government's budget process.

Article II has always been vague on just what the institution of the presidency should be. The men at the Philadelphia Convention, as well as the citizens who ratified the Constitution, assumed that George Washington would be the first president and would shape the office as he saw fit, and that indeed happened. But between Washington and Roosevelt relatively little changed in the office of the chief executive, even while Congress, especially in the Progressive era and then in the New Deal, created one new governmental agency after another, all supposedly under the supervision of the president. The 1939 reforms finally gave the president the capacity to manage government and hastened the advent of what some have termed "the administrative presidency," one that exercises extensive domestic power on behalf of the president through rule making, policy implementation, and budget oversight. It also established a formal apparatus that, according to some critics, short-circuited the separation of powers and ratified the great transfer of authority from Congress to the executive that took place during the New Deal.

A National Labor Policy

Judicial approval of governmental activity also extended to the national labor policy, and the cases upholding the Wagner Act marked only the beginning of the Court's validation of federal power over labor relations. In 1938, the Court extended the reach of the National Labor Relations Board to a fruit-packing company that shipped only a little over one-third of its output in interstate commerce (*Santa Cruz Fruit Packing Company v. N.L.R.B.*). Since the stream of commerce theory admittedly did not fit the facts of the case, Chief Justice Hughes ruled that labor disturbances at the plant could substantially disrupt interstate commerce. He also discarded the old distinction between direct and indirect effects; the involvement of any particular business in interstate activity could be a question only of degree, and no "mathematical or rigid formulas" could determine that degree; the Court's subjective judgment would be the test. In *Consolidated Edison Company v. N.L.R.B.* (1938) and *N.L.R.B. v. Fainblatt* (1939), the Court approved federal control over companies that sold their entire production within one state. In the first case, however, the electric company did sell power to radio stations and other interstate companies, and so a disruption in service caused by a labor dispute would adversely affect those businesses. These cases wiped out all the traditional tests, such as the stream of commerce and direct and indirect effects, and in substance, used the commerce power to justify federal regulation of labor relations in any business that had some relationship, even a remote one, to interstate commerce. Nevertheless, the Court still retained the power to curtail the legislative reach and on rare occasions would do so.

The decisions also prompted Congress to impose national labor criteria in the Fair Labor Standards Act of 1938, the last major piece of New Deal reform legislation before the war. Congress had been disturbed by the large variations in hours, wages, and restrictions (or lack of them) on child labor, all matters that it had first addressed in the National Industrial Recovery Act. The 1938 statute established a national minimum wage, which within two years would be raised to 40 cents an hour, as well as maximum hours, which in the same period would be lowered to forty a week. It also prohibited the shipment in interstate commerce of any goods produced by an establishment employing child labor, the same provision as the one in the 1916 Child Labor Act, which the Court had struck down in *Hammer v. Dagenhart*.

As with the Wagner Act, the Court confirmed the power of Congress to legislate on these matters under the Commerce Clause (*United States v. Darby* [1941]). Congress enjoyed complete authority under that clause, Justice Stone ruled, and could prohibit any type of goods from entering the stream of commerce. The reasons that Congress might choose to do so lay beyond the scope of judicial inquiry; if even a tenuous link to interstate commerce could be established, the federal power existed.

Labor was a major beneficiary of the Roosevelt Court, just as it had been one of the least favored litigants during the Taft era. Within a few years, the Court overruled nearly all its earlier restrictive rulings. In 1940, it removed most union activities from proscription under the antitrust laws in *Apex Hosiery Company v. Leader*. The following year, in *United States v. Hutcheson*, it ruled that the Norris–LaGuardia Act had changed the criminal sections of the Sherman law as they might be applied to labor unions. Justice Frankfurter's opinion in effect overruled the *Duplex Printing* case, and restored Section 20 of the Clayton Act as its drafters had intended—as a prohibition against the use of injunctions in labor disputes except when necessary to prevent irreparable damage to property. He then merged that concept with the Norris–LaGuardia Act's prohibition against enjoining labor union activities through equity proceedings. It would be illogical, he concluded, to allow criminal prosecution for activities that could not be enjoined in equity, and therefore the Norris–LaGuardia Act had effectively canceled out Sherman Act prosecutions for normal union activity. For the first time in a half-century, labor unions could picket, strike, and engage in other activities free from the fear of prosecution under the antitrust laws. As a final grace note, in *Phelps Dodge v. N.L.R.B.* (1941), the Court abandoned the freedom of contract argument it had used to void federal and state prohibitions against yellow-dog contracts, which as a result passed into history.

Nonetheless, the Roosevelt Court did not always make organized labor the victor in cases that came before it. As late as 1941, a majority of the justices did not view picketing as a fully protected constitutional right. In *Milk Wagon Drivers Union v. Meadowmoor Dairies*, Justice Frankfurter held that freedom of speech, while basic to American democracy, could in the context of violence "lose its significance as an appeal to reason and become part of an instrument of force." States could therefore restrain picketing that led to violence or destruction of property. In similar reasoning, the Court refused to exempt public meetings from all state control, although it would intervene when local laws clearly discriminated against groups such as labor (*Thomas v. Collins* [1945]). On the whole, however, organized labor in the late 1930s and early 1940s looked upon the nation's highest court as a friend rather than as the foe it had been before 1937.

The Commerce Power and Agriculture

The extension of the commerce power in labor relations had its counterparts in other fields. In agriculture, for example, the later New Deal legislation found the bench receptive to viewing farming not as a local matter, but as an integral part of the nation's commerce. In 1939, the Supreme Court sustained the Tobacco Inspection Act of 1935 in *Currin v. Wallace*. Chief Justice Hughes noted that Congress had power, under the Commerce Clause, to establish the conditions by which agricultural goods could be sold interstate. The Agricultural Marketing Agreement Act of 1937, which regulated intra- as well as interstate arrangements, received approval in *United States v. Rock Royal Cooperative* (1939). As the courts came to acknowledge the integrated nature of a modern national economy, their interpretations of the Commerce Clause left little beyond the reach of Congress.

The Supreme Court seemed to have come full circle when it validated the second Agricultural Administration Act, with Justice Roberts, whose *Butler* opinion had struck down the New Deal's first effort at farm reform, delivering the majority decision. Congress had enacted this ambitious program in 1938, with the ultimate goal of creating an "ever-normal granary" for the nation by storing surpluses from bountiful crops for use in lean years. The statute authorized crop loans, encouraged soil conservation, and offered crop insurance. But the new measure did not include the processing taxes or quotas on farmers that the Court had objected to in *Butler*. Instead, the law empowered the secretary of agriculture to assign national acreage allotments that would then be subject to approval by farmers through cooperative marketing agreements. In March 1938, farmers began voting on the allotments for the spring planting; cotton growers approved the acreage reductions by a lopsided margin of 1,189,000 to 97,000, and tobacco raisers by 213,000 to 34,000.

Having abandoned the tax rationale, Congress insisted that it could regulate agriculture under the Commerce Clause. Some disgruntled tobacco planters, unhappy over their reduced allotments, sued on the basis that agriculture was a local matter, and that the law thus violated the Tenth Amendment by invading the reserved powers of the state. In *Mulford v. Smith* (1939), Justice Roberts upheld the controls imposed by the law, since Congress could enact "any rule . . . intended to foster, protect and conserve" commerce. The government could regulate how much of a particular commodity could be sold, which had the direct effect of giving Congress the power to control how much could be grown, the most important step in imposing order on the atomistic agricultural sector of the economy. Roberts thus approved, under the Commerce Clause, practically the same type of control he had invalidated four years earlier, when Congress had tried to use the taxing power. Moreover, he abandoned the distinction that the Court had previously drawn in *Hammer v. Dagenhart* between "harmful" and "harmless" objects. It no longer made any difference why Congress wanted to prohibit the interstate movement of particular goods; legislative motive did not matter so long as the power existed. For all practical purposes, the Court had overruled *Butler*.

The Court took one more step in expanding the commerce power when it sustained the wheat quota provisions of the 1938 law in *Wickard v. Filburn* (1942). In a strong opinion by Justice Jackson, the Court abandoned the old distinction between production (essentially a local activity) and commerce. "Whether the subject of the regulation in question was 'production,' 'consumption,' or 'marketing' is, therefore, not material for the purpose of deciding the question of federal power before us." Any activity, no matter how local it seemed to be, could come within congressional reach if it exerted a substantial effect on interstate commerce. Moreover, this effect need not be characterized as direct as opposed to indirect, as Jackson specifically repudiated another ancient test of the commerce power.

The Reach of the Commerce Power

Within a few years, the Court thus reversed more than a half-century of precedent that had imposed a narrow interpretation on the federal commerce power. Justice Jackson characterized the earlier view as aberrant and claimed that the true interpretation of the Commerce Clause should be that of Chief Justice Marshall, who "described the federal commerce power with a breadth never yet exceeded." In *Jones & Laughlin* (1937), the Court had reinvigorated the rationale of "affecting commerce," so that intrastate activities, in that case labor, that affected interstate commerce came within federal reach. Five years later, in *Wickard v. Filburn*, the Court expanded the affecting commerce doctrine so that almost any activity could be so defined. In between, in *United States v. Darby* (1941), the justices approved the so-called commerce prohibiting doctrine, whereby an expanded interpretation of the commerce power allowed Congress regulatory authority over noncommercial activities. *Darby* did not invent this idea, however; it had received initial judicial approval in the Progressive era, but then had been rejected after the invalidation of the first Child Labor Law in *Hammer v. Dagenhart*. A sign of how far the Court had traveled was the unanimity in both *Darby* and *Wickard*. McReynolds, the last of the Four Horsemen (all of whom had dissented in *Jones & Laughlin*), retired a few days before the Court announced the *Darby* decision.

There is little question that the Roosevelt appointees, because of their experience during the Depression, appreciated modern economic theories, which stressed the national character of markets. A century earlier, the emergence of national markets had similarly affected the development of commercial law. National markets did not disappear in the latter nineteenth or early twentieth centuries, but conservative jurists ignored them and created legal fictions that imposed artificial boundaries between so-called local and national business. In *Mulford v. Smith*, Justice Roberts finally acknowledged the national scope of the problems confronting agriculture and the power of Congress to respond to any commercial situation "working harm to the people of the nation."

A quarter-century later, the second Justice Harlan, in *Maryland v. Wirtz* (1968), would claim that *Wickard* did not mean "that Congress could use a relatively trivial impact on commerce as an excuse for broad general regulation of state or private activity." But with the acceptance of a national market theory, it has rarely been difficult to establish the necessary relationship. In fact, the Supreme Court until the era of the Rehnquist Court virtually abandoned any limits on the commerce power, and Congress used it to reach many noncommercial areas, such as criminal activity and racial discrimination. But even when so stretched, the post-*Wickard* theory at least reflected a realistic appraisal of the interconnectedness of local and interstate business.

Similar reasoning could be found in the Court's validation of other New Deal measures. The Public Utilities Holding Company Act of 1935 received its initial judicial blessing in *Electric Bond and Share Company v. S.E.C.* (1938), with only Justice McReynolds dissenting. The act permitted the Securities and Exchange Commission to compel the registration of holding companies and prohibited the use of the instrumentalities of commerce (such as the mails) by unregistered firms. Relying on the lottery case (*Champion v. Ames* [1903]), Chief Justice Hughes ruled that "when Congress lays down a valid rule to govern those engaged in transactions in interstate commerce, Congress may deny to those who violate the rule the right to engage in such transactions."

The more controversial "death sentence" clause, prohibiting the pyramiding of holding companies, did not come before the Court until 1946. In *North American Company v. S.E.C.*, the Court sustained the section that required each holding company to limit its operations to a single integrated public utility system. Justice Murphy found that Congress had adequate cause to condemn nonintegrated systems as inimical to the general welfare and that the commerce power "permits Congress to attack an evil directly at its source, provided that the evil has a substantial relationship to interstate commerce." In the same term, in *American Power & Light Company v. S.E.C.*, the Court upheld another part of the death sentence clause, which gave the Securities and Exchange Commission the power to order the dissolution of "unduly or unnecessarily complicated" structures.

The Demise of "Old Swifty"

In fact, about the only area in which the Court attempted to restrict federal power involved the judiciary itself. Ever since *Swift v. Tyson* (1842), federal courts had been relatively free to ignore state law in diversity suits (cases involving citizens of different states) and to apply a general commercial law or common law. Created by Joseph Story, the rule fostered economic growth because firms dealing in national markets could rely on uniform commercial rules, administered by sympathetic federal courts, which ignored the idiosyncrasies of multiple state statutes.

By the twentieth century, however, many states had either revised their legislation to conform to generally accepted commercial practices or had adopted some of the model codes prepared by the National Conference of Commissioners on Uniform State Laws. The commissioners had promulgated uniform statutes on negotiable instruments (1896), warehouse receipts (1906), sales (1906), bills of lading (1909), stock transfers (1909), conditional sales (1918), and trust receipts (1933), and every state had adopted two or more of these acts. But variations on specific matters still existed among states, and to avoid particular state laws, business continued to resort to federal courts, often manufacturing diversity in order to qualify.

The most notorious abuse can be found in *Black & White Taxicab Co. v. Brown & Yellow Taxicab Co.* (1928). The Brown & Yellow Company, a Kentucky corporation, signed an agreement with the Louisville & Nashville Railroad, also a Kentucky firm, which gave it exclusive rights to solicit business at the railroad's Bowling Green, Kentucky, station. This froze out the Black & White Company, which violated Kentucky common law against monopolies. So the Brown & Yellow reincorporated in Tennessee and executed the contract there; it then invoked its new status as a Tennessee corporation to enter federal court in Kentucky to seek an injunction against Black & White's soliciting passengers at the station. Since the federal common law developed under *Swift* did not prohibit monopolistic contracts, the federal district court issued the injunction, which the Court of Appeals and the Supreme Court later sustained. Holmes, joined by Brandeis, dissented vigorously against this transparent ruse to evade state law. Holmes condemned the *Swift* doctrine as "an unconstitutional assumption of powers by courts of the United States which no lapse of time or respectable array of opinions should make us hesitate to correct."

For the next ten years, Brandeis continued to inveigh against what he considered the abuse of diversity jurisdiction and the invasion of states' rights. Although not unfriendly to a broad use of certain national powers, Brandeis always remained a federalist, and he believed that the states should maintain the powers granted to them under the Constitution. The failure to guard and exercise these powers would lead inevitably to the expansion of federal authority, which he viewed as potentially destructive of liberty. The federal system allowed for differences among state legal codes; that this might inconvenience some businesses mattered far less than the need to sustain the states in their full authority within a federal system. *Swift*, he believed, had upset the balance; worse, it had opened the door to flagrant manipulation, as in the taxicab case, to bypass legitimate state regulation. Federal courts, Brandeis contended, should accept only diversity suits in which compelling reasons required adjudication by federal officials; but even there, state law should apply. Like Holmes, Brandeis objected to the notion of "a transcendental body of law outside of any particular State but obligatory within it."

Brandeis finally won over a majority of the Court to his view in the landmark case of *Erie Railroad Co. v. Tompkins* (1938). Tompkins, a Pennsylvania citizen, had been injured by an Erie freight train as he walked alongside the right of way. He charged negligence on the part of the railroad, claiming that he had been rightfully on the premises because many people used the footpath that ran alongside the tracks. Although the accident had occurred in Pennsylvania, Tompkins sued in federal court in New York, because the Erie held its charter from that state—and because Pennsylvania law deemed pedestrians strolling along the right of way to be trespassers. The federal court denied the railroad plea that Pennsylvania law should apply; relying on *Swift*, it ruled that general law, which federal courts could apply, allowed Tompkins to recover.

In his opinion, Brandeis brought out all the alleged defects of the *Swift* doctrine. Why should federal courts ignore Pennsylvania law in an accident that took place in that state and involved a Pennsylvania citizen and a railroad which, although incorporated elsewhere, did much business there? The Court abandoned *Swift* and promulgated a new doctrine that required that federal courts apply state law as declared by the legislature or interpreted by the highest state court—except when the Constitution or federal statute required otherwise. "There is no federal general common law," Brandeis declared.

Erie required a major rethinking of problems relating not only to the jurisdiction of federal courts, but also to the doctrine of conflicts of law. Prior to *Erie*, federal courts could often ignore the question of which state law to apply by resorting to the so-called general law; now they had to determine which state law would govern in diversity cases—the law of the state in which the federal court heard the case, or that of another state, such as the one in which an accident had occurred or property was located. If Brandeis had hoped that abolishing the *Swift* rule would shift the balance between federal and state jurisdiction toward a greater emphasis on state law, he would have been sorely disappointed.

To begin with, the same day as he handed down *Erie*, Brandeis also delivered the Court's unanimous decision in *Hinderliter v. La Plata River Co.* The case involved an interstate compact between New Mexico and Colorado over division of the waters of the La Plata River. "Whether the waters of an interstate stream must be apportioned between these two States," he declared, "is a question of 'federal common law' upon which neither the statutes nor the decisions of either State are conclusive." So a federal common law did exist, but only in those areas in which state law would be inapplicable because it infringed on federal supremacy; of course, only federal courts could determine where that fine line ran.

Critics of the *Erie* ruling also questioned whether the *Swift* doctrine had ever been so terrible as to warrant its total abolition. The fraudulent creation of diversity did not derive from *Swift* itself and could easily have been cured by statute. In fact, Congress did just that in 1958, when it amended Section 1332(C) of the federal code to define the citizenship of a corporation as that of its principal place of business; under this simple rule, the Brown & White Taxicab Company could never have gotten into federal court. Moreover, if *Swift* had been so wrong, as Brandeis claimed, Congress could have nullified it by changing the Judiciary Act at any time; evidently both Congress and the states approved of the doctrine and its beneficial effects, since it was left alone.

Moreover, the same year as *Erie*, Congress enacted the Federal Rules of Civil Procedure, which streamlined and rationalized procedures in federal courts. Brandeis had said that state law would apply except when a federal statute existed, and the new rules seemed to offer some guidance to the courts. In 1941, the Court declared that federal law should apply in federal courts whenever a procedural question arose but that state law should apply to substantive questions. However, as subsequent cases demonstrated, the line between procedural and substantive law could not always be easily determined; a statute of limitations, for example, is usually a procedural matter, but in some contexts, it may represent a substantive right. Although *Erie* remains the law, so many exceptions and explanations have been created that, according to some commentators, we have in essence adopted a neo-Swiftian doctrine under which federal courts always apply federal law unless there is a compelling reason to use state law—just the opposite of what Brandeis had hoped to accomplish.

The Court and State Powers

While attempting to restructure part of the federal-state balance, *Erie* appears in retrospect as something of an aberration relative to the Court's apparent determination to expand the authority of the federal government. But the Court also expanded the states' police powers, and it would be better to examine the issue less in terms of states' rights than as one in which the courts recognized that modern economic and social problems required greater governmental involvement, be it at the state or federal level. Before *Morehead*, in fact, the Court seemed to have been moving toward a more expansive view of state powers, along the lines Justice Brandeis had called for in his *New State Ice* dissent; *West Coast Hotel v. Parrish*, therefore, represents no sharp departure, but a return to precedent.

With the Court's adoption of a broad view of interstate commerce came the problem of how to handle state regulatory measures that affected interstate activities. The conservatives had seemingly erected a major roadblock to state regulation in *Colgate v. Harvey* (1935). Justice Sutherland found that the Privileges and Immunities Clause of the Fourteenth Amendment, which had lain dormant for six decades since the *Slaughterhouse Cases*, forbade a Vermont state tax on deposits held by its citizens in out-of-state banks. The right to conduct interstate business, Sutherland held, constituted one of the privileges and immunities guaranteed by the Constitution. But only five years later, in *Madden v. Kentucky*, the Court, speaking through Justice Reed, ruled a similar law valid. The states had great freedom to manage their own affairs, he noted, except when the Constitution provided otherwise or when the federal government had preempted an area.

By reviving the commonsense rule of *Cooley v. Board of Wardens* (1851), the Court allowed states a fairly broad play of regulatory power; in the absence of federal legislation, states could exercise their own authority. In *Milk Board v. Eisenburg* (1939), for example, the Court upheld a Pennsylvania law that empowered a state agency to regulate prices and inspect milk, even milk imported from outside the state. Justice Roberts conceded that the law affected interstate commerce, but he did not consider it unreasonable, nor did it discriminate between local and out-of-state producers.

The old dogmas of freedom of contract and substantive due process passed into oblivion at this time, hanging on only in the dissents of the Four Horsemen, soon themselves to be gone. Felix Frankfurter, who as a law professor had severely criticized the conservative members of the Court for writing their personal views into the law, expressed the now dominant doctrine of judicial restraint in *Osborn v. Ozlin* (1940), which upheld a Virginia statute regulating insurance brokerage contracts. It made no difference, he declared, that state legislation

> may run counter to the economic wisdom of Adam Smith or J. Maynard Keynes, or may be ultimately mischievous even from the point of view of avowed state policy. Our inquiry must be much narrower. It is whether Virginia has taken hold of a matter within her power, or has reached beyond her borders to regulate a subject which was none of her concern because the Constitution has placed control elsewhere.

So at least in the area of economic regulation, the Court would defer to the legislature and adopted the low-level test of rational basis. If the legislature had the general power and put forward any rational reason for exercising that power in a particular manner, the courts would not interfere. As Justice Black later declared, courts "may no longer substitute their social and economic beliefs for the judgment of legislative bodies" (*Ferguson v. Skrupa* [1963]).

The Court, however, never wholly adopted such a policy of restraint, because, among other things, the questions that came before it for adjudication could no more be fitted into Frankfurter's mechanistic view of judicial restraint than they could to Roberts's T-square. So the Court never totally abandoned the regulation of state legislation; rather, it moved into the business of drawing lines between state and federal authority. It oversaw the modernization of state tax programs, for example, as the states developed new sources of revenue to replace those that had been depleted by the Depression and widespread unemployment. Sales taxes could affect interstate commerce, as could license fees on chain stores, since both could be used to discriminate against out-of-state businesses. When this happened, the Court quickly intervened. In *Hale v. Bimco Trading Company* (1939), the Court struck down a Florida tax on cement imported into the state, since there was no corresponding levy on locally produced cement. Similarly, in *Best v. Maxwell* (1940), the Court held a North Carolina privilege tax of $250 imposed on traveling salesmen as discriminatory. But a Virginia tax on vehicles used in peddling received the Court's blessing. Although it obviously affected out-of-state salesmen, the tax applied equally to local peddlers, and thus constituted a legitimate state purpose of regulation through taxation (*Caskay Baking Co. v. Virginia* [1941]).

Conclusion: The Crisis Survived

By the time of Roosevelt's third inaugural in 1941, the Court no longer appeared, at least to conservatives, as the protector of property rights, the impartial arbiter protecting vested interests against the jealousies of the masses. Instead of inflexibly applying strict standards of constitutionality, the justices now seemed like just another group of politicians, pragmatically tailoring their decisions to meet the exigencies of the moment. Taking the judicial oath no longer seemed comparable to the anointment of a cardinal or bishop.

From the conservative point of view, the Court no doubt seemed a far different institution in 1940 than it had been a decade earlier. The veneration and mystique had disappeared. Roosevelt had tried to lay his hands on the Holy of Holies, and while the attack had been beaten back, the damage had been done. First Roberts and Hughes had caved in and delivered their votes to the liberals. Then death and retirement had allowed "that man in the White House" to pack the Court with ciphers all too willing to follow the political winds. Having lost the battle, Roosevelt had, as he claimed, won the war.

Such a characterization not only maligns the Roosevelt appointees, but ignores the damage that the conservative jurists, especially the Four Horsemen, had themselves done to the Court. From 1918 to 1936, they ignored the reality of the world outside the judicial cloister; they dismissed precedent when it did not serve their interests; instead of objectively applying neutral rules, they constantly injected their own biases into decisions. Roosevelt's goal of trying to force the Court to take cognizance of contemporary needs did not offend the American people; his too clever political ploy did. The Court had lost a great deal of its prestige before the constitutional crisis of 1937.

But if the Supreme Court could no longer rely on a quasi-reverent basis of public support, it could and did establish a more comprehensive foundation to justify its enormous power. Over a century earlier, the great chief justice, John Marshall, had based the Court's authority on the assumption that in a federal system under a written Constitution, some agency had to serve as the ultimate arbiter of what that Constitution meant and as an adjudicator between competing claims within the system. The modern world, full of challenges never imagined by the Framers, had even more need of a tribunal to serve these functions, a tribunal not of Platonic guardians but of pragmatic and practical persons, learned in the law, but sensitive to the conditions in which people lived and the government functioned.

Marshall had also set an example in his expansive interpretation of the Commerce Clause; supporters of the New Deal claimed, not without some justification, that the post-1937 decisions merely marked a return by the Court to its historically broad view of the commerce power. On the bench, the justices peppered their opinions with references to early nineteenth-century cases to show a connection between their views and those of Marshall and Story. When Justice Murphy declared the federal commerce power "as broad as the economic needs of the nation," supporters hailed the statement as "Marshallian." Off the bench, respected commentators such as Edward S. Corwin, Walton Hamilton, and Douglass Adair provided scholarly support to the claim that the Framers had always intended the Commerce Clause to provide the federal government with extensive powers.

In the 1970s and 1980s, it became fashionable to blame the New Deal for a host of problems afflicting the country, from huge debts to unnecessary welfare programs to a bloated bureaucracy, as well as the alleged collapse of state authority within the federal system. The cave-in of the Court, ran part of this argument, had removed the brakes on the tendency of the national government to expand its authority at the expense of the

> We have behind us eight terrible years of a crisis we have shared with all countries. Here we are, and our basic institutions are still intact, our people relatively prosperous, and most important of all, our society relatively affectionate. No rift has made an unbridgeable schism between us. The working classes and . . . the industrialists are not demanding a Man on Horseback. No country in the world is so well off.
>
> —Dorothy Thompson, *New York Herald Tribune* (9 October 1940)

states, a tendency which the Framers had warned about. This argument is at best misleading, for the federal system has, over two centuries, shifted in favor of central authority for a variety of reasons. If nothing else, the development of a national economy has required greater national powers, a process that was well underway long before Franklin Roosevelt took his first oath of office. The Court, it is true, gave the federal government a broad mandate under the Commerce Clause. Yet one should ask how the United States would have fared if Congress had not had power equal to the country's needs.

One should also note that the Court recognized the necessity for expanding the states' authority under their police powers; it did not enlarge federal control at the expense of the states so much as to make it possible for all levels of government to deal with emergencies. One might well ponder who the real federalists were—the Four Horsemen, who tried to create a no-man's land where neither federal nor state government could act, or the liberals such as Brandeis, Stone, and Cardozo, who saw creative possibilities at both local and national levels.

For Further Reading

General works on this period are listed at the end of the last chapter, but see especially William E. Leuchtenburg, *Roosevelt and the New Deal* (1960); and Arthur M. Schlesinger, *The Politics of Upheaval* (1960). For some of the legislation in the second Hundred Days, see Roy Lubove, *The Struggle for Social Security, 1900–1937* (1968); Thomas McCraw, *TVA and the Power Fight* (1971); Phillip J. Funigiello, *Toward a National Power Policy: The New Deal and Electric Utility Industry, 1933–1941* (1973); Irving Bernstein, *Turbulent Years: A History of the American Worker, 1933–1941* (1970); and Richard D. McKinzie, *The New Deal for Artists* (1973). For some of the radical pressures pushing Roosevelt, see Abraham Holzman, *The Townsend Movement* (1963); David Bennett, *Demagogues in the Depression: American Radicals and the Union Party, 1932–1936* (1969); and Alan Brinkley, *Voices of Protest: Huey Long, Father Coughlin, and the Great Depression* (1982). Labor policy is explored in Christopher L. Tomlins, *The State and the Unions: Labor Relations, Law, and the Organized Labor Movement in America, 1880–1960* (1985).

For the Court fight, Leonard Baker, *Back to Back: The Duel Between FDR and the Supreme Court* (1967), and Joseph Alsop and Turner Catledge, *The 168 Days* (1938), are both competent journalistic accounts, while E. S. Corwin, *Court over Constitution* (1938), is quite perceptive. The so-called standard account is normally attributed to William E. Leuchtenburg. See "The Origins of Franklin D. Roosevelt's 'Court-packing' Plan," and "FDR's 'Court-packing' Plan," in *The Supreme Court Reborn: The Constitutional Revolution in the Age of Roosevelt* (1995). For the political activities of the justices, see Leuchtenburg, "The Nine Justices Respond to the 1937 Crisis," 1997 *Journal of Supreme Court History* 55 (1997). The revisionist view is presented in Barry Cushman, *Rethinking the New Deal Court: The Structure of a Constitutional Revolution* (1998).

The reasons behind Justice Roberts's famous "switch in time" have occasioned several studies. See John W. Chambers, "The Big Switch: Justice Roberts and the Minimum Wage Cases," 10 *LaborHistory* 44 (1969); and Charles A. Leonard, *A Search for a Judicial Philosophy: Mr. Justice Roberts and the Constitutional Revolution of 1937* (1971). Questions about the validity of the Roberts memorandum are dealt with in Richard D. Friedman, "A Reaffirmation of the Authenticity of the Roberts Memorandum, or Felix the Non-Forger," 142 *University of Pennsylvania Law Review* 1985 (1994).

For Roosevelt's efforts at reorganization, see Barry D. Karl, *Executive Reorganization and Reform in the New Deal: The Genesis of Administrative Management, 1900–1939* (1963); Richard Polenberg, *Reorganizing Roosevelt's Government, 1936–1939* (1966); and A. J. Wann, *The President as Chief Administrator: A Study of Franklin D. Roosevelt* (1968).

For the postcrisis cases, see Richard C. Cortner, *The Wagner Act Cases* (1964) and *The Jones & Laughlin Case* (1970); Paul R. Benson, Jr., *The Supreme Court and the Commerce Clause, 1937–1970* (1970); C. Herman Pritchett, *The Roosevelt Court: A Study in Judicial Politics and Values, 1937–1947* (1948); Ashley Sellers and Jesse E. Baskette, Jr., "Agricultural Marketing Agreement and Order Programs, 1933–1943," 33 *Georgetown Law Journal* 123 (1945); and E. S. Corwin, "The Passing of Dual Federalism," 36 *Virginia Law Review* 1 (1950). For efforts to reconcile the Social Security cases with *Butler*, see Thomas R. McCoy and Barry Friedman, "Conditional Spending: Federalism's Trojan Horse," 1988 *Supreme Court Review* 85 (1988) [pg].

The *Erie* case continues to be a major source of debate, much of it technical, but see John Hart Ely, "The Irrepressible Myth of Erie," 87 *Harvard Law Review* 693 (1974); the actual facts behind the case are detailed in Irving Younger, "What Happened in Erie," 56 *Texas Law Review* 1010 (1978).

The changes in federalism wrought by the Roosevelt revolution are explored in William Anderson, *The Nation and the States: Rivals or Partners* (1956); Joseph E. Kallenbach, *Federal Cooperation with the States Under the Commerce Clause* (1942); and John R. Schmidhauser, *The Supreme Court as Final Arbiter in Federal-State Relations* (1958).

32

Civil Liberties and the Roosevelt Court

Rights of Labor • The Bar, the Justice Department, and Civil Liberties • Cardozo and Selective Incorporation • Black and Total Incorporation • Frankfurter and the Limits of Restraint • Labor and the First Amendment • Religion • The Flag Salute Cases • Civil Liberties in Wartime • Treason and Espionage • For Further Reading

ALTHOUGH MOST LIBERALS welcomed the New Deal's activism in combating the Depression, the accompanying growth of government alarmed civil libertarians, who still tended to see strong central authority as inimical to individual rights. Certainly the example of the Fascists in Italy, the Nazis in Germany, and the Communists in Russia gave little reassurance that the growth of national government in the United States would be accompanied by a concern for the Bill of Rights. Yet the Roosevelt administration—with one significant exception, discussed in the next chapter—displayed great sensitivity for civil liberties, not only during the Depression years, but during World War II as well. At the same time, the Supreme Court—again with one major exception—continued and accelerated the nationalization of the Bill of Rights and the expansion of civil liberties and civil rights.

Rights of Labor

The National Recovery Administration's marked bias toward business and its cavalier disregard of Section 7(a) initially seemed to mean that government had lent its authority to management's traditional hostility toward labor and the repressive measures that accompanied it. In its 1934 report, the American Civil Liberties Union noted pessimistically that "alarms are widely expressed over alleged dictatorship by the President, the abrogation of States' rights and the vast economic power of the federal government." By 1936, however, the ACLU recognized that the government had done a complete turnabout; the greatest threat to liberty came not from the government, but from "the resort to force and violence by employers, vigilantes, mobs, troops, private gunmen, and compliant sheriffs and police."

The change in the Roosevelt administration's attitude resulted from its disillusionment with business's actions during the first New Deal. Management had been willing enough to take the benefits offered by the government, but it had not kept its part of the bargain in regard to labor. The second New Deal, with its commitment to labor through the Wagner Act and the National Labor Relations Board, scrutinized far more critically the gross violations of civil liberties that workers suffered at the hands of antiunion management, often aided by state and local authorities.

In early 1936, a Senate subcommittee chaired by Robert M. LaFollette, Jr., of Wisconsin, began to investigate charges that workers' rights, especially free speech and assembly, had been violated. The LaFollette committee detailed the lengths to which management had gone to crush labor, including the use of private armies, spies, intimidation, and *agents provocateurs*, as well as the involvement of corrupt local officials. Following the violence of the Little Steel strike of 1937, the committee publicized how employers had continuously flouted the Wagner Act, broken the laws, and disregarded civil liberties. These practices, of course, had been employed for nearly a half-century, ever since workers had seriously begun organizing into unions. But now, for the first time, workers could look past hostile bosses and uncaring local officials to the federal government for help; the Wagner Act put the law on their side. Moreover, the Depression had led to a loss of faith in business, so that the public now viewed with suspicion management's claims that radicals and subversives caused labor strife.

Much of the civil liberties agitation in the mid- and late 1930s resulted from efforts by American workers to organize and bargain collectively. Unlike previous periods of labor unrest, however, workers now had potent allies. The national government, especially the Department of Labor and the Labor Relations Board, actively supported organized labor, as did much of the Democratic majority in Congress. The Roosevelt appointees to the Court fully sympathized with labor goals, unlike the antiunion justices of the Taft years. Labor in particular and civil liberties in general also received strong support from academics and from younger lawyers who had imbibed the attitudes of the Realists or the civil liberties views of such influential law teachers as Ernst Freund, Felix Frankfurter, and especially Zechariah Chafee, Jr.

The Bar, the Justice Department, and Civil Liberties

Within the legal profession, devotion to civil liberties manifested itself quite clearly in the formation of the National Lawyers Guild. The conservative American Bar Association had abandoned its traditional posture of political neutrality to attack much of the New Deal's legislation, and especially the court-packing plan. In early 1937, liberal lawyers set up their own organization, which had a frenetic career over the next fifteen or so years. The Guild attracted not only liberals, such as Morris Ernst and Frank P. Walsh, but many radicals as well, so that in the early 1950s, the Justice Department sought to label it as a Communist organization. Although this effort failed, the attack, led by Attorney General Herbert Brownell, so tarnished the group's image that it soon slid into oblivion.

The Guild's most lasting achievement may have been the influence it exerted on the American Bar Association (ABA). A number of ABA members, although economically and politically conservative, did support the Bill of Rights and resented being characterized as economic royalists insensitive to personal liberties. Frank Hogan, who became ABA president in 1938, helped steer the organization back to its traditional nonpartisan stance, but he argued that lawyers had to be as alert to infringements by big government on individual freedoms as to attacks on property rights. He persuaded the association to create a Committee on the Bill of Rights, chaired by Grenville Clark of New York, with representatives from both the liberal and conservative wings of the bar. As its first legal action, the committee filed a brief written by Zechariah Chafee, supporting the rights of the Congress of Industrial Organizations (CIO) to speech and assembly in Jersey City, against the depredations of Mayor Frank "I am the Law" Hague. Lawyers with impeccable Republican and conservative credentials, but with a strong attachment to civil liberties, represented Angelo Herndon in *Herndon v. Lowry* (1937).

Although the committee as a whole had a definite commitment to civil liberties, its members had widely divergent views on what policy it should follow. For the most part, however, they supported the traditional view of liberty as a negative, that is, the absence of government restraint. Neither the ABA nor a majority of its Committee on the Bill of Rights thought that government should take a positive role in expanding the meaning of liberty, since to do so might invite government manipulation of those rights toward a specific political end. The examples of Germany and Italy made it all too clear how government could distort law in the name of freedom and wind up destroying liberty.

Within the administration, however, some New Dealers began considering how government could be instrumental in fostering individual freedom. Frank Murphy, the popular governor of Michigan, became attorney general of the United States in January 1939, and he immediately set out to make the Department of Justice into an "aggressive" protector of fundamental rights. In Michigan, Murphy had seen firsthand how powerful corporations could subvert freedom, and he believed that only the government could protect the individual against this. He cleansed the Justice Department of the political hacks appointed by Homer Cummings, created a Civil Liberties Unit, and staffed the department with men and women who were dedicated to, as Murphy put it, having the government serve as both shield and sword. It would not only protect citizens against the arbitrary deprivations of their rights; it would also cut away at both public and private actions that might limit those rights at some future time. "I am anxious," Murphy told civil liberties activist Roger Baldwin, that the Justice Department "should be a force for the protection of the people's liberties."

The Civil Liberties Unit, renamed in 1941 as the Civil Rights Section, assumed that sufficient authority for its program could be found in the three Civil War amendments, as well as in the laws that had attempted to implement them. For example, the unit's lawyers utilized one of the old Ku Klux Klan Acts to prosecute a corrupt New Orleans politico in *United States v. Classic* (1941). The 1870 law had forbidden interference with rights guaranteed by the Constitution, and the Supreme Court agreed that tampering with the ballot box undermined the right to vote. Justice Stone's opinion gave the Justice Department the rationale to protect individuals not only against private abuses of their rights, but against state and local authority as well. Such a concept had been out of political favor since the waning days of Reconstruction.

Cardozo and Selective Incorporation

The most important federal agency to advance civil liberties proved to be the Supreme Court. There is a certain irony that the Roosevelt appointees, even as they sanctioned the enormous expansion of governmental power over the nation's economic life, moved to create a new and potent civil liberties jurisprudence that limited governmental control over the individual and yet gave the government powerful tools to protect the basic rights of its citizens. Moreover, this happened in the midst of depression and war, a time when one would hardly expect any great concern for the individual, especially if he or she happened to be out of step with majoritarian sentiments. Although the arrival of the Roosevelt nominees triggered this constitutional upheaval, as with most radical transformations, there had been earlier portents. Holmes and Brandeis, of course, had led the way in the 1920s, but even the conservatives had shown considerable sensitivity to individual rights. By 1937, the question seemed, at least to some members of the Court, less one of expanding rights than of finding the proper criteria and limits for doing so.

Benjamin Nathan Cardozo, the shy, retiring successor to the flamboyant Holmes, shared Holmes's devotion to free expression, but he also saw the need to draw some boundary lines. While he did not oppose the nationalization of civil liberties standards, he believed that a blanket application of the Bill of Rights to the states would destroy an important aspect of federalism and deprive the nation of the opportunity for the experimentation in the states that Brandeis had lauded in his *New State Ice* dissent. In late 1937, Cardozo delivered the majority opinion in *Palko v. Connecticut*, one of the crucial cases in civil liberties history, and in doing so, he defined much of the judicial debate for the next generation. The case involved a relatively limited question: did the Fourteenth Amendment incorporate the guarantee against double jeopardy in the Fifth Amendment and apply it to the states? Cardozo answered that it did not, for the Fourteenth Amendment did not automatically subsume the entire Bill of Rights. This implied that it did incorporate some rights, but which ones? Cardozo included all the protections of the First Amendment, for freedom of thought and speech "is the matrix, the indispensable condition, of nearly every other form of [freedom]." But as for the Second through Eighth amendments, the Court should apply only those that are "of the very essence of a scheme of ordered liberty" and "so rooted in the traditions and conscience of our people as to be ranked as fundamental."

This doctrine of "selective incorporation" lodged enormous power and discretion in the Court. Nothing in the Constitution provided guidance; rather, the justices had to modernize the Bill of Rights and decide which parts of it applied to the states, based on their own views (guided in some small degree by history and precedent) of what constituted a fundamental right.

Palko had an immediate effect on Harlan Fiske Stone, who had also given a great deal of thought to how the Court's expansion of the commerce power and abandon-

> There may be narrower scope for operation of the presumption of constitutionality when legislation appears on its face to be within a specific prohibition of the Constitution, such as those of the first ten Amendments, which are deemed equally specific when held to be embraced within the 14th. . . .
>
> It is unnecessary to consider now whether legislation which restricts those political processes which can ordinarily be expected to bring about repeal of undesirable legislation, is to be subjected to more exacting judicial scrutiny under the general prohibition of the 14th Amendment than are most other types of legislation. . . .
>
> Nor need we enquire whether similar considerations enter into the review of statutes directed at particular religious, national, or racial minorities; whether prejudice against discrete and insular minorities may be a special condition, which tends seriously to curtail the operation of those political processes ordinarily to be relied upon to protect minorities, and which may call for a correspondingly more searching judicial inquiry.
>
> —Harlan Fiske Stone, *United States v. Carolene Products Co.* (1938), footnote 4.

ment of substantive due process affected individual liberties. A former attorney general and confidant of President Hoover, Stone recognized the need to expand those rights that were directly connected to the political process, so that all groups could participate fully; the freedom to influence political activities, he believed, lay at the heart of democracy. *Palko* made it possible to expand constitutional safeguards without having to amend the document, but the Court would have to do what Cardozo had suggested, that is, develop some hierarchy of values. In a noncivil liberties case, *United States v. Carolene Products Company* (1938), Stone added what is certainly the most famous footnote in American constitutional history. While the Court should certainly defer to the legislature in economic matters, he proposed that it should impose higher standards of review in areas of civil liberties and civil rights. Practically ignored at the time, the *Carolene Products* note laid the basis for differentiated review, one of the contemporary Court's strongest weapons in its defense of individual rights.

Black and Total Incorporation

Roosevelt's first appointee, Hugo LaFayette Black of Alabama, initially subscribed to Cardozo's *Palko* opinion. Black's intuitive commitment to civil liberties derived from his populist background, and his rise from police court judge to U.S. Senator left him convinced that democracy could work only if the people had control of their government. Courts had to ensure that the people would not be frustrated by the machinations of powerful interests, be they private or entrenched in local government.

Before long, Black began to expound his own position in civil liberties cases. He seemed to have little use for precedent, contending that *stare decisis*, while useful in common law, had only limited value in constitutional adjudication. Despite his occasionally rough-hewn law, Black's instincts for fair play and justice could not be denied, and Brandeis, who always displayed great sensitivity to the nuances of tradition, applauded Black's opinion in *Johnson v. Zerbst* (1938). Johnson had been convicted of passing counterfeit money, and at the time of his trial had been indigent and unable to afford a lawyer. Black's opinion, for a 6–2 majority, held that federal courts could not deprive an accused of life or liberty unless providing counsel or determining that the defendant had intelligently and competently waived this right.

Not until he had sat on the bench for ten years did Black finally reach the position he had been seeking. In *Adamson v. California* (1947), the majority utilized the *Palko* approach to rule that although the Fifth Amendment prohibited the prosecution from making comments on the failure of a defendant to take the stand in his own defense in federal cases, the Fourteenth Amendment did not require a similar rule in the states. Black's dissent set forth the fullest exposition of his "total" incorporation theory. He rejected Cardozo's criteria as too vague, since they allowed the courts too much discretion; the only way to ensure uniformity in both state and federal courts would be to apply all the rights in the first eight amendments to the states through the Due Process Clause of the Fourteenth Amendment. In an extensive appendix, Black presented historical evidence that the framers of the Fourteenth Amendment had intended to extend the Bill of Rights to the states. The Court never adopted Black's total incorporation theory, but adhered, at least in theory, to Cardozo's doctrine of "selective" incorporation. In the 1960s, however, the Warren Court, without formally overruling *Palko*, adopted the Black position in practice; it selectively incorporated nearly all the Bill of Rights, and even expanded it.

Black found his companion in arms when Roosevelt named William Orville Douglas to replace Brandeis in the spring of 1939. The brilliant Douglas had worked his way through Columbia Law School and, after a brief stint in a Wall Street firm, had gone on to teach at the Yale Law School, where he came under the influence of the Legal Realists. His pioneering work in business law led to an appointment to the Securities and Exchange Commission, and when he became chairman in 1937, he used the agency to force reforms on the management of investment houses and the Stock Exchange itself. Although Douglas idolized Brandeis and paid devotional service to Brandeis's philosophy of judicial restraint, he would stray far from the limits Brandeis had preached. Later one of the most activist of all judges in expanding the reach of constitutionally protected liberties, Douglas reached that position slowly. Often lumped with the "left wing" of the Court because of his voting record on civil liberties, Douglas did not develop any identifiable judicial philosophy in these early years.

Strong support for civil liberties also came from Frank Murphy, named to replace Pierce Butler in 1939. Although Stanley Reed and Robert H. Jackson proved supportive of the Court's general direction, neither could be characterized as activists along the lines of Black, Douglas, or Murphy. Reed, for example, even though he wrote the landmark opinion in *Smith v. Allwright* (1944), advancing the cause of civil rights, normally opposed the argument that civil liberties required extraordinary constitutional protection. Jackson, as Murphy's successor as attorney general, had had responsibility not only for the civil liberties program but also for internal security as America prepared for war. Once on the bench, Jackson, like Reed, tended to vote with the libertarian majority although rarely taking a leading role in that area.

Frankfurter and the Limits of Restraint

The greatest surprise and disappointment to civil libertarians proved to be Felix Frankfurter, who had assumed the seat previously held by Holmes and then Cardozo, in February 1939. Frankfurter had influenced a generation of students at the Harvard Law School, instructing them in the virtues of judicial restraint and railing against the iniquities of the Taft Court. He had won the enmity of conservatives and the praise of liberals for his defense of radical I.W.W. leader Tom Mooney and later of Sacco and Vanzetti. Brandeis had called him the most useful lawyer in America, and defenders of civil liberties expected him to pick up the banner of their heroes.

But Frankfurter fastened on judicial restraint as the great legacy of Holmes and Brandeis and turned it into a fetish. Neither Holmes nor Brandeis had ever intended the Court to abdicate its role of judicial review; they merely wanted the judiciary to stop acting as a superlegislature, second-guessing the people's elected representatives as to the wisdom of their policy. Moreover, both Holmes and Brandeis saw a crucial difference between the review of economic legislation and that of statutes affecting individual liberties; the courts should always block legislative efforts to restrict civil liberties except under the exigencies of a clear and present danger. Moreover, in suggesting that the Bill of Rights, especially the First Amendment, should be nationalized, Brandeis had clearly indicated that judges ought not be too restrained in protecting freedom.

Frankfurter, the "scholar on the bench," ultimately came to argue that courts ought to show as much deference to legislation in matters of civil liberties as they showed in economic matters. The Constitution, he believed, left legislatures pretty free to develop policies in accord with the will of the people. If these policies proved restrictive, the courts should do no more than ensure that nothing blocked the avenues of political participation, for the solution to restrictive policies lay at the polls and not in the courtroom. Only when legislatures exceed the bounds of common decency did Frankfurter believe courts should interfere directly. He did assert that courts might take a more activist role in protecting procedural rights, however, for procedural due process made other liberties possible. Yet even here, he claimed only a limited role for the courts.

It came as no surprise, therefore, when Frankfurter filed a concurring opinion in 1947, defending the majority's selective incorporation approach in *Adamson* and sharply attacking Black's view of total incorporation. Only those rights that were necessary to ensure due process ought to be incorporated, and he provided relatively flexible guidelines to determine what that meant. The Frankfurter approach, while picking up the Cardozo argument, still had the problems that Black complained about, for it left judges free to determine what, at any given moment, constituted due process. The *Adamson* debate indicated the cleavage among the Roosevelt appointees, one that would grow deeper within a few years, as the Warren Court tackled a number of highly volatile issues.

Labor and the First Amendment

Both Cardozo in *Palko* and Stone in his *Carolene Products* footnote invited dissident groups and individuals to seek out a broader interpretation of constitutionally guaranteed rights. Labor groups initiated one series of cases testing the reach of the First Amendment's protection of free speech. Brandeis, as in so many areas, had pointed the way in *Senn v. Tile Layers' Protective Union* (1937), when he intimated that picketing, aside from its value as a tool in labor disputes, might also be a form of speech. The case involved the validity of a Wisconsin law making peaceful picketing lawful and nonenjoinable, and also providing for publicity in labor disputes. Union members did not have to rely on such a statute to make the facts of a labor dispute public, Brandeis declared, "for freedom of speech is guaranteed by the Federal Constitution." To the contractor who had brought the suit and claimed that the union's rules and actions interfered with his right to earn a living, Brandeis replied: "One has no constitutional right to a 'remedy' against the lawful conduct of another."

As the labor movement gained strength, its frequent resort to litigation amplified the meaning of the First Amendment. In *Hague v. CIO* (1939), labor challenged a Jersey City ordinance requiring permits for public meetings. Under Mayor Frank Hague, Jersey City police had frequently broken up union meetings, destroyed their literature, and run union organizers out of town. By a vote of 5 to 2, the Court found the ordinance unconstitutional, although the majority disagreed as to why. Justice Roberts, joined by Black, found that access to public streets and parks for peaceable assembly had "from ancient times been a part of the privileges, immunities, rights and liberties of citizens." While such use might be regulated in the public interest, it could not, "under the guise of regulation, be abridged." Justices Stone and Reed objected to the privileges and immunities rationale, preferring to support the result through the Due Process Clause. Chief Justice Hughes thought the new labor laws by themselves protected the organizers, though he tended to agree with Stone's opinion. Justice McReynolds, joined by Butler in dissent, called for judicial restraint, since "the management of such intimate local affairs, generally at least, is beyond the competency of federal courts."

Neither *Senn* nor *Hague* determined conclusively whether the First Amendment provided special protection for labor activities, and the Court itself could not seem to make up its mind just what it meant. In 1941, the Court categorized picketing as speech in striking down an Illinois law prohibiting picketing by persons not directly involved in the labor dispute; the following year, it ruled that a union could not be prohibited from peaceful picketing even in the absence of a normal type of labor dispute. A majority of the Court did not view picketing *per se* as a fully protected constitutional right, however. In another 1941 opinion, Justice Frankfurter noted that freedom of speech, although basic to American society, can in the context of violence "lose its significance as an appeal to reason and become part of an instrument of force." States could, therefore, restrain picketing that caused violence or the destruction of property. Joined by Reed and Douglas, Black dissented, concerned that the injunction went beyond merely prohibiting violence to stopping public discussion of important issues.

Similarly, the Court refused to exempt public meetings from all state control, although it did intervene where local laws clearly discriminated against certain groups. In *Thomas v. Collins* (1945), for example, Justice Rutledge voided a Texas statute requiring labor union officials to secure an organizer's card from local town officials before soliciting for members. (In this case, a CIO organizer had addressed a mass meeting of oil workers and had openly sought members, despite a restraining order from a local court.) Rutledge held that the law was an invalid interference with free speech and assembly, which, as part of the First Amendment, had "a sanctity and a sanction not permitting dubious intrusions." Significantly, Justice Roberts, joined by Frankfurter, Stone, and Reed, dissented; they claimed that a state could license public meetings so as to maintain peace and order, provided it did so in a neutral manner. Within a few years, the dissenters would gain a majority on the Court.

Religion

Even more than labor, dissident religious groups benefited enormously from the Roosevelt Court's concern with civil liberties. The First Amendment provides that "Congress shall make no law . . . prohibiting the free exercise" of religion, but practically no case law on the subject existed prior to the 1930s. As John Adams had so fervently wished, Congress had paid no attention to religion, except for laws passed after the Civil War attacking the Mormon practice of bigamy in the Utah Territory. A Mormon challenge on the grounds that the ban interfered with free exercise of religion received no sympathy from the Court (*Reynolds v. United States* [1879]). A few years later, a unanimous court in *Davis v. Beason* (1890), upheld the Idaho Territory's disenfranchisement of those who advocated or practiced plural marriage. Although nearly every state's bill of rights had some guarantee of religious freedom, dissident sects complained that a variety of police laws in effect denied them religious freedom.

Jehovah's Witnesses, for example, included household solicitation, sale of publications, parades, and public meetings to gain new adherents as part of their religious practices. None of these activities by themselves seemed noxious to local authorities, but all of them fell under either state or local regulations that were long accepted as part of the police power. Although there is no reason to assume that the Witnesses could not have secured the necessary permits (many of which required no more than simple registration with a clerk), they refused to apply, since they denied the legitimacy of temporal authorities in this area. The Witnesses read the *Palko* decision as an invitation to nationalize all the First Amendment freedoms.

The first Witness case came before the Court in *Lovell v. Griffin* (1938), and Chief Justice Hughes, for a unanimous Court, struck down a city ordinance that prohibited the distribution of pamphlets or other literature without permission from the city manager. Hughes hardly even mentioned religious freedom, but declared the ordinance "invalid on its face . . . [because] it strikes at the very foundation of the freedom of the press by subjecting it to license and censorship." The following year, in *Schneider v. Irvington*, the Court extended the *Lovell* ruling to set aside several ordinances prohibiting door-to-door solicitation or distribution without permission of the local police. Once again, the majority, this time through Justice Roberts, decided the case on the more established rules of press freedom rather than on the Free Exercise Clause. But Roberts did take the first step in implementing Stone's *Carolene Products* note, calling on courts to scrutinize any regulation of personal rights with heightened attention.

The Court finally gave the Witnesses a victory based on the Free Exercise Clause in *Cantwell v. Connecticut* (1940). The state prohibited solicitation of money for any charitable or religious cause without approval by the secretary of the public welfare council, who had the power to determine if the applicants represented a legitimate religion before granting approval. Justice Roberts, for a unanimous bench, invalidated the law as a violation of religious liberty under the Due Process Clause of the Fourteenth Amendment, another step in incorporating the Bill of Rights. The state certainly had the power to license solicitors, Roberts ruled, even for religious causes; but the arbitrary power of the secretary created a censorship over religion inconsistent with religious freedom.

Cantwell also expanded the doctrine, first enunciated in the 1879 Mormon case, differentiating between belief and action. In the earlier case, Chief Justice Waite had declared that Congress could pass no law attempting to restrict belief, but that it could limit conduct if such behavior threatened public order or safety. As an example, Waite suggested that if people wanted to believe in human sacrifice, they could do so; but the state certainly had the power to prevent their conducting such a rite. Roberts confirmed that freedom to believe came totally within the protection of the First Amendment, but that freedom to act had to be balanced against social needs. Where no compelling reason existed to limit conduct, believers should be free to act. Although this distinction, which remains a core principle of free exercise jurisprudence, made a good deal of sense, it left the determination of priorities to the subjective judgment of the courts, and in the next few years, Jehovah's Witnesses saw how much this judgment could fluctuate.

The Flag Salute Cases

Two weeks after *Cantwell*, Justice Frankfurter balanced the need for religious freedom against the community's needs and found for the latter in *Minersville School District v. Gobitis* (1940). Two Witness children had refused to salute the flag, since the Witnesses considered such an act proscribed by the biblical command against worshiping graven images. The local board of education then expelled the Gobitis children, and since their parents could not afford to enroll them in a private school, they stood in violation of the state's compulsory education law. Frankfurter admitted that the case posed a dilemma between community interests and individual rights, but he apparently had little trouble choosing. With Europe already at war and Americans worried that the United States would soon be involved, the government had the right, indeed the duty, to foster "national unity [as] the basis of national security." Such unity could be strengthened by symbols such as the flag, which "transcended all internal differences, no matter however large." The state had chosen to emphasize the importance of the flag, and the courts should accordingly defer to that judgment.

The *Gobitis* case, one of the earliest examples of Justice Frankfurter treating civil liberties in the same manner as economic legislation, drew a sharp and anguished retort from Justice Stone. In his lone dissent, Stone charged that the mandatory flag salute suppressed freedom of speech as well as religion and coerced children "to express a sentiment violative of their deepest religious convictions." Here the political processes, which Frankfurter depended on to rectify repression, would never afford the Witnesses relief, especially in the light of the patriotic fervor sweeping the country; only the courts could protect minority rights in such a situation. This last comment apparently came in response to a letter from Frankfurter, explaining that the majority opinion would

> To stigmatize legislative judgment in providing for this universal gesture of respect for the symbol of our national life in the setting of the common school as a lawless inroad on that freedom of conscience which the Constitution protects, would amount to no less than the pronouncement of pedagogical and psychological dogma in a field where courts possess no marked and certainly no controlling competence. . . . To the legislature no less than to courts is committed the guardianship of deeply cherished liberties.
>
> —Felix Frankfurter, *Minersville School District v. Gobitis* (1940)

preach "the true democratic faith of not relying on the Court for the impossible task of assuring a . . . tolerant democracy," a task that properly belonged to "the people and their representatives."

The Witnesses, however, refused to compromise their beliefs, even in the face of public scorn and judicial rebuffs. The following year, in *Cox v. New Hampshire*, a unanimous Court, speaking through Chief Justice Hughes, upheld a state regulation requiring a permit for parades. Regulation of street use had long been a traditional power of local government, and the New Hampshire statute did not vest arbitrary power in the licensing board; it merely provided for regulation in order to prevent traffic congestion and other inconveniences.

In *Chaplinsky v. New Hampshire* (1942), the Court unanimously sustained the conviction of a Witness who had gotten into a fight after calling a city marshal "a God damned racketeer" and "a damned Fascist." The statute in question had enacted the old common law "fighting words" doctrine: "No person shall address any offensive, derisive or annoying words to any other person who is lawfully in any street or other public place, nor call him by any offensive or derisive name." The state court had interpreted this to mean "words likely to cause an average person to fight," and the Supreme Court, through Justice Murphy, agreed that Chaplinsky's words would likely "provoke the average person to retaliation." Murphy went on to point out that the First Amendment's protection of free speech had never been intended to cover certain types of speech. "These include the lewd and obscene, the profane, the libelous, and the insulting or 'fighting' words. . . . Such utterances are no essential part of any exposition of ideas."

That same year, in *Jones v. Opelika*, a majority of the Court upheld the validity of municipal license fees imposed on transient merchants or book peddlers. Since the Witnesses sold books and the law imposed a fee on all peddlers, Justice Reed saw no reason to exclude those whose product had a religious message. Once again Stone, now chief justice, dissented, terming the Opelika ordinance worse than the Connecticut law that had been voided in *Lovell*, since there one did not have to pay money to exercise one's freedom of speech. Significantly, Justices Black, Douglas, and Murphy joined in Stone's dissent, and took the extraordinary step of repenting their vote in *Gobitis*.

By then, despite the general popular hostility toward the Witnesses, many within the legal profession had begun to rethink the implications of the flag salute case, especially after the United States entered the war against fascism. The flag salute could hardly compare to the thought control and repression practiced in Nazi Germany, but any unwarranted intrusion on personal liberty in the name of the state struck many people as totally unjustified. On the Court, sentiment also began to swing the other way. James Byrnes, after a brief and undistinguished year on the bench, gladly resigned to take up duties as an administrative assistant in the White House. To replace him, Roosevelt named Wiley Rutledge, a member of the Court of Appeals for the District of Columbia who had a definite sympathy for civil liberties and free speech.

In May 1943, Rutledge joined the four dissenters in *Opelika* to reverse that ruling in *Murdock v. Pennsylvania*. Justice Douglas, in the majority opinion, claimed that a tax on peddling religious tracts too closely resembled a tax imposed on a preacher for "the privilege of delivering a sermon." Douglas also advanced the preferred freedoms doctrine by categorically stating that "freedom of press, freedom of speech, freedom of religion, are in a preferred position."

The climax came in June 1943, when the Court reversed *Gobitis* in *West Virginia State Board of Education v. Barnette*. The earlier case had led to numerous instances of persecution, including some physical assaults, inflicted on Witness children because of their devotion to their faith, a situation that could hardly win approval as news leaked out about Hitler's "Final Solution" to the "Jewish problem." Both the ABA Committee on the Bill of Rights and the ACLU filed briefs supporting the Witnesses, and Justice Jackson, normally an ally of Frankfurter, joined the liberals and wrote one of the most eloquent opinions of his judicial career.

Much to Frankfurter's anger, Jackson, who found the central issue to be less one of religious liberty than of freedom of speech, used Holmes's clear and present danger test to justify his decision. The Witnesses' refusal to salute the flag hurt no one, it did not violate the rights of other people, and it posed no danger to public order or to the state. To sustain the requirement of the flag salute would be to pervert the meaning of the Bill of Rights, whose whole purpose, he claimed, had been to place essential freedoms such as speech, press, and religion beyond the reach of the legislature.

The swing over to the side of individual rights did not go unprotested. The minority in *Murdock* and in another 1943 Witness case, *Martin v. Struthers* (in which the Court by a 5–4 vote struck down a local ordinance prohibiting door-to-door campaigns to distribute religious tracts), emphasized the need of the state to preserve public order, and they took a relatively restricted view of the reach of the Bill of Rights. Justice Reed, for example, argued in his *Murdock* dissent that the Framers had intended freedom of speech to ensure the right to be heard, and freedom of religion to protect ritual; the First Amendment ought not be interpreted to exclude speech, press, or religion from the general rules of society. Jackson, aside from the second flag salute case,

> The very purpose of the Bill of Rights was to withdraw certain subjects from the vicissitudes of political controversy, to place them beyond the reach of majorities and officials and to establish them as legal principles to be applied by the courts. . . . If there is any fixed star in our constitutional constellation, it is that no official, high or petty, can prescribe what shall be orthodoxy in politics, nationalism, religion or other matters of opinion or force citizens to confess by word or act their faith therein.
>
> —Robert H. Jackson, *West Virginia Board of Education v. Barnette* (1943)

also found himself with the minority. The Constitution, he asserted in his dissent in *Douglas v. Jeannette* (1943), did not allow one religious group to ride "roughshod over others simply because their consciences told them to do so." Sharp dissents also came from Frankfurter, who urged restraint upon the Court. In terms that the Four Horsemen would have approved, he cautioned that the legislature had to have the greatest possible discretion to protect the community against abuse.

Civil Liberties in Wartime

Civil libertarians, remembering the Wilson administration's attacks on speech and press and the Palmer campaign against aliens, dreaded the prospect of American involvement in another war. The fact that war required some limits on individual rights could hardly be denied, although opinions varied widely on where to draw the line. Many people wanted to shut down the activities of American fascist groups, and the administration did investigate, harass, and suppress the speech of pro-Nazi speakers. As historian Richard Steele noted, "the dozens victimized for their utterances and associations during World War II did not approach the thousands prosecuted for sedition during World War I." But the memory of the excesses of the earlier war remained vivid in the minds of Justice Department officials, and for the most part they refused to prosecute all but the most pro-Nazi groups.

The example of the European dictatorships provided a salutary warning of what should not be allowed to happen here. Despite the Dies Committee's calls to act against dissidents (see the next chapter), the president's public promise to sustain free speech and press, the definite civil liberties commitment of Attorney General Francis Biddle, and the absence (except on the West Coast) of the antialien hysteria that had swept the country in 1917–1918, all contributed to sustaining a relatively healthy civil liberties climate during the war.

The Supreme Court shared these concerns. Even before the war broke out it had sent signals that it would not contemplate state disregard of essential personal liberties. In *DeJonge v. Oregon* (1937), the Court unanimously struck down the state's criminal syndicalism law after local police, at the instigation of conservative government officials, had broken up a peaceful meeting sponsored by the Communists. In that same term, a divided Court reversed the conviction of Angelo Herndon, a black Communist party organizer attempting to organize integrated workers, who had been charged with attempting to overthrow the government of Georgia. The evidence, according to Justice Roberts, showed no clear and present danger, nor did it even show any tendency toward violence. The statute merely served as a "dragnet which may enmesh anyone who agitates for a change of government" (*Herndon v. Lowry* [1937]).

Since many of the worst abuses during World War I had resulted from prosecutions of alleged subversives under state criminal laws, the Roosevelt administration moved quickly to assert sole federal control over internal security, mainly through the Alien Registration Act of 1940. At the 1940 Governors' Conference, the states acceded to the administration's request that all enforcement of internal security essentially be left in the hands of the federal government. A few months later, the Supreme Court confirmed federal supremacy in *Hines v. Davidowitz* (1941). The Court overturned a

Pennsylvania alien registration law on the grounds that the federal statute had preempted the field. Attorney General Biddle promoted a policy of cooperation between federal and state law enforcement agencies, but he made it clear that the states should leave alien control, sedition, and other security-related matters to the national government.

The justices, while recognizing the need of the government to protect itself, wanted to ensure that there would be no repetition of the earlier wartime excesses. The Justice Department, for example, sought to control the activities of naturalized citizens of German and Italian origin who had manifested either disloyal or merely dissident behavior. The government sought to revoke their citizenship on the grounds that current disloyal behavior proved they had secured citizenship either illegally or under false pretenses. Within a year of American entry into the war, the Justice Department had initiated over 2,000 investigations, and had secured the denaturalization of forty-two people.

As it turned out, the case testing this campaign, *Schneiderman v. United States* (1943), involved neither a Nazi nor a Fascist sympathizer, but a Communist; the government based its case on the claim that his Communist party membership proved that the defendant did not have the "true faith and allegiance to the United States" which citizenship demanded. Wendell Willkie, the 1940 Republican candidate for president, represented Schneiderman and eloquently pleaded with the Court not to establish the principle that a person could be punished for alleged adherence to abstract principles. For a 6 to 3 majority, Justice Murphy rejected the government's case. While naturalization constituted a privilege granted by Congress, once a person became a citizen, he or she enjoyed all the rights guaranteed by the Constitution, especially freedom of thought and expression. Membership in the Communist party had not been illegal at the time Schneiderman had taken out his papers, nor had it been established that current membership was "absolutely incompatible" with loyalty to the Constitution. In order to denaturalize a person, the government had to provide "clear, unequivocal and convincing evidence" of illegality or fraud, a burden it had failed to carry. Surprisingly, Chief Justice Stone dissented, finding Communist membership proof of disloyalty; less surprisingly, justices Frankfurter and Jackson joined in the dissent.

Only a year later, the Court reversed another denaturalization order, this time unanimously (*Baumgartner v. United States* [1944]). The Justice Department thought it had met the *Schneiderman* test in a case involving a naturalized German, who had embraced Nazi doctrines of racial superiority after he had become an American citizen in 1932. Although Justice Frankfurter delivered the Court's decision, the concurring opinion of Justice Murphy, joined by Black, Douglas, and Rutledge, indicated how far the nation had progressed from the antialien madness of the first war. Murphy noted that the gift of citizenship is not granted on condition that the new citizen forego any future criticism of his newly adopted land; nor can he or she be punished for later criticism, even if it involves vituperative or defamatory language. "The naturalized citizen has as much right as the natural-born citizen to exercise the cherished freedoms of speech, press, and religion." Not until *Knauer v. United States* in 1946 did the Court uphold a denaturalization order. In this case, however, the government presented conclusive evidence that at the time he had sought American citizenship, Knauer had been seeking to promote Nazism in the United States.

The Court also proved cool to prosecutions arising under the old Espionage Act of 1917, with its laundry list of subversive activities apparently aimed as much at punishing deviant behavior as at catching spies or traitors. In *Hartzel v. United States* (1944), a 5 to 4 vote overturned the conviction of a man who had distributed racist literature vilifying Jews, Englishmen, and the president and calling on the United States to form an alliance with Nazi Germany. Although the literature had reached the hands of army officers, Justice Murphy ruled that the government had failed to prove that the petitioner had intended to subvert the war effort. Murphy insisted on a literal application of the clear and present danger test, and despite the scurrilous nature of the material, he pointed out that Hartzel's activities had posed no real danger. The Court's insistence in this and other cases that the government show a clear and present danger, with clear, unequivocal and convincing evidence, for the most part discouraged the Justice Department from prosecuting persons merely for voicing unpopular or even noxious doctrines.

Treason and Espionage

When it came to real spies and traitors, the Court still insisted that the spirit and letter of the law be maintained; but it also recognized that such cases might properly belong within the realm of military justice, in which different criteria of evidence, procedure, and guilt prevailed. The first case, *Ex parte Quirin* (1942), arose out of the arrest of eight Germans put ashore from submarines on Long Island and Florida, with orders to sabotage industrial plants. The Federal Bureau of Investigation and the Coast Guard quickly arrested all eight, a military tribunal tried them for violating the rules of war, found them guilty, and sentenced six of them to death. In the midst of the trial, however, seven of the Nazis sought writs of habeas corpus, and the Supreme Court agreed to hear arguments at a special session convened during its summer recess. After hearing the arguments, the Court promptly denied the appeal without explaining its reasons; three months later, when the Court convened for the October 1942 term, Chief Justice Stone delivered a written opinion joined by all his brethren.

The rather elaborate opinion said, in essence, that under the war powers, the president could establish military commissions that had the appropriate jurisdiction to try such cases. But Stone went far beyond restating what by then amounted to a truism; he also rebutted all the points raised by the Nazis' counsel, pointing to thirteen separate clauses in the Constitution that undergirded the war powers. He did imply, however, that even spies and prisoners of war had some rights under the Constitution. This last assumption had no legal basis at all, for nowhere in English or American legal history could one find evidence that enemy military personnel had any of the rights belonging to citizens. Ever since the American Revolution, the United States had always tried enemy personnel in wartime by summary military procedures, a fact known to and accepted by the Framers of the Constitution.

Perhaps in the midst of a war against totalitarianism, the Court wanted to make a statement that even with the nation under attack, Americans would not ignore the Constitution and its safeguards. As it turned out, the Court never developed the implications of *Quirin*, such as the possibility that the Constitution would follow the flag and

> Constitution makes President Supreme Commander and Congress can carry on war. Time out of mind it is within the power of Commander-in-Chief to hang a spy. Articles of War recognize that there is a law of war. He would say the whole history of army shows there is a law (common) of war—waging war—by all usages they were not prisoners of war. Bound to give some play to Executive as to an administrative agency.
>
> —Hugo L. Black, memorandum on *Ex parte Quirin* (1942)

extend its protections into captured Axis territory. In 1946, the Court backed away from this possibility in *In re Yamashita*. A Japanese general appealed his military conviction for war crimes, claiming that his summary military trial did not meet the requirements of the Fifth Amendment. Chief Justice Stone, speaking for a 7 to 2 majority, declared that Yamashita had no constitutional rights at all, nor any standing in American civil courts; his conviction could only be appealed to a higher military authority.

The Court also had to deal with a handful of treason cases. No case involving treason had previously come before the high court, although ever since the Burr trial, it had been an accepted principle of American law that only the relatively narrow definition in Article III, Section 3—"levying War against [the United States], or in adhering to their Enemies, giving them Aid and Comfort"—could be applied, and, as constitutionally mandated, confirmation by two witnesses or open confession was required for conviction.

The first two cases grew out of the saboteurs incident. Two of the eight Nazis had managed, before their arrest, to make contact with two Americans, who they hoped would assist in their plans. The FBI arrested the two Americans, one a friend and the other the father of one of the Nazis, and charged them with treason. At the trial of the friend, Cramer, two FBI agents testified that they had witnessed Cramer meeting with the saboteurs, that he had taken a meal with them, and that he had offered to handle their money. The government claimed that these acts constituted giving aid and comfort to the enemy and that the testimony of the FBI agents met the constitutional requirement of two witnesses. The trial judge agreed and so interpreted the law to the jury, which returned a verdict of guilty.

By a 5 to 4 vote, the Supreme Court reversed the conviction in *Cramer v. United States* (1945). According to Justice Jackson, the overt act had to be traitorous in intent by itself, and not merely appear traitorous because of surrounding circumstances; meeting the saboteurs did not, by itself, manifest treason. Jackson's opinion included a lengthy scholarly summary of the law of treason, from the early days through World War I; he concluded that the Founding Fathers had intended a restrictive definition. Jackson certainly had some authority to support this view, but as Justice Douglas's dissent pointed out, it added another layer to the proof for treason. Two witnesses had to testify not only to the act, but also to the intent as well. Douglas claimed that Marshall's opinion in the Burr trial and Jackson's in the *Cramer* case had practically eliminated treason as a crime.

Two years later, in *Haupt v. United States* (1947), the Court reviewed the case of the other American, Hans Haupt, the father of one of the saboteurs, and upheld his conviction by an 8 to 1 vote. The evidence showed that Haupt had sheltered his son, gotten a car for him, and arranged for a job in a factory that manufactured the Norden bombsight. Under the *Cramer* criteria, Haupt's counsel argued, none of these acts were traitorous in themselves, but merely manifested the natural desire of a father to help his son. But Justice Jackson disagreed and described Haupt's activities as "steps essential to his design for treason," which "forward[ed] the saboteur in his mission." Only Justice Murphy dissented, claiming—correctly—that the Court had moved away from the strict tests it had earlier enunciated in *Cramer.*

The *Haupt* case, the first in which the Supreme Court sustained a treason conviction, permitted the government to prosecute other Americans who had aided the enemy during the war, such as Douglas Chandler, who had broadcast English-language programs from Berlin during the war. The Chandler case raised the issue of whether treason could take place only within the territorial limits of the United States; in *Kawakita v. United States* (1952), the Court ruled that treason encompassed activities by American citizens anywhere.

For Further Reading

There are a number of works that provide good introductory overviews to the growth of civil liberties jurisprudence in this era, including Paul L. Murphy, *The Constitution in Crisis Times, 1918–1969* (1972); Milton R. Konvitz, *Fundamental Liberties of a Free People: Religion, Speech, Press, Assembly* (1957); and Henry J. Abraham, *Freedom and the Court: Civil Rights and Liberties in the United States* (4th ed., 1982). Melvin I. Urofsky, *Division and Discord: The Supreme Court under Stone and Vinson, 1941–1953* (1997), provides a larger context in which to evaluate the Court's activities in this area.

The work of the La Follette committee is detailed in a fine monograph by Jerold S. Auerbach, *Labor and Liberty: The La Follette Committee and the New Deal* (1966). Labor and speech rights are explored in two articles by Joseph Tanenhaus, "Picketing as Free Speech: The Growth of the New Law of Picketing from 1940 to 1952," 38 *Cornell Law Quarterly* 1 (1952), and "Picketing as Free Speech: Early Stages in the Growth of the New Law of Picketing," 14 *University of Pittsburgh Law Review* 397 (1953).

For the incorporation controversy, see Richard C. Cortner, *The Supreme Court and the Second Bill of Rights* (1981). For the Cardozo and Frankfurter view, see Felix Frankfurter, "Memorandum on 'Incorporation' of the Bill of Rights into the Due Process Clause of the Fourteenth Amendment," 78 *Harvard Law Review* 746 (1965). For the differences between Black and Frankfurter see James F. Simon, *The Antagonists: Hugo Black, Felix Frankfurter and Civil Liberties in Modern America* (1989). For Justice Stone and the *Carolene Products* note, see Louis Luskin (Stone's clerk that term), "Footnote Redux: A Carolene Products Reminiscence," 82 *Columbia Law Review* 1093 (1982).

There are a number of biographies of Cardozo and the Roosevelt appointees that explore the question of incorporation as well as other important issues. For Cardozo see Andrew Kaufman, *Cardozo* (1998), which covers his entire life, and Richard Polenberg, *The World of Benjamin Cardozo: Personal Values and the Judicial Process* (1997), which examines key elements of his jurisprudence. Hugo Black is well served in both Roger K. Newman, *Hugo Black: A Biography* (1994), and Tinsley E. Yarborough, *Mr. Justice Black and His Critics* (1988). To understand Frankfurter on the bench, one has to start with his earlier career, which is excellently handled in Michael E. Parrish, *Felix Frankfurter and His Times: The Reform Years* (1982); for the Court years see Melvin I. Urofsky, *Felix Frankfurter: Judicial Restraint and Individual Liberties* (1991). Two provocative psychological interpretations are Harry N. Hirsch, *The Enigma of Felix Frankfurter* (1981), and Robert A. Burt, *Two Jewish Justices: Outcasts in the Promised Land* (1988).

William O. Douglas is one of the few members of the Court to have written memoirs; see his *Go East, Young Man: The Early Years* (1974) and *The Court Years, 1939–1975* (1980), as well as the fine biography by James F. Simon, *Independent Journey* (1980). See also Melvin I. Urofsky, "William O. Douglas as a Common Law Judge," 41 *Duke Law Journal* 133 (1991), and the large number of essays collected in Stephen L. Wasby, ed., *"He Shall Not Pass This Way Again": The Legacy of Justice William O. Douglas* (1990). Eugene Gerhart, *America's Advocate: Robert H. Jackson* (1958) is uncritical, and a good biography of this fascinating and important figure is needed. See also Glendon Schubert, *Dispassionate Justice: A Synthesis of the Judicial Opinions of Robert H. Jackson* (1969), and the symposium, "Mr. Justice Jackson," 8 *Stanford Law Review* 3 (1955). A recent work that places his judicial career in context is Jeffrey D. Hockett, *New Deal Justice: The Constitutional Jurisprudence of Hugo L. Black, Felix Frankfurter, and Robert H. Jackson* (1996).

The Jehovah's Witness cases are examined in Leo Pfeffer, *Church, State and Freedom* (rev. ed., 1967); Harry Kalven, "The Concept of the Public Forum," 1965 *Supreme Court Review* 1 (1966); and David Manwaring, *Render unto Caesar: The Flag Salute Controversy* (1962). Frankfurter's mindset is discussed in Richard Danzig, "Justice Frankfurter's Opinions in the Flag Salute Cases: Blending Logic and Psychologic in Constitutional Decisionmaking," 36 *Stanford Law Review* 675 (1984). Civil liberties in wartime in general are assessed in E. S. Corwin, *Total War and the Constitution* (1947). The prosecution of Nazi sympathizers is told in Richard W. Steele, *Free Speech in the Good War* (1999).

For treason, see the excellent survey by J. Willard Hurst, *The Law of Treason in the United States* (1971). The Nazi invasion case is analyzed in Cyrus Bernstein, "The Nazi Saboteur Trial: A Case History," 11 *George Washington Law Review* 131 (1943). The question of the reach of the Constitution is discussed in A. Frank Reel, *The Case of General Yamashita* (1949).

33

World War II

Neutrality Legislation • The Ludlow Amendment • Internal Security • Executive Agreements • Presidential Power • Organizing for War • The Court and Wartime Regulations • Anti-Japanese Sentiment • Japanese Relocation • The Relocation Cases • Milligan *Redux • The Judgment of History • The War Crimes Trials • The United Nations • For Further Reading*

FROM THE EARLY days of the republic, the major responsibility for the conduct of foreign affairs has belonged to the president. While Congress has a constitutional role to play, prior to the 1930s it had, with a few exceptions, deferred to executive leadership. But then the debate over American foreign policy in light of the growing Fascist menace led Congress to take unprecedented steps in that area, setting up a potential confrontation between the executive and legislative branches of government. The outbreak of war shifted power back to the White House, but in a new and vastly more expanded manner that reflected the complexities of modern life and also raised serious questions about traditional constitutional directives.

Neutrality Legislation

The shadow of World War I hung heavily over the New Deal; most Americans wanted nothing at all to do with Europe and argued that the country should not repeat the mistake of getting involved in a European war. As a result, Roosevelt discovered that his enormous political influence over Congress on domestic issues had no counterpart when it came to foreign policy. At the beginning of 1935, the president proposed that the United States join the World Court, a relatively innocuous suggestion that had more symbolic than real significance. Both Coolidge and Hoover had espoused a similar proposal, and with sixty-eight Democrats in the Senate, Roosevelt felt confident that the measure would pass easily. Instead, the isolationists mounted a full-scale campaign against the protocols. In the Senate debate, Thomas Schall of Minnesota shouted: "To hell with Europe and the rest of those nations!" Thousands of telegrams flooded the Senate, and when the vote came in February, the treaty failed by seven ballots, with twenty Democrats deserting their president.

Part of the defeat can be attributed to the Nye Committee's lurid exposés of how arms manufacturers and bankers had allegedly secured American intervention in the European fray in 1917. Instead of going to war to save the world for democracy, the committee concluded, the United States had entered the fighting "to save the skins of American bankers who had bet too boldly on the outcome of the war and had two billions of dollars of loans to the Allies in jeopardy." The Nye hearings did not create isolationism, but intensified determination that the errors of 1914–1917 would not be repeated. After Hitler announced plans to rearm Germany and Italy invaded Ethiopia in 1935, a concerned Congress enacted a series of neutrality laws to ensure that the United States would not get enmeshed in foreign wars.

Roosevelt did not necessarily oppose neutrality legislation, but he did want to preserve as much flexibility as possible. Instead of the total embargo of arms shipments that the isolationists demanded, Roosevelt wanted the discretion to decide whether an embargo should be imposed and against which nations. Congress, however, saw this as too akin to the old Wilsonian distinction between "good" and "bad" nations, and refused to give the president what he wanted. The 1935 Neutrality Act required an embargo on implements of war (but not all war materials) whenever the president found that a state of war existed; it also warned Americans traveling on the ships of belligerent nations that they did so at their own risk. Never before had Congress so shackled the executive's hands in the conduct of foreign policy. It marked a complete reversal of the traditional division of responsibilities, in that the legislative branch had defined the nation's foreign policy—at least for the time being.

Many isolationists, however, proved as troubled as the president by the statute's lack of discretionary authority, especially after Roosevelt, following the precise letter of the law, imposed a blanket arms embargo after the Italian invasion of Ethiopia and the outbreak of the Spanish Civil War. When the 1935 act expired the following year, isolationists in Congress differed so much among themselves that for the moment they could only agree on extending the earlier legislation. Yet despite the growth of fascism, isolationist sentiment peaked in 1937, and Congress passed a new law further restraining arms sales and bank loans to belligerents, forbidding American travel on belligerent ships, and prohibiting the arming of American merchant ships trading with warring nations. But the statute at least gave the president some leeway in that goods other than munitions could, at his discretion, be exported to belligerents on a cash-and-carry basis.

The Ludlow Amendment

The most extreme effort by isolationists came after the *Panay* incident. On December 12, 1937, Japanese planes bombed an American gunboat, clearly marked with American flags, lying at anchor in the Yangtze River. Fighter planes then strafed the ship, killing three men and seriously wounding eleven more. Two hours later, the *Panay* sank. Japan quickly apologized, and the administration found the American people preferred to withdraw our forces from China rather than make Japan respect our rights there.

Worried that Roosevelt would use the incident to provoke a war, congressional isolationists revived a proposal that Representative Louis Ludlow had introduced earlier, a constitutional amendment to prevent the United States from going to war, except in case of invasion, unless a majority of the people voted to do so in a referendum. The proposal had been bottled up in the House Judiciary Committee, but two days after the *Panay* sank, a discharge petition mustered enough votes to bring it to the floor of the House. Roosevelt sent a strongly worded letter to the Speaker of the House warning that the amendment "would cripple any President in his conduct of our foreign relations." By bringing enormous pressure on Democratic members, the president in late January 1938, managed to prevent the amendment from being brought to the floor of the House, by a vote of 209 to 188

The victory indicated the reappearance of a chief executive intent on regaining control of foreign policy, but the closeness of the vote showed the strength of the isolationist bloc. Although Roosevelt had staved off a complete crippling of executive authority, he could not secure the revisions he wanted in the Neutrality Act. When Hitler invaded Poland in September 1939, the 1937 law was still on the books. The president, as required by the statute, declared that a state of war existed and imposed an arms embargo on the Allies as well as on the Axis.

On September 21, Roosevelt called Congress into special session and asked it to amend the Neutrality Act. This time he got what he wanted. Under the 1939 Neutrality Law, the Allies could buy war goods for cash and take them home on their own ships; American vessels remained prohibited from the war zones. "What the majority of the American people want," *The Nation* noted, "is to be as unneutral as possible without getting into the war." The isolationists had tried as hard as possible to keep the United States out of the fray; the Congress they controlled had temporarily wrested direction of foreign policy out of executive hands. As American involvement in the war loomed closer, the executive not only regained what had been lost, but also began expanding presidential power.

Internal Security

Despite the neutrality legislation, Roosevelt had not been altogether passive. In the summer of 1936, the president had met with J. Edgar Hoover, director of the Federal Bureau of Investigation, who told him that the government had no intelligence data on either Communist or Fascist activities in the country. Acting on the president's orders, the bureau, in cooperation with the Department of State, began secretly collecting data on potential subversives. In the next few years, the government secured important information on the identities and activities of foreign agents and made good use of those files when the nation later went to war.

Congress had similar concerns about subversion, but patriotic zealots there acted with little sense of restraint. In May 1938, the House created a special Committee on Un-American Activities under the chairmanship of Martin Dies of Texas. The highly partisan committee charged that the national government had been riddled with Communists, radicals, and other dangerous persons, whom only a thoroughgoing exposure would eliminate. Despite promises from Dies to observe fundamental procedural rights, the committee rode roughshod over civil liberties in its headlong rush to ferret out alleged radicals. It accomplished nothing in terms of identifying subversives, and like other witch hunts, it often smeared innocent people.

Roosevelt, disgusted with the Dies Committee from the start, took much of the wind out of its sails by openly authorizing the FBI to investigate the German-American Bund and other groups, under the Foreign Agents Registration Act. Through executive order, he also gave the bureau official supervision of all espionage investigations. As the threat of war increased, congressional concern led to other action, some of it of dubious value. In 1939, Congress tacked on to the Hatch Act a provision prohibiting the employment of Communists by the government. In March 1940, Congress updated the 1917 Espionage Act by adding penalties for peacetime violations. In June, an Alien Registration Act aimed primarily at Communists included a section allowing the Justice Department to prosecute not only those actually conspiring to overthrow the government, but also anyone who advocated or conspired to advocate its overthrow. Although the government registered and fingerprinted five million aliens, it did so courteously and sympathetically. The two attorneys general responsible for alien registration, Robert Jackson and Francis Biddle, tried not to offend the rights and sensibilities of these persons, the large majority of whom proved completely loyal to the nation.

The fact that the FBI had taken effective steps against subversion did not appease congressional critics. Even after the country declared war, Dies continued his tirades against alleged Reds in government; in 1943, he attached a rider to an important appropriations bill barring three supposed Communists, Goodwin B. Watson, William E. Dodd, Jr., and Robert Morss Lovett, from the federal payroll. Roosevelt denounced the rider as a bill of attainder, but because the money bill could not be delayed, he reluctantly signed it. In 1946, a unanimous Court struck down the provision in *United States v. Lovett*. Justice Black ruled that Congress had plainly tried to punish the three men without a judicial trial, and he ordered the government to reimburse them for back pay.

Executive Agreements

Roosevelt had never been afraid to exercise power, and as the international situation worsened, he assumed that the Constitution gave him powers as commander-in-chief to meet the emergency. Despite the isolationists' efforts to prevent involvement in foreign wars, no one seriously challenged the idea that the president had primary responsibility for directing foreign policy. The Supreme Court, in *United States v. Curtiss-Wright Export Corporation* (1936), had noted the "plenary and exclusive power of the President as the sole organ of the federal government in foreign relations," a phrase reminiscent of John Marshall's description many decades earlier. In addition, Justice Sutherland ruled that the president's control over foreign relations did not rely on any act of Congress, but derived independently from the Constitution.

There has been considerable criticism of *Curtiss-Wright*, both for its logic and its history. The case arose after Congress had delegated authority to the president to declare an arms embargo in Latin America if he found that to do so would "contribute to the reestablishment of peace" between belligerents. The previous year, the Court had twice struck down what it termed excessive delegation in domestic matters, and the only question the Court faced involved whether Congress could delegate more broadly in international affairs. The case never should have involved the existence of an independent presidential power, since the litigants raised only the question of whether Congress had exceeded its powers.

Sutherland's opinion closely tracks an article he had written as a senator in 1910 and published in his 1919 book, *Constitutional Power and World Affairs.* There and in other places, Sutherland advocated a vigorous—even belligerent—diplomacy that unceasingly asserted American rights. In the opinion, Sutherland claimed that only the federal government had any control over foreign affairs, and with the exception of the advise and consent powers of the Senate, all foreign powers resided in the executive branch. Scholars have attacked both the history on which Sutherland relied, showing that the states did not give up all of their powers following the Revolution and that the Constitution grants Congress a large voice in foreign policy, including the power of the purse. The Framers, it is claimed, made no such distinction between foreign and domestic affairs, and certainly in modern times, the line is often difficult to discern.

Roosevelt began to expand his foreign policy prerogatives in the mid-1930s by negotiating a set of secret executive agreements with Great Britain and France to establish cooperative defense arrangements. After the outbreak of the war in 1939, he used executive agreements to fashion foreign policy and avoid confronting isolationist opposition in the Senate. In October 1939, the United States and nineteen Latin American countries agreed to the Declaration of Panama, which established a "neutrality belt" around the western hemisphere. In August 1941, Roosevelt and British Prime Minister Winston Churchill issued the famous Atlantic Charter, which set out the war aims of the United Nations.

The most famous executive agreement involved an exchange of destroyers for naval bases in September 1940. Britain had lost nearly half the ships it needed to defend her home waters, and Churchill pleaded with the president for some fifty or sixty "over-age" World War I destroyers to use against Nazi submarines. Roosevelt wanted to help, but he worried not only that the ships might be needed for American defense, but that providing warships to a belligerent would violate international law and be seen as an act of war. Moreover the Walsh Act, passed in June 1940, allowed the sale of older vessels only if the navy certified them as useless for defense; naval officers, in order to prevent Congress from scrapping the destroyers, had just testified that the ships still had defense value. If Roosevelt sought approval for the deal from Congress, isolationists might easily have blocked the sale.

Roosevelt bypassed the Congress by negotiating an executive agreement in which the United States traded fifty old destroyers for the use of British bases in Newfoundland, Bermuda, and the Caribbean. Attorney General Robert Jackson prepared a memorandum assuring military leaders that they could certify the ships as nonessential to national security, since the bases the nation would receive in return would be far more valuable for that purpose. Although most Americans approved of the deal—even some of the isolationists welcomed the expanded control over nearby waters that the bases made possible—critics attacked Roosevelt for the method he had chosen. He had, they

> Suppose my neighbor's home catches fire, and I have a length of garden hose four or five hundred feet away. If he can take my garden hose and connect it up with his hydrant, I may help him to put out his fire. Now what do I do? I don't say to him before that operation, "Neighbor, my garden hose cost me $15; you have to pay me $15 for it." What is the transaction that goes on? I don't want $15—I want my garden hose back after the fire is over.
>
> —Franklin D. Roosevelt, Explaining Lend-Lease (1940)

claimed, flouted the congressional will, transgressed international law, and ignored the public. "Mr. Roosevelt today committed an act of war," fumed the *St. Louis Post-Dispatch.* "He also became America's first dictator." But the president's supporters applauded his willingness to bypass outmoded conventions of international law when Britain's very survival depended on quick action. To them, he had displayed statesmanship of the highest order.

The constitutional questions surrounding the destroyer-bases deal have been largely ignored due to the brilliant success of the scheme. A case can be made, however, that the transfer violated the intent of Congress as statutorily expressed in the Walsh Act. Attorney General Jackson had to distort words in the law that were otherwise plain in meaning to conclude that the destroyers could be disposed of if more valuable properties for the national defense could be secured. The possibility that the delivery of warships, even overage ones, to a belligerent might involve the United States in war would, on its face, seem sufficient justification to have the matter approved either by Congress through statute or at least by the Senate through treaty ratification. In fact, Roosevelt hesitated a long time before consenting to the transfer by executive agreement, because he feared that it might prove constitutionally defective.

Presidential Power

By the fall of 1940, many Americans considered the United States a nonbelligerent rather than a neutral nation, involved in everything except the actual fighting. Roosevelt had declared a limited national emergency on September 8, 1939, to, as he put it, "make wholly constitutional and legal certain necessary measures." In May 1941, he proclaimed an "unlimited" emergency to justify additional measures for the defense of the Western Hemisphere.

What these declarations meant, and what constitutional basis they relied on, remained uncertain. After the first decree in 1939, the Senate asked the attorney general to explain what, if any, additional executive powers the president now had. Frank Murphy refused to be specific but maintained that "the constitutional duties of the Executive carry with them the constitutional powers necessary for their proper performance." And so the "adequacy of the Constitution" theory, which had justified Lincoln's conduct of the Civil War, reappeared in modern garb. Roosevelt had argued from his very first day in office that the Constitution's broad and flexible grants of power gave the

American government in general—and the executive in particular—more than sufficient authority to meet any crisis.

Like Lincoln and Wilson before him, Roosevelt's assumption of broad authority under the war powers relied less on constitutional clauses than on public approval. So long as the citizenry perceived him as acting in the best interests of the country, they would support him regardless of what constitutional theories he invoked to justify his policies. If, however, the president lost this broad-based political support, it mattered little what he claimed the Constitution said. Roosevelt's extensive use of executive agreements and executive orders, revolutionary by themselves, masked the fact that more often than not he sought—and received—legislative authorization for his policies.

Much of the president's policy, in fact, could be constitutionally justified by the broad grants of authority that Congress delegated to the executive. The Neutrality Act of 1939 gave him the discretion he had sought in imposing embargoes, and the peacetime draft legislation passed in September 1940 expanded executive policy-making powers. The Lend-Lease Act of March 1941 not only repealed the cash-and-carry provisions of the 1939 Neutrality Act, but authorized the president to manufacture or procure any article needed for the defense of any country he deemed vital to American interests, and then to sell, lend, lease, exchange, or otherwise supply that article in any way that he thought proper. When he first proposed Lend-Lease, a reporter asked whether the concept would require congressional approval. "Oh, yes," the president replied, "this would require various types of legislation, in addition to appropriation."

In April of 1941, Roosevelt chose to ask Congress for authority to allow him to confiscate and make use of foreign merchant vessels in American ports. At the time, about 80 foreign ships lay idle in American ports, and another 150 in other ports in the hemisphere. Declining to act under his powers as commander-in-chief, the president stated that he lacked authority to seize the ships; Congress quickly provided the necessary legislation. Throughout the war, Roosevelt always preferred congressional validation and authority, but he had no hesitation in acting on what he perceived to be the broad powers of the presidency.

Some of Roosevelt's most important activities lacked statutory authorization. He utilized executive orders to embargo the shipment of aviation fuel and scrap metals to Japan and to freeze Japanese assets in the United States. His order in October 1939, establishing a "Neutrality Patrol" in the western Atlantic, derived from the traditional powers of the commander-in-chief to use the navy as an instrument of foreign policy, a tradition that went back to John Adams. Roosevelt ignored a seeming proscription in the Lend-Lease Act and ordered the navy to convoy merchant ships carrying war goods to Great Britain. In July 1941, the president sent American troops to Iceland as a result of an executive agreement with the new Republic of Iceland. Roosevelt now had to arrange for convoys for the supply ships to Iceland, convoys that also protected the delivery of Lend-Lease goods that were headed farther east.

As some critics warned, convoys meant shooting. In September 1941, in response to an alleged U-boat attack on the destroyer *Greer*, Roosevelt used his own authority as commander-in-chief to order the navy to hunt down German submarines. To some people, this appeared that the president, and not Congress, had declared war; whatever the technicalities may have been, no one doubted that a de facto state of hostilities existed between the two countries, without formal constitutional requirements having been met. Isolationists later charged that Roosevelt had deceitfully and unconstitutionally involved the country in war, by subverting the express will of Congress that the nation should remain neutral. Yet, like Lincoln before him, Roosevelt believed that the Constitution gave him the authority he needed to act; moreover, between 1939 and 1941, the mood of Congress shifted dramatically. The isolationists, triumphant in 1937, had the ground cut out from under them as Americans came to understand—and fear—the menace of fascism. Roosevelt may have been ahead of Congress on some issues, but the conflict that marked the prewar years soon dissipated. If Congress had really opposed Roosevelt's policy, it could have refused his requests on the draft or Lend-Lease and nullified his executive orders by legislation. Instead, public and congressional opinion endorsed his policies. How long this type of foreign policy management could have continued is difficult to say, but the Japanese attack on Pearl Harbor on the morning of December 7, 1941, focused all attention on the president, with both Congress and the nation looking to him for leadership.

Organizing for War

Less than two weeks after the attack on Pearl Harbor, Congress enacted the first War Powers Act, essentially reinstating the Overman Act of World War I and authorizing the president to reorganize the government almost any way he saw fit. Roosevelt had already created, by administrative order, the Office of Emergency Management in May 1940; it now became the coordinating agency for the vastly expanded wartime executive. All together, Roosevelt created some twenty-nine separate agencies to prosecute the war, such as the War Production Board, the Office of Civilian Defense, the War Manpower Commission, the Office of Defense Transportation, and others. These were counterparts of the Wilsonian war agencies, although on a vastly larger scale, and for the most part they ran fairly efficiently. Unlike 1917, the government now had a large body of experienced bureaucrats, and the statistics that had been collected by the National Recovery Administration and other New Deal agencies provided for the first time a detailed picture of the nation's manufacturing capacity. The United States could and must, in Roosevelt's words, become "the arsenal of democracy."

Direction of the government assumed a certain pattern. Congress passed legislation delegating broad authority to the president, often without the direction or restraints that the Supreme Court had declared necessary in the *Schechter* case. Roosevelt then

> It will not be sufficient for us and the other United Nations to produce a slightly superior supply of munitions to that of Germany, Japan and Italy. The superiority of the United Nations in munitions and ships must be overwhelming . . . a crushing superiority of equipment in any theater of the world war.
>
> —Franklin D. Roosevelt to Congress (1942)

established agencies or did whatever he thought was needed to further the war effort. The War Powers Act of December 1941, and a similar measure in March 1942, provided catchall authority for a variety of executive functions, from regulating production to impounding enemy property, from censoring overseas communications to requisitioning entire factories. The Emergency Price Control Act of January 1942 and the War Labor Disputes Act of June 1943 addressed more specific issues, but they too gave the commander-in-chief broad discretion in exercising vast powers.

Roosevelt not only exercised the powers Congress gave him, but, as he told the nation, he would utilize whatever powers he considered necessary to the successful prosecution of the war. At one point, Roosevelt warned that if Congress failed to repeal a portion of the Price Control Law, "I shall accept the responsibility, and I will act. . . . The President has the power, under the Constitution, and under Congressional acts, to take measures necessary to avert a disaster." But, he assured the people, he would always act with due regard to the Constitution, and "when the war is won, the powers under which I act automatically revert to the people—where they belong."

The Court and Wartime Regulations

Among the wartime agencies, the Office of Price Administration (OPA) had been created to carry out provisions of the Emergency Price Control Act of 1942. Congress had delegated sweeping power to set prices; it had also created an Emergency Court of Appeals with exclusive jurisdiction over challenges to OPA policies on price fixing, rationing, salary limits, and other controls. In *Yakus v. United States* (1944), the Supreme Court approved the creation of the Emergency Court and also validated the wide discretionary powers that Congress had delegated to the executive. Justices Rutledge and Murphy, however, argued that by denying the regular Title III courts authority to review the constitutionality of the regulations, Congress in effect had asked the judiciary to act unconstitutionally. The dissenters could not accept the majority argument that Congress had the power to limit appeals, both in terms of timeliness and venue, that is, which courts could hear an appeal and when. Shortly after the decision, Congress decided that perhaps the dissenters had been right and repealed the time and venue restrictions in the Stabilization Extension Act of 1944.

For the most part, however, the Roosevelt Court gave Congress and the administration an almost unrestricted power to regulate the wartime economy. In *Steuart and Company v. Bowles* (1944), the Court approved OPA sanctions that had suspended allotments of fuel oil to dealers who violated the rationing scheme. The failure to allow for any sort of judicial review obviously ran afoul of normal standards of procedural due process, but Justice Douglas interpreted the OPA order not as a punishment, but as a means to promote more efficient distribution of scarce resources. A little earlier in the year, in *Bowles v. Willingham* (1944), the Court had also sustained an OPA order freezing rental rates on apartments. When the nation calls on men and women to sacrifice their lives in war, it is not constitutionally obligated to "assure each landlord a 'fair return' on his property."

The sanctity of property rights, still a powerful doctrine in 1936, was replaced less than five years later by the view that property had to give way to other priorities established by the state and had to be subject to the state's police powers, or in case of war, to the war powers. The Court refused to second-guess the executive or legislative branches on what had to be done to win the war, and it sustained all challenges to the Price Control Act.

The most extreme exercise of federal authority over private property—presidential seizure of industrial plants—never came before the Supreme Court. Both Lincoln and Wilson had exercised similar authority; Lincoln had taken over some railroad and telegraph lines, while Wilson had acted when labor problems or managerial inefficiency had threatened war production. Neither president had specific statutory authority, but had relied on the constitutional powers allegedly available to the commander-in-chief in wartime.

Roosevelt invoked a similarly vague justification when he seized a California plant of the North American Aviation Company in June 1941—six months *before* Pearl Harbor—to break a strike that had crippled production of badly needed planes. He took over a half dozen other plants under the same war powers claim, until Congress granted him statutory authority in the War Disputes Act of 1943. Nearly forty additional seizures occurred under color of this act, but only one—the well-publicized takeover of nine Montgomery Ward plants—led to litigation in the lower courts. The government returned the property before an appeal could be carried to the high court.

If anything, the enormous authority wielded by the federal government between 1939 and 1945 proved again the marvelous elasticity of the Constitution. As in 1861 and 1917, tensions arose between the need to secure near dictatorial authority to prosecute the war and formal constitutional limitations on government—separation of powers and protection of individual rights. At every turn, the former won out over the latter, but neither Roosevelt nor Congress wanted to subvert civil liberties or destroy property rights. At all times, they justified their actions not just in light of wartime exigencies, but in constitutional terms as well. Like Lincoln and Wilson, Franklin Roosevelt had to bend the Constitution, but he did not break it.

Anti-Japanese Sentiment

As noted in the previous chapter, overall, the Supreme Court and the Roosevelt administration received high marks from civil libertarians during the war except in one area—the internment of Japanese-Americans. In the worst violation of civil liberties in American history, the government forcibly transferred 112,000 persons of Japanese origins—70,000 of them American citizens—away from their homes, jobs, and property, locked them in detention centers, and kept some of them there up to four years.

Immediately after the Japanese attack on Pearl Harbor in 1941, the general attitude toward the Japanese-American population, nearly all of whom lived on the West Coast, remained fairly tolerant. "Let's not get rattled," urged the *Los Angeles Times;* most of the Japanese in this country were "good Americans, born and educated as such," and the paper urged its readers that "there be no precipitations, no riots, no mob law." General John L. DeWitt, head of the Western Defense Command, termed the idea of evacuating Japanese from the coastal areas as "damned nonsense!"

But prejudice against the Japanese dated back decades before the war. After Congress passed the Chinese Exclusion Act in 1882, Californian nativists began a campaign to keep the Japanese out of the country too. Because of their small numbers, however, the Japanese initially attracted little attention, although they began to buy up small farms in supposedly barren areas, which through hard work they made enormously productive. Papers soon carried headlines and editorials on "the Yellow Peril," and in 1906, the San Francisco school board agreed to transfer all Japanese students to the segregated school already reserved for the Chinese.

Two years later, Theodore Roosevelt negotiated a "Gentlemen's Agreement," in which Japan agreed to limit the flow of male workers to the United States if Congress did not legislate to that effect. Exemptions in the agreement, however, allowed another 118,000 immigrants, including thousands of so-called mail-order or picture brides, to enter the country between 1908 and 1924. Anti-Japanese organizations now sought to bar further land purchases, and in 1913, the California legislature passed an Alien Land Law, prohibiting further purchases or leasing of land by aliens ineligible for citizenship.

Although Congress had never specifically excluded Asians from naturalization, it had referred in various laws to whites and Africans. Lower court judges had on a number of occasions interpreted the law as allowing the naturalization of Japanese immigrants. In *Ozawa v. United States* (1922), however, the Supreme Court unanimously put an end to this practice, ruling that Congress, by the wording of the statute, had not intended persons of other than white or of African ancestry to be eligible for naturalization. When Congress passed the Immigration Restriction Act of 1924, which reduced the quotas on nearly all groups, it singled out the Japanese for total exclusion, despite the protests of the State Department.

Given this background, it was little wonder that within six weeks of Pearl Harbor, the initial tolerance had given way to a full-throated cry to get Japanese-Americans, all of whom allegedly might be saboteurs or spies, away from the West Coast, which alarmists claimed would soon be invaded by the Emperor's forces. Although the government had no evidence of even a single instance of sabotage by a Japanese-American, public hysteria demanded that the military do something. General DeWitt, now eager to accommodate, began a campaign to secure approval for the mass removal of the Japanese, the same idea that he had recently denounced. The respected columnist Walter Lippmann, after a talk with DeWitt, informed his readers that "nobody's constitutional rights include the right to reside and do business on a battlefield. There is plenty of room elsewhere for him to exercise his rights." A few days later, the less restrained columnist Westbrook Pegler called for every Japanese man and woman to be put under armed guard, "and to hell with habeas corpus until the danger is over."

In fairness, one should note that responsible military analysts at this time viewed the Pacific as a Japanese lake, and in fact, until the Battle of Midway in June 1942, it appeared that nothing could stop the Imperial Fleet or prevent an invasion of the West Coast. One should also recall that the treatment of Japanese-Americans, unfair as it was, came nowhere close to the way the Japanese and Germans treated minority groups in the countries they occupied.

Japanese Relocation

On February 19, 1942, without discussing it with his cabinet, President Roosevelt signed Executive Order 9066. Some critics of the relocation have claimed that Roosevelt himself should bear little responsibility, since he had no part in originating or developing the program, and, with so many other war-related demands on his time and energy, he did not recognize the problem. But while presidents ought not to be blamed for every act of their subordinates, the person in the White House is, under the Constitution, the chief executive of the United States and therefore is responsible for what executive agencies and officers do. Protests against 9066, including warnings from his own attorney general, ought to have alerted the president to the danger; furthermore, he augmented and continued the program through other executive orders and personally prohibited its discontinuation until after the election.

Executive Order 9066 authorized the secretary of war and certain military officers to designate parts of the country as "military areas" from which any and all persons might be excluded, and in which travel restrictions might be imposed. Roosevelt issued the order solely on his power as military commander-in-chief, but army lawyers feared the actions that were necessary to implement 9066 might not withstand court scrutiny on such a narrow base. They wanted more authority, and got it on March 21, when Congress enacted the major provisions of 9066 into law and added stringent penalties for those who resisted relocation.

General DeWitt had already begun the program on March 2, 1942, designating the entire Pacific Coast as a military area because of its susceptibility to attack. This initial proclamation made no reference to any personal restrictions, but noted that future notices would set out particulars. On March 24, with congressional authority having been added to that of the president, DeWitt established a curfew along the coastal plain between 8:00 P.M. and 6:00 A.M. for German and Italian nationals and for all persons of Japanese ancestry. Three days later, military officials prohibited not only Japanese nationals (Issei) but American citizens of Japanese ancestry (Nisei) from leaving the military areas. Then on May 9, the army excluded all Japanese-Americans, both Issei and Nisei, from the West Coast military zones. Japanese-Americans could comply with these contradictory orders only by reporting to designated central locations, from which they would be transported to "relocation centers" in the interior. The War Relocation Authority, which had been established under Executive Order 9102 for the sole purpose of helping the military in its evacuation program, operated these centers, which amounted to nothing more than detention camps.

Although relocated families could stay together, they had to leave homes and jobs; property owners suffered enormously because they had to dispose of their holdings in a matter of days and accept whatever price they could get. Inside the camps, despite a variety of busywork activities, they had little to do. Amazingly, the 110,000 men, women, and children responded cooperatively for the most part. A number of younger Nisei volunteered to serve in the army, and their unit, the 442nd Regimental Combat Team, turned out to be among the most highly decorated in the European theater of operations.

The relocation program constituted the most serious invasion of individual rights by the federal government in the history of the country. The entire operation proceeded on racist assumptions and brought forth such astounding statements as that of Congressman Leland Ford of California that "a patriotic native-born Japanese, if he wants to make his contribution, will submit himself to a concentration camp." Despite the absence of even a shred of evidence of disloyalty, the entire Japanese-American population—including native-born citizens—stood condemned, because, as General DeWitt so eloquently put it, "A Jap is a Jap."

In contrast to the treatment of Japanese on the West Coast, it is instructive to see what happened to Italians on the East Coast. After Mussolini's declaration of war against the United States in December 1941, some 600,000 Italians—more than ten percent of the entire Italian-American community—remained Italian citizens and were automatically labeled as "enemy aliens." But the Roosevelt administration had been actively cultivating Italian voters, and the president instructed Attorney General Nicholas Biddle to cancel that designation. The announcement was made to a cheering 1942 Columbus Day crowd in Carnegie Hall, New York, just weeks before the congressional elections.

The Relocation Cases

The constitutional basis for both Roosevelt's executive orders and congressional legislation left much to be desired, but they nonetheless received the imprimatur of the nation's highest tribunal. The first case resulting from the internment program to reach the Court was *Hirabayashi v. United States* (1943). Gordon Hirabayashi, a University of Washington senior and a native-born citizen, had been arrested for failing to report to a control center and for violating the curfew. The Court sustained the legitimacy of the curfew, but evaded any ruling on the wider implications of the relocation program. Chief Justice Stone, for a unanimous Court, held that the power to impose a curfew in wartime clearly lay within the presidential war powers, as well as congressional authority. He noted the gravity of the situation (which no one questioned) and the possible disloyalty of some Japanese-Americans (which no one could prove), and said that the Court ought not challenge the discretion of the military in interpreting the war powers broadly. Any discrimination based on race, while "odious to a free people," had clearly been relevant to the situation, and Congress had properly taken it into account.

Justices Murphy, Douglas, and Rutledge entered concurring opinions, which practically amounted to dissents. This proved especially true of Murphy's remarks, in which he objected to any invasion of rights based on race, even in wartime. The curfew or-

> Do you think it is conducive to the things you care about, including the great reputation of this court, to suggest that everybody is out of step except Johnny, and more particularly the Chief Justice and seven other Justices of this Court are behaving like the enemy and thereby playing into the hands of the enemy. Compassion is, I believe, a virtue enjoined by Christ. Well, tolerance is a long, long way from compassion—and can't you write your views with such expressed tolerance that you won't make people think that when eight others disagree with you, you think their view means that they want to destroy the liberties of the United States and "lose the war" at home.
>
> —Felix Frankfurter, pleading with Frank Murphy not to dissent in *Hirabayashi v. United States* (1943)

der, he noted, had "a melancholy resemblance" to the way Jews were being treated in Germany and Nazi-occupied Europe. But the three men reluctantly consented to what they considered an unconstitutional program because of the allegedly critical military situation.

The Court heard two other cases the following year, testing the relocation program, and in both, they shied away from dealing with the central issue. In *Korematsu v. United States* (1944), an American citizen, turned down because of ulcers after he had volunteered for the army, had refused to leave the war zone. Justice Black's opinion for the majority separated the exclusion issue from that of detention, and found the war power of Congress and the president sufficient to sustain the order. In wartime, civilians had to defer to military judgment and bear the resulting hardships that had always accompanied war. Somewhat disingenuously, Black denied that race had anything to do with Fred Korematsu's arrest; he had been ordered to leave the war zone not because of his race, but because of military necessity.

This time three justices, Murphy, Roberts, and Jackson, entered strenuous dissents. Justice Jackson wrote that Korematsu had been convicted of nothing more than "being present in the state whereof he is a citizen, near the place where he was born, and where he lived all his life." Jackson also attacked the cruel quandary that the military proclamations had created. On the one hand, they forbade Japanese-Americans from leaving, and on the other, forbade them from remaining, with the only option left open being "submission to custody, examination, and transportation out of the territory, to be followed by indeterminate confinement in detention camps."

Justice Roberts proved even blunter in his dissent, charging that Korematsu had been convicted "for not submitting to imprisonment in a concentration camp." Justice Murphy also dissented eloquently "from this legalization of racism" and exposed the central problem of the relocation program: it had been based solely on prejudice, on unproven fears that some members of one group, identifiable because of their ethnicity, might be disloyal. No similar action had been taken against German-Americans or Italian-Americans, despite the fact that some German-Americans and German nationals were arrested for espionage and treason.

On the same day, the Court unanimously authorized a writ of habeas corpus for Mitsuye Endo, a citizen whose loyalty had been clearly established. Although the American Civil Liberties Union, which filed an amicus brief in all three cases, had hoped to make *Ex parte Endo* a challenge to the entire detention program, Justice Douglas carefully skirted that issue and confined his ruling to the single question of whether the War Relocation Authority could detain persons whose loyalty had been confirmed. He held that it could not, but he had difficulty with the opinion, since this case came perilously close to the larger issue raised in the minority opinions in *Korematsu*—whether a person accused of no crime could be detained by military officials outside a combat zone. In *Ex parte Milligan* (1866), decided *after* the fighting in the Civil War had stopped, the Chase Court had said no, but Douglas now tried to distinguish between the two; Milligan had been held by the army, whereas Endo had been detained by a civilian agency. Douglas ignored the fact that the War Relocation Authority had been created for no purpose other than to assist the military to carry out the evacuation. In concurrences that nonetheless attacked the majority opinion, Murphy and Roberts decried the Court's refusal to resolve an important constitutional issue that had properly come before it—whether a loyal citizen who had committed no crime could be deprived of her liberty.

There has been a general condemnation of the internment program, and of the Supreme Court's condoning it, ever since. Recent evidence indicates that the solicitor general knew that no military necessity justified the relocation and that he deliberately misled the Court in this area. Perhaps it is too much to expect the Court to remain free of the passions that inevitably sweep a nation during wartime, but there is a bitter irony in comparing Stone's *Carolene Products* footnote, which called for a "more exacting judicial scrutiny" of racially directed legislation, and his *Hirabayashi* opinion, which condemned discrimination in general, but then approved of it in this application. Nor can one find much evidence of the concern for rights that later marked the careers of Black and Douglas in their *Korematsu* and *Endo* opinions. Only Murphy seemed fully consistent between his earlier opinions and his position in the Japanese cases, but even he bowed to what the Court, and much of the nation, took to be military necessity.

Milligan Redux

In *Ex parte Milligan* (1866), decided after the Civil War had ended, the Supreme Court had ruled that persons accused of crimes could not be tried before military tribunals as long as civilian courts remained open. That issue came before the Court again in the Second World War, and once again the justices reached the same conclusion. Shortly after the attack on Pearl Harbor, the government had imposed martial law on the Hawaiian Islands, and a comprehensive suspension of constitutional protections lasted until October 1944. Unlike the West Coast detention scheme, martial law in the islands applied to the entire population of 465,000, of whom slightly more than a third were of Japanese origin.

In February 1944, a civilian shipyard worker, Lloyd Duncan (a Caucasian), got into a fight with military sentries, who promptly arrested him. A military court tried and convicted him and sentenced him to six months in prison. Duncan's civilian attorney then sought a writ of habeas corpus in federal district court, claiming that since the civilian courts had remained open, the provost's court had no jurisdiction. The government put General Robert Richardson and Admiral Chester Nimitz on the stand to testify that a Japanese military menace, although weakened, still existed and thereby justified martial law. The local judge ordered Duncan freed on the basis of *Milligan* and that martial law had been illegal since at least March 1943.

The Supreme Court accepted the case for review and heard oral argument on December 7, 1945, four years to the day after the attack on Pearl Harbor. By a 7–2 vote the Court, speaking through Justice Black, upheld the lower court in *Duncan v. Kahamamoku* (1946). Black, who had been the author of *Hirabayashi*, had to distinguish between why the Court had accepted the military's rationale in 1943 but refused to do so now. Black did this by ignoring the constitutional implications of martial law, and writing what amounted to a historical treatise on habeas corpus; the great writ had been created to fight the type of tyranny that army rule often brought. What Black did not say was that in the midst of war, he stood ready to believe what the military authorities had told him; in 1946, with the war over, he sat as an historian and found the army version unconvincing.

The Judgment of History

The decisions on Japanese-Americans so jarred the legal community that they quickly came under universal attack. Historian Eugene V. Rostow summarized this judgment in the title of an article he wrote in 1945: "The Japanese American Cases—A Disaster." Since then, no reputable scholar has defended the decisions. Some members of the Court later admitted that the Court had erred badly; "the evacuation case was ever on my conscience," Justice Douglas declared in his memoirs.

The internment has continued to haunt the nation's conscience as well. In 1948, Congress took a first step toward making amends with enactment of the Japanese American Evacuation Claims Act. Although the Federal Reserve Bank estimated the loss of property at $400 million, the statute limited compensation to claims that could be verified by written records, a burden most of the internees could not meet. As a result, the Treasury paid out $37 million on claims of $148 million. Then in 1980, Congress established the Commission on Wartime Relocation and Internment of Civilians, with a mandate to "review the facts and circumstances" that had led to Executive Order 9066 and the resultant internments. Between July and December 1981, approximately 750 witnesses testified, many of them internees who told for the first time of the trauma they had suffered and the psychological scars they still bore; the commission also heard from some of the architects of the policy that had put those people behind barbed wire.

In its report in February 1983, *Personal Justice Denied*, the commission condemned the internment as a "grave injustice," which resulted from decisions "conceived in haste and executed in an atmosphere of fear and anger at Japan." The commission unanimously agreed that 9066 had not been justified by military necessity, but, as Frank Murphy had argued nearly forty years earlier, was the result of "race prejudice, war hysteria and a failure of political leadership." The commission also concluded that the Supreme Court decisions on relocation had been "overruled in the court of history." But those decisions are still on the books, and the fear remains that in some future crisis the argument of military necessity might again be used to limit the rights of citizens. The argument is not that farfetched. At the Relocation Commission hearings, Wall Street attorney John J. McCloy, still unrepentant over his role in shaping the internment program as assistant secretary of war, pointed out that a major threat to American security existed less than 90 miles from the Florida coast and urged the commission not to recommend any restrictions that might hamper the government from responding to the threat of fifth columnists.

At the same time that the Relocation Commission began its hearings, lawyers for Gordon Hirabayashi, Fred Korematsu, and others began the lengthy process in federal district courts on the West Coast to have their convictions overturned. Utilizing evidence uncovered by Peter Irons in researching his book on the relocation cases, they asked for the ancient and little-used writ of *coram nobis*, a final avenue of relief for persons who have been convicted of a crime and served their sentence, but who seek reversal of the judgment on the grounds that the original conviction had been tainted by governmental misconduct. Irons had found evidence that not only did General DeWitt know that the Japanese-Americans posed no security threat, but so did the government lawyers, especially John Fahy, who argued the cases before the Supreme Court.

> They did me a great wrong.
>
> —Fred Korematsu, deciding to seek reversal of his conviction (1982)

In 1984, the district court vacated Korematsu's conviction, and the other trials also resulted in a resounding defeat for the government. The Justice Department appealed one of the reversals, but ran into a stone wall in the Ninth Circuit, which upheld the lower court's decision. In response to the government's claim that so much time had passed as to make the issue moot, Judge Mary M. Schroeder declared: "A United States citizen who is convicted of a crime on account of race is lastingly aggrieved." At that point the government decided not to appeal to the Supreme Court.

In August 1988, Congress passed a redress bill that provided $20,000 to each internment camp survivor, and on August 10, President Ronald Reagan signed the bill into law. The law included a national apology as well as money for an educational fund to instruct future generations of Americans about the lessons of the internment . By the time the law's ten-year limit for applying had run out, some 60,000 survivors had entered claims totalling $1.2 billion.

The War Crimes Trials

When news of German atrocities against Jews and other groups reached the West in 1942, both Roosevelt and Churchill warned that those perpetrating the "Final Solution" would be held responsible for "crimes against humanity" after the war. Later, the Allies issued a similar warning to the perpetrators of Japanese atrocities. Although international law contained no provisions covering the extermination of millions of innocent civilians, Harry S. Truman, who succeeded to the presidency on Roosevelt's death in April 1945, also believed that the Nazi war criminals had to be punished. He agreed to the establishment of an International Military Tribunal to meet in Nuremberg, Germany, composed of representatives from the United States, Great Britain, France, and the Soviet Union. To present the case against the Nazis, the president asked Associate Justice Robert H. Jackson to serve as the American special prosecutor in the hearings, which eventually sentenced twelve Nazis to death and seven others to imprisonment. The Nuremberg trials established a precedent for additional prosecutions of Nazis involved in the "Final Solution." Some 2,000 trials have been held in Western Europe, the United States, and Israel, as Nazi officials in hiding have been located and exposed; an unknown number of similar trials were held in the U.S.S.R. and other east bloc countries.

Very few people objected to the Nuremberg trials; the Nazis had murdered six million men, women, and children for no reason other than their religion, and had also killed hundreds of thousands of gypsies, people with mental or physical infirmities, and political opponents. Crimes so heinous could not go unpunished, yet as Senator Robert A. Taft of Ohio pointed out, the Nuremberg tribunal punished men for offenses that had never been part of accepted international law. In addition to adjudication, the tribunal in essence legislated ex post facto laws. Although some constitutional scholars agreed with Taft's contention, the general public believed that the Nazis received far fairer treatment than they deserved or had given to their victims. Defenders of the trials relied on such international agreements as the Pact of Paris outlawing war, the Geneva Convention's rules for the care of sick and wounded prisoners, and the Hague declarations on the rules of war, as general justifications for the trials, as well as on the fact that murder, pillage, and rape constituted crimes in every country that the Germans had occupied. None of the Nazis convicted at Nuremberg sought review of their verdicts from the U.S. Supreme Court or from appellate tribunals in Britain, France, or the Soviet Union.

However, some Japanese war criminals tried by an international military court in Tokyo did seek writs of habeas corpus from the Supreme Court. Their lawyers claimed both that the military court lacked proper jurisdiction and that the Constitution followed the flag, an idea intimated at but not fully articulated in *Ex parte Quirin* in 1942. In 1946, the Court backed away from this possibility in the case of the "Tiger of Malaya," Japanese general Tomoyuki Yamashita. Shortly after the Japanese surrender, General Douglas MacArthur had established a special military commission to try Yamashita for crimes committed during the Japanese occupation of the Philippines. At the trial, the prosecution accused Yamashita of violating the rules of war by permitting his troops to commit brutal atrocities, although no charge was made that he had himself participated in the atrocities or had even ordered them. The military court nonetheless found him guilty and sentenced him to death.

With the war now over, the justices did not feel the haste they had in the Nazi saboteur case; they ordered a stay of execution and heard arguments in early January 1946. Chief Justice Stone wrote a narrow opinion upholding the authority of the military tribunal and also backed away from the implications of the *Quirin* decision. Both justices Rutledge and Murphy dissented, claiming that the Constitution did in fact follow the flag and that even defeated enemies, once in the hands of American troops, enjoyed minimal constitutional protection.

The two decisions, *Quirin* and *Yamashita*, raise a number of questions that Stone did not answer clearly, mainly because no clear line of authority of precedent governs this area. The wording of the Constitution does not clearly delineate military from civilian courts, but historically, there have always been sharp distinctions between the two. Justice Black, in a draft opinion, suggested that military court decisions should be reviewed only by appellate military courts, and eventually the government did set up a procedure for appellate review of military justice.

> The grave issue raised by this case is whether a military commission . . . may disregard the procedural rights of an accused person as guaranteed by the Constitution. The answer is plain. The Fifth Amendment guarantee of due process of law applies to "any person" who is accused of a crime by the Federal Government or any of its agencies.
>
> —Frank Murphy, dissenting in *In re Yamashita* (1946)

The United Nations

Following World War I, isolationists had blocked American involvement in the League of Nations because they claimed that the League charter would impinge on American sovereignty. Sentiment for a new world body, with the United States as an active member, grew throughout the war. (The League had collapsed at the outbreak of hostilities.) Roosevelt and Churchill had agreed in the 1941 Atlantic Charter to establish "a permanent system of general security," and in January 1942, twenty-six countries at war with the Axis signed the declaration of the "United Nations" in Washington. Both houses of Congress agreed in the fall of 1943 to a resolution introduced by J. William Fulbright, favoring "international machinery with power adequate to establish and maintain a just and lasting peace."

Two weeks after Roosevelt's death, delegates from fifty nations met in the San Francisco Opera House and drew up the charter of the United Nations. The organization would consist of a General Assembly composed of all members (those signing the charter as well as those admitted in the future) and a Security Council with responsibility "for the maintenance of international peace and security." The eleven-nation council would have five permanent members—the United States, the United Kingdom, France, China, and the Union of Soviet Socialist Republics—and six other members elected for rotating two-year terms. In addition, there would be an International Court of Justice in The Hague; a Trusteeship Council to oversee the former Italian and Japanese colonies, as well as the mandates that had been issued by the League of Nations; an Economic and Social Council to coordinate the Food and Agricultural Organization, World Bank, and other specialized agencies; and a Secretariat to administer the business of the United Nations. In sharp contrast to the bitter debate over the League of Nations in 1919, the Senate ratified the U.N. charter, 89 to 2, after six days of debate.

Despite the general sentiment in favor of the United Nations, some of the constitutional questions raised about the League of Nations remained unresolved with regard to the new organization. The U.N. charter forbids member states from using or threatening force against other states; in effect, if the United States took this agreement seriously, it would give up a right inherent in sovereignty, the right to go to war by its own will. The United States has not, however, given up the *power* to do so, but has voluntarily pledged not to use war as an instrument of foreign policy. The charter also prohibits member nations from sending troops overseas for purposes inconsistent with those of the United Nations, another limitation on sovereignty. All treaties, of course, involve self-denial by the signatories, and as has happened countless times in history, nations have broken treaty obligations when it suited them to do so. In the four decades since the United Nations came into being, the United States, under a succession of presidents, has often sent troops overseas on a unilateral basis in technical violation of the charter, as have other countries. The charter provisions do little more than inject another consideration in deciding whether or not to employ force in a particular situation.

What has been much more troubling is the commitment of the United States to participate in collective action by the United Nations. Under the charter, member nations agree to apply military sanctions against aggressor states. Approval of these sanctions rests in the Security Council, where the American delegate may consent to this country's participation in the sanctions, or even veto them. In effect, an executive appointee, acting under direction of the president, may commit the United States to military conflicts without the congressional approval called for in the Constitution. Congress, however, agreed to this provision in the act, approving American membership in the United Nations and authorizing the president to negotiate agreements with the Security Council for the use of American military forces. Although Congress reserves the power to approve the agreements, it has left the president free, on his own authority, to commit troops for fighting.

The United Nations cannot, of course, force the United States to act against its will. For one thing, the United States retains a veto power in the Security Council. But even without the veto, so-called Article 43 agreements are only as binding on the signatories as they want them to be. The ultimate decision to go to war rests with the United States, although that decision could, under certain circumstances, be made unilaterally by the president.

For Further Reading

For a general constitutional framework, see William C. Banks and Peter Raven-Hansen, *National Security Law and the Power of the Purse* (1994); Gary M. Stern and Morton H. Halperin, eds., *The U.S. Constitution and the Power to Go to War* (1994); and Louis Henkin, *Constitutionalism, Democracy and Foreign Affairs* (1990).

American foreign policy in the 1930s is explored in Selig Adler, *The Uncertain Giant: American Foreign Policy Between the Wars* (1966); and John E. Wiltz, *From Isolation to War, 1931–1941* (1968). For Roosevelt's leadership, see Robert Dallek, *Franklin D. Roosevelt and American Foreign Policy, 1932–1945* (1979); James MacGregor Burns, *Roosevelt: Soldier of Freedom* (1970); and Eric Larabee, *Commander in Chief: Franklin Delano Roosevelt, His Lieutenants and Their War* (1987). For Truman and foreign policy, see Norman A. Graebner, *The Age of Global Power: The United States Since 1938* (1979); Bert Cochran, *Truman and the Crisis Presidency* (1973); and Richard F. Haynes, *The Awesome Power: Harry S. Truman as Commander in Chief* (1973). Executive authority in wartime is examined in Louis Fisher, *Presidential War Power* (1995).

Neutrality is examined in the older but still authoritative two volumes by William Langer and S. Everett Gleason, *The Challenge to Isolation 1937–1940* (1952), and *The Undeclared War, 1940–1941* (1953). See also, Robert Divine, *The Illusion of Neutrality* (1962); and Wayne S. Cole, *Gerald P. Nye and American Foreign Relations* (1962). For internal security matters in the early years of the war, see August R. Ogden, *The Dies Committee* (1945); and Telford Taylor, *Grand Inquest: The Story of Congressional Investigations* (1955). Francis Biddle, *In Brief Authority* (1962), and Eugene C. Gerhart, *America's Advocate: Robert H. Jackson* (1958), examine the role of two attorneys general in balancing security against liberty. The Lovett episode is analyzed in Frederick L. Schuman, "'Bill of Attainder' in the Seventy-Eighth Congress," 37 *American Political Science Review* 819 (1943).

The growth of governmental—and especially presidential power—is well detailed in E. S. Corwin, *Total War and the Constitution* (1947); and Clinton Rossiter, *Constitutional Dictatorship: Crisis Government in the Modern Democracies*; (1948), which, despite its title, approves of Roosevelt's wartime leadership. Organizing the economy for war is examined in Eliot Janeway,

The Struggle for Survival: A Chronicle of Economic Mobilization in World War II (1951). Studies of governmental organization include Nathan Grundstein, "Presidential Subdelegation of Administrative Authority in War-time," 16 *George Washington Law Review* 301, 478 (1948); D.D. Holdoegel, "The War Powers and the Emergency Price Control Act of 1942," 29 *Iowa Law Review* 454 (1944); and Leonard Boudin, "The Authority of the National War Labor Board over Labor Disputes," 43 *Michigan Law Review* 329 (1944). Clinton Rossiter, *The Supreme Court and the Commander-in-Chief* (1951), looks at the Court's response to war regulations.

Japanese relocation and the resultant cases are criticized in Eugene V. Rostow, "The Japanese-American Cases—a Disaster," 54 *Yale Law Journal.* 489 (1945); Morton Grodzins, *Americans Betrayed: Politics and the Japanese Evacuations* (1949); and especially, in the withering indictment by Peter Irons, *Justice at War* (1983). The report of the Commission on Wartime Relocation, *Personal Justice Denied* (1983), is also well worth perusing. The critical documents are provided in Peter Irons, *Justice Delayed* (1989), which details the fight for *corum nobis*. A recent book by Page Smith, *Democracy on Trial: The Japanese American Evacuation and Relocation in World War II* (1995), takes a less hostile approach and tries to put the internment into the larger context of a nation at war. For military rule in Hawaii, see Harry N. Scheiber and Jane L. Scheiber, "Constitutional Liberty in World War II: Army Rule and Martial Law in Hawaii, 1941–1946," 3 *Western Legal History* 341 (1990).

On presidential control over foreign affairs, see Louis Henkin, ed., *Foreign Affairs and the U.S. Constitution* (1990); and Charles Lofgren, "*United States v. Curtiss-Wright Export Corporation*: An Historical Reassessment," 83 *Yale Law Journal* 1 (1973). For executive agreements, see Craig Matthews, "The Constitutional Power of the President to Conclude International Agreements," 64 *Yale Law Journal* 345 (1955); and Elbert M. Byrd, Jr., *Treaties and Executive Agreements in the United States: Their Separate Roles and Limitations* (1960). For the postwar trials, see Arieh J. Kochavi, *Prelude to Nuremberg: Allied War Crimes Policy and the Question of Punishment* (1998); William J. Bosch, *Judgment on Nuremberg: American Attitudes Toward the Major War-Crimes Trials* (1970); and the highly critical and polemical Richard H. Minear, *Victor's Justice: The Tokyo War Crimes Trial* (1971).

For postwar problems related to international treaties, see Ruth B. Russell, *A History of the United Nations Charter* (1958); Edwin Borchard, "The Charter and the Constitution," 39 *American Journal of International Law* 767 (1945); and Jacob Hyman, "Constitutional Aspects of the Covenant," 14 *Law & Constitutional Problems* 451 (1949).

34

Fair Deal and Cold War

Conservative Reaction • The Taft–Hartley Law • Government Loyalty Programs • Smith Act Prosecutions • Dennis v. United States *• Justice Harlan's Solution • The McCarran Act • McCarthyism • The North Atlantic Treaty Organization • The Bricker Amendment • The Korean Police Action • Civilian Control of the Military • The Steel Seizure Case • For Further Reading*

POSTWAR ERAS ARE often marked by conservatism, as turmoil gives way to a desire for what Warren Harding called "normalcy." After twelve years of upheaval, of depression followed by a world conflict, it would not have been surprising to find the American people seeking respite from turbulence. But the forces unleashed during that time could not easily be quieted. The massive planning that had accompanied the New Deal and War Deal could not be abandoned; even conservatives recognized that it would be disastrous to return to pre-1929 policies. Similarly, the responsibilities that the United States had assumed as a world power in the fight against fascism could not be laid down; too many nations looked to America as a bulwark against aggression. And the fear of communism abroad poisoned domestic tranquility in another postwar Red Scare.

Conservative Reaction

Franklin Roosevelt had indicated that he had ambitious plans to expand New Deal reforms after the war; Harry Truman, in calling for a "Fair Deal," intended to follow that plan. But in the postwar reaction against the party in power, the Republicans won control of both legislative chambers in 1946, for the first time in sixteen years. Eager to reestablish its power, a conservative Congress promised little hope of extending reform under presidential leadership.

Congressional conservatives had succeeded even before the election in watering down Truman's proposal for what became the landmark Full Employment Act of 1946.

Nevertheless, the statute still declared the nation's economic policy to be the utilization of government resources and the power to provide maximum employment, production, and purchasing power. The act created a Council of Economic Advisers to monitor the economic health of the nation and to make recommendations to the president on appropriate monetary and fiscal policies. The Employment Act, even in its watered-down form, nonetheless represented a significant step in the direction of governmental responsibility for economic welfare, a principle that would have been deemed revolutionary as recently as the 1920s.

In constitutional terms, the act marked a breathtaking reversal. In 1936, the Supreme Court still proclaimed the belief that government could best maintain the free enterprise system by keeping out of business affairs, and that it had no authority to impose market controls or force a redistribution of resources. But if Congress had adopted Truman's more ambitious program—which would have given the government even more direct control of the economy—the law would have withstood review by the courts. Conservatives may have quibbled over the proper amount of governmental intervention, but they no longer doubted its legality or economic necessity in the modern world.

Even as Congress was seeking to reassert its authority, it found that it had approved several measures that required further expansion of the executive. By January 1947, the president had to send Congress three separate annual messages—the constitutionally mandated State of the Union, as well as the budget and economic reports required by the Employment Act of 1946, which were prepared by augmented presidential staffs. Congress unified the military branches under a single Department of Defense and created the Atomic Energy Commission, both of which vested significantly enhanced authority in the White House. The Taft–Hartley Act bolstered presidential power over the nation's labor relations. To help him make better use of all these powers, Truman reorganized parts of the executive to make them more efficient, in accord with recommendations from a commission headed by former Republican president Herbert Hoover. Harry Truman revered the presidency, and he resisted congressional encroachment on presidential prerogatives. He vetoed more bills in his nearly eight years than any of his two-term predecessors, determined to pass the office on to his successors unimpaired.

The Congress, however, had other ideas. The Republicans never forgave Franklin Roosevelt for running and winning a third and then a fourth term, and they took their revenge in the Twenty-second Amendment, which limited future presidents to two terms. Ratified in 1951, it is one of the more ill-advised alterations to the Constitution, and it has the potential, as Truman predicted, "for making a 'lame duck' out of every

> This amendment grows directly out of the unfortunate experience we had in this country in 1940 and again in 1944 when a President who had entrenched himself in power by use of patronage and the public purse refused to vacate the office at the conclusion of two terms, but used the great powers of the Presidency to perpetuate himself in office.
>
> —Karl Mundt (Rep., S.D.), during Senate debate on Twenty-second Amendment (1947)

second-term President for all time in the future." Dwight Eisenhower, the first chief executive to whom it applied, condemned the amendment as "an act of retroactive vindictiveness" against Roosevelt rather than the product of "judicious thinking about the institutions of the Republic."

One can hardly dispute that the Twenty-second Amendment represents the most blatantly partisan alteration in the Constitution since the Civil War. Every Republican who cast a ballot in either house of the Congress voted for it, and they got the needed two-thirds from conservative, anti–New Deal Democrats who, within a few years, would leave the party entirely. Republican-dominated state legislatures raced to ratify the proposal in the spring of 1947. Nineteen of the twenty-six legislatures in which Republicans held majorities in both houses were in session when Congress submitted the amendment; all but one ratified in less than two months. Hatred of Franklin Roosevelt seemed to unify the Republican party more than anything else that year. Of 1,571 Republicans in state legislatures voting on the amendment, only eleven opposed it.

Southern Democrats joined in the feeding frenzy, especially after Truman's Committee on Civil Rights issued its report (see Chapter 35). Determined to protect Jim Crow and uncomfortable with much of the New Deal, Southern leaders saw the amendment as a tool to reduce presidential power. Although temporarily delayed by Truman's upset win in 1948, Southern resentment gave the Republican sponsors of the amendment the additional states needed for ratification, which took place in February 1951.

Since then, Republicans and Democrats have both criticized the amendment. With the popular Dwight Eisenhower in office in the 1950s, Republicans realized that the term limit cut both ways. When Congress held hearings in 1959, former president Truman declared that the "Roosevelt haters got busy and sold the country a bill of goods." Even some Roosevelt "haters," like Illinois Republican Everett Dirksen, who had been a strong supporter of the amendment in 1947, agreed. Term limits, Dirksen said, like national Prohibition, represented an undemocratic restriction; the people ought to be trusted to make wise choices. Despite bipartisan condemnation of the Twenty-second Amendment, inertia remains a powerful force, and periodic efforts at repeal have never cleared committee.

The Taft–Hartley Law

Conservatives did manage to roll back a few of the gains made by labor during the New Deal. Republicans as well as many conservative Democrats had always opposed the Wagner Act, and a series of disruptive strikes after the war strengthened their case for imposing restrictions on labor unions. The Taft–Hartley Act, certainly the most important piece of conservative legislation after the war, gave management greater rights in labor disputes and curtailed some of organized labor's power. Adopted over Truman's veto, the statute prohibited secondary boycotts, the closed shop (in which only union members could work), and jurisdictional walkouts; increased the legal responsibility of unions for their actions; and authorized the president to seek injunctions to delay strikes eighty days if the work stoppage would adversely affect the nation. Similar antiunion sentiment led thirty states to take advantage of Section 14b and adopt laws restricting union power, the most common being the so-called right to work statutes, which prohibited making union membership a condition of employment.

For all the conservative exultation about the law, it did little to change the course of federal labor policy. The Wagner Act, to ensure the right of labor to organize and to bargain collectively, had set out a list of practices in which management could not engage; perceiving that the balance had swung too far over, the Taft–Hartley bill set up a comparable list of practices forbidden to labor. But both bills aimed at creating a fair environment in which labor-management relations could take place. Taft and others wanted to diminish the discretion of administrative agencies, such as the National Labor Relations Board, by establishing explicit procedural rules. Many on the labor side, such as union leader William M. Lieserson, also wanted more precision in federal labor law so that both sides would know their duties and rights. Taft himself had never expressed any intention to undermine the principle of collective bargaining, and on more than one occasion he claimed that the Taft-Hartley Act did little more than correct the procedural deficiencies of the Wagner Act. The law, he claimed, was no more than "a revision of elaborate existing laws, such as the Wagner Act," all of which had been "written on sound principles." The basic theory of Taft–Hartley, he declared in 1948, "is the same as the theory of the Wagner Act."

While one might dismiss some of this as political rhetoric aimed at assuaging union members, the fact remained that after Taft–Hartley the government's basic labor policy remained the support and protection of collective bargaining. Some of the abuses of organized labor had been corrected, but that by itself could hardly be labeled antilabor or antiunion. The strictures placed upon the NLRB did not introduce any radical changes in the board's regulatory behavior, but it did ensure that the board would follow even more closely the legal models and procedures that had been part of its operations since its inception. Only in refusing to enforce a closed shop could Taft–Hartley be said to be a step back from Wagner, and even there, many people did not consider this necessarily an antiunion provision.

Taft–Hartley, like many postwar statutes, had little regard for civil liberties, and it required union officials to file affidavits that they were not members of the Communist party nor any other subversive organizations. In many ways, this provision can be said to mark the beginning of the postwar Red Scare, and it was among the first to reach the Supreme Court. In 1950, the Court upheld Section 9(h), denying access to the National Labor Relations Board to those unions whose officers had refused to swear that they were not Communists. In *American Communications Association v. Douds*, Chief Justice Vinson admitted that the statute discouraged the lawful exercise of political freedom by requiring oaths related to individual political beliefs. This abridgment of free speech, however, had to be weighed against the government's power to regulate commerce.

This proved too much for Justice Black, who declared that the Commerce Clause does "not restrict the right to think." Even justices Frankfurter and Jackson, while concurring in the result, objected to imposing a test on beliefs. "Under our system," Jackson wrote, "it is time enough for the law to lay hold of the citizen when he acts illegally, or in some rare circumstances where his thoughts are given illegal utterance. I think we must let his mind alone." But Vinson, a cold warrior from the start, could only square the overly broad sweep of Section 9(h) with the First Amendment by ignoring it, and trying to ground the power in the Commerce Clause. It proved an ominous start to the Court's response to the postwar hysteria.

Government Loyalty Programs

Although tension between the president and Congress is normal within the system of checks and balances, Congress launched a particularly vicious attack against the executive branch in its efforts to root out alleged security risks. While Communist spying certainly did take place during the cold war era, the Red Scare of the late 1940s and early 1950s subverted civil liberties, destroyed the reputation of many innocent persons, and gave congressional investigations a bad name that lasted for years.

The Dies Committee had declined after Pearl Harbor, but in January 1945, Representative John Rankin of Mississippi—racist, anti-Semitic, conservative, and bitterly anti-Roosevelt—secured House approval for the creation of a permanent Committee on Un-American Activities. When the Republicans took over the House two years later, J. Parnell Thomas became the committee's chairman, and in a quest to expose alleged Communists and Communist sympathizers in the government, he used the committee as a bludgeon against the Truman administration. Before long, the committee had expanded its search into labor unions, colleges and universities, and even Hollywood. Any group, in fact, that committee members or staff suspected of being too liberal became a target.

Communism certainly posed a danger to the United States, as one could plainly see in the arrests and trials of Julius and Ethel Rosenberg, Judith Coplin, Klaus Fuchs, and others, as spies. But with the exception of Alger Hiss (who was convicted for perjury, not spying), the committee contributed nothing to the exposure of espionage or subversion. The FBI and not the committee uncovered the major postwar spy rings. The committee, however, kept repeating undocumented charges that Communists had infiltrated government and society, and demanded that the president "do something."

The FBI, while certainly far more effective than congressional committees, also had a dark side. J. Edgar Hoover had been obsessed about subversives since his days under Wilson's attorney general, A. Mitchell Palmer, the chief sponsor of the 1919 Red Scare. While he eliminated the corruption in the FBI when he took it over in 1924, the bureau, in addition to fighting crime, began collecting enormous amounts of data about suspected Communists. Hoover set up a vast network of informants and undercover agents, and every rumor, no matter how trivial, went into secret files. Truman complained privately about Hoover and the danger of the FBI becoming a "Gestapo

> Once they get the movies throttled, how long will it be before we're told what we can say and cannot say into a radio microphone? If you make a pitch on a nationwide radio network for a square deal for the underdog, will they call you a Commie? . . . Are they going to scare us into silence?
>
> —Frank Sinatra, on the House Un-American Activities Committee hearings (1947)

or Secret Police." But neither he nor any of his successors tried to fire the FBI director. Hoover had secret files on many political figures; he had mastered the art of public relations—nearly everyone in America saw him as the nation's number one crimefighter—and he controlled information that many people needed, or thought they needed.

Truman tried to act sensibly. He had access to FBI reports showing that the Communist party of the United States had been largely discredited; it had fewer than 20,000 members, many of whom might have been better described as inactive sympathizers. But common sense and caution merely infuriated the witch hunters. When the president named a Temporary Commission on Employee Loyalty in November 1946, conservatives attacked it as a cover-up of previous sins and also as an admission that there were Communists in the government; otherwise why establish a commission?

Four months later, in response to this pressure, Truman issued Executive Order 9835, instituting the Federal Loyalty and Security Program. The attorney general would compile a list of subversive organizations, defined as "totalitarian, Fascist, Communist or subversive . . . or approving the commission of acts of force or violence to deny to others their constitutional rights." Membership in any group on the attorney general's list by itself constituted "reasonable doubt" as to an employee's loyalty and could be grounds for dismissal. The massive investigation of federal workers that followed included the collection of a great deal of unverified information from numerous sources, which could be the basis for an individual's dismissal as a security risk. In the end, the attorney general's office named eighty-two organizations, and although the list carried a disclaimer that the government of the United States did not believe in "guilt by association," right-wing groups and private employers often considered membership in any one of the proscribed organizations as evidence of disloyalty. The House Un-American Activities Committee condemned the attorney general's list as wholly inadequate; it issued its own report, naming 624 organizations that were allegedly communistic or dedicated to the overthrow of the government.

Truman's loyalty program paid little attention to civil liberties. The very word "loyalty" was problematic, encouraging zealots to bring charges on the flimsiest of evidence, as well as allowing people with grudges to file unfounded charges. While employees had a right to hear the charges against them, they did not have a right to confront their accusers, even at public hearings to determine guilt or innocence. So-called evidence produced by the FBI and other sources often amounted to little more than a file full of rumors and innuendo that the loyalty boards read, but which remained closed to the accused. Many so-called subversives had done nothing more than belong to one or more left-leaning or even simply liberal organizations named by Red hunters as Communist.

> [J. Edgar Hoover]'s use of gossip, rumor, slander, backbiting, malice and drunken invention, which, when it makes the headlines, shatters the reputations of innocent and harmless people. . . . We are shocked. We are scared. We know that the thing stinks to heaven, that it is an avalanching danger to our society.
>
> —Bernard De Voto, on the FBI accumulation of information

One should note that Truman's program in many ways did little more than expand the loyalty program established during the war. The attorney general's list of subversive organizations had then focused mainly on Fascist organizations, but had included Communist groups as well. Roosevelt had hoped to fend off right-wingers in Congress who charged the New Deal with being soft on communism. Roosevelt, recognizing J. Edgar Hoover's obsessions, kept the loyalty program out of the FBI's hands by assigning the work to the Civil Service Commission, a slight Hoover never forgave. Truman thus expanded a set of flawed procedures, and in the hysteria of the late 1940s, government employees became easy targets for the Red baiters.

Despite its abuses, the presidential security program never deteriorated to the mudslinging that characterized the congressional hearings. Between 1947 and 1951, the Civil Service Commission, charged with conducting the initial probes under rules of basic fairness, gave more than three million federal employees a clean bill of health. Some 14,000 "doubtful" cases went to the FBI. Of these, 2,000 persons left government service, although the evidence indicates that few of the resignations resulted from the investigation. All told, the FBI recommended that only 212 people be discharged as possible security risks, hardly the numbers expected in a bureaucracy allegedly "honeycombed" by subversives.

Smith Act Prosecutions

To demonstrate its opposition to communism, the administration did prosecute twelve leaders of the American Communist party under the Smith Act of 1940. The statute made it a crime to conspire to teach or advocate the overthrow of the government by force, or to belong to a group advocating such overthrow; it thus departed drastically from the classical civil liberties position of proscribing only those words or actions presenting a clear and present danger to society. Before 1948, the government had invoked the Smith Act only twice, once against a Trotskyist faction of a Teamsters Union local in Minnesota, and once against a group of thirty-one alleged Fascists. But as early as 1945, the FBI had begun compiling information on the Communist party; its dossier reached over 1,800 pages within two years. Under pressure from the House Un-American Activities Committee, Attorney General Tom Clark finally initiated prosecution. In July 1948, a federal grand jury returned indictments against twelve national leaders; because of ill health, the case of one of the Communist officials was severed from the others. The nine-month trial of the other eleven—the "Battle of Foley Square"—began in January 1949.

> . . . to organize as the Communist Party of the United States, a society, group, and assembly of persons who teach and advocate the overthrow and destruction of the Government of the United States by force and violence, and knowingly and willfully to advocate and teach the duty and necessity of overthrowing and destroying the Government of the United States by force, which said acts are prohibited by . . . the Smith Act.
>
> —Indictment against Eugene Dennis, William Z. Foster and others (1948)

Intense antagonism between the five defense lawyers and presiding judge Harold Medina marked the often explosive proceedings. The FBI secretly put the attorneys, all of whom belonged to the liberal National Lawyers Guild, under surveillance, even eavesdropping on their conferences and strategy sessions. Although this certainly tainted the trial, it probably made no difference to the outcome. The defense lawyers never had control of their clients, who insisted on using the trial as a forum to air standard Marxist-Leninist formulas. On October 14, 1949, as expected, the jury found all eleven guilty. Before sentencing the defendants, however, Judge Medina issued contempt citations against the five lawyers (as well as against one of the defendants who had insisted on representing himself), charging them with deliberately conspiring to obstruct the trial, provoke incidents, and impair his health in order to secure a mistrial.

Although the defense attorneys had overstepped the bounds of propriety, Medina's fifty counts of contempt and the accompanying jail sentences, ranging from one to six months, seemed not only excessive, but patently vindictive. Such penalties, if nothing else, chilled the opportunity of unpopular defendants to secure adequate counsel, though even the attorney general of the United States did not seem to find that prospect displeasing. In an address to the Chicago Bar Association in 1946, Tom Clark had warned against lawyers getting involved in defense of those who would destroy American liberties. In the midst of the Smith Act trial, and just after his appointment to the Supreme Court, he again questioned the right of Communists either to practice law or to have counsel; those who stood outside the consensus of shared values did not deserve the benefits of those values, Clark said.

In *Sachar et al. v. United States* (1952), a majority of the Supreme Court upheld the contempt convictions, noting that the lawyers had violated professional decorum in the face of repeated warnings from the bench. Justice Black, joined by Douglas, entered a short dissent, focusing on Medina's prejudices: he had called the lawyers "brazen," "mealy-mouthed," and "liars," and no one should be tried by a judge who had so publicly attacked them. The lawyers had, in effect, been found "guilty by representation" of their clients. Justice Frankfurter entered a separate dissent that alone dealt with the real issue. The lawyers had been abusive, but "the contempt of the lawyers had its reflex in the judge," and he laid out a bill of particulars against Medina's conduct of the trial that, Frankfurter charged, made him totally unfit to pass on the lawyers' contempt.

In the meantime, the eleven defendants had been pursuing their appeals, claiming that the government had not proven that either their words or deeds met the clear and present danger test. They had good reason to believe that they could win on this argument, since the Supreme Court had used it frequently in the 1940s to strike down a variety of restrictions on various forms of speech. There had, however, been growing criticism of that standard from a number of sources. Strict advocates of free speech protested the "balancing" of speech against other, and supposedly lesser, values. Some critics believed that the test restricted the government too much and prevented it from taking the necessary measures to protect against subversion. A middle position condemned clear and present danger as oversimplified, since the whole problem of freedom and order required the consideration of many other variables.

Judge Learned Hand had wrestled with this problem ever since World War I. Despite his skepticism that substantive constitutional rights could be judicially enforced, he had tried to articulate judicial standards for speech cases. Now, as chief judge of the Second Circuit, he heard the initial appeal of the Smith Act defendants in 1950, and he tried to distinguish their situation from former cases, such as *Gitlow v. New York* (1925), which dealt primarily with verbal protests against some governmental activity. "It is one thing to say that the public interest in keeping streets clean, or in keeping a register of union leaders, or in requiring solicitors to take out licenses, will not justify interference with freedom of utterance," he wrote upholding the convictions. "It is quite another matter to say that an organized effort to inculcate the duty of revolution may not be repressed." Although some of Hand's defenders have argued to the contrary, Hand seems to have retreated from his original speech protective stance in the 1917 *Masses* case and even to have diluted the speech protective aspects of Holmes's clear and present danger test.

Dennis v. United States

The Supreme Court had entered the postwar era with relatively little Speech Clause jurisprudence, aside from the "clear and present danger" test developed by Holmes and Brandeis in the 1920s. (The full implications of Brandeis's opinion in *Whitney v. California* would not be recognized and developed until the Warren era.) But Holmes's famous aphorism about falsely shouting fire in a theater is not a very useful analytical tool to determine when a danger is real, and if real, when it is proximate, and if proximate, if it is of the magnitude that justifies state intervention.

Justices Black and Douglas had become increasingly unhappy with the test, especially as applied by the conservative majority after the war. Douglas believed that had Holmes and Brandeis had the opportunity to develop their ideas more fully in additional cases, they would have abandoned the clear and present danger test in favor of free and unrestricted speech in all but the most dire emergencies. Black began developing a new jurisprudence that viewed the First Amendment, especially the Speech Clause, as occupying a "preferred" position among constitutionally protected rights. He and Douglas also argued for an "absolutist" interpretation of the First Amendment's prohibitions against the abridgment of speech. In their view, the First Amendment barred all forms of governmental restrictions on speech, and no place existed in the regime of the First Amendment for any clear and present danger test.

For Frankfurter, the balancing implicit in the clear and present danger test fitted perfectly with his conception of the judicial function. Even while recognizing that a conservative majority might read their own views into the test, he believed that by applying rigorous tools of analysis and clearheadedly evaluating the circumstances, judges could determine when a danger existed and when it did not. By this view, explicating First Amendment issues did not differ at all from explicating Commerce Clause questions. There is much truth in Douglas's charge that Frankfurter saw the First Amendment not as a shield against state regulation of speech, but as an invitation to limit speech.

The two opposing views clashed in *Dennis v. United States* (1951). A majority of the justices sustained the lower courts, as Chief Justice Fred M. Vinson (appointed by Truman following Stone's death in 1946) expanded on Hand's theme. There is no

> When one talks about "preferred," or "preferred position," one means preference of one thing over another. Please tell me what kind of sense it makes that one provision of the Constitution is to be "preferred" over another. . . . The correlative of "preference" is "subordination," and I know of no calculus to determine when one provision of the Constitution must yield to another, nor do I know any reason for doing so.
>
> —Felix Frankfurter to Stanley Reed, 7 February 1956

"right" to rebellion where means for peaceful and orderly change exist. "We reject any principle of governmental helplessness in the face of preparation for revolution. No one could conceive that it is not within the power of Congress to prohibit acts intended to overthrow the Government by force and violence." As for the Smith Act's alleged infringement of speech, Vinson noted that the law aimed to outlaw "advocacy, not discussion." The clear and present danger test, according to the chief justice, obviously did not mean "that before the Government may act, it must wait until the putsch is about to be executed, the plans have been laid and the signal is awaited." The Court found Hand's new test—the gravity of the evil discounted by its improbability—to be better than the old Holmes formula. In this case, the "gravity of the evil" meant the overthrow of the government, an evil so great that in all instances it could be used to trump the improbability of the danger, no matter how remote.

Both Hugo Black and William Douglas dissented. Black reasserted his belief in the preferred position of First Amendment rights and recalled Brandeis's earlier warning of the difficulty in determining the limits of free speech when popular emotions run high. Douglas, who in later opinions would frequently criticize the *Dennis* decision, pointed out that the Smith Act required the element of intent; one not only had to say something, but had to believe it as well, so that "the crime then depends not on what is taught but on who the teacher is. That is to make freedom of speech turn not on what is said but on the intent with which it is said."

The *Dennis* decision came at the height of the anti-Communist sentiment sweeping the nation, and it immediately ran into criticism from civil libertarians and legal scholars. Both Holmes's clear and present danger test and Learned Hand's refinement of it assumed that only speech or related action that posed an immediate danger could be limited and that speech that sought to bring change at some unspecified future time

> Some nations less resilient than the United States, where illiteracy is high and where democratic traditions are only budding, might have to take drastic steps and jail these men for merely speaking their creed. But in America they are miserable merchants of unwanted ideas; their wares remain unsold. The fact that their ideas are abhorrent does not make them powerful. . . . The First Amendment reflects the philosophy of Jefferson "that it is time enough for the rightful purposes of civil government, for its officers to interfere when principles break into overt acts against peace and good public order."
>
> —William O. Douglas, dissenting in *Dennis v. United States* (1951)

remained fully protected. *Dennis* removed this temporal element, so that the government could now reach not only an actual effort to overthrow, but a conspiracy to do so, or even advocacy of such a conspiracy, an act twice removed from actual danger. Moreover, in *Dennis* the Court made no distinctions between theoretical and concrete advocacy.

The noted constitutional scholar Harry Kalven wondered why the Court had to "work so hard to affirm the convictions." After all, the trial court had determined the factual basis for guilt, and the highly respected Second Circuit had upheld the verdict. The Smith Act had been modeled after laws upheld by earlier courts, and the defendants were hardly nonentities; they were, in fact, the leaders of the Communist party of the United States, a group admittedly dedicated to the overthrow of the government. Kalven suggested that the high profile of the original trial made it look to many people that the United States had engaged in exactly the same type of political trial it had condemned in the Soviet Union; Dennis and his cohorts had not been tried for their actions but for their ideas, and Chief Justice Vinson had to labor mightily to try and make it look as if this had not been a political trial.

But the justices also had to wrestle with the stringent criteria that Brandeis had elaborated upon Holmes's clear and present danger test, and in fact it could not square the *Dennis* verdict with those standards. Vinson's opinion is so strained and illogical because he worked very hard to prove something impossible to prove—namely, that thinking about ideas, or even thinking about teaching and discussing ideas, without anything else, without any overt action, constitutes a clear and present danger to the state. To do this he had to read evil intent into the record, a notion that Holmes and Brandeis had specifically disavowed. The illogic of the majority opinion marked a low point in the Court's cold war record, and even the majority members realized they would have to rethink the issue.

Justice Harlan's Solution

The Court, in fact, did show itself more sensitive to free speech and security issues in subsequent Smith Act prosecutions. In *Yates v. United States* (1957), the Court set aside the conviction of fourteen middle-level Communist leaders. Justice Harlan ruled that the trial court had given too broad a meaning to the term "organize," and he limited *Dennis* in claiming that the Smith Act proscribed advocacy "to do something, now or in the future, rather than merely to believe in something." The Court sustained the part

> Public opinion being what it now is, few will protest the conviction of these Communist petitioners. There is hope, however, that in calmer times, when present pressures, passions and fears subside, this or some later Court will restore the First Amendment liberties to the high preferred place where they belong in a free society.
>
> —Hugo L. Black, dissenting in *Dennis v. United States* (1951)

of the Smith Act that made membership in any organization advocating the overthrow of the government by force or violence a felony in *Scales v. United States* (1961). Yet in a companion case, *Noto v. United States*, Justice Harlan invalidated such a conviction on the grounds that the evidentiary test had not been met; the prosecution had failed to show that the Communist party actually advocated forceful or violent overthrow of the government.

Later commentators have praised Harlan, a conservative Republican appointed by Eisenhower, for reinvigorating free speech protection and curtailing Smith Act prosecutions, even though the Court had held the act constitutional in *Dennis*. By "interpreting" *Dennis* and finding judicially manageable standards, he led the Court in a new direction; by imposing strict evidentiary criteria, Harlan in fact reestablished the Hand test. It would have been politically troublesome to a Court already charged with being too liberal and "soft on criminals" to have reversed itself on *Dennis*; Harlan's approach avoided that danger, while strengthening protection of speech. A similar pattern can be found in the Court's treatment of other anti-Communist legislation of the period.

The McCarran Act

Congress enacted the Internal Security Act, also known as the Subversive Activities Control Act or McCarran Act, in the spring of 1950. Through a number of highly complicated provisions, it required Communists and other "subversive" groups to register with the attorney general. To justify this admitted infringement on the First Amendment, Congress declared the existence of an international Communist conspiracy that constituted a clear and present danger to the United States. For enforcement of the law, Congress created a Subversive Activities Control Board, which, despite broad administrative discretion, remained answerable for its decisions to the courts. President Truman vetoed the bill, calling it "the greatest danger to freedom of speech, press, and assembly since the Sedition Act of 1798." But Congress, fearful of being considered soft on communism in an election year, promptly overrode the veto by large margins in both houses.

The Court, by a 5 to 4 vote, sustained the registration provision in *Communist Party v. S.A.C.B.* (1961). Justice Frankfurter denied that the First Amendment prevented Congress from requiring registration of membership lists of "organizations substantially dominated or controlled by that foreign power controlling the world Communist movement." However, the Court did put aside convictions for refusing to register, on the grounds that the wording of board orders constituted a violation of the Fifth Amendment's prohibition against self-incrimination (*Albertson v. S.A.C.B.* [1965]).

Since Section 6 of the act prohibited any member of a Communist organization from using a passport, the State Department now tried to revoke the passports of two party leaders. In *Aptheker v. Secretary of State* (1964), the Court invalidated that section because it "too broadly and indiscriminately restricts the right to travel and thereby abridges the liberty guaranteed by the Fifth Amendment." Another section made it a criminal offense for a member of a Communist organization to work in any defense facility. In *United States v. Robel* (1967), the Court declared that section unconstitutionally overbroad as well, but this time because it violated the First Amendment right of association.

By the time Congress enacted the Communist Control Act of 1954, the Red Scare had ebbed considerably, and the statute's sweeping provisions had few practical consequences. Only one case ever reached the Supreme Court, *Communist Party v. Catherwood* (1961), and the Court gracefully sidestepped the constitutional questions by declaring that this particular case raised interesting questions of state law, which had to be resolved in state courts.

The Court's policy of upholding the antisubversion statutes in general, but then severely restricting their application, also allowed it to invalidate state efforts to penalize allegedly subversive activities. In *Pennsylvania v. Nelson* (1956), the Court overturned a conviction under a state law for conspiring to overthrow the government of the United States by force and violence. Chief Justice Earl Warren held that the Smith Act, the McCarran Act, and the Communist Control Act had created a "pervasive" federal scheme that allowed no room for state interference. The decision effectively nullified the use of laws in forty-two states against sedition and criminal anarchy to prosecute alleged Communist plots to overthrow the federal government; theoretically, states could still prosecute efforts to undermine state governments. A decade later, however, the Court ruled that a Louisiana subversive activities law was void because of vagueness. Finally, in *Brandenburg v. Ohio* (1969), the Court struck down all laws penalizing advocacy of ideas, no matter how radical, as contrary to the First Amendment's guarantee of free speech.

McCarthyism

The worst aspect of the Red Scare, and the greatest abuse of power, involved the activities of the Republican senator from Wisconsin, Joseph R. McCarthy. "McCarthyism," as *Washington Post* cartoonist Herbert Block labeled the phenomenon of undocumented defamation of character, soon affected nearly every aspect of national life. The junior senator knew how to exploit the media with his constant accusations of treason in high places and his tirades against "State Department perverts," the "bright young men who are born with silver spoons in their mouths," and who now were "selling the Nation out."

The Republican victory in 1952 made McCarthy chairman of the Senate Committee on Government Operations, and he used the forum as a bludgeon against various foreign affairs agencies. For a while, he seemed undefeatable, and those who opposed him wound up labeled as traitors or worse. Men and women appeared before his committee to answer charges of disloyalty, without any opportunity to know who had accused them or the basis of the charges. Those who dared to invoke their rights, such as refusing to answer under the Fifth Amendment's protection against possible self-incrimination, found themselves accused by McCarthy as traitors.

McCarthy demanded access to employees in the army and elsewhere, and a number of key Republican senators backed him. Dwight Eisenhower, who privately detested McCarthy but had kept silent about his activities, now felt the junior senator from Wisconsin had gone too far. "I will not allow people around me to be subpoenaed," he told party leaders, and when they pressed him to cooperate, he stood firm. In addition, he made sure his cabinet officers understood his resolve and directed the secretary of defense to withhold sensitive information from McCarthy and his committee. "It is essential to efficient and effective administration that employees of the Executive Branch be in a position to be completely candid in advising with each other on official matters." It followed that "it is not in the public interest that *any* of their conversations or communications, or *any* documents or reproductions, concerning such advice be disclosed."

In terms of constitutional prerogatives, Eisenhower here asserted what some scholars claim is the most absolute assertion of the presidential right to withhold information from Congress that had ever been uttered in American history. Previous presidents had claimed that discussions in cabinet meetings should be confidential, but no chief executive had ever claimed that all of the business of the executive branch should fall under the umbrella of executive privilege, a concept at that time untested in the courts. While some contemporaries doubted the constitutionality of Eisenhower's action, no one challenged it. As for McCarthy, without access to the information he wanted, he could not provide any data to support his charges of numerous subversives in the executive.

Because congressmen and senators are immune from criminal and civil liability for anything they say in the course of their duties, people smeared by McCarthy had no legal redress against him. He cannily refused to be specific when outside the capital, and although his daily accusations grabbed the headlines, his victims' denials invariably wound up on the back pages. The turning point came when the courageous newscaster Edward R. Murrow exposed McCarthy's tactics on his widely viewed television show, "See It Now."

Soon afterward, the senator overreached himself. Failing to get preferential treatment from the army for a young protege, G. David Schine, McCarthy decided to investigate the armed services for alleged Communist influences. The televised portion of the "Army-McCarthy hearings" ran from April 22 to June 17, 1954. For the first time, instead of hearing McCarthy's accusations on the evening news or reading about them in the morning paper, Americans saw the man in action; it proved a revelation. His bullying, his disdain for procedural fairness, and the obvious falseness of his accusations all left a sour taste.

The Democratic victory in that fall's election deprived him of the committee chairmanship, but even his Republican colleagues had finally grown weary of his indiscriminate attacks. On December 2, 1954, by a vote of 67 to 22, the Senate condemned him for affronting the dignity of the chamber. As much as anything, that event marked the end of the Red Scare. The McCarthy hearings, like those of the House Un-American Activities Committee, had not uncovered a single subversive in high places. The job of catching spies reverted to the FBI, which had continued that function despite the interference of congressional committees. On the positive side, perhaps one can credit congressional leaders with a heightened sensitivity to the fact that the investigatory power, although an essential tool of legislative activity, could in the wrong hands turn into a terrible weapon against the people's rights.

The North Atlantic Treaty Organization

The concern over Communist subversion did not grow in a vacuum. In the years immediately after World War II, the Soviet Union had gained control over most of Eastern Europe. People feared that Moscow intended to advance communism through outright aggression and fifth column activities in other countries, as well. In the "Truman Doctrine," the president had declared it the nation's policy to oppose Soviet aggression; Congress had backed that policy through the Marshall Plan of economic aid to Western Europe and had applauded the Berlin airlift when Russia had tried to freeze the Western powers out of that city. In 1949, the United States signed the most extensive collective security agreement in its history, the North Atlantic Treaty.

The Senate, although highly favorable to the idea behind NATO (North Atlantic Treaty Organization), recognized constitutional problems with the treaty similar to those raised by the United Nations treaty. Under Article 5, an attack against any member is considered an attack against all of them. The provision does not automatically trigger a war, but it calls for each member to take "such action as it deems necessary, including the use of armed force." Perhaps aware of the concern raised by the United Nations charter, the drafters of the North Atlantic Treaty added that such action shall be "carried out by the Parties in accord with their respective constitutional processes."[1] The phrase is useful more as a reassurance than anything else. Constitutional authorities agree that while nothing in the Constitution prohibits a treaty from committing the United States to go to war, a clause that would automatically send American troops into battle would probably not withstand judicial scrutiny. In fact, in the fifty years since the signing of the North Atlantic Treaty, its members have gone to war only once, and then not in defense of a fellow NATO country but against Serbia's attack on Kosovo, technically still a part of Yugoslavia. Congress never fully approved of U.S. participation in the air strikes, and the Republican-dominated Congress reluctantly acquiesced after it became clear that President Clinton's gamble to force the Serbs out had paid off.

Considering the speed with which modern attacks can be launched and the need for an equally rapid response, it is conceivable that military commanders in the field, acting with the approval of the president, could involve the nation in a conflict within a matter of minutes, without a congressional declaration. This possibility led Senator Arthur Watkins of Utah to propose a reservation to the North Atlantic Treaty, denying that the United States owed military assistance to its allies, even when attacked, unless Congress approved the action by a joint resolution. The Senate voted down the proposal by a lopsided margin, delegating to the president the right to commit troops under the treaty as he found necessary. Secretary of State Dean Acheson, testifying before the Foreign Relations Committee, assured the senators that the treaty would not put the United States automatically at war. "Under our Constitution," he said, "the Congress alone has the power to declare war."

But despite these assurances, the balance of power had in fact shifted, and Congress had played no small role in amplifying the authority of the presidency at its own

1. Similar provisions are in the Rio Treaty of 1947, involving the United States and eighteen Latin American countries, and the Southeast Asia Treaty of 1954.

expense. The cold war required a rethinking of traditional American policy and especially of the role the military would play in containing Communist expansion. To this end, Congress, working with Harry Truman, reorganized the military, and while the army and navy kept their separate identities, leadership now came from a unified Department of Defense. The Strategic Air Command received the job of patrolling American skies on a continuous basis. The atomic bomb had been developed during World War II; now the country began work on thermonuclear hydrogen bombs. New advisory bodies charged with developing and coordinating American policy, such as the Joint Chiefs of Staff and the National Security Council, reported directly to the president. And despite wording to the contrary, the NATO and SEATO (South East Asia Treaty Organization) treaties gave the president, not the Congress, greater power in determining American foreign policy.

The Bricker Amendment

Despite Acheson's assurances that only Congress had the power to declare war, many conservatives recognized and feared the shift in power from the legislative to the executive. Several states petitioned Congress for a constitutional amendment to limit the presidential treaty power, and in February 1952, the American Bar Association recommended that the Constitution be amended so that treaties in conflict with "any provision of this Constitution shall not be of any force or effect." Senator John Bricker of Ohio introduced a proposal that not only limited the treaty power, but also imposed constraints on executive agreements. The Bricker Amendment struck at the strong foreign policy leadership of a president like Roosevelt; it also sought to overturn the Court's ruling in *Missouri v. Holland* (1920) that treaty obligations overrode state constitutions and laws.

The debate over the Bricker Amendment continued for two years, as opponents and advocates argued over its potential effect on foreign policy. Defenders claimed that Roosevelt and Truman had overstepped the bounds of their constitutional powers and that the Supreme Court had opened the door to a total destruction of states' rights. Opponents replied that the president needed a free hand in foreign affairs and that sufficient safeguards already existed to prevent any president from exceeding legitimate authority. The amendment, strangely enough, made no reference to the presidential power as commander-in-chief, and so did not restrict the executive use of military force.

By January 1953, on the eve of Dwight Eisenhower's inauguration, Bricker claimed to have sixty-four senators ready to vote for his amendment. But Eisenhower and his secretary of state, John Foster Dulles, both opposed the measure, as did most leading constitutional scholars. When the test vote came in February 1954, a watered-down version failed by one vote in the Senate, and after the Democrats regained control of Congress later that year, the issue faded away entirely.

Today there are relatively few constraints on presidential conduct of foreign policy. The War Powers Act of 1973, passed in response to Richard Nixon's abuses, is considered by many to be a dead letter (see Chapter 39). For example, no declaration of war has accompanied any of the military incursions ordered by American presidents in the last five decades. Collective security agreements have not been the problem; instead, presidents have insisted on their rights, as commander-in-chief, to use military force as an instrument of foreign policy whenever, in their judgment, American interests are threatened.

Harry Truman committed American troops to support United Nations action after the invasion of South Korea. Dwight Eisenhower sent troops to Lebanon in 1958; John Kennedy imposed a naval quarantine around Cuba in 1962 and that same year initiated the American involvement in Vietnam, which Lyndon Johnson greatly expanded. Johnson also sent troops to the Dominican Republic; Richard Nixon bombed Cambodia without congressional approval; Gerald Ford used troops in the Mayaguez incident; and Jimmy Carter risked war by sending in troops in an ill-fated effort to rescue American hostages in Iran. Ronald Reagan similarly saw no need to consult Congress when he dispatched troops to Lebanon, or ordered the invasion of Grenada and the bombing of Libya, even though by then Congress had enacted statutory restrictions on presidential use of troops. George Bush in the Gulf War and Bill Clinton in Somalia and Kosovo secured a form of congressional approval that hardly amounted to a declaration of war. The Korean conflict well illustrated this point.

The Korean Police Action

When the allies liberated Korea from Japanese occupation at the end of World War II, they "temporarily" divided the country along the 38th parallel: by 1950, the Communist north had come under the influence of China, while South Korea had allied itself with the United States. In June 1950, North Korean troops invaded the south, which immediately appealed for help to the United Nations. Because the Soviet Union had temporarily walked out of the United Nations, its representative was not present to veto a Security Council resolution that branded North Korea as the aggressor, called for the withdrawal of its forces, and asked United Nations members to render assistance. Two days later, on June 27, President Truman ordered American troops into battle in Korea. Termed a "police action," the Korean conflict cost 33,000 American lives, 104,000 Americans wounded or missing, and billions of dollars, yet it never constituted a war in a formal sense, since Congress did not declare war. By enacting empowering legislation, as well as appropriating funds to support the military operations, Congress de facto approved presidential policy, much as it would a decade and a half later in Vietnam.

Critics then and later complained that the executive had usurped congressional authority in violation of the Constitution. Truman, they claim, disregarded the unambiguous statutory language and legislative history of the United Nations Participation Act. He ordered troops into Korea without any congressional approval and ignored the various agreements that had been made between his administration and the Congress to assure advance legislative approval of military action. In fact, Truman had already ordered American sea and air forces to assist South Korea before the UN Security Council requested military assistance.

If the Congress had truly wanted to stop American involvement, however, it could have done so. Troops could not have stayed in Korea one extra day if Congress had voted to cut off funds. In the end, Congress adopted a weak resolution in April 1951, agreeing to Truman's policy, but urging that "in the interests of sound constitutional process, and of national unity and understanding, Congressional approval should be obtained on any policy requiring the assignment of American troops abroad."

Truman justified his decision on the basis of American treaty obligations to the United Nations, although this country had never signed an Article 43 agreement for troops to be used in peacekeeping operations. Whether constitutional support for this position existed has never been settled, since the debate has focused more on the wisdom of the Korean policy than on its constitutionality. Opponents of the war initiated a number of court cases to test the legality of American involvement in Korea in the absence of a congressional declaration, but the Supreme Court refused to hear any of them.

Civilian Control of the Military

There is one constitutional doctrine on which Harry Truman had no doubts; an avid student of history, he firmly believed that the Founding Fathers had intended the military to be at all times under the control of elected civilian officials. He had agreed to support the United Nations in a limited action to remove North Korean troops from South Korea. The commander of the United Nations and American forces, General Douglas MacArthur, saw the Korean operation as part of a greater anti-Communist crusade, however. After China entered the war on the side of North Korea, MacArthur, without clearing his statements with the Joint Chiefs of Staff, began calling for massive bombings of China and the use of atomic weapons. When MacArthur refused to obey orders to keep quiet, Truman, with the unanimous concurrence of the Joint Chiefs, removed him from command in April 1951.

Legitimate policy disputes separated the general from the president, but Truman did not emphasize them. He fired MacArthur because he wished to preserve what he considered one of the most important of constitutional principles—civilian control over the military. MacArthur had been insubordinate and had directly challenged the authority of the commander-in-chief. When later on people praised him for his courage in standing up to the five-star general and war hero, Truman snapped to a reporter that "courage had nothing to do with it. He was insubordinate, and I fired him."

Rarely had the country witnessed such outpourings of emotion, both the adulation accorded to MacArthur on his return to the United States, and the opprobrium heaped

> It seems strangely difficult for some to realize that here in Asia is where the Communist conspirators have elected to make their play for global conquest, and that we have joined the issue thus raised on the battlefield; that here we fight Europe's war with arms while the diplomats there still fight it with words; that if we lose the war to Communism in Asia the fall of Europe is inevitable; win it and Europe most probably would avoid war and yet preserve freedom. As you point out, we must win. There is no substitute for victory.
>
> —Douglas MacArthur to House Republican Leader Joseph Martin (20 March 1951)

on "Captain Harry" for daring to fire one of the great American military heroes. The Joint Chiefs of Staff, all respected military men, testified in the widely publicized Senate hearings on MacArthur's dismissal that the general had repeatedly and publicly challenged the administration's policy in Korea and thus violated a basic constitutional principle that the military had to remain subordinate to civilian authority. As this message sunk in, people began to appreciate Truman's position. MacArthur had come as close as any American since George McClellen to being a political general, and his attack on his commander-in-chief's policy justified Truman's dismissal of him.

The Steel Seizure Case

The year after he dismissed MacArthur, Truman shocked the nation again. The Korean conflict, no matter what one called it, constituted a real war, and administration officials believed that they had the same broad powers to mobilize the country as Roosevelt had enjoyed from 1941 to 1945. When the United Steel Workers threatened to strike after the Wage Stabilization Board had been unable to negotiate a settlement, Truman decided to act. In early April 1952, he issued Executive Order 10340, directing Secretary of Commerce Charles Sawyer to seize and operate the nation's steel mills to assure continued production of steel for defense needs.

Although Truman had no statutory authority for this action, he had another option, one with express statutory authority, to forestall the strike. The Taft-Hartley Law of 1947 included procedures whereby the government could secure an eighty-day "cooling off" period to postpone any strike that would adversely affect the public interest. Truman had vetoed the measure, only to have the Republican Congress override the veto. Taft-Hartley would not have provided a permanent solution, but at the least it enjoyed statutory justification and would have bought time in which a settlement might be reached—or, failing that, Congress could have imposed a solution through legislation. Truman, however, chose not to invoke the law. Instead, he simply seized the mills, informed Congress of what he had done, and invited its astounded members to take legislative action if they thought it necessary.

Although Truman based his order on his authority as commander-in-chief, the government's lawyers later argued that the president had acted solely on inherent executive power, without the need for statutory support. At a news conference on April 17, a reporter asked Truman, if he could seize the steel mills under his inherent powers, could he also seize the newspapers and the radio stations. Truman answered that "under similar circumstances the President of the United States has to act for whatever is for the best of the country." Recognizing that this theory of virtually unlimited presidential power offended many people, Truman began back-pedaling. He wrote a letter to the Senate stating that Congress could, "if it wishes, reject the course of action I have followed in this matter." In a further effort to defuse criticism, Truman said that all presidential powers are derived from the Constitution and are limited by that document's provisions.

Despite the president's unparalleled action, most contemporary commentators believed that the steel companies could not win their appeal to the judiciary before a Supreme Court composed entirely of men appointed by either Roosevelt or Truman.

Moreover, the manner in which the steel companies had framed their argument allowed the Court an easy way to avoid the issue. The companies conceded that an emergency existed and that the government had the right to take over their businesses during an emergency; but they objected that the wrong branch of government had proceeded against them. In essence, they complained that the privileges of the legislative branch had suffered as a result of the executive's unconstitutional acts. Rarely does a private party sue on behalf of one branch of government, and the Court could have dismissed the suit for lack of standing. But by a vote of 7 to 2, the justices agreed to hear the case, and in *Youngstown Sheet & Tube Company v. Sawyer*, they ruled 6 to 3 that the president had acted unlawfully.

Justice Black delivered the majority opinion, which flatly denied that the president had authority under any statute, under any express provision of the Constitution, or even by any implied power as commander-in-chief to seize the steel mills. Without specific constitutional permission, the president can act only if there is express or clearly implied authorization by Congress; if the legislature remains silent, then no power is granted. Justice Frankfurter's concurring opinion agreed with the result, but he offered somewhat more leeway for the executive. The president could act, Frankfurter argued, even in the face of congressional silence, if it could be shown that historically, the legislative branch had acquiesced in similar actions. Justice Jackson moved even further along the spectrum in his concurrence, arguing that Congress had not been silent, but in its debates over the Taft-Hartley Act and the Defense Production Act had considered giving the president such power and had decided not to do so. The Court, looking at the legislative history, could reasonably believe that Congress did not want the president to have this power.

Chief Justice Vinson had privately assured Truman before the president had acted that the seizure would be legal and, if challenged in the courts, would be upheld. Now Vinson, joined by Reed and Minton, dissented and argued for an extensive interpretation of presidential authority. Where Black had claimed the president could act only if empowered by Congress, Vinson asserted that the president could act in every instance except where limited by express congressional refusal. Vinson's opinion implied a practically unlimited executive power, a position Truman had not even asserted.

The *Youngstown* decision triggered a fifty-three-day strike in the steel industry. Although the Court had clearly intimated that Congress and the president had ample statutory means to avert the strike, the political sensitivities of an election year prevented either from acting. From a constitutional standpoint, *Youngstown* remains one of the "great" modern cases, in that it helped redress the balance of power among the three branches, a balance that had been severely distorted by the enormous growth of executive authority first in the New Deal and then during the war and the postwar search for global security.

For Further Reading

An excellent general introduction to the period is James T. Patterson, *Grand Expectations: The United States, 1945–1974* (1996). Alonzo L. Hamby, *Beyond the New Deal: Harry S. Truman and American Liberalism* (1973) is one of the best works on the Truman years; see also the two volumes by Robert J. Donovan, *Conflict and Crisis: The Presidency of Harry S. Truman, 1945–1948* (1977) and *The Tumultuous Years: The Presidency of Harry S. Truman, 1949–1953* (1982); and R. Alton Lee, *Truman and Taft–Hartley* (1967). There are two fine biographies of Truman, David McCullough, *Truman* (1992), and Alonzo L. Hamby, *Man of the People: A Life of Harry S. Truman* (1995).

For labor and the Taft-Hartley Act, see Melvyn Dubofsky, *The State and Labor in Modern America* (1994); Christopher L. Tomlins, *The State and the Unions: Labor Relations, Law, and the Organized Labor Movement in America, 1880–1960* (1985); and James Patterson, *Mr. Republican: A Biography of Robert A. Taft* (1972).

There are many works on the anti-Communist drives of this period, but by far the best single volume is Stanley I. Kutler, *The American Inquisition: Justice and Injustice in the Cold War* (1982). Other worthwhile studies include Michal R. Belknap, *Cold War Political Justice: The Smith Act, the Communist Party, and American Civil Liberties* (1977); David Caute, *The Great Fear: The Anti-Communist Purge Under Truman and Eisenhower* (1978); Alan Harper, *The Politics of Loyalty: The White House and the Communist Issue, 1946–1952* (1968); and Morton Grodzins, *The Loyal and the Disloyal* (1956). For McCarthyism, see Richard Fried, *Nightmare in Red: The McCarthy Era in Perspective* (1990); David Oshinsky, *A Conspiracy So Immense: The World of Joe McCarthy* (1983); Thomas Rosteck, *See It Now Confronts McCarthyism* (1994); and Ellen Schrecker, *Many Are the Crimes: McCarthyism in America* (1998).

Specialized studies include Eleanor Bontecou, *The Federal Loyalty–Security Program* (1953); Walter Goodman, *The Committee: The Extraordinary Career of the House Committee on Un-American Activities* (1968); John P. Sullivan and David N. Webster, "Some Constitutional and Practical Problems of the Subversive Activities Control Act," 45 *Georgetown Law Journal* 299 (1957); E. S. Corwin, "Bowing Out Clear and Present Danger," 27 *Notre Dame Law Review* 325 (1952); and Robert Mollan, "Smith Act Prosecutions: The Effect of the Dennis and Yates Decisions," 26 *University of Pittsburgh Law Review* 705 (1965). A good discussion of Hand's efforts to develop a viable speech test is in the absorbing study by Marvin Schick, *Learned Hand's Court* (1970); in this connection, see also Gerald Gunther, "Learned Hand and the Origins of Modern First Amendment Doctrine: Some Fragments of History," 27 *Stanford Law Review* 719 (1975); as well as the relevant sections of Gunther's *Learned Hand: The Man and the Judge* (1994).

For foreign affairs and presidential power, see Melvyn Leffler, *A Preponderance of Power: National Security, the Truman Administration, and the Cold War* (1992), as well as Louis Fisher, *Presidential War Power* (1995). See also Loch K. Johnson, *The Making of International Agreements: Congress Confronts the Executive* (1984). For the NATO treaty, see Richard H. Heindel et al., "The North Atlantic Treaty in the United States Senate," 43 *American Journal of International Law* 633 (1949). The Bricker Amendment is the subject of a number of articles; see especially, Arthur E. Sutherland, "Restricting the Treaty Power," 65 *Harvard Law Review* 1305 (1952); and Glendon Schubert, "Politics and the Constitution: The Bricker Amendment During 1953," 16 *Journal of Politics* 257 (1954).

On Korea, see Burton Kaufman, *The Korean War: Challenges in Crisis, Credibility, and Command* (1986); and A. Kenneth Pye, "The Legal Status of the Korean Hostilities," 45 *Georgetown Law Journal* 45 (1956). The firing of MacArthur is the subject of a fine monograph by John W. Spanier, *The Truman-MacArthur Controversy* (1965). For the steel seizure, see E. S. Corwin, "The Steel Seizure Case—A Judicial Brick Without Straw," 53 *Columbia Law Review* 53 (1953); there are several books on the episode, but the excellent volume by Maeva Marcus, *Truman and the Steel Seizure Case: The Limits of Presidential Power* (1977) is definitive.

35

The Struggle for Civil Rights

Truman and the First Steps • The NAACP Intensifies Its Efforts • The Vinson Court and Civil Rights • Enter Earl Warren • The Five School Cases • Brown v. Board of Education *• The Reaction to* Brown *• Implementation • "All Deliberate Speed" • Eisenhower and Little Rock • For Further Reading*

NO OTHER SET of decisions by the U.S. Supreme Court has so altered the social fabric of the nation as those involving the civil rights of African Americans. Though the Civil War erased legal bondage, Reconstruction failed to wipe out other badges of discrimination, and the entire nation acquiesced as the South created a complex legal and social system designed to keep blacks in separate and inferior status. But eight decades of tradition began to crumble after World War II, and in *Brown v. Board of Education* (1954), the Court sounded the death knell of legally enforced racial discrimination. The case did not mark the triumph of equality, however, but merely the end of legally imposed inequality. *Brown* was only the first stage in a continuing campaign to end racism and discrimination in America.

Truman and the First Steps

During World War II, the nation's declared aim of fighting intolerance abroad led black Americans to renew their demands for the end of racial injustice at home. In response, President Roosevelt issued an executive order on June 25, 1941, directing that blacks be accepted into job-training programs in defense plants. The order also forbade discrimination by employers holding defense contracts and set up a Fair Employment Practices Commission (FEPC) to investigate charges of racial discrimination. But aside from this step, civil rights remained a low priority of the war administration.

President Harry S. Truman, beset by a multitude of crises after taking office, put up no protest when Congress killed the wartime agency. Later on, however, he asked Congress to create a permanent FEPC, and in December 1946, he appointed a distinguished panel to serve as the President's Commission on Civil Rights to recommend "more adequate means and procedures for the protection of the civil rights of the people of the United States." The commission's report, "To Secure These Rights," issued in October 1947, defined the nation's civil rights agenda for the next generation. The commission noted the many restrictions on blacks and urged that each person, regardless of race, color, creed, or national origin, should have access to equal opportunity in securing education, decent housing, and jobs. Among its proposals, the commission suggested antilynching and antipoll tax laws, a permanent FEPC, and the strengthening of the civil rights division of the Justice Department.

In a courageous act, the president sent a special message to Congress on February 2, 1948, calling for prompt implementation of the commission's recommendations. The Southern delegations promptly blocked any action by threatening to filibuster. Unable to secure civil rights legislation from Congress, Truman moved ahead by using his executive authority. He bolstered the civil rights section of the Justice Department and directed it to assist private litigants in civil rights cases. He appointed William Hastie, the first black judge of a federal appeals court, and named several African Americans to high-ranking positions in the administration. Most important, by executive orders later in the year, the president abolished segregation in the armed forces and ordered full racial integration in the services.

The achievements of the Truman administration fell far short of the promises. While Southern control of key congressional committees blocked legislative action, the president never made civil rights a top priority of his administration. Aware that he had limited political capital, Truman chose not to expend it on an issue whose outcome remained uncertain. Nonetheless, black Americans had gotten the attention of the nation's political leaders; not until they learned to exert political force of their own would they be able to move civil rights to the top of the country's agenda.

While Congress refused to create a federal agency, a number of states set up their own FEPCs. New York acted first in 1945, establishing the State Commission Against Discrimination to investigate and stop prejudice in employment. In the next decade, other Northern states passed similar laws, so that nearly two-thirds of the entire population of the country came under some form of governmental protection against bias in hiring.

The NAACP Intensifies Its Efforts

Against this backdrop the National Association for the Advancement of Colored People (NAACP) resumed its campaign, or to be more precise, intensified its efforts, because even during the war it had not been quiescent. In 1941, the Court for the first time had upheld a black plaintiff's challenge to segregated transportation. Congressman Arthur W. Mitchell of Illinois had been ejected from a Pullman car when the train crossed into Arkansas. Mitchell filed a complaint, not in court, but with the Interstate Commerce Commission, claiming he had been discriminated against in violation of the Interstate Commerce Act. When the ICC upheld the railroad, Mitchell appealed to the high court, which upheld his claim (*Mitchell v. United States* [1941]). The Mitchell decision gave the NAACP hope that the Court stood ready to review its earlier transportation holdings that had sustained segregation.

In another important wartime case, the NAACP had gotten the Court to strike down the all-white primary in *Smith v. Allwright* (1944). The organization had always had as its goal the defeat of the separate-but-equal doctrine, but its leaders, especially Thurgood Marshall, realized that in terms of tactics, it would have to begin by attacking the South's failure to provide equal facilities. In a wide range of cases, decided primarily in the lower courts on the basis of Chief Justice Hughes's opinion in *Gaines*, Marshall and his colleagues forced Southern states to improve the physical facilities of all-black schools and to pay black teachers on a par with whites.

In the spring of 1946, Marshall and William Hastie came to Washington to argue a transportation rather than a school case. Irene Morgan, a black woman, had boarded a bus in Richmond to go to Baltimore, and she had been ordered to the back of the bus as Virginia law required. Morgan refused, claiming that as an interstate passenger Virginia law did not apply to her. After her arrest and conviction, the NAACP took the case on appeal.

The NAACP relied on an 1878 decision, *Hall v. DeCuir,* in which the Court had invalidated a Louisiana Reconstruction statute prohibiting discrimination on account of race as a burden. Chief Justice Morison Waite had ruled that railroads needed a uniform policy throughout the country, but that only Congress could make such a policy through its control of interstate commerce. However, a few years later, the Court refused to void a Mississippi law requiring segregation, in *Louisville, New Orleans & Texas Railway Co. v. Mississippi* (1890). In the transportation cases that followed, leading up to *Plessy*, the Court validated the doctrine of separate-but-equal. It did not, however, ever overrule *Hall v. DeCuir's* holding regarding the supremacy of Congress in interstate transportation.

In *Morgan v. Virginia* (1946), Justice Reed, for a 7–1 majority, followed the reasoning in *DeCuir,* but stood it on its head. Claiming that railroads needed a uniform policy, he held that in interstate travel, rail and bus lines could not discriminate on the basis of race. Reed very carefully made it clear that the opinion did not affect state law regulating intrastate commerce.

Two years later, the Court ignored both *DeCuir* and *Morgan* to uphold a Northern state's antidiscrimination law, even though it clearly affected interstate and foreign commerce. A Detroit amusement park company operated a steamboat to an island on the Canadian side of the Detroit River. The company had refused to allow a young black woman to go on an outing with a number of white classmates and claimed that the Michigan Civil Rights Act had no applicability since the steamboat ran in foreign commerce.

> Today we are just emerging from a war in which all of the people of the United States were joined in a death struggle against the apostles of racism. . . . How much clearer, therefore, must it be today than it was in 1877, that the national business of interstate commerce is not to be disfigured by disruptive local practices bred of racial notions alien to our national ideals, and to the solemn undertakings of the community of civilized nations as well.
>
> —NAACP brief in *Morgan v. Virginia* (1946)

In *Bob-Lo Excursion Company v. Michigan* (1948), Justice Rutledge evaded the precedents by ruling that the commerce, although technically foreign, was actually "highly local," since the island, except for its foreign ownership, for all practical purposes was part of Detroit. The case indicated the problems the Court would have if it tried to decide race discrimination suits on the basis of the commerce power. Justice Douglas pointed the way to the future in his concurrence, suggesting that the Equal Protection Clause would give the courts a far more flexible tool; he also intimated that as far as he was concerned, one could not square the separate-but-equal doctrine with the constitutional mandate of equal protection.

The Court had still one more chance to abandon separate-but-equal in transportation, in *Henderson v. United States* (1950). Elmer Henderson had been traveling from Atlanta, Georgia to Washington, D.C. in May 1942, and had wanted to eat dinner. Upon reaching the dining car, he found ten tables reserved for white passengers and one, shielded by a curtain, set aside for blacks. Although the "black" table was full, the conductor refused to allow Henderson to occupy an empty seat at one of the white tables. Henderson filed a complaint with the ICC, which still proved timid in attacking discrimination, and the Supreme Court unanimously struck down the practice on the same grounds as *Mitchell*, namely, such arbitrary arrangements interfered with the equal access of passengers in violation—not of the Constitution—but of the Interstate Commerce Act. By relying on *Mitchell*, the Court did not attack separate-but-equal, but made it far more difficult for the carriers to meet the standard. *Plessy* remained alive, but somewhat restricted.

The Vinson Court and Civil Rights

The Vinson Court proved equally reluctant to confront the separate-but-equal rule in education, but it continued on the path laid out in *Gaines* before the war. Although it decided only a handful of cases in this area and took a very cautious approach, it anticipated some of the Warren Court's landmark decisions.

In 1948, two cases reached the Court involving restrictive covenants, which denied blacks access to housing in white neighborhoods. The covenants had become widespread after the Court, in *Buchanan v. Worley* (1917), had struck down local ordinances enforcing residential segregation; as "private agreements," the covenants presumably did not come within the reach of the Fourteenth Amendment. But all six members of the Court who participated in *Shelley v. Kraemer* agreed that state action existed. Chief Justice Vinson explained that so long as the discriminatory intent of the covenants could be enforced in state courts, then the states were sanctioning racial discrimination in violation of the Fourteenth Amendment. The Court was careful not to declare the covenants themselves illegal, since private discrimination continued to be constitutionally permissible, but it did make them unenforceable. In a companion case, *Hurd v. Hodge*, Vinson applied the holding to covenants in the District of Columbia. Although the Fourteenth Amendment did not apply to the national government, the chief justice found that such actions violated the 1866 Civil Rights Act and that it went against public policy to allow a federal court to enforce an agreement that was unenforceable in state courts.

> These are not cases . . . in which the States have merely abstained from action, leaving private individuals free to impose such discriminations as they see fit. Rather, these are cases in which the States have made available to such individuals the full coercive power of government to deny to petitioners, on the grounds of race or color, the enjoyment of property rights.
>
> —Fred M. Vinson, *Shelley v. Kraemer* (1948)

The Court also took a few hesitant steps against racial segregation in education. In *Missouri ex rel. Gaines v. Canada* (1938), Chief Justice Hughes had startled the South by insisting that if it wanted to keep segregated schools, then it had to provide some form of similar or equal opportunity. The Court did not have a chance to show how seriously it meant this until after the war. The first case involved Ada Sipuel, who after compiling an excellent record at the State College for Negroes in Langston, had applied to the University of Oklahoma Law School, the only one in the state. The school refused to admit her and told her a separate law school with "substantially equal" facilities would soon open. She sued for immediate admission, and Thurgood Marshall, chief counsel for the NAACP, knew he would lose in the lower courts. But he prepared the ground for his appeal, and four days after the Court heard arguments in *Sipuel v. Board of Regents of the University of Oklahoma* in 1948, it issued a unanimous *per curiam* order directing Oklahoma to provide Ms. Sipuel (by then Mrs. Fisher) with a legal education "in conformity with the equal protection clause of the Fourteenth Amendment and to provide it as soon as it does for applicants of any other group." The board of regents angrily created a law school overnight, roping off a small section of the state capitol in Oklahoma City and assigning three teachers to attend to the instruction of Ada Sipuel and "others similarly situated." When Marshall appealed to the Supreme Court, the justices, with only Murphy and Rutledge dissenting, refused to consider whether the state had in fact established an equal facility.

A few years later, the state again tried to get around the rules. The University of Oklahoma had grudgingly admitted sixty-eight-year-old George W. McLaurin to its graduate school, where he hoped to earn a doctorate in education. But McLaurin had to sit in the corridor outside the regular classroom, use a separate desk on the mezza-

> I was saying to [Mac Q. Williamson, attorney general of Oklahoma] how I thought that even if they were eventually able to persuade the Supreme Court that the facilities of the Negro school were equal, what was the state going to do when a Negro applied for a medical education—build him a whole medical school? He suddenly saw a flash of light, I guess, and struck his forehead with his palm as the revelation hit him. "Oh, my God," he said, "suppose one of them wanted to be a petroleum engineer! Why, we've got the biggest petroleum-cracking laboratory in the country here." And I think the fire went out of his case after that.
>
> —Walter Gellhorn, NAACP expert witness in *Sipuel v. Oklahoma Board of Regents* (1948)

nine of the library, and eat alone in a dingy alcove in the cafeteria. When the NAACP challenged these rules, the university allowed McLaurin inside the classroom but surrounded his seat with a railing which said "Reserved for Colored." For a unanimous bench, Chief Justice Vinson struck down these rules in *McLaurin v. Oklahoma State Regents* (1950) as imposing inequality on the petitioner even though he physically attended the same school as whites. The Vinson Court refused to overrule *Plessy*, but consciously or not, the chief justice had provided a clue to the NAACP on how it might attack segregation in the future.

The same day as *McLaurin*, the Court handed down its decision regarding efforts to keep blacks out of the University of Texas Law School in Austin. After Heman Marion Sweatt applied in 1946, the district court gave Texas six months to establish a law school. The state created the School of Law of the Texas State University for Negroes; a makeshift classroom in an Austin basement marked the beginning of the allegedly equal black law school, although before long the state did appropriate a significant sum to upgrade it. While the physical plant and library had grown by the time Thurgood Marshall carried the case to the Supreme Court, Marshall felt confident he could show that the absence of a good library, well-known faculty, and all the other intangibles that made the University of Texas Law School a topflight institution denied Sweatt an equal education.

If nothing else, the members of the Supreme Court—especially Tom Clark, a graduate of the Texas Law School—knew what made a good law school, and in *Sweatt v. Painter*, they unanimously rejected the Texas claim that it had provided equal facilities. Chief Justice Vinson ordered Sweatt admitted to the Austin school, the first time the Supreme Court had ever ordered a black student admitted to a previously all-white school on grounds that the state had failed to provide equal separate facilities. But despite the steps taken in all three cases, the *Plessy* rule of separate-but-equal remained the law of the land.

Enter Earl Warren

When Chief Justice Fred Vinson died unexpectedly of a heart attack on September 8, 1953, speculation about his successor quickly focused on Earl Warren, the popular Republican governor of California. In fact, Dwight Eisenhower had already promised Warren the first vacancy on the bench, although at the time, the president did not ex-

> The University of Texas Law School possesses to a far greater degree those qualities which are incapable of objective measurement but which make for greatness in a law school. Such qualities, to name but a few, include reputation of the faculty, experience of the administration, position and influence of the alumni, standing in the community, traditions and prestige. It is difficult to believe that one who had a free choice between these law schools would consider the question close.
>
> —Fred M. Vinson, *Sweatt v. Painter* (1950)

pect it to be the center chair. Admirers would later call Earl Warren "Superchief" and "the greatest Chief Justice since John Marshall," but there was little in his previous record to foreshadow his extraordinary tenure as the nation's highest judicial officer. Warren had no prior judicial experience, and many observers viewed his appointment as a piece of political patronage.

Yet political savvy on the bench is not a quality to be despised. William Howard Taft had used his political talents during the 1920s to expand the power of the Court, and his successor, Charles Evans Hughes, had skillfully averted permanent damage to the Court during the tumultuous New Deal era. Although Harlan Fiske Stone had been greatly respected as a judge, he had not been a successful chief justice, and the personality and ideological cracks on the Court had opened up even wider during Fred Vinson's tenure. Beyond his ability to establish peace and manage the Court effectively, Warren understood the necessity of making controversial decisions acceptable, if not palatable, to the public at large. A lifelong public servant, he saw the bench not as a hermitage or an ivory tower, but as a vital part of daily government.

The Five School Cases

The new chief would preside over the rehearing of arguments in five potentially explosive suits challenging racial segregation in public schools. The justices had been anticipating a direct attack on the separate-but-equal doctrine, especially after the decisions in *McLaurin* and *Sweatt.* For Thurgood Marshall, the Texas opinion was "replete with road markings telling us where to go next." Seventeen Southern and border states, as well as Washington, D.C., legally required segregation in public schools; another four states permitted it. The attack on segregation per se and not just on the lack of equal facilities had been the goal of the NAACP for years, but in deciding to take on these cases, Marshall and his legal team knew they would face formidable obstacles.

In June 1952, the Court had announced that it would hear arguments the following December in cases challenging school segregation laws in Delaware, Virginia, South Carolina, Kansas, and the District of Columbia. The Court had consolidated the cases, with the Kansas appeal as the lead case so that, according to Justice Clark, "the whole question would not smack of being a purely Southern one."[1]

The Court, as an *amicus* brief from the Justice Department pointed out, had several options. It could avoid overruling *Plessy* by the simple expedient of finding the colored schools unequal and ordering either integration or another remedy. But the two

1. In the same term that the brethren wrestled with the school cases, they also heard another challenge to the South's white primary system. For fifty years, the Jaybird Democratic Association of Fort Bend County, Texas, had been holding a May primary separate from the official one run by the county the following month. The criteria for voting in the Jaybird primary were the same as those for voting in the regular election, except blacks could not vote (as they could in the county election, thanks to *Smith v. Allwright*). In Court, Jaybird officials acknowledged that they intended to exclude blacks and claimed they could so as a private club. But as Justice Black noted in *Terry v. Adams* (1953), the Jaybird primary served as a subterfuge, since whoever won the Jaybird balloting in effect won not only the official primary but the general election as well.

lawyers who drafted the brief, Philip Elman and Robert Stern, urged that a significant body of precedent warranted the abandonment of separate-but-equal, which they condemned as a contradiction in terms. In what may have been one of the most influential suggestions made during the entire litigation, they noted that even if the Court chose to strike down racial segregation in the schools, it did not have to do so immediately; a "reasonable period of time will obviously be required to permit formulation of new provisions," and implementation could well be left to the lower courts.

The brethren had been unable to reach agreement after the initial argument, and in the spring of 1953, they asked counsel to reargue the case the following fall. Specifically, they wanted both sides to discuss whether Congress in proposing, and the states in adopting, the Fourteenth Amendment had intended to ban racial segregation in schools. Further, if the Court ruled against continued segregation, how should the decision be put into effect?

Until recently, scholars had believed that the Court in Vinson's last term stood deeply divided over whether to reverse *Plessy*. Supposedly Black, Douglas, Burton, and Minton wanted to overrule *Plessy* outright, while Vinson, Reed, and Clark believed segregation constitutional. Frankfurter and Jackson opposed racial discrimination, but questioned whether the Court had the power to interfere in what had traditionally been a local matter. Recent scholarship, as well as common sense, tells us that the supposed divisions on the bench in 1952 could not have been concrete, since with the exception of one person, the Court that handed down the unanimous decision in *Brown* in 1954 was the same Court that first heard the five cases in 1952. It now appears that once Vinson died, Stanley Reed was the only justice who supported segregation and believed it constitutional.

The Court, with Earl Warren presiding, heard reargument in the cases beginning December 7, 1953. Instead of the usual hour or two permitted oral presentation, the justices sat through an unprecedented ten hours spread over three days. The redoubtable John W. Davis, a former solicitor general of the United States, represented South Carolina, and he defended racial segregation in an emotional coda to a long and distinguished career. He denied that the Court had any authority to intrude in an area reserved for the states alone, or interfere with practices hallowed by the usages of time. "To every principle," he intoned, "comes a moment of repose when it has been so often announced, so confidently relied upon, so long continued, that it passes the limits of judicial discretion and disturbance."

For Thurgood Marshall, leader of the NAACP legal team, the moment was equally dramatic; his very presence in the courtroom symbolized what he demanded of the Court and of the nation—equality for all people regardless of the color of their skin.

> We recognize that there are a great many people of the highest character and position who disapprove of segregation as a matter of principle or as ethics. We think that most of them really do not know the conditions, particularly in the South, that brought about that situation.
>
> —T. Justin Moore, attorney for the Commonwealth of Virginia, in oral argument (1953)

> I got the feeling on hearing the discussion yesterday that when you put a white child in a school with a whole lot of colored children, the child would fall apart or something. Everybody knows that is not true.
>
> Those same kids in Virginia and South Carolina—and I have seen them do it—they play in the streets together, they play on their farms together, they go down the road together, they separate to go to school, they come out of school and play ball together. They have to be separated in school.
>
> There is some magic to it. You can have them voting together, you can have them not restricted because of law in the houses they live in. You can have them going to the same state university and the same college, but if they go to elementary and high school, the world will fall apart.
>
> —Thurgood Marshall, attorney for the NAACP, in oral argument (1953)

He condemned school segregation laws as nothing but Black Codes, which could be sustained only if the Court found "that for some reason Negroes are inferior to all other human beings." To buttress his case, Marshall argued that segregation not only violated the Constitution, but had adverse and lasting psychological effects on black children who were consigned to an obviously inferior position. The NAACP submitted a "Brandeis brief," citing the latest social science research to support this contention.

Brown v. Board of Education

The decision on segregation in education did not come down until the following spring. Part of the delay may be attributed to the fact that Warren, who held only an interim appointment, did not receive Senate confirmation until March. But the chief justice used that time to "mass the Court," so that when he began reading the opinion in *Brown v. Board of Education* at 12:52 P.M. on May 17, 1954, he spoke for a unanimous bench.

Considering its epochal significance, the *Brown* decision was deceptively simple, running only eleven pages; Warren intended it to be short enough so that the nation's newspapers could run it in its entirety. The history of the Fourteenth Amendment and its relation to education, which the Court had asked both sides to argue, had been "inconclusive"—in part because public education in the South in 1868 had been so primitive that no one had bothered to think about it. Warren then briefly examined the *Plessy* doctrine and noted the extent of segregation in Northern as well as Southern states. Times had changed, Warren declared, and "in approaching this problem, we cannot turn the clock back to 1868 when the Amendment was adopted, or even to 1896 when *Plessy v. Ferguson* was written. We must consider public education in the light of its full development and its present place in American life throughout the Nation." Education played a crucial role in training people to become productive members of society; even more important, it prepared them to be citizens and to participate in the critical political choices facing the country. When the state undertook to provide education, it had to do so on equal terms to all.

By now, Warren had read through two-thirds of the opinion, and he finally reached the crucial question: "Does segregation of children in public schools solely on the basis of race . . . deprive the children of the minority group of equal educational opportunities?" Pausing for a moment, Warren said "We unanimously believe it does." Reaffirming the eloquent dissent of the first Justice Harlan in *Plessy*, that separate could never be equal, Warren declared that to segregate black schoolchildren

> from others of similar age and qualifications solely because of their race generates a feeling of inferiority as to their status in the community that may affect their hearts and minds in a way unlikely ever to be undone. . . . Segregation with the sanction of law, therefore, has a tendency to retard the educational and mental development of Negro children.

As a result, the Court concluded "that in the field of public education the doctrine of 'separate-but-equal' has no place. Separate educational facilities are inherently unequal." When Warren announced that the decision was unanimous, he later recalled, "a wave of emotion swept the room."[2]

Each member of the Court understood the importance of the decision and knew that the opinion would be widely and closely read. They knew they did not have to convince black Americans and the many Northern whites who already believed the Fourteenth Amendment prohibited official racism, and they also recognized that unregenerate racists would not agree no matter what the Court said. But the Court hoped to reach those who could be persuaded, and who could be brought to understand the need to do away with state-sanctioned segregation. In a memorandum accompanying a draft of the *Brown* opinion, Earl Warren explained that he had operated on "the theory that the opinions should be short, readable by the lay public, non-rhetorical, unemotional and, above all, nonaccusatory." He saw this as the one chance to bring as many Southern whites as possible to understand and support the decision.

The last paragraph of the *Brown* opinion showed Warren's famed political astuteness. Noting the wide applicability of the decisions and the complexity of devising an appropriate solution, he invited the parties to assist the Court in fashioning a proper remedy and declared that arguments would be heard that fall. The "wide applicability" phrase broadcast the intention of the Court to order desegregation in all school districts, North and South, urban and rural. The reference to the complexity of the problem and the delay in issuing implementing orders signaled to the South that the justices recognized the emotional crisis that the decision would cause and that they would allow time for the states to accustom themselves to the idea. By inviting the different parties to join in fashioning a remedy, the Court hoped that the Jim Crow states would cooperate and thus avoid the imposition of harsher solutions should they refuse. Finally, Warren carefully framed the opinion to apply to only one area, the legal segregation of children by race in primary and secondary public schools, the group most likely to win public sympathy as victims of racism. The decision did not strike down all Jim Crow laws, nor did it declare all discriminatory statutes unconstitutional. Crit-

---

2. In the companion case of *Bolling v. Sharpe*, the Court struck down segregation in the District of Columbia as well. Finding that segregation deprived the plaintiff of "liberty under law," the Court ruled that such discrimination violated the Fifth Amendment. The Constitution could not permit the federal government to operate segregated schools when it forbade the states to do so.

ics might predict that such would be the logical extension of *Brown*, but for the moment, the Court concerned itself only with education.

The Reaction to *Brown*

Within an hour of the opinion, the Voice of America beamed news of the decision around the world in over thirty languages. Northern newspapers for the most part hailed the decision as "momentous." What the justices have done, declared the *Cincinnati Enquirer*, "is simply to act as the conscience of the American nation." Within the black community, reaction was mixed, as leaders waited to see how the lofty words would be translated into action. The *Chicago Defender*, a leading black newspaper, called the decision a "second emancipation proclamation . . . more important to our democracy than the atomic bomb or the hydrogen bomb." Local black columnist Nat Williams, writing in Memphis, said "there was no general 'hallelujah, 'tis done' hullaballoo. Beale Streeters are sorta skeptical about giving out with cheers yet." Such skepticism, unfortunately, proved well founded.

Initially, the South heard voices of moderation, more so than one might have expected. The governor of Virginia, Thomas Stanley, called for "cool heads, calm study, and sound judgment." Governor "Big Jim" Folsom of Alabama declared that "When the Supreme Court speaks, that's the law." The governor of Arkansas promised that "Arkansas will obey the law. It always has." The respected *Louisville Courier-Journal* assured its readers that "the end of the world has not come for the South or for the nation. The Supreme Court's ruling is not itself a revolution. It is rather acceptance of a process that has been going on for a long time." The editors urged Southerners to follow the Court's example of moderation, advice akin to that of the *Atlanta Constitution*, which called on Georgians "to think clearly."

The Court had expected criticism of the decision not only from the South, which would naturally defend its way of life, but from the scholarly community as well. The chief justice's insistence that the opinion be "short, readable by the lay public, nonrhetorical, unemotional and, above all, nonaccusatory," had been a brilliant political stroke, papering over theoretical differences among the justices, but it robbed the decision of intellectual force and authority. The Court's dismissal of the background and relevance of the Fourteenth Amendment as "inconclusive," for example, led to charges that the Court had misunderstood history. One group argued that the amendment had been designed to ensure black equality, and therefore that the Framers had intended it to prevent segregation in the schools and elsewhere. Another faction weighed in with convincing evidence that the "original understanding" of those responsible for the Fourteenth Amendment did not encompass regulation of race relations.

> The Negroes did not themselves instigate the agitation against segregation. They were put up to it by radical busybodies who are intent upon overthrowing American institutions.
>
> —Senator James Eastland of Mississippi, on the *Brown* decision (1954)

The famous footnote 11 elicited a far more serious and enduring attack. In its "Brandeis brief," the NAACP had cited whatever material it could find to support the claim that segregation hurt black children. The chief justice, to buttress his finding that segregation psychologically harmed black children, cited a number of works, including Gunnar Myrdal's classic study of racism, *An American Dilemma* (1944) and Kenneth B. Clark's highly controversial studies of negative self-image among black children. Warren himself later said, "It was only a note," but critics seized on it as proof that the Court had not interpreted law but had applied its own sociological views. Former associate justice and now governor of South Carolina, James F. Byrnes, derided footnote 11 as Communist inspired. The temerity of the bench in citing a foreigner, the Swede Gunnar Myrdal, raised Southern hackles; the Georgia attorney general denounced Myrdal because one of his teachers had been black radical W.E.B. DuBois, "who sent a message of condolence on the death of Stalin."

At the time, social science research in this area could best be described as limited and social science methods as still primitive. Indeed, as sociological and psychological studies have become more sophisticated, Clark's studies have been increasingly dismissed as simplistic and methodologically flawed. The contradictory findings of subsequent social science studies on the effects of segregation only confirm the argument that while courts have to acknowledge facts, they should be extremely leery of accepting the interpretation of those facts by social scientists.

Critics also accused the Court of excessive judicial activism. Whether one agreed with *Brown* or not, the Court had obviously departed dramatically from its previous rulings in this area. It had admittedly been chipping away at *Plessy* for some time, but its recent decisions had given little indication that it would abandon the fifty-year-old doctrine of separate-but-equal so precipitately. Unlike most Court opinions, the decision contained practically no citations to precedents, because so few existed. Critics charged the Court with engaging in the same type of policy-making activism as in *Lochner*, *Adair*, *Adkins*, and the anti–New Deal cases. In *Brown*, however, the Court overturned its own prior ruling in *Plessy*, a decision that today nearly everyone agrees had been wrongly decided; in the reform cases, the Court interposed its own views over that of the legislature. Granted, the whole edifice of segregation statutes relied on that decision, but if *Plessy* was wrong, then so too were the laws that resulted from it.

Warren also presented two very different and contradictory ideas of constitutional interpretation in the opinion. When he announced that "separate educational facilities are inherently unequal," he seemed to be saying that racial segregation violated the constitutional mandate at all times and in all places. In essence, he intimated that constitutional meaning is unchanging and that the Equal Protection Clause had always meant what the Court now said it meant, that racial discrimination had been unconstitutional since 1868 and that cases to the contrary, such as *Plessy*, had been wrongly decided.

But Warren also implied an opposing view of constitutional interpretation, that constitutional meaning changes with changing times and circumstances. Chief Justice John Marshall had lectured the American people always to remember that the Constitution is intended "to be adopted to the various crises of human affairs." This notion of a "living Constitution" could be seen in Warren's dismissal of what the framers of the Fourteenth Amendment had intended regarding schooling, since public education

> If *Brown v. Board of Education* reflected a change in the American civic culture, it also generated further changes. *Brown* was the Supreme Court s most important decision of the twentieth century. Today it stands as much more than a decision about schools, or even a decision about segregation. *Brown* is our leading authoritative symbol for the principle that the Constitution forbids a system of caste.
>
> —Kenneth L. Karst, *Belonging to America: Equal Citizenship and the Constitution* (1989)

had been practically nonexistent in the South in 1868. By this view, although the Court overruled *Plessy*, one could argue that at the time it had been correctly decided.

Defenders of the Court conceded most of these points, but insisted that the justices had followed the right moral as well as legal course. One did not need fancy studies to see what must be plain to everyone, that "racial segregation under government auspices inevitably inflicts humiliation." In response to Southern charges that the Court had promulgated a lawless decision, some scholars responded that massive racial discrimination constituted so great a violation of moral law as to make lawful a court ruling against it. Since neither Congress nor the states showed any inclination to promote civil rights, the Court's action may have been the only way to get the country moving on the road toward full racial equality. While that path has at times been painful and even violent, without *Brown* it is doubtful if legal segregation could have been ended except through massive protest and violence, such as afflicted South Africa in the 1980s.

J. Harvie Wilkinson, now a federal judge on the Court of Appeals for the Fourth Circuit, dismisses much of this criticism when he reminds us that *Brown* "was humane, among the most humane moments in all our history. It was, with the pardonable exception of a footnote, a great political achievement, both in its uniting of the Court and in the steady way it addressed the nation." That it had flaws and might have been a more passionate document will continue to be debated, but this misses the point. Instead of grieving for what it might have been, "better we be thankful for what it was."

Implementation

Warren's strategy assumed that the states would accept the inevitability of desegregation by the time the Court handed down the implementation decree, and initial signs seemed encouraging. Some Southern communities did not wait for the Court to act, but began desegregating schools by the time the 1954 academic year began. Baltimore adopted a freedom of choice plan, which enabled 3,000 blacks to attend previously all-white schools that September. Louisville changed over its school system within a semester, while St. Louis initiated a two-year plan. Counties in West Virginia, junior colleges in Texas, and public schools in Washington, D.C., and Wilmington, Delaware, all enrolled blacks in previously segregated schools.

Ominous signs soon appeared, however. Governor Stanley abandoned his earlier moderation and announced in June that he would do everything he could to continue segregation in Virginia. In Mississippi, White Citizens Councils began to form in July, pledged to total war in defense of segregation. For the most part, though, a wait-and-see attitude in the South marked the twelve months following *Brown*. After all, no one knew exactly what the Court would order, and until then the schools would remain racially segregated.

The Court heard arguments on proposed remedies that winter and again in April. The subject was controversial enough on its own, but the justices realized that they also had to decide whether to abandon, at least in this area, the Court's traditional policy of ruling only on the case before it. Normally, if someone raises a valid claim that his or her constitutional rights have been violated, the decree is directed only to that petitioner's case; other persons "similarly situated" do not immediately gain the benefit of the decision. Lower federal courts then take notice of the ruling and apply it prospectively to future petitioners raising the same issue. In the school cases, however, this would mean that every black child wishing to enroll in a previously all-white school would have to go to court to secure the same rights that Linda Brown now enjoyed in Topeka. Determined states and localities, armed with sufficient resources, could tie up the desegregation process for years by litigating every such claim.

Moreover, the Court usually takes little notice of practical matters of implementation. Once a right has been defined, it has to be available to all citizens, despite any institutional dislocations. But circumstances in public education varied enormously, and the Court understood that in some schools desegregation would mean a few blacks sitting in predominantly white classrooms and in other schools just the opposite—and it made a difference. Finally, how long could the Court give the South? Every day that black children continued to attend segregated schools they suffered a loss of their constitutional rights in violation of the Fourteenth Amendment's assurance of the equal protection of law. But too precipitate an order might lead to widespread obstruction, perhaps even violence.

The NAACP pushed for full integration in the shortest possible time; blacks had been waiting three and a half centuries to be treated as equals and should not have to wait any longer to claim their constitutional rights.

The South seemed equally intransigent. Virginia urged the Court to face the "reality" of major differences between the two races and offered statistics to prove the inferiority of blacks. Florida had commissioned a poll and ominously informed the Court that only one out of seven police officers would enforce attendance at racially mixed schools. The state also put forward such a complicated plan that, according to Richard Kluger, "the most ungainly camel in Islam would have had an easier time passing through the eye of a needle than a black child getting into a white school in Florida."

The federal government, appearing as *amicus* at the request of the Court, urged a middle position between "integration now" and "segregation forever." The states should submit timetables within ninety days, and implementation should be supervised by the local district courts. The courts would have the discretion to make adjustments in the schedules depending on local conditions. Communities would thus have a chance to change their attitudes and accept desegregation as necessary in order for all Americans to enjoy their full constitutional rights. An immediate start would have to be made, however, and the decision would have to be enforced by federal, state, and local officials, all of whom had taken an oath to support the Constitution.

On May 31, 1955, Chief Justice Warren, again for a unanimous Court, handed down a seven-paragraph implementing decision, commonly known as *Brown II*. School segregation had to be ended everywhere, but the Court recognized that varying local conditions required different solutions. Local school districts must "make a prompt and reasonable start toward full compliance," and oversight would be lodged in the federal district courts. The local judges should exercise the "practical flexibility" traditionally associated with equity, but delay and noncompliance should not be contemplated. Desegregation of public schools should proceed "with all deliberate speed."

The Court did not fix a date for the end of segregation, nor even require that initial plans be filed within ninety days, as the federal government had suggested. In fact, it gave the South far more than the segregationists had expected, raising hopes that the actual implementation of the decree could be delayed indefinitely. Assignment of primary responsibility to the local district courts led some Southerners to assume that the decree could be completely ignored. Lieutenant Governor Ernest Vandiver of Georgia rejoiced when he heard the news. District judges, he declared, "are steeped in the same traditions that I am. . . . A 'reasonable time' can be construed as one year or two hundred. . . . Thank God we've got good Federal judges."

"All Deliberate Speed"

Within a short time, many federal judges in the South made it quite clear that they took their oath to support the Constitution seriously. John Minor Wisdom, John R. Brown, Elbert Tuttle, and Richard Rives of the U.S. Court of Appeals for the Fifth Circuit, as well as district court judges Frank Johnson of Alabama and J. Skelly Wright of Louisiana defied friends and associates to become forceful advocates of integration. By January 1956, federal judges had rendered opinions in nineteen cases, and in every one, they reaffirmed the Supreme Court's ruling that segregation denied equal protection of the law. School segregation laws fell in Florida, Arkansas, Tennessee, and Texas. District Judge J. Skelly Wright, born and educated in New Orleans, struck down a Louisiana plan that would have retained completely segregated schools. He expressed his sympathy for all the problems white state officials faced and spoke of the need for "the utmost patience" on everyone's part. "But the magnitude of the problem may not nullify the principle. And that principle is that we are, all of us, freeborn Americans, with a right to make our way unfettered by sanctions imposed by man because of the work of God" (*Bush v. Orleans Parish School Board,* E.D. La, 1956). Inspired by such victories, the NAACP filed additional petitions for desegregation of 170 school districts in seventeen states.

Some Southern judges, however, found integration distasteful and believed the Supreme Court had decided *Brown* wrongly. With neither the Congress nor the president eager to push desegregation, they tended to emphasize the "deliberate" rather than the "speed," and perhaps little more could have been expected of them. For a few, their devotion to segregation proved stronger than their oath of office. In Dallas, Texas, for example, the NAACP started a suit in September 1955, and Judge William Atwell, an outspoken defender of segregation, refused to act for two years. Time and again, the NAACP had to appeal to the Fifth Circuit Court of Appeals, which consistently overruled Atwell and ordered him to move ahead with desegregating the city's school system. Atwell finally retired, but another segregationist took over the case. T. Whitfield

Davidson admonished blacks to recognize "that the white man has a right to maintain his racial integrity and it can't be done so easily in integrated schools." Again, the NAACP had to appeal over and over again to get around Davidson's obstructionary tactics.

A major problem facing the NAACP involved the local nature of public education. Local school boards, not the states, controlled the schools and determined policy, and this made it especially difficult and expensive to press for desegregation. Most small black communities could not afford to undertake a desegregation suit. Even when local attorneys volunteered their services or the NAACP Legal Defense Fund sent in one of its lawyers, it cost plaintiffs approximately $15,000 (the equivalent of $55,000 in current dollars) to take a desegregation suit through federal courts. As a result, as late as 1961, few school districts in the Deep South had faced a school desegregation suit.

Encouraged by all these obstacles to implementing desegregation, the South dug in its heels. Presses ground out articles and books purporting to demonstrate not only the error of footnote 11, but how "science" proved the basic inferiority of black people. The Citizens Council movement spread and soon claimed 500,000 members in eleven states. Whites and blacks who signed desegregation petitions lost their jobs and found they could not get credit from stores or banks. In 1956, 101 members of Congress, including all but three of the senators from the former Confederate states, signed a belligerent "Southern Manifesto," opposing the Court's decision, thus giving an imprimatur of respectability to segregationist resistance.

In Virginia, usually seen as moderate in its race relations, Senator Harry F. Byrd called for "massive resistance" to desegregation, and soon after, political leaders resurrected the long-discarded theories of John C. Calhoun. Alabama claimed that it had the right of interposition to protect its citizens from unconstitutional federal action, and the state legislature resolved *Brown* to be "null, void and of no effect." Georgia adopted a similar resolution, adding that it intended to ignore the Court. Mississippi condemned *Brown* as "unconstitutional and of no lawful effect," and set up a commission to prohibit compliance. Although avoiding the word "nullification," South Carolina protested against "the illegal encroachment of the central government." Both houses of the Louisiana legislature unanimously endorsed interposition, while North Carolina adopted a "resolution of protest."

Aside from the rhetoric, Southern states enacted measures designed to thwart the courts and prevent compliance. Georgia, for example, made it a felony for any school official to use tax money for mixed-race schools, while Mississippi declared it unlaw-

> The inept fraternity of politicians and professors known as the United States Supreme Court chose to throw away the established law. These nine men repudiated the Constitution, spit upon the Tenth Amendment, and rewrote the fundamental law of this land to suit their own gauzy concepts of sociology. If it be said now that the South is flouting the law, let it be said to the high court, *You taught us how.*
>
> —*Richmond News Leader* (1956)

ful for the races to attend school together at the high school level or below. Several states adopted plans to evade integration by substituting some form of private school system. Mississippi and South Carolina actually amended their constitutions to abolish public schools. Some states set up grant programs to support private schools, and nearly all of them amended their laws to shift full responsibility for pupil placement to local school boards, thus making it necessary to sue each district separately, rather than entering a single suit against the state. Because *Brown* proscribed segregation based only on race, states instituted all sorts of other health and welfare criteria, which could be manipulated to keep white and black children in separate classes. "There is not one way, but many," John Temple Graves of Alabama proclaimed. "The South proposes to use all of them that make for resistance. The decision tortured the Constitution—the South will torture the decision."

When school opened in September 1956, 723 school districts in the seventeen border and Southern states had accomplished some measure of desegregation, 186 more than the previous year. But 3,000 school districts remained totally segregated. About 300,000 blacks went to school in so-called integrated situations, which could mean many things; 2,400,000 remained entirely segregated. In Alabama, Florida, Georgia, Louisiana, Mississippi, North and South Carolina, and Virginia, total segregation remained the rule. In that fall's election, candidates who had urged moderation went down to defeat in one state after another. When the new state legislatures met in early 1957, they passed dozens of additional measures to cause delay. In the wake of the *Brown* decision, the Ku Klux Klan came alive again, and bombings, beatings, murders, and cross burnings spread across the Southern states. In Mississippi, three prominent civil rights activists were murdered during the summer and fall of 1955, and in 1957, a group of whites in Birmingham, Alabama savagely beat and castrated a black man and then told him, "This is what will happen if Negroes try to integrate the schools." All over the South, as the noted Southern-born scholar C. Vann Woodward lamented, "the lights of reason and tolerance began to go out under the insistent demand for conformity [and] a malaise of fear spread over the region."

Eisenhower and Little Rock

As has often been noted, the Supreme Court has the power neither of sword nor purse and can rely for implementation of its decisions only on the moral authority that it

> I am convinced that the Supreme Court decision set back progress in the South at least fifteen years. . . . It's all very well to talk about school integration—if you remember that you may also be talking about social disintegration. Feelings are deep on this, especially where children are involved. . . . We can't demand perfection in these moral things. All we can do is keep working toward a goal and keep it high. And the fellow who tries to tell me that you can do these things by FORCE is just plain NUTS.
>
> —Dwight Eisenhower to Emmet John Hughes, reported in Hughes, *Ordeal of Power* (1963)

commands, or on the aid of Congress and the president. In the years immediately after *Brown*, such assistance failed to materialize. In the White House, Dwight Eisenhower lamented his appointment of Earl Warren to the Court as "the biggest damn fool mistake I ever made," and complained that *Brown* had set back the cause of racial progress in the South by fifteen years; the appropriate thing would have been to educate people to understand the necessity for change.

Yet Eisenhower's record is mixed. He had, after all, signed off on the Justice Department's brief urging the Court to overrule *Plessy*. The day after the *Brown* decision, the president ordered the District of Columbia Board of Commissioners to set an example of peaceful desegregation. Over the next five years, Eisenhower made four more appointments to the high court and made no effort to select men who might question *Brown*. Despite his private views that prejudice could not be overcome by law, his justice and state departments strongly applauded the decision. Nonetheless, one of the most beloved and respected presidents of the century failed to use his high office, with its enormous potential for moral leadership and public education, to guide the South away from intransigence. When officials at the University of Alabama defied a court order to admit Authorine Lucy, Eisenhower said, "I certainly hope that we could avoid any interference." The university remained segregated for seven more years.

But finally, events forced Eisenhower to act. In the fall of 1957, the Little Rock, Arkansas, school board agreed to a court order to admit nine black students to Central High School. Governor Orville Faubus, previously considered something of a moderate, called out the national guard to prevent the blacks from entering. He withdrew the troops on a court order, but when the black students again tried to attend, a mob attacked the school and drove them off. Eisenhower, who only two months earlier had said he could not envision any situation in which he would use federal troops, could no longer passively sit by and watch federal authority flouted. He ordered 1,000 paratroopers into Little Rock and federalized 10,000 Arkansas national guardsmen to protect the black students and maintain order in the schools. The chief executive who had desperately wanted to avoid the entire civil rights issue, and who for three years had failed to provide leadership, outraged the South by becoming the first president since Reconstruction to use federal troops to enforce black rights.

Eisenhower withdrew the troops at the end of the school year, and the Supreme Court, for the first time since *Brown II*, spoke out on desegregation in a case arising out of the Arkansas turmoil. In *Cooper v. Aaron* (1958), for the first time in its history, the Court issued a unanimous *per curiam* decision *signed* by all nine justices. (Felix Frankfurter infuriated his colleagues when he insisted on adding a separate concurrence of his own.) *Cooper* not only affirmed the *Brown* ruling, but reasserted the Court's authority as the ultimate interpreter of the Constitution. Arkansas claimed not to be bound by *Brown*, since it had not been a party to that suit. The Court could have limited itself to a sharp reminder that state officials have no power to nullify a federal court order. Instead, it reminded Arkansas—and the nation—that ever since 1803 it had been, in Chief Justice Marshall's phrase, "the province and duty of the judicial department to say what the law is." That principle, the Court continued, "has ever since been respected by this Court and the Country as a permanent and indispensable feature of our constitutional system. It follows that the interpretation of the Fourteenth

Amendment enunciated by the Court in the *Brown* cases is the supreme law of the land," binding not only the federal government but state officials as well.

Rather than obey the Court, Faubus shut down the Little Rock schools altogether in 1958 and 1959; he reopened them only in response to another court order. In Virginia, three cities and two counties also closed their schools to prevent integration, and the General Assembly provided funds to promote private schools. The pace of desegregation slowed to a crawl: only thirteen additional school districts in 1958, nineteen the following year, and seventeen in 1960. In Congress, both houses considered and passed separate bills to restrict the Court's power or nullify its decisions, but no one measure passed in both chambers. Six years after *Brown v. Board of Education*, thousands of school districts in the South remained segregated, moderate voices had been muted, and politicians loudly claimed that Supreme Court decisions need not be obeyed as the law of the land.

For Further Reading

For the FEPC and the beginnings of civil rights, see Louis Ruchames, *Race, Jobs, and Politics* (1953); and Samuel Krislov, *The Negro in Federal Employment: The Quest for Equal Opportunity* (1967). Integration of the armed services is examined in Richard Dalfiume, *Desegregation of the U.S. Armed Forces: Fighting on Two Fronts, 1939–1953* (1969). For the Truman administration in general, see Donald R. McCoy and Richard T. Ruetten, *Quest and Response: Minority Rights in the Truman Administration* (1973); and William C. Berman, *The Politics of Civil Rights in the Truman Administration* (1970). The spread of antibias laws into the states is detailed in Duane Lockard, *Toward Equal Opportunity: A Study of State and Local Anti-Discrimination Laws* (1968).

For the Shelley case, see Clement E. Vose, *Caucasians Only: The Supreme Court, the N.A.A.C.P. and the Restrictive Covenant Cases* (1959); Louis Flenkin, "Shelley v. Kraemer: Notes for a Revised Opinion," 110 *University of Pennsylvania Law Review* 473 (1963); and Mark V. Tushnet, "*Shelley v. Kraemer* and Theories of Equality," 33 *New York Law School Review* 383 (1988). For other pre-*Brown* decisions, see Daniel T. Kelleher, "The Case of Lloyd Lionel Gaines: The Demise of the 'Separate-but-Equal' Doctrine," 56 *Journal of Negro History* 262 (1971); Loren Miller, *The Petitioners: The Story of the Supreme Court of the United States and the Negro* (1966); Darlene Clark Hine, *Black Victory: The Rise and Fall of the White Primary in Texas* (1979); Irving F. Lefborg, "Chief Justice Vinson and the Politics of Desegregation," 24 *Emory Law Journal* 243 (1975); and Catherine A. Barnes, *Journey from Jim Crow: The Desegregation of Southern Transit* (1983).

The NAACP strategy is explicated in two books by Mark V. Tushnet, *The NAACP's Strategy Against Segregated Education, 1925–1950* (1987), and *Making Civil Rights Law: Thurgood Marshall and the Supreme Court, 1936–1961* (1994). See also, Jack Greenberg, *Crusaders in the Courts* (1994), the story of the NAACP legal challenge to segregation by one of the then young legal staff. For more on Marshall, see Juan Williams, *Thurgood Marshall: American Revolutionary* (1998).

For civil rights and black status in general during the 1940s and 1950s, see Donald G. Nieman, *Promises to Keep: African-Americans and the Constitutional Order, 1776 to the Present* (1991); Harvard Sitkoff, *The Struggle for Black Equality, 1954–1992* (1993); and Taylor Branch, *Parting the Waters: America in the King Years, 1954–1963* (1988). A good overview of the period in general is James T. Patterson, *Grand Expectations: The United States, 1945–1974* (1996).

The literature on *Brown* is massive, but the definitive analysis is Richard Kluger, *Simple Justice: The History of* Brown v. Board of Education *and Black America's Struggle for Equality* (1976). Kluger covers all the cases leading up to *Brown*, the divisions on the Court, as well as the litigation strategies on both sides. Other useful works on the case include Daniel M. Berman, *It Is So Ordered: The Supreme Court Rules on School Segregation* (1966); Alfred H. Kelly, "The School Desegregation Case," in John Garraty, ed., *Quarrels That Have Shaped the Constitution* (1964); Charles L. Black, Jr., "The Lawfulness of the Segregation Decisions," 69 *Yale Law Journal* 421 (1960); and Ira M. Heyman, "The Chief Justice, Racial Segregation, and Friendly Critics," 49 *California Law Review* 104 (1961). The question of how the justices divided before the opinion is discussed in Mark V. Tushnet and Katya Lezin, "What Really Happened in *Brown v. Board of Education*," 91 *Columbia Law Review* 1867 (1991); while the unanimity matter is examined in Dennis J. Hutchinson, "Unanimity and Desegregation: Decision-making in the Supreme Court, 1948–1958," 68 *Georgetown Law Journal* 1 (1979).

The relevance of the Fourteenth Amendment to the case is discussed in Alfred H. Kelley, "The Fourteenth Amendment Reconsidered: The Segregation Question," 54 *Michigan Law Review* 1049 (1955); and Alexander M. Bickel, "The Original Understanding and the Segregation Decision," 69 *Harvard Law Review* 1 (1955), originally prepared as a research memorandum when Bickel clerked for Justice Frankfurter. The problem of social science data is touched on in I.A. Newby, *Challenge to the Court: Social Scientists and the Defense of Segregation, 1954–1966* (1967), most of which is an attack on scientific racism.

Other works dealing with Southern resistance to desegregation include Benjamin Muse, *Virginia's Massive Resistance* (1961); C. Vann Woodward, *The Strange Career of Jim Crow*. 2nd ed. (1966); Bob Smith, *They Closed Their Schools: Prince Edward County, Virginia, 1951–1964* (1965); Numan V. Bartley, *The Rise of Massive Resistance: Race and Politics in the South During the 1950s* (1969); Neil R. McMillan, *The Citizens Councils: Organized Resistance to the Second Reconstruction, 1954–1964* (1971); and Charles Fairman, "The Attack on the Segregation Cases," 70 *Harvard Law Review* 83 (1956). Southern constitutional theory is presented in James J. Kilpatrick, *The Southern Case for School Segregation* (1962). A good overview is Benjamin Muse, *Ten Years of Prelude: The Story of Integration Since the Supreme Court's 1954 Decision* (1964). A unique study is Jack W. Peltason, *Fifty-eight Lonely Men* (1961), a sympathetic examination of federal judges in the South who enforced the desegregation decisions. On Arkansas, see the excellent case study by Tony Freyer, *The Little Rock Crisis: A Constitutional Interpretation* (1984). The debate over *Brown* and the actual effect it had are discussed in James T. Patterson, *Brown v. Board of Education: A Civil Rights Milestone and Its Troubled Legacy* (2001).

The literature on the Warren Court is growing rapidly. An excellent book placing the Court and its decisions within the larger political context of the times is Lucas A. Powe, Jr., *The Warren Court and American Politics* (2000). A short introduction is Morton J. Horwitz, *The Warren Court and the Pursuit of Justice* (1998). Two useful collections of essays are Mark V. Tushnet, ed., *The Warren Court in Historical and Political Perspective* (1993); and Bernard Schwartz, ed., *The Warren Court: A Retrospective* (1996). The older Alexander M. Bickel, *Politics and the Warren Court* (1965) is still pertinent. Warren has been the subject of numerous books and articles, but see especially G. Edward White, *Earl Warren: A Public Life* (1982); Bernard Schwartz, *Super Chief: Earl Warren and His Supreme Court—A Judicial Biography* (1983); and Ed Cray, *Chief Justice: A Biography of Earl Warren* (1997).

36

"We Shall Overcome!"

The Civil Rights Movement Begins • Early Civil Rights Legislation • The Kennedy Commitment • "The Schoolhouse Door" • The 1964 Civil Rights Act • The Court Loses Patience • Attacking Segregation Everywhere • State Action and Racial Classification • Civil Rights and the First Amendment • The Sit-In Cases • The Court and the 1964 Civil Rights Act • Voting Rights • The 1965 Voting Rights Act • South Carolina v. Katzenbach *• New Uses for Old Laws • What Has Been Accomplished • Conclusion: An Unfinished Agenda • For Further Reading*

THE TURMOIL CREATED by Southern intransigence after *Brown* forced both the executive and legislative branches to take action. The three Civil War amendments gave Congress power to enforce the provisions through "appropriate legislation," although what that meant had not been tested in the courts for three-quarters of a century. The federal judiciary did not stop with school desegregation, but expanded the meaning of the Fourteenth Amendment's Equal Protection Clause to invalidate all forms of state-sponsored or protected discrimination. Meanwhile, black Americans began to exert their own pressure to hasten the pace of desegregation, often with tragic results. But despite the many obstacles, the country moved steadily toward the long-deferred ideal of a society free of the badges of racial discrimination; and civil rights workers—blacks and whites—sang joyously that they would overcome the legacy of slavery and discrimination.

The Civil Rights Movement Begins

There are two different facets of the civil rights movement. One is epitomized by Thurgood Marshall and his colleagues at the NAACP Legal Defense Fund, committed to eradicating racial discrimination through litigation. The other is that of Martrin Luther King, Jr., Rosa Parks, and those who took to the streets to demand that segregation be ended. The two often cooperated, sometimes competed, and very often wound up at the same place—the U.S. Supreme Court. The litigation strategy began with the founding of the NAACP and its careful work in the late 1930s and early 1940s that led to the *Brown* decision. Many historians date the activist beginnings to December 1, 1955, when Rosa Parks, a black seamstress, refused to move to a seat in the back of a Montgomery, Alabama bus. When the bus driver had her arrested, the black community mounted a boycott against the bus company that soon brought international attention. It also brought to the fore a new black leader, Martin Luther King, Jr., whose philosophy and tactics squarely confronted Jim Crow law.

The tactics of the activist civil rights movement, ranging from boycotts to sit-ins to mass demonstrations produced several cases that went to the Supreme Court. The mass marches unleashed fears of social breakdown, while the boycotts and sit-ins challenged traditional rights of private property owners. Dr. King, a great admirer of Mahatma Gandhi, wanted to use peaceful civil disobedience as a device to force white racists to think about the nature of their oppression of black people. While admirable in the abstract as an alternative to the type of violence that marked South Africa's turmoil of apartheid, it did create a tension within the civil rights movement between those who insisted on obedience to the law and to the Constitution and those who claimed a moral duty to disobey immoral laws. King in many ways resurrected the "higher law" philosophy of William Lloyd Garrison, the fiery abolitionist leader who condemned the Constitution as "an agreement made in hell," and demanded that man's law had to give way to God's law.

King's tactics often angered Thurgood Marshall, and the Legal Defense Fund, who understood the role of the Constitution as a form of civil religion in American life. By laying claim to constitutional legitimacy in his attack on segregation in the courts, Marshall also in some ways appealed to a higher law, and he worried that the boycotts and mass demonstrations would undercut what he saw as black America's best hope for justice: judicial acknowledgment that the Equal Protection Clause prohibited any form of state discrimination based on race.

The Montgomery boycott went on for almost a year, and while King organized blacks to operate car pools and make-shift jitney services, the NAACP carried the battle to the courts. On November 13, 1956, the high court in *Gayle v. Browder* affirmed a lower court ruling that the city ordinance requiring segregated seating on public transportation violated the Constitution and must stop no later than December 20. In effect, the Court had finally overruled *Plessy.* On December 21, Martin Luther King sat down next to a white man at the front of a bus. Thurgood Marshall's comment highlighted

> We are tired—tired of being segregated and humiliated, tired of being kicked around by the brutal feet of oppression. If we will protest courageously and yet with dignity and Christian love, when the history books are written in future generations the historians will pause and say, "There lived a great people—a black people—who injected new meaning and dignity into the veins of civilization."
>
> —Martin Luther King, Jr., at a rally in Montgomery, Alabama (1956)

the difference between the two sides of the movement. "All that walking for nothing. They might as well have waited for the Court decision."

Early Civil Rights Legislation

With pressure mounting both in the courts and on the streets, President Eisenhower took a few cautious steps against racial discrimination in early 1957. He proposed legislation creating a bipartisan civil rights commission with power to investigate violations, especially abridgment of the franchise. He also strengthened the civil rights division of the justice department, empowering the attorney general to bring suits to protect any rights, including voting and attendance at desegregated schools. Southern congressmen immediately set about to kill the bill, or at least to weaken it in order to make it useless. In the end, the Civil Rights Act of 1957 set up the commission and authorized suits to protect voting rights, but did not give the Justice Department a wide-ranging mandate to protect civil rights.

For all Eisenhower's reluctance to back civil rights, he would not allow the recalcitrant Southern state governments to challenge federal authority, as they had at Little Rock, so he asked Congress for further legislation. The 1960 Civil Rights Act emphasized protection of voting rights and authorized judges to appoint referees to help blacks register and vote. In response to the growing violence against civil rights demonstrators and activists, the measure provided criminal penalties for bombing or mob action to obstruct court orders. The act passed despite a Southern filibuster of 125 consecutive hours, and most people credited its passage to the Senate majority leader, Lyndon B. Johnson of Texas, one of only three Southern senators who had not signed the Southern Manifesto. Although hailed as landmark pieces of legislation, the 1957 and 1960 statutes gave relatively little aid to civil rights activists except in regard to voting, and they did not mention segregation at all. Nevertheless, for the first time since Reconstruction, Congress had attempted to protect the rights of black people.

The Kennedy Commitment

John F. Kennedy entered the White House in 1961, amid high hopes from blacks that he would provide the moral leadership and governmental support of civil rights that had been so painfully absent during the Eisenhower years. The new president could hardly have ignored the issue. Just a week following his election, the Supreme Court handed down a major decision, *Gomillion v. Lightfoot*, which struck down an Alabama gerrymandering law designed to negate black voting. Soon after the inauguration, Roy Wilkins of the NAACP called for immediate action to promote voting, education, and employment opportunities for blacks, and the Rev. Martin Luther King, Jr., handed Kennedy a nearly 100-page memorandum outlining the civil rights agenda.

Because of Southern strength in Congress, Kennedy decided to act initially by executive order, and on March 6, 1961, he created a presidential Commission on Equal Employment Opportunity, whose energy quickly won the plaudits of civil rights leaders. Administration officials set an example in testing color barriers, especially in Washington; they refused to speak to segregated audiences, boycotted private clubs that discriminated because of race, and pressured federal employee groups to abandon discriminatory practices. The Justice Department informed all federal judges that the administration intended to carry out the Constitution and would enforce their decisions in regard to civil rights. In late 1962, Kennedy signed an executive order prohibiting racial and religious discrimination in housing built or purchased with federal assistance.

But Kennedy had items other than civil rights on his agenda, and he could not afford to alienate the powerful Southern bloc in Congress. When young black activists began so-called freedom rides in the summer of 1961, the administration showed its reluctance to intervene. In December 1960, the Supreme Court had ruled that the Interstate Commerce Act forbade discrimination in bus terminals serving interstate carriers (*Boynton v. Virginia*). Starting in May, members of the Congress of Racial Equality (CORE) and the Southern Non-Violent Coordinating Committee (SNCC) left Washington, D.C. on bus trips to the Deep South to test local compliance with the Court's ruling. The Kennedy administration refused to endorse the rides, although Attorney General Robert Kennedy tried to work behind the scenes to ensure the freedom riders' safety. Only after lengthy negotiations had failed and Southern state officials looked the other way at the violence inflicted on the riders did the federal government send U.S. marshals into Alabama. Kennedy managed to reach an agreement with Mississippi officials, that if the state would protect the riders from the mobs, the Department of Justice would not interfere with local prosecution of persons who violated state segregation laws.

While unsympathetic to direct action, the Kennedy brothers understood the demands of the black community. While the president moved slowly—much too slowly for some black leaders—he gradually endorsed civil rights as a cause of his own. He appointed blacks to high governmental positions; Thurgood Marshall, for example, became a U.S. circuit court judge. Kennedy also used executive orders to align the federal government with the civil rights movement, and under Robert F. Kennedy the Justice Department became an outspoken ally and champion of civil rights. Both Kennedys crossed a Rubicon of sorts in October 1962, when James Meredith sought to enter the University of Mississippi on a court order.

"The Schoolhouse Door"

State courts, the state legislature, and Governor Ross Barnett had all promised that the Mississippi government would prevent integration, which they termed "unconstitutional." On September 24, Barnett issued a gubernatorial proclamation directing the arrest of any federal official attempting to enforce Meredith's court order. The next day, Barnett stood "in the schoolhouse door" and personally blocked Meredith from registering. A few days later, the Justice Department sent 320 federal marshals to the Ole Miss campus at Oxford, and that evening President Kennedy went on national television to appeal for reason and patriotism in Mississippi.

It was too late. Armed mobs attacked the marshals, while state police, whom Barnett had promised would keep order, stood by watching. This was far more than an attack on civil rights workers. It constituted an insurrection against the lawful authority of the U.S. government, and Kennedy answered it promptly. The president federalized the Mississippi National Guard and brought in regular army troops to restore and maintain order. Only after two people had been killed and 375 wounded (about half of them marshals) did James Meredith enroll.

The following spring, a similar situation threatened to explode at the University of Alabama, after a federal judge ordered the admission of two blacks. Governor George C. Wallace, who in his inaugural earlier in the year had promised "segregation now, segregation tomorrow, segregation forever," vowed to block their way, but Kennedy warned the governor that he would take immediate action. Wallace stood theatrically in the schoolhouse door and made his speech before television cameras, and then quickly gave in when Kennedy nationalized the guard. That fall, Wallace tried again, ordering the guard to prevent the opening of schools on an integrated basis in Birmingham and two other cities. Kennedy again took over the guard, but this time he ordered them back to their barracks so that the schools could open. For five days, nothing happened, and then a horrible wave of violence erupted. By the end of 1963, a nation exhausted by senseless bloodshed finally began to make some progress in civil rights.

The 1964 Civil Rights Act

Kennedy eventually concluded that the government needed additional statutory authority; large areas of discrimination lay beyond the reach of a federal remedy, either judicial or executive. The government, Kennedy explained, wanted to provide civil rights workers with a legal outlet, "a remedy other than having to engage in demonstrations which bring them into conflict with the forces of law and order in the community."

On June 11, 1963, as George Wallace prepared to block a black student from entering the University of Alabama, Kennedy announced he would ask Congress for legislation to provide "the kind of equality of treatment which we would want ourselves." The measure would promote civil rights on two broad fronts. First, it would ban discrimination in public accommodations, on grounds that businesses serving the public

> It ought to be possible for American students of any color to attend any public institution without having to be backed up by troops. It ought to be possible for American consumers of any color to receive equal service in places of public accommodation, such as hotels and restaurants and theaters and retail stores, without being forced to resort to demonstrations in the street, and it ought to be possible for American citizens of any color to register and to vote in a free election without interference or fear of reprisal. . . . In short, every American ought to have the right to be treated as he would wish to be treated, as one would wish his children to be treated. But this is not the case.
>
> —John F. Kennedy, Address to Nation on Civil Rights (June 11, 1963)

lost their private nature and became public. Second, the attorney general would be able to seek desegregation of public education on his own authority, especially when he had reason to believe that fear of reprisal prevented parents or students from initiating action themselves. For the first time, in effect, the national government announced that it would enforce *Brown* on its own, rather than rely on those who, although affected by segregation, could not do it by themselves.

Black leaders immediately hailed Kennedy's speech as a "Second Emancipation Proclamation," and a coalition of Northern and Western congressmen and women rallied to sponsor the necessary legislation. To show that the bill had widespread support, civil rights leaders called for a massive march on Washington that summer. On August 28, 200,000 people, black and white together, gathered in front of the Lincoln Memorial in the greatest civil rights demonstration of our time. Millions more watched in awe on television and listened as Mahalia Jackson sang and Martin Luther King told of his dream, that "one day on the red hills of Georgia, the sons of former slaves and the sons of former slave-owners will be able to sit together at the table of brotherhood." The "sweet reasonableness" of that crowd stood in marked contrast to the violence that soon followed. In September, a bomb exploded at a black Sunday school in Birmingham, killing four children, and two months later, John Kennedy himself lay dead of an assassin's bullet.

Few black leaders expected much of the new president. Since Lyndon Johnson was a Southerner and the likely Democratic presidential nominee in 1964, they doubted he would risk alienating Southern support by embracing civil rights. Johnson, however, was determined to be president of all the people, and he proved an effective champion of the cause. In his first address to Congress on November 27, 1963, he stated simply and effectively: "We have talked long enough in this country about equal rights. We have talked for one hundred years or more. It is time now to write the next chapter, and to write it in the books of law." With the help of Democrat Hubert Humphrey of Minnesota and Republican Everett Dirkson of Illinois, Johnson guided an expanded version of Kennedy's bill through both houses of Congress, broke a Southern filibuster, and signed it into law on July 2, 1964.

The Civil Rights Act of 1964 had eleven titles—or sub-sections—covering education, public accommodations, expanded powers for the attorney general, and voting

> When the architects of our republic wrote the Declaration of Independence and the Constitution, they were signing a promissory note to which every American was to fall heir. This note was a promise that all men would be guaranteed the unalienable rights of life, liberty, and the pursuit of happiness.
>
> It is obvious today that America has defaulted on this promissory note so far as her citizens of color are concerned. Instead of honoring this obligation, America has given the Negro people a bad check; a check which has come back marked "insufficient funds." But we refuse to believe that the bank of justice is bankrupt. . . . So we have come to cash this check—which will give us the riches of freedom and the security of justice.
>
> —Martin Luther King, Jr., speech in front of Lincoln Memorial, August 28, 1963

rights; it also coordinated different federal agencies to promote desegregation. Under the threat of losing federal aid if they failed to make a "good faith, substantive start," hundreds of Southern school districts finally began to desegregate. Using its commerce authority, Congress prohibited racial discrimination in restaurants, hotels and motels, filling stations and soda fountains, and required equal access to parks, pools, and stadiums. The bill also strengthened the earlier voter registration protections and established a sixth-grade education as a presumption of literacy.

The Court Loses Patience

The Supreme Court, with the exception of *Cooper v. Aaron,* had remained silent since *Brown*, leaving implementation of desegregation to the lower courts. But the justices ran out of patience in the early 1960s. For example, Justice Arthur Goldberg, appointed by Kennedy in 1962, commented in *Watson v. Memphis* (1963), that *Brown II* had "never contemplated that the concept of 'deliberate speed' would countenance indefinite delay in elimination of racial barriers in schools." As a result, at the same time that the Kennedy administration was stepping up its civil rights activities, the Court accepted more segregation cases, and its unanimous rulings added to the sense of urgency that the time had come to act.

The Court also began addressing itself to specifics. In *Goss v. Board of Education* (1963), it struck down plans that permitted students in schools in which their race was a minority to transfer to schools where they would be in a majority. Justice Clark's opinion held that transfer plans based solely on racial factors "inevitably lead toward segregation by race" and therefore could not stand under *Brown II.* The following year, the Court attacked massive resistance in Virginia in *Griffin v. Prince Edward County School Board.* It ordered public schools in Prince Edward, which had been closed for five years, to reopen. Justice Black declared that the Constitution did not permit the abolition of public schools in one county of a state while they remained open elsewhere. Black also warned that the Court had grown impatient; ten years had been long enough for the South to reconcile itself to desegregation.

The impatience could also be seen in the executive branch and in the lower courts. The Department of Health, Education and Welfare (HEW) issued new guidelines in March 1966 stipulating that in order to receive federal funds, school districts would be judged on their actual progress toward desegregation, including goals and timetables to speed up the process. The agency would no longer settle for token integration.

Federal courts reinforced this message. So-called freedom of choice plans had become fairly common across the South and supposedly allowed students of either race to attend the school of their choice. Local officials defended the plans as good-faith efforts to comply with *Brown,* but critics charged that they discouraged blacks from attending white schools and had no significant effect on segregation. In December 1966, Judge John Minor Wisdom of the Court of Appeals for the Fifth Circuit shocked Southern school officials with his decision in *United States v. Jefferson County Board of Education.* Wisdom endorsed the HEW guidelines and directed all federal district judges in the Fifth Circuit to follow them in their decrees in school desegregation suits. Al-

> If school officials in any district should find that their district still has segregated facilities or schools or only token integration, their affirmative duty to take corrective action requires them to try an alternative to freedom of choice plans, such as a geographic attendance plan . . . or some other acceptable substitute.
>
> —John Minor Wisdom, *United States v. Jefferson County Board of Education* (1966)

though Wisdom did not disallow freedom of choice plans, he emphasized that district judges should allow them only if they led to actual integration. When the school board appealed and asked for a rehearing, all twelve judges of the Fifth Circuit heard the case *en banc* and endorsed Wisdom's decision. No clearer message could be sent to the school districts in the Deep South, most of which fell within the geographic boundaries of the Fifth Circuit.

Green v. County School Board (1968) marked a major shift in the Court's role. After three years of freedom of choice, not one white child had chosen to attend a formerly black school, and 85 percent of black students still went to all-black schools. For the Court, Justice William Brennan (appointed by Eisenhower in 1956) indicated that results, not good faith, would henceforth be the mark of an acceptable plan. In footnotes, the Court took the unusual step of indicating specific plans that would meet the Court's requirements, such as dividing the district geographically, with all students in each half attending the school in that half.

Green proved to be the Court's last easy school case, in which the justices had the fairly straightforward task of overturning a scheme patently designed to avoid the *Brown* mandate. It also marked the end of the first stage of school desegregation, the gradualist period in which the courts seemed willing to accept "tokenism" and so-called good-faith efforts in the hope that the South would eventually come around. That process had yielded nothing near what the Court or the black community wanted.

No doubt a gradualist approach had been necessary, and "all deliberate speed" had been a legitimate starting point. Perhaps if the Court had pushed for more sooner, the reaction might have been far more violent and bloody. But some critics have charged that the Supreme Court failed to provide sufficient leadership and thus must carry some of the burden for the tokenism, the uneven results, and even the breakdown of lawful authority. For ten years, from *Brown* to *Griffin,* the Court said almost nothing, allowing time for the lower courts to implement the desegregation decision. After setting in motion one of the major social upheavals of this century, perhaps the Court should have monitored more closely the change it had mandated. While it never defined "all deliberate speed," it complained that the phrase meant far more than the states had offered. The justices declared what they considered unconstitutional, but did not inform Southern officials what would meet the constitutional test. Perhaps, given the deeply embedded patterns of racial discrimination in the South, little more could have been expected at first. As we shall see later, the Burger Court inherited this problem, and in the 1970s, it had to confront the larger issue of not only striking down school segregation, but also seeking to replace it with a true integration.

Attacking Segregation Everywhere

Brown had specifically been limited to the problem of segregation in public schools, but as the South had realized, its logic dictated an end to legally enforced racial segregation in other areas as well. The NAACP Legal Defense Fund, even as it continued its attack on school segregation, launched a flurry of lawsuits against other practices designed to keep blacks separated from whites. Compared with the rate of desegregation in the schools, barriers to blacks in other public facilities seemed to collapse overnight.

Typically, a local federal district judge would rule that the old *Plessy* doctrine of separate but equal no longer applied after *Brown,* and that segregation of public facilities therefore violated the Equal Protection Clause of the Fourteenth Amendment. An appeal to the Supreme Court invariably resulted in *per curiam* affirmations of the lower court rulings. In those few cases in which the lower courts sustained segregated facilities, the Court remanded with directions to proceed in a manner "not inconsistent with *Brown.*" Thus the high court affirmed the end of segregation on public beaches,[1] buses,[2] golf courses,[3] and parks.[4] In *Johnson v. Virginia* (1963), it reversed a black man's contempt conviction for refusing to comply with a state judge's order to move to a section of the courtroom reserved for blacks. "Such a conviction cannot stand," the Court declared, "for it is no longer open to question that a State may not constitutionally require segregation of public facilities."

A somewhat more complex issue arose over segregation in private facilities. Ever since the *Civil Rights Cases* (1883), the Court had held private discrimination beyond the reach of the Fourteenth Amendment. In *Shelley v. Kraemer* (1948), however, state enforcement of restrictive covenants had been deemed state action and prohibited. The Warren Court used this distinction to void the exclusion of blacks from a private theater located in a public park[5] and from a private restaurant in a court house.[6] In 1961, Justice Clark emphasized that totally private activities remained immune from the reach of the courts under the Fourteenth Amendment, but that a connection to governmental authority brought such discrimination within the definition of "state action." As a result, in *Burton v. Wilmington Parking Authority* (1961), a private restaurant located in a municipally owned and operated parking garage had the necessary connection, and could not discriminate on the basis of race.

In modern days, however, there is very little private business activity that does not have some nexus to public authority, and the Court indicated in *Burton* that the state action doctrine had limits. The state, according to Justice Clark, had to be involved "to some significant extent," and over the next two decades, several cases came before the Court testing what constituted a "significant" level of state involvement.

---

1. *Mayor of Baltimore v. Dawson* (1955).
2. *Gayle v. Browder* (1956).
3. *Holmes v. Atlanta* (1955).
4. *New Orleans City Park Improvement Assn. v. Detiege* (1958).
5. *Muir v. Louisiana Park Theatrical Assn.* (1955).
6. *Derrington v. Plummer* (1957).

State Action and Racial Classification

State laws regulating private conduct obviously constituted state action. Nearly all Southern states had some sort of antimiscegenation laws on their books, which prohibited sexual relations, cohabitation, or marriage between members of different races. In the only previous case on this subject to reach the high court, *Pace v. Alabama* (1883), the Court had sustained a state law imposing higher penalties on adultery or fornication between a white person and a black person than between members of the same race, because the higher penalty applied equally to both offenders. Since sexual relations between the races remained one of the great fears of the South, the Court had avoided taking challenges to the antimiscegenation laws. But in *McLaughlin v. Florida* (1964), the Court invalidated a criminal statute prohibiting cohabitation by interracial married couples as a violation of the Equal Protection Clause. Justice White's majority opinion declared any racial classification constitutionally suspect and subject to the most rigid scrutiny. Justice Stewart, in his concurrence, concluded that "it is simply not possible for a state law to be valid under our Constitution which makes the criminality of an act depend upon the race of the actor."

Sixteen states still had laws prohibiting and punishing marriage between the races. Challenges to such laws had twice been carried to the Supreme Court, but had been dismissed in 1955 and 1956 as lacking any federal question. After *McLaughlin,* the Court could not help but find that such an issue existed, and in *Loving v. Virginia* (1967), it struck down a prohibition against interracial marriage as a violation of the Fourteenth Amendment. "Restricting the freedom to marry solely because of racial classification," declared Chief Justice Warren, "violates the central meaning of the Equal Protection Clause."

In his famous dissent in *Plessy,* the first Justice Harlan had declared that "Our Constitution is color-blind," and some members of the Warren Court suggested a *per se* rule to invalidate all legislative distinctions requiring racial classification. Although not going that far, the Court did place a heavy burden of proof on the states to show that a racial classification fulfilled some compelling governmental interest. It is a difficult burden to carry, but in a few instances, states have been able to show that racial classification will not be used for invidious discrimination and is consistent with permissible state objectives. In *Tancil v. Wools* (1964), the Court approved a requirement that divorce decrees indicate the race of the parties for record-keeping purposes, and in *Lee v. Washington* (1968), it noted that prison authorities, "acting in good faith and in particularized circumstances," could take racial hostility into account to maintain order.

Civil Rights and the First Amendment

As part of its resistance to the logic of *Brown*, Southern states tried to clamp down on what they saw as the chief instigators of the unrest, the civil rights organizations, and in particular, the NAACP. Several states passed laws to suppress these groups, which immediately challenged them on First Amendment grounds. The Court's broad interpretation in these cases of the rights subsumed under the First Amendment presaged its broad reading of these rights in other areas (see next chapter).

Initially, Southern states demanded to see the NAACP's membership lists. Once having secured that information, all members holding state or local government jobs would have been fired, while those in the private sector would have faced various forms of economic intimidation, and all would have been subject to the depredations of night-riders and other terrorist activities. In *NAACP v. Alabama* (1958), the Court recognized the reason behind the law and abandoned a longstanding practice of deferring to states in regulating organizations.

In *Shelton v. Tucker* (1960), the Court struck down an Arkansas law requiring the names of members in various organizations, and in *NAACP v. Button* (1963), the Court reversed an attempt by Virginia to prosecute the NAACP for improperly soliciting blacks to serve as plaintiffs in civil rights suits. The state attacks on civil rights organizations resembled the federal government's attack on Communists a decade earlier, but in these cases, the Court resolutely protected the First Amendment right of association, and in doing so, began to backtrack on its more flagrant cold war decisions. The justices began to see the contradiction between according civil rights groups the rights of privacy and association, while denying them to groups labeled by right-wing organizations and federal red-hunters as subversive, without any supporting proof.

The greatest First Amendment case involving civil rights came when the commissioner of police and fire in Montgomery, Alabama, filed a libel suit against *The New York Times* for running an ad soliciting funds for civil rights work. While the case is discussed more fully in the next chapter in terms of the Warren Court's general approach to the First Amendment, *The New York Times v. Sullivan* (1964) arose out of the civil rights movement, but then forced the courts, normally unsympathetic to antigovernment criticism, to rethink the parameters of accepted public discourse.

The Sit-In Cases

The state action cases, for the most part, proved fairly easy once the Court had decided on a general rule to govern them. Far more complex issues reached the Court in those cases resulting from the sit-in movement and other demonstrations by civil rights activists protesting continued discrimination.

In February 1960, four neatly dressed students from the all-black Agricultural and Technical College in Greensboro, North Carolina, politely asked for coffee at a Woolworth's lunch counter; refused service, they remained in their seats until arrested. Within a short time, militant black youths took up the sit-in tactic, and by the end of the year, they had desegregated lunch counters in 126 cities. They soon turned the weapon against other areas of discrimination, with "kneel-ins" at churches and "wade-ins" at public pools. Boycotts supplemented the sit-ins, bringing economic pressure on white merchants to support civil rights demands.

The sit-ins marked a turning point in the movement, and in response to this new militancy, more than 200 Southern cities began to desegregate their public accommodations. The small cities and towns in the Deep South refused to budge, but in the upper South and border states, the pace of desegregation picked up sharply. Students boasted that they had done more to unseat segregation in six months than the federal courts had done in the six years after *Brown*.

> We cannot tolerate, in a nation professing democracy and among people professing Christianity, the discriminatory conditions under which the Negro is living today. We do not intend to wait placidly for those rights which are already legally and morally ours to be meted out to us one at a time.
>
> —Atlanta sit-in leaders (1960)

Prior to the Civil Rights Act of 1964, restaurants had been considered private, and in the absence of any state law commanding segregation, they retained the right to grant or refuse service to anyone they chose. A protester sitting in at a lunch counter or in a restaurant therefore violated the owner's property rights and could be prosecuted for trespass or disturbing the peace.

Although obviously in sympathy with the protesters, the Court failed to develop a rule to cover the situation. Justice Douglas alone appeared willing to eliminate the distinction between state action and private discrimination, but his colleagues believed that some forms of private discrimination are permissible in a free society. People have the right, providing they do not use the power of the state, to associate with whom they please, and private clubs or organizations can define their membership as they desire. Douglas received more support when he suggested that restaurants and hotels should not be seen as totally private, but as a type of public activity, and therefore subject to law. Under the old common law, common carriers, for example, had to offer their services without discrimination. A third approach conceded that although restaurants had the right to refuse service, for the state to arrest the protesters involved state action to enforce discrimination. A broad reading of *Shelley* would have prohibited the state's enforcement of trespass laws against persons excluded from private property on racial grounds, and this would have provided a consistent doctrinal approach to sit-in cases.

The Court, however, set aside all the convictions without, in most instances, even citing *Shelley,* perhaps thus signaling that unconstitutional state action had to involve more than even-handed enforcement of private biases. In the first sit-in case, *Garner v. Louisiana* (1961), the majority dismissed the disturbing the peace conviction for an alleged lack of "evidentiary support." The following year, in *Taylor v. Louisiana,* the Court overturned the breach of peace convictions of blacks who had "invaded" an all-white waiting room in a bus station. The protesters had been orderly and polite, and in any event, segregation in an interstate transportation facility violated federal law.

When it could, the Court invoked the First Amendment to protect the right of peaceful protest. In *Edwards v. South Carolina* (1963), the Court reversed the breach of peace convictions of 187 black students who had gathered at the state capitol to protest continued racial discrimination. When a large crowd of onlookers assembled, police ordered the students to disperse within fifteen minutes and then arrested them when they remained. Justice Stewart ruled that South Carolina had violated the protesters' constitutionally protected rights of speech and assembly.

More sit-in cases reached the Court in 1963 and 1964, and the justices continued to vacate convictions on narrow technical grounds. In only one case, *Bell v. Maryland,* did six of the justices reach the broader *Shelley* issue, and they divided 3 to 3. The case arose from the conviction of twelve sit-in demonstrators under Maryland's criminal trespass law. After their conviction, however, the state enacted a public accommodations law, forbidding restaurants and similar facilities from refusing service because of race, so that the offense for which the twelve had been convicted no longer constituted a crime in Maryland. Justice Brennan's opinion for the Court simply vacated the lower court ruling and remanded the case for further consideration in light of the new state law.

But Justice Black would have none of this, and initially he had managed to cobble together a 5–4 majority to keep the protesters in jail. The man from Alabama who had been one of the strongest supporters of the decision to end segregation now feared that militant civil rights activism could trigger anarchy and social disorder. Eventually he lost his majority, but for the first time, members of the Court actually addressed the substantive issues in the sit-in cases.

Justice Douglas entered a lengthy opinion, joined by Justice Goldberg and Chief Justice Warren, arguing that restaurants constituted businesses dealing with the public, and therefore came within the *Shelley* doctrine. Justice Black, joined by justices Harlan and White, took a far narrower view of both *Shelley* and Section 1 of the Fourteenth Amendment. By itself, he claimed, Section 1 did not forbid owners of property, including restaurants, to ban people from entering or remaining on that property, even if the owners acted out of racial prejudice. Bigots also had the right to call on the state to protect their legitimate property interests.

Shortly afterward, the Court ruled in *Hamm v. Rock Hill* (1964) that enactment of the Civil Rights Act abated prosecutions against persons, who, if the act had been in force at the time they had been arrested for sitting in, would have been entitled to service. This did not, however, put an end to the sit-in cases, since despite its broad wording, the 1964 act did not reach all the types of establishments that protesters wanted desegregated.

Black wound up in the minority in several of these cases, but then managed to muster a majority in *Adderley v. Florida* (1966). Thirty-two students from Florida A&M University had been arrested outside the county jail while protesting the arrest of some of their comrades, and for the first time since *Brown,* the Court upheld criminal convictions against civil rights protesters. The following year Black again broke with the liberals to uphold a contempt of court conviction against Martin Luther King in *Walker v. City of Birmingham*, and struck fear into the entire movement.

> It is high time to challenge the assumption in which too many people have too long acquiesced that groups that think they have been mistreated or that have actually been mistreated have a constitutional right to use the public's streets, buildings, and property to protest whatever, wherever, whenever they want, without regard to whom such conduct may disturb. . . . But I say once more that the crowd moved by noble ideals today can become the mob ruled by hate and passion and greed and violence tomorrow. . . . The peaceful songs of love can become as stirring and provocative as the Marseillaise did in the days when a noble revolution gave way to rule by successive mobs and chaos set it.
>
> —Hugo L. Black, dissenting in *Brown v. Louisiana* (1966)

> I submit that an individual who breaks a law that conscience tells him is unjust, and willingly accepts the penalty by staying in jail to arouse the conscience of the community over its injustice, is in reality expressing the very highest respect for law."
>
> —Martin Luther King, Jr., "Letter from Birmingham Jail" (1963)

King had been leading a nonviolent campaign to desegregate public accommodations in Birmingham, Alabama and, at the same time, to draw attention to the fact that ten years after *Brown,* many areas of Southern life remained completely segregated. After a series of sit-ins and marches, the city obtained an injunction from an Alabama lower court judge forbidding any further demonstrations. Believing the injunction immoral and unconstitutional, King went ahead with demonstrations on Good Friday and Easter Sunday. Police promptly arrested him, and the court found him guilty of contempt of court for violating the injunction. The case came to the Supreme Court four years later, and his attorneys argued that if King had immediately appealed the injunction it would have been overturned as an unconstitutional limitation on First Amendment rights. The only question, then, was whether King could disobey an admittedly unconstitutional judicial order without bringing an appeal; could he, in the name of conscience, circumvent the judicial process?

The long history of the injunction compounded the difficulties. Conservative federal judges had long issued injunctions against labor unions until finally stopped by the Norris-LaGuardia Act of 1932. Progressives detested the injunction because it could be issued by a judge upon petition by one side and did not require an open hearing on the merits of the dispute. By the time the aggrieved party could appeal the injunction, weeks and perhaps months might have gone by in which they could not engage in the proscribed activity, even if it were a legal activity. Certainly members of the Supreme Court, a number of whom had been veterans of the prolabor New Deal, remembered this history. And all of the Court knew the recalcitrance of Southern judges who had done everything they could to block implementation of the *Brown* decision. To appeal an injunction through a hostile state judiciary could take years; in fact, the appeal in *Walker* had taken four years.

Nonetheless, the Court is always reluctant to find against the judiciary, even when, as in this case, it recognized that the lower courts wanted to thwart the protesters' constitutional rights. "It cannot be presumed," wrote Justice Potter Stewart for the majority, "that the Alabama courts would have ignored the petitioners' constitutional claims." The dissenters pointed out the illogic of this sentiment, and Justice Brennan spoke to a broader issue in his dissent. "We cannot permit fears of 'riots' and 'civil disobedience,' "he declared, "to divert out attention from what is here at stake." But the fact of the matter is that the Court fully recognized those fears, and like the country at large, had become more intolerant of social protest.

The Court and the 1964 Civil Rights Act

The Supreme Court had paid close attention to the progress of the 1964 Civil Rights Act, recognizing that its passage would mark the alignment of all three branches of the federal government in strong advocacy of civil rights. Within six months after the president signed the law, the Court heard challenges seeking to prevent enforcement of the public accommodations section of Title II. In both cases, a unanimous Court sustained the law.

In *Heart of Atlanta Motel v. United States* (1964), the Court upheld congressional power under the Commerce Clause, the Equal Protection Clause, and Section 5 of the Fourteenth Amendment. According to Justice Clark, "Congress possessed ample power" to reach such discrimination, and the fact that it used commerce powers to deal with a moral issue made no difference. In legislating under the Commerce Clause, Congress had on numerous occasions chosen to resolve moral questions. If Congress had the power, how it chose to use that power did not concern the Court. Clark rejected out of hand the claim that a motel located in a city did not fall within the meaning of interstate commerce; the record clearly showed that the hotel advertised along interstate highways, that it catered to conventions, and that approximately 75 percent of its registered guests came from out of state. Although Clark contended that such a broad interpretation had been accepted by the Court for 140 years, in fact the decision marked one of the most expansive views of the Commerce Clause ever offered by a federal court.

In the companion case of *Katzenbach v. McClung,* the Court unanimously sustained the law as it applied to restaurants. Ollie's Barbecue in Birmingham, Alabama, did not solicit interstate business, it was not located near an interstate road or bus or train connections, and it served primarily local customers. But approximately half of the food it bought each year came from outside the state and that provided a sufficient nexus to interstate commerce. Since Congress had conducted extensive hearings into the effect of racial discrimination on interstate commerce and had concluded that such discrimination had a direct and adverse effect on the free flow of such commerce, the Court saw no reason to challenge that finding.

Voting Rights

Although the 1964 Civil Rights Act had a profound impact in many areas, the section on voting rights was not fully effective, and hundreds of thousands of blacks remained disenfranchised. The total of registered blacks in Alabama, for example, had risen from 6,000 in 1947 to 110,000 in 1964, but not a single one had registered in Lowndes and Wilcox counties, where blacks outnumbered whites 4 to 1. Nonetheless, although still relatively small in the South, the number of blacks who were registered and able to vote had been climbing steadily, and a variety of forces came together in 1965 to provide the greatest advance for black suffrage since the Fifteenth Amendment.

Just as in the school cases, a series of Supreme Court decisions stretching back three decades had already chipped away at Jim Crow restrictions. Although the Court had seemingly validated black disenfranchisement in primaries in *Grovey v. Townsend* (1935), it had soon reversed itself. In *United States v. Classic* (1941), it held that Congress could regulate a primary where it constituted part of the overall machinery for choosing elected federal officials. A few years later, in *Smith v. Allwright* (1944), Justice Reed specifically rejected the *Grovey* ruling, and held instead that whether or not the state designated a political party as a private organization, the primary remained part of the electoral process. Exclusion of blacks, therefore, violated the Fifteenth Amendment. The issue of a "private" primary came back before the Court in *Terry v. Adams* (1953), in which blacks had been excluded from the "preprimary" elections of the Jaybird Democratic Associations in Texas, voluntary clubs of white Democrats. Winners of the Jaybird contest usually ran unopposed in the regular Democratic primary and often at the general election as well. Although the Court could not agree on a single opinion, eight justices did find the preprimary exclusion a violation of the Fifteenth Amendment.

The Court also attacked many of the other devices designed to exclude blacks from voting. In *Schnell v. Davis* (1949), the high court invalidated an Alabama law requiring would-be voters to understand and be able to explain any section of the state constitution in order to register. Local registrars would ask black applicants to explain the most complicated sections, but rarely challenged whites at all. Then in *Gomillion v. Lightfoot* (1960), the Court struck down an Alabama law that, in Justice Frankfurter's words, redrew "the shape of Tuskegee from a square to an uncouth twenty-eight-sided figure." In doing so, it had excluded all but four or five black voters out of 500, but not a single white voter. Even normal standards of gerrymandering paled before this crude attempt to "fence" blacks out of the town.

Other longtime barriers also began to fall, such as the poll tax, which had proven one of the most effective means of disenfranchisement. Efforts to have Congress repeal the tax for federal elections under its Article I, Section 4 powers had hitherto proved unsuccessful, although by 1948, only seven Southern states still retained the tax. Under the impetus of the civil rights movement, Congress finally approved a constitutional amendment barring poll taxes in federal elections, and the required number of states ratified the Twenty-fourth Amendment early in 1964. (Poll taxes in state elections continued for another two years; see below.)

The 1965 Voting Rights Act

Civil rights leaders knew that blacks would have to gain greater access to the ballot if they wished to achieve greater political and economic equality. In the spring of 1965, Martin Luther King, Jr., organized a march from Selma, Alabama, to the state capital in Montgomery to protest the barriers still facing black voters in that state. Although African Americans made up about half of Alabama's population, they accounted for only 1 percent of the registered voters. Governor Wallace forbade the march, and when King defied the order, Wallace refused to provide protection for the marchers. On Sunday, March 7, 1965, Alabama state troopers attacked unarmed and defenseless men, women, and children, using bullwhips, clubs, and tear gas, as television cameras broadcast the sickening spectacle to the nation and to the world.

Lyndon Johnson federalized the Alabama National Guard to protect the demonstrators, and on March 15, he went before Congress to deliver one of the greatest addresses ever made by an American president. Speaking simply and powerfully, he vowed to use the full resources of the presidency to wipe out the prejudice that he had seen scar the small children he used to teach in a tiny Mexican-American school. To ensure equality, all Americans had to be able to enjoy and use their constitutional right to vote, but local officials in the South employed "every device of which human ingenuity is capable" to deny that right. Existing laws had proven inadequate in the face of such systematic discrimination, and so he proposed "a simple, uniform standard which cannot be used, however ingenious the effort, to flout the Constitution." The president then paused, and looking out at Congress and the nation, said emphatically: "And we *shall* overcome."

Utilizing all his famed persuasive skills, Johnson steered the 1965 Voting Rights Act through Congress; he signed it into law on August 6. The measure authorized the attorney general to send federal registrars into any county that he suspected of discrimination, in particular those counties where 50 percent or more of the voting-age population had failed to register and vote in 1964. Local voting regulations and procedures could be suspended, as could literacy tests and any other devices used to preclude otherwise eligible voters from registering. Attorney General Nicholas Katzenbach soon issued a proclamation identifying Alabama, Alaska, Georgia, Louisiana, Mississippi, South Carolina, Virginia, 34 counties in North Carolina, and isolated counties in Arizona, Hawaii, and Idaho as meeting the criteria for federal action, and now, for the first time, federal law would protect the integrity of the registration and voting processes in the South. Unlike the first Reconstruction, during which the executive, legislative, and judicial branches had been at odds and states were allowed to defy the constitutional mandate, the so-called second Reconstruction saw the president, Congress, and the Supreme Court united in their determination to protect voting rights against racial discrimination.

More than any other statute, the Voting Rights Act gave blacks real power. Two months after a federal registrar arrived in Selma, the percentage of voting-age blacks on the rolls rose from 10 to 60; within a year after passage of the law, 166,000 blacks registered for the first time in Alabama, and within five years, the total number of registered blacks in the South more than doubled. Between 1964 and 1969, black registration in the Deep South almost doubled, increasing from 36 to 65 percent of the black adults in the region. Before long, these figures translated into elected black legislators, sheriffs, and mayors, more than 500 in the lower South alone by 1969. The fact that blacks now had a significant voice in the election of sheriffs significantly affected the way law enforcement officials treated African Americans, who, if mistreated by these officials, could conceivably vote them out of office at the next election.

South Carolina v. Katzenbach

The Southern states quickly challenged the Voting Rights Act, and the Supreme Court agreed to take *South Carolina v. Katzenbach* on original jurisdiction. In particular, South Carolina objected to the provisions dealing with literacy tests and the powers of federal registrars, as well as the length of time Congress permitted the attorney general to suspend local procedures. Some question existed as to whether South Carolina had proper standing to sue, since *Massachusetts v. Mellon* (1923) had held that a state could not bring suit to shield its citizens from the operation of a federal statute. However, the Court had ignored this ruling whenever it considered state interests sufficiently affected. After watching Southern states flout desegregation rulings for a decade, no doubt the justices wanted to resolve the constitutionality of the Voting Rights Act as quickly as possible, so that a sympathetic administration could continue to enforce it.

South Carolina's long and involved brief boiled down to three main challenges to the law. First, the state claimed that Section 2 of the Fifteenth Amendment gave Congress power to forbid violations of Section 1 only in general terms; specific remedies had to be left in the hands of the judiciary. Next, the formula for determining which areas fell within coverage violated the constitutional guarantee that all states had to be treated equally. Finally, the provision barring court review of administrative findings constituted a bill of attainder and infringed on the separation of powers.

For a nearly unanimous court (Justice Black dissented on only one point), Chief Justice Warren dismissed all the state's challenges and sustained the major provisions of the act. Going back to *McCulloch v. Maryland* and *Gibbons v. Ogden,* he held that Congress had a full range of means to choose from in carrying out any legitimate ends. Congress "may use any rational means to effectuate the constitutional prohibition of racial discrimination in voting." As for the areas to which Congress applied these remedies, the Court noted that Congress had studied the problem at length and had taken note of information provided by the Civil Rights Commission and the Justice Department as to where the greatest impediments existed and that it had properly chosen "to limit its attention to the geographic areas where immediate action seemed necessary." Warren also gave short shrift to the equality of states argument, which he interpreted to mean only that all states had to be admitted into the Union on an equal basis; afterward nothing prevented the treatment of localized evils by discrete remedies.

The Court also dismissed the separation of powers claim. Prescribing remedies "which go into effect without any need for prior adjudication is clearly a legitimate response to the problems, for which there is ample precedent under other constitutional provisions." Congress had determined that case-by-case litigation would only delay remedy of the evil and would "shift the advantage of time and inertia from the perpetrators of the evil to its victims." The "specific remedies," the chief justice concluded, are "appropriate means of combatting the evil."

Soon afterward, the Court overturned the use of poll taxes in state elections in *Harper v. Virginia Board of Elections* (1966). Since the Twenty-fourth Amendment applied to federal elections only, Justice Douglas, speaking for a 6 to 3 majority, invoked the Equal Protection Clause of the Fourteenth Amendment to finally inter the tax. Justices Black and Harlan (joined by Stewart) entered vigorous dissents. Despite Black's willingness to expand Bill of Rights protection through the Fourteenth Amendment to the states, he and Harlan both took a fairly conservative approach in requiring a textual basis for constitutional coverage, and neither subscribed to the idea of constant reinterpretation of constitutional terms. Both dissents attacked the majority's use of equal protection as akin to earlier Courts' use of due process "to write into the Constitution its notions of what it thinks is good governmental policy."

A few weeks later, the Court upheld another part of the Voting Rights Act in *Katzenbach v. Morgan.* Section 4(e) held that anyone who had successfully completed sixth grade in a Spanish-language Puerto Rican school could not be denied the right to vote because of inability to read or write English. New York, which had a large number of Spanish-speaking citizens, required literacy in English as a condition for voting. There had been no claims that New York used its literacy test in a discriminatory manner; any person of Puerto Rican background or ancestry who could pass the relatively simple test could vote. A lower court had ruled Section 4(e) unconstitutional as an invasion of powers reserved to the states.

Justice Brennan's 7 to 2 opinion dismissed almost out of hand all previous decisions upholding literacy tests as legitimate conditions for voting, such as *Lassiter v. Northampton County Board of Elections* (1959), since no federal legislation had been in effect at that time. He then read an extremely expansive interpretation of congressional power that, as the dissenters Harlan and Stewart noted, essentially handed over what had previously been a judicial function of regulating and interpreting congressional powers to the legislature itself.

Morgan generated enormous criticism, and not only from people who believed citizens ought to be able to speak and write the language of the country in order to vote. In effect, Brennan said that Congress, with its greater resources to investigate and determine facts, was better able than the courts to perceive discrimination and to prescribe a remedy. The courts should defer to Congress, because of the latter's fact-finding ability, and impose only a low level of scrutiny, a simple, rational basis test. Section 5 of the Fourteenth Amendment had been designed to give Congress remedial powers to enforce the substantive rights embodied in Section 1, and Congress had broad discretion as to the choice of remedies. But it had always been the judiciary that had defined what the substantive rights in Section 1 had meant, and now, according to Brennan's opinion, that function could also be exercised by Congress. By this logic, Congress could make a factual determination concerning any controversial issue, and the courts would be bound by that decision and unable to exercise independent judgment.

New Uses for Old Laws

The civil rights movement not only affected school desegregation, public accommodations, and voting rights, but touched all areas of modern life in which people are discriminated against because of their skin color. Attorneys for civil rights groups developed fresh interpretations of constitutional provisions, and they even dusted off some old Reconstruction-era laws that had never been purged from the statute books. For example, the 1866 Civil Rights Act included a provision guaranteeing "all citizens" the same rights to buy, hold, and convey property "as is enjoyed by citizens" and that now appears as 42 U.S.C. 1982. In *Jones v. Alfred H. Meyer Co.* (1968), the Court ruled that §1982 derived its legitimacy from the Enforcement Clause of the Thirteenth Amendment and that it therefore prohibited racial discrimination in the sale or rental of all property, private as well as public. The decision came only a few weeks after the passage of the Civil Rights Act of 1968, which finally provided a federal fair housing law.

Of even more importance is 42 U.S.C. 1983, derived from the Civil Rights Act of 1871, and which reads:

> *Civil action for deprivation of rights.* Every person who, under color of any statute, ordinance, regulation, custom, or usage, of any State or Territory, subjects, or causes to be subjected, any citizen of the United States or other persons within the jurisdiction thereof to the deprivation of any rights, privileges or immunities secured by the

> Constitution and laws, shall be liable to the person injured in any action of law, suit in equity, or other proper proceedings for redress.

The widespread use of §1983 was derived from *Monroe v. Pape* (1960), which permitted a damage suit against police officers for an unlawful invasion of the petitioner's home and a subsequent illegal search, seizure, and detention. Justice Douglas's majority opinion in that case had imposed a strict liability standard "that makes a man responsible for the natural consequences of his actions." Although there are limits to §1983 liability, Douglas's interpretation gave civil rights advocates a potent weapon to use against individuals, including some government officials, who could no longer claim immunity because they acted under color of law.

Other sections from the old laws that have enjoyed a new lease on life include §1985, imposing tort liability on any two or more persons convicted of conspiring to deprive the injured party of his or her civil rights; §1343, giving federal courts original jurisdiction in civil rights cases; and §1443, permitting defendants to remove certain civil rights cases to federal courts. Moreover, the criminal provisions of 18 U.S.C. 241 and 242, which provide penalties and fines for conspiracy and deprivation of civil rights under color of law, were derived from the 1870 and 1866 Civil Rights Acts, respectively. They received confirmation as having contemporary force in *United States v. Guest* (1966) and *United States v. Price* (1966). The first case involved private persons who had conspired to prevent blacks from using public facilities in Georgia; the latter case grew out of the murder of the three civil rights workers in Mississippi.

What Has Been Accomplished

Nearly a half-century after the Court handed down its historic decision in *Brown v. Board of Education*, it is unclear how much the decision accomplished in improving the education of African Americans. There is no question legalized segregation has disappeared. Walk through any Southern town or city, even in the Deep South, and one sees blacks and whites intermingling, shopping in the same stores, seated side-by-side at lunch counters, and standing in line to vote. At schools that die-hard segregationists vowed would remain all-white, students now gather at football and basketball games to cheer on black athletes. Where the face of Southern law and order had once been overwhelmingly white, today one finds black sheriffs, judges, city officials, and state legislators; in 1989, Virginia elected a black governor.

But what about school desegregation? The greatest progress seemed to have taken place between 1968 and 1980. The percentage of black students in public schools that were more than 90 percent minority declined from 62.9 percent in 1968 to 34.8 percent in 1980, and 34.1 percent in 1992. The percentage of white students in schools 90 percent or more non-Hispanic white declined in the same period as well—77.8 percent in 1968, 60.9 percent in 1980, 48.9 percent in 1992. Progress toward desegregation since then has been glacial.

The greatest change, of course, came in the South. In 1954, 100 percent of black children in the South attended predominantly black schools; by 1968, this had dropped to 77.5 percent of black students, while 68.8 percent of white students still went to to predominantly white institutions. These percentages fell sharply in the 1970s, to 24.6

and 32.2 percent, respectively, and then dipped only slightly afterwards. By contrast, the percentage of blacks in the Northeast who went to predominantly black schools rose during these years from 42.7 percent in 1968 to 49.9 percent in 1992. In big cities like New York, Philadelphia, and Washington, most black children attend predominantly black schools.

In part, the overwhelmingly black nature of public schools in big cities throughout the country is due to the growth of suburbs and to so-called white flight, in which financially able white parents either moved out of the cities or placed their children in private schools. In Summerton, South Carolina, where the Legal Defense Fund began its battles in the 1940s, the public schools in 1979—a quarter-century after *Brown*—were almost entirely black; one white student went to school with 2,029 blacks. The other white students went to the private Clarendon Academy or schools outside of town. When a reporter asked Harry Briggs, the plaintiff in *Briggs v. Elliot* (one of the companion cases to *Brown*), what he had accomplished, he replied "Nothing!" But, he added, the fight had been necessary. Linda Brown-Thompson showed only a little more hope. In 1984, when as a parent she had become involved in another school desegregation suit, she expressed dismay at how long the fight had been going on. "It was not the quick fix we thought it would be."

But the story is not all one sided. Black teenagers are staying in school longer and are almost as likely to complete high school as their white peers. This has led to a rapid rise in the number of blacks attending public colleges and universities, as well as to the expansion of a black middle class. Nor should one discount the psychological value of an educational system that no longer systematically classifies blacks as second-class citizens.

The extent of change, especially in the South, has been phenomenal, but at the turn of the century, the debate is not over legalized apartheid, but whether black children would be better off in primarily black schools. Many black intellectuals doubted the virtues of desegregated schools, despite the fact that the achievement scores of black students have risen far more significantly in integrated schools than in predominantly black schools. Black students in desegregated schools are more likely to stay out of trouble with the law, avoid out-of-wedlock pregnancy, and go on to college. Critics, however, claim that these achievements are class related. Most of the children attending desegregated schools come from middle-class homes, while poorer children go to predominantly black urban schools or small country schools.

Behind the debate over the effects of desegregation looms a larger question, and that is whether courts can in fact initiate social change. There is no question that the Warren Court's decisions in *Brown* and its progeny led to the end of legalized segregation, but the record is far from clear whether the end result will be the better education of black children, nominally the reason the NAACP went to court as well as the chief justification for the *Brown* decision. Much of the debate in the 1980s and 1990s over the efficacy of courts acting as agents of change grew out of the efforts, as the first Justice Harlan put it, to make a Constitution that is truly race blind.

It was perhaps inevitable that *Brown* raised hopes it could not fulfill. No one case—not even a series of cases—could overcome the deep-seated racism that has become institutionalized in American society. Jack Greenberg, who worked with Thurgood Marshall on *Brown* and who succeeded him as head of the Legal Defense Fund, wrote

> I'm a firm believer that you support the school that's within your community. I'm from the segregation time, back in the '50s and '60s, so coming from that background I felt that my children would have a better opportunity to interact socially in an integrated situation. That's where it turned out to be a mirage. It proved to me that educationally and socially your children can learn just as much in a predominantly black situation as opposed to an integrated situation.
>
> —Brenda Jackson, black parent (1992)

on the fortieth anniversary of the landmark decision that "altogether, school desegregation has been a story of conspicuous achievements, flawed by marked failures, the causes of which lie beyond the capacity of lawyers to correct. Lawyers can do right, they can do good, but they have their limits. The rest of the job is up to society." One can easily substitute "courts" for "lawyers"; the conclusion is the same.

Conclusion: An Unfinished Agenda

The fifteen years following *Brown v. Board of Education* marked a major constitutional revolution, a second Reconstruction, which many people hoped would finally carry out the promises of racial justice and equality deferred from the first Reconstruction. But in 1969, when Earl Warren retired from the Court and Richard Nixon entered the White House, no one could claim that the revolution had been completed. De jure segregation in the South had begun to recede, but de facto segregation, North as well as South, remained a major problem. Similarly, although outward forms of racial discrimination had been outlawed, more subtle biases still excluded blacks from economic and social opportunity in many areas. Could the legal system reach this type of prejudice, and could it—or should it—attempt to compensate for the effects of past discrimination? Analysts saw the Nixon election of 1968 as a "blacklash," with the white majority allegedly upset that blacks had come too far too fast in their drive for equality. Numerous issues of civil rights, therefore, remained on the agenda of the country and of the Supreme Court as the nation entered the 1970s.

But for one brief moment in our history, the three branches of government, as well as the American people, stood united in their determination to wipe away the shame of segregation. In 1964, despite the longest filibuster in the Senate's history, the Civil Rights Act passed by large majorities in both houses of Congress. That fall, Senator Barry Goldwater, the Republican candidate for the presidency, denounced the Court as out of step with the country and with the other branches of government. Goldwater's resounding defeat pointed out the falsity of that statement. All three branches of government supported civil rights, and polls showed that a large majority of Americans did as well. Despite the difficulties with the sit-in cases, the Warren Court itself remained unified. Voting records for the term ending June 1964 showed a high level of agreement within the Court. Brennan had agreed with the majority 96 percent of the time, Warren 93 percent, Goldberg, Douglas, and White over 85 percent, Black, Clark, and Stewart over 83 percent. Only Justice Harlan seemed out of step, and yet he, too, agreed with the majority in two-thirds of the cases. Soon that internal harmony, like the seeming agreement of the nation, would come to an end.

For Further Reading

Nearly all of the works listed in the previous chapter are relevant to this one as well. In addition, a better understanding of what the legal battles were all about requires knowledge of the civil rights struggle itself. Some well-balanced accounts include Taylor Branch, *Parting the Waters: America in the King Years, 1954–1963* (1988); Hugh Davis Graham, *The Civil Rights Era: Origins and Development of National Policy* (1990); Harvard Sitkoff, *The Struggle for Black Equality, 1954–1992* (1913); and John Higham, ed., *Civil Rights and Social Wrongs: Black-White Relations Since World War II* (1997). For a look at how the movement played out in local areas, see William H. Chafe, *Civilities and Civil Rights: Greensboro, North Carolina and the Black Struggle for Freedom* (1980); John Dittmer, *Local People: The Struggle for Civil Rights in, Mississippi* (1994); and the dramatic story that Russell H. Barrett tells in *Integration at Ole Miss* (1965).

For the status of civil rights legislation in the mid-1960s, see Donald B. King and Charles W. Quick, eds., *Legal Aspects of the Civil Rights Movement* (1965); the work of the commission established in the 1957 law is analyzed in Foster Rhea Dulles, *The Civil Rights Commission, 1957–1965* (1968). For the Kennedy administration, see Carl N. Brauer, *John F. Kennedy and the Second Reconstruction* (1977); Southern opposition is examined in J. B. Martin, *The Deep South Says Never* (1957); and Anthony Lewis, *Portrait of a Decade: The Second American Revolution* (1964).

The Court's growing annoyance with Southern delay is covered in J. Harvie Wilkinson, III, *From Brown to Bakke: The Supreme Court and School Integration, 1954–1978* (1979). For case studies on the attack on segregated schools, see Liva Baker, *The Second Battle of New Orleans: The Hundred-Year Struggle to Integrate the Schools* (1996); Frye Gaillard, *The Dream Long Deferred* (1988), which deals with Charlotte, North Carolina; and Bob Smith, *They Closed Their Schools: Prince Edward County, Virginia, 1951–1964* (1965).

The expansion of the attack on racial segregation is looked at in Catherine A. Barnes, *Journey from Jim Crow: The Desegregation of Southern Transit* (1983); and Thomas P. Lewis, "Burton v. Wilmington Parking Authority—A Case Without Precedent," 61 *Columbia Law Review* 1458 (1961). For the miscegenation cases, see Harvey M. Applebaum, "Miscegenation Statutes: A Constitutional and Social Problem," 53 *Georgia Law Review* 49 (1964); and Peter Wallenstein, "Race, Marriage, and the Supreme Court: From *Pace v. Alabama* (1883) to *Loving v. Virgin*ia (1967)," 1998 *Journal of Supreme Court History* 65 (#2).

The concept of state action is discussed in Charles L. Black, Jr., "The Constitution and Public Power," 52 *Yale Review* 54 (1962); and Thomas P. Lewis, "The Meaning of State Action," 60 *Columbia Law Review* 1083 (1960). The applicability of the doctrine to the sit-in cases is analyzed in Kenneth L. Karst, "Foreword: Equal Citizenship Under the Fourteenth Amendment," 91 *Harvard Law Review* 1 (1977); see also, Monrad G. Paulson, "The Sit-In Cases of 1964: 'But Answer Came There None,'" 1964 *Supreme Court Review* 137 (1964).

Harry T. Quick, "Public Accommodations: A Justification of Title II of the Civil Rights Act of 1964," 16 *Western Reserve Law Review* 660 (1965) is a fine analysis not only of the provisions of the law, but also of the legislative history leading up to it and its subsequent judicial approval. For voting rights, Donald S. Strong, *Negroes, Ballots, and Judges* (1968) is an indictment of Southern judicial and legislative resistance to the first three civil rights acts. David Garrow, *Protest at Selma: Martin Luther King, Jr. and the Voting Rights Act of 1965* (1978) ties the genesis of the act to civil rights activities. Analyses of the 1965 law and subsequent cases include Alexander M. Bickel, "The Voting Rights Cases," 1966 *Supreme Court Review* 79 (1966); L. Thorne McCarty and Russell B. Stevenson, "The Voting Rights Act of 1965: An Evaluation," 3 *Harvard Civil Rights-Civil Liberties Review* 357 (1968); and Ward Y. Elliott, *The Rise of Guardian Democracy: The Supreme Court's Role in Voting Rights Disputes, 1848–1969* (1974). Steven F. Lawson, *Black Ballots: Voting Rights in the South, 1944–1969* (1976) is an excellent study, as is his *In Pursuit of Power: Southern Blacks and Electoral Politics, 1965–1982* (1985).

There is a growing body of material on the long-term effects of *Brown* and its progeny on education and race relations. A good synthesis is James T. Patterson, *Brown v. Board of Education: A Civil Rights Milestone and Its Troubled Legacy* (2001). See also, David Armor, *Forced Justice: School Desegregation and the Law* (1995); Lino Graglia, *Disaster by decree: The Supreme Court Decisions on Race and the Schools* (1976); Andrew Kull, *The Color-Blind Constitution* (1992); and Gerald Rosenberg, *The Hollow Hope: Can Courts Bring About Social Change?* (1991). The long-term debate can be examined in such books as Orlando Patterson, *The Ordeal of Segregation: Progress and Resentment in America's "Racial" Crisis* (1997); and Andrw Hacker, *Two Nations: Black and White, Separate, Hostile, Unequal* (1992); a contrary and more upbeat view can be found in Abigail and Stephan Thernstrom, *America in Black and White: One Nation Indivisible* (1997).

37

The Warren Court and the Bill of Rights

The First Amendment • The Overbreadth Doctrine • Symbolic Speech • Libel and the First Amendment • Obscenity • The Religion Clauses • Prayer, Bible Reading, and Evolution • Aid to Schools • Search and Seizure • Self-Incrimination • The Right to Counsel • The Right to Privacy • Conclusion: Judicial Activism and Civil Liberties • For Further Reading

FROM THE MID-1920s on, the Court had been involved not only in the question of whether the Due Process Clause of the Fourteenth Amendment applied the Bill of Rights to the states, but also whether the meaning of those rights had changed since they were first enunciated in the eighteenth century. In the 1950s, the Court took the lead in championing social justice through a reinterpretation of constitutional protections that vastly expanded individual liberties for all Americans. By steering a middle course between the activism of Hugo Black and William O. Douglas and the restraint of Felix Frankfurter, Earl Warren and his chief lieutenant, William Brennan, managed to utilize the methods of the latter to support the goals of the first two. The chief justice skillfully utilized his political talents to forge a majority on the bench that favored the fullest constitutional protection of individual rights.

One needs to see the Warren Court decisions in the areas of civil liberties as closely related to those protecting civil rights. Some of the key speech and association decisions, such as *New York Times v. Sullivan* and *NAACP v. Button*, grew directly out of the civil rights conflict. Blacks also suffered greatly from the inequities of the criminal justice system, and justice for unpopular minorities accused of crime related closely to the Court's overall search for a living Constitution that provided justice to all citizens.

The First Amendment

Scholars consider the Warren Court among the most speech protective in the nation's history; parties invoking free speech claims won nearly three-fourths of their cases before the Warren Court, as opposed to less than half before the Burger Court. But the Court's contribution to speech jurisprudence lay less in the number of cases it decided but in the broad vision of the First Amendment that informed its decisions. Above all, a majority of the justices saw free speech as holding a preferred position among constitutional values. They subscribed to Benjamin Cardoza's view that freedom of speech and thought "is the matrix, the indispensable condition, of nearly every other form of [freedom]." In addition, they saw that speech could be attacked not just directly, but indirectly, and that could not be allowed either. In *Bates v. City of Little Rock* (1960), the Court held that First Amendment freedoms "are protected not only against heavy-handed frontal attack, but also from being stifled by more subtle governmental interference."

Even if one does not ascribe a preferred position to the First Amendment, it is clear that some of our most important rights are located in its clauses—freedom of speech, press, religion, assembly, and petition. In the 1950s and 1960s, the Court expanded the concept of free expression in cases growing out of the civil rights movement, the protest against the Vietnam War, and the continuing problem of internal security.

Two related themes run throughout these cases. One was the debate over the preferred position of First Amendment rights advocated by Justices Black and Douglas; the other was whether these rights are "absolute" or require "balancing" with competing interests. For Black, the preferred position doctrine led naturally to the absolutist view, while Frankfurter, joined by John Marshall Harlan, advocated balancing. How difficult the issue could be was seen in *Konigsberg v. State Bar of California* (1961), a 5 to 4 opinion in which the Court sustained the state's denial of bar admission to an applicant who had refused to answer questions on Communist party membership. Harlan's majority opinion carefully explored how society had differing interests, none of which could be allowed to override all others. While people had a right to say whatever they wished, in some instances society had an equally compelling reason either to limit that speech or to punish the speaker if the speech had incited certain results. Harlan detailed a lengthy list of cases in which the Court had approved limits on speech to show that historically the Court had always balanced these various interests. Justice Black's eloquent dissent acknowledged these cases, but he believed that, in the area of speech, any whittling away of liberty would lead to its eventual loss. Balancing required establishing criteria for evaluating the government's intent as well as that of the speaker, which meant that the most important of all freedoms rested on the subjective judgment of courts. He believed it was much better to take an absolutist stance. "The First Amendment's unequivocal command that there shall be no abridgement of the rights of free speech and assembly show that the men who drafted our Bill of Rights did all the 'balancing' that was to be done."

The absolute/balancing dichotomy, however, can be misleading. Black never advocated unconditional freedom of speech, and Harlan always considered speech as one of the most precious of freedoms. In fact, all modern justices, even those labeled as "conservative," have agreed that the First Amendment is "special" in some sense. The debate is not between opposing doctrines, but about where, in a relatively limited part of the spectrum, the line should be drawn. The absolutists want to go farther in protecting all kinds of speech than the balancers, but both place the line well on the side of free speech as against control.

The Overbreadth Doctrine

"Overbreadth" became a key idea informing the Warren Court's speech decisions. The doctrine acknowledged that speech and other First Amendment rights might be restricted, but required that the government show a compelling need to do so. Judges could thus use the test to keep interference as minimal as possible. It provided the balancers with a means to achieve the goals of the absolutists, while at the same time retaining flexibility to meet emergencies.

In *Brandenburg v. Ohio* (1969), the Warren Court responded to the criminal syndicalism statutes that Holmes and Brandeis had protested against in the 1920s. Brandenburg, the leader of a Ku Klux Klan group, had been convicted for advocating terrorism as a means of political reform. Much of the prosecution's case rested on a videotape showing two Klan meetings, one of six persons and the other of twelve, in which the speaker mumbled obscenities against blacks, Jews, and other groups and then urged "caucasians" to fight for their rights. In the *per curiam* opinion, the Court voided the statute because its overly vague definition of criminal activities unduly restricted both advocacy and the right to assembly.

Brandenburg has been described as combining the best of Holmes, Brandeis, and Learned Hand, in that it makes freedom the rule and restraint the exception, permits restriction only where a clear connection between speech and legitimately proscribed actions can be established, and requires that the government spell out its rules clearly and in the least restrictive manner. The problem with clear and present danger—that judges had to guess at the probability of danger—is replaced with a clearer and more easily ascertainable test: will these words, in this context, incite action *now*. The so-called harmless inciter, one whose inflammatory words will not cause present action, is let alone.

Overbreadth proved a useful doctrine in the various Vietnam War protest cases. In *Bond v. Floyd* (1966), for example, the Court ruled that black activist Julian Bond's First Amendment rights had been violated by the Georgia House of Representatives, which had excluded him from membership because, it claimed, Bond could not conscientiously take the required oath to support the Constitution, given his antiwar sentiments. In the unanimous opinion, Chief Justice Warren ruled that neither public officials nor private persons could be punished for their opinions if they did not violate the law. Bond's statements, in which he expressed his admiration for those who opposed the draft, could not be construed as a violation of 50 U.S.C. 462(a), which made it an offense to counsel, aid, or abet a person to refuse or evade registration for the draft. Warren assumed the legitimacy of that provision, but he held that it had to be interpreted narrowly. Expressing admiration for those who had the courage of their convictions did not constitute "counseling, aiding or abetting."

Symbolic Speech

Speech may take several forms, and the Court has consistently ruled that symbolic speech also comes under the First Amendment umbrella. In *Tinker v. Des Moines School District* (1969), the Court overturned the expulsion of three students for wearing black armbands to symbolize their opposition to the war. School officials claimed that the wearing of armbands interfered with proper discipline and might be disruptive. Justice Abe Fortas (appointed by Johnson in 1965) rejected this argument and held that students do not lose their constitutional rights when they enter the schoolhouse. School officials had shown no proof that any disruption had occurred. In fact, the record showed that the three students had been especially circumspect, explaining the armbands to those who asked without trying to impose their views on others. Fear that a disturbance might occur could not justify repression. "Our history says that it is this sort of hazardous freedom—this kind of openness—that is the basis of our national strength, and of the independence and vigor of Americans who grow up and live in this relatively permissive, often disputatious, society."

Symbolism had its limits, however, as the Court made clear in *United States v. O'Brien* (1968). David O'Brien and three others had burned their draft registration cards at an antiwar rally. They admitted they knew that the law prohibited mutilation or destruction of the cards, but they claimed protection under the First Amendment: the card burning symbolized their opposition to the Vietnam War. The Court, according to the chief justice, refused to accept "the view that an apparently limitless variety of conduct can be labeled 'speech' whenever the person engaging in the conduct intends thereby to express an idea." The government had a legitimate interest in preserving the cards, since the draft played an important role in providing manpower for the nation's defense. Only Justice Douglas dissented, but not on First Amendment grounds; he wanted the Court to deal with what he termed the underlying issue, "whether conscription is permissible in the absence of a declaration of war," a question that the Court consistently refused to hear.

The overbreadth doctrine, despite some whittling down during the 1970s, remains a core ingredient of First Amendment law; its importance lies not just in these few cases, but in its wider application. It is a present-oriented doctrine, requiring judges to look not at some horrid future possibility, but at what happened in a specific set of circumstances. Courts can also indicate to legislators whether certain restrictions might be valid if drafted more carefully and with the restrictions more tightly drawn. This satisfies the balancers, who believe that some restrictions may be valid and that courts should give guidance in this area.

Libel and the First Amendment

While developing particular tests for different rights protected by the First Amendment, modern courts have not tried to maintain strict distinctions between them. Speech, press, religion, assembly, and petition are all part of the larger freedom of expression that is the essence of the amendment. As result, one hears phrases like "clear and present danger" in religion cases and arguments about the nature of speech in press and assembly decisions.

Expression, however, is an amorphous concept. Different people "express" themselves in a variety of ways, and the Court has not always been able to accommodate them all within manageable and consistent parameters. Yet the Warren Court constantly expanded the limits of protected speech, and in doing so, the justices undoubtedly broadened freedom of expression. But this expansion led to confusion regarding the location of those limits. Not even Justice Black ever claimed that all forms of expression came within First Amendment protection, but now one could not be sure what remained excluded.

As late as 1942, in *Chaplinsky v. New Hampshire*, a unanimous Court had confidently listed "fighting words," obscenity, and libel as examples of expression outside First Amendment protection. The United States had long ago done away with the English common law on libel and defamation of character, in which the mere publication of a defamatory statement—whether true or not—could be punished. American law allowed the defendant to offer evidence of the truth of the statement, which, if accepted by judge or jury, served as a complete defense. All states, however, still permitted civil actions in tort for false or malicious statements, and wide gradations existed among the jurisdictions. Some states differentiated degrees of malice; others distinguished between simple errors and more serious distortions of truth. Who was being defamed made a difference; the Supreme Court of Kansas formulated a rule in *Coleman v. McLennan* (1908) that allowed almost unlimited criticism of public officials, except where the publisher employed "deliberate falsehood and malice." Because the jury usually determined "truth," "falsehood," "deliberate," and "malice," local passions rather than objectivity often governed the outcome of libel suits.

The Supreme Court had, with few exceptions, left libel a matter for state law. In 1952, a closely divided Court upheld a state statute prohibiting the libel of any group in *Beauharnais v. Illinois*. Justice Frankfurter denied that libel came within the constitutional protection of speech; the state legislature had as good a reason to try to prevent defamatory attacks on groups as on individuals, and he saw no reason for the courts to interfere. Justices Black, Douglas, Reed, and Jackson all entered dissents, ranging from Black's absolutist view of criminal libel laws as unconstitutional to Jackson's anticipation of the overbreadth doctrine. Despite the closeness of the vote, the Court did not return to the libel issue for a dozen years: *Beauharnais* itself has never been overruled.

In this context the Court handed down one of the most important First Amendment cases, *New York Times v. Sullivan*, in 1964. An advertisement in the *Times* signed by dozens of clergy and other civil rights advocates charged the police and city officials of Montgomery, Alabama, with unleashing "an unprecedented wave of terror" against blacks engaged in nonviolent demonstrations against discrimination. Sullivan, Montgomery's police and fire commissioner, sued the newspaper and several of the black clergymen who had signed the ad, and won a $500,000 judgment under Alabama law. The ad contained several factual errors, such as the claim that the Rev. Martin Luther King, Jr., had been arrested seven times; he had, in fact, been arrested four times. Alabama law held publications "libelous per se" if the words tended "to injure a person [in] his reputation" or "to bring [him] into public contempt." The statute re-

> In Montgomery, Alabama, after students sang "My Country 'Tis of Thee" on the State Capitol steps, their leaders were expelled from school, and truckloads of police armed with shotguns and tear-gas ringed the Alabama State College Campus. When the entire student body protested to state authorities by refusing to re-register, their dining hall was padlocked in an attempt to starve them into submission. . . .
>
> Again and again the Southern violators have answered Dr. King's peaceful protests with intimidation and violence. They have bombed his home almost killing his wife and child. They have assaulted his person. They have arrested him seven times—for "speeding," "loitering," and similar "offenses. . . . Obviously their real purpose is to remove him physically as the leader to whom the students and millions of others—look for guidance and support. . . .
>
> We urge you to join hands with our fellow Americans in the South by supporting, with your dollars, this Combined Appeal for all three needs—the defense of Martin Luther King—the support of the embattled students—and the struggle for the right-to-vote.
>
> —"Heed Their Rising Voices," advertisement in *The New York Times*, 29 March 1960

tained many elements of the old common law, and although the defendant could offer truth as a defense, doing so was a heavy burden.

The nexus between the First Amendment and civil rights could not have been clearer. If Alabama could force the *Times* to bankruptcy (and $500,000 was an enormous judgment in the 1960s), it could insulate itself from public scrutiny of its treatment of blacks. Criticizing the South, or even just reporting what happened, could prove too expensive for news organizations. One did not even have to have much of a presence in the state to come within its civil jurisdiction—the *Times* distributed only 394 copies of its daily press run of 650,000 in Alabama, and only 35 of them went to Montgomery—and the paper did not have any full-time reporters stationed in the state.

In a unanimous decision, the Court found the statute "constitutionally deficient for failure to provide the safeguards for freedom of speech and of the press that are requirements" of the First Amendment. Justice Brennan's opinion carefully explained that there is always a balancing test between unlimited speech and the legitimate interests of the state; in matters of public interest and concerning public officials, he struck that balance on the side of free speech, with the exception of "recklessly false statements" made with "actual malice." The Court considered the case, Brennan wrote, "against the background of a profound national commitment to the principle that debate on public issues should be uninhibited, robust and wide-open, and that it may well include vehement, caustic, and sometimes unpleasantly sharp attacks on government and public officials."

Why should libel—a false and defamatory statement—be accorded constitutional protection? According to Brennan, who quoted the nineteenth-century English philosopher John Stuart Mill, "even a false statement may be deemed to make a valuable contribution to public debate," since in the exchange of views this may help bring out the truth. Under the First Amendment, there is no such thing as a false idea; there are, of course, false facts, and there is no constitutional value attached to them. But since false statements are inevitable in public debate, if the Court drew the line only at truth, people would say less, there would be less debate, and consequently less exchange of ideas. As Brennan wrote in another libel case, *Garrison v. Louisiana* (1964), "speech concerning public affairs is more than self-expression; it is the essence of self-government." In effect, the Court proposed a strategy, which has governed ever since, that extended the line of protection past the constitutional minimum all the way to facts, even false facts, to encourage the debate that we deem valuable.

Within a few years of this case, the law of libel had been effectively nationalized. While states could still control the procedural aspects of actions for libel, the substantive criteria had to conform to the Court's ruling in *New York Times* and subsequent cases. If speech dealt with public officials and their conduct, it came within constitutional protection.

A few years later, a majority of the Court applied the *Times* rule to public figures as well as to officials in *Curtis Publishing Co. v. Butts* and *Associated Press v. Walker*, decided together in 1967. The *Butts* case grew out of a *Saturday Evening Post* article that asserted that the University of Georgia coach had attempted to fix a game. In the other case, Walker, a retired general, had sued the Associated Press for a report that he had led a mob in opposition to enforced desegregation during the riots at the University of Mississippi.

Although the Court divided sharply in its reasoning, all the justices agreed that the press enjoyed greater freedom in its treatment of public figures than of private citizens. Only Justice Harlan, however, dealt with the troubling question of where to draw the line between *public* action and persons, who are legitimate subjects for journalistic criticism and investigation, and *private* acts and persons, who should be able to enjoy undisturbed privacy. The clear cases are easy, such as a mayor's management of city affairs, or a student's taste in soap operas. But does the private life of the mayor, for example, deserve protection of a different order from his official conduct? Is the public entitled to know whether one public official is faithful to his wife, or if another drinks too much Scotch from her teacup after hours? The question of so-called newsworthiness would be left for the Burger Court to settle much later.

Obscenity

Obscenity, like libel, had long been considered outside First Amendment protection and subject to state control. The Supreme Court's first encounter with obscenity came in a little noticed case at the beginning of the 1956 term, *Butler v. Michigan*, in which Justice Frankfurter threw out a state statute as a violation of freedom of the press. The law banned books containing obscene, immoral, or lewd language for their potentially harmful effect on youth. "Surely this is to burn the house to roast the pig," wrote Frankfurter. The law "would reduce the adult population of Michigan to reading what is fit for children." Although the case put forward no judicial standards by which to judge the obscene, it did make clear that the older, Victorian values could not be sustained in a First Amendment challenge.

The following year, the Court did try to establish a new standard in *Roth v. United States*, decided with *Alberts v. California*. Roth had been convicted under a federal statute prohibiting the mailing of obscene materials; the *Alberts* case involved a state obscenity law. Justice Brennan, for a majority of the Court, noted that "obscenity is [historically] not within the area of constitutionally protected speech or press," but any idea having "the slightest redeeming social importance" could claim First Amendment protection. He drew a distinction between sex and obscenity, defining the latter as material "which deals with sex in a manner appealing to prurient interests." The Court rejected the earlier test for obscenity, developed in the 1868 English case of *Regina v. Hicklin*, which judged the material by the effect of selected passages on particularly susceptible persons. In its place, the Court adopted a standard already in use in some American courts: "Whether to the average person, applying contemporary community standards, the dominant theme of the material taken as a whole appeals to prurient interests."

Justices Douglas and Harlan in their separate opinions both pinpointed the key problem as being how to identify obscene material. The Brennan test, although more liberal and fairer than the *Hicklin* standard, still required subjective judgment as to whether the allegedly prurient material had any redeeming social value. There had been many examples in the past of new and shocking art forms that were initially attacked as obscene. When James Joyce's *Ulysses* had first been published, staid critics had condemned it, and the federal government had refused to allow its importation into the country. Yet within a few years, writers and scholars were hailing *Ulysses* as a masterpiece, and in the famous case of *United States v. One Book Called "Ulysses"* (1933), Judge John M. Woolsey of the federal district court in New York relied on expert witnesses to sustain the literary value of Joyce's novel; in doing so, Woolsey anticipated much of the *Roth* test.

The determination of what constituted obscenity troubled the Court for the next two decades. As Justice Harlan noted in 1968, the subject had produced a variety of views "unmatched in any other course of constitutional adjudication." Thirteen obscenity cases between 1957 and 1968 elicited a total of fifty-five separate opinions. The justices seemed preoccupied with the question of "What is obscenity?" instead of conducting the type of inquiry normal to First Amendment litigation, "What state interests justify restraint?" Brennan's flat-out "obscenity is not speech" put it into a separate category apart from the well-defined analyses that the Court developed in other speech issues. Not until the Burger Court refined the *Roth* test in 1973 did the justices finally confront the question of why the states had an interest in such controls.

Because obscenity, like beauty, is often in the eye of the beholder, the Warren Court never established manageable tests to separate obscenity from other sexually oriented but constitutionally protected speech. Although a majority of the Court subscribed to Brennan's abstract *Roth* standard, agreement on what it meant never crystallized in practice. Justices Black and Douglas, occasionally joined by Fortas, argued that the state should not censor speech at all. Justice Harlan wanted a double standard, with the states having far greater power in this area than the federal government. The chief justice introduced the question of motive by the merchandiser. The variables in the *Roth* test wound up being manipulated in dozens of ways.

In December 1959, in a rare unanimous opinion, the Court invalidated a California law punishing a bookseller for the mere possession of obscene literature (*Smith v. California*). The decision reflected Warren's belief, endorsed by the American Law Institute, that unless the seller had a clear idea of the contents of the allegedly obscene merchandise, he could not be accused of pandering. Earlier in the year, the Court had applied the *Roth* test to movies in *Kingsley Pictures Corp. v. Regents*, throwing out a New York ban on a film version of D. H. Lawrence's novel *Lady Chatterley's Lover*. State officials had condemned the film for allegedly extolling wrong values, such as adultery, as "desirable."

The growing range of sexual expression in movies brought more and more cases of film censorship before the courts. In *Time Film Corp. v. Chicago* (1961), the Court ruled that states could license movies for exhibit, although this obviously put film in a second-class status as compared to other forms of expression and subjected them to prior restraint. The Court tried to establish some standards to govern movie licensing in *Jacobellis v. Ohio* (1964), involving the Louis Malle film "Les Amants" (The Lovers). The film had been shown nationwide without incident and had been favorably reviewed; at least two major critics ranked it among the best films of the year. A single scene toward the end of the film provided Ohio's sole reason for finding the film obscene. A badly fractured Court suggested amplifying the *Roth* test, but using as a base the standards of a "whole national community." How far the judges had failed to articulate a manageable standard can be seen in Justice Stewart's concurrence, in which he discussed hard-core pornography: "I shall not today attempt further to define the kinds of material I understand to be embraced within that shorthand description; and perhaps I could never succeed in intelligibly doing so. But I know it when I see it, and the motion picture involved in this case is not that."

This still left state-appointed movie censors with enormous control over film standards. The Court tried to rectify this somewhat in *Freedman v. Maryland* (1965), ruling that censors had the burden of proving a film should not be shown, rather than the distributor having to prove it should. This decision did much to cut down the arbitrary power of censors, and the Court also insisted that censors had to follow strict standards of procedural due process in their efforts to prevent film showings.

Chief Justice Warren, along with justices Brennan and Fortas, tried to refine the *Roth* test in *Memoirs v. Massachusetts* (1966), a case dealing with the purported recollections of an eighteenth-century prostitute, Fanny Hill. Three elements had to "coalesce" to warrant governmental regulation: "(a) the dominant theme of the material taken as a whole appeals to prurient interest in sex; (b) the material is patently offensive . . . ; and (c) the material is utterly without redeeming social value." This reformulation still left the bench divided on a number of issues. Should the community standards under which material would be judged be local or national in scope? Should prurient appeal be determined by "straight" or deviant groups? Did the word "utterly," as Justice Clark claimed, make it impossible to declare anything obscene? This divergence of opinion led the Court to adopt the practice in *Redrup v. New York* (1967) of reversing obscenity conviction on a *per curiam* basis if five or more judges, each applying his own interpretation of the *Roth* test, believed that the material was not obscene. Over the next six years, the Court disposed of thirty-one cases in this manner.

Although the Court reversed most of the convictions it reviewed, it still held obscenity outside constitutional protection, and in several noted cases it upheld either the convictions or the statutes that had been challenged. In *Ginzburg v. United States* (1966), the Court sustained publisher Ralph Ginzburg's conviction for violating the federal postal censorship laws. Justice Brennan avoided the defense claim that the material—erotic magazines and *The Housewife's Handbook on Selective Promiscuity*—standing alone did not meet the *Roth* test. Instead, he relied on the pandering aspect of Ginzburg's operation, pointing out that the "leer of the sensualist" permeated the advertising. So a new feature entered the calculus—the manner of distribution.

The Court also approved the constitutionality of a state law to protect children from pornography in *Ginsberg v. New York* (1968). The statute prohibited the sale of any material to children under seventeen that presented a salacious view of nudity, sexual relations, or abuse. Justice Brennan came as close as anyone during the Warren era in attempting to explain why the government should regulate obscenity, when he claimed that the state had always had a special interest and obligation to protect the well-being of youth. Justices Black, Douglas, and Fortas dissented, the first two on their usual argument that the government had no business censoring any form of speech or press. Fortas also expressed concern over the impact these cases would have on future decisions. He charged that the Court had adopted a theory of "variable obscenity," which would keep booksellers guessing whether or not they violated the law. "Bookselling," he claimed, "should not be a hazardous profession."

A dozen years and even more cases after the Court entered this thicket, the Warren Court had still not managed to solve what Justice Harlan called "the intractable obscenity problem." If a majority of the justices agreed that obscenity enjoyed none of the usual protection afforded to speech, they could not agree on what constituted obscenity. Brennan's *Roth* test had not worked, nor had the Warren revision in *Memoirs*. Justice Stewart's "I know it when I see it" summed up the Court's failure, which reflected that of the larger society in trying to deal with the sexual revolution. By the end of the 1960s, Victorianism had been abandoned, replaced by a belief in sex as the source of all personal meaning. In 1967, *Newsweek* ran a lead story entitled "Anything Goes: Taboos in the Twilight," noting the absence of any consensus on sexual issues.

By Warren's retirement in 1969, obscenity law had been clearly liberalized, protecting almost anything on the open market as long as children and nonconsenting adults were protected. The *Roth* test, if nothing else, did provide a basis for protecting serious art and literature, while the decisions regarding state censorship forced the bureaucracy out of the closet and imposed procedural requirements. What one needs to keep in mind is that what we would label "hard-core pornography" did not hit the market until the 1970s, and today viewers of prime-time network shows can watch scenes far steamier than any of the materials with which the Warren Court had to wrestle.

The Religion Clauses

The Court's libertarian reading of the First Amendment's freedom of expression infused new vigor into the Jeffersonian philosophy of the two religion clauses. Modern jurisprudence on these two clauses had begun rather tentatively during the Vinson years. The "wall of separation" formula had first been utilized by Justice Black in *Everson v. Board of Education* (1947), a strange opinion in which Black had written an eloquent essay on the historical reasons for separation of church and state, going all the way back to the 1786 Virginia Statute for Religious Freedom. He quoted Jefferson, stating that the clause had been intended to erect "a wall of separation between church and State," a wall, Black claimed, that had to be sustained; the Court "could not approve of the slightest breach." He then turned around and sustained a New Jersey statute allowing school districts to reimburse parents of parochial school students for costs in transporting them to class.

Four justices had dissented, and in an often quoted sentence, Justice Jackson pointed out that Black's entire opinion pointed exactly in the opposite direction to his conclusion. "The case which irresistibly comes to mind as the most fitting precedent is that of Julia who, according to Byron's reports, 'whispering "I will ne'er consent"—consented.'"

Although Catholics had applauded the decision, many Protestant denominations, as well as civil liberties groups, had condemned it. The Court then managed to offend several religions when it struck down an Illinois released-time program in *McCollum v. Board of Education* (1948). The law permitted representatives of different denominations to come into the public schools and provide religious instruction for students of their faith who voluntarily chose to attend the weekly sessions. Response to the barrage of criticism may have played some role in leading the Court to back down somewhat in its next religion case, *Zorach v. Clausen* (1952). By a 6 to 3 vote, the Court sustained a New York released-time program that differed from that of Illinois in that students left the school building and attended religious instruction in churches or synagogues. Justice Douglas went out of his way to show that the Court did not oppose religion.

> We are a religious people whose institutions presuppose a Supreme Being. . . . When the State encourages religious instruction or cooperation with religious authorities by adjusting the schedule of public events to sectarian needs, it follows the best of our traditions. For it thus respects the religious nature of our people and accommodates the public service for their spiritual needs.

The inconsistencies between *McCollum* and *Zorach* could not be ignored, but the Warren Court avoided taking any more religion cases during the 1950s. Its activism in civil rights and liberties, however, invited a reexamination of several religion-related questions.

The first significant religion cases came before the Court in 1961 and involved Sunday closing laws. In *McGowan v. Maryland*, the Court upheld a state law that required most retail stores to close on Sunday, but permitted a number of exceptions for resorts and entertainment businesses. The policy, long established not only in Maryland but elsewhere, had the support of Christian groups as well as established businesses, which did not want to compete with newer and aggressive retailers offering longer hours of service. A strict reading of the First Amendment would have required the Court to strike down these laws, since, as Chief Justice Warren conceded, "the original laws which dealt with Sunday labor were motivated by religious forces."

The Court sidestepped the problem by claiming that over the years, the original religious purpose of the blue laws had given way to a secular rationale, and that therefore the laws bore "no relationship to establishment of religion as those words are used in the Constitution." The present purpose, according to Warren,"is to provide a uniform day of rest for all citizens; the fact that this day is Sunday, a day of particular significance for the dominant Christian sects, does not bar the State from achieving its secular goals. Sunday is a day apart from all others. The cause is irrelevant; the fact exists."

The Christian plaintiffs in *McGowan* could raise only the establishment argument, but Jewish merchants could object to the Sunday laws on free exercise grounds as well. In *Braunfeld v. Brown*, Orthodox Jewish merchants pointed out that under rabbinic law they could not keep their stores open on Saturday, and since Pennsylvania forbid them to do business on Sunday, they were in a cruel situation in which they had either to violate their religious beliefs or suffer severe economic hardships. The chief justice again sidestepped the real issue by claiming, as in *McGowan*, that the Sunday laws served only a secular purpose. Although the state could never regulate religious *belief* in any form, Warren cited a long string of precedents in which the Court had approved limits on *action*. Laws that had a primarily secular purpose but that imposed an indirect burden on religion did not violate the Constitution.

Warren's opinions in *McGowan* and *Braunfeld* elicited strong dissents from Justice Douglas; the fact could not be avoided, he declared, that all blue laws were derived from the Fourth Commandment and not from the Constitution; in his view, they all violated both the establishment and free exercise prohibitions. In a separate dissent in *Braunfeld*, Justice Brennan asked the questions that Warren had so carefully evaded, and yet are essential in First Amendment cases. "What, then, is the compelling state interest which impels the state to impede appellants' freedom of worship? What overbalancing need is so weighty in the constitutional scale that it justifies this substantial, though indirect, limitation of appellants' freedom?" Even granting the Court's depiction of Sunday laws as essentially secular in nature, what great state need prevented exemption for those who would take their day of rest, their religious sabbath, on another day? Brennan pointed out that twenty-one of the thirty-four states with blue laws allowed such exemptions, evidently without hurting the secular purpose of a day of rest, and he charged the Court with exalting "administrative convenience" above religious freedom.

The dissenters' arguments had a surprisingly swift impact, for two years later the Court handed down a decision that in effect negated *Braunfeld*. A Seventh-Day Adventist had been discharged from her job because she would not work on Saturday, her sabbath; she could not find other work because she would not accept any job requiring Saturday work. South Carolina rejected her claim for unemployment compensation because state law barred benefits to workers who failed, without good cause, to accept "suitable work when offered." After the South Carolina Supreme Court upheld the denial of benefits, Sherbert appealed, claiming interference with her free exercise of religion. In *Sherbert v. Verner* (1963), the Court, through Justice Brennan, agreed with her.

Brennan applied the traditional analysis he had urged in his *Braunfeld* dissent—what compelling state interest required an infringement on religious freedom?—and he could not find any. He did not believe that granting benefits to Adventists on slightly different grounds than to Sunday worshipers constituted an establishment in favor of the Adventists. Rather, it ensured that the government would act neutrally toward all groups and not penalize one because it had a different day of rest from the others.

By this case, the Court had already begun moving toward a more activist view of the religion clauses. In *Torcaso v. Watkins* (1961), it upheld an individual's right not to believe in God by striking down test oaths in Maryland. Nearly all states had had some form of test oath prior to the Civil War, requiring an affirmation of religious belief, but most had either been wiped off the books or allowed to stagnate in the latter nineteenth century. Because the First Amendment had not applied to the states until 1925, no cases testing such oaths had come before the Court prior to *Torcaso*, which in essence administered the *coup de grace* to a moribund practice.

Prayer, Bible Reading, and Evolution

Prayer in public schools, however, was far from moribund when the Court declared the practice unconstitutional in *Engel v. Vitale* (1962). The New York Board of Regents had prepared, for use in public schools, a "nondenominational" prayer, which read: "Almighty God, we acknowledge our dependence upon Thee, and we beg Thy blessings upon us, our parents, our teachers and our country." Many local school boards required that the prayer be recited daily in each class, but a number of parents challenged it as "contrary to the beliefs, religions, or religious practices of both themselves and their children." The state's highest court upheld the rule so long as the schools did not compel students to join in the prayer when parents objected. By a 6 to 1 vote (justices Frankfurter and White did not participate), the Supreme Court held the practice "wholly inconsistent with the Establishment Clause." The prayer, according to Justice Black, could not be interpreted as anything but a religious activity, and the Establishment Clause "must at least mean that it is no part of the business of government to compose official prayers for any group of American people to recite as a part of a religious program carried on by government." Only Justice Stewart dissented. He considered that the practice did no more than recognize "the deeply entrenched and highly cherished spiritual tradition of our Nation."

Not since *Brown* had the Court come under so much public criticism, much of it stemming from a misunderstanding of what the Court had said. Conservative religious leaders attacked the decision for promoting atheism and secularism. Southerners saw *Engel* as proof of judicial radicalism. "They put the Negroes in the schools," Representative George W. Andrews of Alabama lamented, and "now they have driven God out." Senator Robert C. Byrd of West Virginia summed up the feelings of many when he complained that "someone is tampering with America's soul."

The Court had its champions as well as its critics. Liberal Protestant and Jewish groups interpreted the decision as a significant move to divorce religion from meaningless public ritual and to protect its sincere practice. The National Council of Churches, a coalition of Protestant and Orthodox denominations, praised *Engel* for protecting "the religious rights of minorities," while the Anti-Defamation League, a Jewish organization, applauded the "splendid reaffirmation of a basic American principle." President Kennedy, the target of religious bigotry in the 1960 campaign from many of the sources now attacking the Court, urged support of the decision even if one disagreed with it. As he told a news conference:

> We have, in this case, a very easy remedy. And that is, to pray ourselves. And I would think that it would be a welcome reminder to every American family that we can pray a good deal more at home, we can attend our churches with a good deal more fidelity,

> and we can make the true meaning of prayer much more important in the lives of all of our children.

Kennedy's commonsense interpretation of what the *Engel* decision meant captured the Court's intent. The justices did not oppose prayer or religion; the Framers had gone to great lengths to protect individual freedom in this area. But to protect *individual* freedom, the state could not impose any sort of religious requirement, even an allegedly nonsectarian prayer. When the power and prestige of government is placed behind any particular belief, Justice Black argued, "the inherent coercive pressure upon religious minorities to conform to the prevailing officially approved religion is plain." The Founding Fathers understood that "governmentally established religion and religious persecutions go hand in hand."

One year later, the Court extended this reasoning in *Abington School District v. Schempp*, ruling that the Establishment Clause prohibited required reading of the Bible. A Pennsylvania law provided for the reading of at least ten verses of the Bible each day, as well as the recitation in unison of the Lord's prayer. The Schempp family, members of the Unitarian Church, challenged the law, claiming that the practice constituted a religious exercise.

In his opinion for the majority, Justice Clark spoke of the "wholesome neutrality" of the Constitution toward religion, and set forth specific standards by which to judge whether the government had violated the First Amendment:

> The test may be stated as follows: what are the purpose and the primary effect of the enactment? If either is the advancement or inhibition of religion then the enactment exceeds the scope of legislative power as circumscribed by the Constitution. That is to say that to withstand the strictures of the Establishment Clause there must be a secular legislative purpose and a primary effect that neither advances nor inhibits religion.

Again, conservatives misinterpreted and attacked the Court's decision, claiming that the justices had now expelled the Bible from school, along with God. The Rev. Billy Graham professed himself "shocked," and claimed that "prayers and Bible reading have been a part of American public school life since the Pilgrims landed at Plymouth Rock." Justice Clark, however, had made it quite clear that classes could still study the Bible as literature or as a religious document; it just could not be used for proselytizing purposes or in any manner that partook of a religious exercise.

Prayer and Bible reading had been largely an Eastern and Southern experience; in the Midwest only about one-third of the schools engaged in the practice, and only about one-sixth of the schools in the West. After *Engle* and *Schempp*, religious practices vanished in the East and West, but continued in a more muted form in the Midwest. Opposition to the decisions centered in the South, where many school districts completely disregarded the rulings. The state superintendent of education in South Carolina told school boards to ignore *Schempp*, while Governor George Wallace of Alabama threatened to stage a "pray-in" at public schools. Critics of the Warren Court, especially in the South, objected to far more than the civil rights decisions.

Opponents of the prayer and Bible reading decisions attempted to override the Court by amending the Constitution. From 1963 until the present, almost every session of Congress has seen the introduction of a proposed amendment to permit Bible reading or prayer in the public schools. Senator Everett Dirksen of Illinois led the campaign in the 1960s, claiming that the "common man" wanted his children to pray in school, but it soon became apparent that most religious leaders not only understood what the Court meant but approved the two rulings. When Dirksen finally brought his prayer amendment to the floor of the Senate in September 1966, it fell nine votes shy of passage. In the early 1980s, resurgent Christian fundamentalists and Ronald Reagan again called for prayer in the schools, only to discover that a majority of Americans still supported the Court's argument that religious freedom required the maintenance of the wall of separation.

A third case following *Engel* and *Schempp* also aroused the ire of religious conservatives. The conviction of John Scopes for teaching Darwin's theory of evolution in 1927 had not reached the Supreme Court on appeal because the Tennessee high court had dismissed the case on a technicality. As a result, the antievolution statutes in Tennessee and other states had never been subjected to constitutional scrutiny. Finally, in *Epperson v. Arkansas* (1968), a unanimous Court, speaking through Justice Fortas, found the Arkansas antievolution statute in conflict with the Establishment Clause. "Arkansas did not seek to excise from the curricula of its schools and universities all discussion of the origin of man. The law's effort was confined to an attempt to blot out a particular theory because of its supposed conflict with the Biblical account, literally read."

Aid to Schools

At about the same time that the Court was expanding the reach of the Establishment Clause in regard to state laws, the federal government raised new problems through its greatly increased aid to education programs. In January 1965, Lyndon B. Johnson proposed $1.5 billion in grants to primary and secondary schools, both public and private, secular and parochial. With Johnson exerting all of his famed political arm-twisting, the Elementary and Secondary Education Act passed both houses of Congress by wide margins, and the president signed it into law in April. By 1968, Congress was funneling more than $4 billion a year into elementary and secondary schools. Part of it went to church-related schools with high percentages of children from low-income families. That aid immediately drew criticism as a violation of the First Amendment, and opponents set about finding a way to challenge it in the courts.

The Supreme Court had first encountered the problem of federal aid to religious institutions in *Bradfield v. Roberts* (1899), in which it had sustained a federal appropriation for the construction of a public ward in a hospital owned and operated by a nursing order of the Roman Catholic Church. The Court did not address the issue of whether aid to religious institutions is permissible, because it held the hospital did not constitute a religious body. In the 1947 *Everson* case, the Court had upheld a form of state aid, since the primary purpose had been to benefit children. The Johnson administration hoped to prevent a challenge to the act from even coming before the Court, and it defeated an effort by Senator Sam Ervin of North Carolina to amend the measure so as to allow taxpayer suits to test its constitutionality. (Under the doctrine of *Frothingham v. Mellon* [1923], taxpayers lacked standing to challenge the government's disposition of its tax revenues.)

In *Flast v. Cohen* (1968), however, Chief Justice Warren reversed a lower court ruling based on *Frothingham* and permitted a taxpayer to initiate a suit against the law. The policy considerations behind the earlier decision no longer applied, and in any event, the "barrier should be lowered when a taxpayer attacks a federal statute on the ground that it violates the Establishment and Free Exercise Clauses of the First Amendment." By this decision, the chief justice ensured that the Supreme Court would have a significant voice in the debate over educational policies. Although most of those cases would not reach the Court until after Earl Warren retired, the late 1960s saw the enactment of dozens of state and federal programs to aid education, and many of them included parochial schools as beneficiaries. In the cases testing these laws, opponents would argue that they violated the Establishment Clause, while supporters would rely on the child benefit theory that had been enunciated in *Everson*.

Search and Seizure

Aside from the desegregation rulings, few decisions of the Warren Court aroused such public debate as those nationalizing the Fourth, Fifth, and Sixth amendments and then expanding their reach. These three articles of the Bill of Rights deal with criminal procedure and protect against arbitrary action by government officers. The Warren Court not only made these protections applicable to the states through the Fourteenth Amendment's Due Process Clause, but also fortified the rights of accused persons when confronted by the power of the state.

The Fourth Amendment expressed the Framers' opposition to the offensive practices of the British prior to the Revolution, and it governs how police may carry out one of their major responsibilities, gathering evidence during the investigation of crimes. While it sets limits on what the police may do, the amendment recognizes the legitimacy of reasonable search and seizure and does not erect insurmountable obstacles to that process. To secure a warrant, investigating officers need merely show "probable cause" and spell out with some precision the places to be searched and the type of evidence sought.

Because the Fourth Amendment applied directly to the national government, federal law enforcement officers and federal courts had developed a fairly coherent policy on the need for warrants and the grounds necessary to procure them. Yet as late as 1947, in *Harris v. United States*, a majority of the Court, including Black and Douglas, joined in Chief Justice Vinson's opinion that if police entered an apartment with a valid warrant to seek one kind of evidence and discovered another, they could use this material in prosecuting a different offense. Justices Frankfurter, Murphy, Jackson, and Reed dissented, claiming that this doctrine violated the intent of the Fourth Amendment and, in essence, gave police a roving warrant. Frankfurter's dissent, one of his best, laid out in careful detail the history of the warrant in common law and the background of the Fourth Amendment. This argument won over Justice Douglas a year later in *Johnson v. United States*, which considerably narrowed *Harris* and strongly implied the need of specific warrants for police searches.

The Vinson Court also took the step of applying the Fourth Amendment to the states in *Wolf v. Colorado* (1949). But the justices split, 6 to 3, over whether the exclusionary rule, which had been the remedy for federal violation of the warrant since 1914, should also apply to the states. In his majority opinion, Justice Frankfurter argued that the exclusionary rule, as a judge-made remedy, did not constitute part of the Fourth Amendment and therefore could not be imposed by federal courts on the states. Justice Murphy dissented, claiming that the Fourth Amendment made no sense without the exclusionary rule; he saw the rule as implicit in the amendment.

When the Warren Court came to consider this issue again in *Mapp v. Ohio* (1961), it adopted Murphy's argument. To say that the Fourth Amendment applied to the states, wrote Justice Clark, but to deny the only means of enforcing it, "is to grant the right but in reality to withhold its privilege and enjoyment." Clark noted the controversy over the exclusionary rule and admitted that in some cases the criminal might go free because the police had blundered. But a higher consideration existed, "the imperative of judicial integrity." The government had to set an example of fidelity to the law, for if its officers ignored the law, the public would eventually do so as well.

Critics who attacked the *Mapp* decision for handcuffing the police ignored the fact that by 1961, roughly half the states had already adopted the exclusionary rule. As Justice Roger Traynor of the California Supreme Court explained, he had reversed his own thinking on the subject, because without the rule the "princely rights" of the Fourth Amendment had no remedy. If police could use evidence that they had seized without a warrant, or with an improper warrant, then why should they bother getting a warrant at all? The states had been going in the direction of *Mapp* for several years, he claimed; the Supreme Court had merely accelerated the process.

Chief Justice Warren delivered the Court's 8 to 1 opinion in the other major Fourth Amendment case decided during his tenure, *Terry v. Ohio* (1968). An experienced police officer observed three men who appeared to be "casing" a store. He stopped them and, dissatisfied with their answers to his questions, frisked them. He found revolvers on two of the men and arrested them. Counsel for the men claimed that because the officer had no warrant, he had no right to search them and that the revolvers could not be introduced as evidence. In a long and rambling opinion, the chief justice upheld the police officer, ruling that if the police had reasonable grounds and needed to act promptly, they could stop and frisk suspects without a warrant.

Self-Incrimination

Public controversy over the Warren Court's criminal cases dwelt less on its Fourth Amendment decisions than on how it interpreted the Fifth and Sixth. The Fifth includes what has sometimes been called "the Great Right," that no person "shall be compelled in any criminal case to be a witness against himself." The origins of the right go back to objections against the inquisitorial proceedings of the medieval ecclesiastical tribunals, as well as of the Courts of Star Chamber. By the late seventeenth century, the maxim of *nemo tenetur prodere seipsum*—no man is bound to accuse himself—had been adopted by common law courts and had been expanded to mean that a person did not have to answer any questions about his or her actions. The state could prosecute a person, but could not require that he or she assist in that process. The colonies carried this doctrine over as part of the received common law, and many states wrote it into their early bills of rights. Madison included it as a matter of course when he drafted the federal Bill of Rights.

The privilege came under heavy criticism during the Red Scare of the 1950s, as witnesses refused to answer Senator McCarthy's questions on grounds of possible self-incrimination. "Taking the Fifth" became associated with Communists, and critics charged that a truly innocent person should not hesitate to take the stand and tell the truth in criminal trials or before investigating committees. Legal journals and the popular press carried articles on whether this constitutional right, which allegedly sheltered only guilty persons, ought to be amended.

The Court had taken an expansive view of this right since the latter nineteenth century. In *Boyd v. United States* (1886) and *Counselman v. Hitchcock* (1892), it had expanded the privilege against self-incrimination to apply to any criminal case, as well as to civil cases in which testimony might later be used in criminal hearings. In 1967, the Court expanded the concept of a "criminal case" to include juvenile delinquency proceedings in *In re Gault*. The privilege is not absolute; persons may not refuse to be fingerprinted, to have blood samples, voice recordings, or other physical evidence taken, or to submit to intoxication tests—even though all these may prove incriminating. But at a trial, the accused has the right to remain silent, and any adverse comment on a defendant's silence, by either judge or prosecutor, violates the constitutional privilege.

Although an accused person may not be forced to testify, he or she may voluntarily confess, and the confession may be used in evidence. The old common law rule against confessions obtained by torture, threats, inducements, or promises had been reaffirmed as part of constitutional law by the Court in 1884. In modern times, there have been three distinct phases in the Court's determination of the admissibility of a confession.

From 1936 to 1964, the due process clauses of the Fifth and Fourteenth amendments provided the standard by which to judge voluntariness. In *Brown v. Mississippi* (1936), the Court threw out confessions obtained by whipping. Over the next three decades, the justices refined the concept of voluntariness to include not only freedom from outright physical abuse, but also from more subtle abuses such as denial of food or sleep. They also ruled that psychological brutality could invalidate a confession, as in *Payne v. Arkansas* (1958), in which police told an illiterate suspect that thirty to forty people were waiting to "get" him if he did not confess. The Court never developed any clear, objective test, but on a case-by-case basis looked at whether the "totality of circumstances" offended a sense of fairness.

From 1964 through 1966, the Court tied the Fifth Amendment privilege to the Sixth Amendment's right to counsel, on the grounds that only if the accused had been properly informed of his or her rights, including the right to remain silent, could an ensuing confession be admissible. The key case was *Massiah v. United States* (1964). The defendant had been indicted for violating federal drug laws; he had retained a lawyer, pleaded not guilty, and been released on bail. Federal agents trailed Massiah and electronically eavesdropped on a private conversation, thus securing incriminating evidence that led to his conviction at the trial. The Court, through Justice Stewart, threw the verdict out; once the accused had a lawyer, the police could not use anything he said unless he had been advised by counsel as to the effects of those words.

Later that year, the Court ruled that the Fifth Amendment's privilege against self-incrimination applied to the states (*Malloy v. Hogan*). Shortly afterward, in *Escobedo v. Illinois*, the Court overturned the conviction of Danny Escobedo because police would not allow him to see the attorney he had asked for until after they had secured a confession to the crime. As Justice Goldberg wrote:

> Our Constitution strikes the balance in favor of the rights of the accused to be advised by his lawyer of his privilege against self-incrimination. . . . No system worth preserving should have to *fear* that if an accused is permitted to consult with a lawyer, he will become aware of, and exercise, these rights. If the exercise of constitutional rights will thwart the effectiveness of a system of law enforcement, then there is something very wrong with that system.

In 1966, a seriously divided Court handed down the landmark ruling of *Miranda v. Arizona*. Chief Justice Warren finally gave police and the lower courts a clear test to help them determine voluntariness. A person had to be informed in clear and unequivocal terms of the constitutional right to remain silent, and that anything said could be used in court. In addition, the officers had to tell the suspect of the right to counsel and that if he or she had no money to hire a lawyer, the state would provide one. If the police interrogation continued without a lawyer present, the chief justice warned, "a heavy burden rests on the Government to demonstrate that the defendant knowingly and intelligently waived his privilege against self-incrimination and the right to counsel." The four dissenters, Harlan, White, Stewart, and Clark, protested against replacing the flexible totality of circumstances approach with what they considered to be rigid and inappropriate rules.

The *Miranda* decision unleashed a storm of criticism of the Court for its alleged coddling of criminals, and some scholars shared the minority's view that *Miranda* represented a radical break, in which the Court had made a "new law and new public policy." In 1968, Congress responded by adding section 3501 to Title 18 of the U.S. Code, which set out far more lenient criteria by which federal courts could determine the admissibility of confessions. Interestingly enough, the courts have for the most part ignored §3501 and followed the more stringent rules of the Supreme Court. Despite the law and order mentality that informed national politics during the late 1960s and early 1970s, the basic soundness of *Miranda* became clear.

The more progressive police departments in the country lost little time in announcing that they had been following similar practices for years, and that doing so had not undermined their effectiveness in investigating or solving crimes. Felons who wanted to confess did so anyway; in other cases, the lack of a confession merely required more efficient police work to find and convict the guilty party. As to charges that the decision encouraged crime, Attorney General Ramsey Clark explained that "court rules do not cause crime." Many U.S. attorneys agreed, and one commented that "changes in court decisions and procedural practice have about the same effect on the crime rate as an aspirin would have on a tumor of the brain."

After *Miranda,* the Court retreated somewhat from its emphasis on the right to counsel in confession cases and based its decisions on whether the suspects had made a knowing waiver of their rights. Police still could not coerce a confession; they still had to inform suspects of their rights. If a person wanted to confess, however, the record had to show that a knowing and voluntary waiver of *Miranda* rights had taken place. The introduction of inexpensive and portable videotaping equipment has provided police with a simple means of showing that they have met this test. When a suspect wishes to confess, the police make a tape showing a police officer reading the *Miranda* warning, and then asking the suspect if he or she understands these rights, and if so, still wants to confess. The confession is then recorded, and judge and jury can easily see if all the criteria have been met.

The Right to Counsel

The right to counsel grew phenomenally during the Warren years. The American right to have assistance of counsel in *all* criminal cases marked a significant departure from the earlier English practice, which allowed lawyers only in some misdemeanor cases; in ordinary felonies, England had not permitted counsel at all until 1836, although judges evidently often bent this rule. Twelve of the original thirteen states rejected the English common law doctrine and extended the right to all criminal cases; the Judiciary Act of 1789, the Federal Crimes Act of 1790, and the Sixth Amendment followed this pattern. Although the amendment makes no reference to providing counsel for indigents, the federal government did appoint lawyers in serious cases, and a number of states also provided counsel for poor defendants in felony trials.

The right to counsel had been one of the first to be nationalized in *Powell v. Alabama* (1932). Ten years later, however, in *Betts v. Brady,* the Court backed off and declared that the Fourteenth Amendment had not incorporated the specific guarantees of the Sixth. A majority held that counsel for indigent defendants did not constitute a fundamental right essential to a fair trial. Rather, the justices would make a case-by-case inquiry into the totality of circumstances to see if the lack of counsel had deprived the defendant of a fair trial. Over the next twenty years, the Court heard many special circumstances, and in most of the cases, it determined that a lawyer should have been provided to ensure fairness. In *Chewning v. Cunningham* (1962), for example, the Court reversed a conviction under a recidivist statute, holding that due process had been denied because the legal questions in the case presented too great a potential for prejudice without a lawyer's assistance.

The following year, in the great case of *Gideon v. Wainwright*, a unanimous Court, speaking through Justice Black (who had dissented in *Betts*), did away with the cumbersome case-by-case adjudication and ruled that the presence of counsel was a fundamental right essential to a fair trial. As Warren biographer Ed Cray wrote, "No tale so affirmed the American democracy. No story broadcast around the world so clearly proclaimed that not just the rich received justice in American courts." The Court also took the unusual step of applying *Gideon* retroactively, so that states that had not originally provided counsel in felony cases now had either to retry the defendants properly, or, as often proved the case, with witnesses dispersed and evidence cold, let them go.

Gideon applied only to felony trials; not until 1972 did the Court expand the right to include misdemeanors as well. But in 1967, the Court did expand the right to counsel to include a far greater part of the criminal process. In *United States v. Wade*, the Court extended the right back to the lineup, ruling that the wording of the Sixth Amendment required the assistance of counsel from the time when the police investigation shifts from a general seeking after facts to an accusatory proceeding. The decision reflected the Court's concern over growing evidence of the shoddiness and unreliability of police identification techniques. Later that year, the Court extended the right in the other direction, past the determination of guilt to the sentencing phase of a trial in *Mempa v. Rhay*.

The whole rationale behind the Warren Court's decisions in criminal cases reflected the belief that exercise of constitutional rights ought not to depend on a person's wealth or education. Poor people have the same rights under the Constitution as the rich, but often they do not know about them. In *Miranda* and other cases, the Warren Court basically said that all Americans must know, at a minimum, that they have rights and that police cannot trick them into forfeiting those rights by withholding that information.

The Right to Privacy

The Court's expansion of enumerated liberties encouraged litigation by parties with special interests, hoping that the mantle of constitutional protection might spread even farther. In the spring of 1965, the Court decided one of a handful of cases that can truly be said to have established a new area of constitutional law. In *Griswold v. Connecticut*, the Court resurrected substantive due process to establish a constitutionally protected right of privacy.

Various privacy rights existed within the common law, but often they were attached to property, such as in the old adage that "a man's home is his castle." In the United States, the law of privacy remained poorly defined; commentators believed that a right existed, but there was practically no case law on the subject. In 1890, Louis Brandeis and his law partner, Samuel D. Warren, Jr., had published a pioneering article on the subject in the *Harvard Law Review*, a piece later credited with launching American law on this subject.

Civil libertarians believed that privacy could be brought under constitutional protection through implied guarantees in the Bill of Rights and through implicit and explicit dicta in various Court rulings. The First Amendment, for example, protected various forms of freedom of expression; the Fourth limited government search and seizure

> If an obscure Florida convict named Clarence Earl Gideon had not sat down in his prison cell with a pencil and paper to write a letter to the Supreme Court . . . the vast machinery of American law would have gone on functioning undisturbed. But Gideon *did* write that letter, the Court *did* look into his case; he *was* retried with the help of a competent defense counsel, found not guilty and released from prison after two years for a crime he did not commit—and the whole course of American legal history has been changed.
>
> —Attorney General Robert F. Kennedy, Address to New England Law Institute, 1 November 1963

of person or property; the Fifth barred self-incrimination; the Ninth provided a catchall for nonenumerated rights; and the Fourteenth applied all of them to the states. In addition, the Third forbade the quartering of soldiers; Justice Story had written in his *Commentary* on the Constitution that the Third had the "plain object . . . to secure the perfect enjoyment of that great right of the common law, that a man's house shall be his castle, privileged against all civil and military intrusions."

The Court had previously indicated the existence of nonenumerated rights that were embodied in so-called personal liberties. Over the years, these had been held to include a right to educate one's child, to marriage and procreation, travel, and choice of association. The most striking statement on privacy could be found in Brandeis's great dissent in the wiretap case, in which he declared that the Framers had "conferred, as against the government, the right to be let alone—the most comprehensive of rights and the right most valued by civilized men" (*Olmstead v. United States* [1928]).

The *Griswold* case involved an 1879 statute prohibiting the use of any drug or device to prevent conception and penalizing any person who advised on or provided contraceptive materials. Civil libertarians had tried to get the Supreme Court to review this law twice before, most recently in *Poe v. Ullman* (1961). Justice Frankfurter had then written a plurality opinion denying review for lack of justiciability, noting that there had been only one prosecution in eighty years. With such a tacit understanding between the police and the public to leave people alone, the Court need not interfere. Justices Douglas and Harlan entered strong protests: Douglas wanted to know what lawyer would advise clients to rely on a "tacit agreement" that police would not enforce a criminal statute, while Harlan suggested that a liberty interest (a personal right that came within the protection of the Fourteenth Amendment) existed that deserved protection.

Shortly after *Poe*, New Haven officials did prosecute Estelle Griswold, the executive director of the Connecticut Planned Parenthood League, along with one of the doctors in the League's clinic who had prescribed contraceptives to a married person. With Frankfurter's argument of nonjusticiability thus destroyed, the Court accepted the case, and Justice Douglas delivered one of the most creative and innovative opinions in his thirty-six years on the bench. Most of the references to privacy in earlier cases had relied on a liberty embodied in substantive due process, which in the mid-1960s still suffered from the bad odor of Lochnerism. Douglas did not want to invoke substantive due process, so he cobbled together justifications from various parts of the Bill of Rights. The amendments "have penumbras, formed by emanations from those guarantees that help give them life and substance." These emanations together (joined in what one wit described as Amendment 3½) form a constitutionally protected right of privacy; and no privacy could be more sacred, or more deserving of protection from intrusion, than that of the marital chamber.

Justice Goldberg, joined by Brennan and the chief justice, concurred, relying on the rarely cited Ninth Amendment, which reserves to the people all nonenumerated rights. The right to privacy, Goldberg maintained, predated the Constitution, and the Framers intended that all such ancient liberties should also enjoy constitutional protection. Justice White concurred on due process grounds, while Justice Stewart dissented, claiming that the Court had exceeded the limits of judicial restraint. Stewart

> We deal with a right of privacy older than the Bill of Rights—older than our political parties, older than our school system. Marriage is a coming together for better or for worse, hopefully enduring, and intimate to the degree of being sacred. The association promotes a way of life, not causes; a harmony in living, not political faiths; a bilateral loyalty, not commercial or social projects. Yet is an association for as noble a purpose as any involved in our prior decisions.
>
> —William O. Douglas, in *Griswold v. Connecticut* (1965)

thought the statute "an uncommonly silly law," but he could find nothing in the Bill of Rights forbidding it.

The dissent by Justice Black and Justice Harlan's concurrence are of special interest because they illustrate two major theories of constitutional interpretation. Although Black advocated total incorporation of the Bill of Rights, he remained in many ways a strict constructionist; he would only incorporate those rights specified in the first eight amendments. He dismissed Goldberg's Ninth Amendment opinion scornfully, declaring that "Every student of history knows that it was intended to limit the federal government to the powers granted expressly or by necessary implication."

Justice Harlan did not fear the idea of substantive due process and based his concurrence on that theme. Due process, he claimed, reflects fundamental principles of liberty and justice, but these change over time as society progresses. The Court has the responsibility of reinterpreting phrases such as "due process" and "equal protection" so that the Constitution itself may grow with the times. Harlan saw Black's view as too rigid; both the states and the federal government needed the flexibility to experiment in means to expand the protection of individual rights.

Douglas's result—the creation of a constitutionally protected right to privacy—and Harlan's substantive due process rationale established the basis for the expansion of autonomy rights in the 1970s. *Griswold* is the forebear of *Roe v. Wade* (the case that legalized abortion) and many other cases enlarging personal freedoms. *Griswold* became the launching pad for the new substantive due process and a progenitor of the fundamental interest interpretation of the Due Process Clause.

The Warren Court decided one other noteworthy privacy case, one that involved the search of a man's home for bookmaking evidence. The police discovered several pornographic films, and prosecuted Robert Stanley under a statute prohibiting the "possession of obscene materials." Georgia defended the law on the basis of *Roth*, and argued that if it could protect the physical well-being of its citizens, it could also protect their minds. Justice Thurgood Marshall (appointed by President Johnson in 1967) disagreed, and in *Stanley v. Georgia* (1969), he declared that the right "to receive information and ideas, regardless of their social worth, is fundamental to our free society." The state conceded that Stanley did not sell the films, but merely owned them, presumably for his own viewing. Marshall dismissed the conviction with a ringing affirmation of the right to privacy: "If the First Amendment means anything, it means that a State has no business telling a man, sitting alone in his own home, what books he may read or what films he may watch."

Conclusion: Judicial Activism and Civil Liberties

The activism of the Warren Court upset many people, including some who sympathized with the goals of its decisions. Such astute and respected commentators as Alexander Bickel of the Yale Law School still adhered to the doctrine of judicial restraint as expounded by Felix Frankfurter, whose law clerk he had been. Activism on behalf of any program, no matter how attractive, suffered from the same problems that had beset the Court during the *Lochner* era: judges ought to leave policymaking to the political branches. But neither Frankfurter nor other advocates of judicial restraint seemed to recall the important distinction that Justice Brandeis, himself a great apostle of restraint, had made between economic regulation and statutes affecting fundamental rights. The courts should defer to legislative will regarding the former, asking only if Congress or a state assembly had the constitutional power to pursue the goal. But when it came to individual liberties such as speech, the courts had a special responsibility to ensure that legislatures stayed within the narrow parameters allowed by the Constitution. Such a role requires far more than a passive judiciary; in the area of civil liberties, at least, a strong case can be made for an activist Court.

Moreover, there is the simple question that one must always ask about any judicial opinion—did the Court get it "right?" In some cases it is hard to tell, but the Warren Court produced a string of great cases matched by no other court in our history, not even that of John Marshall. In *Brown v. Board of Education* (1954), it struck down Southern apartheid; in *New York Times v. Sullivan* (1964), it established freedom of the press as a central component of American democracy and took the idea of freedom of expression further than it had ever gone before; despite the controversy engendered by *Engele v. Vitale* (1962) and *Abington School District v. Schempp* (1963), the Court's insistence on a wall of separation between church and state clearly mirrored the intention of the Framers; *Gideon v. Wainwright* (1963) is one of the foundation stories of American Constitutional history, while *Miranda v. Arizona* (1966) provided the prophylactic test for how police may treat persons suspected of crimes; *Griswold v. Connecticut* (1965) established a right that nearly all Americans hold dear, the right of privacy; while *Baker v. Carr* (1962) and *Reynolds v. Sims* (1964) redrew the political map of the United States to ensure democratic representation. Some of these cases have drawn intense criticism, yet no one denies their great and lasting impact on American life. Moreover, despite the pledges of conservative presidents to undo the actrivist record of the Warren Court, three decades after Earl Warren retired, all of these landmark opinions are still in force.

> Where there is injustice, we should correct it; where there is poverty, we should eliminate it; where there is corruption, we should stamp it out; where there is violence, we should punish it; where there is neglect, we should provide care; where there is war, we should restore peace; and wherever corrections are achieved we should add them permanently to our storehouse of treasures.
>
> —Earl Warren, inscription on his tombstone

For Further Reading

There has been a great deal of recent scholarly interest in the Warren Court, its decisions and its justices. The best single volume, placing the Court in the context of its times, is Lucas A. Powe, Jr. *The Warren Court and American Politics* (2000). Bernard Schwartz, ed., *The Warren Court: A Retrospective* (1996), and Mark V. Tushnet, ed., *The Warren Court in Historical and Political Perspective* (1993) are both collections of papers delivered at conferences on the Court. A good short overview is Morton J. Horwitz, *The Warren Court and the Pursuit of Justice* (1998).

Frederick P. Lewis, *The Context of Judicial Activism* (1999) is the most recent work dealing with the Court's activism, this time from a sympathetic viewpoint. Raoul Berger, *Government by Judiciary: The Transformation of the Fourteenth Amendment* (1977) is a strong polemic claiming that the Court expanded civil liberties through a totally erroneous reading of the Fourteenth Amendment. Berger's "clause-bound literalism" is effectively attacked in John Hart Ely, *Democracy and Distrust: A Theory of Judicial Review* (1980). One of the most thoughtful critics of judicial activism was Alexander M. Bickel; see his *The Least Dangerous Branch* (1962), *Politics and the Warren Court* (1965), and *The Supreme Court and the Idea of Progress* (1970).

For issues concerning speech, a good place to begin is Alexander Meikeljohn's philosophic analysis of the types of speech and the need to protect certain types, such as "public" speech more than others, in *Free Speech and Its Relation to Self-Government* (1948). In this connection, see William J. Brennan, Jr., "The Supreme Court and the Meikeljohn Interpretation of the First Amendment," 79 *Harvard Law Review* 1 (1965); and Lillian BeVier, "The First Amendment and Political Speech: An Inquiry into the Substance and Limits of Principle," 30 *Stanford Law Review* 299 (1978). Harry Kalven, Jr., *A Worthy Tradition: Freedom of Speech in America* (1988), sums up a lifetime of scholarly exploration of free expression and is particularly sympathetic to the Warren Court decisions. An excellent case study is Anthony Lewis, *Make No Law: The Sullivan Case and the First Amendment* (1991); see also, the broader context presented in Lucas A. Powe, Jr., *The Fourth Estate and the Constitution* (1991).

For the special problems of obscenity, see David Lowenthal, *No Liberty for License: The Forgotten Logic of the First Amendment* (1997), Part II. See also Harry M. Clor, *Obscenity and Public Morality: Censorship in a Liberal Society* (1969); Richard S. Randall, *Censorship of the Movies* (1968); Charles Rembar, *The End of Obscenity: The Trials of Lady Chatterly, Tropic of Cancer, and Fanny Hill* (1968); and C. Peter Magrath, "The Obscenity Cases: Grapes of Roth," 1966 *Supreme Court Review* 7 (1967). See also, David Richards, "Free Speech and Obscenity Law: Toward a Moral Theory of the First Amendment," 123 *Universitry of Pennsylvania Law Review* 45 (1974), which emphasizes the importance of private liberty in a free society; and Harry Kalven, Jr., "The Metaphysics of the Law of Obscenity," 1960 *Supreme Court Review* 1 (1961), which also questions the intrusion of the state in such an unmanageable area.

The cases and problems arising from the two religion clauses are examined in John T. Noonan, Jr., *The Lustre of Our Country* (1998); Richard E. Morgan, *The Supreme Court and Religion* (1972); Frank J. Sorauf, *The Wall of Separation: The Constitutional Politics of Church and State* (1976); and Philip Kurland, ed., *Church and State* (1975). See also John H. Laubach, *School Prayers: Congress, the Court, and the Public* (1969); Kenneth M. Dolbeace and Phillip E. Hammond, *The School Prayer Decision: From Court Policy to Local Practice* (1970); and Candida Lund, "Religion and Commerce—The Sunday Closing Cases," in C. Herman Pritchett and Alan F. Westin, eds., *The Third Branch of Government* (1963).

For the Warren Court and reform of criminal procedure in general, see Fred Graham, *The Due Process Revolution: The Warren Court's Impact on Criminal Law* (1970); and A. E. Dick Howard, ed., *Criminal Justice in Our Time* (1965). See also, Claude R. Sowle, *Police Power and Individual Freedom: The Quest for Balance* (1962); Arnold N. Enken and Sheldon H. Elsen, "Counsel for the Suspect: Massiah v. United States and Escobedo v. Illinois," 49 *Minnesota Law*

Review 47 (1964); and Yale Kamisar, "A Dissent from the Miranda Dissents," 65 *Michigan Law Review* 59 (1966). Liva Baker, *Miranda, Crime, Law and Order* (1983), examines both the case and its context. A study indicating that the *Miranda* decision did not affect conviction rates is Seeburger and Wettick, "Miranda in Pittsburgh—A Statistical Study," 29 *University of Pittsburgh Law Review* 1 (1967). For the right of counsel, see the classic study by Anthony Lewis, *Gideon's Trumpet* (1964).

For privacy, see the seminal work by Louis D. Brandeis and Samuel D. Warren, "The Right to Privacy," 4 *Harvard Law Review* 193 (1890). A survey of the situation toward the end of the Warren era is Alan F. Westin, *Privacy and Freedom* (1967). See also, Robert G. Dixon, "The Griswold Penumbra: Constitutional Charter for an Expanded Law of Privacy?" 64 *Michigan Law Review* 197 (1965), and Note, "The Uncertain Renaissance of the Ninth Amendment." 33 *University of Chcago Law Review* 814 (1966); as well as David J. Garrow, *Liberty and Sexuality* (1994).

38

A Nation in Turmoil

Internal Security • The Decline of HUAC • Reapportionment • Opposition to the Apportionment Rulings • The Great Society • Johnson and Presidential Prerogatives • Vietnam and the Tonkin Gulf Resolution • War Issues and the Court • Impatience over Civil Rights • Criminal Law • The Commission on Law Enforcement • The Omnibus Crime Control Act • The Fortas Affair • Warren's Final Term • Conclusion • For Further Reading

IN THE PREVIOUS two chapters, we have seen the constitutional revolution wrought by the Warren Court in civil rights and liberties. By themselves, the cases in these areas ensured that the 1950s and 1960s would be remembered as a period of upheaval. But other issues contributed to the national turmoil. The war in Vietnam, for example, raised a number of constitutional questions, and far more than usual the justices found themselves enmeshed in political matters. The Court remained activist, however, and by the time a weary Earl Warren retired from the bench in 1969, he had seen the nation's highest court through its most tumultuous years since the Civil War era.

Internal Security

The Kennedy administration harbored no illusions about the menace of communism, but it did not see conspiracies and spies behind every tree. The new attorney general, Robert Kennedy, possibly because of his earlier role as an assistant to Senator Joseph McCarthy wanted to bury the last vestiges of the 1950s Red Scare. The Kennedys made clear that they did not view the American Communist party as a political danger to the country, and they sought to abolish unnecessary loyalty tests and to end the rash of unsupported "security risk" charges against government employees. Robert Kennedy, who had recently returned from an extensive trip overseas in 1962, also wanted to correct the impression he had found among many foreigners who believed that the United States imposed police-state regulations because of its obsession with security.

Liberals on the Court, who had grown increasingly uncomfortable with the 1950 McCarran Act, welcomed this change in attitude. Although the Court upheld the registration provisions of the statute in January 1961, and aspects of the government's security program a few weeks later, all the decisions elicited strong dissents from the chief justice, Black, Douglas, and Brennan. Black especially protested "the dangerous venture of outlawing groups that preach doctrines nearly all Americans detest," a policy he condemned as a gross violation of the First Amendment (*Communist Party v. SACB* [1961]).

The following year, Kennedy made two appointments to the bench, Byron R. White, to replace the ailing Whittaker in April, and Arthur J. Goldberg, who took Frankfurter's seat in the fall. The liberals now had a majority, and they managed to find a fatal constitutional flaw in nearly all the internal security measures that subsequently came up for review. In February 1963, with Justice Goldberg delivering the opinion, the Court struck down sections of both the 1940 and 1952 Nationality Acts in *Kennedy v. Mendoza-Martinez*. The sections had stripped Americans of citizenship without judicial trial if they stayed out of the country in time of war to evade military service. A year later, with Goldberg again speaking for the Court, Section 6 of the McCarran Act fell. American Communists could travel abroad for "wholly innocent purposes" without fear of losing their passports. To deny this right, Goldberg said in *Aptheker v. Secretary of State*, violated the Fifth Amendment. When the Subversive Activities Control Board (SACB), which had been created by the McCarran Act, tried to force so-called Communist front organizations to register, on the basis of dubious testimony about their activities, the Court overruled it in *American Committee for Protection of the Foreign Born v. SACB* and *Veterans of the Abraham Lincoln Brigade v. SACB* (both in 1965). The Court termed the evidence, much of it dating back more than ten years to unnamed sources, as "stale" and therefore inadmissible.

As the decade wore on, the Court's concern with civil liberties also informed its decisions on state and federal security programs. Justice Black, for example, took special satisfaction in *Lamont v. Basic Pamphlets* (1965) when, for the first time, the Court relied on the First Amendment to void an act of Congress. The Court ruled unconstitutional a rider to the 1962 Federal Employees Salary Act requiring persons to whom "Communist political propaganda" had been addressed to file a written request to have the material delivered.

After initial deference to congressional investigating agencies, the Court took a much stricter view of their methods. As late as 1961, with Frankfurter and Whittaker still on the bench, the Court had sustained the House Un-American Activities Committee's contempt citations for witnesses who refused to answer questions concerning their membership in the Communist party. But Justice Stewart, who often gave the Frankfurter bloc its fifth vote, changed his position, and in *Deutsch v. United States* later in the year, he cast his ballot to void a conviction when the committee had sought information totally irrelevant to the investigation. Bernhard Deutsch had agreed to answer any questions about his activities, but not about what others might have done.

Stewart wrote the majority opinion soon afterward, voiding for vagueness a Florida law requiring public employees to swear that they had never lent "aid, support, advice, counsel or influence to the Communist Party" or face possible dismissal from their jobs. Stewart questioned the wisdom of anti-Communist statutes "so vague that men of common intelligence must necessarily guess at its meaning and differ as to its application" (*Cramp v. Board of Public Instruction* [1961]). The decision encouraged public employees in other states to attack what they considered demeaning loyalty requirements on similar vagueness grounds, and the Court struck down security statutes from Washington, Arizona, New York, and Maryland.

The Decline of HUAC

The Warren Court also reined in the activities of the House Un-American Activities Committee (HUAC) and its state counterparts by requiring greater adherence to procedural fairness, analogous to its new interpretation of what the Bill of Rights required in criminal trials. The Court never questioned the right of Congress through its committees to investigate whatever it pleased, so long as it spelled out precisely the nature and scope of the investigation. In *Watkins v. United States* (1957), the Court overturned a contempt conviction of a committee witness who had refused, on the basis of the First Amendment, to answer questions about Communist party associates. The Court ruled that the House resolution creating the committee and HUAC's own definition of its investigation failed to meet constitutional requirements for specificity. The contempt citation, as a result, suffered from the "vice of vagueness," and violated due process. In his somewhat rambling opinion, Chief Justice Warren warned Congress that its broad investigatory powers had limits. Its committees had no right to expose an individual's private affairs without legitimate justification, or to punish those who refused to cooperate in this invasion of privacy, without proving that the inquiry related to some specific and legitimate purpose.

The justices seemed to back away from the *Watkins* ruling in the next few years, as Frankfurter led a 5 to 4 majority in a series of cases deferring to congressional authority; the chief justice, Black, Douglas, and Brennan continued to criticize HUAC for its denial of First Amendment rights. When Frankfurter and Whittaker departed in 1962, the tide swung the other way. *Russell v. United States* (1962) dismissed the convictions of six persons who had refused to cooperate with HUAC and the Senate Internal Security subcommittee, in what the Court characterized as a fishing expedition. Again, the Court did not deny Congress's power to investigate, but demanded that it specify clearly the subject of an investigation and that its committees desist from harassing persons who refused to cooperate in unauthorized Red-baiting.

By the end of the 1960s, HUAC had lost nearly all the power that it had wielded a scant decade earlier. The Court's insistence on due process had contributed to the decline, as had the opinion of the Kennedy and Johnson administrations that the internal Communist menace had been greatly exaggerated. Liberals in the press, in the universities, and in Congress attacked the committee's Red-baiting, and although they could never get the full House to abolish it, they managed to have HUAC's appropriations cut sharply and its mandate narrowed considerably.

At the same time, the Court took steps to curtail state legislative committees imitating HUAC-type investigations. In *Sweezy v. New Hampshire* (1957), the Court applied the *Watson* rationale to reverse the conviction of a college professor who, on First Amendment grounds, had refused to answer questions about his activities. Chief Justice Warren condemned the legislative charge to the committee as being so vague that it might better be considered "an absence of authority." A few years later, the Court again upheld First Amendment rights in *Gibson v. Florida Legislative Investigating Committee* (1963), overturning the conviction of an NAACP official who had refused to provide membership lists. (The committee allegedly wanted to find out if Communists belonged to the civil rights organization.) In 1965, in *Dombrowski v. Pfister*, the Court struck down portions of two Louisiana antisubversive laws and thus allowed federal courts to enjoin the witch-hunting tactics of that state's un-American activities committee. The Red Scare of the 1950s had finally petered out.

Reapportionment

Outside the areas of civil rights and liberties, the Warren Court's greatest impact on American life came from its highly controversial rulings on legislative apportionment. The Constitution is clear that each state is to have two senators and that members of the House of Representatives are to be apportioned according to the state's share of the population as determined by a required decennial census. But there is no guidance as to how these representatives are to be assigned within each state. Madison had implied that the arrangement should be equitable, so that a man's vote would have approximately the same weight as his neighbor's in both state and federal elections.

Some states periodically redrew the lines of their congressional districts, as well as their state assembly districts, to ensure at least a rough equity among voters. In fact, during the 1950s, three-fifths of all the states reapportioned one or both of their legislative chambers. But despite major population shifts, twelve states had not redrawn their districts for more than three decades; Tennessee and Alabama had not reapportioned their legislatures since 1901, and Delaware since 1897. Amazing discrepancies existed in a number of states: in Vermont, for example, the most populous assembly district had 33,000 persons, the least populous 238, yet each had one representative. The distortions ran even higher in state senate districts that, like the federal model, often followed geographical lines. In California, the Los Angeles senatorial district included six million people; in a more sparsely populated rural section of the state, the senate district had only 14,000 persons. Distortions such as these grossly undervalued urban and suburban votes and overvalued the ballot in older rural districts. Naturally, the rural minorities who controlled state government had little incentive to reapportion, because to do so would mean giving up their power.

Unable to secure change from the legislatures themselves, reform groups turned to the courts, invoking the constitutional guarantee of a "Republican Form of Government" (Article IV, Section 4), but the Supreme Court initially refused to get involved. Challengers of an Illinois law prescribing unevenly apportioned congressional districts brought their suit to the high court in *Colgrove v. Green* (1946). Only seven justices heard the arguments; of these, justices Reed and Burton joined in Frankfurter's opinion for the Court. "The petitioners ask of this Court what is beyond its competence to grant," declared Frankfurter in holding the issue to be a political question and therefore nonjusticiable. "From the determination of such issues the Court has traditionally remained aloof." Frankfurter relied on *Luther v. Borden* (1849), the case that arose from Dorr's Rebellion, to hold that the Constitution conferred on Congress "exclusive authority to secure fair representation. . . . Courts ought not to enter this political thicket." Justice Black, joined by Douglas and Murphy, dissented; they thought the complaint presented a justiciable controversy. Justice Rutledge agreed with the dissenters on the justiciability issue, but he concurred in the result, since he shared Frankfurter's view that the courts should not get involved. "The right is not absolute," he wrote, "and the cure may be worse than the disease." Four years later, the Court again refused to enter the "political thicket" and affirmed a lower court's dismissal of a challenge to the Georgia system of apportioning assembly seats by counties.

The first hint of a change came in *Gomillion v. Lightfoot* (1960), when the Court, through Justice Frankfurter, struck down a blatant gerrymandering scheme in Alabama designed to disenfranchise black voters. Frankfurter relied on the Fifteenth Amendment and carefully avoided any mention of expanding the Court's ruling to other situations, but reformers thought they now had an opening through which to resume their battle for reapportionment. In March 1962, the Court accepted a suit brought by urban voters in Tennessee, where there had been no redistricting since 1901, even though the state constitution required reapportionment every ten years.

Baker v. Carr, decided later that year, took the Court away from its traditional policy of avoiding questions of legislative representation. Justice Brennan, for a 6 to 2 majority, ruled only that such issues were justiciable and that citizens who believed their vote had been diluted had standing to bring suit in federal district court. But he did not prescribe any particular remedy. "We have no cause at this stage to doubt the District Court will be able to fashion relief if violations of constitutional rights are found," and the high court would wait to see what happened. The Court thus assigned the power and responsibility to afford relief from malapportionment to the lower courts, much as they had already been mandated to remedy voting discrimination based on race.

Brennan could not simply ignore the political question doctrine, so he drew a careful distinction between recognized political questions and apportionment. In all other cases, either the Constitution explicitly or implicitly assigned the issue to another branch of government, or the Court had refused jurisdiction because the question lacked "judicially discoverable and manageable standards for resolving it." In *Colgrove*, Brennan correctly noted, a majority of the Court had believed the issue justiciable, and in *Gomillion*, it had specifically asserted judicial power and ability to resolve such problems.

Predictably, the Court's two leading advocates of restraint, Frankfurter and Harlan, entered bitter protests. Justice Frankfurter accused the majority of risking the Court's prestige in an area that assuredly should be left to the political process. "In a democratic society like ours," he argued, "relief must come through an aroused popular conscience that sears the conscience of the people's representative." Justice Harlan thought the system might be better, but he found nothing in the Constitution to prevent a state "acting not irrationally, from choosing any electoral structure it thinks best suited to the interests, tempers and customs of the people." Both men ignored the heart of the complaint—that a majority of the people could not adopt the system "best suited" to their needs because of an entrenched minority.

Baker v. Carr led many legislatures to redistrict voluntarily; elsewhere, reformers launched dozens of suits in state and federal courts to force reapportionment. One-half of the states reapportioned at least one house, but there was confusion over what the Court considered proper standards. Did the districts have to be mathematically equal in population, or would the Court permit some variance? Could one house of a bicameral legislature be apportioned on other grounds, such as geography? Could a state recognize certain historic divisions as a factor in drawing lines? If a plan had some questionable features, yet a majority of the electorate approved it in a referendum, would this meet judicial approval? Obviously the high court would have to hear more cases, and it would also have to determine what Justice Brennan had implied existed on this issue, "judicially discoverable and manageable standards."

In fact, the criterion adopted by the Court proved remarkably clear and relatively easy to apply—one person, one vote. In March 1963, with Attorney General Robert F. Kennedy arguing the case for the federal government as *amicus*, the Court heard a challenge to the Georgia county unit system, the same system it had refused to look at more than a dozen years earlier. The system assigned each county a number of units, and successful candidates for state offices had to poll a majority of units in statewide primaries. Population was only one factor in the distribution of units, which gave rural counties more units than the heavily populated urban areas. The district court had ruled the system, as it stood, unconstitutional in 1962; it ordered a redistribution of units so that the disparities would be no greater than those existing between states in the electoral college system. Justice Douglas, speaking for all the brethren save Harlan, ruled that the entire county unit system violated the Fourteenth Amendment's Equal Protection Clause; he also overturned the district court's proposed solution.

Gray v. Sanders technically dealt with voting rights rather than with apportionment, but Douglas—despite Harlan's assertion that a "one man, one vote rule flies in the face of history"—had happily hit on a formula that not only provided judicial guidance, but caught the popular imagination as well. All other formulations of the issue appeared to pit one group against another—rural versus urban, old settlers against newcomers—but "one person, one vote" (or, in the coinage of the time, "one man, one vote") had a democratic ring to it. Who could object to assuring every person that his or her vote counted equally with those of others? To support this formula meant upholding democracy and the Constitution; to oppose it seemed mean and petty.

In June 1964, the Court handed down decisions in six cases, involving apportionment schemes in Alabama, Colorado, New York, Maryland, Virginia, and Delaware. Two of the decisions deserve special consideration. Chief Justice Warren delivered the Court's opinion in the lead case of *Reynolds v. Sims*, which invalidated an Alabama plan that involved a complex formula utilizing both population and a "federal" arrangement. The state claimed that since the Constitution permitted disparities between the states, each state should be allowed similar deviations within its borders. Warren dismissed the federal analogy as inapposite and irrelevant and declared one man, one vote would now be the rule for all state legislative bodies, including upper houses.

Warren dismissed any and all formulas that attempted to weight certain factors:

> To the extent that a citizen's right to vote is debased, he is that much less a citizen. The weight of a citizen's vote cannot be made to depend on where he lives. . . . A citizen, a qualified voter, is no more nor no less so because he lives in the city or on the farm. This is the clear and strong command of our Constitution's Equal Protection Clause.

> Neither history alone, nor economic or other sorts of group interests, are permissible factors in attempting to justify disparities from population-based representation. . . . Citizens, not history or economic interests, cast votes. People, not land or trees or pastures vote. As long as ours is a representative form of government, and our legislators are those instruments of government elected directly by and directly representative of the people, the right to elect legislators in a free and unimpaired fashion is a bedrock of our political system.
>
> —Chief Justice Earl Warren, *Reynolds v. Sims* (1964)

The Colorado case, *Lucas v. Forty-Fourth General Assembly of Colorado*, presented a unique problem. The electorate, by a 2 to 1 vote, had approved a plan that had a fairly clear population ratio for the lower house, but greater variance for the senate, so as to give rural areas some weighted power, although far from a controlling voice. The state made much of the fact that a majority of the voters had agreed to the dilution of their voting power in order to protect the minority. The chief justice dismissed the argument out of hand; the Court dealt here not with the rights of minorities but with the rights of individuals. "It is a precept of American constitutional law," he declared, "that certain rights exist which a citizen cannot trade, barter, or even give away. . . . A citizen's constitutional right can hardly be infringed simply because a majority of the people choose that it be."

Justice Harlan dissented in all six cases. The chief justice's opinion, he charged, rested on bad history and bad law and undermined the essence of a federal system. In a pluralistic society, Harlan would have allowed apportionment formulas to take into account a number of considerations, including history, economics, geography, adequacy of representation for sparsely settled areas, theories of bicameralism, urban-rural balance, and the preference of a majority of voters for a particular scheme.

On Justice Douglas's urging, the Court had decided the six cases at the end of the term, rather than holding them over until the fall, so that reapportionment could take place before that year's elections. Despite the sweep of the rulings, the Court indicated that it expected rapid compliance. It eschewed anything resembling an "all deliberate speed" formula, and urged that unless the district courts could be convinced by un-

> These [apportionment] decisions give support to a current mistaken view of the Constitution and the constitutional function of this Court. This view, in a nutshell, is that every major social ill in this country can find its cure in some constitutional "principle," and that this Court should "take the lead" in promoting reform when other branches of government fail to act. . . . The Constitution is not a panacea for every blot upon the public welfare, nor should this Court, ordained as a judicial body, be thought of as a general haven for reform movements.
>
> —Justice John Marshall Harlan, dissenting in *Reynolds v. Sims* (1964)

usually strong reasons to the contrary, they should allow no more state elections to be held under invalidated plans.

Opposition to the Apportionment Rulings

Not everyone eagerly embraced the "one person, one vote" doctrine. Rural legislators proved less than enthusiastic about giving up their power, and in Congress, representatives from these areas tried to remove apportionment questions from federal court jurisdiction. Senate minority leader Everett Dirksen of Illinois went so far as to introduce a constitutional amendment to override the Court's decisions and allow a state to employ criteria other than population in determining the makeup of one house. After the Dirksen proposal failed to win Senate approval on two successive votes, conservatives initiated a drive to call a constitutional convention by petition of two-thirds of the states. By mid-1967, thirty-two states had petitioned for a gathering to deal with the apportionment issue, only two shy of the required number. But the drive then stalled as new legislatures, elected under court-ordered redistricting plans, took control of the state houses. In addition, legal scholars pointed out that the wording of the petitions varied from state to state, so one could not be sure just what the states had asked. Senator Paul Douglas of Illinois, who led the opposition to the Dirksen amendment, announced that in his opinion, Congress would still have discretion as to whether it should convene a convention even if the necessary number of states approved the petition. Because the convention route had never been followed, no one had any idea how the body might be structured. Would the states have the same representation that they had in the electoral college, or would the one person, one vote rule apply?

Before long, the Court's opponents found themselves on the defensive. Influential groups such as the League of Women Voters endorsed *Reynolds v. Sims* and conducted educational campaigns explaining the ruling. Once implemented, of course, reapportionment faced little opposition, as formerly dominant minorities could no longer block the will of the majority. No state, once reapportioned, sought to return to the old system. The only further questions that the Court had to answer involved how precisely the formula had to be applied. In *Swann v. Adams* (1967), the Court invalidated a Florida plan that had relatively minor deviations. Justice White conceded that the Court did not require absolute precision, but he noted that the statute failed to provide an adequate explanation for certain significant deviations. The Court recognized the impossibility of perfect compliance, but it would impose strict scrutiny on any plan that failed to approximate that standard. The following year, in *Avery v. Midland County*, city and county governments came under the one person, one vote rule as well.

The apportionment decisions fitted in with the Warren Court's general determination to expand and protect individual rights and to promote equality before the law. Fairness in voting seemed of a piece with fairness in criminal procedures and in the treatment of Americans of different races or religion.

The civil rights cases, the expansion of rights for the accused, and the reapportionment decisions made the Warren Court a target of conservative resentment. The Wyoming legislature adopted a resolution in 1963 calling for the abolition of the Supreme Court and its replacement by a "Court of the Union" consisting of the fifty state chief justices. Billboards popped up all over the country bearing the motto "Impeach Earl Warren," a sentiment also found on placards at the Republican convention in San Francisco in 1964. Senator Barry Goldwater of Arizona, the conservatives' hero and the Republican standard-bearer that year, called for a return to basic American values and blamed the Court for much of the nation's confusion. In his view, the Court, instead of serving as a balance wheel against excess, had become an agent for unthinking change. The landslide victory of Lyndon B. Johnson that fall repudiated the Goldwater program, at least temporarily, but it could hardly be viewed as an endorsement of the Warren Court's activism. For the next few years, however, Johnson's domestic program and the war in Vietnam diverted attention from the judiciary.

The Great Society

Between early January and mid-April 1965, the president sent ninety-seven messages and seventy-eight bills to Capitol Hill, and the Eighty-ninth Congress wiped clean the slate of unfinished New Deal and Fair Deal business. The list of Great Society measures is staggering: the Appalachian Regional Development Act launched a major assault on poverty in that area; the Housing and Urban Development Act authorized federal support for 240,000 units of low-rent public housing; health care legislation established Medicare for the elderly, mental health facilities, and aid for handicapped and retarded citizens; an overhaul of the immigration laws led to the abolition of national origins quotas; federal aid was provided for elementary and secondary education; voting rights were extended; and much more.

A few of these laws, those involving voting rights and education, led, as we have seen, to litigation in the courts; in every instance, the Supreme Court upheld the power of the government. Lyndon Johnson saw himself as the successor to Franklin D. Roosevelt and the Great Society as the culmination of the New Deal. It is one mark of how much constitutional thought had changed that no one on the Warren Court questioned the government's power to engage in all these activities.

Lyndon Johnson had a chance to go down in history as one of the great presidents of the twentieth century. Inheriting the office in the wake of a presidential assassination, he had moved effectively to assure the continuity of government and to calm a troubled people. A Southerner, he was a great champion of civil rights; he not only secured important legislation, but his administration enforced those laws and worked assiduously to bring African Americans into full equality in American society. In 1967, he named Thurgood Marshall, the NAACP's chief architect of *Brown*, as the first black person to sit on the Supreme Court. Great Society legislation marked a major step in

> From your committees and both your houses have come the greatest outpouring of creative legislation in the history of this nation.
>
> —Lyndon Johnson to the Eighty-ninth Congress (1965)

fighting poverty, improving the nation's cities, upgrading education, and in general making the United States a better place for all its citizens. Nevertheless, Johnson's programs and his reputation would ultimately founder on America's involvement in the Vietnam quagmire.

Johnson and Presidential Prerogatives

As was the case with his domestic programs, Johnson's foreign policy reflected his experiences in the 1930s and 1940s. He remembered vividly how his idol, Franklin Roosevelt, had been hamstrung by Congress and unable to respond to Fascist aggression until 1941. Johnson also remembered conservative charges that Roosevelt had "sold out" at Yalta, and that Truman had "lost" China to the Communists. Johnson wanted to be remembered for a strong and successful foreign policy as well as for the Great Society, and he understood how in the last quarter-century, Congress had increasingly deferred to the executive in foreign affairs. As a leader in the Senate, Johnson had contributed to that policy. He had backed Truman's decision to send troops to Korea in 1950; while he later came to believe that Truman should have asked for a congressional resolution, Johnson saw this as a political and not a constitutional error. He had backed Eisenhower's overseas policies, claiming that he had no desire to take responsibility and authority from "the constitutional leader."

Now that he was the constitutional leader, Johnson made no secret of his belief that the president had practically sole power over all aspects of foreign policy. "There are many, many, who can recommend, advise and sometimes a few of them consent. But there is only one that has been chosen by the American people to decide." This marked a complete turnaround from Madison's *Helvidius* attack on "the extraordinary doctrine that the powers of making war, and treaties, are in their nature executive. . . . It would never do for a democracy; it smacked of monarchy," and even from the view of the strongest of nineteenth-century presidents, Abraham Lincoln, who, commenting on Polk and the Mexican War, claimed that "*no one man* should hold the power of bringing the nation into war."

The country got its first glimpse of the Johnson style in foreign policy in the spring of 1965, when he sent 22,000 American troops to the Dominican Republic, without asking for congressional authorization. The president claimed that he had acted to save American lives threatened by the civil war there, and as this had been a traditional prerogative of the commander-in-chief, he did not need legislative approval. But if Johnson had wanted only to protect American lives, he could have sent in far fewer marines, just as Ronald Reagan could have done twenty years later in Grenada. Johnson soon conceded his real motive: "We don't propose to sit here in our rocking chair with our hands folded and let the Communists set up any government in the Western Hemisphere." To use American troops for political purposes, however, raised just those types of questions that the Founding Fathers had clearly intended for congressional deliberation and participation. Although critics from both parties denounced the Dominican intervention, Johnson ignored them; at the same time, he began the Americanization of the war in Vietnam.

Vietnam and the Tonkin Gulf Resolution

The United States had been concerned with events in Indochina since 1945, especially after French forces pulled out following their defeat in 1954 at Dienbienphu. Communist North Vietnam supported the Vietcong guerrilla campaign against the pro-Western government in South Vietnam, and to aid that government, President Kennedy had sent the first American "advisers" to train South Vietnamese (ARVN) troops. By the fall of 1963, the number of American advisers had reached 16,000; since some went regularly into battle with ARVN forces, there had been American casualties. But a few months before his death, Kennedy had made clear that he viewed Vietnam as "their" war; the Vietnamese "are the ones who have to win it or lose it." Unfortunately, Lyndon Johnson felt compelled to make major decisions on future policy in Southeast Asia before he had a chance to settle in to his new responsibilities. Pentagon officials convinced him that with sufficient American aid, the ARVN could defeat the Vietcong, and Johnson declared that "I am not going to be the President who saw South Vietnam go the way China went."

Johnson's resolve not to "lose" Vietnam stiffened under attacks from Barry Goldwater, who during the 1964 campaign continuously assailed the administration's "no win" policy. Johnson denounced the Republican candidate for wanting to enlarge the conflict, but at the same time he promised not to abandon Vietnam and leave it for a Communist takeover. Then in August 1964, North Vietnamese gunboats reportedly fired on American destroyers in the Gulf of Tonkin. Johnson called in congressional leaders and, reminding them of the earlier criticism of Truman for not seeking congressional approval of his Korea decision, asked their advice about getting some sense of Congress on American policy. The delegation thought that would be a fine idea, and Johnson pulled out of his pocket a resolution that had been drafted months before, authorizing the commander-in-chief to "take all necessary measures to repel any armed attack against the forces of the United States and to prevent further aggression."

The Gulf of Tonkin Resolution passed the House of Representatives unanimously. In the Senate, Daniel Brewster of Maryland and Gaylord Nelson of Wisconsin tried unsuccessfully to add some safeguards to what they saw as a blank check to the president. When the vote came, only Wayne Morse of Oregon and Ernest Gruening of Alaska voted no. In an election year, no one wanted to appear less than 100 percent supportive of a president seeking to protect American lives.

The resolution had important constitutional as well as political significance. Congress had, in fact, written the president a blank check; it had handed over one of its most important powers and one of the few designated roles it has in foreign affairs—the power to declare war. Yet neither the House nor the Senate seemed to worry about this abdication of responsibility, possibly because no one anticipated the extent to which the United States would become involved in the war. The document left somewhat unclear whether Congress had in fact delegated its own war power to the executive, or had merely confirmed the president's independent authority as commander-in-chief to respond as he saw proper to attacks on American lives or interests.

During the brief Senate debate, John Sherman Cooper of Kentucky asked whether "if the President decided that it was necessary to use such force as could lead into war,

> In adopting a resolution with such sweeping language, however, Congress committed the error of making a *personal* judgment as to how President Johnson would implement the resolution when it had a responsibility to make an *institutional* judgment, first, as to what *any* President would do with so great an acknowledgment of power, and, second, as to whether, under the Constitution, Congress had a right to grant or concede the authority in question.
>
> —Senate Report No. 129, 91st Congress, 1st Session (1969)

we will give that authority by this resolution?" The floor leader for the resolution, J. William Fulbright of Arkansas, answered "that is the way I would interpret it." But, he added, "I have no doubt that the President will consult with Congress in case a major change in present policy becomes necessary." The power to make war is vested in Congress and not in the president, declared Wayne Morse. "Congress has no constitutional authority to grant such authority to the President."

A few years later, after Lyndon Johnson had escalated American involvement to nearly a half-million ground troops and extensive bombing of North Vietnam, critics charged that the Gulf of Tonkin Resolution had never been intended as a declaration of war, but merely as an affirmation of the president's power to take limited retaliatory action to protect American forces. During the debate, Senator Fulbright had assured the Senate that "the last thing we would want to do" is authorize a large war on the Asian mainland. When Fulbright later led a 1968 investigation into the events in the Gulf of Tonkin, he found evidence that the incident might have been manufactured by the administration to provoke a military response and provide an excuse to expand American involvement. The Defense Department branded the charge as "monstrous," but refused to let the Foreign Affairs Committee see any information that might have shed light on what had happened. Fulbright complained that "every thing related to the Tonkin incident is secret except that which the Pentagon deems should be made public." By then, however, antiwar critics had accepted as a truism the charge that President Johnson had misled Congress and the nation, using what had been intended as a statement of limited support to escalate the war.

Yet Sam Ervin of North Carolina, respected by his fellow senators as a knowledgeable constitutionalist, described the Gulf of Tonkin Resolution in 1970 as "clearly a declaration of war." In addition to granting the president broad authority, the document specifically announced that "the United States is prepared, as the President determines, to take all necessary steps, including the use of armed force, to assist any member or protocol state of the Southeast Asia Collective Defense Treaty requesting assistance in defense of its freedom." One has to assume either enormous stupidity or naivete on the part of over 500 congressmen and senators to believe they did not know what they had approved. While the wording of the resolution may have been ambiguous as to how much authority Congress had delegated, no one could have interpreted it as anything less than a war declaration, even if Congress had meant only a limited war. Moreover, in subsequent years, Congress voted billions of dollars for the war, a declaration every bit as effective as one having the magic words missing from the Gulf of Tonkin document—"We hereby declare that a state of war exists."

The president could easily have secured a more precise and much stronger authorization from Congress for a limited war, and probably could have secured a formal declaration. But Johnson preferred not to call the Vietnamese venture a "war," and he felt no need for a formal statement. Although he used to flaunt the Gulf of Tonkin Resolution before congressional critics, he never really believed that it provided legitimacy for his policies. As the "imperial president rampant," Johnson interpreted the Constitution as giving the *executive* the power to make war, while Article I, Section 8 allowed Congress to support presidential decisions, not to initiate or even sanction a war. For all his "consulting" with Congress, the president rarely asked for advice from the Hill; instead, he informed congressional leaders what he intended to do or had already done. "Such acts of courtesy are always to be welcomed," a Senate Foreign Relations Committee report noted; "the Constitution, however, envisages something more."

The State Department, unlike the White House or the Pentagon, cared a great deal about presenting a legitimation of American involvement. Under-secretary Nicholas Katzenbach, a former attorney general, described the Gulf of Tonkin Resolution, along with the SEATO (Southeast Asia Treaty Organization) treaty, as the "functional equivalent" of a war declaration. Congress had approved both, and therefore the president had given Congress "a full and effective voice." Moreover, Katzenbach argued in 1967, the president had the constitutional authority with or without the resolution or treaty. The reasoning behind this bold assertion of presidential power was set out in a memorandum from the State Department's legal adviser, Leonard C. Meeker, which claimed for the president a "constitutional power" to repel any attacks. While the Framers had meant direct attacks on American territory, in the modern world the United States had global interests, and an attack on any of them could threaten the nation's security. According to Meeker, the Constitution left it wholly to the president to determine when and if such an attack had taken place, what the proper response should be, and whether or not to consult with Congress.

War Issues and the Court

During the 1964 debate, Wayne Morse had suggested that if the Gulf of Tonkin Resolution ever came before the Supreme Court, the justices would declare it unconstitutional. Morse, however, doubted that the high court would ever review the resolution, and as a former law teacher, he knew modern precedents went against him. Ever since the 1930s, the Court had validated broad delegations of authority from Congress to the president and had held that the president had inherent powers to act in foreign affairs without congressional approval. The central constitutional issues of the Vietnam War—the absence of a formal declaration of war and the extent of presidential power—never came directly before the bench, since the justices denied certiorari whenever they could. But a number of peripheral issues could not be ignored, and the fact that the Court recognized the intensity of the public debate could be seen in several dissents.

Mention has already been made of the Court's unanimous opinion in *Bond v. Floyd* (1966) that the Georgia legislature could not deprive a duly elected member of his seat because of antiwar statements. Legislators, declared Chief Justice Warren, must "be given the widest latitude to express their views on issues of policy." The majority proved far from consistent in other dissent cases, however. In *Turner v. New York* (1967), they refused to take the appeal of seventeen antiwar demonstrators, who had been arrested and convicted of disorderly conduct at a rally, on the grounds that the case lacked sufficient merit. Justices Fortas and Douglas dissented, claiming that the case raised important First Amendment issues. Douglas also noted the presence of other significant questions "and I would resolve them."

The Court, however, refused to get sucked into the debate on American foreign policy. In several cases involving resistance to the draft on grounds of the war's unconstitutionality, the Court denied certiorari, always with a dissent from Douglas and often from one or two other members of the Court. In *Mora v. McNamara* (1967), Justice Stewart dissented from the denial of certiorari and stated what he and Douglas considered important constitutional issues raised by the case that the Court ought to adjudicate:

> I. Is the present United States military activity in Vietnam a "war" within the meaning of the Constitution?
> II. If so, may the Executive constitutionally order the petitioners to participate in that military activity, when no war has been declared by the Congress?
> III. Of what relevance to Question II are the present treaty obligations of the United States?
> IV. Of what relevance to Question II is the Joint Congressional Resolution of August 10, 1964?

These are "large and deeply troubling questions," Stewart declared. "We cannot make these problems go away simply by refusing to hear the case of three obscure Army privates. I intimate not even tentative views upon any of these matters, but I think the Court should squarely face them by granting certiorari."

That same term, the Court refused to take *Mitchell v. United States*, in which the protesters had invoked the so-called Nuremberg defense to justify their resistance to the Vietnam War. The claim of Nazi war criminals that they had no personal responsibility for the Holocaust, but had merely been following orders, had led to clauses in the 1945 London agreement that "wars of aggression" imposed a responsibility on individuals to resist. In his dissent, Justice Douglas noted the considerable body of opinion that viewed American policy in Vietnam as constituting a war of aggression, which raised several important questions that the Court ought to answer: Did Vietnam qualify as a war under the Treaty of London? Did that treaty constitute the supreme law of the land? Did it make the nature of the war a justiciable issue? Did the defendants have standing to invoke the treaty provisions? Although these were sensitive and delicate matters, Douglas contended, the Court should deal with them.

When the Court did accept a case, it shied away from the larger issues to concentrate on narrow questions. In *United States v. O'Brien* (1968), it upheld a 1965 law prohibiting the destruction of draft cards on the grounds that the government had a sufficient interest to warrant this suppression of symbolic speech. In *O'Brien* and another card-burning case later that term, *Holmes v. United States*, Douglas again dissented and urged his brethren to stop avoiding important issues that the public had a right to have decided. "The question whether there can be conscription when there has not been a declaration of war has never been decided by this Court," he said. "I think we owe to those who are being marched off to jail . . . an answer to this important undecided constitutional question." But the Court continued to avoid the matter, deciding a few draft resistance cases on statutory or due process grounds, but never referring to the issues that Stewart and Douglas raised.

Impatience over Civil Rights

The violent opposition in the South in 1964 and 1965 presented not only a crisis of conscience for the nation, but also raised issues of federal-state relations. Traditionally, the maintenance of order had been a state and local police function, but Southern officials seemed disinclined to exercise that role in protecting civil rights advocates. In the summer of 1964, three college students, James Chaney, Andrew Goodman, and Michael Schwerner had been brutally murdered, and evidence suggested collusion in the crime by local authorities. When federal investigators sought prosecutions in the case, Mississippi courts refused to return indictments. The following year, a similar incident occurred in Alabama, when a federal official witnessed the shooting of Viola Liuzzo as she drove home from the Selma march: Alabama courts refused to convict the assailant of murder. The Selma march led to still another dispatch of federal troops, after Governor George Wallace had promised that he would protect the demonstrators and then announced he could not.

Federal law and court precedent allowed the federal government to protect individuals from "state action" that infringed on their civil rights, but it could not pursue a similar policy against individuals. In two important 1966 cases, the Court extended the umbrella of federal protection against private individuals. *United States v. Price* arose out of the Mississippi murders; after the state had refused to act, the federal government had sought indictments against the Nashoba County sheriff, deputy sheriff, a policeman, and fifteen individuals under 18 U.S.C. sections 241 and 242, which derived from the 1866 and 1870 Civil Rights Acts. The district court had dismissed most of the charges on the grounds that the Fourteenth Amendment did not reach individuals, but the Supreme Court, speaking through Justice Fortas, reversed all the dismissals. He declared that the case involved only issues of statutory construction, and not of constitutional power. The involvement of any public official brought the activity within the under color of law definition of section 242. Fortas noted that the state officials had not stood by passively, but "the brutal joint adventure was made possible by an officer of the State. . . . It was a joint activity, from start to finish." In *United States v. Guest*, decided the same day, the Court reversed an earlier interpretation of section 241; through Justice Stewart, it upheld the power of the federal government to reach wholly private conspiracies.

The two decisions, however, revealed the Court's dissatisfaction with the inability of the federal government to protect the lives and rights of its citizens. Six justices entered concurring or partially dissenting opinions complaining about the limited reach of sections 241 and 242 and indicating to Congress that stronger legislation protecting basic rights would be appropriate under the Fourteenth Amendment. Although President Johnson announced the next day that the Justice Department would draft such a law, Congress did not act until after the assassination of Martin Luther King, Jr., in

> To do little to relieve the agony of Negro life is as inflammatory as inciting a riot. To put an Asian war of dubious national interest far above domestic needs in the order of priorities and to pit it against reforms that were delayed a century is worse than a blind policy; it is a provocative policy.
>
> —Martin Luther King, Jr. (1966)

April 1968. The day after King's funeral, the House of Representatives passed and sent to the White House the Civil Rights Act of 1968. The measure banned racial discrimination in the sale or rental of most housing in the country, provided criminal penalties for interference with the civil rights of individuals, protected civil rights workers as they sought to enroll voters and in other activities, and imposed heavy penalties for interstate travel and transportation of explosives for the purpose of civil disorder.

The Court in the meantime, impatient with the slow pace of Congress, the executive, and the states, exercised its own powers to strike at civil rights violations. In two 1967 cases, *Whitus v. Georgia* and *Coleman v. Alabama,* it ruled that a fair trial had been denied if blacks had been consistently excluded from grand and petit jury rolls. The Court interpreted another section of the Reconstruction laws to give Congress power under the Thirteenth Amendment to prohibit all racial discrimination, private as well as public, in the sale or rental of property (*Jones v. Alfred H. Mayer Co.* [1968]). In several school cases in 1968, the Court invalidated freedom of choice and free transfer plans that it believed had been used to thwart real desegregation. The Court threw out a freedom of choice plan in Virginia's New Kent County (*Green v. County School Board* [1968]) because it put the onus for achieving integration on black children. "The burden on a school board today," Justice Brennan announced, "is to come forward with a plan that promises realistically to work, and promises realistically to work *now*." In a footnote, the Court went much further than it had in previous school cases by suggesting possible solutions; instead of merely declaring what was impermissible, henceforth the Court would often indicate what would be acceptable.

The Warren Court left a significant legacy to the country in its civil rights decisions, yet discrimination proved far more pervasive in the nation's social and economic fabric than some optimists had thought. Although the Warren Court decisions struck down the most obvious forms of segregation, the Burger Court would have to confront the far more difficult question of how far the Equal Protection Clause reached into private and semiprivate areas and determine the limits of judicial activism in seeking equality.

Criminal Law

The Court appeared a bit more hesitant in deciding how far to push its new doctrines involving criminal procedure. After the controversy over the 1965 *Miranda* decision, the Court seemed to pull back, as if to reassure the nation that it had no intention of curbing legitimate police procedures. It ruled that the constitutional prohibition against

> A legal system is simply a mature and sophisticated attempt, never perfected, to institutionalize a sense of justice and to free men from the terror and unpredictability of arbitrary force.
>
> —Chief Justice Earl Warren, interview (1964)

double jeopardy did not apply to the states,[1] limited the reach of the Fourth Amendment,[2] and approved the use of undercover agents and their right to make narcotics arrests once they were invited into a dealer's home.[3] The Court also extended the right against self-incrimination to police officers accused of ticket fixing; the officers had been given the choice of testifying and thus incriminating themselves, or losing their jobs and pension rights. Such confessions, according to Justice Douglas, could not be used since they had been involuntarily given.[4] Prosecutors applauded the Court's decision in upholding the Texas habitual criminal statute; Justice Harlan ruled that informing a jury of a defendant's past record at the sentencing phase of the trial did not violate due process.[5] Later that year, the Court upheld warrantless arrests under certain circumstances.[6]

Critics of the judiciary remained unappeased, however, and claimed that the Court still coddled criminals, charges that gained in intensity as the Court swung back to concern for individual rights in the 1967 and 1968 terms. A majority threw out a conviction in which a first offender had confessed after nine days of intermittent but unrelenting interrogation without the benefit of counsel[7] and then reaffirmed an old doctrine that the state could not secure a conviction based on evidence it knew to be false.[8] In other cases that term, the Court required states to provide trial transcripts for indigent defendants seeking appeal,[9] insisted that confessions be truly voluntary,[10] reaffirmed the right to a speedy trial,[11] and denied that sex offenses comprised a special category of crime in which defendants could be denied their full constitutional rights.[12] In a highly controversial decision, *In re Gault*, the Court managed to offend both law-and-order groups and advocates of special youth courts by insisting that juvenile offenders be accorded full procedural rights.

Police groups attacked two other cases that elevated individual rights and restricted police procedures. In *Berger v. New York*, the Court invalidated a state eavesdropping law so broadly drawn as to allow an almost unlimited power to wiretap. Police could

---

1. *Clichos v. Indiana* (1966).
2. *Lewis v. United States* (1966).
3. *Hoffa v. United States* (1966); *Osborn v. United States* (1966).
4. *Garrity v. New Jersey* (1967).
5. *Spencer v. Texas* (1967).
6. *McCray v. Illinois* (1967); *Warden v. Hayden* (1967).
7. *Clewis v. Texas* (1967).
8. *Miller v. Pate* (1967).
9. *Enstminger v. Iowa* (1967); *Gardner v. California* (1969).
10. *Sims v. Georgia* (1967).
11. *Klopfer v. North Carolina* (1967).
12. *Specht v. Patterson* (1967).

secure a warrant without any proof that a crime had been or would be committed, could keep the tap in place as long as they pleased, and could use the information they gleaned any way they wanted. That same day, in *United States v. Wade*, the Court ruled that although participation in a police line-up did not constitute self-incrimination, a defendant had the right to counsel at the time of the line-up.

The following term, with Thurgood Marshall replacing Tom Clark, the Court continued to expand its protection of accused persons. In his first opinion, Justice Marshall extended the *Gideon* ruling to require counsel at posttrial hearings in which revocation of probation could lead to further imprisonment.[13] The Court also delivered its broadest interpretation yet of the Fourth Amendment in reversing a conviction based on a wiretap. "The Fourth Amendment," Justice Stewart proclaimed, "protects people, not places." He explained that the ruling did not invalidate all wiretaps, but henceforth, police would have to secure a proper warrant just as they did in any other type of search.[14] Despite mounting criticism of the *Miranda* rule, the Court reaffirmed that decision and applied it to Internal Revenue Service investigations as well.[15]

The Commission on Law Enforcement

In response to the growing demands for law and order, President Johnson had appointed a Commission on Law Enforcement and Administration of Justice, which handed in its report, "The Challenge of Crime in a Free Society" early in 1967. According to statistics for 1965, the latest year available to the commission, police had apprehended 457,000 adults as suspects in index crimes (those crimes included in national reports). Formal charges had been brought against 177,000; of these, the courts had dismissed charges in 9,000 cases; 38,000 persons had gone to trial, resulting in 30,000 convictions and 8,000 acquittals. Statistically, therefore, only 8 percent of those arrested had been processed fully through the formal steps of prosecution. As to what happened to the other 92 percent, the commission noted that though there was inadequate information about the disposition of many cases, it seemed clear that in many instances, defendants had either pleaded guilty to or been convicted of a less serious crime than the one originally charged. In an overwhelming number of cases—130,000—the accused had simply pleaded guilty to the original charge. If nothing else, these figures emphasized that the traditional view of a litigatory criminal justice system had to be replaced by the more accurate portrait of an administrative system.

In such a system, the various rules handed down by the Court did not cripple police. As the report noted:

> Policemen cannot and do not arrest all the offenders they encounter. It is doubtful if they arrest most of them. A criminal code, in practice, is not a set of specific instructions to policemen but a more or less rough map of the territory in which policemen work. How an individual policeman moves around that territory depends largely on his personal discretion.

---

13. *Mempa v. Ray* (1967).
14. *Katz v. United States* (1967).
15. *Mathis v. United States* (1968).

The criminal procedure decisions of the Warren Court altered that rough map a little and required police to make some adjustments; but the rulings did not, nor had the Court intended them to, rob the police of that discretion. They did ask that the government take seriously the rights guaranteed in the Constitution.

The Omnibus Crime Control Act

By 1968, public opinion had swung sharply to the right on many domestic issues. The growing opposition to the Vietnam War among the young, with their new and strikingly different lifestyles, triggered a reaction among both blue-collar workers and affluent business and professional people. Conservatives blamed many of the nation's ills on the "permissiveness" that they claimed the Supreme Court had helped foster through its "softness" on criminals and pornography. In the election campaign that year, both major parties, as well as George Wallace's American party, emphasized law and order.

The Congress took this as a signal to transform Lyndon Johnson's call for a progressive reform of federal criminal law into a much harsher measure, part of which clearly aimed to rein in the judiciary. The Omnibus Crime Control and Safe Streets Act of 1968 marked a defeat for Johnson and congressional liberals, while Title II specifically overrode a number of Supreme Court decisions. Police could hold a suspect for six hours (more in certain situations) without arraignment; "voluntary" confessions would be admissible even if arresting officers had not followed *Miranda* guidelines strictly; and trial judges could determine the issue of voluntariness in a "totality of circumstances" context. The provisions on wire tapping allowed judges to authorize taps to cover a very broad range of activities and permitted police almost unrestricted use of any information secured in this manner.

Liberals in Congress managed to delete a section forbidding appellate review of trial court judges' decisions on confessions, but they had little other success in revising the bill. During the debate, they charged that the measure constituted a "cruel hoax" that would be "destructive of the tenets of our liberty," without doing anything to reduce crime. The respected Representative Emanuel Celler believed the criminal law sections unconstitutional, but in an election year, Congress wanted to appear tough on crime. Gerald Ford, the Republican leader of the House, made quite clear that the bill struck not only at criminals but at courts as well. "I refuse to concede," he announced, "that the elected representatives of the American people cannot be winners in a confrontation with the Supreme Court." Congress sent the measure to the White House on June 6, the day after Robert Kennedy had been shot after winning the California primary. Although Johnson considered some of its features questionable, the president signed the bill into law on June 19.

The Fortas Affair

The prime target of anti-Court sentiment, Chief Justice Earl Warren, would not be around when challenges to the Omnibus Crime Control Act reached the high court. On

June 13, he had gone to the White House and handed the president two letters. One read, "I hereby advise you of my intention to resign as Chief Justice of the United States effective at your pleasure." The other note explained that the seventy-seven-year-old Warren was not retiring because of health, or personal or professional problems, but solely because of age. A memorandum of the meeting by a White House aide recorded that the chief justice told the president that he wanted Johnson "to appoint as his successor someone who felt as Justice Warren did." At an unusual press conference a few weeks later, the chief justice explained that he had left the date open because of the work of the Court: "if I selected a particular day and the vacancy was not filled it would be a vacuum." When a reporter asked what would happen if the Senate failed to confirm his successor by the beginning of the October 1968 term, Warren conceded, "I suppose I would be obliged to act as Chief Justice."

Much to Warren's satisfaction, Johnson nominated Abe Fortas to the center chair and circuit court judge Homer Thornberry to fill Fortas's position as associate justice. Before announcing the appointments, Johnson reportedly secured the approval of James Eastland, the powerful chairman of the Senate Judiciary Committee, Richard Russell, the senior Democrat in the Senate, and Everett Dirksen, the minority leader. Thornberry, an old friend of Johnson's from Texas, had served in Congress for fourteen years and had easily been confirmed when first named to the district court and then to the Fifth Circuit Court of Appeals.

But despite the Democratic majority in the Senate, the Fortas nomination immediately ran into trouble. Republicans smelled victory in the upcoming election, and they wanted to preserve these most prestigious of all presidential appointments for the new, probably Republican, chief executive. Critics also charged "cronyism"; in the hearings, Fortas admitted that he had given advice to his old friend the president on a number of issues, a practice dating back many years and which had continued even after he had gone onto the bench. The timing of Warren's resignation also caused resentment. Since the Republicans would probably nominate his old political enemy, Richard Nixon, it appeared somewhat unethical for the chief justice to try to influence the choice of a successor. "What business did Warren have to say anything about his successor?" Senator Robert Griffin of Michigan complained. "It smacked of collusion." Because Warren had not given a definite date when he would step down, Senator Sam Ervin took up the whole first day of hearings with questions on whether, within the meaning of the Constitution, a "vacancy" actually existed.

The Senate adjourned for the political conventions and its summer recess without taking action, and by the time the hearings resumed after Labor Day, Fortas's prospects had worsened. The Democratic convention in Chicago had been marred by clashes between police and demonstrators; opposition to the war had increased; and Nixon, in his acceptance speech, had attacked certain courts for going "too far in weakening the peace forces, as against the criminal forces." Fortas now suffered because of his close identification with two unpopular agencies, the Johnson presidency and the Warren Court.

Then came the revelation that Fortas, while on the bench, had accepted $15,000 from American University for some summer law school seminars. The Senate Judiciary Committee discovered that the money had been raised by Fortas's former law partner, Paul Porter, from five men, three of them his clients who might well be involved in future litigation in the federal courts. The charges of cronyism increased, and on October 2, Fortas asked Johnson to withdraw the nomination. On October 10, the president asked Earl Warren to stay on the Court "until emotion subsides."

After Nixon's election, Warren sent word to the president-elect that he still intended to resign, but did not want to leave in the middle of the term and thus throw additional administrative burdens on the Court. Nixon indicated his acceptance, and on December 5 came the announcement that the chief justice would step down at the end of the term. By then, Nixon would have another vacancy in hand. *Life* magazine reported that Justice Fortas had accepted a $20,000 fee from a foundation established by financier Louis Wolfson, who had been convicted of securities violations and was then appealing the case. Moreover, the $20,000 constituted only the first payment in a series that was to last all of Fortas's life and then go to his widow for as long as she lived. Although Fortas had returned the money and canceled the arrangement, the news cast an additional shadow on his integrity. Rumors flew that the Justice Department had even more incriminating evidence that could lead to impeachment, and so, to avoid further embarrassment to himself and the Court, Fortas resigned on May 14, 1969.

Warren's Final Term

A "lame-duck" chief justice, unlike a president, suffers little diminution of power. His vote has always been, and remains, one of nine; as "first among equals," his added influence derives less from title than from force of character. Warren's brethren continued to hold him high in their affection and esteem; to William Douglas, for example, Warren would always be "*the* Chief." And so in this last year of tenure, the Court continued to uphold civil rights and liberties, and in his last opinion, Warren reaffirmed the supremacy of the Court as the chief interpreter of the Constitution.

The Warren Court remained activist to the end. In April, it struck down one-year state residency requirements for welfare eligibility because, according to Justice Brennan, such regulations violated the freedom to travel and denied equal protection.[16] In June, the Court refused to allow localities to reinstate literacy tests in a challenge to a section of the 1965 Voting Rights Act. Justice Harlan declared that since the district had not yet integrated its schools, a literacy test in the face of unequal education could not be allowed.[17] Shortly afterward, the Court invalidated an Ohio criminal syndicalism law, finally overturning the 1927 *Whitney* precedent.[18] It also overruled the 1937 decision in *Palko v. Connecticut,* by extending the Fifth Amendment protection against double jeopardy to the states and striking down multiple punishments for the same offense.[19]

On June 16, Earl Warren delivered his valedictory as chief justice in *Powell v. McCormack*. Adam Clayton Powell, Jr., the flamboyant congressman from Harlem, had been reelected to the House in 1966. Although he met the age, citizenship, and

---

16. *Shapiro v. Thompson* (1969).
17. *Gaston County v. United States* (1969).
18. *Brandenburg v. Ohio* (1969); see p. 819.
19. *Benton v. Maryland* (1969); *North Carolina v. Pearce* (1969).

residency requirements for membership detailed in Article I, Section 2, the House refused to let him take his seat. A select committee had reported that Powell had "wrongfully diverted House funds . . . and that he had made false reports on expenditures." Article I, Section 5 provides that "Each House [of Congress] shall be the Judge of the . . . Qualifications of its own Members" and may "expel a Member" with the concurrence of a two-thirds majority. The House did not vote to *expel* Powell, however; by a vote of 307 to 116, it *excluded* him from membership in the Ninetieth Congress.

Powell then sued the House, seeking his salary for the duration of the Ninetieth Congress and a declaratory judgment that the House had no constitutional power to deny him his seat. In circuit court, Judge Warren E. Burger ruled that Powell had no standing and the court no jurisdiction, since the matter constituted a political question. Judicial intervention, according to Burger, would violate the doctrine of separated powers. Following Burger's ruling, Powell's district reelected him in 1968, and the House in the Ninety-first Congress permitted him to take his seat, thus mooting a major part of his suit.

A nearly unanimous Court (only Justice Stewart thought the case should have been dismissed for mootness) not only took the case, but ruled in Powell's favor. Although a "textually demonstrable constitutional commitment" gave each House the power to judge its members' qualifications in Article I, Section 5, this power, according to Chief Justice Warren, related only to the qualifications listed in Article I, Section 2, namely, age, citizenship, and residency. By this reading, the House had no power to expel for any reason other than failure to meet the three criteria. "The Constitution leaves the House without authority," Warren wrote, "to *exclude* any person duly elected by his constituents, who meets all the requirements for membership expressly prescribed in the Constitution." Any other rule, he held, would deprive people of the right to elect their own representative.

The political question boundary had been considerably narrowed in *Baker v. Carr*, and some commentators believed that it vanished completely in *Powell*. Warren took the old *Marbury v. Madison* syllogism and reasserted the Court's role as the ultimate arbiter of constitutional issues. Is there a constitutional question? If so, then the Court is the appropriate body to make constitutional interpretations, and the Supreme Court decides *all* constitutional questions. Even if another branch has authority under the Constitution to decide the merits of an issue (the "who decides" question), the Court has the power to determine if in fact that other branch does have the authority ("who decides who decides") and the ultimate appellate power to review the decision to see if that other branch got it right.

One week later, on the final day of the term, President Nixon paid an unprecedented visit to the Court to introduce the new chief justice and to pay tribute to Earl

> The Court is a leader of opinion, not a mere register of it; but it must lead opinion, not merely impose its own; and—the short of it is—it labors under the obligation to succeed.
>
> —Alexander Bickel, *The Least Dangerous Branch* (1962)

Warren. The man who had attacked Warren so often in the 1968 campaign now praised him for helping "to keep America on the path of continuity and change, which is so essential for our progress." In response, Warren expressed his hope that the justices would never agree on all matters, since then the Court would lose its vitality and influence in national affairs.

Conclusion

The debate over the Warren Court's activism did not fade with the chief justice's retirement, but has remained a prominent issue for analysis, discussion, and disputation in law schools, at government and history seminars, and in the political arena. The furor has faded on some decisions, such as reapportionment, and although there is still some criticism of the reasoning in *Brown*, few people will deny that equality for black Americans had been long overdue. If the federal courts had not taken the lead, it is unlikely that Congress, the president, or the state legislatures would have moved in the matter. In the controversial decisions on civil liberties and criminal procedure—for all the political opposition, the furor from the law-and-order groups, the proposed constitutional amendments, and the refinement of some issues in later cases—the core ideas remain intact.

Professor Joseph Bishop of Yale, in a perceptive article entitled "Warren Court Is Not Likely to Be Overruled," written shortly after Warren's retirement, remarked that nothing would have made the Court's major decisions in such sensitive areas as electoral equality, race relations, and criminal procedure "palatable to a large segment of the population, including a great many highly vocal politicians. . . . But in these areas it is my judgment . . . that (1) the Court was right, and (2) most people knew it was right."

For Further Reading

Good introductions to the era are Alan J. Matusow, *The Unraveling of America* (1984); William L. O'Neill, *Coming Apart: An Informal History of America in the 1960s* (1971); and William E. Leuchtenburg, *A Troubled Feast: American Society since 1945* (1979). The decline of internal security as a major issue and the fading of HUAC are examined in Jerold H. Israel, "Elfbrandt v. Russell: The Demise of the Oath?" 1966 *Supreme Court Review* 193 (1967); and Walter Goodman, *The Committee: The Extraordinary Career of the House Committee on Un-American Activities* (1968).

The historical background and broader issues of apportionment are well examined in Richard C. Cortner, *The Apportionment Cases* (1970). See also, Robert G. Dixon, Jr., *Democratic Representation: Reapportionment in Law and Politics* (1968); Carl A. Auerbach, "The Reapportionment Cases: One Person, One Vote—One Vote, One Value," 1964 *Supreme Court Review* 1 (1965); and Robert McCluskey, "Foreword: The Reapportionment Case," 76 *Harvard Law Review* 54 (1962). For resistance to the decision and its ultimate impact, see Nelson W. Polsby, ed., *Reapportionment in the 1970s* (1971); and Robert McKay, "Reapportionment: Success Story of the Warren Court," 67 *Michigan Law Review* 223 (1968).

The growth of presidential power in domestic as well as foreign affairs is the subject of Arthur

M. Schlesinger, Jr., *The Imperial Presidency* (1973). Prior to the Johnson and Nixon administrations, many scholars approved the idea of a strong executive to overcome what they perceived as the structural weaknesses of American government inherent in the Constitution. See, for example, Harold Laski, *The American Presidency: An Interpretation* (1940); Richard Neustadt, *Presidential Power: The Politics of Leadership* (1956); and James MacGregor Burns, *Presidential Government: The Crucible of Leadership* (1965). Opposing views can be found in E. S. Corwin, *The Presidency: Office and Powers* (1957); and Herman Finer, *The Presidency: Crisis and Regeneration* (1960).

For the Vietnam War in general, see James Herring, *America's Longest War* (1979). For the constitutional issues, see Louis Fisher, *Presidential War Power* (1995); Francis Wormuth, *The Vietnam War: The President vs. The Constitution* (1974); W. Taylor Reveley, III, *War Powers of the President and Congress* (1981); David W. Robertson, "The Debate Among American International Lawyers About the Vietnam War," 46 *Texas Law Review* 898 (1968); and Stanley Faulkner, "Congress, the President, and the Power to Commit Forces to Combat," 86 *Harvard Law Review* 1771 (1968).

For the general controversy over the law-and-order issue, see V. A. Leonard, *The Police, the Judiciary, and the Criminal* (1969). The presidential commission, *The Challenge of Crime in a Free Society: A Report* (1967), is critiqued by one of its dissenting members, Isidore Silver, in "The President's Crime Commission Revisited," 43 *New York University Law Review* 916 (1968). The impact of Court decisions on police work is dealt with in several of the articles in Theodore L. Becker, ed., *The Impact of Supreme Court Decisions* (1969).

The *Powell* case is explored in Kent M. Weeks, *Adam Clayton Powell and the Supreme Court* (1971). The issue of judicial control over legislatures is examined in C. P. Kindregan, "The Cases of Adam Clayton Powell, Jr., and Julian Bond: The Right of Legislative Bodies to Exclude Members-Elect," 2 *Suffolk University Law Review* 58 (1968); and Note, "Legislative Exclusion: Julian Bond and Adam Clayton Powell," 35 *University of Chicago Law Review* 151 (1968).

39

Richard Nixon and the Corruption of Power

A Moderate Start • Powers of the Commander-in-Chief • The Cambodian Rider • The War Powers Act of 1973 • Expansion of Domestic Powers • The Pocket Veto • Budgets and Impoundments • The Congressional Budget Act • Watergate • Executive Privilege • Spiro Agnew Departs • United States v. Nixon *• Resignation • The Lessons of Watergate • The "Plebiscitary Presidency" • For Further Reading*

IN 1968, REPUBLICAN Richard Milhouse Nixon squeaked past Hubert Humphrey, Johnson's vice president, to win the presidential election. His 43.4 percent of the popular vote, only seven-tenths of 1 percent more than Humphrey, was the smallest share for a winner since that of Woodrow Wilson in 1912. Four years later, Nixon crushed George McGovern at the polls, capturing 60.8 percent of the popular vote, losing only Massachusetts and the District of Columbia in the electoral college, and apparently smashing the remnants of the great Roosevelt coalition. On August 8, 1974, a disgraced Nixon, facing certain impeachment, became the first president to resign from office. In his five-and-a-half-year tenure, Richard Nixon upset the traditional balance of powers and attempted to expand an already swollen executive to the point where it alone controlled government policy. Then, in a drama with all the hallmarks of Greek tragedy, he overreached himself, and the system he had attempted to corrupt pulled him down. Some viewed the Nixon years as the greatest threat to the Constitution since the Civil War; others saw his downfall as a triumph of law and constitutional government.

However we interpret these events, they do illustrate what scholars such as Bruce Ackerman and Mark Tushnet have been pointing out, that not all constitutional decisions are made in the Supreme Court. While the justices did have a role to play in the drama, it proved a minor one. The Congress and the executive squared off to redetermine one of the oldest questions in American constitutional history, the proper division of power among the branches.

A Moderate Start

The political system withstood the tumult and violence of the 1968 campaign, and power passed peaceably on January 20, 1969. Defying the expectations of both his critics and supporters, the thirty-seventh president did not immediately try to undo the reform programs set in place by Roosevelt, Truman, Kennedy, and Johnson. Instead, he deliberately sought the center and consciously attempted to foster a spirit of moderation. In his inaugural, he stated that "We cannot learn from one another until we stop shouting at one another—until we speak quietly enough so that our words can be heard as well as our voices." Nixon spoke to the desire of "Middle America"—the "unyoung, unblack, and unpoor"—for peace and stability after the turmoil of the Johnson administration.

Certainly conservatives expected something different in light of Nixon's campaign rhetoric; yet in his first term, he displayed a far broader view of public affairs than his opponents had been willing to credit to him. In January 1971, he proposed a sweeping overhaul of the welfare system, with a national minimum of $2,460 annually in cash and food stamps for a family of four—a significant improvement over the $468 that a family then received in Mississippi and more than nineteen other states paid. Nixon scrapped a few Great Society programs, but the administration worked with Congress to expand Social Security benefits, regulate federal campaign spending, provide assistance to the working poor, extend the right to vote in federal elections to eighteen-year-olds (which led to the Twenty-sixth Amendment), ban cigarette commercials on radio and television, and on the eve of the 1972 election, establish a groundbreaking, revenue-sharing plan that returned millions of dollars of federal monies to the states.

Overseas, Nixon cut back American troop strength in Vietnam, which had reached a record 543,000 when he took office. The former Cold Warrior, who had denounced Democratic efforts to improve relations with the Communist bloc, ushered in the age of "détente," signed a treaty with the Soviet Union limiting land- and sea-based missiles, and, most amazingly of all, journeyed to Beijing to open diplomatic relations between the United States and China.

Not everyone rejoiced. The economy turned sour, drugs became a problem in the suburbs as well as in the ghettos, violence seemed more widespread, the war continued in Vietnam, and the administration appeared indifferent if not hostile to civil rights. The president put some members of the White House staff in costumes reminiscent of a Victor Herbert operetta, and underneath the laughter at this foolishness could be heard the anxiety over the extent to which Nixon was trying to amass power.

No more than Johnson, Nixon did not create the "imperial" presidency, and he cannot be blamed for the accretion of great power to the office. Since Washington's time, both the Constitution and political events have demanded that the chief executive take the lead in foreign policy. Though the Constitution is far more explicit in its division of power and responsibility between legislative and executive branches in domestic policymaking, since 1933, there has been growing pressure on the president to take the lead role there too. Modern communications have also contributed to the shift of attention from the Capitol to the White House. Reporters find it far easier to seek comments from the president or his aides than from 500 members of Congress; they expect the executive to have something to say on every issue and a solution to every problem.

By the time Nixon took office, the federal government had grown so large that it could not be effectively managed. In 1965, Senator Abraham Ribicoff counted 150 federal agencies and more than 400 regional and area field offices servicing outside agencies through 456 different "program channels." Nixon initially had little interest in management and told a reporter that he intended to coordinate domestic policy through regular cabinet meetings. "All you need is a competent Cabinet to run the country at home." Within a year, he had abandoned this view, and he began a campaign to take back control of the agencies from the bureaucrats.

As one scholar noted, Nixon "fulfilled" several trends of the modern presidency, trends that had begun in Franklin Roosevelt's tenure. He secured presidential control over policy-making, especially in foreign affairs. The State Department, which had often treated the president as a temporary nuisance, lost nearly all of its power in shaping foreign policy. Just before taking office, Nixon asserted that "You need a President for foreign policy; no Secretary of State is really important; the President makes foreign policy." Nixon and his national security advisor, Henry Kissinger, ran high-level diplomacy from the White House, leaving minor matters and the provision of technical advice to the bureaucrats. After Kissinger became secretary of state, Nixon continued to rely on him, as an individual, but did not trust the State Department for policy development. While subsequent presidents would rely more on their secretaries of state, the department would never again enjoy the great influence it had once had over foreign policy.

Similarly, power over domestic policy also shifted from agencies to the Office of the President, and White House staff took on administrative functions previously exercised by line agencies. Critics cried "imperial presidency," but from a historical viewpoint, Nixon actually continued in the tradition of Roosevelt, Kennedy, and Johnson.

Powers of the Commander-in-Chief

Nixon indicated how far he believed his powers as commander-in-chief went in his conduct of the continuing war in Vietnam. During the 1968 campaign, he had claimed to have a secret plan to bring "peace with honor." Although the Pentagon began to pull troops out soon after the new administration took over, withdrawal proved far more difficult than Nixon or his chief foreign policy adviser, Henry Kissinger, had anticipated. Between January 1969 and the final settlement in 1973, another 20,000 American soldiers died.

The plan for extricating the United States from Southeast Asia involved direct negotiations in Paris with the North Vietnamese and their Vietcong allies, as well as "Vietnamization" of the war, by which American troops would leave and be replaced by strengthened ARVN forces. To pressure the enemy to come to the bargaining table, the administration expanded the war. On March 14, 1969, American planes began fourteen months of bombing Communist sanctuaries in neighboring Cambodia. The president did not inform Congress of this operation, which involved four times the total bomb tonnage that had been dropped on Japan during the Second World War; the legislature did not learn about it until newspaper reporters broke the story. Then, on April 30, 1970, Nixon went on national television to announce an "incursion" by American troops into Cambodia to "clean out" Communist camps and staging areas. By this time, the administration had disowned the Gulf of Tonkin Resolution (Congress revoked it in January 1971), so the continued war in Vietnam, the bombing and invasion of Cambodia, the so-called Christmas bombing of Hanoi and Haiphong in December 1972, and the mining of North Vietnamese harbors all rested on Nixon's claims of unilateral authority as commander-in-chief. The legal justification, he explained, "is the right of the President of the United States under the Constitution to protect the lives of American men." He compared the situation to the Cuban missile crisis of 1962 and concluded that "in the modern world, there are times when the Commander-in-Chief . . . will have to act quickly."

The analogy to Kennedy's response fails to be convincing. The discovery of missile sites in Cuba took place only days before Russian ships were scheduled to deliver the weapons; the Vietcong and the North Vietnamese had been using bases in Cambodia for more than four years before Nixon ordered the bombing. A few days' delay would hardly have affected the course of the war, and Nixon could have consulted with congressional leaders. Instead, he chose to keep "Operation Menu" secret from the Congress and even from all but his closest advisers within the White House. Kennedy had set up an "executive committee" to seek out and discuss different opinions and options; Nixon and Kissinger acted as a law unto themselves.

Constitutional considerations mattered little. The president did not even ask the State Department (which normally handles questions of international law) to prepare a legal case for the Cambodian incursion until four days after it had begun. He turned to assistant attorney general William H. Rehnquist to justify his right to act as commander-in-chief. In a brief entitled "The President and Cambodia: His Constitutional Authority," Rehnquist claimed that the Constitution gave the commander-in-chief "a grant of substantive authority" that had allowed presidents throughout American history to send troops "into conflict with foreign powers on their own initiative," and to deploy "armed forces outside the United States." According to Rehnquist, Congress had confirmed this power by acquiescing in presidential policies. President Nixon, he claimed, had done nothing new or radical, but had made "precisely the sort of tactical decision traditionally confided to the commander-in-chief in the conduct of armed conflict."

The argument that once in a war a president had full power to direct its military course amounted to little other than common sense. Rehnquist, however, claimed much more; he asserted that the Constitution gave the commander-in-chief far-ranging, substantive powers that lay beyond the check of Congress, such as expanding the war zone to a neutral country if he thought it necessary to protect American lives. To "prove" his argument, Rehnquist relied on two cases that in fact had little if any relevance to the situation: *Durand v. Hollins* (1860), in which Justice Nelson on circuit confirmed the country's power to use force in order to protect American citizens abroad, and the Civil War *Prize* cases. But in the first case, President Pierce had used a navy gunship to rescue Americans caught in a Nicaraguan civil war, and not to involve the United States in the fighting, and Rehnquist did not explain how Cambodia could be compared to a rebellious Confederate state in the second case.

The Cambodian Rider

The bombing of Cambodia led to increased student protests and the closing of many U.S. colleges and universities in May 1970, as well as the killing of students at Kent State and Jackson State universities. It also led to confrontations between Nixon and the Congress over the meaning of legislation and whether the legislature had any discretion in directing the use of appropriated funds.

In early 1970, President Nixon told the nation that after July 1, the only air missions over Cambodia would be for the purpose of interdicting the movement of enemy men and material in order to protect the lives of American troops. In response, Congress wrote in section 601 of the military authorization bill for 1971, declaring it the policy of the United States to terminate "at the earliest practical date" all military operations in Southeast Asia and to provide for the prompt and orderly withdrawal of American forces. The language of the statute placed the responsibility for establishing the final date for withdrawal on the president. In signing the bill, Nixon declared that section 601 "does not represent the policies of this Administration" and was "without binding force or effect."

When a congressman sued the president, a federal district judge admonished Nixon for his statement, noting that when the president signed the bill, including §601, "it established 'the policy of the United States' to the exclusion of any different executive or administrative policy, and had binding force and effect on every officer of the Government. No executive statement denying efficacy to the legislation could have either validity or effect" (*DaCosta v. Nixon* [E.D.N.Y. 1972]).

Cambodia also brought into question the claim that Congress, by appropriating money, thus sanctioned the war. In 1970, a federal district judge had declared that "the entire course of legislation [providing funds] shows that Congress knew what it was doing, and that it intended to have American troops fight in Vietnam" (*Berk v. Laird* [E.D.N.Y. 1970]). The notion that Congress had approved the Vietnam War by its continued funding had been a staple of Johnson and Nixon spokespersons, but by the beginning of 1973, members of Congress, the public, scholars, and federal judges had begun to question that assumption. In January, the Paris peace agreement provided for the withdrawal of all American forces by March, and the president could no longer

> [Judges can no longer] be unmindful of what every schoolboy knows: that in voting to appropriate money or to draft men a Congressman is not necessarily approving the continuation of a war no matter how specifically the appropriation or draft act refers to that war. A Congressman wholly opposed to the war's commencement and continuation might vote for the military appropriations and for the draft measures because he was unwilling to abandon without support men already fighting. An honorable, decent, compassionate act of aiding those already in peril is not proof of consent to the actions that placed and continued them in that dangerous posture. We should not construe votes cast in pity and piety as though they were votes freely given to express consent.
>
> —Judges Charles Wyzansky and David Bazelon, *Mitchell v. Laird* (D.C. Cir. 1973)

justify military operations as directed toward protecting American soldiers. Nixon, however, continued the massive bombing of Cambodia.

When a supplemental appropriation bill reached the floor of the House, Congressman Clarence Long offered an amendment to prohibit the use of any funds authorized by the bill to support continued American operations in Cambodia. Nixon vetoed the bill, claiming that the "Cambodian rider" would destroy any chance for a negotiated settlement in that country. He also noted that the nine agencies covered by the bill would soon run out of operating funds, implying that the wheels of government would grind to a halt if Congress persisted in its attitude.

To Congress, Nixon had not only challenged its judgment, but also its explicit constitutional power of appropriation. Indeed, one could argue that Congress had done exactly what the Constitution provided, decide whether or not to spend money on a specific program. If Nixon refused to acknowledge the congressional power of the purse, the legislators could easily have held him accountable for any governmental shutdown. But Congress backed off. It failed to override the veto, and a revised bill included a compromise delaying the cutoff of funds from June 30 to August 15, 1973, in effect giving Nixon permission to bomb Cambodia for forty-five more days. Even so, by finally exercising the power of the purse, Congress managed to end American military operations in Southeast Asia.

The compromise aborted several cases that had been filed in federal courts. On July 25, a federal judge in New York held that Congress had not authorized the bombing in Cambodia, and the fact that Congress had been unable to override the president's veto should not be seen as an affirmation of authority. The Court of Appeals for the Second Circuit reversed on the grounds that the August 15th compromise did in fact constitute congressional approval.[1] Other courts quickly adopted this rationale to avoid having to decide between legislative and executive claims.

The War Powers Act of 1973

An aroused Congress had already begun to reassert its authority before Nixon's election. After Johnson's attorney general, Nicholas Katzenbach, told the Senate Foreign Relations Committee that "the expression of declaring a war is one that has become outmoded in the international arena," the committee had prepared a "sense of the Senate" resolution late in 1967, rejecting that point of view. The "National Commitments" resolution, as it came to be called, reaffirmed the importance and necessity of the congressional war power and denied that the executive could "alter on its own authority" any provision of the Constitution that it considered obsolete. The Congress had gone along with the Vietnam policy because it lacked "guidelines of experience" in meeting the demands of the nation's new role as a world power and had too readily been "overawed by the cult of executive expertise." In the future, Congress planned to make explicit limits on any powers it granted the president. Originally scheduled for a vote in April 1968, Senate lead-

1. *Holtzmann v. Schlesinger* (E.D.N.Y. 1973), stayed by the Supreme Court before being reversed by the second circuit later in the year.

ers deferred bringing the resolution to the floor after Lyndon Johnson announced at the end of March that he would not be a candidate for reelection and called a halt to the bombing of North Vietnam. But in June 1969, by a vote of 70 to 16, the Senate adopted the resolution over the objections of the new Nixon administration.

The resolution merely said that the Senate believed commitments made without congressional approval were invalid and had no legal force until Congress passed enabling legislation. The Senate realized that in the past it had not insisted on the executive informing the legislature of exactly what it did overseas, so in early 1969, a Foreign Relations subcommittee began a two-year investigation to learn the extent of existing public and secret commitments. By midsummer, senators were expressing shock at the level of American involvement in Laos and Thailand. In effect, Stuart Symington of Missouri told his colleagues, "the United States had been at war in Laos for years," and had six major bases and 45,000 troops in Thailand to support the secret operations in Laos. Senators John Cooper (Rep., Kentucky) and Frank Church (Dem., Idaho), in order to prevent Laos from escalating into another Vietnam, introduced a bipartisan amendment to a foreign aid bill to prohibit using any money to send any combat troops into Laos and Thailand. The White House strenuously opposed the resolution, and administration supporters such as Strom Thurmond (Rep., S. Carolina) urged their colleagues "to stand behind our President and show unity." But the Cooper-Church amendment passed the Senate 80 to 9, and the House added its approval, the first time since before World War II that Congress had asserted any control over foreign military operations.

Congress next turned to what Johnson spokesmen had called the "functional equivalent" of a war declaration, the Gulf of Tonkin Resolution. Senator Charles Mathias (Rep., Maryland) introduced a proposal for repeal, and the Foreign Relations Committee held hearings in February and March 1970. The administration withdrew its initial opposition, claiming that it had more than sufficient authority under the Constitution and the SEATO treaty. Before the committee could report to the full Senate, however, the president announced the Cambodian incursion.

Faced with a strong, albeit controversial presidential action, a Congress tentatively reasserting its authority lost its nerve. Senator Jacob Javits (Rep., New York) protested that the president had so defined his power as "to intrude upon, and even preempt, the powers reserved so explicitly to the Congress." But majority leader Mike Mansfield (Dem., Montana), one of the cosponsors of the Cooper-Church amendment, now defended the president and said that the "power was his to reach under the Constitution." Mississippi Democrat John Stennis, the powerful chairman of the Senate Armed Services Committee, declared that as long as the commander-in-chief "is exercising a judgment that is within reason . . . he is the only one that we have to make decisions. We have no one else."

Senators Cooper and Church now introduced a second proposal, to cut off funds for troops in Cambodia after June 30, the day Nixon had promised that they would be withdrawn. Sam J. Ervin, Jr. (Dem., N. Carolina), one of the most knowledgeable and respected constitutionalists in the upper house, opposed the new resolution. "The Founding Fathers were not foolish enough to place the command of American troops engaged in combat operations in a Congress of the United States which is now composed of 100 Senators and 435 Representatives." A war council of that size, Ervin warned, would be "bedlam." Even those who opposed the Nixon policies and believed that the executive had arrogated too much power had to recognize the force of Ervin's argument. They would have to come up with legislation specific enough to curb the president and reestablish congressional authority, yet would not curtail his legitimate powers as commander-in-chief or hamper his carrying out an effective foreign policy.

In June 1970, Democratic Representative Dante B. Fascell of Florida and Senator Jacob J. Javits of New York introduced measures that they believed would resolve this difficulty. As Javits explained, the Framers had never intended congressional power to restrict the executive in responding to attack, in protecting American lives and property abroad, or in carrying out commitments previously approved by the treaty process. Moreover, in an age of nuclear missiles, Congress might not have time to declare war; the president properly had to initiate defensive measures immediately. Both bills allowed the president full discretion under existing treaty obligations, but if he chose to use American forces in any other context, he had to report their use to Congress and seek its approval for continuation of the operation. The Fascell bill called for the president to report to Congress within twenty-four hours; the Javits bill forbade the president from continuing any armed operation for more than thirty days without legislative approval. The Nixon administration opposed any restraint on what it considered the unrestricted powers of the commander-in-chief, and working through its allies in the House of Representatives, it managed to weaken the proposal so as to make it practically meaningless. Twice the House passed a relatively innocuous bill, but the Senate refused to go along.

Nixon broke the deadlock in December 1972, by ordering massive bombardment of Hanoi and Haiphong in North Vietnam. Although the bombing had been halted by the time the Ninety-third Congress convened in January 1973, the mood of Congress had shifted perceptibly. Javits introduced his resolution again, this time with fifty-seven cosponsors. The War Powers Act, Senator Edmund Muskie (Dem., Maine) declared, would be the first step in ending the "White House monopolization of our foreign affairs." The bill, he said, did not alter the Constitution, but only "fulfills" its intent. The Senate passed the measure easily, and, with minor adjustments, the House also agreed. Although the fighting in Vietnam had ended early in the year, a shocked Congress discovered in March that the bombing of Cambodia had continued. When pressed for the constitutional justification of the bombing, deputy assistant secretary of state William H. Sullivan informed the Foreign Relations Committee that lawyers had begun work on the question; in the meantime he would "just say the justification is the reelection of President Nixon."

The War Powers Act of 1973 required the president "in every possible instance" to consult with Congress before committing American forces to hostilities. If that was not practical, he had to report in writing within forty-eight hours to the Speaker of the House and the president pro tem of the Senate the movement of troops, the circumstances requiring American action, the authority for the decision, and the expected scope and duration of the operation. If Congress did not approve of the president's decision by a declaration of war or some other resolution within sixty days, he would have to withdraw the troops at once, or within thirty days if he certified it would take that long to effect a safe withdrawal. Even if Congress initially approved the president's actions, it could terminate American involvement within sixty days by concur-

> The President is to be commander-in-chief of the army and navy of the United States. In this respect his authority would be nominally the same with that of the King of Britain, but in substance much inferior to it. It would amount to nothing more than the supreme command and direction of the military and naval forces, as first General and Admiral of the Confederacy; while that of the British king extends to the *declaring* of war and to the *raising* and *regulating* of fleets and armies,—all of which, by the Constitution under consideration, would appertain to the Legislature.
>
> —Alexander Hamilton, *Federalist No. 69* (1788)

rent resolution. Despite the House language watering down some provisions, most members of Congress believed that the bill accomplished its main purpose of checking unbridled presidential power; they wanted to send a message.

Richard Nixon did not want to hear it. Despite the large majorities behind the bill in both houses, he vetoed the measure in October 1973. The Founding Fathers, he claimed, had deliberately given the commander-in-chief broad and flexible powers. The bill would seriously "undermine this Nation's ability to act decisively and convincingly in times of international crisis," and would "strike from the President's hand . . . his ability to exercise quiet diplomacy backed by subtle shifts in our military deployment." Congress easily overrode the veto, 284 to 135 in the House and 75 to 18 in the Senate, and took what many hailed as the first significant step in reining in the imperial presidency.

American constitutional doctrine requires that every exercise of government power be accountable. Presidents Eisenhower and Kennedy began America's commitment to the war in Vietnam without congressional authorization. Lyndon Johnson expanded the war with indirect approval, as Congress passed the Tonkin Gulf Resolution and approved constantly growing spending for the war. Nixon secretly expanded the war. Congress is the only body that could have acted, both because of its express constitutional powers, as well as the fact that the judiciary has throughout our history refused to serve as a recourse in this area. Suits to test the legitimacy of the war proved unavailing, whether brought by young men seeking to avoid service in an undeclared war or by members of Congress claiming that their constitutional prerogatives had been usurped by the president.

How effective the War Powers Act of 1973 has actually been is far from clear, and every president since its passage has claimed that it unconstitutionally restricts the

> If the people ever let command of the war power fall into irresponsible and unscrupulous hands, the courts wield no power equal to its restraint. The chief restrain upon those who command the physical forces of the country, in the future as in the past, must be their responsibility to the political judgments of their contemporaries and to the moral judgments of history.
>
> —Justice Robert H. Jackson, *Korematsu v. United States* (1944)

power of the commander-in-chief. Proponents of the measure argued that it would not hamper a president in carrying out any legitimate policy, but only required that responsibility and authority be shared with the legislative branch, as constitutionally mandated. The resolution did not deny—to the contrary, it affirmed—the president's prerogative to take the nation into war without a congressional declaration. Supporters saw it as a clarification of constitutional provisions relating to warmaking, an acknowledgement that even if the old-style declaration of war no longer made sense, the Constitution still required some form of congressional oversight and approval. The symbolic nature of the bill appeared far more significant at the time—a triumph of Congress over a president who had, in its opinion, aggrandized the powers of the commander-in-chief.

Expansion of Domestic Powers

Nixon also confronted Congress on domestic issues. On taking office, he faced the perennial difficulty of trying to gain control over the permanent bureaucracy and force it to carry out his policies. In 1969, this problem seemed greater than usual. Lyndon Johnson had expanded the federal bureaucracy to implement Great Society programs and had staffed the new agencies with men and women committed to liberal programs who enjoyed protection in their jobs under the civil service laws. Unable to exercise direct control over the bureaucrats, the president chose to increase the size and influence of the White House staff, which would be personally loyal to him and to his policies, and which he could use to bypass or override the agencies.

His first step was to bring the Bureau of the Budget under closer presidential supervision. Renamed the Office of Management and Budget in the executive reorganization of 1970, it became not only more responsive to presidential control, but a much more political agency as well, tied to White House policymaking at several levels. Within the White House, Nixon relied on the National Security Council rather than on the State Department for advice on foreign affairs, and he created a Domestic Council as a counterpart to shape domestic policy. In every secretariat and in many agencies, the president appointed political operatives at the deputy level to preclude policy decisions being made independently of the Oval Office.

The White House payroll more than doubled to 3,500 persons during Nixon's first term, and the nature of the immediate staff changed dramatically. Presidential aides had long been important because of their access to the chief executive. But under Nixon, aides like H. R. Haldeman and John Ehrlichman wielded unprecedented personal power; they not only helped administer the Office of the President, but played key roles in determining policy.

With Congress still under Democratic control, Nixon could not secure legislative repeal of the Kennedy-Johnson programs; so he adopted various stratagems to subvert them. In July 1969, the administration informed the nation that it would no longer enforce Title VI of the 1964 Civil Rights Act, which prohibited discrimination based on race, color, creed, or national origin in any program receiving federal aid. The attorney general and the secretary of the Department of Health, Education and Welfare (HEW) issued a joint statement interpreting the requirement for cutting off funds as permissive, but first a district judge and then a unanimous Court of Appeals ruled in *Adams v. Richardson* (1973) that the law required HEW to carry out congressional intent.

Thus deterred by the courts from carrying out a policy of selective implementation, Nixon sought other means to kill off programs he did not like. At the start of his second term, buoyed by his huge electoral majority, he started to cancel programs outright. In the Department of Agriculture, he terminated the Rural Environmental Assistance Program (which dated back to 1936), the Water Bank Program to preserve waterfowl wetlands, the rural electrification loan agency, disaster loans, and other programs. He declared an eighteen-month moratorium on certain federal housing programs, and in January 1973, he omitted any request for funds for the Office of Economic Opportunity (OEO) in the 1974 budget.

The OEO, created by Johnson to coordinate the Great Society's "war on poverty," had been a special target of Nixon's during the campaign, and as president, he had the right to recommend discontinuance of its funding. Before Congress could act on this proposal, Howard Phillips, the acting director of OEO, announced that the president's proposed budget superseded the current congressional authorization still in force, and he set about dismantling the agency.

Once again, the courts ruled against the administration's interpretation of unrestrained executive authority. To allow a proposed and unapproved budget proposal to take precedence over a duly enacted appropriation, District Judge William B. Jones ruled in *Local 2677 v. Phillips* (1973), "would in effect give the President a veto power through the use of his budget message," and the Constitution had not given the chief executive that power. The executive budget constituted nothing more than a proposal until Congress acted on it, and Congress could act on it as it pleased. In the meantime, the president had the constitutional obligation to enforce the law, and the president may not "refuse to execute laws passed by Congress with which he disagrees."

The Pocket Veto

Nixon's continuing battle with Congress also led him to use a recognized power in a new and questionable manner. In addition to the normal provision for veto and override, the Constitution provides in Article I, Section 7, for the so-called pocket veto—"If any Bill shall not be returned by the President within ten Days (Sunday excepted) after it shall have been presented to him, the Same shall be a Law, in like Manner as if he had signed it, unless the Congress by their Adjournment prevent its Return, in which Case it shall not be a Law."

In the early days of the republic, presidents had rarely utilized pocket vetoes; there had only been eighteen before the Civil War. In fact, there had only been sixty-four pocket vetoes altogether before Nixon, more than half of them during the Truman administration. About two-thirds of all pocket vetoes had been of private bills, and there had been none of a major piece of legislation. Moreover, the practice of adjournment *within* a session had also been rare; Congress did so only five times before 1941, three of these in 1867, during the strife with Andrew Johnson. There had been only one instance of a pocket veto during an adjournment of less than ten days, when Lyndon

Johnson had pocket-vetoed a private relief bill during a nine-day adjournment in 1964. Congress had never confronted the president on intrasession pocket vetoes because the bills had not involved important policy issues.

The Supreme Court had spoken only twice on this issue. First, in *Okanogan Indians v. United States* (1929), it held that the pocket veto provision applied at the end of a session of Congress as well as at the end of the Congress. The second case arose when Franklin Roosevelt vetoed a private bill and sent it to the secretary of the Senate with a regular veto message at a time when the upper house had recessed for three days. The beneficiary of the measure went to court and claimed that the bill had become law because the Senate had not been in session and therefore could not receive the veto message. In *Wright v. United States* (1938), Chief Justice Hughes held that the secretary of the Senate could receive a veto message for that body and intimated that a pocket veto might be valid for a prolonged intrasessional adjournment, but certainly not for a three-day break.

In December 1970, Congress passed the Family Practice of Medicine Act authorizing $225 million for hospitals and medical schools to promote and train family practitioners; the vote in the Senate had been 64 to 1, and in the House 345 to 2. On December 22, with two of the president's ten days of consideration remaining, Congress adjourned for a five-day Christmas break. Before it left, however, the Senate made provision for its secretary to receive any communications from the president during that time. Both by the terms of the *Wright* decision and by the Senate's own precautions, the conditions for a pocket veto did not exist. Nonetheless, on December 24, Nixon announced a pocket veto of a major bill that had overwhelming support in Congress.

Senator Edward Kennedy of Massachusetts promptly took the administration to court. In a civil action, he argued that "If the pocket veto clause applies to a five-day adjournment, why should it not also apply to an adjournment of three days, or a weekend, or one day, or even overnight?" The purpose of the veto provisions of the Constitution had been to create a balance of responsibility and power between the executive and legislative branches. Congress could pass a bill; the president could veto it; the Congress would then have a chance to reconsider, and if a sufficient majority still approved the measure, it could override the veto. The pocket veto had obviously been meant to apply only to a specific situation, when Congress had adjourned, and common sense as well as the Supreme Court had interpreted that to mean more than just a brief recess. Senator Jacob Javits charged that Nixon had "illegally vetoed" the measure, and in 1971 and 1972, the Senate approved appropriations for the program. Interestingly, James Madison once wrote: "An abuse on the part of the President . . . in a case of sufficient magnitude to deprive Congress of the opportunity of overruling objections to their bills, might doubtless be a ground for impeachment." Congress did not take up this suggestion, because at the time it found itself engaged in still another confrontation with Nixon on control of the budget.

Budgets and Impoundments

Budget leadership began shifting from Congress to the executive during the Eisenhower administration, and the trend accelerated during the Kennedy–Johnson years.

The executive, with responsibility for developing the budget and with enhanced tools for statistics gathering and analysis, seemed to know more than the legislature about the economy's needs. While Congress could, and often did, object to particular measures, the prevailing pattern saw the president propose and Congress dispose much as he suggested. Congress did not have the staff expertise to develop an independent budgetary process, nor did it seem inclined to do so. At the same time, however, congressional leaders began expressing their resentment at executive presumptions about the budget. Lyndon Johnson, who initially got Congress to give him almost anything he requested in the way of tax adjustments and Great Society expenditures, found that by 1967, the leaders of the money committees were opposing him on nearly everything. Wilbur Mills of Arkansas, chairman of the House Ways and Means Committee, led the fight against Johnson's budget that year and forced the president to cut several billions in expenditures. When he reluctantly signed the bill, Johnson blamed Congress for failing to do its duty. Congress ought not "shift to the President the responsibility for making reductions in programs which the Congress itself is unwilling to do."

Economic demons loosed by the Vietnam War came home to roost in the early years of the Nixon administration. Inflation rose to more than 6 percent a year, and Congress, instead of proposing its own program, called on the president to act. House majority leader Carl Albert demanded that "the vast and influential powers of the Office of the President must be brought to bear against these sharply rising price increases." Senator William Proxmire, vice chairman of the Joint Economic Committee, also asked for "leadership from the White House." Although some congressmen, such as Wright Patman, chairman of the Joint Economic Committee, said that Congress should stop waiting for Nixon and "assert its constitutional powers," most legislators believed only the president could take the necessary steps.

To force Nixon to act, and also to make clear that the president and not Congress bore the blame, the Democratic-controlled legislature began delegating even more economic power to the executive. Republicans objected to this obviously political ploy, but they could not water down proposals to give the president blanket authority to establish wage and price controls. They labeled the measures "buck passing," as did Nixon, who could not veto the measure, since it had been tacked on as a rider to defense appropriations. He charged Congress with abdicating its responsibility; if it believed such controls were necessary, Congress "should face up to its responsibilities and make such controls mandatory."

Congress lacked the will to develop an independent fiscal policy; worse yet, it lacked the means to do so. The Reorganization Act of 1946 had tried to impose some order on the literally dozens of budgetary amendments passed since the original Budget and Accounting Act of 1921. The system, chaotic as it seemed, actually worked fairly well when the president came from the same party as the majority in Congress, since both branches had a political incentive to cooperate. But the increasingly common situations in which the Democrats controlled Congress and the Republicans held the White House revealed congressional ineffectiveness. Eisenhower frequently vetoed money bills sent by the Democratic Congress during the last six years of his tenure. Congress rarely overrode the vetos, not only because the Democrats lacked the necessary majority, but because Congress did not have a system in place to propose an alternative budget. When Nixon and the legislature came to loggerheads over economic policy in 1972, he issued an ultimatum that if the Congress could not get its house in order and develop a sensible program, it should give him power to do so. Congress did neither, so he chose to overrule the legislature when it appropriated money against his wishes and imposed his own policy by the device of impounding funds.

As Nixon frequently pointed out, he was not the first to impound funds, citing Jefferson's alleged refusal to spend $50,000 in 1803 that Congress had voted for gunboats. In fact, Jefferson had done nothing of the sort; as he told Congress, the Louisiana Purchase had made the immediate deployment of the vessels unnecessary, and he had therefore *deferred* spending the money until a better design had been developed. A year later, he reported that such a design had been approved and construction had begun. The only other case of presidential impoundment during the nineteenth century came during the Grant administration, when the president refused to spend river and harbor funds in 1876, claiming that the appropriations bill did not make the expenditure "obligatory." In view of the depression, Grant announced he would not spend money "upon work not clearly national."

Other presidents had occasionally refused to spend part of an appropriation. In early 1941, Franklin Roosevelt began withholding public works money from projects not directly related to national defense. He explained that he considered this as nothing more than an emergency measure, which should not become a regular practice "to set aside or nullify the expressed will of Congress." President Truman impounded air force funds in 1949, but he did so under an option that Congress itself had provided. In 1961, John F. Kennedy refused to spend an extra $180 million voted for the B-70 bomber, basing his decision on his right as commander-in-chief. To reduce inflationary pressure during the Vietnam War, Lyndon Johnson postponed spending over $5 billion, but only after meeting with congressional leaders and securing their assent.

Congress has, in fact, occasionally provided statutory authority for impoundment. The Anti-Deficiency Acts of 1905 and 1906, and the 1951 amendments, permitted impoundment to effect savings and set up contingency reserves, provided that the purpose of the programs for which the monies had originally been appropriated could still be carried out. The Civil Rights Act of 1964 directed the withholding of federal funds when localities failed to desegregate their schools. Other bills from time to time permitted the president to withhold funds if he determined that certain conditions existed.

No president, however, had ever claimed to have constitutional authority to defy Congress through impoundment. When he was urged by civil rights leaders to deny Mississippi federal funds, John Kennedy flat out declared, "I don't have the power." So when Richard Nixon first began exploring impoundment, he asked the Justice Department to justify such a policy in terms of latent executive authority. Assistant attorney general William Rehnquist responded: "With respect to the suggestion that the President has a *constitutional* power to decline to spend appropriated funds, we must conclude that the existence of such a broad power is supported by neither reason nor precedent." Rehnquist doubted the possibility of formulating any constitutional theory to "justify a refusal by the President to comply with a Congressional directive to spend."

Despite this advice, midway in his first term Nixon began to withhold funds in a manner and to an extent far beyond that of all of his predecessors combined. Where previous presidents had nearly always limited their impoundment to a single item, Nixon attacked numerous programs, especially those in health, housing, and other human services. Of $7 billion appropriated, for example, for conservation and to clean up the nation's air and water, the president withheld $1 billion. By 1973, Nixon's policy had affected over 100 federal programs and totaled $15 billion, almost one-fifth of all controllable funds.

The president claimed practically an unlimited executive power. "The constitutional right of the President of the United States," he told a news conference, "when the spending of money would mean either increasing prices or increasing taxes . . . is absolutely clear." The constitutional issue, when framed this way, could no longer be ignored: Either the executive had to comply with legislative spending directives or he could ignore them; if the latter, this meant the president had supreme power within the government. Senator Sam Ervin, chairman of the Senate Judiciary Subcommittee on the Separation of Powers, opened hearings in March 1971 by announcing that the Constitution required the president to "execute all laws passed by the Congress. . . . He has no authority under the Constitution to decide which laws will be executed or to what extent they will be enforced." Many of the witnesses agreed, but the president's men defended his action. Caspar Weinberger, the deputy director of the Office of Management and Budget (OMB), asserted that the president's responsibility to execute the laws authorized and might even require impoundment, because he had to look beyond the particular statute to assess its impact as part of all the laws. Only the president, Weinberger claimed, had the overall knowledge and the overall responsibility to do this.

As the hearing made clear, Nixon was using impoundment not as a budget management tool, but for policy purposes. One OMB official, when asked why the president had withheld funds for urban renewal and model cities programs, candidly replied: "Nixon doesn't believe in them." The president used impoundment as an item veto, a power not given to the executive in the Constitution. There was a case to be made for the item veto; over forty states have it, and several presidents, including Roosevelt and Eisenhower, had requested it. But the Constitution only permits the executive to veto entire bills. If Nixon could impound at his will, he would not only exceed the limits of presidential power, but drastically upset the balance between the branches by impinging on legislative prerogatives. The president could veto a bill; Congress could override the veto; the president could then in effect veto the program a second time by impounding funds, and the Congress would be unable to respond. Just this happened with the Water Pollution Control Act, which the Congress passed over Nixon's veto; the president then refused to execute the law by impounding the funds.

The Congressional Budget Act

Although Congress has often delegated its powers willingly, it resists having power taken without asking. Following the hearings on impoundment, Senator Ervin introduced a bill requiring the president to report all impoundments, with the reason for his action, and permitting Congress to override his decision within sixty days. The bill, however, died in the midst of wrangling over a federal budget ceiling. Almost as if courting disaster, Nixon stepped up his withholding. He began canceling entire programs, while his Justice Department claimed that a so-called executive power gave the president all the constitutional authority he needed.

More than fifty suits attacked impoundment in federal court, although Nixon resigned before most of them had been decided. Only one, *Train v. City of New York* (1975), reached the Supreme Court. With Nixon by then out of office, the government avoided any claim that the Constitution permitted impoundment and instead argued that the 1972 amendments to the Water Pollution Control Act gave the president wide discretion to control the rate of spending. A unanimous Court rejected this view, and lower courts did not treat similar claims any more sympathetically.

The Ervin bill surfaced again in 1973, but this time it enjoyed a broad range of support. Fiscal conservatives concerned with budget deficits wanted to restrain the growth in government spending and believed a congressional budget would force greater restraint on members of Congress. Liberals also supported the measure, believing that a congressional budget would require serious policy debates in place of haphazard decision making.

After extensive negotiations in Congress, the Ervin proposal finally emerged as the Congressional Budget and Impounding Act of 1974. Unlike most laws, which deal with programs, this one defined basic relationships between the executive and legislative branches through an elaboration of structure and process. It imposed substantial restraints on presidential impoundment and required legislative approval of executive efforts to curtail or end programs that had already been funded. The law distinguished between two types of impoundment. Where the president simply wished to *defer* spending, he could do so unless Congress initiated action; either house might prevent his deferring the spending by adopting a simple majority resolution. If the executive wanted to *impound* funds to terminate or cut approved spending, he had to seek explicit congressional approval. If Congress failed to rescind the original appropriation within forty-five days, the president had to spend the money. As a control, the president also had to report all withholding of both types.

To increase its capability to deal with budget problems, Congress also established new budget committees in both houses to prepare tentative budget recommendations to be presented and adopted as concurrent resolutions every May. This would serve as an alternative to the presidential budget and allow Congress to initiate fiscal policy rather than merely respond to executive recommendations. To provide budget expertise comparable to that in the executive branch, the law created the Congressional Budget Office, with a full staff and the capacity to coordinate the various Senate and House committees. The target goals established by the concurrent resolution would serve other committees in evaluating and preparing program legislation. To adjust to the presidential budget, as well as to change economic conditions, Congress could pass a second concurrent resolution later in the year. How effective the new law would prove to be would not be known for a while, but like the War Powers Act, it marked a successful effort by Congress to reassert what it considered its legitimate authority vis-à-vis the executive branch.

Watergate

In setting executive power against legislative power, Richard Nixon followed the path of his modern predecessors in testing the limits of presidential authority. He claimed more than they did—far more—and eventually he forced Congress to stiffen its resistance and reclaim some of the powers it had lost or delegated to the executive branch over the previous forty years. For the most part, even those members of Congress who opposed Nixon's policies and denied his arguments for unlimited presidential power saw this conflict as within the broad parameters of the political and constitutional process. But then came the Watergate scandal, and as Senator Ervin's committee uncovered details of White House abuse of power, a consensus developed that Nixon had gone beyond the limits of acceptable presidential behavior.

The story of Watergate must be seen as part of Nixon's broader efforts to aggrandize the powers of the presidency, in which he ignored not only Congress but also the law. His claims for unlimited discretion in foreign affairs and in the impoundment dispute and his efforts to bypass Congress by unilaterally canceling programs through the pocket veto all reflected his belief that the president of the United States had been endowed by the Framers with absolute authority. In the debates over his nomination of G. Harrold Carswell to the Supreme Court, Nixon several times spoke of himself as "the one person entrusted by the Constitution with the power of appointment," and totally ignored the very specific words of Article II, Section 2, that the president only had the power of *nomination,* which required the "Advice and Consent of the Senate."

Still, the Watergate scandal did not arise from any of Nixon's public acts or pronouncements, but from the clandestine activities he had approved. Always fearful of conspiracies and of reporters, Nixon attempted early in his administration to plug leaks of confidential information to the press. Previous presidents had used the FBI for security work, and its chief, J. Edgar Hoover, had not been unwilling to have the bureau collect political intelligence as well. Nixon, however, did not trust Hoover or the bureau, so in July 1970, he approved a secret memorandum by White House aide Tom Huston for comprehensive surveillance of all Americans who "pose a major threat to our internal security." The plan envisaged warrantless searches of mail; infiltration by secret government agents into allegedly subversive student groups; the monitoring of overseas mail, cable, and telephone calls; and, if necessary, burglaries of private homes and offices. Unhappy over disclosures in the press of information about supposedly secret conversations, Nixon also ordered warrantless taps on the phones of more than a dozen members of the National Security Council, as well as those of several newspaper reporters.

The Huston program so obviously violated the Constitution that any president, much less one who had been a practicing lawyer, should have denounced it on the spot and fired the person who proposed it. Even J. Edgar Hoover, who had never been regarded as particularly sensitive to civil liberties, condemned it as illegal. Nixon decided not to implement the full plan, but he did permit parts of it, including mail searches and occasional break-ins. Needless to say, he had absolutely no statutory authority for any of this.

The publication of the so-called *Pentagon Papers* in 1971 seemingly confirmed the administration's worst fears about security leaks. The Pentagon had undertaken an extensive review of the decisions leading to American involvement in Vietnam, and Daniel Ellsberg, an antiwar civilian employee, had copied the report and sent it to *The New York Times* and other major newspapers. Soon after, the president established a special White House unit—known later as "the Plumbers"—with the authority to engage in any espionage it considered necessary to protect national security interests. The

Plumbers embarked on a series of escapades that, if they had not been so blatantly illegal, might have become comic opera. Within a few months, the White House staff dissolved the unit, fearful that exposure of its antics could harm Nixon in his campaign for reelection. But the Plumbers remained available, and the White House hired some of them to work for the Committee to Re-elect the President (CREEP), the agency Nixon and his aides had created to bypass the Republican National Committee. It was a CREEP unit that attempted to break in to the Democratic National Committee headquarters in Washington's Watergate apartment complex on June 17, 1972, seeking information that might be damaging to the Democratic candidate, George McGovern. The bungling of that burglary led to the eventual resignation of Richard Nixon from office.

Although George McGovern tried to make campaign issues of the Watergate burglary, the cloudy finances of CREEP, the administration's disregard of civil liberties, and Nixon's usurpation of power, he could not interest the electorate in any of these matters. Not until after the election did allegations about a White House connection to the burglary and millions of dollars in money laundered by CREEP begin to catch public attention—thanks in large measure to the investigative work of two *Washington Post* reporters, Bob Woodward and Carl Bernstein, and the insistence of District Judge John J. Sirica that the Watergate burglars had not told the whole story at their trial. In February 1973, the Senate appointed a select committee chaired by Sam Ervin of North Carolina to look into alleged illegal activities during the 1972 campaign.

Within a short time, Watergate became a national obsession, grabbing the morning's headlines and dominating the evening news. Former attorney general John Mitchell acknowledged that he had met with the conspirators before the break-in, although he claimed to have opposed the plan. L. Patrick Gray III, acting director of the FBI, had to resign after he admitted destroying documents related to the case on orders from the White House. Information about White House espionage plans, as well as about presidential finances, became public. Nixon had falsely dated a gift of papers to the National Archives to secure tax deductions, had been negligent on his tax returns, and had used government money to improve his homes in Key Biscayne and San Clemente. "It's beginning to be like Teapot Dome," declared an astonished Barry Goldwater, a conservative ally of Nixon.

At first, the president tried to ignore the allegations, and the White House staff maligned efforts to link them or Nixon to "this grubby business." Then on April 18, 1973, the president referred to Watergate for the first time and claimed that an internal investigation had cleared everyone presently employed in the White House. Less than two weeks later, Haldeman, Ehrlichman, and Attorney General Richard Kleindienst all resigned. In a nationally televised address, Nixon declared his own innocence in a speech that even his supporters could not help but describe as obfuscating and self-serving.

Whatever the public thought of Richard Nixon's guilt or innocence at this time, the president did little to help his reputation by attempting to block the work of the Senate Select Committee. Ervin, the avuncular but highly respected senator from North Carolina, opened the public phase of his investigation on May 17, 1973. Every day, the nationally televised hearings brought new and astounding evidence of other burglaries, illegal wiretaps, laundered money, blackmail, and intimations that the White House, indeed the president himself, had known about and had authorized grossly illegal activities. In early July, White House aide Alexander Butterfield inadvertently revealed the existence of a secret tape recorder in the Oval Office that taped the president's private conversations. Nixon, who had so often ignored the right of privacy of others, had bugged himself, and in the end, it would be his undoing. As Nixon well knew, the tapes connected him to Watergate, and he embarked on a desperate struggle to keep them out of the hands of congressional investigators.

Executive Privilege

Watergate involved not only violations of criminal law and unethical behavior by government officials; at its highest level, it raised important constitutional questions about executive privilege and the nature of the impeachment power. From the first, Nixon had attempted to thwart the work of the investigators by denying the Senate committee access to executive branch employees who might have relevant information. Attorney General Kleindienst, before his resignation, claimed that the president could bar any of the 2.5 million employees of the executive agencies from testifying before Congress. Unable to sustain this implausible argument, the administration retreated to what it considered the more defensible grounds that executive privilege allowed a president to withhold documents from the legislative and judicial branches.

History provided numerous incidents of chief executives refusing to turn over certain papers to Congress. Washington had first asserted this privilege in 1792, when the House of Representatives had wanted to examine materials in the president's possession relating to General St. Clair's defeat by the Ohio Indians; a few years later, he refused to produce documents relating to Jay's Treaty. Jefferson actually defied a subpoena during the Burr trial. Harry Truman had ignored a House resolution, saying that he would determine which, if any, papers he would deliver to Congress or its committees. Most presidents claimed, and legitimately so, that their effectiveness in executing sensitive matters would be compromised unless they could assure those with whom they dealt of confidentiality. For its part, the Congress asserted that its investigatory power extended into any area relating to the public interest. Dwight Eisenhower was the first to use the actual phrase "executive privilege," and its existence or extent, especially vis-à-vis the legitimate claims of the other branches, had never been adjudicated. Most commentators considered this a political question of the purest sort, one that should be resolved directly between Congress and the president, and not by the courts.

During the Watergate hearings, presidential representatives constantly claimed executive privilege in refusing to produce documents. Once the existence of the tapes was revealed, however, the Ervin Committee knew that the tapes could provide evidence that could finally prove—or disprove—a connection between Nixon and the Watergate burglary. When the president refused to hand over five tapes on grounds of executive privilege, the committee sought a *subpoena duces tecum,* ordering Nixon to hand the tapes over to committee investigators. Judge Sirica, however, denied the request, and upheld the president's claim of executive privilege in withholding documents from Congress.

Under prodding from the Ervin Committee, Nixon had agreed in May 1973 to establish the Office of Special Prosecutor to investigate allegations of misconduct in the executive branch. After Kleindienst's resignation, the president had named Elliot L. Richardson as attorney general, and Richardson recommended his old teacher,

Archibald L. Cox of the Harvard Law School, as special prosecutor. Armed with a broad mandate to discover the truth behind Watergate and with a pledge from Nixon that he would have "complete independence," Cox began his work. Cox soon determined that he would have to examine White House tapes of certain conversations; when Nixon refused to release them, he secured a *subpoena duces tecum,* directing the president to deliver the tapes to a grand jury. When Nixon refused, Cox went into federal court, and this time Judge Sirica ordered the president to comply with the subpoena. By now desperate to avoid producing the tapes, the president appealed to the circuit court, invoking executive privilege and claiming that Sirica's order "threatened the continued existence of the presidency as a functioning institution."

In October, the circuit court decided against the president, in *Nixon v. Sirica,* and directed him to produce the tapes. The 5 to 2 majority ruled that while executive privilege existed, it did not provide blanket coverage for all presidential documents: In a variation of the *Marbury* question of "who decides who decides," the circuit court declared that the judiciary would determine in what circumstances executive privilege shielded documents and when it did not. In response to an implied threat that the president, representing a coequal branch of government, was not amenable to judicial process, the majority insisted that a president, like anyone else, remained "legally" bound by an order enforcing a subpoena, even if a court lacked physical power to enforce its decision. "The courts in this country always assume that their orders will be obeyed, especially when addressed to responsible government officials."

Nixon now tried to deal with Cox, promising him summaries of the nine tapes in question, but the special prosecutor refused. The president then ordered Cox, as an employee of the executive branch, to cease his efforts to secure the tapes through court orders. Cox called a press conference and pointed out that the president of the United States, the chief law enforcement official of the country, had refused to carry out a direct order of a federal court. An exasperated Nixon ordered Attorney General Richardson to fire Cox; Richardson refused and resigned in protest; the assistant attorney general, William Ruckelshaus, followed suit. Finally, the solicitor general, Robert Bork, carried out the presidential directive.

Technically, Nixon may have been well within his rights to fire an employee of the executive branch, a power that the Supreme Court had upheld in the *Myers* case nearly a half-century earlier. But the "Saturday Night Massacre"—as the firing and resignations were dubbed by the press—destroyed Nixon's pledge of an independent investigation. Many Americans who had been willing to take the president's word on his innocence now had second thoughts. For the first time, a majority of the country suspected that Richard Nixon had indeed been involved in the Watergate scandal. The House of Representatives soon after began looking into whether grounds existed for impeachment. Meanwhile, in the face of the public uproar over the firing of Cox, Nixon named a new special prosecutor, Leon Jaworski of Texas.

Spiro Agnew Departs

Until then, Nixon had felt fairly immune from impeachment, believing that Congress did not want Vice President Spiro Agnew in the White House. Agnew had been the hatchetman for Nixon in two campaigns, lashing out at "effete, impudent intellectuals," "ideological eunuchs," and the "tiny and closed fraternity of privileged men" of the network news programs. Few people believed Agnew capable of serving as president. Then on October 10, Agnew resigned.

Attorney General Richardson had earlier informed Agnew that the Justice Department had evidence that would likely lead to his indictment for income tax evasion. Agnew had then asked congressional leaders to seek his impeachment in order to test his guilt or innocence, and he put forward the questionable constitutional claim that a vice president enjoyed immunity to ordinary criminal process. When the House leaders refused, Richardson worked out a bargain in which Agnew pleaded *nolo contendere,* tantamount to a confession of guilt. To evade a jail sentence, Agnew also agreed to resign the vice presidency.

Agnew's departure triggered the first use of the Twenty-fifth Amendment, which had been ratified in 1967 and had resulted in part from John Kennedy's assassination. (Lyndon Johnson had served without a vice president from November 1963 to January 1965.) Under its terms, when a vacancy occurred in the vice presidency, "the President shall nominate a Vice President who shall take office upon confirmation by a majority vote of both Houses of Congress." Nixon named Gerald Ford of Michigan, the lackluster minority leader of the House, who enjoyed a reputation for personal integrity as well as the respect of his colleagues. Congress confirmed him without difficulty within a few weeks.

For the next several months, the country underwent the agony of watching the Senate committee uncover more bizarre stories and more evidence linking Nixon to the scandals. The president, in the meantime, declared his innocence on the one hand, while trying to thwart all efforts to reach the truth on the other. On television, Senator Howard Baker of Tennessee asked one witness after another, "What did the president know and when did he know it?" In his State of the Union message in January 1974, Nixon tried to tough it out. "One year of Watergate is enough," he told the country; he urged Congress and the people to pay attention to more important business. He also assured them that he had "no intention of walking away from the job that the American people elected me to do." In April, the White House released hundreds of pages of tape transcriptions that, although carefully edited, shocked the nation by their depiction of the gutter mentality of the president and his men. If Nixon had hoped that the transcripts would clear his name, he soon found out otherwise.

United States v. Nixon

On March 1, 1974, a federal grand jury indicted former Attorney General John Mitchell, White House aides Haldeman and Ehrlichman, and four other members of the president's staff or employees of CREEP on various charges of conspiracy to defraud the United States and to obstruct justice. (Ultimately, twenty-five members of the Nixon administration would go to prison.) The grand jury named Richard Nixon, the president of the United States, as an unindicted coconspirator. On April 18, the new special prosecutor, Leon Jaworski, as part of the prosecution against Mitchell, sought a *subpoena duces tecum* from Judge Sirica, directing the president to produce certain documents and tapes. The president provided only edited transcripts of the tapes and then moved to quash the subpoena on grounds of executive privilege. The district court denied the motion, and the president appealed to the circuit court. Because of what he termed the public importance of the issues, Jaworski took the unusual step of asking the Supreme Court to grant certiorari immediately; he argued that whichever side lost in the circuit court would appeal, and the public needed to have the question settled as quickly as possible.

On July 24, 1974, Chief Justice Warren Burger spoke for a unanimous bench in *United States v. Nixon* (Justice Rehnquist did not participate). He declared that the president had to obey the special prosecutor's subpoena. Nixon had argued the nonjusticiability of the case, claiming that courts had no jurisdiction in a dispute between the president and a member of the executive branch; he had also raised the defense of executive privilege. While admitting that a conditional privilege existed, Burger denied that the president had blanket coverage. As the lower court had ruled earlier in *Nixon v. Sirica,* Burger said that the courts would decide which materials could ultimately be retained under executive privilege. The rule of law, however, required courts to balance this "presumptive privilege" against the need to protect the integrity of the criminal justice system.

Resignation

In the meantime, the House Judiciary Committee began hearings to determine whether Nixon's activities constituted impeachable offenses. As in the earlier case of Andrew Johnson, no clear answer existed as to what Article I, Section 4 meant when it listed "other high Crimes and Misdemeanors." Restudy of the Johnson case, however, had led many scholars to dismiss the older argument that a president or other federal official could be impeached only for an indictable criminal offense. Rather than viewing impeachment as a form of judicial process, which required the full panoply of criminal procedure, rules of evidence, and the like, they claimed that the Framers had intended impeachment as a political measure. It provided a constitutional safety valve when political misconduct, even if not criminal, exceeded the bounds of acceptable behavior and threatened to wreck the system. Andrew Johnson had done nothing criminal; yet he had paralyzed the government of the United States in its Reconstruction policy by his refusal to accept the will of Congress expressed through duly enacted legislation. President Nixon's lawyers argued just the opposite, that only a criminally indictable offense could warrant impeachment. Many allegations had been made about Nixon's behavior, but the president had broken no law. "Where," they asked, "is the smoking gun?"

The House Judiciary Committee had begun hearings on the possibility of impeachment in April 1974, but had been reluctant to act in the absence of hard evidence. The Supreme Court handed down its decision in *United States v. Nixon* on July 24, and three days later, the committee voted out three articles of impeachment against the president. Article I charged Nixon with obstructing the administration of justice in violation of his constitutional duty to see that the laws were faithfully executed; it reflected bipartisan anger and disgust over Nixon's involvement in Watergate. Article II focused on the president's abuse of power, including his use of the Internal Revenue

Service, FBI, and CIA to harass citizens, as well as the activities of the Plumbers, all of which "violate the Constitutional rights of citizens, impair the due and proper administration of justice . . . [and] contravene the laws governing agencies of the executive branch."

Article III proved the most questionable from a constitutional point of view. It charged that the president had violated his oath of office by refusing to produce documents in response to subpoenas from the House Judiciary committee on four separate occasions. By this action, Nixon,

> substituting his judgment as to what materials were necessary for the inquiry, interposed the powers of the Presidency against the lawful subpoenas of the House of Representatives, thereby assuming to himself functions and judgments necessary to the exercise of the sole power of impeachment vested by the Constitution in the House of Representatives.

This article carried fewer votes than did the first two, because in *United States v. Nixon,* the Court had acknowledged the existence of executive privilege (which the president had claimed as the basis for withholding materials from Congress) and had avoided ruling on the dispute between the executive and legislative branches. Moreover, the committee had voted 32 to 6 not to go to court in an effort to enforce the subpoenas.

When talk of impeachment began, Nixon received strong support from party loyalists. But one of the tapes Nixon had been forced to turn over to Jaworski on order of the Supreme Court showed him deeply implicated in the Watergate cover-up from the very beginning. On June 23, 1972, the president had directed his aides to use the Central Intelligence Agency (CIA) to terminate the Watergate investigation. News of this came shortly after the House Judiciary Committee recommended impeachment, and these same loyalists now privately advised the president to resign, based on their belief that the full House of Representatives would certainly impeach him and that the Senate would most likely convict. By early August, Nixon had lost almost all Repub-

> Using the powers of the office of President of the United States, Richard M. Nixon, in violation of his constitutional oath faithfully to execute the office of President of the United States, and to the best of his ability preserve, protect and defend the Constitution of the United States, and in disregard of his constitutional duty to take care that the laws be faithfully executed, has repeatedly engaged in conduct violating the constitutional rights of citizens, impairing the due and proper administration of justice in the conduct of lawful inquiries, of contravening the law of governing agencies in the executive branch and the purposes of these agencies. . . .
>
> [List of specific violations follows]
>
> In all of this Richard M. Nixon has acted in a manner contrary to his trust as President and subversive of constitutional government to the great prejudice of the cause of law and justice and to the manifest injury of the people of the United States.
>
> Wherefore, Richard M. Nixon by such conduct warrants impeachment and trial and removal from office.
>
> —Impeachment Article II, Adopted by House Judiciary Committee, 24 July 1974

lican support in Congress after he released tapes showing he know about and participated in the Watergate cover-up. On August 8, 1974, Richard Milhouse Nixon resigned as president, and Gerald Ford took office as the thirty-eighth president, the first not to be elected in his own right as president or vice president. "I am acutely aware," he told the American people the next day, "that I have received the votes of none of you." He promised an open and candid administration and proclaimed that "our long national nightmare is over." Such optimism proved somewhat premature, but it was a good beginning.

The Lessons of Watergate

Watergate put immense strain on the Constitution and the political system, because Richard Nixon, like Andrew Johnson, ignored the rules. Some historians have defended Johnson's views on Reconstruction policy; there are those who now praise Nixon for some parts of his foreign and domestic programs and are even sympathetic to his views on relations between the executive and legislative branches. But it is unlikely that anyone will applaud his shameful role in the Watergate scandals, his perversion of governmental agencies to serve narrow personal and partisan purposes, or his degradation of the office of the presidency.

The constitutional system survived and may even have been strengthened by the ordeal. Congress, which had already started to reassert its authority, began its investigations reluctantly, unwilling to believe that the man who held the nation's highest office had engaged in criminal activities. But once begun, Sam Ervin's Senate committee and Peter Rodino's House Judiciary Committee acted diligently and with a keen sense of history and propriety. The openness of the inquiry impressed many normally anti-American critics abroad, who contrasted the public airing and ultimate cleansing of dirty laundry with the cynicism and repression they saw at home.

There are several lessons that can be gleaned from the Watergate affair. First, the hearings showed that investigations are an essential part of legislative responsibility. The Supreme Court had recognized this earlier in *Watkins v. United States* (1957), when it held that "the power of the Congress to conduct investigations is inherent in the legislative process. That power is broad. . . . It comprehends probes into departments of the federal Government to expose corruption, inefficiency or waste." But, as Chief Justice Warren had then noted, it is not an unlimited power. Congress must play by the rules and obey the strictures of procedural due process.

Another lesson of Watergate was the limited nature of congressional investigation. The subpoena power, for example, is effective when directed at ordinary citizens, but how far will it carry into the executive branch? For the most part, lower officials agreed to heed the subpoenas, but when Alexander Butterfield balked at testifying in public, Senator Ervin reportedly sent him a message: "Tell Mr. Butterfield that if he is not here this afternoon, I will send the sergeant at arms to fetch him." Butterfield appeared, much to everyone's relief, since as Senator Baker noted, the sergeant at arms could not have got past the White House gate.

Senate Resolution 60, establishing the Select Committee, authorized it to subpoena "any . . . officer . . . of the executive branch of the United States Government." The Nixon administration denied that the committee could subpoena a president, but Senate Resolution 194, as well as a district court decision (*Nader v. Butz* [1974]) held otherwise. Still, it is unclear whether such a subpoena can be enforced and whether the courts will intervene. The reluctance regarding the third impeachment article stemmed from uncertainty over whether one branch of the government could exercise such power over another. Both Judge Sirica and Chief Justice Burger supported, at least in part, a claim of executive privilege against the legislature; only when Nixon defied the judiciary did the courts declare that he had to obey the subpoenas.

Executive privilege proved the most controversial and least understood of all the Watergate issues. Law professor Raoul Berger, the most pugnacious of the commentators, declared flat out that executive privilege was a "myth," with no foundation in the Constitution, which had been created only by unchallenged actions of successive presidents. The Court disagreed, as we have seen, and so have most scholars. Even ardent champions of the legislature concede at least a limited protection of executive privacy.

The Constitution, it is true, does not mention executive privilege, but neither does it mention judicial review or the power of Congress to investigate. All have evolved through usage. If a constitutional justification is necessary, one could argue that the general grant of the executive or legislative or judicial authority subsumes all the normal powers and responsibilities necessary to carry out those functions. Common sense, as well as historical usage, support the necessity for confidentiality in several instances. Discussions between a president and his advisers, if they are to be candid, should be assured privacy. Military and diplomatic information should also be limited to only those with official responsibility. But what about general information that, if made public, might prove inconvenient or embarrassing to the president and his staff? Is there a "right" of either Congress or the public to know about this material for its own sake? There are certainly no constitutional or statutory grounds either to admit or deny access; perhaps the best argument one can make is that without access, there is no congressional oversight and no accountability of key White House figures, who are neither elected nor confirmed by the Senate. A little more than a decade later, these issues would appear again in the Iran-Contra scandal.

In 1971, upset by the Nixon administration's refusal to inform Congress of its military operations in Southeast Asia, the Senate Subcommittee on Separation of Powers had held hearings on executive privilege. The bill it produced called for the executive agencies to provide any data that Congress demanded "unless executive privilege is invoked" by the president in writing, with reasons why the material should not be produced. A number of senators also suggested that if the legislative and executive branches came to an impasse, the matter should be referred to the courts for arbitration. Fortunately, this proposal quickly died; if it had been enacted, it would have put the courts in an untenable situation. One should recall that in most instances, a request from a congressional committee is respected by the executive agencies or by the White House; the problem arises only in the relatively few cases when the president, for whatever reasons, believes that Congress should not have access.

The courts consistently refused to enforce congressional subpoenas against the president. The select committee got nothing it requested when it resorted to the courts, nor did the committee really expect the courts to enforce its requests; to have done so would have plunged the judiciary into a political battle from which it could not hope to emerge unscathed. The doctrine of separation of powers is not precise, and little in the way of history or law can serve as guideposts to delimit executive or legislative powers when they come into conflict. There is no doubt that Congress could have conferred jurisdiction on the courts to determine such issues; that it would have been wise to do so is questionable.

On the other hand, the courts gave the special prosecutor nearly everything he wanted, because, although technically within the executive branch, he served as an officer of the law and therefore as a representative of the judiciary's commitment to justice. In a conflict of wills between Congress and president, the issue of justice might be confused by partisanship; between the president and the special prosecutor, especially one as respected as Archibald Cox or Leon Jaworski, there could be no question but that the courts would enforce the criminal process. The president, as the chief law enforcement official in the country, could not claim to be above the law. Nevertheless, like Congress, the federal courts had no real power over the president; the bailiff of the court would have had no more chance of getting through the White House gate than the Senate's sergeant at arms. The courts put their prestige on the line, gambling that the president would not dare ignore their orders while attempting to portray himself as an honest man.

The judiciary emerged the stronger for the ordeal. In the extremely delicate question of executive privilege, it confirmed the existence of a presidential right, but then arrogated the power to determine if and to what extent the privilege could be invoked. What is lost in the turmoil over Watergate is the fact that in *United States v. Nixon,* the Supreme Court established a certain hegemony over the executive branch comparable to what it had achieved in *Powell v. McCormack*: it would decide the critical question of "who decides who decides."

The great unanswered question about Watergate concerned impeachment. Nixon did the country and himself a great favor by resigning rather than forcing a national trauma of impeachment and trial. There is general agreement that the House would have voted one or more articles of impeachment, and with the production of the smoking gun, the Senate would probably have convicted. But on what grounds? The debate in 1974 repeated many of the questions raised when the Jeffersonians attacked the courts and when Andrew Johnson stood trial—namely, does impeachment require criminal action, or can it also serve as a safety valve for political malfeasance? Two decades later, a president would be impeached for alleged moral misconduct and for obstructionist tactics in a civil law suit.

Despite the claims of Nixon's attorneys and some less-involved commentators that only an indictable offense justifies removal, there is abundant evidence that the Framers meant impeachment to serve as a solution to a political impasse as well. The Constitution specifically provides that the penalty shall be removal from office—a political punishment—and allows further prosecution for criminality, wholly apart from impeachment and removal. The nineteenth-century English legal historian F. W. Maitland argued that the English constitution allowed Parliament to make impeachable offenses mean whatever the members want them to mean, and the Founding Fathers certainly had the English practice in mind when drafting the American procedure.

Some scholars suggest that revulsion against his criminal acts drove Nixon from office, and that as a result, the indictable offense theory has gained the upper hand, at least temporarily. Such a conclusion may be unwarranted, since the full extent of Nixon's perversion of executive agencies did not become fully known until after his resignation.

The "Plebiscitary Presidency"

A final note on the significance of Watergate involves the so-called plebiscitary presidency. Attempting to provide some sort of rationale for the Nixon presidency, some scholars have suggested that Nixon found the old constitutional system of checks and balances inadequate to provide the majority with legitimate representation in government. Congress, fragmented among numerous interest groups, had lost the will to govern and surrendered or delegated its most important powers to the executive. Thus the government of the United States now resided in the presidency. A model could be found in the France of Louis Napoleon or Charles De Gaulle, both of whom assumed near-dictatorial power on behalf of and with the blessing of the people. So long as the leader has the backing of a majority, he can do no wrong and cannot be held to any other standard than popular approval.

Nixon himself seemed to agree with this view. In his famous television interview with David Frost in 1977, Nixon announced that the president can do no wrong! He claimed that actions that might be criminal when committed by others are legal when committed by the president or by those acting under his orders for the sake of the general good. Some liberal political analysts had been pointing in this direction for a long time, although they never claimed that a president could wantonly break the law. They approved a strong presidency as being necessary for democratic societies in the modern age—but they had a Franklin Roosevelt or a John Kennedy in mind, not a Richard Nixon. The presidency is, after all, the only office that can claim to speak for all the American people, and reformers had long argued that only a strong president could effectively translate the national will into action. Such assumptions, of course, relied on a noble, or at least an honest, president, as well as some form of accountability to prevent the abuse of power. Congress, therefore, would serve less as a coequal branch helping to develop national policy than as a check to keep the president from overstepping the very broad parameters of executive power.

The plebiscitary president may well be necessary in a modern society; possibly some aspects of the constitutional system, such as congressional declarations of war, are outmoded in an age of intercontinental ballistic missiles. It may also be that the modern political system places greater responsibility, as well as the burden of leadership, in the presidency than in Congress. But if nothing else, Watergate demonstrated that the system works only as well as the people who occupy the nation's highest offices. Nixon, Mitchell, and Kleindienst debased their offices; Sam Ervin, Archibald Cox, and Elliot Richardson fulfilled the trust placed in them. For a while it seemed as if the system had broken down, but in the end, it proved to be far more resilient than many people had suspected.

For Further Reading

The literature on Nixon continues to grow, but a good balanced biography is Herbert S. Parmet, *Richard Nixon and His America* (1990). Garry Wills, *Nixon Agonistes* (1970), and Allen Drury, *Courage and Hesitation: Inside the Nixon Administration* (1972), were both written before the scandals erupted. For a defense of his policies and actions, see *RN: The Memoirs of Richard Nixon* (1978).

The expansion of executive power is detailed in William M. Goldsmith, *The Growth of Presidential Power: A Documented History*. 3 vols. (1974). Warren W. Hassler, Jr., *The President as Commander in Chief* (1971), provides a brief overview of how various presidents from Washington to Nixon exercised this power. For a broader context, see Louis Fisher, *Presidential War Power* (1995); and David Gray Adler and Larry N. George, eds., *The Constitution and the Conduct of American Foreign Policy* (1996). The sources on Vietnam that are cited in Chapter 38 are relevant here as well, as is John Norton Moore's brief in support of presidential policy, *Law and the Indo-China War* (1972).

For the struggle over control of spending, see Howard E. Schuman, *Politics and the Budget: The Struggle Between the President and the Congress* (3rd ed., 1992). Louis Fisher, *Presidential Spending Power* (1975), claimed that a variety of schemes such as impoundment had effectively shifted budgetary control to the executive and administrative agencies. See also Warren Archer, "Presidential Impoundment of Funds," 40 *University of Chicago Law Review* 328 (1973). The pocket veto is well analyzed in John W. Dumbrell and John D. Lees, "Presidential Pocket-Veto Power: A Constitutional Anachronism?" *28 Political Studies* 109 (1980).

The literature on Watergate is large and still growing. The best book on the subject is Stanley I. Kutler, *The Wars of Watergate: The Last Crisis of Richard Nixon* (1990); along with this, see the documents Kutler has collected in *Watergate: The Fall of Richard M. Nixon* (1996). Earlier but still useful works include two books by the reporters who broke the story in the *Washington Post,* Robert Woodward and Carl Bernstein, *All the President's Men* (1974), and *The Final Days* (1976); as well as Theodore H. White, *Breach of Faith* (1975). The impact of the scandal on the presidency is examined in Thomas E. Cronin, *The State of the Presidency* (1975). Constitutional aspects are analyzed in Philip S. Kurland, *Watergate and the Constitution* (1978), and Ralph K. Winter, *Watergate and the Law: Political Campaigns and Presidential Power* (1974).

James Hamilton, *The Power to Probe: A History of Congressional Investigations* (1976) is weak on history, but as the assistant chief counsel to the Ervin committee, Hamilton provides a fine account of its activities. Another useful first-hand account is Leon Jaworski, *The Right and the Power: The Prosecution of Watergate* (1976). An excellent symposium on the Supreme Court case is "*United States v. Nixon*: Presidential Power and Executive Privilege Twenty-Five Years Later," 83 *Minnesota Law Review* 1061 (May 1999). The question of executive privilege is also dealt with by Archibald Cox, "Executive Privilege," 122 *University of Pennsylvania Law Review* 1383 (1984); and Paul A. Freund, "Foreword: On Presidential Privilege," 88 *Harvard Law Review* 13 (1974); Raoul Berget's study, *Executive Privilege: A Constitutional Myth* (1974), often becomes polemical. One should also see U.S. Senate, Committee on the Judiciary, Subcommittee on Separation of Powers, *Executive Privilege: The Withholding of Information by the Executive* (1971).

The renewed controversy over the criteria for impeachment is examined in Michael J. Gerhardt, *The Federal Impeachment Process: A Constitutional and Historical Analysis* (1996); Raoul Berger, *Impeachment: The Constitutional Problem* (1973); Charles L. Black, Jr., *Impeachment: A Handbook* (1974); and John R. Labovitz, *Presidential Impeachment* (1978). Presidential abuse of power did not, of course, start with Nixon; see Barton J. Bernstein, "The Road to Watergate and Beyond: The Growth and Abuse of Executive Power since 1940," 40 *Law & Contemporary Problems* 58 (1976); and Victor Navasky's muckraking polemic, *It Didn't Start with Watergate* (1977).

The resurgence of Congress triggered by Johnson and Nixon is examined in James L. Sundquist, *The Decline and Resurgence of Congress* (1981); and Harvey Mansfield, ed., *Congress Against the President* (1976).

40

The Burger Court and Equal Protection

The Burger Court Forms • Continuing Desegregation • Busing • Desegregation in the North • Bakke *and Affirmative Action • Gender Discrimination • The Equal Rights Amendment • Poverty and Disability • The Abortion Decisions • Post-*Roe *Decisions • For Further Reading*

IN 1968, RICHARD Nixon had campaigned as much against the Warren Court as against his Democratic opponent, pledging to remake the Court into a more conservative institution, one supporting the "peace forces" rather than the criminals. Nixon filled four seats on the bench, and Gerald Ford another one; all five of the new justices easily met conservative criteria. Yet the Burger Court did not overthrow the major doctrinal decisions of its predecessor. The Court made some modifications here, retrenched a little there, and advanced in other areas. The men Nixon appointed struck down state abortion laws; restricted capital punishment; fought gender discrimination, and during the Watergate crisis, told the president that they, not he, would decide when and if executive privilege applied. But Warren Burger proved unable to do one thing that Earl Warren had done so well—mass the Court. In its major decisions, and in many of its less important cases as well, the Court spoke with a multitude of voices, creating confusion about exactly what it meant.

Scholars have had difficulty assessing the Burger Court because contradictions abound. What might be said is that in large part these inconsistencies resulted from the fact that the Burger Court inherited the problems that the Warren Court had created. In many ways, the Warren Court had the easy cases, both in the area of equal protection as well as civil liberties. By the 1950s, few Americans outside the South could justify a system of state-sponsored racial segregation, and the cases the Court heard in the Warren years had a relatively easy framework. Did a law cause or support racial discrimination? If so, then the statute would be struck down as a violation of the Fourteenth Amendment's Equal Protection Clause. But once past this level, once the Court began grappling with secondary effects, then the justices found no easy answers, and the disarray and multiple voices in their decisions reflected the confusion over these matters in the larger society. In addition, the Warren Court steadfastly refused to get involved in questions of gender discrimination; by the 1970s, no court could evade that issue.

The Burger Court Forms

Nixon took office in January 1969, knowing that he had one vacancy already in hand, since Earl Warren had announced that he would step down in June, at the end of the term. The president chose as the new chief justice Warren Earl Burger of the Court of Appeals for the District of Columbia. The D.C. Circuit is the most visible and arguably the most important of the circuit courts, since by law and location many of the cases challenging government rulings go there. In the 1960s, under Chief Judge David L. Bazelon, it also had a reputation as one of the most liberal of the federal courts. Burger, an Eisenhower appointee, had caught the attention of newspapers, as well as conservatives by his vocal law-and-order dissents against what he considered to be liberal judicial activism. The president saw in Burger the tough-minded, firm, yet fair type of conservative that he had promised to appoint to the bench. Newspaper columnist James Reston characterized Burger as "experienced, industrious, middle-class, middle-aged, middle-of-the-road, Middle-Western, Presbyterian, orderly, and handsome," all of which, in Nixon's view, made Burger the ideal person to head the nation's highest court. Despite fears that liberals would try to torpedo the nomination, the Senate judiciary committee approved Warren Burger unanimously on June 3, and the full chamber confirmed his nomination four days later by a vote of 74 to 3.

The president had more difficulty filling the seat Abe Fortas had vacated. Nixon had courted Southern votes during the election by strongly implying that the federal government would ease off in its enforcement of civil rights legislation and that he would appoint conservative judges sympathetic to the Southern view. The president first named South Carolinian Clement F. Haynsworth, Jr., chief judge of the Court of Appeals for the Fourth Circuit. Several members of the Court, including Brennan and Black (who disagreed with his philosophy), thought Haynsworth would make a fine justice, given the solid reputation he had earned on the Fourth Circuit. But labor and civil rights groups attacked the nominee, citing what they depicted as a string of antiunion, anti-integration decisions. Moderate Republicans withdrew their support when they learned that Haynsworth had participated in a case that indirectly concerned a company in which he held stock. There had been no serious breach of ethics, but together with his poor testimony at the confirmation hearings, it led the Senate to reject him by a vote of 55 to 45 on November 21, 1969.

The following April, the Senate rejected Nixon's next appointee, G. Harrold Carswell of the Fifth Circuit, whom Burger had recommended to the president as a solid conservative worthy of promotion. Investigators discovered that Carswell had once declared that "segregation of the races is proper and the only practical and correct way of life in our states." Although he had later retracted this sentiment, researchers also learned that Carswell had been involved in an effort to use a federally financed public golf course as a private segregated club. Moreover, unlike Haynsworth, Carswell did not enjoy a good reputation in the legal community. The dean of the Yale Law School asserted that Carswell had "the most slender credentials" for the Court of any nominee in this century. Senator Roman Hruska of Nebraska dismissed these attacks by noting that "there are a lot of mediocre judges and lawyers, and they are entitled to a little representation, aren't they?" The Senate turned Carswell down, 51 to 45. An angry Nixon declared that he would not appoint another Southerner and "let him be subjected to this kind of malicious character assassination."

Over a year had now passed since the Fortas resignation, and the brethren still worked shorthanded. More than 200 petitions for certiorari had been put in a file marked for "Justice X." Since many of them already had three votes for review, the new justice would have an immediate impact on the Court's calendar by his decisions on whether to cast the fourth, decisive vote for review. Nixon finally found a judicial conservative whom he thought could get Senate confirmation, Harry A. Blackmun of the Eighth Circuit, an old friend of Warren Burger. Modest and soft-spoken, Blackmun had impeccable academic credentials, had practiced law for sixteen years, and had built a solid reputation as a moderate judge who believed in judicial restraint and strict construction of the Constitution.

Two years later, Hugo Black and John Marshall Harlan retired because of ill health, and Nixon named two more men whom he considered reliable conservatives. To fill Black's seat, Nixon turned to the South and chose Lewis F. Powell, Jr., a former president of the American Bar Association. Although some blacks protested the appointment, others testified on Powell's behalf about the efforts that he had made to ensure peaceful integration when he had been president of the Richmond School Board and the Virginia State Board of Education. Although personally opposed to integration, Powell had refused to go along with "massive resistance" and had managed to keep Richmond's schools open during the desegregation crisis. He thought the obstructionist tactics of Virginia's Byrd machine counterproductive, but more important, Powell believed in the rule of law. One might see Powell's role in the Virginia school crisis as evolutionary, in which he moved away from the old system of state-endorsed discrimination toward a realization that segregation could not be sustained on constitutional grounds. This evolutionary attitude would also mark Powell's career on the Court, and despite the president's characterization of Powell as a conservative, the nominee himself eschewed labels. "My views may be liberal on one issue and conservative on another," he told a reporter. He did, however, believe in judicial restraint, which, as he informed the Senate Judiciary Committee, derived from his having studied with Felix Frankfurter at Harvard Law School.

To fill Harlan's seat, Nixon chose assistant attorney general William H. Rehnquist, then only forty-seven years old. The administration expected that Rehnquist might face opposition in the Senate. He had provided legal justification for some of the more unpopular Nixon policies in crime control and civil rights, and unlike the moderate Powell, advocated a hard-line conservatism. Rehnquist had been a law clerk to Robert Jackson during the October 1953 term, and during the Court's consideration of *Brown v. Board of Education,* had written a memorandum urging Jackson not to overturn the *Plessy* decision. Rehnquist claimed that Jackson had asked him to argue that position in order to help him make up his mind, but later scholarship has suggested that this may not have been true. Despite some stiff questions at the committee hearings, however, the Senate approved Rehnquist only a few days after Powell.

Had Nixon not been forced to resign, he would have had another appointment to make in 1975, when the man he detested as the most liberal member of the Court, William O. Douglas, finally stepped down because of ill health, after a record tenure of thirty-six years. Gerald Ford, who had tried to impeach Douglas for alleged misconduct six years earlier, worried that the Democratic Senate might make the nomination a political issue. He knew that trying to replace the outspokenly liberal Douglas with a rigid conservative in an election year would only cause trouble. So he turned to a solid but noncontroversial federal judge, John Paul Stevens of the Seventh Circuit. As a practicing attorney, Stevens had been considered a lawyer's lawyer, and his supporters claimed that his reasoned opinions on the bench made him a judge's judge. Moreover, Stevens had neither partisan ties nor skeletons in the closet, and the Senate unanimously confirmed him.

No vacancies occurred on the high court for several more years, robbing Jimmy Carter of the opportunity to make any appointments to the Supreme Court, the only president elected in his own right to serve out a full term denied that chance. Rumor had it that Carter intended to appoint a woman, and his successor did. When Potter Stewart resigned in 1981, Ronald Reagan kept a campaign promise and named Sandra Day O'Connor, a state court judge from Arizona who had placed second to William Rehnquist at Stanford Law School. Although she had conservative economic views, some Republican senators considered her "too soft" on abortion and too much in favor of equal rights for women.

Thus the Burger Court took shape. With the appointment of Justice O'Connor, the bench appeared divided into three groups. The chief justice, along with Rehnquist and O'Connor (often joined by White) constituted the conservative bloc. Brennan and Marshall consistently supported the liberal tradition, while Powell, Blackmun, and Stevens (occasionally joined by White) held the middle position.

The greatest difference between the Court that sat from 1953 to 1969 and the one that followed it involved the occupant of the center chair. As chief justice, Earl Warren had led the Court and used his political skill to make the Court a potent voice in American life. Even when the Warren Court split on an issue, as it often did in the area of rights of the accused, one never had the sense of a fragmented bench. Warren Burger, although establishing better relations with Congress than did his predecessor, lacked the political acumen to lead the Court, and his colleagues often looked down on Burger as a judicial lightweight.

Far more than during Earl Warren's tenure, the Supreme Court divided in its decisions, and it became common to see three, four, or even five opinions in a case. The Court decided a number of important cases by 5 to 4 votes; in a large number of them, Lewis Powell cast the swing vote. The man who had told the Senate Judiciary Committee that he eschewed labels, that he could be liberal on some issues and conservative on others, had told the truth.

Continuing Desegregation

The Burger Court inherited a number of unresolved issues, especially the complex problem of desegregation. The Warren Court had moved from the "all deliberate speed" formula of *Brown II* to a demand for immediate results in *Green*, and a mark of its impatience with continued Southern delay had been the unusual step of suggesting specific remedies. In *United States v. Montgomery County Board of Education* (1969), one of the last Warren Court decisions, Justice Black set down guidelines to achieve racial mixes of faculty at each school that reflected the ratio of white to black teachers in the entire system. For the first time, the Court endorsed numerical goals as a remedy; it thus ushered in one of the more controversial issues of the 1970s—minimum racial quotas.

In the summer of 1969, while Warren Burger made plans to refurbish the Supreme Court building and to modernize its antiquated administrative system, Richard Nixon began to play out his Southern strategy. Secretary of Health, Education and Welfare Robert Finch wrote Chief Judge John Brown of the Fifth Circuit asking for a delay in desegregation rulings for thirty Mississippi school districts. On August 18, after a special appearance by the Justice Department in support of the request, the Fifth Circuit granted a three-month delay. The action sparked a revolt among government attorneys in the Civil Rights Division. In many cities, they refused to defend the Nixon policies, secretly passing information to civil rights attorneys working for the NAACP Legal Defense Fund.

The Fund appealed to the Supreme Court, and in *Alexander v. Holmes County Board of Education* (1969), the Court issued a one-paragraph *per curiam* order reversing the delay and admonishing the Fifth Circuit for granting it. "The obligation of every school district is to terminate dual school systems at once." When the Fifth Circuit, which had been quite diligent in enforcing desegregation, granted another delay to avoid disruption during the school year, the Supreme Court again reversed. Over the next ten months, the Fifth Circuit issued 166 desegregation orders in school cases, and no one could doubt the impact these had on schools. By 1971, 44 percent of black pupils were attending majority white schools in the South, compared with only 28 percent in the North and West. Unfortunately, *Alexander* also triggered what came to be known as "white flight," a mass exodus of white pupils from public to private schools, and from the cities to predominantly white suburbs. In some Mississippi districts, over 90 percent of white students left the public schools.

The midyear "integration now" order triggered some violence as well. In Lamar, South Carolina, a mob attacked two buses carrying black students to previous all-white schools; the children escaped only because of the quick action by the police. Segregationists used the Lamar incident to condemn the Court for interfering in the South's traditional way of life, but moderates compared the trouble to what had happened in Little Rock. There, Governor Faubus had winked at the resistance; in South Carolina, Governor Robert E. McNair did his duty and sent state police to protect blacks and enforce the law. But if reasonable Southern leaders stood ready to heed the law, questions still remained about just what the law required.

At least part of the answer came in the new chief justice's second term, when the Court handed down its last unanimous school segregation decision in *Swann v. Charlotte-Mecklenburg Board of Education* (1971). Prior cases had for the most part dealt with rural school districts, where blacks and whites lived in relatively close proximity and remedies could be easily devised. In the cities, school officials could claim that segregation resulted from residential patterns: children went to the schools that were

> The neighborhood school is not a constitutional requirement if departure from it is necessary to disestablish a segregated system. . . . Busing is not an impermissible tool.
>
> —Justice John Marshall Harlan, in conference discussion of *Swann* (1971

nearest to where they lived, and so all-black neighborhoods would have all-black schools even in the absence of state laws mandating segregation. This argument, of course, ignored decades of de jure segregation (required by law) and the fact that school boards had often gerrymandered district lines to ensure racially uniform schools—a form of de jure segregation, since it involved state action.

Speaking for the Court, Chief Justice Burger declared that current segregation resulted from past misconduct. He affirmed the district court's order requiring the school board not only to redraw attendance zones, but to bus students in order to achieve a racial mix at each school approximating the racial composition of the entire district. In a companion case, *North Carolina State Board of Education v. Swann* (1971), the Court invalidated North Carolina's antibusing statute, which prohibited school assignments on the basis of race; the Court ruled that such a racially "color-blind" law actually operated to prevent integration.

Busing

Busing, which affected Northern as well as Southern schools, urban as well as rural districts, proved an explosive issue. Mobs firebombed buses in Denver, Colorado, and Pontiac, Michigan, and parents boycotted schools in many districts. Congress bowed to white resistance by including in the Higher Education Act of 1972 a moratorium on court orders directed to "achieving a balance among students with respect to race, sex, religion, or socioeconomic status." In *Drummond v. Acree* (1972), however, Justice Powell as circuit justice, refused to stay a busing decree that he characterized as designed to end segregation and not to achieve a racial balance, dismissing the 1972 statute as inapplicable. If Congress had wanted to end busing, he noted, "it could have used clear and explicit language appropriate to that result."

Under President Nixon's prodding, Congress then enacted in the 1974 Educational Amendments a "priority of remedies" that federal courts and agencies could use to implement desegregation, and it barred any order requiring "the transportation of any student to a school other than the school closest or next closest to his place of residence." But the law also included a provision stating that nothing in it had been intended to diminish federal courts' authority to enforce the Fifth and Fourteenth amendments. Later on in the 1970s, Congress barred the use of federal funds to force desegregated school districts to bus students.

In 1982, the Court decided two cases involving state measures aimed at curbing mandatory busing. In *Washington v. Seattle School District No. 1*, a 5 to 4 majority struck down a state initiative law that prohibited school boards from requiring students to attend any school other than the nearest or next nearest to their homes (the law did not bar judicial orders requiring busing to eliminate de jure segregation). Justice Blackmun held that a majority could not use the machinery of government to place impediments in the path of minorities seeking equal rights, especially when such laws relied on racial classification. The initiative law, according to Blackmun, reallocated governmental power to the disadvantage of racial minorities.

That same day, Justice Powell, who had dissented in the *Seattle* case, wrote the 8 to 1 majority opinion in *Crawford v. Los Angeles Board of Education*, sustaining a California initiative prohibiting court-ordered busing to end de facto segregation. State courts had been active in trying to achieve full integration, even when there was no evidence of past discrimination on the part of the government. Proposition I limited the state courts' power to order busing to the same level that federal courts exercised under the Fourteenth Amendment. A state, Powell wrote, may do more than the Equal Protection Clause mandates, but it is only required to do no less. He rejected the argument that once a state had done more, it may not recede.

Desegregation in the North

By the time the Court heard these cases, it had been involved for a decade in the complex problem of racial segregation in the North. Unlike Southern school districts, where state and local laws had required separation of the races, Northern school patterns had usually resulted from de facto segregation in residential patterns. In *Keyes v. Denver School District No. 1* (1973), the Court heard a challenge to a school system that had never been statutorily segregated, but that was nonetheless de jure segregated because the school board had used race as a determinant in drawing attendance zones and in siting new schools. In a highly fragmented decision requiring desegregation of the system, Justice Brennan spoke for himself, Douglas, Stewart, Marshall, and Blackmun; the chief justice concurred in the result; Powell concurred in part and dissented in part; Rehnquist dissented totally; and White did not participate.

Brennan purported to adhere to the Court's previous distinction between de jure and de facto segregation, with the former defined as involving purpose or intent to segregate by the state, and therefore a violation of the Equal Protection Clause. Brennan actually blurred any differences; energetic plaintiffs could always find evidence that a school official had done something that could be interpreted as purposefully or intentionally fostering segregation. Justice Powell's concurrence suggested that the distinction be dropped altogether and that the Court adopt a single standard for all schools throughout the country. Powell failed to win support of this position from his brethren; only Justice Douglas agreed with the contention that the de jure/de facto distinction no longer made sense.

While Powell's effort to abandon the de jure/de facto distinction appealed to those opposed to discrimination in any form, it contained an internal inconsistency that made it unacceptable to the brethren. While wiping away the necessity to prove the cause of discrimination, it would have also meant the end of busing as a remedy. Segregation of any kind would have been subject to uniform treatment, North and South, but the courts would have been unable to order transportation to further integration. Justice Brennan recognized this and in response to Powell's suggestion, wrote that while he shared the view that de jure and de facto segregation should receive the same constitutional treatment, he disagreed with what that treatment would be and believed that Powell's approach would end the twenty-year effort to advance integration and end segregation.

The Court extended the logic of *Keyes* in two 1979 Ohio cases, *Columbus Board of Education v. Penick* and *Dayton Board of Education v. Brinkman*. Although Ohio schools had not been segregated by statute, the Court found evidence that parts of each city's school system had been deliberately segregated at the time of *Brown,* and therefore, the school boards had an affirmative constitutional duty, which they had not met, to desegregate. The majority opinion in both cases rested on a finding of continued intentional segregation, a finding disputed in both instances by some members of the Court. Justice Rehnquist's dissent charged that the Court's "cascade of presumptions . . . sweeps away the distinction between de facto and de jure segregation." One could not ignore history and dismiss the fact that some segregation resulted not from state action or evil intent, but from other considerations that the courts had neither the power nor the jurisdiction to change.

Opposition to integration and busing led many people to withdraw their children from public schools and enroll them in white private schools, or to move from racially mixed cities to predominantly white suburbs. The Court responded by limiting state aid to racially restrictive private schools, forbidding textbook loans (*Norwood v. Harrison* [1973]) and exclusive temporary use of public facilities (*Gilmore v. Montgomery*[1974]). Moreover, by a 7 to 2 vote, the Court sustained a Section 1981 civil rights suit against a segregated private school in *Runyon v. McCrary* (1976). According to Justice Stewart, parents had a First Amendment association right to send their children to schools promoting the idea that racial segregation is desirable. But it did not follow that the principle protected the *practice* of excluding racial minorities from such institutions. (Private individuals and organizations, such as clubs, may discriminate, since the Court has repeatedly held that private discrimination is not controlled by the Fourteenth Amendment. In this case, however, the Court gave a broad reading to Section 1 of the 1866 Civil Rights Act, which forbids the making of private contracts that discriminate on the basis of race. These contracts, if enforced in state courts, would be considered state action, and therefore in violation of the Fourteenth Amendment.)

Where the Burger Court found positive evidence of state-sponsored or endorsed discrimination, it acted as energetically as the Warren Court in striking it down. But the Burger Court showed more reluctance to intrude where segregation resulted from historic patterns rather than from statutory requirements. And even while sternly re-

> I take it as a postulate that differences in treatment of individuals based on their race or ethnic origin is at the bull's eye of the target at which the Fourteenth Amendment's Equal Protection Clause was aimed. . . . Certainly the cases are too numerous to require citation that differentiation between individuals on this basis is "suspect," subject to "strict scrutiny," or whatever equivalent phrase one chooses to use.
>
> —Justice William H. Rehnquist, Memorandum to Court, 11 November 1977

quiring the end of de jure segregation, the justices could not agree on how far the Constitution required society to go to achieve full integration. A good example was the Court's response to white flight to the suburbs.

Civil rights advocates claimed that the whole purpose of *Brown* would be frustrated if whites could escape integration by moving to the suburbs, where most blacks could not afford to live or could not buy housing because of covert discrimination. They maintained that suburbs and their core cities constituted economically unified metropolitan areas that more and more shared gas, water, sewer, police, and other services; separate school districts, therefore, served no other purpose than to foster segregation. The argument made sense to one district judge, who found Detroit schools unconstitutionally segregated. Since desegregation of the 64 percent black system of the city would cause white flight, the court ordered fifty-three surrounding suburban school districts unified with that of Detroit to prevent resegregation. The plan extended the logic of *Keyes* and *Dayton*, by which de jure segregation in one part of a system justified sweeping remedies for the entire system.

The Supreme Court, however, would not go this far. By a 5 to 4 vote in *Milliken v. Bradley* (1974), it held that federal judges could not order multidistrict remedies without proof that the district lines had originally been drawn in a racially discriminatory manner. "The scope of the remedy," Chief Justice Burger wrote, "is determined by the nature and extent of the constitutional violation." The Constitution spoke only to purposeful and intentional discrimination and could not be invoked to ameliorate problems that were not caused by official action. For some, *Milliken* marked the triumph of an antiblack strategy. For the first time since *Brown*, civil rights lawyers had lost a case, and Justice Marshall lamented in his dissent that the Court, after twenty years of small steps forward, had taken a great step backward. But for many, the case provided relief. Segregation in the cities, whatever its cause, had not been the creation of the suburbs, and the courts would not require the suburbs to bear the burden of integration. The Supreme Court had affirmed that although the Constitution called for racial equality, other traditions also deserved consideration, and "no single tradition in public education," according to the chief justice "is more deeply rooted than local control over the operation of the schools."

Bakke and Affirmative Action

In nonschool discrimination cases, the Burger Court took a broader view than many people had expected. The justices not only held all de jure discrimination constitutionally impermissible, but they interpreted civil rights legislation to prohibit discriminatory effects as well. In *Griggs v. Duke Power Company* (1971), one of the early cases testing the Title VII employment provisions of the 1964 Civil Rights Act, the chief justice spoke for a unanimous Court in holding that an employer could not require job applicants to take intelligence tests or have a high school diploma if the consequences of testing would be discriminatory and if the tests were unrelated to the job requirements. The tests, although racially neutral, had no bearing on job performance, but kept poorly educated blacks, no matter what their abilities, from advancing beyond the lowest-paid jobs.

> One may accept the consequences of the fact that the average adult Negro, because of poorer educational opportunities and other environmental circumstances, is unable to compete for the more remunerative jobs in much the same way that one recognizes differences within the white group which likewise are due to different educational opportunities. Such an attitude can be coupled with a demand for equal economic chances for Negroes and whites who have the same abilities and qualities as workers, citizens, and consumers.
>
> —Richard Sterner, *The Negro's Share: A Study of Income . . .* (1943)

Civil rights groups and some lower courts mistook *Griggs* to mean that the Court had erected a constitutional barrier to practices that led to discriminatory results, and some courts began disallowing all employment tests. But *Griggs* had involved a test that even the company had conceded had no relation to the job. In *Washington v. Davis* (1976), black plaintiffs challenged a verbal ability test that had kept them off the District of Columbia police force. For a 7 to 2 Court, Justice White upheld the test, which had been developed by the Civil Service Commission and had a direct bearing on the work to be performed.

By the mid-l970s, civil rights activists were calling not only for the end of racial bias, but also for affirmative programs to help minority groups overcome the effects of past discrimination. The medical school at the University of California at Davis had just such an affirmative action program. It set aside 16 of its 100 openings each year for minority students, who could be admitted even if they had grades and test scores lower than rejected majority applicants. Alan Bakke, a white male, had scores just below the cutoff point for majority applicants, but high enough to have assured him acceptance if he had been black, Chicano, or Native American. His suit charged that the minority quota system denied him equal protection; the California Supreme Court agreed, and the university appealed.

The Supreme Court had ducked the question of affirmative action a few years earlier in *DeFunis v. Odegaard* (1974), on the grounds that DeFunis, who had been allowed to attend law school during adjudication, was about to graduate and thus the case had been mooted. But by the time *Regents of the University of California v. Bakke* reached the Court in 1978, debate over affirmative action in society and the government had reached a point at which the issue could no longer by evaded. Advocates defended the constitutionality of affirmative action and praised a society in which a majority could voluntarily disadvantage itself to compensate minorities for previous injustices. Critics, on the other hand, attacked any plan that used race as a determinant as offensive to the Constitution. Although quotas benefit one group, they argued, they disadvantaged majority individuals who cannot be held responsible for society's past sins.

If the contestants expected a clear-cut answer from the Supreme Court, *Bakke* disappointed both sides; like society at large, the justices split over the matter. The chief justice, along with justices Stevens, Stewart, and Rehnquist, condemned the Davis admission plan as violating Title VII of the 1964 Civil Rights Act, basing their view completely on statutory construction of the law. Justices Brennan, White, Marshall, and

> If you view the [affirmative action] programs as admitting qualified students who, because of this Nation's sorry history of racial discrimination, have academic records that prevent them from effectively competing for medical school, then this is affirmative action to remove the vestiges of slavery and state imposed segregation by root and branch. If you view the program as excluding students, it is a program of quotas which violates the principle that the Constitution is color-blind.
>
> —Justice Thurgood Marshall, Memorandum on *Bakke*, 13 April 1978

Blackmun believed the Davis program did not violate either the statute or the Constitution. In a compromise—and deciding—opinion, Justice Powell sided with the chief justice's group in holding that Alan Bakke had been illegally discriminated against by the Davis scheme, but he then joined with the Brennan bloc to rule that race could be a factor in admissions programs if used to secure a more diversified student body. Numerical quotas based on race, even if established for benign purposes, would not be acceptable, however.

Some commentators praised Powell for striking a politically necessary compromise; others attacked the decision for its failure to provide a clear standard for the lower courts to use in evaluating other programs. The ability to take race into account at all opens a Pandora's box. How much of a consideration should it be? How can one determine when it ceases to be but one factor among many, and when a quota has been established? The case was "music to our ears," said John Harding, counsel to Columbia University. "Now we can continue to do what we are already doing."

In partial response to such criticism, the Court took a more definite stance the following year in *United Steelworkers Union v. Weber* (1979), ruling 5 to 2 that a voluntary affirmative action program did not violate Title VII. An agreement between the employer and the union reserved half of the openings in an in-plant craft-training program for blacks until the percentage of black craftworkers reached the percentage of blacks in the local labor force. According to Justice Brennan, the Civil Rights Act left the private sector free to take such race-conscious steps to eliminate racial imbalances in traditionally segregated job categories.

A year later in *Fullilove v. Klutznik* (1980), the Court upheld the Minority Business Enterprise (MBE) clause of the Public Works Employment Act of 1977, which required that 10 percent of federal funds appropriated for local public works projects be subcontracted for goods or services supplied by minority-owned businesses, even if they did not enter the lowest bid. The six members of the Court who voted to sustain the MBE clause in *Fullilove* could not agree on a single rationale. The chief justice, along with White and Powell, relied primarily on Congress's power to adopt reasonable programs to overcome the results of past discrimination; Marshall, Brennan, and Blackmun believed the quota could be sustained because of an important governmental objective. Rehnquist, Stewart, and Stevens agreed that a race-conscious remedy was permissible if "its sole purpose is to eradicate the actual effects of illegal race discrimination," but objected to the MBE clause because it went beyond this goal and sought a particular racial balance as a goal in and of itself.

After *Bakke*, *Weber*, and *Fullilove*, proponents believed the Court had endorsed the basic constitutionality of affirmative action. But in *Firefighters v. Stotts* (1984), the Court surprised observers by ruling in another fragmented opinion that a bona fide seniority system took precedence over an affirmative action plan. In the early 1970s, Memphis had adopted a seniority system for all city workers. Later, a suit by black employees led Memphis to agree to a program to increase the number of blacks on the city payroll. When budgetary problems required layoffs of some workers in 1981, the city, relying on the seniority system, applied the "last hired, first fired" rule. The seniority plan had not been adopted with an intent to discriminate, but it had had that effect, since in many departments blacks had been the last hired. The lower court enjoined Memphis from using the last hired rule because of this racially discriminatory effect. Justice White vacated the injunction and ruled that Title VII could not displace a legitimate seniority system; "it is inappropriate to deny an innocent employee the benefits of his seniority in order to provide a remedy" for unintended racial discrimination. The decision left the fate of many affirmative action programs in the air, since their champions claimed that in order to overcome past discrimination, not only should minorities be favored, but their new status protected. Since seniority in nearly all instances would favor white males, minorities would lack job protection in times of economic distress, when they needed it most.

In the 1985 term, the last over which Burger presided, the Court heard three affirmative action cases that elicited a variety of opinions but no consensus. It reaffirmed that a legitimate seniority system could not be displaced by an affirmative action plan, although only four members joined in Justice Powell's opinion. Powell intimated that an affirmative action plan *might* take precedence if strong evidence of prior discrimination existed (*Wygant v. Jackson Board of Education* [1986]). On practically the last day of the term, however, the Court also reaffirmed that lower courts could, given evidence of past discrimination, mandate affirmative action plans that included hiring goals, even if these worked to the disadvantage of some majority members; again, only four members of the Court joined in Justice Brennan's lead opinion (*Local 28, Sheet Metal Workers' International Union v. EEOC* [1986]). Brennan managed to garner six votes, however, to sustain a consent decree setting hiring goals to overcome the results of previous bias (*Local 93, Int. Assoc. of Firefighters v. Cleveland* [1986]). The issue would obviously return to the Court. In fact, as one of its last orders at the end of the term, the Court set down two affirmative action cases for the Rehnquist Court to hear.

> A racial quota derogates the human dignity and individuality of all to whom it is applied; it is invidious in principle as well as in practice. Moreover, it can easily be turned against those it purports to help. The history of the racial quota is a history of subjugation, not beneficence. Its evil lies not in its name, but in its effects; a quota is a divider of society, a creator of castes, and it is all the worse for its racial base, especially in a society desperately striving for an equality that will make race irrelevant.
>
> —Alexander Bickel, *The Morality of Consent* (1975)

Affirmative action is a good example of the argument some scholars put forth that the Burger Court, if it did not have more difficult cases than its predecessor, had more nuanced and complex issues to deal with. Certainly the Warren Court's decisions in *Brown* and *Loving* were politically difficult to make at the time, but in retrospect, a majority of Americans today would agree that state laws segregating school children by race or banning interracial marriage are flat out wrong. Affirmative action, on the other hand, generated controversy when the first cases came down, and it continues to do so. The public policy debate on this issue has been at times vehement, with people polarized as to whether or not racial or gender preferences ought to be allowed. Should some sort of recompense for the years of persecution suffered by minorities as a group be at the expense of individuals who may never have discriminated at all. The Reagan administration took a strong stance against affirmative action, and Attorney General Edwin Meese tried to influence both localities and courts to reverse the trend toward minority preferences in employment and academic admissions. It is little wonder that one finds inconsistencies in the Court's opinions; they reflect the confusion of the larger society.

Gender Discrimination

Despite its general expansion of equal opportunities, the Warren Court had paid no attention to gender discrimination. Until 1971, the Supreme Court repulsed every effort to overcome legal handicaps imposed on women. At a time when the Court struck down one racially discriminatory practice after another, the brethren found no constitutional reason why women could not be kept off juries. The state could rationally find, the Court explained in *Hoyt v. Florida* (1961), a necessity to spare women from this obligation in light of their place at "the center of home and family life."

Thus it was the Burger Court—with a majority of appointees supposedly chosen for their devotion to judicial restraint and strict construction—that forged ahead to make sex discrimination constitutionally suspect. The women's movement had won its first major victory in 1964, when Title VII of the Civil Rights Acts prohibited employment discrimination on the basis of race, religion, national origin, and sex. Throughout the sixties, the media carried one story after another on the women's movement and its efforts to achieve sexual equality. The chief justice first entered the Court in the lists in the unanimous opinion of *Reed v. Reed* (1971), which invalidated an Idaho estate law giving men preference over similarly situated women as administrators of decedents' estates. This radical departure of the Court from its previous position occurred in the context of two significant steps then being debated by Congress. Within a few months,

> The paramount destiny and mission of a woman are to fulfill the noble and benign offices of wife and mother. This is the law of the Creator.
>
> —Justice Joseph Bradley, *Bradwell v. Illinois* (1873)

> Our Nation has a long and unfortunate history of sex discrimination. Traditionally, such discrimination was rationalized by an attitude of "romantic paternalism" which, in practical effect, put women, not on a pedestal, but in a cage. As a result of notions such as these, our statute books gradually became laden with gross, stereotyped distinctions between the sexes. . . . It is true, of course, that the position of women in America has improved markedly in recent decades. Nevertheless, it can hardly be doubted that, in particular because of the high visibility of the sex characteristic, women still face pervasive, although at times more subtle, discrimination in our educational institutions, in the job market and, perhaps most conspicuously, in the political arena.
>
> —Justice William Brennan, *Frontiero v. Richardson* (1973)

in early 1972, Congress would overwhelmingly approve the Equal Rights Amendment and send it to the states, and the following year it passed the Equal Pay Act of 1973, mandating equal pay for equal work.

The Court heard its second Title VII case in 1971, *Phillips v. Martin Marietta Corporation*. The *per curiam* decision held that firms willing to hire fathers, but not mothers, with preschool children engaged in sex discrimination prohibited by the law. Both *Reed* and *Phillips* relied on statutory interpretation. Even in the important case of *Frontiero v. Richardson* in 1973, the Court shied away from declaring sex a *constitutionally* suspect classification akin to race. In *Frontiero*, an 8 to 1 Court struck down provisions of the Equal Pay Act and Title VII exempting the military; it held that the armed services could not deny to married women the same fringe benefits paid to their male counterparts. Under the existing law, men automatically received a housing allowance and health care benefits for their civilian wives; women received these benefits only if they supplied three-fourths of the family's support (all of their own and one-half of their husband's). Justice Brennan, along with Justices Douglas, White, and Marshall, declared his willingness to bring gender discrimination within the reach of the Equal Protection Clause and to make classifications based on sex as suspect as those based on race, but he lacked one vote in support of this position.

Nonetheless, *Frontiero* constituted a major step forward for women: Despite its unwillingness to invoke the equal protection doctrine, the Court did not invalidate the legislation, but corrected it. Instead of saying that Congress could not provide benefits to the families of married men, it directed that similar benefits go to women's families. Moreover, by striking down the requirement for women to be the main provider of support in order to receive benefits, the Court began its assault on long-held stereotypes regarding women's roles. It would be a while, however, before the Court would reach the conclusion that equality demanded equal treatment, and nothing less.

Like other sections of society, the Court grappled with the problem of trying to achieve equality before the law for both men and women, while recognizing that differences did exist that might justify the retention of some paternalistic measures, even if they violated a strict equal protection standard. Where no valid reason justified discrimination, however, the Court moved to end it quickly. It struck down a jury selection scheme identical to the one approved by the Warren Court (*Taylor v. Louisiana*

> I would think that sex is a suspect classification, if for no other reason than the fact that Congress has submitted a constitutional amendment making sex discrimination unconstitutional. I would remain of the same view whether the amendment is adopted or not. . . . Of course, the more of this we do on the basis of suspect classifications not rooted in the Constitution, the more we approximate the old substantive due process approach.
>
> —Justice Bryan White to Justice William Brennan, 15 February 1973

[1975]), and unanimously invalidated several sex-based differentials in Social Security benefits (*Weinberger v. Weisenfeld* [1975]).

In 1977, the Court adopted a higher standard of review for sex discrimination cases. Until 1971, the Court had employed the simple rational basis test in evaluating state laws employing sex classifications. In 1948, for example, Justice Frankfurter upheld a Michigan law excluding women from bartending, on the grounds that the state had good reason in wanting to keep women out of saloons. In race classifications, the Court had developed the doctrine that Justice Stone had suggested in his *Caroline Products* footnote, and it employed a strict scrutiny standard of review. It considered any racial classification as suspect; the state had the burden of proving that a compelling state interest required such classification. So long as the Court did not rely on the Equal Protection Clause in gender discrimination suits, it could avoid the imposition of strict scrutiny. In *Califano v. Goldfarb* (1977), the Court placed gender cases in an intermediate level of heightened scrutiny, requiring more than a rational basis for discrimination, but allowing somewhat greater leeway than the strict scrutiny of race cases.

Goldfarb raised problems similar to those in *Frontiero* and *Weisenfeld*. The Social Security law granted a widow survivor's benefits automatically; for a widower to receive the same benefits, he had to prove that his wife had contributed all of her own support and half of his. Four members of the Court found the distinction reasonable and accepted the government's argument that the classification reflected the real world, in which most women depended on their husbands for support. The majority, however, saw this as stereotyped thinking. Congress, Justice Stevens claimed, had ordered differential treatment out of "habit," an "accidental by-product of the traditional way of thinking about females." Three years later, all but Justice Rehnquist had come around to this point of view. *Wengler v. Druggists Mutual Insurance Company* (1980) presented virtually the identical problem as *Goldfarb*, this time in connection with death benefits under a state workers' compensation plan. By then the justices, as well as government and society, had learned of a quiet revolution that had been going on since World War II. There had been a steady increase in the number of women working full time outside the home, so that in the early 1980s, an estimated two-thirds of all women between twenty-five and fifty-four were employed. This fact required a rethinking not only of the economic relationships between the sexes, but also of the so-called women's place in society.

In two 1979 decisions, the Burger Court took decisive steps to make the Constitution as gender-neutral as it is supposed to be race-blind. In *Orr v. Orr*, the Court struck down an Alabama law under which husbands but never wives might be required to pay alimony. Such classifications must fall, according to Justice Brennan, whenever they reflect the "baggage of sexual stereotypes," especially that men have a duty to work and support their wives, whose responsibility is centered on the home. In *Califano v. Westcott*, the Court struck down provisions of the Aid to Families with Dependent Children program that allowed benefits to be paid to a family when an employed father lost his job, but not when a working mother became unemployed. Although the justices split over the appropriate remedy, all nine—including Justice Rehnquist—agreed that the provision violated the Equal Protection Clause.

The justices recognized that gender did make some undeniable differences, and they tried to develop a rational doctrine to deal with such situations as pregnancy. In *Cleveland Board of Education v. LaFleur* (1974), the Court ruled that school teachers may not arbitrarily be dismissed or placed on involuntary leave if pregnant. In *Nashville Gas Company v. Satty* (1971), it held the practice of stripping pregnant women of accumulated job seniority a violation of Title VII. But if a woman could not be penalized for being pregnant, the employer did not have to reward her either. Pregnancy is not a disability, and state disability income plans could exclude pregnancy without violating equal protection (*Geduldig v. Aiello* [1974]); similarly, private employers could omit pregnancy from their disability coverage (*General Electric Co. v. Gilbert* [1976]). Congress later reversed these last two rulings through statute.

The Court also accepted legitimate differences between the sexes following the reinstitution of selective service in 1980. Congress had explicitly limited the draft to males, despite feminist protests, and in 1981, the Court heard an equal rights challenge to the law. In *Rostker v. Goldberg*, the Court rejected the claim by a 6 to 3 vote. According to Justice Rehnquist, although military considerations alone may not negate constitutional guarantees, congressional judgment in this area carried great weight, to which the Court deferred. Applying the heightened scrutiny that had become the norm in gender discrimination cases, he found that the government had an important interest in protecting the country. Since neither side questioned the Defense Department policy of excluding women members of the armed services from combat, the nation's need for male combat troops allowed Congress to limit the draft to men only.

In July 1982, the Court reaffirmed the heightened scrutiny test in a controversial 5 to 4 decision, *Mississippi University for Women v. Hogan*. A traditionally all-women nursing school had denied admission to a male nurse seeking additional training, although it would have allowed him to audit some courses. The state did provide comparable programs elsewhere that accepted men, but Joe Hogan wanted to attend MUW, the school closest to where he lived. Justice O'Connor declared that none of the state's justifications for maintaining an all-women enrollment could disguise the fact that the school rejected male applicants solely on the basis of gender. In a strained argument, she also claimed that Title IX of the 1972 Education Amendments Act, which exempted traditionally single-sex schools from the prohibition against gender discrimination, had no force. Section 5 of the Fourteenth Amendment gave Congress the power to enforce equal protection, not to dilute it. Justice Powell's dissent made out a convincing case for traditional single-sex education as an alternative that should be supported. He found the burden on Joe Hogan—the inconvenience of attending a school other than one near where he currently lived—insufficient to disturb educational programs that provided additional opportunities for women.

The Equal Rights Amendment

The *Mississippi University* decision came down on July 1, 1982, one day after the extended deadline for ratification of the proposed Equal Rights Amendment (ERA) expired. The amendment provided that "equality of rights under the law shall not be denied or abridged by the United States or by any State on account of sex," and authorized Congress to enact enforcing legislation. Congress had originally sent the amendment to the states in early 1972; within a few months, about half the states had ratified it. Then opposition groups began to lobby intensively, and the amendment stalled. Proponents managed to get an extension of the ratification deadline from 1978 to the end of June 1982, but even then only thirty-five states had approved, three short of the necessary margin.

Opposition to the amendment ranged from outright male chauvinism to claims that it would hurt women by vacating protective legislation; hysterics warned that the ERA would require unisex bathrooms, while states' rights advocates feared that it would give the federal government still another club with which to bludgeon the states. Some critics also saw the ERA as a stalking horse for gay rights, as well as a tool for supporters of abortion rights. In constitutional terms, it is unclear just how an equal rights amendment would affect existing law. It would certainly raise gender to a suspect classification akin to race and thus require strict rather than merely heightened scrutiny. But would it affect areas where the Court had said valid differences justify gender distinction, such as in the armed services? Would it require the abrogation of all legislation designed to protect women? In *Michael M. v. Superior Court* (1981), the Court had upheld a California statutory rape law that punished the male participant in intercourse when the female was under eighteen, but did not work reciprocally. The plurality opinion admitted trouble in fitting the statute into normal gender discrimination analyses, but believed that the legislature had acted rationally in recognizing differences between the sexes. Under the ERA, could such a law stand?

Some people claim that for all practical purposes, the Burger Court legislated the ERA judicially. It struck down invidious distinctions based on sex and held that stereotyped generalizations of sexual differences must fall. The Court also ruled that the truth of generalizations, even when based on fact, did not justify different treatment. In *Los Angeles Department of Water Power v. Manhart* (1978), the Court conceded the fact that statistically, as a class, women lived longer than men. Working on that fact, the city required a larger contribution from female employees for their pension plans, with the result that women took home less pay than men earning the same gross pay. As Justice Stevens explained, the generalization, while "unquestionably true," described the group—but individuals did not necessarily follow the group characteristic. Some women live longer than the male average, and some die at an earlier age. Although the case involved a statutory construction of Title VII, Stevens emphasized that rights are protected for the enjoyment of individuals and not of groups. Applying this same principle in *Arizona Governing Committee v. Norris* (1983), the Court struck down a state plan that required equal contributions from men and women, but paid out a lower pension to women.

Poverty and Disability

In the absence of a constitutional amendment, the Court did not make gender a fully suspect classification, nor did it accept any invitation to extend this category to the poor and handicapped. In *San Antonio Independent School District v. Rodriguez* (1973), the petitioners attacked the Texas system of financing public schools, which relied primarily on local property taxes. As a result, rich districts, those with factories, prosperous businesses, and expensive housing, spent considerably more than poorer areas on schools. Many of these poor districts had overwhelmingly Hispanic populations and also some of the highest tax rates in the state. They taxed themselves as much as they could, but could not raise anything near the amounts generated by wealthy districts with lower tax rates. Parents of Mexican-American children initiated the suit on behalf of all children residing in districts with a low property tax base, claiming violation of equal protection. The District Court accepted the argument, and, exercising strict scrutiny, ruled poverty a suspect classification and education a fundamental right. By a 5 to 4 vote, the Supreme Court reversed.

Justice Powell denied that poverty constituted a suspect classification, and he distinguished the case from earlier decisions that had led some to see the Court as in fact moving in that direction. The Court had held that fundamental interests, such as securing a divorce or the right of appeal after a criminal conviction, could not be denied simply because a person lacked money. But education, while certainly important in American life, "is not among the rights afforded explicit protection under our Federal Constitution." Justice Marshall entered an impassioned dissent against what he termed the Court's "rigidified approach to equal protection analysis"; he saw the majority decision as a retreat from the Court's earlier stance on civil rights.

The Court also refused to extend suspect classification status to the disabled and retarded, even while it expanded the definition of minimum care and training they could demand from the state. In *Youngburg v. Romeo* (1982), Justice Powell found a constitutional right to "minimally adequate and reasonable training" for the mentally retarded; but although this constituted a "liberty interest," it was not absolute and had to be balanced against "the relevant state interest." The Court also read the Education for All Handicapped Children Act of 1975 in an extremely narrow manner, again denying that the disabled had any special constitutional status [*Hendrick Hudson Central School District v. Rowley* (1982)].

It came as something of a surprise, then, when the Court ordered Texas to admit children of illegal aliens into public schools in *Plyler v. Doe* (1982). By a 5 to 4 vote, the Court, speaking through Justice Brennan, held that denial of a free public school education to undocumented alien children violated the Equal Protection Clause. Brennan applied the strict scrutiny analysis, since alienage had long been accepted as a suspect classification, but he implied that education might be viewed as a fundamental interest, an assertion that left Justice Powell, who concurred in the result, uncomfortable. Powell's opinion is, in fact, somewhat strange for him, and in many ways reads more like a social tract than a judicial statement. He sharply criticized Congress's failure to establish an effective system of immigration control, and he expressed sympathy with states like Texas that bore the brunt of the problems. But children should not be punished for their parents' behavior, and he could find no adequate state interest to justify dening these children the benefit of an education. It cannot be argued rationally, he declared, "that anyone benefits from the creation . . . of a subclass of illiterate persons, many of whom will remain in the state." The five separate opinions filed in this case left many questions open regarding the constitutional status, if any, of equal access to public education and of qualitative differences among schools.

The Abortion Decisions

Whatever its uncertainties about affirmative action, women's rights, and educational opportunity, the Burger Court left no doubt that it considered personal autonomy a fundamental interest, as it made clear in its most controversial decision. *Roe v. Wade* (1973), along with the companion case of *Doe v. Bolton*, invalidated all state antiabortion statutes. Justice Blackmun's opinion for the 7 to 2 Court did not rely on equal protection analysis, but on the concepts of privacy and autonomy first suggested in *Griswold v. Connecticut*. In *Roe*, however, Blackmun boldly ventured to do what Douglas had skirted in *Griswold*; he identified a new substantive due process as the basis of noneconomic individual rights. The right of privacy, he asserted, "is broad enough to encompass a woman's decision whether or not to terminate her pregnancy," and the choice is best left to the woman and her physician. But the right is qualified, and Blackmun utilized a trimester approach to define when the state's interest overtook those of the woman. In the first three months of pregnancy, the woman had an absolute right to an abortion. In the second trimester, when the risks of abortion procedures to the woman increased and there was a chance that the fetus might be viable, the state could not deny an abortion, but could regulate the conditions under which it took place. In the last months of pregnancy, the state's interest in the potential life of the fetus took precedence over the woman's privacy rights, and the state could prohibit abortions completely.

Roe touched off a public uproar nearly as great as the segregation decision, and one that may prove more enduring. When Earl Warren left the Court fifteen years after *Brown*, the principle that racial segregation was wrong and immoral had been accepted by a vast majority of the American people. The reaction to *Roe*, far from quieting down, has remained vehement, "Right to Life" groups continue to picket abortion clinics, petition legislatures and Congress for a constitutional amendment to forbid abortions, seek state and federal laws defining when life begins so as to undercut *Roe*, and in some cases, resort to violence by bombing clinics, harassing those who work there, physically intimidating women who seek abortions, and even murdering doctors.

Catholic religious doctrine holds that life begins at conception, and many non-Catholics believe that a fetus, from its earliest cell multiplication, is a living person. On the other hand, some religions require an abortion to save a mother's life. Scientists, however, differ over when life begins, and English common law held that legal life did not begin until birth. "Pro-choice" advocates take a similar view, and argue that the primary right is that of the woman to control her own body and not be forced to endure unwanted pregnancies. Some opponents of abortion concede that when conception results from rape or incest, or when a pregnancy threatens the life of the mother, an abortion is permissible; but the purist wing deems all life sacred and therefore protected.

If it is impossible to resolve the question of when life begins in moral or scientific terms, then one can begin to understand the criticism that has been heaped on the Court for trying to impose a legal solution—an effort, some say, akin to *Dred Scott* and equally doomed to failure. Even among those who agree that women should be able to secure safe and legal abortions, commentators believe that the Court overreached itself and intruded without constitutional justification into an area in which it had no business.

Although some states still had late nineteenth-century laws on their books, others had instituted reforms that, while not making abortion as freely available as *Roe* did, nonetheless marked a significant step in that direction. In New York, for example, there were more abortions than live births in the year preceding *Roe.* According to some critics, the Court interfered too soon and should have given the states time to work the problem out on their own. Unlike racial segregation, where the Court had been chipping away at separate but equal for decades, abortion had no precedential history: *Brown* marked a logical culmination of a reasoned judicial process, whereas *Roe* appeared as a bolt from the blue. Other critics depict *Roe* as the liberal equivalent of *Lochner*, with the Court misusing substantive due process to impose its own values on society.

There have been defenders of the abortion decision, both in public and in the law schools. Proponents of judicial activism argue that it is the Court's responsibility constantly to reexamine constitutional provisions of due process, equal rights, and the unenumerated rights of the Ninth Amendment to determine if they need updating and to articulate what these rights mean in the light of current needs. The judiciary has a right to intervene, they claim, when moral consensus is in flux; by taking bold steps, courts assist a new consensus to develop.

Because of the inflammatory nature of its subject, *Roe* attracted the greatest attention, but it was only one of several decisions by the Warren and Burger Courts to figure in the most recent cycle of debate over the power of judicial review. That debate is now phrased in terms of "interpretivism," which holds that judges can only enforce ideas that are clearly stated or strongly implied in the Constitution itself, and "noninterpretivism," which allows courts to range in other sources, so as to articulate what contemporary society sees as its most fundamental values. Proponents see noninterpretive review as a crucial "agency of moral evaluation and growth," by which courts engage in an open-ended quest for the current meaning of natural rights. Opponents, on the other hand, condemn noninterpretivism as little more than an invitation to judges to write their own moral values and prejudices into law; they insist that judges be bound by the original intent and words of the Constitution and such original sources as *The Federalist* and Madison's notes of the Philadelphia Convention. Some scholars have sought a middle position, in which judges begin with the original sources, but avoid a "clause-bound literalism" that fails to recognize that changes in society since 1787 require corresponding changes in judicial thinking. Yet, even those advocating a middle ground worry about judges writing their personal values into law.

Post-*Roe* Decisions

Despite the criticism provoked by *Roe*, the justices did not back down from their assertion of personal autonomy as a fundamental right; but neither did they expand the right to abortion. In the first major post-*Roe* case, *Planned Parenthood of Missouri v. Danforth* (1976), the Court by a 6 to 3 vote invalidated a state law barring a woman from securing an abortion during the first trimester without spousal consent. According to Justice Blackmun, the state did not have the power to forbid the abortion and therefore could not delegate it to the husband, despite his "deep and proper concern and interest in his wife's pregnancy."

The question of parental authority over pregnant minors came before the court several times. In *Bellotti v. Baird* (1976), a companion case to *Danforth*, the Court struck down a requirement for written parental permission on similar grounds; the state could not delegate power it did not have itself. But Justice Blackmun's opinion intimated that in the case of a minor, some restrictions might be permissible if they did not "unduly burden" the right to seek an abortion. Three years later, in *Bellotti v. Baird* (*Bellotti II*), the Court again struck down a law limiting minors' access to abortion, this time by an 8 to 1 vote. The Massachusetts law in question required an unmarried minor to obtain the consent of both her parents; if they refused, a state judge could authorize the abortion if he or she believed that good cause had been shown. Justice Powell's opinion set out guidelines for the states: minors had to have alternative procedures; if they feared their parents or did not want to inform them of their pregnancy, they must be allowed to go directly to an appropriate judicial or nonjudicial authority; if the young woman demonstrated her maturity and that she was well informed about the nature of the choices open to her, the third party had to give the permission she sought. But, Powell made clear, while the state may intervene in cases in which the minor is immature or there is evidence that she is incapable of acting responsibly, the presumption is on the side of the woman.

In 1981, the Court narrowly approved a parental notice requirement in *H.L. v. Matheson*, in which physicians had to "notify if possible" the parent or guardian of a minor seeking an abortion if she lived at home, was economically dependent, or otherwise not legally emancipated. In subsequent decisions on this issue, the Court failed to develop a clear policy and evaluated each case on its particular circumstances.

In its last term, the Burger Court struck down a highly restrictive Pennsylvania statute, whose provisions on informed consent, public disclosure of information, and regulation of medical care, according to Justice Blackmun, disguised the obvious policy of discouraging abortions (*Thornburgh v. American College of Obstetricians and Gynecologists* [1986]). The 5 to 4 vote led some antiabortion groups to cheer that the Court had changed its mind and had begun a retreat from *Roe* and that one or two new appointments would lead to a complete overturn of that case. A closer reading of the opinions did not justify that view; seven members of the Court still stood by the *Roe* decision, but obviously they differed over where they would draw the line between the women's right to an abortion and the state's legitimate interests in medical supervision and protection of the fetus in the third trimester.

Although feminists claimed that *Roe* would end the terrible dangers of back alley abortions, poor women could still not afford either the doctors' fees or medical insurance to cover the procedure. While many clinics did offer abortion and family planning services to the poor at little or no cost, prochoice advocates sought government assistance, arguing that lack of funds should not be an impediment to exercising personal autonomy. If state and federal programs covered the costs of childbirth, then under equal protection these programs ought to pay for the choice of not having a child. Antiabortion forces in Congress and in a number of state legislatures disagreed and cut funding for abortions from Medicaid and other medical assistance programs.

In *Maher v. Roe* (1977), the first major abortion funding case, a 6 to 3 Court sustained a Connecticut law that excluded nontherapeutic, medically unnecessary abortions from a Medicaid program. Justice Powell rejected the claim that if the government funded a woman's choice to have a baby, it had to fund the equally valid choice of an abortion. In an argument that appeared in several cases, Powell denied that withholding funding constituted an intrusion by the government on women's choices. *Roe*, he explained, had prohibited the states from barring access to abortion for those who could pay for it; it did not require the states to support abortion by underwriting its costs. Government could, it if chose, encourage childbearing as a policy, even if such a policy had a disproportionate effect on the poor.

Three years later, the Court narrowly sustained the Hyde Amendment, which drastically limited the use of federal funds for abortion. In *Harris v. McRae* (1980), a 5 to 4 majority approved the denial of funds even for medically necessary abortions. Justice Stewart again explained that "although government may not place obstacles in the path of a woman's exercise of her freedom of choice, it need not remove those not of its own creation. Indigency falls in the latter category." Although this argument squared with the fact that the Court had refused to consider poverty a suspect classification, it ran counter to a whole string of cases in which the Court had held that the state could not deny fundamental rights to people merely because they could not afford them. One suspects that the Court beat a tactical political retreat here, more concerned with quieting some of the criticism than in maintaining doctrinal consistency.

The 1980 election of Ronald Reagan, an open foe of abortion, and the increased political militancy of religious fundamentalists led to a rash of state laws attempting to circumvent *Roe*. In 1983, the Court dealt with a number of these in *Akron v. Akron Center for Reproductive Health* and *Planned Parenthood Assoc. of Kansas City v. Ashcroft*. It struck down regulations designed to put abortion clinics out of business, restrict second trimester procedures to hospitals, and require detailed explanations to women of what would happen to the fetus—all intended, according to the Court, to make access to abortions more difficult and to pressure women into foregoing the procedure. Only a Virginia statute requiring all abortions to be performed in a hospital met with the Court's approval, because the Virginia law defined "hospital" to include clinics and left "the method and the timing of the abortion precisely where they belong—with the physician and the patient" (*Simopoulos v. Virginia*).

Despite the reintroduction of a constitutional amendment to ban abortions, the proposed statute by which Congress would declare that life begins with conception, and the continued vociferous opposition to abortion by Right to Life groups, some evidence suggested that public opinion had begun catching up with the Court. Polls showed that well over half the people favored the right of a woman to secure an abortion, even if the respondents would not have one themselves. Congress, ever alert to such trends, undoubtedly saw bumper stickers proclaiming "I Am Pro Choice and I Vote!" and it refused to pass either the antiabortion amendment or the conception statute. But even if the country should "catch up" with the Court, a significant question remains. If the Court had been denounced in *Lochner* for being so far behind the times, did it act any more correctly in *Roe* by being so far ahead?

For Further Reading

There have been a number of collected essays on the Burger Court, starting with Vincent Blasi, *The Burger Court: The Counter-Revolution That Wasn't* (1985); followed by Herman Schwartz, ed., *The Burger Years: Rights and Wrongs in the Supreme Court, 1969–1986* (1987); Charles M. Lamb and Stephen C. Halpern, eds, *The Burger Court: Political and Judicial Profiles* (1991); and Bernard Schwartz, ed., *The Burger Court: Counter-Revolution or Confirmation?* (1998). Melvin I. Urofsky, *The Continuity of Change: The Supreme Court and Individual Liberties, 1953–1986* (1991); Bernard Schwartz, *The Ascent of Pragmatism: The Burger Court in Action* (1990); and Frederick P. Lewis, *The Context of Judicial Activism: The Endurance of the Warren Court Legacy in a Conservative Age* (1999), all emphasize the continuity between the Warren and Burger courts. A popular look at the inner workings of the Court in these years is Bob Woodward and Scott Armstrong, *The Brethren* (1979).

For the development of equal protection doctrine in regard to school cases, see J. Harvie Wilkinson, III, *From Brown to Bakke: The Supreme Court and School Integration* (1979). Pessimistic views of the courts' role in school affairs include Raymond Wolters, *The Burden of Brown: Thirty Years of School Desegregation* (1984); and Lino A. Graglia, *Disaster by Decree: The Supreme Court Decisions on Race and the Schools* (1976). George R. Metcalf, *From Little Rock to Boston: The History of School Desegregation* (1983), takes just the opposite view, expressing a strong faith in the courts and busing. The latter issue is examined in Gary Orheld, *Must We Bus? Segregated Schools and National Policy* (1978). A balanced synthesis is James T. Patterson, *Brown v. Board of Education: A Civil Rights Milestone and Its Troubled Legacy* (2001).

Studies of specific cases include Bernard Schwartz, *Swann's Way: The School Busing Case and the Supreme Court* (1986); Edward W. Kitch, "The Return of Color-Consciousness to the Constitution: Weber, Dayton, and Columbus," 1979 *Supreme Court Review* 1 (1980); Frank Goodman, "De facto School Segregation: A Constitutional and Empirical Analysis," 60 *California Law Review* 275 (1972); Kenneth L. Karst, "Not One Law at Rome and Another at Athens: The Fourteenth Amendment in Nationwide Application," 1972 *Washington University Law Quarterly* 383 (1972); Leonard P. Strickman, "School Desegregation at the Crossroads," 70 *Northwestern University Law Review* 725 (1975).

Good starting points for affirmative action are Paul D. Moreno, *From Direct Action to Affirmative Action: Fair Employment Law and Policy in America, 1933–1972* (1997), which provides a useful historical overview; and Kenneth L. Karst, *Belonging to America: Equal Citizenship and the Constitution* (1989), which offers a larger constitutional context. For arguments in favor of affirmative action, see Boris I. Bittker, *The Case for Black Reparations* (1973); and Ronald J. Fiscus, *The Constitutional Logic of Affirmative Action* (1992). Opposing arguments can be found in Herman Belz, *Equality Transformed: A Quarter-Century of Affirmative Action* (1991); and Thomas Sowell, *Affirmative Action Reconsidered: Was It Necessary in Academia?* (1975). For the cases, see Allen P. Sindler, *Bakke, De Funis and Minority Admissions: The Quest for Equal Opportunity* (1978), and Bernard Schwartz, *Behind Bakke: Affirmative Action and the Supreme Court* (1988). See also, "Symposium," 67 *California Law Review* 1 (1979); and John

Hart Ely, "The Constitutionality of Reverse Racial Discrimination," 41 *University of Chicago Law Review* 723 (1974).

For the new departure regarding gender discrimination, see Kenneth L. Karst, "Foreword: Equal Citizenship Under the Fourteenth Amendment," 91 *Harvard Law Review* 1 (1977); and "Women's Constitution," 1894 *Duke Law Journal* 477 (1984); Ruth Bader Ginsburg, "Gender and the Constitution," 44 *University of Cincinnati Law Review* 1 (1975); and Ann E. Freedman, "Sex Equality, Sex Differences, and the Supreme Court," 92 *Yale Law Journal* 913 (1983). The hesitant steps taken by the Court in expanding equal protection to other fields are examined in Gerald Gunther, "Foreword: In Search of Evolving Doctrine on a Changing Court: A Model for a Newer Equal Protection," 86 *Harvard Law Review* 1 (1972); and Tinsley E. Yarbrough, "The Burger Court and Unspecified Rights: On Protecting Fundamental and Not-So-Fundamental 'Rights' or 'Interests' Through a Flexible Conception of Equal Protection," 1977 *Duke Law Review* 143 (1977).

The story of *Roe* is told in David J. Garrow, *Liberty and Sexuality: The Right to Privacy and the Making of Roe v. Wade* (1994); and also by the plaintiff's counsel in Sarah Weddington, *A Question of Choice* (1992). An historical overview of changes in public attitudes is Nanette J. Davis, *From Crime to Choice: The Transformation of Abortion in America* (1985). The abortion decisions are discussed in Lawrence H. Tribe, *Abortion: The Clash of Absolutes* (1990); and also in Michael Perry, "Abortion, the Public Morals, and the Police Power: The Ethical Function of Substantive Due Process," 23 *UCLA Law Review* 689 (1976); John Hart Ely, "The Wages of Crying Wolf: A Commentary on Roe v. Wade," 82 *Yale Law Journal* 920 (1973); Richard E. Epstein, "Substantive Due Process by Any Other Name: The Abortion Cases," 1973 *Supreme Court Review* 159 (1974); and Sylvia A. Law, "Rethinking Sex and the Constitution," 132 *University of Pennsylvania Law Review* 955 (1984).

The debate over interpretivism and noninterpretivism is generating a growing literature. The strongest proponent of interpretivism is Raoul Berger, in such books as *Government by Judiciary* (1977); a controversial argument for noninterpretive review appears in Michael Perry, *The Constitution, The Courts, and Human Rights* (1982). A middle way, but one much closer to the noninterpretivists is suggested by John Hart Ely in *Democracy and Distrust: A Theory of Judicial Review* (1980). Some useful articles include Mark Tushnet, "Following the Rules Laid Down: A Critique of Interpretivism and Neutral Principles," 96 *Harvard Law Review* 781 (1983); Richard Posner, "The Meaning of Judicial Restraint," 59 *Indiana Law Journal.* 1 (1983); and Thomas Grey, "The Constitution as Scripture," 37 *Stanford Law Review* 1 (1984).

41

The Burger Court and Civil Liberties

Obscenity • Commercial Speech • Campaign Funds as Political Speech • Freedom of the Press • A Right of Access • Reporter's Privilege • Church and State • The Drive to Reinstate School Prayer • Free Exercise of Religion • Rights of the Accused: Search and Seizure • The Exclusionary Rule • Miranda Warnings • The Death Penalty • Conclusion • For Further Reading

IN THE AREA of Bill of Rights guarantees, as in the equal protection cases, the Warren Court blazed a path, but left its successor to deal with difficult questions of interpretation and implementation. One finds a mixed record, and while civil libertarians criticized some decisions as a retreat from Warren era doctrine, they praised others for breaking new ground. Despite what some people had predicted, the Burger Court did not adopt a hostile attitude toward free thought and expression or the rights of the accused, although it displayed a greater sympathy to claims that freedom, in some instances, had to be balanced against the needs of the state. As we have seen, there has always been such balancing, even by those advocating an "absolutist" interpretation of the First Amendment. The question is how far the Burger Court shifted the line at which it struck the balance.

One also must read the Court's opinions in the 1970s and 1980s against a startlingly different social context than had existed in the fifteen or so years following *Brown*. The civil rights movement, the political triumphs of liberalism, and the antiwar protests led to a significant backlash and a tendency to blame many of society's supposed ills on the permissive attitude of liberalism, especially as it had manifested itself in the Warren Court. Although there is not a shred of evidence that the Warren Court's criminal justice decisions led to more crimes, there could be little doubt that the incidence of crime, and especially violent crime, increased significantly in the 1970s and 1980s. The war on drugs launched by the Reagan administration had its echoes within the Marble Palace, as the justices struggled to maintain basic constitutional rights and at the same time give police greater flexibility in their daily work. Similarly, the growth of an organized, conservative religious bloc demanding a greater role for religion in public life, found sympathetic ears among the newer and more conservative appointees, who saw the wall of separation erected by the Warren Court as a mistake, and wanted instead to create an accommodation between church and state.

But the Burger Court did not respond just to pressures on the right, some of which they embraced and some they resisted; they also responded to pressures on the left, and some of these they also embraced, while resisting others. The women's movement, which had started in the 1960s, had gained significant power by the 1970s, and the nine gentlemen of the Court could hardly have been unaware of women's demands for equal treatment. If nothing else, they read the papers and watched television; they were all married, and several had daughters. It would have been impossible for them to be unaware that women had adopted the strategies of the civil rights movement and that their issues would soon be before the Court. In terms of women's rights, the members of the Burger Court, supposedly appointed because they would eschew judicial activism, proved to be just as activist as their predecessors.

There is a continuity as well as a discontinuity between the Warren Court and the Burger Court. The latter did not turn its back on the precedents of the former, and in several areas actually extended ideas that had initially been articulated during the Warren years. But the Burger Court functioned in a different social and political context, and these led it to follow other paths as well.

Obscenity

The Warren Court never resolved the problem of obscenity. Although a majority of the Court always agreed that First Amendment protection did not cover obscene materials, it could never settle on a definition of what constituted obscenity. Then, in 1970, the U.S. Commission on Obscenity and Pornography issued its report, which concluded that pornography had little effect on sexual behavior or crime and that exposure to erotica had "little or no effect" on attitudes toward sexuality or sexual morality. It recommended that laws governing the sale and distribution of sexual material to adults be repealed and that restrictions be imposed only on public display of explicit material and on sales to juveniles.

In two 1973 decisions, with the four Nixon appointees in place, the Court tried to articulate new standards to allow state legislatures to develop acceptable restrictions. In *Miller v. California*, Chief Justice Burger reaffirmed that obscene material lacked constitutional protection. In lieu of the older definition of obscenity as material "*utterly* without redeeming social value," he suggested that it be defined as "lacking serious literary, artistic, political or scientific value." The trier of fact, be it a judge or a jury, would evaluate the material applying "contemporary community standards." In a companion case, *Paris Adult Theatre I v. Slaton*, the same 5 to 4 majority held that a state had power to regulate the showing of obscene material in places of public accommodation.

Justice Brennan entered a long and thoughtful dissent covering both cases in which he reviewed the Court's troubled efforts to secure a workable definition of obscenity and to draw the proper line between free expression and order. He reluctantly concluded that the effort could never succeed, and he suggested that the Court essentially adopt the majority report of the Commission on Obscenity. Except for obtrusive advertising and distribution to minors, First Amendment protection should prevent the government from trying to suppress allegedly obscene materials; the state would, however, retain the power to regulate the manner of distribution. Brennan also warned that the definition provided by the majority opinions merely shifted the emphasis and that obscenity cases would continue to haunt the Court.

Events confirmed Brennan's prediction. Lower courts remained enmeshed in efforts to distinguish the obscene from material that met, in one form or another, the *Miller* criteria. The Burger Court refused to take as many cases on appeal as its predecessor had, but still had to do so on occasion and floundered when it did. Within a year after *Miller*, a unanimous Court ruled (1974) that jury decisions declaring material obscene could be reviewed; it had never meant them to be considered final. A local jury in Georgia had found the film *Carnal Knowledge* obscene, and the appellate court, according to Justice Rehnquist, had misunderstood *Miller* in believing that it could not overturn jury determinations (*Jenkins v. Georgia* [1974]). Yet in a companion case, the Court by a 5 to 4 vote held that juries could apply local rather than statewide or national standards (*Hamling v. United States* [1974]). It is difficult to decide what message the Court was trying to send that day. In the one case, it allowed local standards to prevail, no matter how provincial; in the other, it said that if appellate courts thought the local standards "wrong," they could reverse. The Court, instead of instructing lower court judges on the law, sowed confusion instead.

A good part of the problem is that the Court never asked the right questions, namely what interest did the states have in regulating allegedly obscene material. The one case in which it did ask this question proved relatively easy to decide. Child pornography appeared as the only area in which the justices agreed. In *New York v. Ferber* (1982), a unanimous Court upheld a state law prohibiting the distribution of materials depicting children engaged in sexual conduct, whether or not the material had been defined as obscene. Here the Court did ask the right question, and Justice White found that the state had a compelling interest in safeguarding children and had enacted appropriate legislation to effect that end. Child pornography constituted "a category of material outside the protection of the First Amendment."

The Burger Court's path on obscene material proved almost as serpentine as that of its predecessor. In 1976, for example, the Court upheld a Detroit ordinance prohibiting the concentration of so-called adult theaters in order to prevent the deterioration of commercial areas into skid rows or "combat zones"; the ordinance clearly identified sexually explicit "adult" films as its target. In *Young v. American Mini Theatres* (1976), Justice Stevens introduced a new variable into First Amendment balancing—a hierarchy of values. Some speech, such as political expression, is fully protected; some, like fighting words, are unprotected. Between these extremes, some types of speech are less valuable than others, although they are still entitled to some protection. These categories, such as sexually explicit material that is not excluded as obscene, warrants a lower standard of review and is subject to more stringent governmental regulation. Justice Stevens applied the same criteria to uphold the Federal Communications Commission ban against playing George Carlin's "Filthy Words" on the radio (*FCC v. Pacifica Foundation* [1978]).

The Court could not, however, define precisely what this lower-value approach required. As a result, in most cases involving so-called obscene speech, the majority consistently reversed convictions based on speech deemed offensive to some people. In *Cohen v. California* (1971), for example, the defendant had worn a jacket with the words "Fuck the Draft" clearly visible, and had been convicted of disturbing the peace by "offensive conduct." In a 6 to 3 opinion, Justice Harlan ruled the wearing of the jacket to have been primarily speech rather than conduct. Although the state had some power to control offensive speech, free expression constituted so "powerful a medicine in society as diverse and populous as ours" that it should be limited as little as possible. As for those offended by the slogan, Harlan pointed out that Cohen had not forced anyone to look at him; people could easily have avoided the message by looking away.

The Court's willingness to permit some limitations on obscene materials, even if ill defined, aided the passage of some local ordinances inspired by women's groups who attacked pornography on the grounds that it promotes sex discrimination and violence against women. In 1984, Indianapolis adopted such an ordinance on the constitutional grounds that promoting civil rights and equality, both guaranteed in the Fourteenth Amendment, is a "compelling" interest that allows a limited restriction on the First Amendment. The ordinance was part of an attack on free speech and press by a militant and, in this case, feminist left, a group that in the past had often wrapped itself in the blanket of free speech. The strange combination of social conservatives and radical feminists reflected no real commonality of interests but a new paradigm in American politics, in which the old definitions of "left" and "right" no longer applied.

In November 1984, U.S. District Judge Sarah Barker struck the ordinance down in *American Booksellers Association v. Hudnut.* Although noting her agreement with the city's concern and reaffirming that pornography enjoyed no constitutional protection, she found the general goal of preventing undefined sociological damage to women unconvincing and not specific enough to warrant intrusion on free speech. The Circuit Court affirmed the decision, and Judge Frank Easterbrook, a conservative Reagan appointee, noted that some speech is more insidious in its effect than others, but any effort to mitigate that effect "leaves government in control of all of the institutions of culture, the great censor and director of which thoughts are good for us." The Supreme Court confirmed the ruling without hearing arguments.

In an effort to clear up the legal and political confusion surrounding the subject, Attorney General Edwin Meese appointed a Commission on Pornography in May 1985 to determine "the nature, extent, and impact on society of pornography in the United States"

> For, while the particular four-letter word being litigated here is perhaps more distasteful than most others of its genre, it is nevertheless true that one man's vulgarity is another's lyric. Indeed, we think it is largely because governmental officials cannot make principled distinctions in this area that the Constitution leaves matters of taste and style so largely to the individual.
>
> —Justice John Marshall Harlan, *Cohen v. California* (1971)

and to make specific recommendations to the attorney general on how the spread of pornography might be contained, consistent with constitutional guarantees. After a year of hearings, the commission issued its highly controversial report in July 1986. It concluded that a causal link existed between violent pornography and aggressive behavior toward women, including rape and physical abuse. The report thus reached conclusions diametrically opposite to those of the 1970 Presidential Commission's report. A number of social scientists, including some who had been consulted by the Meese Commission, charged that it had misused and misinterpreted the data to reach the answers it wanted.

Although the commission proved unable to develop an acceptable legal definition of obscenity, it did propose that Congress enact legislation making it easier to prosecute and seize the assets of those engaged in the business. The attorney general, acting on the authority of his office, attempted to implement at least part of the commission's recommendations by creating a special task force in the Justice Department to prosecute the purveyors of obscene material.

On the last day of his tenure, Chief Justice Burger delivered two opinions that expanded the powers of the states to reach obscene speech and conduct. The Court allowed New York to close an adult bookstore under a public health statute permitting closure for one year of any business where prostitution or lewdness had occurred. In his opinion, Burger noted that a deputy sheriff had personally witnessed patrons engaging in sexual acts; such activity did not fall within the protection afforded by the First Amendment (*Arcara v. Cloud Books, Inc.* [1986]). In the other case, the Court upheld a school board's suspension of a student who had given a sexually suggestive speech in nominating another student for office in the school government. The chief justice distinguished this case from earlier ones involving student speech, in that those had been directly related to political activity, whereas in this case, the speaker's emphasis had been on the innuendo (*Bethel School District No. 403 v. Fraser* [1986]).

Commercial Speech

Before the 1970s, commercial speech—particularly advertising—had been considered outside First Amendment protection. In *Valentine v. Chrestensen* (1942), the Court had ruled almost casually that the First Amendment imposed no restrictions on governmental regulation of commercial advertising, which the Court viewed as commerce

> I do not like pornography. In fact, I think it probably does harm people. . . . Probably all those ugly pictures do encourage violence against women. What should we do about it? Well, my answer is: not a goddamn thing. The cure for every excess of freedom of speech is more freedom of speech. . . . I need the First Amendment so that I'll be able to say to people who say things I do not agree with, "Look, you yellow-bellied son of a bitch—you run on all fours, you molest small children, you have the mind of an adolescent tyrant." I need to . . . be able to answer them back. That's what the whole fuss is about."
>
> —Columnist Molly Ivins, "Havin' Fun Fighting for Freedom" (1995)

rather than as speech. *Valentine* did not mean that all commercial expression went unprotected; *New York Times v. Sullivan*, it will be recalled, involved a paid advertisement, whereas movies and books, which are also commercial ventures, have First Amendment coverage. As late as 1973, though, Justice Powell sustained a local order barring gender designations in certain types of help-wanted advertisements. He described the ads as "classic examples of commercial speech" and therefore not protected by the First Amendment.

One year later, in *Bigelow v. Virginia* (1975), the Court did a complete about-face. In a challenge to the state's attempt to regulate advertising of abortion services, the Court held that commercial speech merited some constitutional protection, the precise level depending on a balance between the public's interest and the state's need to regulate. Then in *Virginia Pharmacy Board v. Virginia Consumer Council* (1976), Justice Blackmun spoke for an 8 to 1 Court in striking down a ban on the advertising of prescription drug prices. The state had argued that such ads constituted "unprofessional conduct" and could therefore be restricted. Although conceding that some types of commercial speech, such as false or deceptive advertising, could be regulated, the Court ruled that even speech that does "no more than propose a commercial transaction" is entitled to protection. Society benefited from having consumers know what items would cost, so they could weigh the merits of different products, services, and providers. The following year, a 5 to 4 Court threw out a longstanding ban against advertising by lawyers.

The Court's expansion of commercial speech protection drew fire from critics who claimed that the First Amendment protects only politically related expression. According to this line of reasoning, the Framers never intended the First Amendment to cover all forms of expression, but only those that contributed to public policy discussions essential to the functioning of a democratic society. Speech that patently has no political content—such as libel, obscenity, and advertising—has no special protection and may be regulated as any other activity, with the courts applying only a rational basis test. The commercial speech cases, they charged, had done no more than create a new property right; the Court had resuscitated *Lochner* and tied it to freedom of speech.

Justice Powell, who wrote many of the commercial speech opinions, emphasized that only a limited First Amendment protection extended to commercial expression, and it therefore deserved a lower level of scrutiny than did regular speech cases. In *Central Hudson Gas & Electric Corp. v. PSC* (1980), an 8 to 1 Court invalidated a ban on utilities advertisements. Powell put forth a four-part test to measure the legitimacy of commercial speech regulations. The material may not be false or misleading; the state has to have a "substantial" interest in regulation; the regulatory technique must be proportional to the interest; and the limitation must be the most minimal possible. Although Justice Blackmun, in concurrence, described Powell's test as "intermediate scrutiny," Justice Rehnquist, in his lone dissent, saw no substantive difference between this test and the standards the Court applied to judge other restrictions on speech. Rehnquist ignored the fact that in the political arena, "false" speech is protected.

One complicated issue of commercial speech involved the various restrictions imposed by the Securities and Exchange Commission. The SEC undeniably had the power to restrict a false or misleading prospectus for stock issue, but should the courts review the commission's determinations to ensure that legitimate speech had not been restricted? In *Lowe v. SEC* (1985), the Court heard a First Amendment challenge to SEC authority. The commission had revoked Lowe's registration as an investment adviser for a variety of offenses, including theft and misappropriation of client funds, and it had issued a permanent injunction against his publishing an investment newsletter. The Court avoided the constitutional question by ruling, through Justice Stevens, that the Investment Advisers Act had provided an exception for such newsletters and that the SEC had therefore exceeded its statutory authority. Joined by the chief justice and Justice Rehnquist, Justice White concurred in the result, but argued that the First Amendment did apply; he saw the injunction as a classic example of prior restraint.

So long as control of advertising remained under the general category of economic regulation, the courts had ignored the matter and deferred to the legislative judgment. By granting commercial speech a constitutional status requiring, at the least, heightened scrutiny, the Court may well have wandered into a morass akin to pornography, in which a state interest in regulation is recognized as legitimate, but confusion reigns over where the boundary line should be drawn. Legal scholars and tobacco manufacturers have raised the question of whether the proposed bans on advertising of cigarettes and other allegedly harmful products runs afoul of First Amendment protection of commercial speech.

Campaign Funds as Political Speech

Related to the commercial speech cases were those dealing with limitations on political campaign funds. Following the Watergate scandals and the disclosure of massive misuse of campaign contributions, Congress amended the Federal Election Campaign Act in 1974. The new statute limited an individual's contributions to $1,000 per candidate per election, with an annual maximum of $25,000 for all federal candidates. It set spending limits on parties and candidates for federal office, required detailed reports of campaign expenditures, and created a system for public funding of presidential campaigns. In *Buckley v. Valeo* (1976), the Court upheld the limits on individual contributions, the reporting provisions, and the public financing scheme. But it struck down all limits on expenditures by candidates or political action committees (PACs) on First Amendment grounds. According to the Court, the spending of money in a campaign constitutes a form of expression, since it buys space or time in public forums to get across ideas; limiting expenditures, therefore, limits speech. The Court rejected a similar argument against contribution limits, even though this imposed some restric-

> Perhaps the most important beneficial consequence of unregulated expression is simply the stimulation individuals receive from a diverse reading and listening fare; this stimulation may contribute to human happiness directly, and hence be thought to have value quite apart from its relationship to the search for truth.
>
> —Vince Blasi, "The Checking Value in First Amendment Theory," *ABA Research Journal* (1977)

tions on expression; it accepted the government's argument of a compelling interest in preventing corruption and maintaining the integrity of the political process.

Since corporate speech and political speech occasionally dovetail, the Court struck down a Massachusetts prohibition against expenditures by banks and businesses to influence political referendums in *First National Bank of Boston v. Bellotti* (1978). Speaking for a bare 5 to 4 majority, Justice Powell tried to avoid the problem of defining commercial speech by declaring that "the proper question [is] not whether corporations 'have' First Amendment rights and, if so, whether they are coextensive with those of natural persons. Instead, the question must be whether [the statute] abridges expression that the First Amendment was meant to protect." Focusing on the activity rather than the actor, Powell converted the issue to simple restriction of political speech and then imposed strict scrutiny. By that standard, the state could not prove that its desire to avoid corruption of the political process by wealthy corporations "buying" referendums constituted a compelling interest strong enough to limit speech.

The right to spend for political purposes received further validation in *FEC v. National Conservative Political Action Committee* (1985). Justice Rehnquist spoke for a 7 to 2 majority in invalidating the $1,000 limit on political action committee expenditures on behalf of presidential candidates receiving public financing. He emphasized that such committees allowed donors to pool their resources in order to amplify their individual voices; to put a limit on these expenditures would penalize "those of modest means as opposed to those sufficiently wealthy to be able to buy expensive media ads with their own resources." By this reasoning, however, where would the Court draw the line between contributions, which it says may be regulated, and expenditures, which may not? The only distinction seemed to be whether a person gave his or her money to a candidate or a committee, or spent it directly.

There is a widespread view that the Court decided wrongly in *Buckley v. Valeo*, and did not understand the extent to which money had distorted the political process. Efforts to reform campaign financing in the 1990s ran aground on the expected opposition of politicians who did not want to give up the millions of dollars of so-called soft money, which could be used for a variety of political activities, many of them unregulated. But at the same time, even ardent supporters of campaign finance reform recognized that unless the *Buckley* decision could be overturned, or at least modified, then no law that placed a limit on spending could survive constitutional scrutiny.

Freedom of the Press

In addition to speech, the First Amendment specifically protects freedom of the press, and in *New York Times v. Sullivan* (1964), the Warren Court had practically immunized the media from libel suits. Ten years after Warren Burger took the center chair, however, the president of the American Newspaper Publishers Association called on his fellow publishers to "fight to rescue, defend and uphold the First Amendment." He charged that "the imperial judiciary . . . is bending the First Amendment at every turn," creating an "atmosphere of intimidation for the press." It is difficult to reconcile the Burger Court's overall record in press cases with this near hysteria.

The idea that because the press is mentioned separately it enjoys some special protection under the First Amendment is one that publishers and reporters have long pushed to have adopted. Justice Potter Stewart argued in a 1974 speech that the "Free Press guarantee is, in essence, a *structural* provision of the Constitution. [It] extends protection to an institution." Stewart believed that the Constitution recognized the press as an additional check on the other three branches of government and that therefore its freedom went beyond the general freedom of expression contained in the Speech Clause. A few years later, Justice Brennan also referred to the structural role that a free press plays in "securing and fostering our republican system of self-government." However, neither scholars in general nor the Court in particular has adopted the view that the press constitutionally enjoys special treatment or protection.

One of the first press cases to reach the Burger Court grew out of the public controversy over American participation in the Vietnam War, the so-called Pentagon Papers case, or, more formally, *New York Times Co. v. United States* (1971). Portions of secret Defense Department studies and reports had been illegally copied and provided to newspapers; *The New York Times* began publication on June 13, 1971; the *Washington Post* followed on the 18th. Both newspapers had carefully investigated their legal rights before commencing publication. The Nixon administration immediately sought injunctions to restrain publication, and between June 15 and 23, the case went through two district and two circuit courts, one of which issued an injunction and the other did not.

Because of this disagreement, and in view of the significance of the documents, the Supreme Court granted certiorari on June 25, heard arguments the next day, and issued its opinion on June 30. The *per curiam* decision vacated all injunctions as unconstitutional prior restraints, which had been held impermissible since *Near v. Minnesota* four decades earlier. Six of the justices concurred in the result, which held that the government had not met the "heavy burden of showing justification for the imposition of such a restraint." Only Harlan, Burger, and Blackmun dissented; they objected to the feverish pace of the case, as well as to the results. All believed that the government had legitimate reasons to suppress the material; the First Amendment did not provide a license for the press to print anything it pleased.

Although a victory for the press, the Pentagon Papers case really broke no new ground. The opinion did little more than reaffirm *Near*'s ban on prior restraint, and only Black and Douglas took an absolutist position. When and if government could prove that publication would harm national interests, it could secure a restraining order—and that is exactly what happened in *United States v. Progressive, Inc.* (1979), a few years later. The district court judge, relying on the Pentagon Papers ruling, granted the government an injunction to restrain the *Progressive* from publishing an article on how to build an atom bomb. Although the government conceded that the scientific information was no longer classified, the judge agreed that publication would allow medium-sized countries an easier and faster route to developing nuclear bombs.

The high court itself upheld a type of prior restraint in *Snepp v. United States* (1980). A number of federal agencies, including the CIA and the defense and state departments require their employees, as a condition of employment, to sign an agreement not to publish any information relating to the agency, either during or after employment, without specific approval. The Court had twice refused appeals in another case, in which a former CIA employee had submitted a manuscript, and the agency had insisted on 168 deletions. Snepp, also a former CIA man, had published *Decent Interval*, a critical account of America's last days in Vietnam, without CIA approval. The government sought an order requiring Snepp to submit any future writings to the CIA for clearance. It also called for a constructive trust (a trust established so that the gains of illegal acts will not go to the perpetrator) to divert any book profits from Snepp to the government. Snepp asserted, and the government conceded, that the book contained no classified information.

In a controversial ruling, the Court—without briefs or oral arguments—sustained a lower-court injunction and imposed the constructive trust. The majority's only mention of the First Amendment came in a footnote; even in the absence of an express agreement, the government could impose "reasonable restrictions on employee activities that in other contexts might be protected by the First Amendment." Justice Stevens, joined by Marshall and Brennan, entered a strong protest against the result, which they denounced as approving prior restraint, and against the majority's hasty and unusual manner of handling the case.

Snepp led to some complaints that in a conflict between the press and the government over issues of national security, the Burger Court would give the press little support. The Court, however, always advocated a balancing interpretation of the First Amendment. In the Pentagon Papers case it had decided for the press because the government could not meet the burden of proving that publication would endanger national security. In two cases not involving national security, the Court struck down restrictions on reporting of governmental activities.

In *Landmark Communications, Inc. v. Virginia* (1978), a newspaper, utilizing lawful methods to gather information, published an accurate report of a pending inquiry by the Virginia Judicial Inquiry and Review Commission and identified the state judge under investigation. A state law classified all information before the commission as confidential and made disclosure a crime. Chief Justice Burger held that this type of information, concerned with the probity of governmental conduct, was near "the core of the First Amendment." The commission's activities, like those of courts themselves, were matters of great and legitimate public interest, and therefore the newspaper had every right to publish information concerning its actions. In *Smith v. Daily Mail Publishing Co.* (1979), the chief justice, again for a unanimous Court, invalidated a state law prohibiting the publication of the name of any youth charged as a juvenile offender. The newspaper, after lawful investigation, had printed the picture and name of a high school student charged with shooting one of his classmates to death. "If a newspaper lawfully obtains truthful information about a matter of public significance," he wrote, "then state officials may not constitutionally punish publication of the information, absent a need to further a state interest of the highest order."

A Right of Access

Even in conflicts between the press and the judiciary, whose interests have always been jealously guarded by the high court, the press fared well. In several cases in which trial courts attempted either to impose prior restraint or ban reporters from the courtroom, allegedly to preserve the integrity of the criminal justice process, the Supreme Court upheld the press and its right to gather news. In *Nebraska Press Association v. Stuart* (1976), the Court for the first time considered the permissibility of a press gag order to ensure a fair trial. A state court, anticipating the sensationalism that would surround the trial of an accused mass murderer in a small town, issued an order prohibiting publication of the accused's confessions, admissions, and any other evidence presented by the prosecution at the preliminary hearing. In a narrowly focused opinion, the chief justice found that the facts did not warrant such prior restraint, and he reiterated the Court's strong presumption against it. Trial courts have various tools available if a judge believes that media publicity may affect the fairness of the proceedings. Judges can order a change of venue, postponement, careful screening of jurors, sequestration of the jury, and restrictions on statements by the lawyers, police, and witnesses, all of whom come within the power of the court.

In the 1979 case of *Gannett Co. v. DePasquale*, a badly divided Court rejected a publisher's attack on a court order closing the courtroom to the press and public during a pretrial hearing on the suppression of evidence. In the majority opinion, Justice Stewart hardly mentioned the First Amendment, but concentrated on the meaning of the Sixth Amendment's right to a public trial. He concluded that it did not mean that the public had a right to insist on an open trial, for that right accrued solely to the defendant. Justice Powell, although concurring in the result, did examine First Amendment implications. He suggested that public confidence in the fairness and efficacy of the criminal justice system depends, at least in part, on receiving accurate information about its workings, information that the press provides.

The following year, in the landmark case of *Richmond Newspapers, Inc. v. Virginia* (1980), a 7 to 1 Court adopted Powell's reasoning. The trial judge, exasperated after three mistrials on a murder charge, had closed the court at the defendant's request and without objection from the prosecution. The judge had acted without giving his reasons, but relied solely on the broad discretion allowed him by Virginia law. Chief Justice Burger emphasized the First Amendment right of the public to know, not the Sixth Amendment, in granting the press access. Seven of the eight participating justices wrote separate opinions (Justice Rehnquist dissented); each had a different view of how the First and Sixth amendments intersected. Only two other members of the Court subscribed fully to Burger's opinion, and both wrote concurring opinions differing significantly from his reasoning.

In 1982, the justices did manage to agree on an opinion in *Globe Newspaper Co. v. Superior Court*, which tested the meaning of *Richmond Newspapers.* A Massachusetts law had been interpreted to *require* exclusion of press and public from the courtroom during the testimony of a minor who had allegedly been the victim of a sex crime. The state court had upheld the law since cases involving sex crimes and minors had traditionally been areas involving "sensitivity to the needs of the victims." But Justice Brennan found that the law violated the First Amendment, which he boldly proclaimed included a right of access to criminal trials. He conceded that the state's desire to protect the psychological well-being of the victims from further trauma was compelling, but he ruled that the law went much further than necessary. It allowed the trial judge no discretion, and all of the testimony could later be secured from the transcript, which constituted a public document.

During the 1970s, media litigants began to urge a new approach to the meaning of the Press Clause. They argued that the clause served not only as a shield to protect the press from governmental interference, but also as a sword to permit the press access to newsworthy events. Embroidering upon Justice Stewart's notion of the press as a fourth branch of government, they proclaimed that the press had not only a duty but a right to gather newsworthy material, because only by gaining access to and publishing this information would the public have the information it needed. To bolster this argument, advocates constantly pointed to the investigative reporting that had uncovered the full extent of the Watergate scandals.

The Supreme Court, however, refused to grant the press such a preferred status. In a number of cases, it ruled that the press enjoyed access equal to that granted the public, but that it had no right to anything more. In the companion cases of *Pell v. Procunier* and *Saxbe v. Washington Post Co.* (1974), the Court rejected attacks on state and federal laws barring press interviews with prisoners. These regulations did not violate the First Amendment, Justice Stewart explained, since they imposed no greater restriction on the press than on the public at large. Four justices—Powell Brennan, Marshall, and Douglas—dissented and argued for some form of access as a press right.

Reporter's Privilege

The refusal of the Court to grant the press special rights of access may, at most, make newsgathering more difficult in certain circumstances—although reporters have been probing into all sorts of places for more than two centuries without any particular constitutional imprimatur. However, reporters often dig up information unavailable to police and other public officials by developing confidential sources, people who will talk to reporters and allow their stories to be printed provided their names are not divulged. Reporters claim that in order to protect these confidential relationships, they should enjoy immunity from having to testify before grand juries or prosecutors about their news sources, a privilege similar to that of a physician and patient or priest and penitent. A number of states have recognized such a privilege, usually by statute, but Congress has not followed suit.

Since 1969, the number of subpoenas to newspersons has increased dramatically. In part, this is due to the rise in political disturbances designed to attract media attention; reporters are invited in to ensure press coverage, and they often have information on the participants that the police want. When faced with a subpoena to testify before a grand jury, reporters have to make the uncomfortable choice of either betraying the confidence of their sources or possibly going to jail on contempt charges. The Supreme Court decided only one case on this issue, *Branzberg v. Hayes* (1972), which combined three separate cases of reporters refusing to testify before grand juries. The three did not claim an absolute privilege, but only that they should not be forced to testify unless the government could make a substantial case that they possessed important information that was not available from any other source.

The Court rejected the claim by a 5 to 4 vote. Justice White acknowledged that newsgathering qualified for First Amendment protection, but he pointed out that the cases did not involve any traditional type of infringement on a free press, such as prior restraint. Rather, they involved a reporter's duty as a citizen to testify before a grand jury probing allegedly illegal activities. Balancing the need to promote effective law enforcement against the burden on newsgathering, White found in favor of law enforcement. Justice Powell, once again the swing vote, concurred in the result, but indicated that at times the balance ought to be struck in favor of the press; he wanted to leave this determination up to the judges in individual cases.

The Burger Court, in sum, refused to grant the press special consideration or create new constitutional guarantees, but otherwise it usually protected the interests of the fourth estate. In other cases, it struck down a state tax imposed solely on newspapers (*Minneapolis Start v. Minnesota Commissioner of Revenue* [1983]), as well as a law requiring that newspapers balance critical stories by printing replies (*Miami Herald Pub. Co. v. Tornillo* [1974]). It backed the press against the federal government in the Pentagon Papers case and even sided with the press against the judiciary to ensure press access to trials. The press as a whole had little to complain about its treatment in the Court during the Burger years.

Church and State

Another area of the First Amendment that the Burger Court had to address was the Establishment Clause. The efforts of the Johnson administration to aid church-related schools under Great Society educational programs brought the issue of church-state separation back into the courts after two decades of relative quiescence. The Warren Court had developed two tests for determining the validity of government programs under the Establishment Clause: the activity must have a secular legislative purpose and a primary effect that neither advances nor inhibits religion. In *Lemon v. Kurtzman* (1971), the Burger Court formally announced a three-pronged standard: the law must have a secular purpose; its primary effect must neither advance nor inhibit religion; it must avoid excessive government entanglement with religion. The Court used the *Lemon* formula to test challenged legislation in practically every subsequent religion case, although it often claimed that it served as no more than a "helpful signpost." According to some critics, both within and outside the Court, that signpost often pointed in different directions.

Purists call for a total wall of separation to forbid any form of governmental aid, even passive support such as tax exemptions. They claim that any aid leads to entan-

> . . . modern governmental programs have self-perpetuating and self-expanding propensities. These internal pressures are only enhanced when the schemes involve institutions whose legitimate needs are growing and whose interests have substantial political support. Nor can we fail to see in constitutional adjudication some steps, which when taken were thought to approach "the verge," have become the platform for yet further steps. . . . The dangers are increased by the difficulty of perceiving in advance exactly where the "verge" of the precipice lies. As well as constituting an independent evil against which the Religion Clauses were intended to protect, involvement or entanglement between government and religion serves as a warning signal.
>
> —Chief Justice Warren Burger, *Lemon v. Kurtzman* (1971)

glement; the government is obliged to ensure that its money is spent lawfully and effectively, and therefore it must be involved in church affairs whenever religiously affiliated agencies receive state or federal aid. At the other end of the spectrum are those who insist that the First Amendment never meant that the government could not aid churches; they see the Establishment Clause as no more than a prohibition against the government favoring one denomination over the others. The "wall of separation," they claim, is no more than Jefferson's personal belief, which the Framers did not adopt. (The phrase appears nowhere in the Constitution or Bill of Rights.) By this view, all state aid to parochial schools is legitimate, provided that it is available on an equal basis to all denominations.

The Burger Court's decisions on state aid to parochial education proved so contradictory that no one—on or off the bench—seemed to know with any certainty what the Constitution permitted or forbade. A quick survey of the decisions highlights the confusion.

The Court held that states cannot lend maps, tape recorders, and other instructional materials to parochial school students (*Wolman v. Walter* [1977]), although it did not overrule the Warren Court's 1968 decision that lending *books* is permissible (*Board of Education v. Allen* [1968]). In 1973, the Court held that states may not reimburse parochial schools for the costs of administering state-mandated but teacher-prepared tests (*Levitt v. Committee for Public Education*) but seven years later, it said that states may subsidize the cost of giving state-prepared tests (*Committee for Public Education v. Regan* [1980]). The Court upheld a Minnesota law allowing taxpayers to deduct some of the costs for parochial education from state taxes (*Mueller v. Allen* [1983]), although it had earlier struck down a similar New York plan of tuition rebates and tax deductions (*Committee for Public Education v. Nyquist* [1973]). The Court also ruled that restrictions that apply to elementary and secondary schools do not necessarily apply to colleges in *Tilton v. Richardson* (1971) and *Hart v. McNair* (1973). Because several of these cases had been reached by 5 to 4 votes, hopes and fears abounded that the Court would soon take a more "accommodationist" view toward aid to parochial education. But in June 1985, the Court reaffirmed the wall of separation, although again only by a 5 to 4 vote. In *Grand Rapids School District v. Ball* and *Aguilar v. Felton*, the justices invalidated both state and federal "shared-time" programs, in which full-time public school teachers taught classes, usually of a remedial nature, in parochial schools.[1]

Some thought the wall had been breached in *Widmar v. Vincent* (1981), when the Court held that a state university that made its facilities available for the activities of registered student organizations could not bar a student group from using rooms for religious worship and discussion. The University of Missouri in Kansas City had a general policy of prohibiting religious meetings in its facilities, but the Court found that the mandate of free speech outweighed that of the Establishment Clause. Justice Powell noted that the university had created a forum that was generally open for student use; by excluding religious discussion, the school had imposed a content regulation that violated the First Amendment. Powell indicated that an "equal access" policy would

1. *Grand Rapids School District v. Ball* (1985); *Aquilar v. Felton* (1985).

be compatible with the Constitution. In 1985, Congress passed the Equal Access Act, which extended the *Widmar* holding to secondary schools receiving federal aid. Some of the law's provisions, such as the requirement that a school official be present in "a nonparticipatory capacity" and that nonschool persons may not direct or attend such meetings, may well lead to constitutional challenges.

The Court's "accommodationist" side also came through in *Marsh v. Chambers* (1983), in which it upheld the Nebraska assembly's practice of beginning every legislative day with a prayer by a paid chaplain. Chief Justice Burger's majority opinion concentrated on the historical prevalence of the practice, which he believed outweighed the minor breach of the Establishment Clause. Then in *Lynch v. Donnelly* (1984), the chief justice delivered a 5 to 4 opinion approving the display of a municipally owned creche in a Pawtucket, Rhode Island, public park at Christmas time. Burger managed to offend both First Amendment purists as well as some Christian groups, the former by his characterization of the wall of separation as little more than a useful metaphor, and the latter by describing the creche, which depicted the biblical story of the birth of Jesus, as only a secular image.

The *Lynch* decision triggered serious criticism of the Court in academic circles, and some scholars charged the chief justice with undermining the Establishment Clause by his willingness to accommodate religious interests. Yet the Court disappointed those who hoped that with the addition of the Nixon appointees it would reverse the *Engel* decision barring school prayer. In fact, the Burger Court's first pronouncement in this area struck down a Kentucky statute requiring the posting of the Ten Commandments, purchased with private funds, in all public school classrooms. The *per curiam* opinion in *Stone v. Graham* (1980) characterized the law as "plainly religious."

The Drive to Reinstate School Prayer

The *Stone* decision revived efforts by conservatives to reverse what they saw as the Court's antireligious nature. Senator Jesse Helms of North Carolina introduced legislation to remove federal court jurisdiction over challenges to voluntary school pro-

> The essence of the crèche's symbolic purpose and effect is to prompt the observer to experience a sense of simple awe and wonder appropriate to the contemplation of one of the central tenets of Christian dogma—that God sent His son into the world to be a Messiah. Contrary to the Court's suggestion, the crèche is far from a mere representation of a "particular historic religious event." It is, instead, best understood as a mystical re-creation of an event that lies at the heart of the Christian faith. To suggest, as the Court does, that such a symbol is merely "traditional" and therefore no different from Santa's house or reindeer is not only offensive to those for whom the crèche has profound significance, but insulting to those who insist for religious or personal reasons that the story of Christ is in no sense a part of "history" nor an unavoidable element of our national "heritage."
>
> —Justice William Brennan, Jr., dissenting in *Lynch v. Donnelly* (1984)

grams. Helms based his proposal on Article III, Section 2, which defines the jurisdiction of the Supreme Court and concludes with the phrase "with such Exceptions, and under such Regulations as the Congress shall make." The Court has on several occasions acknowledged the power of Congress to limit its jurisdiction, but it is unclear whether that power extends to matters of constitutional interpretation. Section 2 deals with appellate and original jurisdiction, that is, the types of cases that the Court can hear only on appeal and those that it may hear directly. It is doubtful if any Court, conservative or liberal, would be willing to accept limitations on its ability to define what the Constitution means.

When Attorney General William French Smith raised questions about the legitimacy of curbing jurisdiction, President Reagan, in May 1982, proposed a constitutional amendment providing that "nothing in this Constitution shall be construed to prohibit individual or group prayer in public schools or other public institutions. No person shall be required by the United States or by any State to participate in prayer." Despite strong pressure from fundamentalist religious groups, the amendment failed to gain many adherents. Opponents argued that introducing any type of prayer approved or led by school authorities carried a strong, even if unspoken, pressure to participate. When the amendment finally came to the floor of the Senate for a vote on March 20, 1984, it fell eleven votes short of passage. The president promised he would carry on the fight, and although he raised the issue several times during the election campaign that year, he did nothing about the matter at the beginning of his second term. Others reintroduced a variety of proposed amendments, however, and Senator Helms sponsored yet another bill stripping the courts of jurisdiction over prayer programs.

Some states attempted to reintroduce prayer into schools by establishing "voluntary" programs or mandating a moment of silence when students could pray or merely meditate. Alabama enacted three such laws. First it provided for a one-minute silent period for meditation in 1978, which it amended in 1981 to authorize "meditation or voluntary prayer"; then in 1982, it directed teachers to lead "willing students" in a prescribed prayer to "Almighty God . . . the Creator and Supreme Judge of the world." Both the district and circuit courts struck down the latter two as invalid, ruling that the sole legislative purpose had been to encourage religious activity in the schools. The Supreme Court affirmed in *Wallace v. Jaffree* (1985), with justices Burger, Rehnquist, and White dissenting. Justice Stevens, for the majority, noted that the moment of silence by itself violated no constitutional provision; it did nothing else than give schoolchildren the right to meditate in silence, "and there is nothing wrong with a little med-

> It is impossible to build sound constitutional doctrine upon a mistaken understanding of constitutional history, but unfortunately, the Establishment Clause has been expressly freighted with Jefferson's misleading metaphor for nearly forty years. . . . The "wall of separation between church and state" is a metaphor based on bad history, a metaphor which has proved useless as a guide to judging. It should be frankly and explicitly abandoned.
>
> —Justice William H. Rehnquist, dissenting in *Wallace v. Jaffree* (1985)

itation and quietness." But the record made clear that the state wanted more, and once it encouraged prayer or had school officials leading prayers, it had gone too far.

The Rehnquist dissent is interesting because for the first time a justice challenged the standard historical interpretation of the Establishment Clause that had prevailed since Justice Black's 1947 opinion in *Everson*. Rehnquist asserted that the Clause did no more than prevent the national government from establishing a single denomination as a "national" church, or to favor one sect over another. Through the incorporation of the Bill of Rights, these prohibitions also applied to the states. But Rehnquist found nothing in the Clause to prevent either the states or the federal government from providing aid to religion, providing it distributed that aid on the basis of neutral principles that did not favor one denomination over another. With his dissent, Rehnquist transformed the accommodationist argument and gave it what it had previously lacked, a claimed historical basis. Most scholars of the First Amendment have disagreed with Rehnquist's historical interpretation, but it has been seized upon and expanded by advocates of governmental support of religious institutions.

Free Exercise of Religion

The Burger Court's record on the Free Exercise Clause proved far more consistent than on Establishment. The Court reaffirmed the basic holding of *Sherbert v. Verner*—that a person may not be denied government benefits due to religious belief—when it reversed, by an 8 to 1 vote, Indiana's denial of unemployment compensation benefits to a Jehovah's Witness who had left his job in a munitions factory because of religious objections to war (*Thomas v. Review Board* [1981]). But although the Free Exercise Clause requires exemption from government regulation under certain circumstances, these are not unlimited. In *United States v. Lee* (1982), the Court refused to exempt the Old Order Amish from paying Social Security taxes on religious grounds, and in *Tony and Susan Alamo Foundation v. Secretary of Labor* (1985), it rejected fundamentalist Christian claims that religious scruples prevented compliance with the minimum wage and other provisions of the Fair Labor Standards Act.[2] The Court also sustained an Internal Revenue Service ruling denying tax-exempt charitable status to schools that practiced racial discrimination. In *Bob Jones University v. United States* (1983), Chief Justice Burger rejected the free exercise claim and found a compelling governmental interest in promoting racial equality.

A state's claim that compulsory education for all children constituted a compelling interest would be approved by most Americans, yet it failed to convince the Court in *Wisconsin v. Yoder* (1972). The Amish objected to provisions of state law requiring attendance past the eighth grade. They believed, and the state did not challenge the sincerity of their belief, that sending adolescent children to high school would endanger their salvation. Although the Court recognized that the Amish marched completely out of step with contemporary society, Chief Justice Burger affirmed their constitutional right to do so. Enforcement of the law would raise "a very real threat of under-

2. *United States v. Lee* (1982); *Tony and Susan Alamo Foundation v. Secretary of Labor* (1985).

mining the Amish community and religious practices as they exist today; they must either abandon belief and be assimilated into society at large, or be forced to migrate to some other and more tolerant region." Given the relatively small number of children involved, the state's interest in educating its citizens would not suffer if it allowed the Amish an exception.

What the *Yoder* majority did not anticipate is that the ruling would provide an impetus for the home schooling movement. While there have always been parents who have taught their children at home, growing dissatisfaction with the nation's public school system, a rising urban crime rate, and the phenomenal growth of the religious right, with its suspicion of all things secular, led to tens of thousands of parents deciding to keep their children out of the public schools. While home schooling is not limited to social and religious conservatives, they have been the backbone of the movement, and their publications have hailed the *Yoder* decision for giving their movement a constitutional imprimatur. It is doubtful if the Burger Court even considered home schooling in its deliberations, since at the time the numbers involved were truly insignificant. One might well point to *Yoder* and the home school movement as a good example of the law of unanticipated consequences.

The mixed record of the Burger Court led to much speculation about the future of the two religion clauses, since a change of only one or two votes might give the accommodationists a majority. Whether the Jeffersonian wall of separation could stand with large sections removed or whether it would just collapse remained a question that the post-Burger Court would have to consider.

Rights of the Accused: Search and Seizure

If conservatives expected anything from the Burger Court, it was that it would reject its predecessor's alleged "softness" on criminals and, in Richard Nixon's words, redress the balance in favor of the "peace forces." However, despite the uproar over cases like *Miranda*, the Warren Court had never attempted to alter significantly American criminal justice. In most of its criminal procedure cases, it had either endorsed police tactics or imposed minor modifications. Even the holdings in some "great" cases like *Gideon*—entitling indigents to counsel—and *Katz*—requiring a search warrant for a wiretap—had already been accepted in principle. The allegedly radical decisions came early; by the mid-1960s, the Warren Court had begun to reexamine and consolidate its earlier rulings.

At first, the Burger Court seemed intent on restricting the rights of the accused, but over the course of the seventeen terms that Warren Burger sat in the center chair, the word that best describes his Court's decisions on criminal procedure is "fluid." The initial effort to cut back on Warren Court decisions passed after a few years, and in the late 1970s, a less police-oriented bench emerged that breathed new life into the substantive and procedural safeguards accorded accused persons. Then in the 1980s, a "tougher" Court began handing down more progovernment decisions, especially in the area of drug enforcement. Perhaps most important, the Burger Court backed away from the absolute prophylactic standards of the Warren Court, and in their place erected a "totality of the circumstances" approach that gave courts much greater leeway in evaluating police procedures.

In one of its first Fourth Amendment cases, the Court rolled back some of the strict standards necessary to secure a search warrant. The Burger Court did not at first abandon the old two-prong test—the reliability of the information and the credibility of its source—but allowed the magistrate to take greater account of the police officer's knowledge of an informant (*United States v. Harris* [1971]). It finally abandoned the test in 1983, replacing it with a "totality of circumstances" approach. According to Justice Rehnquist, who wrote the 6 to 3 majority opinion in *Illinois v. Gates*, reliability and credibility still mattered, but only as factors in a commonsense, practical inquiry into whether evidence or contraband probably could be found in a particular location. Rehnquist emphasized that the new approach was not standardless; the Court had deliberately not spelled out too many details, because it wanted to leave local magistrates with as much flexibility as possible. The Court reaffirmed the totality of the circumstances approach the following year in *Massachusetts v. Upton.*

Critics complained that the Burger Court showed less concern with privacy under the Fourth Amendment than did its predecessor. In several cases, the majority ruled that the police could cast a broad net in their searches and even confiscate some items without a warrant. The Court allowed police who were searching a lawyer's office with a warrant directed to a specific item to take away files, search them at the station, and then return nonrelevant materials (*Andreson v. Maryland* [1976]). A bank depositor, according to Justice Powell, had no reasonable expectation of privacy in his accounts, and therefore a bank could deliver subpoenaed records of transactions without notifying the customer (*United States v. Miller* [1975]) The Court also ruled that police could install a pen register without a warrant. Although a person could expect the contents of a telephone conversation to be private, dialing a number left a record with the telephone company. Therefore, using a pen register to record which numbers a person called did not constitute a search and did not require a warrant (*Smith v. Maryland* [1979]).

The Court, much to the distress of civil libertarians, expanded the doctrine of "consent." No warrant is needed if someone agrees to have a person or premises searched. In *Schneckloth v. Bustamonte* (1973), the majority ruled that police did not have to recite a *Miranda*-type formula informing a person that he or she might refuse police access until they procured a warrant. Police need only demonstrate that consent "was in fact voluntarily given, and not the result of duress or coercion." The Court ignored arguments that some people would agree to an otherwise impermissible search because they did not know their rights.

Although the Burger Court modified (and in the eyes of some, downplayed) Fourth Amendment protection in certain areas, it did not retreat fully, as conservatives had hoped. In fact, the Court expanded some Fourth Amendment rights. In *Gerstein v. Pugh* (1975), for example, the Court dealt with a long-festering problem of detention under warrantless arrest. The Fourth Amendment calls for a warrant before officials may seize a person, but customarily police may arrest persons who are suspected of a felony or caught committing a misdemeanor. Police, however, could often detain suspects several hours or even several days for questioning without formally charging them with any crime. Under *Gerstein*, a person once arrested must be brought before a magistrate within a reasonable time (a few hours); if police cannot make out probable cause for arrest, the person must be released.

The Court did show a strong attachment to privacy of home and person, striking down the widespread practice in many states of allowing police to enter a home and making a warrantless arrest for suspicion of a felony (*Payton v. New York* [1980]). The Court also ruled that a valid warrant to search a tavern and the person of the bartender for drugs gave police no authority to search the patrons. "Mere propinquity to [those] suspected of criminal activity does not, without more, give rise to probable cause to search that person" (*Ybarra v. Illinois* [1980]). And in *United States v. United States District Court* (1972), a unanimous bench held that neither the 1968 federal electronic surveillance law nor the president's inherent powers to protect against domestic subversion "justify departure [from] the customary Fourth Amendment requirement of judicial approval prior to the initiation of a search or surveillance." In a number of other cases, the Burger Court consistently required the procurement of a search warrant in circumstances in which it had not previously been thought necessary, and it declined the opportunity to draw back on some of the Warren Court precedents.

The Court did, however, respond to the public outcry against drug abuse and gave its endorsement to the war against drugs. To some observers it seemed that however protective the Court might be in other areas of Fourth Amendment rights, it seemed willing to permit law officers great leeway in drug-related cases. In *New Jersey v. T.L.O.* (1985), the justices permitted school officials, on reasonable suspicion, to conduct warrantless searches of student belongings for drugs or other proscribed articles. And in one of the last opinions handed down before Burger's retirement, a 5 to 4 Court ruled that aerial surveillance of a person's backyard did not constitute a search, even if police in the airplane photographed marijuana under cultivation and then secured a warrant for an on-ground search. In *California v. Ciraelo* 1986), the facts made clear that "the yard was within the curtilage of the house, that a fence shielded the yard from observation from the street and that the occupant had a subjective expectation of privacy." The majority, however, found this expectation of privacy "unreasonable and not an expectation that society is prepared to honor," although Chief Justice Burger's opinion could provide neither empirical or constitutional reasons why society was not prepared to honor the privacy of a person who put up a high fence around his yard.

The "drug exception" to the Fourth Amendment continued in the early years of the Rehnquist Court. In *Florida v. Riley* (1989), the Court upheld the legality of a helicopter circling above a greenhouse, and with the use of a telephoto lens, observing marijuana growing. The police were able to see through the roof of the greenhouse because two of the panels were missing. This fact gave the majority the opportunity to describe the greenhouse as having "a partially open roof," and therefore subject to aerial surveillance on the basis of *Ciraelo.* Justice Brennan objected strenuously, comparing police tactics to those employed by the brutal dictatorial government in George Orwell's *1984,* and in fact quoted from the novel, BIG BROTHER IS WATCHING YOU!

The Exclusionary Rule

Perhaps the best intimation of the Burger Court's reluctance to assume a strictly law-and-order orientation could be found in its handling of the exclusionary rule—the judge-made ban on using illegally seized evidence. Burger and Rehnquist pushed for a "good-faith" exception, that is, for admitting evidence obtained by "inadvertent" violations, or when police believed in good faith that they had a valid warrant. In 1982, the Court dismissed an argument for such an exception by noting that "to date we have not recognized such an exception, and we decline to do so here" (*Taylor v. Alabama* [1982]). The following term, the Court asked counsel to reargue *Illinois v. Gates* and address the issue of whether changes should be made in the exclusionary rule. When the decision came down in the late spring of 1983, however, Justice Rehnquist apologized for bringing up the good-faith issue and simply noted that the Court was not ready to change the rule.

The Court finally did adopt a very limited good-faith exception in *United States v. Leon* (1984). Police, following up a report by an unproven informer, staked out a house and observed activity indicative of drug trafficking. On this basis, they secured a warrant and arrested a number of persons while seizing a quantity of drugs. Both the district and circuit courts ruled that the warrant had been faulty; it had been issued with less than probable cause, mainly due to reliance on "stale" information and because the police had failed to establish the reliability of the informer. Both lower courts also declined to rule on a good-faith exception in light of *Gates*. But Justice White, speaking for a 6 to 3 majority, used a cost-benefit analysis to uphold the government's claim for a good-faith exception.

The exclusionary rule, he explained, deterred official misconduct and provided a remedy for egregious mistakes. Here the police had followed appropriate procedures; the fault, if any, lay with the magistrate, who possibly misjudged the validity of police information. "When law enforcement officials have acted in good faith or their transgressions have been minor," White explained, "the magnitude of the benefit conferred on such guilty defendants offends basic concepts of the criminal justice system." In a companion case, *Massachusetts v. Sheppard*, the Court applied a good-faith exception when police relied on a warrant that failed to describe specifically the objects to be seized. The police had submitted a sufficiently detailed affidavit, but had used an inappropriate form; both they and the magistrate, however, knew exactly what they wanted. The magistrate had said he would edit the form to make it proper, but then had failed to do so. The police and society should not be penalized, White declared, because the magistrate had made a clerical error.

The two cases provided a relatively narrow exception carved out of the exclusionary rule, and it will take many more decisions to determine how far—if at all—subsequent Courts will widen that exception. The bench is certainly aware of recent studies showing that the exclusionary rule has had little impact on prosecutions. Evidence is excluded as a result of Fourth Amendment violations in only 1.3 percent of cases, and prosecutions have been dropped in less than 0.5 percent of cases because of search and seizure problems. One legacy of the Warren Court is that a strict adherence to constitutional safeguards has made for better police work. Procuring a proper warrant at the start avoids problems later on, and the Burger Court, even in the good-faith cases, emphasized that it would not lower constitutional standards to accommodate sloppy police procedures.

Miranda Warnings

A pattern somewhat similar to that indicated in the good-faith cases appeared in the Burger Court's handling of the most controversial criminal procedure ruling of the

Warren Court—the *Miranda* decision (which required police to advise suspects of their rights and then to desist from questioning if suspects asserted those rights). In a series of rulings in the first half of the 1970s, the Court seemed determined to limit *Miranda*, if not do away with it entirely. In *Harris v. New York* (1971), over a bitter dissent by justices Brennan, Douglas, and Marshall, the Court held that, although statements obtained after a defective Miranda warning could not be used by the prosecution to show guilt, they could be used to impeach the defendant's credibility, which would be just as damaging. Later rulings allowed impeachment use of statements obtained by continued police interrogation, even after the defendant had asserted his or her right to remain silent (*Oregon v. Haas* [1975]), and permitted police to come back and re-question a suspect repeatedly, so long as they recited the Miranda warning each time (*Michigan v. Mosely* [1975]). The doctrine appeared doomed in 1974, when Justice Rehnquist, in *Michigan v. Tucker*, described the Miranda warnings as "not themselves rights protected by the Constitution," but only "prophylactic standards" designed to "safeguard" or to "provide practical reinforcement" for the privilege against self-incrimination.

Nevertheless a few years later, in the controversial case of *Brewer v. Williams* (1977), the Burger Court indicated that the doctrine remained alive and well. Robert Williams, an escaped mental patient, had allegedly abducted and then murdered a ten-year-old girl on Christmas eve in Des Moines, Iowa. Two days later, he called his attorney from Davenport, and upon the lawyer's advice, surrendered to the police there. The attorney also advised Williams not to talk to the police until he arrived back in Des Moines, where the lawyer would be present. The police there promised the attorney they would not interrogate Williams after they picked him up to bring him back to Des Moines. At the start of the 160-mile trip from Davenport to Des Moines, Williams expressed his intent to remain silent. The two police officers, however, aware of his religious beliefs, engaged him in discussions about religious questions and addressed him as "Reverend." It had started to snow, and the police pointed out it would be difficult to find the little girl's body and give her "a Christian burial," a point they made several times. Williams eventually led them to the body.

By a 5 to 4 vote, the Court upheld a lower court ruling that the evidence had been obtained improperly, since the two police officers had in fact interrogated a suspect in custody without benefit of counsel. They also pointed out that the defendant had insisted on his right to have counsel present and that the police had agreed to that request. The Court remanded for a second trial, in which a jury again found Williams guilty. He appealed, but the Court in *Nix v. Williams* (1984) ruled that the tainted evidence had not prejudiced the defense because the body would have inevitably been discovered.

Rhode Island v. Innes (1980) dealt with a similar situation. Innes had been arrested for murder; after he stated in response to a Miranda warning that he wanted to see a lawyer, the police captain told the three patrolmen who took Innes to the stationhouse not to question him. As the car passed a school for handicapped children, one officer expressed concern that a child might find the missing murder weapon, a shotgun, and be injured. Innes then offered to lead them to the gun; they returned to the scene of the arrest, where the captain again read Innes a Miranda warning. Innes said he understood his rights, but wanted to retrieve the shotgun because of the children, and he showed the police its location. The Rhode Island Supreme Court ruled that the gun, as well as the testimony of the officers, had to be excluded because it constituted "custodial interrogation" in violation of *Miranda*.

The Supreme Court reversed, but did so without damaging *Miranda*. Unlike Williams, Innes had not yet been charged with a crime, he had no mental problems, he had received and understood the Miranda warnings, and he had voluntarily agreed to show police the location of the weapon. The Court thus distinguished between "casual questioning," which is allowed, and "custodial interrogation," which is not. The chief justice entered a concurrence in which he declared that he "would neither overrule *Miranda*, disparage it, nor extend it at this late date."

The following year, in *Estelle v. Smith* (1981), the Court gave *Miranda* a generous reading when it ruled that the privilege against self-incrimination applied at the penalty stage of the trial as well as at guilt determination. That same term, in *Edwards v. Arizona*, a unanimous Court held that when a suspect invokes the right to counsel as opposed to the right to remain silent, the police may not "try again."

In its last terms, the Burger Court continued to uphold *Miranda*, although it permitted an exception in a unique emergency. Police apprehended a reportedly armed rape suspect in a supermarket and, before reading him his rights, asked the whereabouts of the gun, to which Quarles replied, "It is over there." The officers retrieved a loaded .38-caliber revolver from an empty carton, formally arrested Quarles, and read him the Miranda warning. The defendant then said he would answer questions without an attorney and identified the gun as belonging to him. The high court, through Justice Rehnquist, agreed by a split vote with the lower court ruling that the questioning constituted custodial interrogation. But the circumstances could not be ignored. There had been a concealed weapon; there might have been an accomplice; and reading the Miranda warning might have led the suspect to remain silent and thus endanger both the police and the public. The police had an obligation to control the situation and retrieving a loaded weapon constituted their highest priority. The Court thus carved out a minor exception in *New York v. Quarles* (1984), one far more limited than it might have been had the case been decided a decade earlier.

The Death Penalty

In a totally unexpected opinion in June 1972, a 5 to 4 Court vacated the death sentences of approximately 600 inmates in prisons across the country. In the one-paragraph *per curiam* opinion in *Furman v. Georgia*, the majority held that imposition of the *then existing* capital punishment schemes violated the ban on cruel and unusual punishment in the Eighth Amendment as applied to the states through the Fourteenth. All nine justices filed separate opinions. Justices Douglas, Stewart, and White emphasized the arbitrary and often capricious manner in which the death penalty had been imposed, and they noted evidence of racial prejudice. Justices Brennan and Marshall alone on the bench believed the death penalty per se violated the Constitution, a position that they held to steadfastly in subsequent capital punishment cases.

Over the next few years, much to the chagrin of opponents of capital punishment, every one of the thirty-seven states that had previously imposed the death sentence rewrote its legislation within a few years in an effort to meet the imprecise constitutional standards implied in the *Furman* opinion. In 1976, the Court began to sort through these new statutes in an effort to articulate workable standards, and it upheld the revised Georgia law in *Gregg v. Georgia*. The new law provided that in a jury trial, the jury would first determine guilt or innocence; if it found the defendant guilty, it would then vote separately on punishment. Both the jury and a judge in a bench trial had to take into account mitigating as well as aggravating circumstances, and the state supreme court would automatically review all death sentences to protect against excessive or disproportionate punishment. Justices Stewart, Powell, and Stevens announced the judgment of the Court. They rejected the argument that modern ideas of human dignity required the abolition of capital punishment. A legislature could, if it chose, justify a death penalty on retribution or deterrence theories, and the sentencing authority could prescribe execution by following clearly stated statutory standards. Justices White, Rehnquist, Blackmun, and the chief justice concurred, whereas Brennan and Marshall reiterated their belief in the unconstitutionality of the death penalty.

The same division of the Court upheld the revised Florida and Texas statutes, but Stewart, Powell, and Stevens joined Brennan and Marshall to strike down the mandatory death sentence provisions enacted by North Carolina and Louisiana. The two states had decided to avoid the problem of capriciousness by requiring imposition of the death penalty as punishment for certain crimes, such as murder of a police officer or murder committed during a felony. Justice White, joined by Rehnquist, Blackmun, and Burger, dissented; they found the mandatory scheme acceptable and would have deferred the sentencing criteria to the state.

Two years later, in *Lockett v. Ohio* (1978), Burger joined the centrist group to strike down a state law as too restrictive of a defendant's ability to introduce evidence of mitigating factors. Sandra Lockett had been sentenced to death as an accessory to a murder committed during a robbery; she did not fire the gun, had not even been in the store, and wanted to testify that she neither knew of nor had approved of the murder. The chief justice called for individualization of sentencing, since unlike other punishments, the death sentence could not be reversed after execution; great care had to ensure that the right decision, taking into account all mitigating circumstances, be reached the first time.

The wide variety of capital punishment schemes, their arbitrary and often discriminatory application (blacks received the death sentence far more frequently than did whites for the same crime, while women convicted of murder rarely received the death sentence), and a lack of applicable standards had led to some support for the Court's original 1972 decision. The majority, however, did not consider capital punishment *per se* unconstitutional, but only the ways in which states imposed this most extreme punishment. The revised statutes avoided many of those problems, and the automatic review now required by all states that impose the death penalty assured some measure of uniformity in application and the avoidance of prejudiced cases.

Yet many of the Court's decisions, such as *Lockett* and *Godfrey v. Georgia* (1980)—which held that a Georgia jury had wrongly applied statutory criteria in sentencing a man to death for shooting his mother-in-law—reintroduced the elements of uncertainty to which the Court had originally objected. Chief Justice Burger was unquestionably correct in asserting that the death penalty is different and therefore must be treated so as to individualize the punishment as much as possible. This requires that judge or jury take full account of a variety of mitigating and/or aggravating conditions. Despite efforts by the states to rationalize this process, in the end this involves a largely subjective determination. If the jury thinks a particular murder is heinous, it will be able to justify the death penalty; if the jury is sympathetic toward a particular defendant, it will find mitigating circumstances to avoid imposing death.

Conclusion

In sum, the Burger Court's record on Bill of Rights issues proved far different from what one might have expected at the time of the new chief justice's appointment. In nearly every area, there is a pattern of initial reaction against earlier liberal doctrine, followed by an acceptance of the need to protect constitutional guarantees, and in some cases, by an expansion of those rights. In questions of women's equality under the Equal Protection Clause, of personal autonomy in the abortion cases, and in capital punishment cases, the Burger Court went far beyond its predecessor.

The Burger Court also continued the Warren tradition of activism in its willingness to decide a wide range of questions, rather than adopting the Frankfurter doctrine of restraint and deference to the legislature. But observers could find no cohesion on the Court, no overriding sense of shared values that had marked so many of the Warren Court decisions, and critics charged the Burger Court with a "rootless activism." Burger could rarely mass the Court; unanimous opinions remained rare, and the volumes of *U.S. Reports* swelled with concurring and dissenting opinions.

Such a condition is a mixed blessing. The unanimity of the Court in the early desegregation decisions, for example, left no doubt that state-sponsored racial discrimination violated the Constitution. But the Supreme Court hears only the complex questions; simple issues are decided at the district and circuit court levels. The diversity of views on the bench reflects that of the population as a whole, an ideal lacking in some earlier courts. One might well applaud the Court for its open-minded approach, its willingness to examine issues on their merits and not through an ideological lens.

> A court that reaffirms and enforces the activist precedents of its predecessor, invalidates the work of its co-equal branches, successfully aborts potential constitutional crises, umpires the systems of federalism and separation of powers, recognizes many new and important individual rights, structures the electoral process, and maintains and develops the jurisdictional and remedial potency of the federal courts is certainly wielding power. That a court's exercise of power seems inspired largely by pragmatic impulses says something about the quality, and possibly the durability, of that court's work. . . . An activist court is one that regularly exercises the power of judicial review to enforce controversial as well as consensual norms. By that standard, the Burger Court has been very much an activist court. Rootless activism is activism nonetheless.
>
> —Vince Blasi, "Rootless Activism," in *The Burger Court* (1983)

Perhaps a good word to describe the Burger Court's record is "pragmatic." It could not develop the overriding jurisprudential themes that had marked the Warren era, in part because the issues had become far more complex. In criminal cases it adopted a "totality of the circumstances" approach, which is very much a pragmatic standard. Perhaps one reason that the Court did almost an about-face in its handling of criminal procedure cases is that it saw "worst case scenarios"—such as a state court judge ruling that a confession obtained from a seriously wounded man in an intensive care unit was "voluntary." An outraged Court threw out the confession in *Mincey v. Arizona* (1978), but it had to notice that the lower court had relied on the rather liberal interpretations it had given to the concept of voluntariness in its own decisions. Such experiences led the justices to a greater appreciation of how fragile constitutional rights are and how they have to be carefully protected.

For Further Reading

A number of sources cited in Chapters 38 and 40 are pertinent here as well. First Amendment decisions of the Burger Court are discussed in Archibald Cox, "Foreword: Freedom of Expression in the Burger Court," 94 *Harvard Law Review* 1 (1980). Frederick Schauer, *Free Speech: A Philosophical Enquiry* (1982), provides a broad context in which to judge governmental efforts to limit expression and is especially good on obscenity problems. See also Stephen Daniels, "The Supreme Court and Obscenity: An Exercise in Empirical Constitutional Policy-Making," 17 *San Diego Law Review* 757 (1980). The feminist arguments against pornography are explicated in Andrea Dworkin, *Pornography: Men Possessing Women* (1981); and rebutted in Nadine Strossen, *Defending Pornography: Free Speech, Sex, and the Fight for Women's Rights* (1995).

For commercial speech, see Daniel A. Farber, "Commercial Speech and First Amendment Theory," 76 *Northwestern University Law Review* 372 (1979); and Thomas H. Jackson and John C. Jeffries, Jr., "Commercial Speech: Economic Due Process and the First Amendment," 65 *Virginia Law Review* 1 (1979). The latter is especially good on the inherent contradictions of the different rationales utilized in these cases. For political expenditures as protected expression, see J. Skelly Wright, "Politics and the Constitution: Is Money Speech?" 85 *Yale Law Journal* 1001 (1976); and Daniel D. Polsby, "Buckley v. Valeo: The Special Nature of Political Speech," 1976 *Supreme Court Review* 1 (1977).

Press issues are discussed in David L. Lange, "The Speech and Press Clauses," 23 *UCLA Law Review* 77 (1975); and Potter Stewart, "Or of the Press," 26 *Hastings Law Journal* 631 (1975). The claim of reporters for special protection is addressed in Harold Nelson, "The Newsmen's Privilege Against Disclosure of Confidential Sources of Information," 24 *Vanderbilt Law Review* 667 (1971); and Vincent Blasi, *Press Subpoenas: An Empirical and Legal Analysis* (1971). The Pentagon Papers case is analyzed in Louis Henkin, "The Right to Know and the Duty to Withhold: The Case of the Pentagon Papers," 120 *University of Pennsylvania Law Review* 271 (1971). See also Jerome A. Barron, *Freedom of the Press for Whom? The Right of Access to the Mass Media* (1973); Note, "The Right of the Press to Gather Information," 71 *Columbia Law Review* 838 (1971); and Anthony Lewis, "A Public Right to Know About Public Institutions: The First Amendment as a Sword," 1980 *Supreme Court Review* 1 (1981).

There has been an enormous outpouring of material on the religion clauses in recent years. See, among many others, Leo Pfeffer, *Religion, State, and the Burger Court* (1984); Leonard W. Levy, *The Establishment Clause: Religion and the First Amendment* (1986); Joseph E. Bryson and Samuel H. Houston, Jr., *The Supreme Court and Public Funds for Religious Schools: The*

Burger Years, 1969–1986 (1990). See also, Jesse Choper, "The Religion Clauses of the First Amendment: Reconciling the Conflict," 41 *U. Pittsburgh Law Review* 673 (1980); Kenneth Ripple, "The Entanglement Test of the Religion Clauses—A Ten Year Assessment," 27 *UCLA Law Review* 1195 (1980); William W. Van Alstyne, "Trends in the Supreme Court: Mr. Jefferson's Crumbling Wall: A Comment on Lynch v. Donnelly," 1984 *Duke Law Journal* 770 (1984); and Norman Redlich, "The Separation of Church and State: The Burger Court's Tortuous Journey," 60 *Notre Dame Law Review* 1094 (1985).

For the historical debate about the meaning of the Establishment Clause, see Levy, cited above, and Douglas Laycock, "'Nonpreferential' Aid to Religion: A False Claim about Original Intent," 27 *William & Mary Law Review* 875 (1986), which argue a historical basis for total separation. Gerard V. Bradley, *Church-State Relations in America* (1987), and Michael J. Malbin, *Religion and Politics: The Intentions of the Authors of the First Amendment* (1978), argue the accommodationist view. Two excellent overviews of the complex issue are Thomas J. Curry, *The First Freedoms: Church and State in America to the Passage of the First Amendment* (1986); and William Lee Miller, *The First Liberty: Religion and the American Republic* (1986).

Leonard W. Levy, *Against the Law: The Nixon Court and Criminal Justice* (1974), expresses liberal perceptions of the Burger Court reversing the advances made under Earl Warren. A more balanced approach is Stephen A. Saltzburg, "Foreword: The Flow and Ebb of Constitutional Criminal Procedure in the Warren and Burger Courts," 69 *Georgetown Law Journal* 488 (1980). Developments in Fourth Amendment law are discussed in Symposium, "The Good Faith Exception to the Exclusionary Rule," 6 *Whittier Law Review* 979 (1984); and Brent R. Appel, "The Inevitable Discovery Exception to the Exclusionary Rule," 21 *Criminal Law Bulletin.* 101 (1985).

The merits of capital punishment are debated in Hugo Bedau, *The Courts, the Constitution, and Capital Punishment* (1977); and Walter Burns, *For Capital Punishment: Crime and the Morality of the Death Penalty* (1979). See also Jack Greenburg, "Capital Punishment as a System," 91 *Yale Law Journal.* 908 (1982); Robert Weisburg, "Deregulating Death," 1983 *Supreme Court Review* 305 (1984); and Charles L. Black, Jr., *Capital Punishment: The Inevitability of Caprice and Mistake* (2nd ed., 1981).

42

The Rehnquist Court: Equal Protection and Individual Autonomy

The Rehnquist Court Forms • Civil Rights • Affirmative Action • Race-Conscious Districting • The Civil Rights Act of 1991 • Gender Discrimination • Sexual Harassment • Abortion • The Right to Die • Conclusion • For Further Reading

IN JULY 1986, Warren Burger stepped down as chief justice of the United States after seventeen terms. The conservative revolution that had been predicted when Richard Nixon appointed him had not come to pass, and in many areas, the Court had been as activist as its predecessor. This resulted, in good measure, from Burger's inability to lead the Court, and he constantly found himself out-maneuvered by Justice William Brennan, who took it on himself to protect the legacy of the Warren Court. Burger had not been a complete failure, and he had done much to modernize the administration of the federal judiciary and to repair relationships between the courts and Congress. But he liked the ceremonial aspects far better than the jurisprudential, and as chair of the commission to celebrate the bicentennial of the Constitution, he found the perfect role for his administrative and ceremonial predilections.

To replace Burger, President Reagan named associate justice William H. Rehnquist, who ever since his appointment to the bench in 1972 had easily been its most conservative member. Liberals feared and conservatives hoped for a full-blown retreat from the patterns of the past three decades, but the record of the Rehnquist Court is far more complex. In some areas, the justices advanced the rights established in the Warren and Burger eras, and in others they trimmed back. The record is mixed, and while clearly the Rehnquist Court stood to the right of its predecessors, it cannot be said that it launched a full-scale assault on the pillars of Warren and Burger era jurisprudence. The Court under Rehnquist also set out to revitalize the notion of federalism, an idea that resonated in the legislative and executive branches as well. In some ways, its key decisions need to be seen less in terms of a particular jurisprudence than in the context of federal and state authority. Decisions that some have criticized as regressive make far more sense if viewed as an effort to shift decision- and policy-making back to the states and to the political branches.

The Rehnquist Court Forms

In 1986, three members of the Warren Court still sat on the bench—William Brennan, Thurgood Marshall, and Byron White. Brennan and Marshall would, until their retirements, constitute the liberal bloc on the Court, two votes that could always be counted on in favor of the individual against the state. White would usually vote with them on matters of racial discrimination, but otherwise favored a moderate to conservative position, especially regarding rights of the accused. Harry Blackmun, appointed by Nixon in 1970, remained a moderate, but as the Court itself became increasingly conservative, he would often vote with Brennan and Marshall. Because of his authorship of *Roe v. Wade*, Blackmun served as the champion of the right to privacy. Lewis Powell, appointed by Nixon in 1970, and John Paul Stevens, appointed by Ford in 1975, also occupied the middle. A 5–4 majority cobbled together by Brennan would include Marshall, Blackmun, Stevens or White, and Powell.

In 1981, Reagan made his first appointment to the Court, and carrying out a campaign promise to name a woman, he appointed Sandra Day O'Connor of Arizona to replace Potter Stewart. O'Connor started out as a solid ally of Rehnquist, who had been her classmate at Stanford Law School, and for a while they constituted a conservative counterbalance to Brennan and Marshall. But over the years, O'Connor moved to a middle position, influenced perhaps by her great admiration for Lewis Powell. While women's groups would have liked a more activist role from her in gender cases, for the most part she did vote in favor of women in most gender discrimination cases, and despite her early hostility to the *Roe* decision, she eventually proved one of the decisive votes that prevented its overturn.

At the same time Reagan promoted Rehnquist to the center chair, he named Antonin Scalia to replace him. Scalia had been a law school professor as well as a member of the court of appeals for the D. C. Circuit, and in both places he had earned a reputation as extremely bright, a personable colleague, and a thoroughgoing conservative. Reagan and others hoped that with Rehnquist leading the Court, Scalia would provide the intellectual muscle to effect the long-sought counterrevolution; in other words, he would play Brennan to Rehnquist's Warren. Scalia remained bright, personable, and conservative, but instead of playing Brennan, he seemed like William O. Douglas, more intent on keeping his jurisprudence pure than on putting together a majority. Scalia showed no inclination to compromise and at times seemed to go out of his way to insult his colleagues by the high level of vituperation in some of his opinions.

Reagan's final appointment was that of Anthony Kennedy to replace Lewis Powell. Reagan originally named Robert Bork, but after a bruising confirmation battle, in which the Senate turned Bork down (see Chapter 44), the president turned to Kennedy, a conservative from the Ninth Circuit. At the time of his appointment, critics claimed that Kennedy shared the same ultraright philosophy as Bork and that he would follow Scalia's lead. In fact Kennedy, while certainly a conservative, tended toward the center. While he often voted with Scalia and the chief justice, in many cases he voted against them, and most often aligned with O'Connor.

Liberals feared the worst when Justice Brennan retired due to ill health in 1990, and President Bush appointed David Hackett Souter, a state court judge from New Hampshire, who had served only seven months on the court of appeals for the First Circuit. Following the Bork debacle, Souter kept a low profile, and critics dubbed him the "stealth nominee" for his evasive answers. But there was little opponents could point to that would in any way disqualify him, and Souter took his seat at the beginning of the fall 1990 term. The first two years proved difficult for him, and he had trouble writing opinions. While conservative in some aspects, he too became a centrist, and along with O'Connor and Kennedy provided the key votes to sustain the abortion precedent. Souter soon emerged as a potentially influential figure, whose careful and thoughtful opinions resembled those of his idol, the second Justice Harlan.

Bush's second appointee, Clarence Thomas, triggered another firestorm in the Senate (see Chapter 44), but because opponents could not prove the truth of the sexual harassment charges, the Senate confirmed him by only four votes. Thomas espoused a jurisprudence as conservative as that of Scalia and Rehnquist, with whom he voted on almost every issue. Beyond that, Thomas argued for a natural rights jurisprudence based more on the Declaration of Independence than on the Constitution and the Bill of Rights, a position that in some areas went beyond even Scalia and the chief justice. Despite the fact that he had benefited from affirmative action policies in getting into Yale Law School, he consistently criticized affirmative action and took the narrowest possible grounds in equal protection cases.

Liberals hoped that when Bill Clinton had openings to fill, he would name liberals of the Brennan-Marshall type, and in this they were disappointed. Clinton, himself a moderate, knew that he would only be able to get moderates confirmed by the Senate. In 1993, he named Ruth Bader Ginsburg as the second woman to the Court, to replace Byron White. A member of the D.C. circuit court, Ginsburg had made her reputation as the lawyer who had developed the strategy for the women's rights cases in the 1970s and who had won six of the seven gender discrimination cases she had argued before the high court. She remained a firm supporter of equal rights, but in most other areas proved a moderate.

When Harry Blackmun stepped down in 1994, Clinton named Steven Breyer to fill his seat. A Harvard law professor who specialized in business law and then a federal court of appeals judge, Breyer had good connections on the Hill because of the years he had worked as an aide to the Senate judiciary committee. Even the conservatives on the committee liked and respected him, and this made his confirmation an easy matter. Breyer, like Ginsburg, tended to gravitate to the center on most matters.

If one had to draw an ideological spectrum of the Rehnquist Court at the end of the twentieth century, one would find a core bloc of conservatives, Rehnquist, Scalia, and Thomas, who tended to vote together on most but not all issues, and whom Kennedy often joined. But Scalia, unlike Thomas and Rehnquist, had a libertarian streak that led him to an active defense of First Amendment values. There was no liberal bloc per se, although within the moderate group Souter, Stevens, and Ginsburg might be termed the most liberal leaning. But for the most part, they gravitated to the center, and from that position one or more would at times join the conservatives. While one might not characterize the Rehnquist Court as ideologically consistent, it tended to favor restriction of state authority at all levels. While its view of federalism often led to decisions striking down federal laws on a states' rights rationale, at the same time, it also curbed the power of the states to act within spheres traditionally ascribed to them. Given this make-up, one is still surprised by the results in cases involving individual liberty and expressive rights.

Civil Rights

In the area of civil rights, affirmative action, and race-conscious districting, critics of the Rehnquist Court see an almost total abandonment of the high standards of equal protection established under Earl Warren and continued in the Burger years. Defenders of the Court believe we are now approaching what the civil rights movement had always declared to be its goal, a color-blind Constitution. The Court's decisions in this area should not be seen as driven by discrimination; rather, they reflect a majority of the justices' views regarding the nature of the federal system, the proper role of the judiciary, and the meaning of the Equal Protection Clause.

The first act of the Rehnquist Court sent civil rights activists to the barricades. Brenda Paterson, a black employee of a credit union in North Carolina, claimed that she had been racially harassed by her supervisor and that she ought to have the right to sue him under 42 U.S.C. Section 1981, a provision derived from the 1866 Civil Rights Act, allowing civil suits to attack racial discrimination in a private setting. That provision had long been moribund, but in 1972, the Court revived it in *Runyon v. McCrary.* The decision filled in interstices of the civil rights laws and gave plaintiffs a legal basis on which to litigate. If a shopkeeper, for example, refused to sell merchandise to someone because she was black, the customer could sue on the basis of Section 1981 and, equally important, collect damages.

Neither side in the litigation had raised the question of whether *Runyon* had been correctly decided, and it came as a bolt out of the blue when the Court announced that in accepting *Patterson v. McLean Credit Union* it would review *Runyon.* In an angry dissent, Justice Blackmun, joined by Brennan, Marshall, and Stevens, wrote that he could not think why the majority wanted to rethink a ruling "that so clearly reflects our society's earnest commitment to ending racial discrimination." Conservative groups that believed private discrimination could not be touched by federal law praised the decision, but the general response was overwhelmingly negative. Dozens of civil rights groups as well as members of Congress rushed to file *amicus* briefs against overruling *Runyon,* and in the face of such massive opposition the solicitor general declined to file a brief in favor of reversal.

When the case actually came before the Court, it unanimously decided that Section 1981 would continue to forbid racial discrimination in the making and enforcement of private contracts, including employment contracts. But then, by a 5–4 vote, the justices ruled that Section 1981 does not provide for a cause of action for racial harassment on the job. In other words, under Section 1981 an employer may be sued for refusing to hire a person because of race, but not if after hiring, the employer treats the person in a discriminatory manner. That type of discrimination, Justice Kennedy declared, can be reached either under state law or Title VII of the Civil Rights Act.

While it would appear that the Court had only held that Ms. Patterson had filed suit under the wrong statute, the difference between Section 1981 and Title VII damages is considerable. Under Section 1981, an aggrieved party may sue for both compensatory and punitive damages, while Title VII suits allow only the recovery of back pay. As the dissenters pointed out, the vitality of Section 1981 as a tool against discrimination, while nominally affirmed by the Court, had been greatly vitiated.

The Court also seemed to back off from judicial involvement in and maintenance of desegregation orders, possibly because by the 1990s, it had become clear that as much desegregation had taken place as would occur without a major change in the nation's socioeconomic fabric. In *Missouri v. Jenkins* (1990), the state of Missouri and the Kansas City school district were found to have operated a segregated school system within the district. A desegregation plan approved by the federal district court required expenditures of $450 million, but various state laws prevented the school district from raising taxes to finance its 25 percent of the costs. The district court judge thereupon ordered a significant increase in the local property taxes despite the state limitations.

Justice White found the district court's actions exceeded its authority, as well as the principles of federal-state comity. The judge, instead of raising taxes on his own authority, should have ordered the school board to do so. White held that the difference involved more than just form. Authorizing and even ordering the school board to act placed the responsibility for implementation on local authorities, where it belonged. Courts should only involve themselves directly as a last resort, and here other options existed.

The Rehnquist Court not only opposed excessive judicial intervention, but it also wanted to end long-term judicial involvement. In the 1950s and 1960s, federal courts entered hundreds of decrees ordering local schools to desegregate. As years passed and overt resistance faded, should the decrees stay in force? What happened if the demographic profile of the school district changed? At what point could one say that a decree originally entered to remedy de jure segregation was no longer necessary?

The Court faced these questions in *Board of Education of Oklahoma City v. Dowell* (1991). At the time of *Brown,* Oklahoma City had operated a segregated school system. In 1971, the district court had ordered systemwide busing as a remedy, and it seemed to work, producing significant integration. As a result, in 1977, the court entered an order terminating the case and its jurisdiction. Then in 1984, as a response to

> How can you have a civil rights law that doesn't cover racial harassment? If you have a right to contract to get a job, don't you have an equal right to work there and not be called a nigger?
>
> —Barry Goldstein of the NAACP, commenting on *Patterson v. McLean Credit Union* (1989)

changing demographics, the school board introduced a plan for neighborhood schools for grades K–4, although allowing any student to transfer from a school in which he or she was in the majority to one in which he or she would be in the minority. A year later, opponents challenged the plan, claiming it would reintroduce segregation, since very few students would avail themselves of the chance to transfer. The district court refused to reopen the case; the court of appeals reversed, holding that the 1972 decree remained in force and imposed a duty on the school system not to take any steps that might reintroduce segregation.

The Supreme Court disagreed. Chief Justice Rehnquist declared that orders entered in desegregation cases had never been intended to be permanent, and common sense dictated that such orders should be dissolved after local authorities had operated in compliance for a reasonable period of time. If the board's new plan violated equal protection, then it should be evaluated under the proper criteria, but not under a decree issued in a different time and under different circumstances.

Justice Marshall, joined by Blackmun and Stevens, dissented and complained that the majority had suggested that after 65 years of official segregation, 13 years of desegregation was enough. But the dissenters seemed to ignore the fact that conditions in Oklahoma City had changed significantly between 1972 and 1984, as well as the fact that in many cities, civil rights groups had begun demanding a return to local schools, with greater parental involvement and control. The majority had not said that outright discrimination would be ignored, but merely that a new program had to be freshly reviewed, and if it violated established equal protection analysis, then a remedy could be imposed.

The Court returned to this issue a year later in *Freeman v. Pitts* (1992), and this time all of the justices approved partial withdrawal of judicial supervision of a school system in DeKalb County, Georgia, which had operated under a consent decree since 1969. Once again, demographics had produced a racial imbalance in the schools, but the district court found that this had resulted from population shifts and not from any overt action by school authorities. The local court had found some areas that still required supervision, but had concluded that in terms of student assignment, the board need no longer work under the judicial eye.

That same year, in a decision hailed by civil rights groups, the Court held that universities, as well as primary and secondary schools, had the same affirmative duty to dismantle dual school systems. Justice White relied heavily on statistics to find that Mississippi still operated a higher education system dominated by racially identifiable institutions. The state had argued that in higher education it had established a true freedom of choice, and therefore if whites went to predominantly white schools and blacks to predominantly black colleges, that represented individual choice and not de jure segregation. The entire Court rejected this argument and mandated that the state had to take steps to do away with this racial separation [*United States v. Fordyce* (1992)].

In 1995, the Missouri case returned to the high court. In *Missouri v. Jenkins*, the chief justice, in a 5–4 decision, ruled that a federal court could not order salary increases and remedial education programs on the ground that student achievement levels were below national norms. The nature of the remedy, he declared, must be shaped by the violation, and in this instance the local court had gone far beyond the mandate of ending racial discrimination. Justice Souter dissented on grounds that the majority had taken on issues not properly presented on the record and, as a result, had sent confusing signals to school districts and the lower courts.

Affirmative Action

The Reagan administration seriously attempted to undo prior civil rights decisions involving affirmative action, arguably the most contentious aspect of the Burger Court's equal protection jurisprudence. In his 1980 presidential campaign, Ronald Reagan had constantly attacked the government for interfering too much in the private sector and made it clear that he opposed employment quotas in any form. In early 1981, Orrin Hatch, scheduled to become chair of the Senate labor and human resources committee, announced that his committee would pressure the Labor Department's office of federal contract compliance to take a softer approach to affirmative action, and if the bureaucrats did not take the hint, Hatch promised to introduce legislation forcing them to do so. The new head of the Justice Department's civil rights division, William Bradford Reynolds, openly attacked affirmative action programs. Yet in 1983, Reagan signed executive order 12432, requiring federal agencies to increase their goals for employment of minority subcontractors by at least 10 percent, at the same time that high officials in the administration denounced all such programs as "illegal."

When Edwin Meese became attorney general in Reagan's second term, he announced that he favored only those programs that sought to widen recruiting and training programs, but expressed his implacable hostility to what he denounced as "quotas." The Justice Department shortly afterward sent out letters to fifty city governments that had signed consent decrees establishing hiring plans for women and minorities, informing them that it considered such plans unconstitutional. The strong reaction to this move seemed to indicate that both public and private sector officials stood diametrically opposed to the administration's policy. Meese stubbornly kept up his attack on any plans that included hiring goals, but the public uproar alerted Reagan's more politically astute advisers to leave the issue alone. Labor secretary William Brock publicly defended affirmative action and his department's enforcement of federal policy, and he managed to stymie Meese's efforts to have Reagan withdraw executive order 12432. When Reagan and Meese left office in January 1989, they left a legacy of eight years of indifference to civil rights, but the various federal regulations concerning affirmative action remained intact.

Meese could look with some satisfaction on the fact that the Reagan appointees to the high court opposed affirmative action, and the justices in the last years of Warren Burger's tenure had begun backing away from the strong statements made in 1970s cases. In the last affirmative action case heard by the Burger Court, *Wygant v. Jackson Board of Education* (1986), the justices began to dismantle the judicial basis for minority preference programs. The Jackson, Michigan school board, in the face of considerable racial tension, had negotiated a contract with the teachers union that in the case of layoffs, seniority would be the guiding rule, but that the percentage of minority personnel (often the last hired) laid off would not exceed the percentage of minorities in the system. As a result of the agreement, during two layoffs in 1976–77 and 1981–82, the school administration retained minority teachers while letting go nonminority teachers with greater seniority. The white teachers sued, not only under Title VII but also under other civil rights statutes and the Equal Protection Clause, which established a high level of scrutiny for racial classification.

Justice Powell spoke for a fragmented Court. Only Chief Justice Burger and Justice Rehnquist joined his opinion fully, while justices White and O'Connor concurred. Because the challenge relied in part on equal protection claims, the school board had to show a compelling state purpose and a means narrowly tailored to meet that goal. Because the school board itself had not caused discrimination, its broad purpose of providing role models for minority students failed the test. While race might be a factor in attempting to remedy past discrimination, the plan had to address discrimination that the agency had itself caused. A legitimate seniority system could not be trumped by an affirmative action program absent this show of specific discrimination.

While most commentators believed that *Wygant*, with its six different opinions, sent a mixed message, Attorney General Ed Meese claimed it as a victory, and in some ways it was. Charles Fried, who served as solicitor general during much of the Reagan administration, declared that the government had no objection to an affirmative action program in which minority members who had been the actual victims of discrimination received some form of preferential and compensatory treatment. But it objected to broad plans involving quotas, in which nonminority members who had never been found guilty of discriminating paid the price for the preferential treatment of minority members who could not prove that they themselves had suffered discrimination.

In the first affirmative action case heard by the Rehnquist Court, the Reagan administration suffered a major setback in its campaign against affirmative action. Santa Clara County in California had adopted a general affirmative action policy and then had sought to apply it in those county agencies that had a statistical record of not hiring minorities or women. The Transportation Agency had very few minorities, and absolutely no woman worked in the 238 higher-paying skilled positions. When an opening for a dispatcher occurred, the county put a woman into the slot, although the supervisors in that division had recommended a man, Paul Johnson. When Johnson learned that gender had been the only reason Diane Joyce had been hired, he sued, claiming that such preferences violated Title VII of the Civil Rights Act.

The high court supported the county's affirmative action plan, with Justice Brennan speaking for a 6–3 court. He argued that Congress, in passing the 1964 measure, had wanted to give employers flexibility to devise programs aiming at discrimination, and there could be no doubt that women had been discriminated against in hiring in the transportation division. Justice O'Connor did not join in the opinion, but concurred in the result, and there is no doubt that the total lack of women in the higher-paid skilled ranks led to her vote.

Justice Scalia, joined by Justice White and the chief justice, filed a strong dissent. Going through all of the Court's prior decisions on equal protection and Title VII, he accused the majority of rewriting the law. Instead of making the law gender-blind and color-blind to do away with all forms of discrimination, the majority had done just the opposite. Now in the name of affirmative action, individuals who had not violated the law in any way would be penalized so that minority members who may never have suffered individual discrimination could receive a preference. In doing this, the Court had ignored the intent of Congress and had engaged in the most blatant form of judicial policy-making. This latest decision went further than any previous case, and henceforth it would be "economic folly" for employers both public and private not to engage in reverse discrimination. And who would suffer? Innocent victims like Paul Johnson, "predominantly unknown, unaffluent, unorganized."

It was a powerful indictment and reflected accurately the outrage of the Reagan administration against racial and gender preferences. However, strong evidence existed that in fact the majority had gotten it right, that it had been congressional intent to allow for preferential programs designed to undo the results of past discrimination against groups. But the oldest members of the Court had joined Brennan's opinion, and within a few years, Powell, Marshall, and Brennan himself would be gone from the bench. Moreover, O'Connor in general did not favor affirmative action, and in this case her vote might be attributed to the fact that the program involved gender rather than race.

The very next term, the roof seemed to fall in on affirmative action. First the Court backtracked on two decades of precedent. Ever since the *Griggs* case in 1971, the Court had permitted statistical evidence of racial imbalance to support a charge of discrimination under Title VII, even if the hiring practices appeared facially neutral. If an imbalance existed, the employer had the burden of proving that the disparity had been caused by the circumstances of the business and not by discrimination. But by a 5–4 vote in *Ward's Cove Packing Co. v. Antonio* (1989), the Court gave companies accused of discrimination an important procedural victory by shifting the burden of proof from the employer to the employee.

The Court then dealt two devastating blows against affirmative action plans. The first involved an archetypical consent decree in Birmingham, Alabama. In response to a discrimination suit by blacks against the city, a federal district court had approved two consent decrees in which the city agreed to hire more African-American firefighters and to arrange promotion goals for them. The court also ruled as untimely efforts by a white firefighters' union as well as some individual white firemen, to intervene in the case. A different group of white firemen who had not been involved in the earlier suit then sued the city under Title VII, claiming they had been denied promotions in favor of less qualified blacks. The city admitted it had made race-conscious decisions, but that such decisions had been permitted—indeed required—under the consent decree and were therefore immune from this type of attack.

The Supreme Court disagreed in *Martin v. Wilks* (1989). Chief Justice Rehnquist rejected the idea that a court-approved consent decree cut off the constitutional rights of those who had not even been a party to the negotiations. The decision raised alarms all over the country in cities that had signed consent decrees in response to antidis-

> A statute designed to establish a color-blind and gender-blind workplace has thus been converted into a powerful engine of racism and sexism, not merely *permitting* intentional race- and sex-based discrimination, but often making it, through operation of the legal system, practically compelled.
>
> —Justice Antonin Scalia, dissenting in *Johnson v. Transportation Agency* (1987)

crimination suits. In nearly all of these situations, there had been people who had not been party to the agreement and who might have been adversely affected by it. Under *Wilks,* any such person could attack the decrees as impinging on his or her rights and then tie up the municipal government for years in expensive and time-consuming litigation. Facing such a threat, local governments would be loath to enter into consent decrees that, instead of reducing their liability to lawsuit, might actually increase the risk.

That same year, the Court voided a Richmond, Virginia set-aside program for minority businesses that had been modeled on the federal program. Congress had established set-asides when it had determined the existence of long-term and widespread discrimination in the construction industry, and it had required that prime contractors on federally financed construction subcontract 10 percent to minority-owned businesses. The Court had approved the set-asides in *Fullilove v. Klutznik* (1980), ruling that Congress had sufficient evidence of discrimination and ample power under the Fourteenth Amendment to enact such remedial legislation.

Following that decision, many state and local governments established similar programs. Richmond, which is 50 percent black, approved a local ordinance in 1983 calling for at least 30 percent of all city-financed prime contracts to go to minority businesses. The problem is that unlike Congress, which held investigatory hearings to establish the existence and extent of discrimination, the city council, dominated by minorities, developed no evidence of bias in the area's construction industry, other than noting that few blacks belonged to the local employer trade groups. The one bit of hard evidence showed that over the previous five years, minority contractors had received only 0.67 percent of the city's prime contracts. When the J. A. Croson Company could not find a minority business that met the city's bonding requirements, it had a contract for plumbing fixtures taken away for rebidding. Croson sued under Section 1983, charging reverse discrimination.

Justice O'Connor, for a 6 to 3 majority, held that the city had not proven a case of prior discrimination and that its 30 percent quota bore no relation to any of the facts submitted in support of the set-aside. "An amorphous claim that there has been past discrimination in a particular industry cannot justify the use of an unyielding racial quota." Unlike the federal government, which had specific power under the Enforcement Clause of the Fourteenth Amendment, racial preference programs undertaken by state and local governments are subject to a strict scrutiny standard, the highest criterion used by courts in racial classification cases.

A close reading of *Croson* indicates that it did not, as many opponents of affirmative action claimed, put an end to set-asides. Rather, Justice O'Connor made clear that for a set-aside to withstand judicial scrutiny, there had to be a solid factual basis to demonstrate a record of prior discrimination that the set-aside addressed. To highlight the difference between the national government and state and local programs, the following year the Court upheld the federal government's power under the Fifth and Fourteenth amendments to authorize set-aside programs in allocating television and radio licenses in *Metro Broadcasting Inc. v. FCC* (1990).

Five years later, however, the Court reversed itself, and in *Adarand Constructors, Inc. v. Pena* (1995), Justice O'Connor, speaking for a highly splintered Court, held that under the Fifth and Fourteenth amendments' due process clauses, any action involving racial classification, including set-asides, by *either* the states or the federal government, would be judged by a standard of strict scrutiny. The greater leeway that the courts had hitherto allowed Congress in affirmative action programs no longer existed. Just as the courts frowned on measures that discriminate because of race, they would now frown with equal fervor on measures that favored on the basis of race. O'Connor again made it clear that this did not make all affirmative action programs automatically unconstitutional; rather the government—be it Congress, the state, or a municipality—would have to show a record of actual prior discrimination in order to justify a narrowly tailored plan.

Nearly five decades after the Court handed down its historic decision in *Brown v. Board of Education*, and four decades after the Civil Rights and Voting Rights Acts, the mood of the country had shifted significantly. A poll around the time of the *Adarand* decision found that 77 percent of the people surveyed believed that affirmative action programs discriminated against whites; even 66 percent of the black respondents answered the same way.

The legal and political future of affirmative action seemed questionable. A ballot measure in California barred state universities from using race as a factor in admissions. In 1996, the court of appeals for the Fifth Circuit struck down the University of Texas affirmative action plan that favored black and Hispanic minorities. In *Hopwood v. Texas*, the appeals court told the University of Texas Law School that it could not use admission standards for minority students different from those it used for white students, a ruling that appeared to run contrary to *Bakke*. The university then appealed to the Supreme Court, which refused to hear the case, thus leaving the Fifth Circuit decision in place. The immediate result of the California initiative and of *Hopwood* was a sharp decline in the number of minority students in the premier public universities in Texas and California. Both states found this situation unacceptable and began seeking some other means to attract minorities. The Texas legislature changed the admissions procedure, providing that the top 10 percent of graduating high school seniors would be automatically admitted to the University of Texas. In California, the number of blacks and Hispanics in higher education has stabilized, and while fewer may attend Berkeley or UCLA, many more are attending the second-tier schools.

Race-Conscious Districting

The Voting Rights Act of 1965 aimed not only at ensuring access to the ballot box, but also that minority votes would count. The statute prohibited any electoral practice that "results in a denial or abridgment" of the right to vote on the basis of race or color. But Section 2 assured racial minorities an equal opportunity to participate in the political process and to elect members of their choice, and under later amendments to the law, a violation of Section 2 could be demonstrated by discriminatory effect alone. In addition, Section 5 provided that in covered jurisdictions, that is, states with a past history of voting discrimination, district lines might be required to give minorities proportional representation in the total make-up of a state's congressional delegation. Thus a state with eight congressional districts and a 25 percent African-American population might be required to draw district lines to create two so-called majority-minority districts in which blacks would constitute a majority of the electorate.

It had, of course, been illegal ever since *Gomillion v. Lightfoot* (1960) to gerrymander districts in order to dilute minority voting strength. In *Rogers v. Lodge* (1982), the Court had approved a court-ordered plan to replace at-large county commissioners with single-district seats. In Burke County, Georgia, blacks constituted a majority of the total population, but only 38 percent of the registered voters. In at-large elections, the white majority easily defeated any black candidates. By ordering single district seats, the district court ensured that in at least some districts blacks would comprise a majority of the voters and thus be able to elect black candidates.

It is one thing to ensure fair apportionment, in which local black majorities form the majority in contiguous and compact districts. But proportional representation had never been a practice in the United States. In many states, the black population is so scattered that even if the total African-American population reached 20 or 25 percent of the population, a fair and race-blind districting scheme might not have a black majority in any district. To ensure at least some minority representation, the Justice Department called upon states in the South to establish districts that had minority domination, even if doing so ran against traditional demands for apportionment based on contiguous and compact district lines.

The Court heard a series of challenges to this practice in the 1990s, and it had to determine, among other questions, whether race-conscious districting affected individual or group rights. The Constitution speaks solely of individual rights, but the Warren and Burger Courts had acknowledged the existence to some extent of group rights in cases like *Bakke.* Moreover, Justice White stated that although cases such as *Rogers v. Lodge* "involved racial groups, we believe that the principles developed in these cases would apply equally to claims by political groups in individual districts." But, he added, proof of vote dilution would have to be quite clear for the Court to approve a group-based remedy. The Reagan administration strongly opposed the notion of group rights, and its antipathy to affirmative action extended to race-conscious districting. However, apportionment is primarily a state function, and in many states civil rights advocates and their allies managed to win significant victories.

In the 1970s and 1980s, the courts turned back a number of challenges to race-conscious districting adopted as a means of redressing past discrimination. Moreover, instead of adopting the strict scrutiny standard normally used in racial classification, they utilized a lower standard, deferring to congressional policy-making power under the Enforcement Clauses of the Fourteenth and Fifteenth amendments. In those years, however, enormous population shifts occurred throughout the country and in the South in particular. The 1990 census required most Southern states to redraw their congressional district lines, and state legislatures, following previous practice, drew minority-majority districts with Justice Department approval to prevent vote dilution among the African-American population. When challenged, states argued that the Justice Department requirements constituted a compelling state interest.

In *Shaw v. Reno* (1993), the Court did not rule on the merits of race-conscious districting or on the state's claim that it had a compelling interest created by the Justice Department requirements, but ruled only that white citizens in North Carolina had a justiciable claim under the Equal Protection Clause to challenge the districting plans, and it remanded the case to the district court for a hearing on the merits. Moreover, Justice O'Connor declared, in a 6–3 opinion, that in reviewing these challenges, courts should adopt a strict scrutiny standard and not defer to congressional authority.

The Court also said that the shape of the district could be the subject of judicial scrutiny. Some states, in order to capture sufficient black population, had drawn districts that the Court claimed practically defied description. One district ran through ten counties, dividing them and even the towns within them. One state legislator remarked that "if you drove down the interstate with both car doors open, you'd kill most of the people in the district." In *Miller v. Johnson* (1995), though, Justice Kennedy held that bizarre shape by itself would not lead to a finding of unconstitutionality. States cannot separate voters on the basis of race alone, he wrote, but the challenger must prove that the legislature deliberately set out to segregate its citizens on a racial basis. Once again, the Court did not reach the merits, but remanded the case for further review.

The following year, the *Shaw* case came back before the justices in the form of *Shaw v. Hunt* (1996). Chief Justice Rehnquist spoke for a 6 to 3 majority in holding that the district court, while following a strict scrutiny standard, had erred in finding that the state had a compelling interest either in establishing majority-minority districts or creating strangely shaped districts. The Court still avoided the key substantive issue: whether, under the proper circumstances, compliance with Section 5 of the Voting Rights Act could be a compelling state interest. That same day, the Court handed down an opinion in *Bush v. Vera*, a Texas redistricting plan. Here it became clear for all to see that the justices held widely divergent views on the subject. Justice O'Connor wrote a plurality opinion joined in whole only by the chief justice and Justice Kennedy, striking down the Texas plan. To iterate her belief that under certain circumstances race-conscious districting could be justified, she had to write a separate concurrence, which led Justice Kennedy to wrote his own concurrence, arguing that whether or not such redistricting would automatically trigger strict scrutiny was still an open question. Justices Thomas and Scalia concurred only in the result, believing that all racially motivated districting required strict scrutiny. Justice Stevens dissented, joined by Ginsburg and Breyer, while Justice Souter dissented on other grounds, also joined by Ginsburg and Breyer. In reading through the tortured opinions, commentators could agree on little except that the Court had not articulated any clear standards to guide lower courts in determining when race-conscious districting triggered strict scrutiny, when it might be justifiable, and what duties the states owed to create such districts under the Voting Rights Act.

> The General Assembly's first redistricting plan contained one majority-black district centered in the [northern] part of the State. This district is somewhat hook shaped. Centered in the northeastern portion of the State, it moves southward until it tapers to a narrow band; then, with finger-like extensions, it reaches far into the southern-most part of the State near the South Carolina border. District 1 has been compared to a "Rorschach ink-blot test" and a "bug splattered on a windshield."
>
> —Justice Sandra Day O'Connor, *Shaw v. Reno* (1993)

The issue came back to the Court only one term later, when the case it had remanded in *Miller v. Johnson* returned on appeal. On remand, the district court in Georgia reconsidered the constitutionality of the 1990 state apportionment plan. After the legislature had failed to develop a scheme that met court approval, the district court fashioned its own plan, one that included only a single majority-minority district. Critics attacked this scheme on the grounds that while the court had the power to draft such a plan, it had failed to follow the rules laid down by the Supreme Court in earlier decisions. More importantly, it had failed to follow the clear mandate of the Georgia assembly that wanted two black-majority districts.

In his dissent in *Bush v. Vera*, Justice Souter had warned that the Court's failure to provide clear guidelines on redistricting would lead to lower courts arrogating unto themselves the power that properly belonged in the legislature. Despite the fact that the Rehnquist Court repeatedly avowed the principle of judicial deference to legislative policy-making, in the case of race-conscious districting, a majority of the justices consistently denied Congress power under the enforcement clauses of the Fourteenth and Fifteenth amendments to impose a plan it deemed necessary to give minorities voting effectiveness. The justices also denied to the states their usual leeway in drawing less than compact or contiguous district lines.

Although the Court never explicitly declared majority-minority districts *per se* unconstitutional, its decision in *Abrams v. Johnson* (1997) made it questionable whether such districts could be created anyplace other than in large cities, where it would be almost impossible not to have them. Justice Kennedy, for a 5–4 majority, reaffirmed that race "must not be a predominant factor in drawing the district lines." While the task of redistricting should always be left to the elected representatives of the people, the high court upheld the district court's plan as necessary, given the inability of the legislature to reach a decision. Kennedy also claimed that neither the Voting Rights Act requirements nor the Enforcement Clauses could be used to justify drawing district lines primarily on the basis of race.

It is possible that states can create majority-minority districts, provided such districts meet the traditional standards of being compact, contiguous, and one-person, one-vote. It is possible that if states do not make race the dominant criterion, they could even stray somewhat from the compact and contiguous standards. Four members of the bench, led by Justice Breyer, dissented in *Abrams,* emphasizing that the lower court should not have been allowed to disregard the legislature's wishes for two majority black districts and that such a wish would not be unconstitutional given the legislature's belief that the Voting Rights Act mandated such a plan. He also reiterated that he and the dissenters—justices Stevens, Souter, and Ginsburg—had consistently argued through all of the districting cases that the majority's rule would prove unworkable and, as a result, would shift responsibility for drawing district lines from the legislature, where it belonged, to the courts, where it did not. This "would prevent the legitimate use (among others, the remedial use) of race as a political factor in redistricting, sometimes making unfair distinctions between racial minorities and others."

That same term, in *Lawyer v. Department of Justice* (1997), a 5–4 majority upheld a Florida redistricting plan in which once again a court had drawn the lines. After the 1990 census, the Florida legislature had drafted a plan that failed to meet Justice Department preclearance under Section 2 of the Voting Rights Act. The legislature then proved unable to come up with a new plan, and the Florida Supreme Court had devised one of its own. The court plan included an irregularly shaped senate district that comprised portions of four counties in the Tampa Bay area and had a 46 percent black voting population. Critics challenged the plan in federal district court on equal protection grounds, and a different plan was fashioned to meet the objections of several of the challengers. The district court then approved the new plan without adjudicating the constitutionality of the state supreme court's proposal.

Justice Souter, joined by all of the dissenters in the *Shaw* line of cases, along with the chief justice, found no procedural problem and no clear error (the traditional standard of review) in the district court's finding. What is of most interest is the majority's rejection of the claim that because the percentage of black voters in the district was higher than in any of the three counties it drew from, it should be invalidated because race had been the primary consideration. (The district had a 36.2 percent black voting-age population.) To this, Souter in essence responded that the Court had never said race could not be a factor, only that it could not be the sole factor. It is hard to see where Souter's opinion provides any more guidance to lower courts and legislatures than did the opinions in the other cases from which he dissented.

The Civil Rights Act of 1991

Several decisions by the Rehnquist Court involving statutory interpretation led Congress to enact a new civil rights act, over the strong objections of President Bush. In effect, in some half-dozen cases involving statutory construction, Congress told the Court: "We didn't mean that. You got it wrong."

In a major provision, the bill reversed the Court's holding in *Ward's Cove Packing Co. v. Antonio* (1989) and allowed plaintiffs to prove discrimination on the basis of statistical evidence, shifting the burden of proof back to the employers in rebutting such evidence. The bill also made it easier for women to collect monetary awards for intentional bias, although the bill set limits, ranging from $50,000 to $300,000, on the amount they could collect. Until this bill, only victims of racial discrimination could sue for cash. Other major provisions spelled out congressional intent that a Reconstruction-era statute applied not only to racial discrimination in hiring but also to harassment on the job, overturning the doctrine in *Patterson v. McLean Credit Union* (1989). The law also greatly curtailed late challenges to consent decrees against discriminatory job practices, reversing the Court's doctrine in *Martin v. Wilks* (1989).

President Bush had attacked the proposal as a "quotas" bill, and had vetoed it when it was first passed by the Congress, despite the fact that both Democratic and Republican moderates had altered the language to ensure that it would not mandate quotas. The bill had support not only from the usual civil rights groups, but also from business leaders, including the prestigious Business Roundtable. Bush, under great political pressure, finally agreed to sign the bill, one that differed only minutely from the one he had earlier vetoed. Whether the measure would, in fact, greatly change civil rights litigation was questionable, given the coolness apparent in a judiciary dominated by Reagan and Bush appointees.

Gender Discrimination

Although feminists had attacked Sandra Day O'Connor for not being more assertive in her defense of women's equality on the Court, the fact remains that the Rehnquist Court did not hand down a single decision against equal protection for women. Beyond that, it defined the jurisprudence on sexual harassment.

Women won their first battle before the Rehnquist Court in 1991, in *United Automobile Workers v. Johnson Controls.* The company operated thirteen factories making different types of batteries. Current medical knowledge recognizes the danger of exposure to lead for women of child-bearing age, dangers that potentially could adversely affect a fetus should pregnancy occur. Men are evidently not similarly affected by lead exposure, and there appears to be no danger of their offspring becoming deformed. At the time of the case, there was no feasible technology to make batteries without lead, and so to avert potential lawsuits of the type initiated by asbestos workers in the 1980s, Johnson Controls adopted a policy of not employing women in jobs involving lead exposure. These jobs, however, were among the better paying in the plant, and women workers sued on the basis of alleged gender discrimination under Title VII of the 1964 Civil Rights Act.

The Court unanimously struck down the company policy. Justice Blackmun, writing for the Court, declared women to be as capable as men in doing the jobs, and the decision about the welfare of future children should be left "to the parents who conceive, bear, support, and raise them rather than to the employers who hire those parents." Justice Scalia concurred in the result, noting only that he would have allowed employers a little more leeway in the rare cases in which health insurance costs for pregnant women would be highly expensive. Scalia had telegraphed his opinion during oral argument, when he attacked the company's lawyer for making a "farce" of the 1978 Pregnancy Discrimination Act.

The next issue to come before the Court involved peremptory challenges to women jurors solely on the basis of gender. In *Batson v. Kentucky* (1986), the Court had struck down peremptory challenges in jury selection when race had been the sole factor; people could not be arbitrarily dismissed solely because of their skin color. In *J.E.B. v. Alabama ex rel. T.B.* (1994), the Court extended that ban against gender challenges. Justice Blackmun wrote for the majority and condemned the stereotyping of women that lay behind the practice. But as Justice O'Connor pointed out in her concurrence, "We know that like race, gender matters. A plethora of studies make clear that in rape cases, for example, female jurors are somewhat more likely to convict than male jurors."

The question that informed both Blackmun's and O'Connor's opinions reveal the difficulty that the Court had distinguishing between "real" differences between men and women and outdated stereotypes. Blackmun's opinion took the view that the Constitution ought to be gender-blind, as it is supposed to be race-blind, and even though the Court never made gender into a suspect classification, he in effect treated it as such. O'Connor's view was more realistic; gender does matter. But she, too, did not want to let these "real" differences be used to support practices that treated women as second-class citizens.

The biggest victory women's rights activists won before the Rehnquist Court involved one of the icons of Southern culture, the Virginia Military Institute, which since its founding had been an all-male institution noted for its rigorous discipline. VMI is a state-supported school, and when women applied there, they were rejected; moreover, Virginia offered no comparable military education to women. The school claimed that its goal of producing citizen-soldiers and its tough disciplinary methods were not suited to women; in particular, it pointed to the spartan barracks, the "adversative model" of training, in which indignities are heaped on "rats" or first-year students, and the lack of privacy. The state offered and in fact set up what it claimed was a comparable training program designed for women at another school, but none of these arguments influenced the Court.

Justice Ruth Bader Ginsburg delivered the Court's opinion in *United States v. Virginia* (1996), in which she ruled that the Commonwealth of Virginia had deprived women of equal educational opportunity and ordered VMI to open its doors to women students. Ginsburg spent a fair amount of her opinion discussion elaborating on the Court's criteria. Although gender did not constitute a suspect classification subject to strict scrutiny standards, it did merit a heightened scrutiny. For Virginia to support its men-only policy, it had to demonstrate an "exceedingly persuasive justification." Moreover, the burden of proof rests upon the state to meet this high standard. In the case of VMI, Virginia had failed.[1]

Sexual Harassment

Although Title VII of the Civil Rights Act prohibits discrimination based on gender, womens rights groups did not know whether this would also apply to a longstanding problem confronting women in the workplace—sexual harassment. The question first came before the high court in the last term of the Burger Court, in *Meritor Savings Bank v. Vinson* (1986). A female bank clerk brought a sexual harassment charge against her superior, claiming that he had threatened to fire her if she did not have sex with him. The defendant responded that it could not be harassment, since the woman had voluntarily gone to bed with him. Justice Rehnquist spoke for a unanimous court in holding that hostile environment sexual harassment is a form of sexual discrimination under Title VII. Moreover, the Court ruled that the proper test is whether the advances were unwelcome, not whether the sexual activity was voluntary. In this case, the employee "voluntarily" agreed to have sex because if she did not, she would have lost her job. Feminists cheered Rehnquist's opinion and the sensitivity it showed to the problems women faced in the workplace.

In 1993, Justice O'Connor also spoke for a unanimous Court in *Harris v. Forklift Systems, Inc.* The lower court had dismissed a sexual harassment suit because the plaintiff could show no physical or psychological injury. O'Connor wrote that to be actionable as a hostile environment, the conduct need not seriously affect the psychological well-being of a woman or lead to physical suffering. Although the Court failed

1. Only Justice Scalia dissented; Justice Thomas, whose son attended VMI, recused.

to give adequate guidance, it clearly implied that a hostile atmosphere by itself could be grounds for a Title VII suit.

Then in 1998, the Court decided a series of cases that hammered home the message that sexual harassment would not be tolerated. In *Gebser v. Lago Vista Independent School District,* a teacher had made sexual advances toward a student, who agreed to go to bed with him. After other students who also had been harassed complained, the school authorities investigated and dismissed the teacher. At that time, Gebser's parents filed suit against the school on her behalf.

Justice O'Connor noted that at the time the incident took place, the school system had no procedures in place for reporting sexual harassment and in fact had no policy on the subject. The plaintiff had not complained to any school authority until after other students had done so and the teacher had been dismissed. By a 5–4 vote, the Court ruled that the school system could not be held liable under Title IX unless a school official who at the minimum had the authority to initiate corrective measures had actual notice of and remained deliberately indifferent to the misbehavior. In this case, the school system had acted promptly once it had notice, and it could not have acted before. The majority refused to extend the old common law doctrine of *respondeat superior*—that an employer is responsible for the misdeeds of an employee when the latter is acting on the job—to the school system in the absence of notice of the employee's misbehavior.

But where supervisors had notice and failed to act, then women who had been sexually harassed had standing to sue. In *Faragher v. City of Boca Raton,* a former city lifeguard brought suit against the city and her immediate superiors for, among other things, creating a "sexually hostile atmosphere" by repeated uninvited and unwelcome touching and crude comments. Speaking for a 7 to 2 majority (Scalia and Thomas dissented), Justice Souter declared that the employer is liable for actionable discrimination caused by a supervisor. In a case decided the same day, *Burlington Industries Inc. v. Ellerth*, Justice Kennedy, for the same 7 to 2 majority, went even further and held that an employer may be held liable for a supervisor's harassing acts even if the employer was not aware of them. In both cases, the Court now seemed willing to apply the agency principle of *respondeat superior*, and it detailed the nature of defenses that employers could utilize, such as the reasonableness of the employer's conduct as well as that of the employee.

Perhaps responding to claims that earlier cases had failed to spell out exactly what constituted a hostile environment, the Court essentially applied the old tort test of the reasonable person. If the factfinder determined that the average woman would find the situation hostile, then it should be considered as such.

That same term, in a case that shocked many conservatives, the Court held that same sex sexual harassment fell under the protection of Title VII. The male plaintiff worked as a roustabout on an oil platform in the Gulf of Mexico, and he alleged that his male coworkers had forcibly subjected him to sex-related humiliations, physically assaulted him in a sexual manner, and had threatened to rape him. The Fifth Circuit summarily rejected his Title VII claim, holding that same-sex sexual harassment could not be actionable.

How far the Court was willing to go to attack sexual harassment became apparent the following term in *Davis v. Monroe County Board of Education* (1999). Relying on the *Gebser* case decided a year earlier, the Court by a 5 to 4 vote determined that schools may be held liable under Title IX for deliberate indifference to complaints about sexual harassment. LaShonda Davis claimed that a male student in her fifth grade class had verbally and physically abused her a number of times, touching her and making crude comments about her body. The girl repeatedly reported these incidents to school authorities, who did nothing; finally, the boy pleaded guilty to sexual battery for his misconduct.

The girl's mother then sued the county school board, alleging they had done nothing to stop the harassment. The court of appeals for the Eleventh Circuit ruled that the student-on-student harassment did not fall within the ambit of Title IX. Writing for the majority, Justice O'Connor first ruled that student-on-student harassment within a school setting did come within the coverage of the Civil Rights Act. She distinguished this case from *Gebser*, in that here the school authorities had been repeatedly told of the abuse and had done nothing about it. She characterized the school board's action, and the test for liability, as a deliberate indifference to known sexual harassment that is "so severe, pervasive, and objectionably offensive that it effectively bars the victims access to an educational opportunity or benefit."

The decision triggered a torrent of criticism, much of it of the kind that "boys will be boys," and jokes about arresting Johnny if he tried to kiss Susie. But the actions of LaShonda Davis's tormentor went well beyond the normal teasing of elementary school students, and as women's groups clearly recognized, were of the type that created and perpetuated an environment in which sexual harassment became a norm, with girls expected to accommodate and learn to live with such behavior as they grew up.

The dissenters did not disagree with this logic, but objected primarily on procedural grounds, namely that school districts had not had notice that they would be responsible for this type of behavior and therefore had not taken adequate precautions to avoid liability. Considering the misbehavior of the boy and the indifference of school authorities, the dissent seemed in some ways to be condoning the lack of action by the school.

The justices also had considerable difficulty dealing with repeated challenges to laws that discriminated against gays and lesbians. Following the decision in *Bowers v. Hardwick* (1986), when by a 5–4 vote the Court had held that laws against sodomy did not violate the constitutional right to privacy, homosexual groups had considered the judiciary hostile to their claimed rights. But then in 1996, the Court had handed gay advocacy groups an important victory. Several cities in Colorado had passed laws banning discrimination in housing, employment, and other areas based on sexual orientation. Antigay groups joined together to back Amendment 2, which precluded all legislative, executive, or judicial action at any level of state or local government intended to protect the status of persons based on their sexual orientation. Amendment 2 passed in a statewide referendum, but the Colorado Supreme Court declared that because it infringed on the fundamental rights of gays and lesbians to participate in the political process, it was subject to strict scrutiny under the Equal Protection Clause of the Fourteenth Amendment. It returned the case to the trial court, which then held that Amendment 2 failed to meet the requirements of strict scrutiny.

Colorado appealed the decision, and in *Romer v. Evans* (1996), Justice Kennedy wrote for a 6–3 majority that no state may "deem a class of persons a stranger to its laws." Justice Scalia, joined by the chief justice and Justice Thomas, angrily attacked the majority for "imposing upon all Americans the resolution favored by the elite class from which the members of this institution are selected." Scalia argued that if states could pass antisodomy laws, they could surely bar legal protection of homosexuals. But the earlier decision had dealt with a specific practice, while *Romer* dealt with a class of people and with their access to economic and political rights that the Court had many times held fundamental to individual liberty, an important distinction by any standard.

Two years later, the Court seemed to hand gay rights groups another victory. In *Oncale v. Sundowner Offshore Services, Inc.* (1998), Justice Scalia, speaking for the Court, noted a number of precedents in which the Court had held that the Civil Rights Act applied to men as well as women. Acknowledging that same-sex harassment "was surely not the principal evil Congress was concerned with when it enacted Title VII," Scalia noted that "statutory prohibitions often go beyond the principal evil to cover reasonably comparable evils, and it is ultimately the provisions of our laws rather than the principal concerns of our legislators by which we are governed."

But if gay rights groups thought the Court had finally come to recognize their claims, they received a rude setback in *Boy Scouts of America v. Dale* (2000). By a 5 to 4 vote, the Court, speaking through the chief justice, held that the Boy Scouts could ban gay members because opposition to homosexuality is part of the organization's expressive message. Application of New Jersey's antidiscrimination law violated the Boy Scouts' right to freedom of association. The logic of the majority received rough handling by the four dissenters, justices Stevens, Souter, Ginsburg, and Breyer. While freedom of association is a hallmark of private groups, claiming that the Boy Scouts constituted a private association stretched the imagination considerably, since up until this case they had taken any boy who had applied for membership. It is clear that the conservative members of the Court are having a difficult time with gay rights, torn on the one hand by the homage to a tradition that excoriates homosexuals and on the other by a commitment to libertarian equality.

Abortion

More than anything else, conservatives wanted the Rehnquist Court to reverse *Roe v. Wade* (1973) and either return control over abortion to state legislatures or ban the procedure altogether on a theory that life begins at conception, and thus the Fourteenth Amendment protects the civil rights of a fetus. Opposition to abortion became the litmus test imposed by the Reagan administration in selecting men and women for the federal bench, and the strategy seemed to be working. In 1987, the court of appeals for the Eighth Circuit, by a vote of 7–3, upheld a Minnesota law requiring women under 18 to notify both parents or secure approval from a judge before getting an abortion. Of the seven judges in the majority, Reagan had appointed six of them. Just four days later, a three-judge panel in the Sixth Circuit struck down a similar Ohio statute as unconstitutional. Both cases would reach the high court on appeal.

The Rehnquist Court handed down its first major abortion decision on the last day of the October 1988 Term. Although some people had anticipated—indeed prayed—

that the Court would overturn *Roe*, the decision did not go that far, thus pleasing neither the supporters nor the opponents of abortion rights. The issue came before the high court in a challenge to a Missouri statute that banned the use of public facilities and public employees in performing abortions, required physicians to perform viability tests on any fetus believed to be at least twenty weeks old, and declared that life begins at conception. Just a few weeks before the Court handed down its decision, more than 300,000 abortion rights supporters marched in Washington, the largest demonstration there since the antiwar gatherings of the early 1970s.

The chief justice spoke for a highly splintered court in *Webster v. Reproductive Health Services* (1989). Joined by justices White, O'Connor, Scalia, and Kennedy, he ruled that the statute's preamble, declaring that life started at conception, amounted to no more than a value judgment by the legislature and could not by itself regulate abortion. The same majority upheld the state's ban on the use of public facilities and employees as consistent with earlier decisions regarding the power of a state to specify its employees duties and restrictions. While an individual woman may have a right to an abortion, the state was not obligated to provide either funds or facilities to help her realize that right.

On the fetal viability section, only White and Kennedy joined Rehnquist in construing the provision to leave its application up to the judgment of the individual doctor. The chief justice used this section, however, to attack the trimester framework of the original *Roe* decision as "unworkable." In a bitter dissent, Justice Blackmun, joined by Brennan and Marshall, defended the trimester scheme and accused the majority of cowardice, deception, and disingenuousness in failing to come to grips with the basic issues involved in the abortion debate. Justice Stevens dissented separately, noting he would have invalidated the testing provision and the preamble, which he claimed violated the Establishment Clause by endorsing particularistic Christian beliefs.

The chief justice did, in fact, recognize the divisive nature of the issue, but pointedly reminded the country that "the goal of constitutional adjudication is surely not to remove inexorably 'politically divisive' issues from the ambit of the legislative process, whereby the people through their elected representatives deal with matters of concern to them." This view had been at the core of conservative criticism of allegedly activist courts for more than four decades. In areas of criminal procedure, civil rights and liberties, as well as privacy and abortion, critics claimed that the courts had usurped the prerogatives of the political branches. They believed that banning abortions, or permitting abortions with restrictions, were policy decisions to be made by the elected representatives of the people and not by the courts. It is a view that Rehnquist held

> The simple truth is that *Roe* no longer survives, and that the majority provides no substitute for its protective umbrella. . . . I rue this day. I rue the violence that has been done to the liberty and equality of women, I rue the violence that has been done to our legal fabric and to the integrity of this Court. I rue the inevitable loss of public esteem for this Court that is so essential. I dissent.
>
> —Justice Harry Blackmun, from unpublished dissenting opinion in *Webster* (1989)

dear, and it also explains his desire to move decision-making away from Washington and from the courts and back to the states.

The next term, the Court heard the cases from the sixth and eighth circuits on parental notification. In *Ohio v. Akron Center for Reproductive Health*, a 6 to 3 majority upheld the Ohio law requiring notice to one parent or a judicial bypass. In contrast, different 5–4 majorities struck down Minnesota's two-parent notification requirement when it did not provide for judicial bypass, but then upheld the same provision when coupled with a bypass in *Hodgson v. Minnesota.* Neither case broke new ground, but many observers noted that it had been Justice O'Connor who provided the critical fifth vote in the Minnesota case and that for the first time, she found that a state restriction unduly burdened a woman's reproductive freedom. The dissenters, led by Justice Marshall, would have found the law, even with the bypass provision, too restrictive. Marshall pointed to the dilemma of a pregnant young woman "in an already dire situation [forced] to choose between two fundamentally unacceptable alternatives: notifying a possibly dictatorial or even abusive parent or justifying her profoundly personal decision in an intimidating judicial proceeding to a black-robed stranger."

Antiabortion activists took heart from these decisions, as well as the Court's upholding the HHS gag rule in *Rust v. Sullivan* in 1991 (see next chapter), and they looked forward confidently to the time in the near future when *Roe* would be overturned. They hoped that the time had come, when the Court heard arguments in *Planned Parenthood of Southeastern Pennsylvania v. Casey,* decided in 1992. The law seemed to include nearly every restriction that abortion opponents could think of to burden the procedure to the point of making it impossible for a woman to elect to have an abortion. The Pennsylvania law required minors to get parental consent and wives to notify their husbands before getting an abortion; doctors had to inform women about potential medical complications; women had to wait 24 hours after requesting an abortion before the procedure could be performed; doctors had to adhere to strict and onerous reporting requirements. A district court had struck the law down, but on appeal, the Third Circuit had upheld all of the provisions except spousal notification. The appeals court also declared that abortion could no longer be considered a fundamental right and, as a result, restrictions on abortion need not be subject to strict scrutiny. The circuit court, in effect, said it would accept any restriction the legislative thought necessary.

The Supreme Court, on the surface, upheld the court of appeals, insofar as it sustained the restrictions, but in its reasoning the majority reaffirmed the "essential holding" of *Roe*. Justices O'Connor, Kennedy, and Souter took the unusual step of coauthoring an opinion, in which justices Blackmun and Stevens joined, in part. The majority opinion reaffirmed three components of *Roe*: (1) the right of a woman to choose to have an abortion before viability and to obtain it without undue interference from the state; (2) the state's power to restrict abortion after viability, providing the law contains exceptions for pregnancies that endanger the woman's life; and (3) the state's legitimate interests "from the outset of pregnancy in protecting the health of the woman and the life of the fetus that may become a child." According to the three coauthors, "These principles do not contradict one another, and we adhere to each." The opinions did not, however, reaffirm the strict scrutiny standard that *Roe* had called for in evaluating restrictions.

> A decision to overrule *Roe*'s essential holding under the existing circumstances would address error, if error there was, at the cost of both profound and unnecessary damage to the Court's legitimacy and to the nation's commitment to the rule of law. It is, therefore, imperative to adhere to the essence of *Roe*'s original decision, and we do so today.
>
> —Justices O'Connor, Kennedy, and Souter in their joint opinion in *Casey* (1992)

Unlike some earlier decisions, which had grounded the right to an abortion in privacy, the majority placed it within the liberty interest of the Fourteenth Amendment's Due Process Clause. Under this reasoning, a "realm of personal liberty" existed that the government may not enter, and this realm protected personal decisions related to marriage, procreation, conception, family relationships, and abortion.

While the majority underscored the Court's obligation to *stare decisis* and the need to make "legally principled decisions," O'Connor, Kennedy, and Souter rejected what they considered *Roe*'s "elaborate but rigid" trimester framework and also rejected the notion that a woman has an unfettered right to choose abortion without interference from the state. Rather, states are free to enact a reasonable framework, in which a woman can "make a decision that has such profound and lasting meaning." Only when these laws "unduly burden" a woman's decision do they violate her personal liberty. By this standard, the Court upheld four of the five Pennsylvania restrictions. The minority of the chief justice, joined by White, Scalia, and Thomas, concurred in the judgment, but dissented from the reaffirmation of *Roe*, which they would have abandoned.

Concurring only in the parts that reaffirmed a woman's basic right to an abortion, Justice Blackmun took the unusual step of praising his colleagues for what he termed "an act of personal courage and constitutional principle." Yet he worried that four members of the Court stood waiting for a fifth vote to overturn *Roe*, and in another unusual statement he noted that "I am 83 years old. I cannot remain on this Court forever, and when I do step down, the confirmation process for my successor may well focus on the issue before us today." When Blackmun did retire two years later, however, the dynamic had changed. Byron White, who had voted against *Roe* in 1973, had retired, and Bill Clinton, a supporter of choice, had nominated Ruth Bader Ginsburg to replace him. At her confirmation hearings, Ginsburg repeated criticism she had made earlier that *Roe* had short-circuited the debate about abortion in the states at a time when many legislatures had begun reforming their abortion statutes. But she made clear that she herself believed in a woman's right to choose. The following year, Clinton named

> The liberty of the woman is at stake in a sense unique to the human condition and so unique to law. The mother who carries a child to full term is subject to anxieties, to physical constraints, to pain that only she must bear. . . . Her suffering is too intimate and personal for the State to insist, without more, upon its own vision of the woman s role.
>
> —Joint opinion, *Planned Parenthood of Southeastern Pennsylvania v. Casey* (1992)

Steven Beryer to replace Blackmun, and it no doubt gave Blackmun great pleasure that his successor also supported choice.

Ginsburg and Breyer quickly aligned themselves with the centrists, and that seemed to give prochoice forces on the Court a clear 6–3 majority. However, in a highly publicized case involving so-called partial-birth abortion, a bare 5–4 majority in *Stenberg v. Carhart* (2000) struck down a Nebraska statute outlawing the procedure and in doing so invalidated similar laws in thirty other states. The majority opinion by Justice Breyer focused on the vague wording of the statute, which opened it to an interpretation that could have restricted all abortions. In the same term, the Court, by a 6–3 vote in *Hill v. Colorado* (2000), held that a state law creating a "no approach" zone outside medical offices did not violate the free speech rights of abortion protesters seeking to deter women from going through with abortions. The "essential holding" of *Roe,* which had looked fairly secure after *Casey,* seemed far more tenuous at the end of the decade.

The Right to Die

In 1990, the Supreme Court confronted an issue it had never heard of before, a claim for a right to die. In fact, it was a relatively new issue for the nation as a whole, arising from the amazing explosion of medical technology in the previous three decades. People who up until the 1960s would have been expected to die from severe accidents or illnesses can now be helped, although there are significant limits on this technology, as well as some unexpected negative effects.

In January 1983, Nancy Cruzan's car swerved on a patch of ice, skidded off the road, and turned over. The 25-year-old woman was thrown from the vehicle and landed face down in a ditch. A medical team arrived in time to save her life, but not fast enough to get oxygen to her brain. She never regained consciousness, and for the next seven years lay in what is known as a permanent vegetative state, awake but totally unaware of anyone or anything. Her autonomous functions, such as heartbeat and breathing, continued without the help of machines, but she received nourishment and water through a tube into her stomach.

Her parents, Joyce and Joe Cruzan, finally gave up hope that their daughter would regain consciousness and went into court to ask that the feeding tube be removed and that Nancy be allowed to die with dignity. Although a local judge granted permission, the Missouri Supreme Court reversed, holding that the state had an important interest in preserving life. In this case, the state's interest had to prevail because Nancy had left no "living will" or other clear and convincing evidence that in such circumstances she would want to have the feeding tube removed. Without this type of evidence, the state court concluded, "we prefer to err on the side of life."

When Chief Justice Rehnquist announced the decision in *Cruzan v. Director, Missouri Department of Health* (1990), he indicated his clear sympathy with the plight of Nancy Cruzan and her parents. He described them as "loving and caring," and if the state of Missouri had to let anyone decide to end medical treatment of their daughter, "the Cruzans would surely qualify." But by a 5–4 vote, the Court upheld the state's interest and found that its demand for clear and convincing evidence of Nancy's wishes to be reasonable.

The vote is misleading, however. Rehnquist, widely recognized as an ardent advocate of judicial restraint and an opponent of court-created rights, carefully declared that there is a right to die. It derives not from any alleged constitutional right of privacy, but rather from the guarantees of personal autonomy embedded in the Fourteenth Amendment's Due Process Clause. A long line of decisions, he held, support the principle "that a competent person has a constitutionally protected liberty interest in refusing unwanted medical treatment." The four dissenters, led by Justice Brennan, agreed that a person has the right to die, but believed that as a federally protected liberty interest it should trump the state's demand for a higher level of evidence.

Had Nancy Cruzan left a living will or other evidence of her desires, there would have been no controversy. But a state also has interests, and the majority did not find a violation of personal autonomy for the state to set a reasonable evidentiary demand. In many ways, this case can also be seen as part of the Rehnquist Court's effort to revive federalism and to shift authority and responsibility away from the federal courts back to the states. Justice Scalia, the only member of the Court opposed to recognizing a right die, bluntly declared that the federal courts "have no business in this field."

In many ways, the *Cruzan* decision is a good example of how the Court should act when confronting a new issue. Having learned its lesson from *Roe*, it chose not to jump ahead of public opinion. The type of decisions that needed to be made were local in nature and should therefore be subject to local discretion. But a long line of common law decisions, as well as some constitutional precedents, did support the right of a person to be let alone, and that included refusing unwanted treatment. The Court acknowledged the liberty interest, which it said the states had to recognize as well; it then left it to the states to determine what should be done.

In fact, the Court played its cards well. Nearly all of the states were in the process of enacting so-called Death with Dignity statutes to provide for living wills, health proxies, and other devices by which people could better control health care decisions. While most states required only a minimum level of evidence to support patient wishes, a few states, such as Missouri, imposed a higher, but not an unreasonable, evidentiary burden. The Court said that in a federal system, such differences between the states did not cause a problem.

Following the decision, the Cruzans went back to local court, this time with additional evidence of their daughter's intent in the form of three new witnesses who testified about a specific conversation in which Nancy had said she would not like to live "like a vegetable." The state of Missouri, having made its point, did not contest the evidence, and on December 5, 1990, the Cruzans received the court order they wanted, directing the Missouri Rehabilitation Center to disconnect the feeding tubes. Twelve days later, Nancy Cruzan died.

Within a few years, the so-called right to die had become statutorily and judicially embedded in the laws of all fifty states, and Congress had passed a patients' rights bill that required hospitals receiving federal funds to obey patient directives in regard to refusal of treatment. But a new problem arose when on June 4, 1990—just three weeks before the Court handed down its decision in *Cruzan*—Dr. Jack Kevorkian hooked up what he called his "mercy machine" to 54-year-old Janet Adkins, a schoolteacher suffering from early stages of Alzheimer's disease. With that single act, the issue of physician-assisted suicide hit the front pages and became a burning issue in public policy debate thereafter.

Although suicide had at one time been considered a felony, all states had wiped that crime off their books. But many states still made assisting in a suicide a crime, and this nominally prevented doctors from helping patients who suffered greatly and wanted to die. *Cruzan* had established the right of a competent person, or a surrogate for an incompetent, to turn off life support and thus hasten death. Both law and ethics reasoned that this did not constitute suicide; death resulted from the underlying illness. Many people, however, could not see why a suffering person on life support could legally elect death, while a suffering person not on life support could not.

Within a few years, courts heard challenges to state proscriptions on assisting suicide. On the West Coast, the court of appeals for the Ninth Circuit struck down Washington state's ban on assisted suicide. The judges read dicta in the *Casey* decision broadly, and found death, like the decision to terminate pregnancy, to be one of those acts "too intimate and personal" to brook interference from the state. Such a right, the court reasoned, constituted a liberty interest protected by the Due Process Clause. On the East Coast, the Second Circuit voided New York's law, but based its decision on the Equal Protection Clause, arguing that the law discriminated between people on life support and others.

The justices, had they agreed with the results of the two appeals courts, could have let the decisions stand, even if the two tribunals disagreed on the constitutional rationale. When the high court announced it would hear the cases, most commentators believed that the conservatives—especially Rehnquist, Scalia, and Thomas, who opposed creating new rights—had granted certiorari for the sole purpose of reversing the appeals courts. The decisions in *Washington v. Glucksberg* and *Vacco v. Quill* came down on the last day of the term in 1997, and while the results may have been what most people expected, the divisions on the Court and the multiple opinions seemed to indicate something else.

The chief justice wrote the opinion for the Court in which justices O'Connor, Scalia, Kennedy, and Thomas joined, and in which all of the justices concurred in the result. But O'Connor, Stevens, Souter, Ginsburg, and Breyer filed concurring opinions that differed significantly from Rehnquist's reasoning and conclusions. Following what was now for him a familiar pattern, Rehnquist asked whether the right claimed—a right to physician-assisted suicide—had existed either at the time of the framing of the Constitution or of the ratification of the Fourteenth Amendment. Since it had not, and given the longstanding legal and moral antipathy to suicide, then there was no historical justification for including it in the liberty interests subsumed under the Due Process Clause. The chief justice also claimed that the lower courts had misread *Casey,* and the reference to "intimate and personal" decisions had never been intended to apply to suicide. The opinion was straightforward and simplistic, and it ignored nearly all of the complex issues that the lower courts had discussed, such as individual autonomy and the lack of distinction between patients who were suffering on life support and those who were not. Rehnquist was consistent though, and the opinion is characteristic of his opposition to the creation of new rights and the desire to leave as much authority in the states as possible.

The fact that a majority of the Court filed concurrences is somewhat unusual, and a close reading indicates that while these five justices might be prepared to accept the results at this time, each indicated that should the states make end-of-life choices too narrow, they would be prepared to revisit the matter. The most elegant and sophisticated of the opinions is that of Justice Souter, who not only indicated his awareness of the human suffering involved, but went into an extended discussion of how new liberty interests may develop under the Due Process Clause. Souter quoted extensively from the second Justice Harlan's dissent in *Poe v. Ullman* (1961), the predecessor case to *Griswold v. Connecticut* (1965). In *Poe*, Justice Harlan laid the basis for a right to privacy grounded in due process rather than in the penumbras and emanations of the Bill of Rights relied upon by Justice Douglas. Using a similar reasoning, Souter showed how one might reach the conclusion that the right to die included a right to assisted suicide. Like the others, he preferred to wait and see what the states would do, a lesson he and the others had learned from *Roe v. Wade*. The state of Oregon had recently passed an initiative allowing physician-assisted suicide, and the Court would wait to see how this state experiment fared. Like Rehnquist, Souter believed it would be best if the states could resolve the issue satisfactorily and in a way that promoted individual autonomy. If not, the Supreme Court had left the door open to revisit this issue.

Conclusion

How can one interpret these decisions and get some sense of a jurisprudential theme for the Rehnquist Court, if in fact one exists? Without question, the justices are very conservative in the sense that they are not eager to create new rights or correct every evil that comes before them, yet at the same time this is the Court that announced that a constitutionally protected right to die exists. If it has not been assertive in defense of minorities, as some civil rights groups have charged, it has certainly not tolerated overt manifestations of racial prejudice. In its antipathy toward affirmative action, there is an irony that the Court is attempting to establish what people like Martin Luther King, Jr., claimed that they wanted—a color-blind Constitution.

If this is a Court that has been unwilling to expand abortion rights, and in fact has tolerated increased restrictions on choice, it is also the Court that reaffirmed the essential holding of *Roe v. Wade,* that a woman has a constitutional right to choose an abortion and that this right cannot be unduly burdened by the state. Women may feel this is unsympathetic to women's rights, but no Court has been as consistent in ruling that women may not be discriminated against because of their gender, in defining in such broad strokes a hostile environment created by sexual harassment, and in giving women substantial legal powers to fight that form of discrimination.

It is, as noted earlier, above all a centrist Court. Part of the reason may be that the Court's leading conservative, Antonin Scalia, has been unable or unwilling to forge the type of coalitions that William Brennan did. Another is that conservatives like justices O'Connor, Kennedy, and Souter take very seriously the conservative doctrine of *stare decisis*, and they are unwilling to overturn long-established doctrines even if they believe the original precedents may have been wrongly decided. But above all, six of the nine justices are jurisprudentially and philosophically moderate conservatives open to the need for change, but not eager to rush in before it is necessary to do so. One may agree or disagree with their decisions in the area of civil rights and individual autonomy, but one can hardly describe them as extremist in any way.

For Further Reading

There are several general works on the Rehnquist Court, which include David G. Savage, *Turning Right: The Making of the Rehnquist Supreme Court* (1992); Stanley H. Friedelbaum, *The Rehnquist Court: In Pursuit of Judicial Conservatism* (1994); Peter Irons, *Brennan vs. Rehnquist: The Battle for the Constitution* (1994); James F. Simon, *The Center Holds: The Power Struggle Inside the Rehnquist Court* (1995); and Tinsley E. Yarbrough, *The Rehnquist Court and the Constitution* (2000).

Portraits written of sitting justices are always incomplete (a caveat that applies to most of the following entries), but see Donald E. Boles, *Mr. Justice Rehnquist: Judicial Activist* (1987); and Sue Davis, *Justice Rehnquist and the Constitution* (1989). Other members of the Rehnquist Court have been written about as well. See Robert Judd Sickels, *John Paul Stevens and the Constitution: The Search for Balance* (1988). Robert W. Van Sickel, *Not a Particularly Different Voice: The Jurisprudence of Sandra Day O'Connor* (1998), finds O'Connor's approach to legal issues "marginalist," while Nancy Maveely, *Justice Sandra Day O'Connor: Strategist on the Supreme Court* (1996), finds her to be a major influence on the bench. For Antonin Scalia, see David A. Schultz and Christopher E. Smith, *The Jurisprudential Vision of Justice Antonin Scalia* (1996); and Richard A. Brisbin, Jr., *Justice Antonin Scalia and the Conservative Revival* (1997). See also the interesting volume consisting of an essay by Scalia as well as the critique by several scholars, *A Matter of Interpretation: Federal Courts and the Law* (1997). The controversial Clarence Thomas is discussed in Scott Douglas Gerber, *First Principles: The Jurisprudence of Clarence Thomas* (1999).

The remaining justices have a tenure so short that there are only some articles available. Among these see Christopher E. Smith, "Supreme Court Surprise: Justice Anthony Kennedy's Move Toward Moderation," 45 *Oklahoma Law Review* 459 (1992); Liang Kan, "A Theory of Justice Souter," 45 *Emory Law Journal* 1373 (1996); Liza W. Hanks, "Justice Souter: Defining 'Substantive Neutrality' in an Age of Religious Politics," 48 *Stanford Law Review* 903 (1996); Ann Baugh et al., "Justice Ruth Bader Ginsburg: Preliminary Assessment," 26 *University of Toledo Law Review* 1 (1994); Amy Walsh, "Ruth Bader Ginsburg: Extending the Constitution," 32 *John Marshall Law Review* 197 (1998); Scott Smiler, "Justice Ruth Bader Ginsburg and the Virginia Military Institute: A Culmination of Strategic Success," 4 *Cardozo Women's Law Journal* 541 (1998); Edward A. Fallone, "The Clinton Court Is Open for Business: The Business Law Jurisprudence of Justice Stephen Breyer," 59 *Missouri Law Review* 857 (1994); and the articles on Breyer and administrative law, at 8 *Administrative Law Journal of American University* 713 (1995).

For civil rights, one should see some of the works on the Reagan administration, including Robert R. Detlefsen, *Civil Rights under Reagan* (1991); and Nicholas Laham, *The Reagan Presidency and the Politics of Race: In Pursuit of Colorblind Justice and Limited Government* (1998). See also, the account by Charles Fried, the solicitor general during much of the administration, of the battle between moderates and extremists in *Order and Law: Arguing the Reagan Revolution—A Firsthand Account* (1991). The Court's record in this area is examined in D.F.B. Tucker, *The Rehnquist Court and Civil Rights* (1995).

For affirmative action in general, see Robert Post and Michael Rogin, eds., *Race and Representation: Affirmative Action* (1998); and Ronald J. Fiscus, *The Constitutional Logic of Affir-*

mative Action (1992); as well as a case study of *Johnson v. Santa Clara,* Melvin I. Urofsky, *A Conflict of Rights: The Supreme Court and Affirmative Action* (1991). See also Paul Brest and Miranda Oshige, "Affirmative Action for Whom?" 47 *Stanford Law Review* 855 (1995); Paul Brest, Jesse Chper et al., "Constitutional Scholars' Statement on Affirmative Action After *Croson*," 98 *Yale Law Journal* 1711 (1989).

The background of race-conscious representation is found in Nancy Maveety, *Representation Rights and the Burger Years* (1991) and in J. Morgan Kousser, *Colorblind Injustice: Minority Voting Rights and the Undoing of the Second Reconstruction* (1999). See also, Note, "The Constitutional Imperative of Proportional Representation," 94 *Yale Law Journal* 163 (1984); Pamela S. Karlan, "Still Hazy After All These Years: Voting Rights in the Post-Shaw Era," 26 *Cumberland Law Review* 287 (1995); Samuel Issacharoff, "The Constitutional Contours of Race and Politics," 1995 *Supreme Court Review* 45 (1996); and Lani Guinier, "(E)racing Democracy: The Voting Rights Cases," 108 *Harvard Law Review* 109 (1994).

For abortion, see Barbara Hinkson Craig and David M. O'Brien, *Abortion and American Politics* (1993); and Lawrence Tribe, *Abortion: The Clash of Absolutes* (1990). See also, Martha A. Field, "Abortion Law Today," 14 *Journal of Legal Medicine* 3 (1993); and Alan Brownstein, "How Rights Are Infringed: The Role of Undue Burden Analysis in Constitutional Doctrine," 45 *Hastings Law Journal* 867 (1994). On the gender cases, see Kathryn Abrams, "An Old Jurisprudence: Respect in Retrospect," 83 *Cornell Law Review* 1231 (1998); and Sarah J. Swisher, "'Georgie Porgie . . . kissed a girl and caused an outrage,'" 26 *Capital University Law Review* 619 (1997).

Peter G. Filene, *In the Arms of Others: A History of the Right-to-Die in America* (1998) is a masterful account of the cultural and political context. For the legal background, see Melvin I. Urofsky, *Letting Go: Death, Dying and the Law* (1993); and for assisted suicide, see by the same author "Leaving the Door Ajar: The Supreme Court and Assisted Suicide," 32 *University of Richmond Law Review* 313 (1998).

43

The Rehnquist Court, Federalism, and Civil Liberties

Federalism • The First Amendment • Speech "Plus" • Flag Burning • Free Exercise of Religion • The Religious Freedom Restoration Act • Church and State • Rights of the Accused • Conclusion • For Further Reading

COMMENTATORS TRYING TO classify the Rehnquist Court often floundered once they had described it as conservative. As noted in the last chapter, despite the existence of a conservative bloc, decisions in the areas of due process and equal protection spanned the jurisprudential spectrum. The same is true for decisions involving individual liberties, but one can discern a thread that does much to explain the Court's overall leanings. In large measure, the Rehnquist Court has tried to devolve power away from itself and from the federal government back to the states. The chief justice and a majority of his colleagues believe that while the Court should not shy away from its role as the authoritative interpreter of the Constitution, it should use that power only when necessary.

Unlike the Warren Court, and even in large measure the Burger Court, the Rehnquist Court appeared uninterested in being a court of last resort for those who claim to have been denied substantive justice in state courts and even rejected claims of actual innocence in a death penalty case. Where the Warren Court had sought out cases like that of Clarence Earl Gideon, the Rehnquist Court did not. It is little wonder then that, unlike the Warren and Burger Courts, which often handed down 150 or more full decisions each term, under Rehnquist that number shrank to 75 or 80.

If we look first at the cases that clearly spell out the Court's proclivities toward a robust federal system, then some of its decisions can be seen as part of a larger pattern. The Court's decisions in the right to die and assisted suicide cases illustrate this pattern clearly. While recognizing a constitutionally protected liberty interest in *Cruzan*, the Court nonetheless placed it within the right of states to regulate. Similarly, while refusing to find a right to assisted suicide, a majority of the Court indicated that states were perfectly free to enact legislation legalizing physician-assisted suicide. But one must keep in mind that given the diverse nature of the nine justices, there can be no uniform pattern imposed on all the decisions. Both conservatives and liberals found decisions of the Rehnquist Court appalling in some instances and exhilarating in others.

Federalism

The concept of federalism is as old as the Republic, but for much of the twentieth century it stood in eclipse. The triumph of the New Deal, the nationalizing effects of World War II, and the continued growth of federal programs well into the 1970s often made the states appear as little more than administrative arms of the government in Washington. Even though Richard Nixon spoke about a new federalism and revenue sharing in the late 1960s, real devolution of power to the states did not take place until the 1980s and 1990s, culminating in the Welfare Reform Act of 1996. The preeminence of the federal government has not been an issue; rather, the question is where one should draw the line between federal and state powers.

The Supreme Court lagged behind both Congress and the executive in the revival of federalism. The men who sat on the Court through the 1970s and into the 1980s for the most part reflected the New Deal vision of a powerful central authority. William Rehnquist almost alone on the Burger Court desired to see state authority augmented and that of the federal government restricted. After becoming chief justice, he continued to push this view—and with increasing success—in part because of the changed personnel on the bench and in part because of the temper of the times. Although many of the decisions have been by narrow 5 to 4 votes, even the dissenters do not support the broad claims of federal authority that the Court had so recently approved as a matter of routine.

Rehnquist won a brief victory in *National League of Cities v. Usery* (1976), in which he patched together a 5–4 majority to hold that the Fair Labor Standards Act could not be applied to state employees performing traditional governmental functions. He argued that the law applied to "States *qua* States," and thus impermissibly interfered with state authority. In the early 1980s, however, the Court began chipping away at *Usery,* and in *Garcia v. San Antonio Metropolitan Transit Authority* (1985), specifically overruled the earlier case. Justice Blackmun declared that it would be almost impossible to utilize the *Usery* criteria to define the line between state and federal authority, and he found the national government's commerce power controlling.

By the early 1990s, however, the conservatives appointed by Reagan and Bush began consistently to limit federal authority. In 1992, the Court struck down the 1985 Low-Level Radioactive Waste Policy Amendments, which imposed upon the states a mandate to act alone or in regional compacts to dispose of waste generated within their borders. Congress offered financial incentives to prod the states into cooperation and also imposed stiff penalties for failure to act. By a 6–3 vote, the Court in *New York v. United States* ruled that the law exceeded congressional power and impinged upon powers reserved to the states under the Tenth Amendment. The three dissenters, White, Blackmun, and Stevens objected to parts of the decision, but concurred in much of it.

The Court also voided the Gun-Free School Zones Act of 1990, which forbade "any individual knowingly to possess a firearm at a place that [he] knows . . . is a school zone." A 12th grade student carried a concealed handgun into his high school and, after arrest and conviction, appealed on the grounds that Congress had exceeded its power. In a 5 to 4 decision in *United States v. Lopez* (1995), Chief Justice Rehnquist ruled that the law exceeded the federal commerce authority, in that in no sense could the possession of a gun in a local school zone be an economic activity that, no matter how often repeated, might affect interstate commerce. The law is nothing other than a criminal statute, the majority held, and to sustain it under the Commerce Clause would make that power into a general police power of the sort held only by the states.

In 1997, the 5 to 4 majority struck down parts of the Brady bill and continued its reinvigoration of the concept of sovereign immunity under the Eleventh Amendment. The Brady bill was the first serious federal effort to control the spread of firearms, and it required state law enforcement officers to receive gun dealer reports and conduct background checks on would-be purchasers as part of the federal program. Justice Scalia, joined by the chief justice, O'Connor, Thomas, and Kennedy, made few references to the Tenth Amendment in his opinion in *Printz v. United States.* Instead, he noted that "there is no constitutional text speaking to" the precise question before the Court, and so the answer had to be "sought in historical understanding and practice, in the structure of the Constitution, and in the jurisprudence of the Court." In those sources he found the requirement that state and local officials carry out a federal program exceeded the authority of Congress and impinged upon powers of the states.

In a move that startled many observers, the Court revived the Eleventh Amendment concept of sovereign immunity. The bar against suing states in federal court had long been thought to be a dead letter, but in *Seminole Tribe of Florida v. Florida* (1996), a 5–4 majority held that Congress lacks the power under the Commerce Clause to subject states to suit in federal court for violations of federally created rights. The majority thus overruled a decision less than seven years old, *Pennsylvania v. Union Gas Co.* (1989), which had given Congress a broad power to enforce its laws by overriding state immunity through suits in federal courts. The Court now held that state sovereign immunity under the Eleventh Amendment completely trumped congressional power under Article I. Although the opinion dealt specifically with suits against states by Indian tribes under the Indian Gaming Regulatory Act, the ruling called into question whether federal courts could entertain suits against states under federal environmental statutes, copyright and patent laws, and the many economic regulations attendant upon a national economy.

The next year, the same 5–4 majority continued to breathe new life into the Eleventh Amendment ban. In *Idaho v. Coeur d'Alene Tribe of Idaho*, the tribe had sued the state to prevent it from interfering with the tribe's use of the banks and riverbeds of Lake Coeur d'Alene. The Indians sought to use the precedent of *Ex parte Young* (1908), which carved out an exception in the Eleventh Amendment to allow federal courts to hear suits against state official for violating federal law.

The majority refused to allow the exception and interpreted the Eleventh Amendment to bar federal courts from asserting jurisdiction over suits against states that go to the heart of a state's interests, even if the complaint is stated in ways that might call into play traditional exceptions. There were in fact possible violations of federal law, but the real question was title to the land, and that remained preeminently a matter of state interest. As such, a suit to quiet title could not be carried forth without the permission of the state itself.

The Court reaffirmed the sovereign immunity doctrine in *Alden v. Maine* (1999). A group of probation officers wanted to sue the State of Maine under the Fair Labor Standards Act. *Seminole Tribe v. Florida* barred the workers from going into federal court, so they sued under the federal statute in state court. The Maine courts dismissed the suit on the grounds of sovereign immunity, the notion that a sovereign state cannot be sued without its consent, and the Supreme Court, by a 5 to 4 vote, agreed. Justice Kennedy for the majority described it as a clear and easy decision, but Justice Souter for the four dissenters argued it was far from clear. The dissenters believed that since the state was being sued under federal law, sovereign immunity did not apply. That same day, in two cases involving the Florida Prepaid Postsecondary Education Expense Board and the College Savings Bank, the Court held, by 5–4 majorities, that sovereign immunity precluded suing the state under the Patent Clause for infringement of patented intellectual property, or under the Lanham Trademark Act of 1946 for infringement of trademark. The minority of Breyer, Stevens, Souter, and Ginsburg vigorously dissented, stating that the decisions deprived Congress of power it legitimately exercised under the Constitution.

In the last term of the century, the Court handed down three opinions reinforcing its views on federalism. Again, by a bare 5–4 majority, the Court struck down the Violence Against Women Act in *United States v. Morrison* (2000). The decision invalidated the law's civil damages provisions, which permitted suits in federal court by victims of crimes "motivated by gender." Chief Justice Rehnquist declared that "the Constitution requires a distinction between what is truly national and what is truly local," repudiating what had been the dominant jurisprudence of the Court for more than a half-century. By a similar 5–4 vote, the Court ruled in *Kimel v. Florida Board of Regents* (2000) that Congress lacked the authority to make the states, as employers, liable to suit under the federal Age Discrimination in Employment Act. Justice O'Connor said that the government's interest in eradicating age discrimination on the job had to yield to the states' sovereign immunity.

However, in a decision that surprised some people, a unanimous Court in *Reno v. Condon* (2000) rejected a states' rights challenge to the Drivers Privacy Protection Act, a federal law that forbade states from selling personal information about licensed drivers and automobile owners. The Court was also unanimous in upholding the supremacy of federal law in two cases with foreign policy implications. In *Crosby v. National Foreign Trade Council* (2000), Justice Souter held that a federal law placing sanctions on Myanmar preempted a Massachusetts law that withheld business from companies doing business with the repressive military regime in the former Burma. In the second case, *United States v. Locke* (2000), the Court invalidated Washington State's safety and environmental regulations for tanker traffic along its coast, on the grounds that federal law superseded.

How far the Court is willing to go in its drive to reinforce a federal scheme is difficult to tell. Almost all the cases have been decided by a narrow 5 to 4 majority, and while Scalia, Thomas, and Rehnquist are reputed to be willing to push this drive quite far, it is not at all certain that Kennedy and O'Connor will be willing to accompany them. Moreover, even the conservatives on the Court recognize that a national, indeed an international, economy and society exist in the twenty-first century and that it would be impossible for the United States to survive without the centripetal regulation of a strong central government.

The First Amendment

An example of the libertarian streak in the Court could be seen in one of its early First Amendment cases, *Hustler Magazine v. Falwell* (1988). *Hustler* ran a spoof about the Rev. Jerry Falwell, a well-known conservative minister and founder of a political organization called The Moral Majority. The spoof portrayed Falwell as a drunkard whose first sexual encounter took place with his mother in an outhouse. Just in case anyone missed the point that this had been intended as humor, small print at the bottom of the page warned the reader "Ad parody—not to be taken seriously." Falwell took it seriously, sued the magazine for libel, invasion of privacy, and intentional infliction of emotional distress, and won on the latter count. The magazine's publisher, Larry Flynt, appealed to the Supreme Court, where, in a unanimous decision, he won.

Speaking for the Court, Chief Justice Rehnquist acknowledged the gross nature of the parody, but declared that for the courts to define and penalize the outrageous would require some very difficult line-drawing and would allow juries to award damages on the basis of their personal dislikes of particular forms of expression. Protecting offensive and vulgar parodies may not be a pleasant task, Rehnquist admitted, but it had to be done to give the First Amendment "breathing space." Using a strongly historical argument, Rehnquist compared the *Hustler* parody to political cartoons portraying George Washington as a jackass or Abraham Lincoln as an ape.

As in so many speech decisions, important principles are often enunciated in a case involving unsavory characters or writings. The *Hustler* case raised no new constitutional issues, but followed and reaffirmed, perhaps even extended, the basic holding of *New York Times v. Sullivan* (1964), which protected the media against libel suits by public figures, subject to the "actual malice" standard. Larry Flynt greeted news of his victory with the comment that "the First Amendment gives me the right to be offensive." As *Time* commented, "and to protect more important things, it does."

The Court, in another strong affirmation of the First Amendment, struck down an ordinance banning cross burnings and other hate crimes, although the justices differed widely on their rationales. A St. Paul teenager, Robert A. Viktora, had burned a cross on the front lawn of a black family and was charged under a city ordinance that prohibited any action "which one knows . . . arouses anger, alarm, or resentment in others on the basis of race, color, creed, religion, or gender." The trial court dismissed the charges and held the ordinance to be overly broad and content based. The Minnesota Supreme Court reversed, holding that states retain their authority to prohibit expressive conduct "likely to provoke imminent lawless conduct," citing the U. S. Supreme Court decision in *Chaplinsky v. New Hampshire* (1942), which sustained restrictions on fighting words.

In *R.A.V. v. City of St. Paul* (1992), Justice Scalia, along with four of his colleagues, disagreed and noted that in any and all instances content-based restrictions on speech are presumptively invalid. The Court had carved out certain exceptions, such as obscenity, defamation, and fighting words, but the lower court had misunderstood how those exceptions should be applied. Those areas are not by themselves constitutionally invalid, but depend on how they are applied. "Thus, the government may proscribe libel; but it may not make the further content discrimination of proscribing *only* libel critical of the government." By focusing on the content, the St. Paul ordinance had become a content-based law, and thus in violation of the First Amendment. All of the justices concurred in Scalia's opinion, but four of them—O'Connor, White, Stevens, and Blackmun—tried to find some way to accommodate so-called hate-crime laws.

R.A.V. came down in the midst of a public debate over hate speech. The St. Paul ordinance and others similar to it had been enacted in response to the documented growth of hate groups in the country, including a resurgence in the Ku Klux Klan and right-wing coalitions that targeted African-Americans, Jews, Asian-Americans, gays, and other minorities. Nearly every state in the union has some form of law aimed at these groups and their activities, and there is a debate both in the academies and among civil liberties groups about the need for and legitimacy of such statutes. On one side, the American Civil Liberties Union argues that once we try to identify certain types of speech as unprotected because they are offensive, we start down a slippery slope that will first ban very offensive speech, then the mildly offensive, and finally speech that a majority does not agree with or like.

Other groups, such as the Anti-Defamation League, believe that the rapidly growing number of hate crimes, as well as the phenomenal growth of right-wing talk show hosts who cultivate minority bashing, requires some restriction in order to protect the victims of these crimes. To allow extremists to hide behind the First Amendment, they claim, is to allow them to destroy our free society, in a manner similar to that in which the Nazis came to power in Germany in the 1930s. (Related to this debate is the demand by some militant feminists, that pornography be classified as a crime against women. See Chapter 41.)

The high court tried to make clear, however, that cities and states did not stand defenseless before this type of conduct. "Let there be no mistake," Scalia wrote, "about our belief that burning a cross in someone's front yard is reprehensible. But St. Paul has sufficient means at its disposal [such as trespass laws] to prevent such behavior without adding the First Amendment to the fire." The very next term, the Court drew a sharp distinction between expression and expressive conduct protected by the First Amendment and conduct it considered criminal.

On an evening in October 1989, a group of young black men had gathered in an apartment in Kenosha, Wisconsin. Several of them began discussing a scene from the movie *Mississippi Burning* in which a white man beat a young black boy who was praying. The group moved outside, and Todd Mitchell asked them: "Do you feel hyped up to move on some white people?" Soon afterwards, they saw a young white man approaching them on the other side of the street. Mitchell said "There goes a white boy; go get him." On Mitchell's urging they ran after the youth, beat him severely and stole his tennis shoes. The boy remained unconscious in a coma for four days.

A jury found Mitchell guilty of aggravated battery, an offense that normally carries a maximum sentence of two years,. But because the jury found that Mitchell had selected his victim because of his race, the maximum was increased to seven years imprisonment. The judge sentenced Mitchell to four years, but an appellate court, rely-

> It is but reasonable that among crimes of different natures those should be most severely punished which are the most destructive of the public safety and happiness.
>
> —William Blackstone, *Commentaries* 16 (1765)

ing on *R.A.V.*, held that the statute that increased penalties if race, religion, and other group characteristics were involved, violated the First Amendment by punishing what the legislature deemed offensive thought.

In *Wisconsin v. Mitchell* (1993), Chief Justice Rehnquist, speaking for the entire Court, reversed, and held that a defendant's motives in committing a crime had traditionally been a factor taken into account in sentencing. The battery had been a criminal act, and by identifying antagonisms based on race, color, religion, or gender as aggravating factors, the state had not violated the First Amendment. The decision permitted the state to enhance punishment for a crime motivated by the victim's race; the law had been passed in the first place to protect blacks against racially motivated attacks. The Court believed that such violence, be it based on race, religion, or gender, has a greater terrorizing effect on society than ordinary violence.

What about indecent speech? The Court had avoided any obscenity cases since the early 1970s, and in any event, it had always drawn a line between the "indecent" and the obscene. The latter enjoyed little or no constitutional protection, while the former might well fit under the First Amendment's umbrella. In 1988, Congress amended the Communications Act to target so-called dial-a-porn, in which one could, for a fee, call numbers that played prerecorded sexually oriented messages. In *Sable Communications, Inc. v. FCC* (1989), the Court, speaking through Justice White, struck down the provisions, but intimated that obscene communications could be restricted. Similarly, in *Denver Area Educational Telecommunications Consortium v. FCC* (1996), the Court voided provisions of the 1992 Cable Television Consumer Protection and Competition Act that required cable companies to block certain indecent programs and authorized the FCC to promulgate regulatory definitions. The Court let stand, however, a provision that authorized a cable operator to enforce prospectively the type of programming it would carry on public access channels.

Perhaps the biggest surprise came when the Court struck down the so-called Communications Decency Act of 1996, in which Congress had made it a crime to send or display sexually explicit material in a manner available to anyone under 18. The bill had barely been signed into law by President Clinton when the American Civil Liberties Union filed a suit in federal court to enjoin enforcement, and a three-judge district court struck down the law on a variety of grounds. The Justice Department, which had in effect admitted that the law violated the First Amendment, nonetheless appealed to the Supreme Court, primarily to appease politically powerful conservative groups.

In *Reno v. American Civil Liberties Union* (1997), Justice Stevens spoke for a unanimous court (Justice O'Connor and the chief justice dissented only on one part) in sustaining the district court's invalidation of the law. In an opinion that clearly showed a far more sophisticated understanding of the Internet than Congress had displayed, Justice Stevens explained the impossibility of setting such restrictions on a new medium, which one of the district court judges had described as "a never-ending worldwide conversation" and a "far more speech-enhancing medium than print, the village green or the mails." Stevens described the World Wide Web as "a vast library including millions of readily available and indexed publications and a sprawling mall offering goods and services." Granted, there are sexually explicit materials on the web, some quite crude, but devices exist that can block these sites. The Court asserted that it is for parents, and not the government, to take the necessary steps to protect their children if they choose to do so. The very chaos of the web—its freedom—makes it impossible to control, for there is no single organization controlling membership in the web, nor any centralized point from which individual web sites or services could be blocked. The Communications Decency Act, in trying to do the impossible, violated several key points of constitutional jurisprudence, including vagueness and overbreadth.

In its last term of the decade, the Court indicated that it might be willing to rethink an earlier decision that held limits on campaign finance to be a violation of free speech. By a 6 to 3 vote in *Nixon v. Shrink Missouri Government PAC* (2000), the Court, speaking through Justice Souter, upheld a $1,000 limit on campaign contributions, and four of the justices indicated that they believed the time had come to rethink the whole issue. In another important speech case, *Board of Regents v. Southworth* (2000), the Court unanimously ruled that universities can collect student activity fees even from students who object to particular activities, as long as the policy is neutral as to the student organizations' viewpoints. While the Court held that cities may adopt general bans on public nudity, including restrictions on erotic dancing at adult clubs (*Erie v. Pap's A.M.*), it struck down a federal law requiring cable television operators to scramble fully the signals of sexually explicit programs (*United States v. Playboy Entertainment*).

Speech "Plus"

For the most part, the Court has taken a decidedly speech protective stance, especially when it has involved pure speech; it has also been solicitous of so-called speech plus, speech tied to some act, although there have been some exceptions. A brief review of some of the cases illustrates this pattern. The Court struck down a New York law designed to prevent criminals from profiting from their crimes at the expense of their victims through books about those crimes. Writing for a unanimous Court, Justice O'Connor in *Simon & Schuster v. New York State Crime Victims Board* (1991), held that the government's ability "to impose content-based burdens on speech raises the specter that the government may effectively drive certain ideas or viewpoints from the marketplace." On the other hand, that same term, although by a bare 5–4 majority, the Court found that an Indiana law requiring dancers in adult bookstores and clubs to wear pasties and a G-string did not violate the dancers' First Amendment right to free expression (*Barnes v. Glen Theatre*).

The Court upheld a Tennessee law prohibiting the solicitation of votes, the display of political posters, or the distribution of political literature within 100 feet of the entrance to a polling place. Justice Blackmun, in *Burson v. Freeman* (1992), found that the state had met the high burden of strict scrutiny review on the grounds that such an ordinance served the compelling interest of preserving the integrity of a secret ballot. But otherwise, efforts to stifle political speech found short shrift with the justices. In *City of Ladue v. Gilleo* (1994), the Court unanimously invalidated an ordinance banning the posting of most signs in order to minimize visual clutter. Ladue, a wealthy and politically conservative suburb of St. Louis, allowed ten exceptions, including for sale signs. Mrs. Gilleo had been fined for putting an $8^{1}/_{2} \times 11$ inch sign in her window saying "For Peace in the Gulf." The lower courts had invalidated the ban on the grounds that the exemptions made it too content based. Justice Stevens went further and argued that the ordinance banned "too much" speech. Ladue, he wrote, "has almost foreclosed a venerable means of communication that is both unique and important. . . . Residential signs play an important part in political campaigns . . . and by eliminating a common means of speaking, such measures can suppress too much speech."

In a 1960 case, *Talley v. California,* the Warren Court had invalidated a Los Angeles ordinance that prohibited the distribution of any handbill in the city unless it had the name and address of the person who prepared, distributed, or sponsored it. In *McIntyre v. Ohio Elections Commission* (1995), a 7 to 2 Court reaffirmed *Talley* in striking down a law common to most states, prohibiting the circulation of anonymous leaflets in connection with political campaigns. Justice Stevens held that "an author's decision to remain anonymous . . . is an aspect of the freedom of speech protected by the First Amendment," and he referred to the great documents published during the debate over ratification signed by "Publius," "Cato," and "the Federal Farmer."

The most speech restrictive decision of the Court came in 1991, when in *Rust v. Sullivan*, a 5–4 majority upheld a regulation issued by the Department of Health and Human Services, prohibiting projects receiving federal family planning funds from counseling or referring women for abortion and from encouraging, promoting, or advocating abortion. Doctors had challenged the regulation, claiming it impinged on the First Amendment right to speech, as well as the right of privacy implicit in the Fifth Amendment. The chief justice held that the federal government had the right to determine how its funds should be used and that people who did not agree with those rules did not have to take the money. Congress immediately declared that it had not intended any such restriction in funding Title X of the Public Health Service Act and immediately passed a bill rescinding the prohibition. George Bush, with an eye to keeping religious conservatives in the Republican camp during an election year, vetoed the measure. In one of his first acts as president, Bill Clinton signed an executive order repealing the regulation.

In still another decision that seemed to cut back on speech-related rights, the Court retreated from the broad-based view of *Tinker v. Des Moines* (1969) that students do not lose their rights when entering the classroom. The case, *Hazelwood School District v. Kuhlmeier* (1988) involved the extent to which school officials could exercise control over a student newspaper produced as part of a journalism class and fully funded by the school. A high school principal had deleted two stories from the paper, one dealing with the impact of parents' divorce on students and the other relating the experience of three students with pregnancy.

Speaking for a 6–3 majority, Justice White immediately denied that a school newspaper constituted a traditional public forum. He then distinguished *Tinker*—in which the school had to *tolerate* particular student speech—from a situation in which the students demanded that the school *promote* particular student speech. Educators, White held, could exercise greater control over student expression in a context in which the speech is part of a formal class and in which the outlet is wholly subsidized by the school. One might also note that in some ways this is a press supportive decision, in that the school itself is the functional equivalent of the publisher, and the Press Clause does not hold that reporters can print anything they want, but that the owners, that is, the publishers of the newspaper, have the freedom to express their views. It is also, in some measure, about restoring authority in public schools, and thus fit in well with the conservative bloc's desire for an orderly society. Justices Brennan, joined by Marshall and Blackmun, dissented, claiming that *Tinker* should have been controlling. "The young men and women of Hazelwood expected a civics lesson," declared Brennan, "but not the one the Court teaches them today."

Flag Burning

One of the most difficult First Amendment issues faced by the Court involved desecration of the American flag, a symbol held in near reverence by most Americans. Next to the abortion decision, no cases generated as much public controversy as those decided by the Court in 1989 and 1990, both by 5 to 4 votes.

Gregory Lee Johnson, a member of the Revolutionary Communist Youth Brigade, had burned an American flag as part of a political protest during the 1984 Republican national convention in Dallas. A Texas jury convicted him under a state statute prohibiting the intentional desecration of a state or national flag. The Texas Court of Criminal Appeals reversed on First Amendment grounds, and the Supreme Court affirmed.

Justice Brennan wrote for himself, Marshall, Blackmun, Scalia, and Kennedy, and he tried to keep the decision as narrow in its scope as possible. Did the burning of the flag constitute expressive conduct, an easy question to answer since the state admitted that it did. If expressive conduct, was it of the type to fall under the First Amendment's protection of political expression. The majority found that it did and that First Amendment values outweighed the state's argument that it needed to protect the symbol of national unity or that it deeply offended people nearby. "If there is a bedrock principle underlying the First Amendment," Brennan wrote, "it is that the Government may not prohibit the expression of an idea simply because society finds the idea itself offensive or disagreeable." No one in the majority approved of the action, and as Justice Kennedy noted in a concurring opinion, "we sometimes must make decisions we do not like. We make them because they are right, right in the sense that law and the Constitution . . . compel the result."

The chief justice, joined by White and O'Connor, wrote a spirited and literate opinion in which he quoted from "The Star Spangled Banner" and John Greenleaf Whittier's "Barbara Fritchie." Justice Stevens dissented separately, arguing that the flag is a unique symbol, "worthy of protection from unnecessary desecration."

The ensuing uproar spilled out over the airways, in hundreds of letters to the editors of newspapers and magazines. The Senate voted 97–3 to express its "profound disappointment" in the decision, and President Bush called for a constitutional amendment, a proposal that appalled almost as many people as the decision itself. In looking over the controversy, constitutional scholar David O'Brien declared that "James Madison, who wrote the First Amendment, would have had his heart warmed by the decision, but he would have been appalled that it was a 5–4 vote." Eventually many people, upon reflection, recognized that the majority had not condoned flag desecration but, as Justice Brennan pointed out, jailing people for burning the flag or forcing them to recite the Pledge of Allegiance is not what patriotism in America is about.

Congress turned down Bush's request for a constitutional amendment, and instead passed the 1989 Flag Protection Act, an antidesecration law that critics claimed could not withstand judicial scrutiny. Within a few weeks of the law's enactment, four demonstrators—including Gregory Johnson—burned an American flag on the steps of the U.S. Capitol.

In *United States v. Eichman* (1990), the same 5–4 majority held the federal statute unconstitutional as an interference with expressive conduct protected by the First Amendment. Justice Brennan rejected the government's argument that Congress could do what the states could not, namely, interfere with a form of political speech. Reiterating that the majority did not care for flag desecration any more than did other Americans, Brennan nonetheless pointed out that "punishing desecration of the flag dilutes the very freedom that makes it so revered." The same four dissenters claimed that the flag could be protected as a symbol of national unity consistent with First Amendment protections.

This time, the decision raised far less of an outcry, perhaps because people had had a chance to think about the majority's reasoning. Republicans tried to make an issue of the case and called for a constitutional amendment to override the Court, an ef-

> As I stepped out of the aircraft [after being released from captivity in Vietnam], I looked up and saw the flag. I caught my breath, then, as tears filled my eyes, I saluted it. I never loved my country more than at that moment. . . . I cannot compromise on freedom. It hurts to see the flag burned, but I part company with those who want to punish the flag burners. . . .
>
> I remember one interrogation [by the North Vietnamese] where I was shown a photograph of some Americans protesting the war by burning a flag. "There," the officer said. "People in your country protest against your cause. That proves that you are wrong."
>
> "No," I said. "That proves I am right. In my country we are not afraid of freedom, even if it means that people disagree with us." The officer was on his feet in an instant, his face purple with rage. He smashed his fist on the table and screamed at me to shut up. While he was ranting I was astonished to see pain, compounded by fear, in his eyes. I have never forgotten that look, nor have I forgotten the satisfaction I felt at using his tool, the picture of the burning flag against him. . . .
>
> We don't need to amend the Constitution in order to punish those who burn our flag. They burn the flag because they hate America and they are afraid of freedom. What better way to hurt them than with the subversive idea of freedom? Spread freedom. . . . Don't be afraid of freedom, it is the best weapon we have.
>
> —James H. Warner, former POW, in letter to *Washington Post*, 11 July 1989

fort that immediately fell flat. A number of conservatives, such as Republican Senator Gordon Humphrey of New Hampshire, opposed the demand for an amendment. "I just don't like tampering with the First Amendment," he declared.

If, as some theorists claim, the First Amendment protects only political speech, and if expressive conduct is part of the speech protected, then there is little doubt that the majority reached the right decision. No one wants to see the flag desecrated, but as the majority pointed out, the First Amendment exists to protect the speakers of unpopular opinions, not to allow opponents to silence them.

Free Exercise of Religion

The Rehnquist Court's record on separation of church and state is far from what conservatives had hoped it would be. Many people expected the Court to be more accommodationist, to allow greater public support of religious education, and at least erode if not completely tear down the metaphorical wall of separation between church and state. Certainly some decisions can be described as accommodationist, yet others ringingly proclaim that the wall is as high and as solid as ever. While the justices have been willing to give a fairly broad interpretation to the Free Exercise Clause, their cavalier dismissal of such claims by Native Americans led Congress to attempt to statutorily overturn some of the Court's decisions. As in other areas, the Rehnquist Court proved both more and less than both its champions and critics claimed.

In its first term, the Rehnquist Court heard a Free Exercise claim involving a challenge to the federal government's plan to build a highway and permit timber harvesting in areas that had sacred value to Indian tribes. In *Lyng v. Northwest Indian Cemetery Protective Association* (1988),[1] Justice O'Connor spoke for a 5–3 majority that conceded that the activities would interfere with tribal pursuit of spiritual fulfillment. But, she argued, the government's plans neither coerced the members into violating any of their religious tenets nor penalized any religious activity. This sophistic reasoning, which ignored the basis of the Free Exercise claim, relied on a 1986 decision, *Bowen v. Roy,* which upheld the government's assignment of Social Security numbers to an Indian child over the protest of her parents, who believed that the number would "rob" the little girl of her soul. In his dissent, Justice Brennan found the majority's reliance on *Bowen* "altogether remarkable." In that case, the issue had been one of internal government record-keeping and had had a limited effect. Logging and road building in or near sacred grounds, on the other hand, had potentially far-reaching negative effects on Indian religions; effects, Brennan warned, that could possibly destroy them. (In the end, the road was not built because the Indians managed to use political influence to stop it.)

Two years later, the Court showed a similar insensitivity to Indian beliefs in *Employment Division, Oregon Department of Human Resources v. Smith* (1990). By a 5 to 4 vote, the Court held that the First Amendment does not bar a state from applying

---

1. Despite the title of the case, there were no burial grounds involved; the area was used traditionally for retreats and rites of passage.

its general criminal prohibition of peyote to individuals who claim to use it for sacramental purposes. In addition, the majority announced that the test balancing governmental action burdening religious practices against a compelling governmental interest, first enunciated in *Sherbert v. Verner* (1963), would no longer apply in cases involving criminal laws of general applicability.

While many western states and the federal government provided exemptions for peyote when used in religious ceremonies, Oregon did not. Two employees in a drug rehabilitation program, Alfred Smith and Galen Black, were fired from their positions because they ingested peyote at a religious ceremony of the Native American Church. The two were then denied unemployment compensation because they had been dismissed for misconduct—the use of a criminally proscribed substance. In a line of cases going back to *Sherbert v. Verner* (1963), the Supreme Court had ruled that state unemployment insurance could not be conditioned on an individual's willingness to forego conduct required by his religion, when that conduct was otherwise legal. Smith and Black argued that the same rule should apply to them, even though the Oregon law made ingestion of peyote illegal, because the Oregon law itself was unconstitutional. The Oregon Supreme Court agreed and overturned the ruling, holding that the First Amendment bars criminal punishment of good-faith religious use of peyote, and the state appealed.

Justice Scalia, writing for a bare majority of the Court, took an extremely narrow view of the Free Exercise Clause. Going all the way back to the 1879 case of *United States v. Reynolds*, he argued that religion could never be used as an excuse for violating "an otherwise valid law regulating conduct that the state is free to regulate." Justice O'Connor, joined in part by Brennan, Marshall, and Blackmun, sharply criticized the Court for abandoning the balancing test. Moreover, by denying the applicants the opportunity to challenge a general criminal law on free exercise grounds, the majority had cut out "the essence of a free exercise claim." Just because this statute involved a criminal statute did not mean that it did not burden religious freedom. Nonetheless, O'Connor joined in the result because she believed the state had a compelling interest under the balancing test, namely its effort to wage a war on drugs.

The Religious Freedom Restoration Act

The general criticism of the *Lyng* and *Smith* decisions led a broad coalition of religious groups to petition Congress for redress, and they asked for a broad federal law that would restore a number of exemptions for religious activities. The coalition garnered strong bipartisan support, and in 1993, Congress overwhelmingly passed and President Clinton signed into law the Religious Freedom Restoration Act (RFRA). The statute contained a number of formal findings that "laws 'neutral' toward religion may burden religious exercise without compelling justification." The law and its accompanying legislative history could not have been blunter in its statement that the Supreme Court had been wrong in *Smith* for eliminating the requirement that government justify burdens on religious exercise imposed by facially neutral laws and that the better interpretation had been the compelling interest test of *Sherbert.* Although popular, RFRA was a sweeping law purporting to bind all government action at all levels—

federal, state, and local. In practical terms, it attempted to overrule a Supreme Court decision by creating a broad federal guarantee of religious freedom greater than that created by the First Amendment.

But where did Congress get its authority to pass RFRA? While Congress can always "overrule" a judicial interpretation of a statute by legislating more precise language, what provision of the Constitution allowed the Congress to override the Court's interpretation of the First Amendment? Congress claimed that it was not actually overturning *Smith,* but merely passing civil rights legislation, in this case religious civil rights. In the past, Congress has passed laws creating greater rights than those embodied in the Constitution, and it claimed the authority to do so from Section 5 of the Fourteenth Amendment: "Congress shall have the power to enforce, by appropriate legislation, the provisions of this article." Since 1803, however, the Court had held itself to be the definitive interpreter of the Constitution. The test case to determine who would prevail arose in the small Texas city of Boerne, located some 28 miles northwest of San Antonio.

The city council had authorized the Historic Landmark Commission to prepare a preservation plan for the downtown area and, in order to maintain the historic look of the area, required anyone seeking to change landmarks or buildings in that area to get preapproval. St. Peter's Catholic Church dated from 1923 and had been built in the mission style of the area's earlier history. The parish was growing, but the sanctuary could hold only 230 worshippers, and on any given Sunday between 40 and 60 people could not be accommodated at some masses. The church sought permission to expand, but the city denied the application on the grounds that the altered structure would damage the integrity of the historic district. The archbishop brought suit, claiming that the denial of the permit violated the RFRA. *City of Boerne v. Flores* (1997) could hardly have been a better test case to demonstrate the weaknesses of the law.

The decision had less to do with religious free exercise than with federalism and the separation of powers. The Court denied that Congress had the power under Section 5 to impose upon the courts a particular constitutional interpretation, and Justice

> Our national experience teaches that the Constitution is preserved best when each part of the government respects both the Constitution and the proper actions and determinations of the other branches. When the Court has interpreted the Constitution, it has acted within the province of the judicial branch, which embraces the duty to say what the law is (*Marbury v. Madison*). When the political branches of the Government act against the background of a judicial interpretation of the Constitution already issued, it must be understood that in later cases and controversies the Court will treat its precedents with the respect due them under settled principles, including *stare decisis*, and contrary expectations must be disappointed. RFRA was designed to control cases and controversies, such as the one before us; but as the provisions of the federal statute here invoked are beyond congressional authority, it is this Court's precedent, not RFRA, which must control. . . . The judgment of the Court of Appeals sustaining [RFRA]'s constitutionality is reversed.
>
> —Justice Anthony Kennedy, *City of Boerne v. Flores* (1997)

Kennedy in essence read a civics lessons to the Congress (see box). The Court would decide what the Constitution meant.

Had the Court sustained RFRA, it would have opened a Pandora's box of litigation and problems. In Boerne, the church was asking for something no one else in the downtown area could get—approval to expand and alter a historic building. Had the church been successful, what would have stopped the hardware store across the street from demanding approval for its plans to expand and arguing under an equal protection claim that it should be treated at least the same as the church? (Justice Stevens in his concurring opinion made this point and claimed that RFRA violated the Establishment Clause by granting preferences for religious groups.) The Court had been insensitive in *Smith* and, for reasons that are unclear, abandoned a perfectly usable balancing test that had been in effect for more than three decades. In their separate opinions, justices O'Connor, Souter, and Breyer indicated that they heard the message and argued that the *Smith* doctrine should be reconsidered.

If the Court would not give religious groups exemptions from general laws, at the same time it would not countenance laws aimed specifically at inhibiting particular practices. The Santeria sect, which originated when the Yoruba people were brought to Cuba as slaves, involved an amalgam of West African religion intermixed with Roman Catholicism. Animal sacrifice (after which the animals were cooked and eaten) constituted an essential part of the group's practices. The animals were not tortured, but killed by a clean cutting of the carotid artery in the neck.

When the Santeria announced plans to open a church in Hialeah, Florida, many residents objected, and the city council quickly passed a series of ordinances effectively preventing animal sacrifice within the city limits and punishing violations with fines not to exceed $500 and/or imprisonment of up to 60 days. Although masquerading as health regulations, the taped sessions of the city council clearly indicated the hostility of officials toward the Santeria, as well as the fact that the ordinances had been passed specifically to keep the Santeria out of Hialeah.

In *Church of the Lukumi Babalu Aye v. City of Hialeah* (1993), the Court unanimously invalidated the regulations as a violation of the Free Exercise Clause, although the justices differed in their reasoning. Justice Kennedy, in his opinion for the Court, called the Hialeah law "religious gerrymandering," and "an impermissible attempt to target petitioners and their religious practices." The law ran afoul not only of the First Amendment but of the Fourteenth as well, in that it violated the Equal Protection Clause by singling out one group's practices.

Church and State

One goal of conservatives in the 1980s had been to get judges on the nation's courts who would reverse what conservatives considered the godlessness of decisions from the Warren and Burger eras and who would tear down the wall of separation between church and state. For these groups, a nation without religion could not survive and prosper, and they read history as "proving" that the Framers had always intended there to be a close relation between religion and the state. In their view, all the Establishment Clause meant was that no one church would receive preferential treatment at the expense of others, and that all religions could receive aid from the state. While the Rehnquist Court in some areas proved receptive to this view, a majority of the Court refused to abandon the notion of separation. To the dismay of strict separationists, the Court allowed some accommodation, but far from what those on the right demanded.

In *Lamb's Chapel v. Center Moriches Union Free Public Schools Dist.* (1993), a local evangelical society had been denied use of school facilities to show a six-part film featuring a psychologist who would argue in favor of "Christian family values instilled at an early age." The district routinely allowed school facilities to be used after school hours by social, civic, and even political groups, but claimed that by allowing Lamb's Chapel access it would be sponsoring a church-related activity. The sect claimed that the school district had opened its buildings to such a wide group of activities that it had become a de facto public forum.

Speaking for a unanimous Court, Justice White rejected the claim that the school had become a public forum. The school district had not been required to open its buildings for any after-school outside activities, he noted, but once it did, denying Lamb's Chapel equal access amounted to content discrimination. The Court held that denial of access had to be "viewpoint neutral," and the school district had failed this test.

Similarly, in *Capitol Square Review Board v. Pinette* (1995), the Court struck down the denial of permission to the Ku Klux Klan to erect a large Latin cross on Capitol Square in Columbus, Ohio. The state had designated the square as a public forum, and the Court assumed that permission had been denied because of the religious symbolism of the cross. The plurality opinion by Justice Scalia rejected the state's contention that permitting the sign would have been a form of establishment. He went on to put the issue in speech terms as well, noting that the activity should be considered private religious expression, fully protected by the First Amendment.

Perhaps the most accommodationist decision of the Court involved funding of a Christian-oriented magazine at a state-sponsored university. Wide Awake Publications sought funding from the University of Virginia, claiming that as a student organization it should not be denied student activity funds merely because it wished to focus on religious rather than secular matters. The university denied the application, arguing that to support a seemingly proselytizing club would violate the Establishment Clause. In *Rosenberger v. Rector and Visitors of the University of Virginia* (1995), the Court, by a 5–4 vote, held that the university could not discriminate against Wide Awake. Justice Kennedy, relying on *Lamb's Chapel,* declared that the case rested more on the Speech than the Establishment Clause, and he held that denying funds to a publication because of its orientation amounted to content discrimination.

> Our precedent establishes that private religious speech, far from being a First Amendment orphan, is as fully protected under the Free Speech Clause as secular private expression. Indeed, in Anglo-American history, at least, government suppression of speech has been so commonly directed precisely at religious speech that a free-speech clause without religion would be *Hamlet* without the prince.
>
> —Justice Scalia, *Capitol Square Review Board v. Pinette* (1995)

But the opinion held more than its share of Establishment Clause comments. In dismissing the university's argument, Kennedy found that the program involved—funding of student activities through student fees—did not require the state in the form of the university to favor or disfavor religion. The program was facially neutral, and the object of student funding is to open a forum for speech and other enterprises. The university's argument also suffered from the fact that while denying funding to Wide Awake, it had given funds to other clearly religious groups, such as the Hillel Society and a Muslim student organization.

Justice Thomas, in his concurrence, sounded a theme that Justice Rehnquist had been arguing for years, namely that the First Amendment did not forbid aid to religion, but merely proscribed the government favoring one denomination over another, and he went into a long listing of historical examples of permissible aid. The dissenters, led by Justice Souter, denied this interpretation, and in his examination of the development of the language in the Establishment Clause, he came to the conclusion that Madison did not intend the clause to mean little more than nonpreference, but wanted to erect a wall of separation.

One could find other examples of accommodation in the Court's decisions both before and after *Rosenberger.* In *Bowen v. Kendrick* (1988), the Court upheld those provisions of the Adolescent Family Life Act of 1982 that authorized federal funds to a variety of public and nonpublic organizations, including those with religious affiliation, for counseling services "in the area of premarital adolescent sexual relations and pregnancy." Opponents labeled the law the "Chastity Act" and claimed that the statute violated the Establishment Clause by providing public funds to promote particular religious views. Speaking for the Court, the chief justice ignored the fact that one of the purposes of the act had been to fund religious groups opposed to abortion and premarital sex and to support their efforts to utilize religion-oriented counseling to attack the problem of teenage pregnancy. He rejected the claim that the law violated the *Lemon* test and that any effect of advancing religion was merely "incidental and remote." To make their case, Rehnquist said, challengers of the law would have to show that federal funds went to organizations that were "pervasively sectarian" and not merely religiously affiliated or inspired.

In *Zobrest v. Catalina Foothills School District* (1993), the Court held that providing a publicly funded sign-language interpreter to a deaf student in a parochial school classroom did not violate the Establishment Clause. The case relied in large measure on an 1986 case, *Witters v. Washington Department of Services for the Blind,* which held that no violation of the First Amendment occurred when a visually handicapped person used state vocational rehabilitation money to pay tuition to a Christian college in order to prepare himself for a career in the ministry. The two decisions, especially *Zobrest,* indicated that the Court might reconsider its opinion in two closely divided 1985 cases, *Grand Rapids School District v. Ball* and *Aguilar v. Felton,* in which the Court had invalidated a popular after-school program of publicly funded remedial sessions that took place in parochial schools.

In *Agostini v. Felton* (1997), the Court by a 5–4 vote declared that the earlier decisions no longer could be squared with intervening Establishment Clause cases that gave a greater flexibility to using public funds in parochial settings. Of the original justices who had decided the case, O'Connor and Rehnquist had been in the minority, but now prevailed with the addition of Scalia, Kennedy, and Thomas. Justice Stevens, the sole remnant of the 1985 majority, now joined in dissent with Souter, Ginsburg, and Breyer.

In her opinion, Justice O'Connor ticked off the assumptions that the earlier Court had made to reach its conclusion that the after-school program had the impermissible effect of advancing religion. First, any public employee who works on the premises of a religious school is presumed to inculcate religion. Second, the presence of public employees on private school premises creates a symbolic union between church and state. Third, any and all public money that directly aids the educational function of religious schools impermissibly finances religious indoctrination.

In the twelve years since *Ball* and *Aguilar*, the Court had abandoned the first presumption; it no longer assumed that if a public employee set foot in a parochial school she automatically inculcated religion. It also no longer presumed that aid to any educational function somehow also served to foster religious indoctrination. With these two assumptions gone, then even using the standard *Lemon* test, the after-school program did not violate the Establishment Clause. The four dissenters, Souter, Stevens, Ginsburg, and Breyer denied that the cases since 1986 meant that the Court's tests for violation had changed. The program had transgressed the First Amendment then, and it still did.

A final example of the accommodationist trend on the Rehnquist Court came in *Mitchell v. Helms* (2000), when a 6–3 majority upheld a federal program that placed computers and other equipment in parochial schools, but the six members who voted for the program splintered over how far down this road they were willing to go. Justice Thomas wrote a plurality opinion joined by the chief justice and justices Scalia and Kennedy, but justices O'Connor and Breyer, who concurred in the result, took a far narrower approach.

Those who demanded that the Court allow some accommodation could look at this series of cases with some satisfaction, but in two areas in which religious conservatives wanted change, they were sorely disappointed.

Although the famous Scopes trial in the 1920s had seemed to discredit those who rejected evolution outright, the belief in a literal reading of the account of creation in Genesis had never died among religious fundamentalists. In the 1960s, they had tried to outlaw the teaching of evolution again, only to be slapped down by the high court in *Epperson v. Arkansas* (1968). A more sophisticated religious bloc hit upon a new tack and labeled the Genesis version "creationism" or "creation science," and in Louisiana passed a so-called balanced treatment act. Schools did not have to teach either creation science or evolution, but if either one was taught, then the other had to be as well.

Nearly all reputable scientists dismiss creationism—which accepts the story of Genesis uncritically—as a fraud, bearing no relation to real science, which questions the validity of everything. With only Justice Scalia and the chief justice dissenting, Justice Brennan spoke for a 7–2 majority in *Edwards v. Aguillard* (1987), striking down the balanced treatment act. While the Court always defers to legislative purpose in secular matters, the debate and legislative record in this instance left no doubt as to the religious purposes behind the statute. The act's primary purpose—to advance a particular religious belief—could not pass the *Lemon* test.

Opposition to the original school prayer decision, *Engel v. Vitale* (1962), had not faded, and with a more accommodationist majority on the Court, advocates of school prayer hoped to see the case overruled. But in *Lee v. Weisman* (1992), the Court, albeit by a slim majority, reaffirmed the vitality of the wall of separation.

The case arose in Providence, Rhode Island, where the school system had for many years invited clergy from various denominations to offer prayers at graduation and promotion ceremonies. When their eldest daughter graduated from middle school in 1986, Daniel and Vivien Weisman (who are Jewish) were offended by the prayer of a Baptist minister, and they protested to school officials. Although they never received an answer to their letter, when their younger daughter was to graduate from the same school, the Weismans learned that a rabbi had been invited to give the blessing, apparently in an effort to appease them. The Weismans, however, had not objected just to the particular prayer, but believed that under *Engel* there should be no prayer in public school. With the aid of the Rhode Island ACLU, they filed suit, and they won both in the district court and the court of appeals. When the Supreme Court granted certiorari, many observers wondered if the conservative majority on the bench now had the votes needed to overturn *Engel*. The Bush administration certainly thought so and filed a brief urging the justices to allow prayer in public school.

By a 5 to 4 vote, the Court not only rejected the Bush administration's plea, it refused to abandon precedent and adopt a new test in lieu of *Lemon* for Establishment Clause cases. The new centrist majority, including justices O'Connor, Souter, and Kennedy, indicated that it saw no need for a new test. Justice Kennedy's opinion reaffirmed previous rulings and held that prayers at public school graduations, no matter how nonsectarian in nature, violated the Constitution.

The fact that Kennedy wrote the opinion surprised many people, since he had given the appearance of being firmly in the conservative camp, and in an earlier case, a dissenting Kennedy had urged the Court to abandon judicially imposed restrictions on religious activities in schools. Many assumed that with Clarence Thomas on the Court, Rehnquist and Scalia would finally be able to implement their First Amendment jurisprudence. Kennedy's opinion indicated that he had changed his mind about the coercive nature of even a supposedly "neutral" prayer, and his opinion here, as in the abortion case, seems to indicate a far stronger middle bloc than had previously been assumed.

That bloc held together in a highly controversial case from a Texas school district where students had voluntarily chosen to have a public, student-led prayer before foot-

> The lessons of the First Amendment are as urgent in the modern world as in the eighteenth century when it was written. One timeless lesson is that if citizens are subjected to state-sponsored religious exercises, the State disavows its own duty to guard and respect that sphere of inviolable conscience and belief which is the mark of a free people. To compromise that principle today would be to deny our tradition and forfeit our standing to urge others to secure the protections of that tradition for themselves.
>
> —Justice Anthony Kennedy, *Lee v. Weisman* (1992)

ball games. The 6–3 majority opinion written by Justice Stevens in *Santa Fe Independent School District v. Doe* (2000), ruled that the prayer, despite its allegedly voluntary nature, nonetheless violated the separation of church and state. Too many people, such as the players, bands, and cheerleaders were required to be at the games, and one could not assume that they all voluntarily agreed to participate in the prayer.

Rights of the Accused

Much of the criticism aimed at the Warren Court focused on its decisions regarding rights of persons accused of crimes. In regard to decisions involving the Warrant Clause and confessions, critics charged the Court with being soft on crime and preventing the police from effectively doing their job. Given the almost total lack of concern by state courts for rights of the accused prior to the 1950s, one can see that the Warren Court, in breathing life back into the Fourth, Fifth and Sixth Amendments, tried to create a set of rigid prophylactic rules which, if followed by police and prosecutors, would meet the basic requirements of the Constitution. The Burger Court began the process, not of repealing Warren Court decisions, but of tempering the rules and replacing absolute standards with a totality of the circumstances test. This trend continued and accelerated in the Rehnquist years, and in the eyes of some observers went so far as to constitute a "revolution on the right."

Miranda v. Arizona remains the most controversial of the Warren-era decisions, and the Rehnquist majority has modified but not abandoned it. In a 1986 case, *Moran v. Burbine*, a 6 to 3 majority that included both Sandra Day O'Connor and William Rehnquist in effect reaffirmed the *Miranda* rule, while giving police somewhat greater lattitude. The following year, Justice Stevens spoke for a 6–2 Court in *Arizona v. Robertson* and held that the general rule against interrogating an in-custody defendant after that person had requested counsel covered all crimes of which the defendant might be suspected. In 1990, the Rehnquist Court reaffirmed an earlier interpretation and expansion of *Miranda.* The 1981 case of *Edwards v. Arizona* held that when a suspect effectively asserts a right to a lawyer (as opposed to a right to remain silent), the suspect cannot be subjected to further police questioning until a lawyer arrives. In 1990, a 7–2 majority of the Rehnquist Court (with the chief justice and Scalia dissenting) upheld and even expanded the *Edwards* rule and in reasoning strikingly similar to the rationale behind *Miranda.* The Court wanted a prophylactic rule to determine the voluntariness of a confession. By adhering strictly to the *Edwards* rule, judicial resources could be conserved. In essence, *Miranda* and *Edwards* serve to make the job of the courts as well as the police easier, by ensuring that confessions are properly made and can therefore be admitted into evidence. In *Withrow v. Williams* (1993), Justice Souter went out of his way to point out that while a prophylactic rule is important, "in protecting a defendant's Fifth Amendment privilege against self-incrimination, *Miranda* safeguards a fundamental trial right."

The Court reaffirmed *Miranda* in a most unusual case. Shortly after the Warren Court had handed down its decision, Congress passed a law in 1968 aimed at overturning the decision. Known as "Section 3501," it essentially provided a very broad and loose definition of what constituted a voluntary confession. No administration has ever tried to use § 3501, or even defend it in court, but a conservative public advocacy group filed a friend of the court brief in the Fourth Circuit, and the justices accepted the argument that § 3501 overrode *Miranda*. In *Dickerson v. United States* (2000), Chief Justice Rehnquist, frequently a critic of *Miranda,* nonetheless, wrote for a 7–2 majority, holding that *Miranda* was a "constitutional rule" and therefore not subject to a congressional override.

But if the Court has not been willing to abandon *Miranda,* it has nonetheless been far stricter than its predecessors in rebuffing appeals, and it has been vigilant against what it views as abuse of the Great Writ. In 1991, the majority lectured lower federal courts against entertaining constitutional claims not raised in accordance with state rules, a decision that can be seen both as part of its push for a stronger federalism as well as a tightening up of habeas procedures. The majority enunciated a general rule that unless the prisoner could both show cause as to why the normal appeal procedures had been flouted as well as prejudice from alleged constitutional violations, the claim should not be heard. This two-pronged test had first been enunciated in *Wainwright v. Sykes* (1977), but lower courts had tended to follow an earlier and more lenient rule propounded by the Warren Court in *Fay v. Noia* (1963). In *Keeney v. Tamayo-Reyes* (1992), the high court indicated that it expected the federal judiciary to toughen up its habeas procedures.

The following year, in *Brecht v. Abrahamson* (1993), the Court made it harder for persons convicted in state courts to obtain habeas relief on the basis of constitutional errors regarding trial type. If deemed harmless error, then even if there had been a constitutional violation, there would be no grounds for habeas. Again, the determination of whether there had been harmless error, like the determination if an exception to the two-pronged rule was justified, would belong to state courts. Rehnquist himself actively lobbied Congress to tighten up habeas procedures, and in 1996, the legislature passed the Antiterrorism and Effective Death Penalty Act, which set up hurdles for state prisoners seeking to obtain relief through a second or successive petition for federal habeas. When prisoners challenged this rule on the grounds that it impermissibly infringed on the Court's appellate jurisdiction, all of the justices united in upholding the new rules (*Felker v. Turpin* [1996]).

In the area of search and seizure, the Court has been less sympathetic to the exclusionary rule than it has to the *Miranda* warning, but it has not rejected it outright. Rather, as in earlier warrant cases, the Court has adopted a totality of the circumstances approach in place of the strict and inflexible rules of the Warren-era decisions. A good example is *Arizona v. Evans* (1995), in which a 7 to 2 majority held that errors caused by a court's clerical employees that result in an unconstitutional arrest do not trigger a Fourth Amendment exclusionary rule. Evans had been pulled over on the basis of a computer error showing an outstanding misdemeanor warrant; in fact the warrant had been quashed seventeen days earlier, but the computer records had not been updated. While being handcuffed, Evans dropped a marijuana cigarette, and a subsequent search of the car turned up a bag of the illicit substance. The state court said that the arrest had been illegal, and therefore the search had been illegal, and it declined to draw a line between police error and judicial error. But the purpose of the exclusionary rule had always been to limit police behavior. In this instance the police, relying on the information they had, had acted appropriately; the conduct of the officer had been reasonable, and therefore the evidence could be admitted. In a companion case, *Wilson v. Arkansas*, Justice Thomas spoke for a unanimous court, holding that the requirement that the police knock and announce their presence is part of the Fourth Amendment's command that searches and seizures be reasonable.

But in criminal procedure as in other areas of jurisprudence, the Rehnquist Court has been far from consistent. While some of its decisions seem to indicate a retreat from earlier precedents, other cases reinforce earlier doctrine. In the October 1999 term, it handed down three search and seizure decisions; one seemed to give the police greater latitude, the other two did not. In *Illinois v. Wardlow* (2000), the Court held that police generally may stop and frisk suspects in a high-crime area simply because they ran at the sight of a police officer. In *Bond v. United States* (2000), however, the Court held that police cannot enter a bus and squeeze the soft-sided luggage of passengers looking for drugs without a search warrant, and in *Florida v. J.J.* (2000), it ruled that police cannot stop and frisk someone based on a general anonymous tip of wrongdoing that has not been independently verified.

Conclusion

All told, the Rehnquist Court as a body is more conservative than any of its predecessors since the reign of the Four Horsemen, but it has not been as reactionary as its foes have claimed. While civil liberties advocates would have preferred the Court to be more solicitous of individual liberties, this is the Court that defended flag burning as protected speech and struck down a clumsy government attempt to censor the Internet. It has been less than friendly to minority religions, but has stood firm against imposed prayer in a school setting. Although unwilling to recognize a right to physician-assisted suicide, it did clothe the right to die in the constitutional mantle. And while "tougher" in its insistence that police be given greater leeway and that the Great Writ not be abused, the Court has not abandoned either the exclusionary rule or the Miranda warning.

That the Court has turned to the right is clear, but a variety of factors have kept it from going as far as its more conservative members might have wanted. The institutional structure of the Court constrains and moderates strong ideological tendencies. One has to win over a majority of the justices to win a case, and to do so one has to compromise. While Rehnquist, Scalia, and Thomas agree on many things, they do not agree on everything, and thus they have to bargain with the moderates to gain a majority.

In addition, a conservative justice often adheres to a jurisprudence of restraint, which may limit his or her desire to follow a more ideological path. The clearest example of this is *Planned Parenthood of Southeastern Pennsylvania v. Casey,* the 1992 abortion case in which justices O'Connor and Kennedy, normally allies of the conservatives, adopted a centrist position because they believed it would be bad to abandon the doctrine of *stare decisis.*

Finally, the very concept of a "conservative judicial ideology" is not as simple as some people believe. Justice Scalia, for example, has a strong libertarian streak, which sometimes leads him to adopt "liberal" positions. And just as no unity existed among the alleged liberals of the Warren era, so there is no uniformity of opinion among the conservatives of the Rehnquist Court. The result has been a modification, but not an abandonment, of rights-oriented principles enunciated in the four decades after World War II. Even the new emphasis on federalism does not necessarily negate that philosophy, but merely gives states and state courts greater leeway and responsibility.

For Further Reading

For the Rehnquist Court in general, see many of the works cited in the previous chapter. Rehnquist's federalist views are explored in Part Four of Sue Davis, *Justice Rehnquist and the Constitution* (1989). See also Martin H. Belsky, ed., *The Rehnquist Court: Farewell to the Old Order in the Court?* (1999).

For the speech cases, see Rodney A. Smolla, *Jerry Falwell v. Larry Flynt—The First Amendment on Trial* (1988); Frank I. Michelson, "Saving Old Glory: On Constitutional Iconography," 42 *Stanford Law Review* 1337 (1990); Gregory Herbert, "Waiving Rights and Burning Flags: The Search for a Valid State Interest in Flag Protection," 25 *Harvard Civil Rights–Civil Liberties Law Review* 591 (1990); and Edward J. Cleary, *Beyond the Burning Cross: The First Amendment and the Landmark R.A.V. Case* (1994).

For religion, see Michael McConnell, "The Origins and Historical Understanding of Free Exercise of Religion," 103 *Harvard Law Review* 1409 (1990); Derek Davis, *Original Intent: Chief Justice Rehnquist and the Course of Church/State Relations* (1991); Gregg Ivers, *Lowering the Wall: Religion and the Supreme Court in the 1980s* (1991).

Rights of the accused are discussed in Yale Kamisar, "Confessions, Search and Seizure and the Rehnquist Court," 34 *Tulsa Law Journal* 465 (1999); Christopher E. Smith, *The Rehnquist Court and Criminal Punishment* (1997); John F. Decker, *Revolution to the Right: Criminal Procedure During the Burger–Rehnquist Court Era* (1992).

44

Constitutional Issues at the End of the Twentieth Century

Congress and Foreign Policy • The Courts and Foreign Policy • The Legislative Veto • Control of the Budget • The Twenty-seventh Amendment • Term Limits • Iran-Contra • The Bork Nomination • The Thomas Nomination • The Line Item Veto • The Role of the Independent Counsel • Clinton's Impeachment • The Election of 2000 • Conclusion • For Further Reading

THE NIXON DEBACLE in the 1970s showed once again that major constitutional issues and decisions can be played out beyond the courtroom or, as in that case, with the judiciary only somewhat involved. In the quarter-century following Richard Nixon's resignation, presidents and congresses began exploring new accommodations in developing the nation's foreign and domestic policies. The nature of politics precludes any eternally fixed arrangement; rather, we can expect continuous adjustments within the broad parameters of the Constitution. But few people expected that so soon after the country had narrowly missed the trauma of a presidential impeachment, it would face that issue once again, although the circumstances surrounding the near impeachment of one president and the actual impeachment of another were vastly different.

Congress and Foreign Policy

At the time of Richard Nixon's resignation in August 1974, relations between the executive and legislative branches had reached a low point unmatched since the days of Andrew Johnson a century earlier. Nixon's departure removed much of the pressure, and the low-key, amiable Gerald Ford did much to restore goodwill between the White House and Capitol Hill. The election of Democrat Jimmy Carter promised even more harmony, since Carter had openly supported a greater role for Congress in policy-making. However, both Ford and Carter soon discovered that an activist Congress could wreak havoc on the normal procedures of making foreign policy.

A major constitutional as well as political problem in the post-Nixon years has been the effort by Congress to carve out a coequal role with the executive in foreign affairs. Nixon's arrogance pushed Congress to enact the War Powers and Budget acts and initiate policies to restrain executive discretion. As a result, during the relatively short Ford administration, Congress and the president clashed on several foreign policy issues.

Late in 1974, the North Vietnamese and Vietcong broke the cease-fire agreement, and the Saigon government failed to respond effectively. President Ford, unable to commit American troops, asked for $300 million to bolster South Vietnam, but Congress refused. When Ford spoke of the nation's "moral obligation," Congress did not yet know about (although many suspected) the secret correspondence between Nixon and Nguyen Van Thieu of November 14, 1972, promising "swift and retaliatory action" if Hanoi broke the Paris accords. But as Senator Henry Jackson noted, Congress had never been notified of any "obligations" and had certainly never been a party to making them. Congress refused to act, Saigon fell, and, as Ford complained to reporters, Congress "took away from the President the power to move in a military way to enforce the agreements." Whether or not anything short of massive American reentry into the war could have affected the outcome is doubtful, but for the first time in decades, a president had been unable to act freely in foreign affairs because of congressional restraints.

Congress used its legislative powers to affect foreign affairs in other ways that the executive resented. The 1974 Jackson–Vanik amendment tied trade concessions for the Soviet Union to continued emigration of Russian Jews, who faced religious persecution in the Soviet Union. The Hughes–Ryan amendment required the CIA to advise eight separate congressional committees about covert operations, an unwieldy arrangement that President Carter later persuaded Congress to change to notification of just the House and Senate intelligence committees. The Turkish invasion of Cyprus in 1974 led to a congressional embargo of aid to Turkey, a move President Ford and Secretary of State Henry Kissinger feared would drive the Turks out of NATO and close key American air bases and surveillance stations near the Soviet Union. Ford twice vetoed the embargo, and he finally won a compromise that delayed action pending negotiations. When the talks failed, however, foreign aid stopped, and Turkey closed some American bases temporarily. The embargo did not lead to withdrawal from Cyprus, for no Turkish leader could give in to such blatant American pressure and hope to remain in office. Finally, President Carter convinced Congress to recognize the failure of its policy and to rescind the embargo in 1978.

A resurgent Congress exercised its newly found muscle in other areas, almost always in opposition to Ford and Kissinger. It stopped covert assistance and anti-Communist FNLA guerrillas in Angola; cut off aid to Chile and Uruguay for human rights violations; denied preferential tariff treatment to OPEC members after the oil embargo; enacted a new trade agreement that severely limited executive discretion by subjecting presidential actions to legislative vetoes; withdrew the United States from the International Labor Organization because of the latter's allegedly radical political stance; and reduced American contributions to the United Nations because it had given the Palestine Liberation Organization observer status. Using the legislative veto, Congress forced the president to withdraw proposed arms sales to Jordan and to cut back the number of missiles he wanted to sell to Saudi Arabia.

Ford battled Congress constantly to preserve presidential prerogatives. In 1976, he vetoed a foreign aid bill that he claimed "would forge impermissible shackles on the President's ability to carry out the laws and conduct the foreign relations of the United States." Congressional efforts "to become a virtual co-administrator," he warned, could lead only to confusion, ineffectiveness, and loss of American influence. Even within Congress, some members began to question the wisdom of the legislature taking so active a role in foreign policy. "Congress cannot and should not run foreign policy," declared Hubert Humphrey. Senator Frank Church of Idaho, soon to head the Foreign Relations Committee, conceded that attempts to make foreign policy by statute, as in the Turkey-Cyprus affair, had been "awkward at best and often unworkable."

Conditions improved somewhat during Jimmy Carter's term, if for no other reason than that party affiliation demanded that a Democratic Congress try to cooperate with a Democratic president. Although Carter had campaigned against the Washington establishment, he believed in sharing information and responsibility with Congress, and he understood that, at least initially, he would have to live within congressional restraints. At first Congress praised Carter's openness and his willingness to keep it informed. Within a short time, however, complaints began mounting on both sides. Congress could not tell what the administration wanted, as differing factions at the state and defense departments fought—often openly—over policy. The administration could not get Congress to loosen its controls over foreign aid, leading Vice President Walter Mondale to complain that the president had been "enfeebled" in running foreign affairs.

Ronald Reagan came into office in January 1981, intent on reversing what he believed to be a decline both in U.S. military power and influence on world affairs. A willing Congress gave Reagan most of what he asked for in terms of enlarging the military, although it balked at funding the strategic defense initiative—or as critics termed it, "Star Wars"—missile defense system. Reagan then used the military on a number of occasions, but never with congressional approval, and he ignored the basic reporting and clearance requirements of the War Powers Act.

Reagan inserted a peacekeeping force in Lebanon in 1982 to disengage the Israeli army and the Palestine Liberation Organization. He ordered the invasion of Grenada to overthrow a pro-Communist faction, claiming that he did so to protect the lives of American medical students on the island. In 1986, he ordered military action against Libya in retaliation for that country's sponsorship of terrorist actions that had claimed the lives of American soldiers in Germany. The following year, the United States favored Iraq in its war with Iran, and the Reagan administration decided to protect the Persian Gulf shipping lanes against Iranian attempts to blockade Iraq and Kuwait. When Kuwait agreed to register its ships as American-flag vessels, the United States sent in ships and planes that sunk Iranian patrol boats and destroyed Iranian oil rigs.

The Lebanon venture eventually ended in failure, when terrorists blew up a marine barrack and killed 250 troops. American troops had been in the country for nearly eighteen months when Reagan and Congress reached an agreement to continue the mission, an agreement that seemingly followed, even if belatedly, the provisions of the

> As I made clear to congressional leaders at the outset, my request for congressional support did not, and my signing this resolution does not, constitute any change in the long-standing positions of the executive branch on either the President's constitutional authority to use the Armed Force to defend vital U.S. interests or the constitutionality of the War Powers Resolution.
>
> —George Bush, signing congressional authorization to proceed against Iraq (1991)

War Powers Act. Yet, Reagan issued a "signing statement," declaring that Congress could not restrict or regulate his powers as commander-in-chief. Congress again invoked the War Powers Act after the invasion of Grenada, calling on the president to issue a report and follow the procedures of the act. But the immediate success of the invasion and its strong public support kept Congress from pushing its request. By the third day of the operation, when it became clear that all goals had been achieved, Republicans and Democrats alike stood applauding the president's decisiveness. The unpopularity of Libya and Iran led only to token gestures in the legislature about the law, and for all practical purposes, both the Reagan administration and Congress considered the War Powers Act a dead letter by the time he left office. President Bush did not follow the law's consultative procedures, nor did Congress when it authorized hostilities against Iraq in 1991. Similarly, President Clinton ignored the act's provisions in the NATO bombings of Serbia during the Kosovo crisis. When members of Congress challenged Bush's and Clinton's activities in federal courts, the judges dismissed the suits, agreeing, in essence, with Clinton's comment that "clearly, the Constitution leaves the President, for good and sufficient reasons, the ultimate decision-making authority [in foreign policy]."

There are both constitutional and practical considerations in determining the proper balance between Congress and the president in foreign affairs. No one questions that in certain areas the president is charged with full responsibility. Ever since the days of George Washington, the president has spoken for the United States to other powers. "The President of the United States," declared House Majority Leader Jim Wright, "is, and must be, the ultimate spokesman of American policy." The president, as commander-in-chief of the armed forces, also has powers that he may use at his discretion under certain circumstances, such as protecting American lives abroad. Hardly anyone doubted President Carter's constitutional power to send in troops in a vain effort to rescue the American hostages in Iran; if anything, critics had wanted him to do so much earlier.

Nor is there much question, even in Congress, that the legislative role must be secondary. Unlike domestic problems, foreign affairs are usually beyond the intimate knowledge of most congressmen. "Congress cannot—nor should it—run foreign policy on a day-to-day basis," declared John Brademas, one of the architects of congressional policy on Turkey. "That is a truism." So congressional leaders in this century have sought some accommodation by which Congress would have a genuine consultative and participatory role in designing policy, which would then be left to the president to execute. The president needs flexibility, but where does one draw the line? Franklin Roosevelt sought congressional approval in 1939 to sell arms to America's allies; thirty years later, Richard Nixon argued that he had no need even to inform Congress of what he intended to do in foreign affairs.

A number of studies show that in most instances the executive does consult with those members of Congress whose committee assignments involve them in foreign matters. But what happens when the branches cannot arrive at a common policy? One or the other branch must prevail if there is to be any policy at all. President Ford claimed that in such an impasse, Congress should defer. "Americans can have only one foreign policy," he declared, and that must be the one articulated by the president. Foreign affairs, according to every president and secretary of state, is a matter of balancing constantly changing variables. To use Vice President Nelson Rockefeller's metaphor, one cannot have "536 individuals' hands on the tiller of the Ship of State."

There are some complaints that an eighteenth-century constitution hampers the foreign policy of a superpower in the late twentieth century. The Constitution does not assign all foreign powers to any one agency, but splits them among the executive and both houses of Congress. In the 1790s, and probably down to World War I, events moved slowly enough to allow resolution of the normal frictions in this multicentric system. Ships took weeks to cross the ocean bearing fresh news from abroad, allowing time for deliberation, consultation, and agreement. Today, cities can be obliterated in a matter of minutes; action, and not deliberation, is the desideratum. Even in less critical situations, a government hampered by an overly deliberative process—or a president restrained by limits imposed by a fearful and jealous Congress—may prove harmful to American interests.

The Courts and Foreign Policy

Foreign policy issues are rarely debated in the courts, and the judiciary has consistently supported the widest authority and discretion for presidential action. Two cases growing out of events during the Carter administration confirmed that pattern.

In December 1978, President Carter announced American recognition of the People's Republic of China as the sole government of China, and it simultaneously withdrew recognition from the Republic of China, often called Taiwan. A week later, the State Department notified Taiwanese officials that the Mutual Defense Treaty of 1955 would end as of January 1, 1980, in accordance with a provision allowing either party to terminate upon one year's notice. Senator Barry Goldwater and other senators opposed to recognition of the Communist government brought suit to enjoin the president from terminating a treaty without Senate concurrence.

The lower courts sustained the president's authority to terminate a treaty without Senate approval, but the Supreme Court in *Goldwater v. Carter* (1979), dismissed the suit without hearing arguments. Justice Rehnquist saw the issue as "political"—because it "involves the authority of the President in the conduct of our country's foreign relations"—and therefore nonjusticiable. The controversy should be left to the two other branches to resolve, since the Constitution is silent. Only Justice Brennan considered the merits. He declared that he would affirm the court of appeals "insofar as it rests upon the President's well-established authority to recognize, or withdraw recognition from, foreign governments," a power that he believed was granted by the Constitution to the president alone.

The other case grew out of the Iranian hostage crisis. In order to secure the release of American hostages, President Carter signed an executive agreement making certain concessions to Iran. To carry out the agreement, the president issued executive orders nullifying prejudgment attachments of Iranian assets and suspending all claims pending against Iran in American courts (these would later be referred to a special Iran–U.S. Claims Tribunal for binding arbitration). Private businesses with claims against Iran protested and brought suit to prevent execution of the agreement, on the grounds that the president had exceeded his authority. The government based its case on the broad, inherent presidential powers under Article II.

Justice Rehnquist's opinion for a unanimous Court in *Dames & Moore v. Regan* (1981) upheld the government's power, but not under the extensive presidential power the Reagan administration (which carried out the Carter agreement) claimed. Instead, the Court relied heavily on the Frankfurter and Jackson opinions in the steel seizure case and noted that Congress had implicitly approved the agreement by its past acquiescence in the settlement of foreign claims through executive agreement. Rehnquist took special care neither to enlarge the Court's recognition of presidential power in foreign affairs nor to grant Congress any previously unrecognized power in that area.

The Legislative Veto

In its efforts to reassert authority, Congress has been on firmer ground when dealing with domestic affairs. No president has ever claimed power over domestic matters comparable to that exercised in foreign policy. Congressmen are fairly well versed in this area, since any federal policy will have some impact on their constituents, and they do not feel at a disadvantage as compared with the executive in terms of knowledge or information. Ideally, Congress and the president work out the details of a specific program; Congress enacts the necessary legislation; the executive branch, through one or more agencies, implements and oversees the program.

In fact, however, Congress tries as much as it can to limit executive discretion in implementation by a mix of how much authority it delegates outright and how much it subjects to what is known as a "legislative veto." Through this device, Congress can require that certain presidential decisions be subject to congressional disapproval, by either both houses or each one alone. Congress has at various times delegated this review function to one or more committees, even to subcommittees, to its Office of Technological Assessment, and in one instance in 1952, to the chairman of the House Appropriations Committee. Although no president likes this device (which is nowhere mentioned in the Constitution), it does serve the useful purpose of allowing Congress to respond to changing circumstances and to make adjustments as a program goes along—rather than try to guess ahead of time what will happen and impose rigid or inflexible statutory controls. Defenders of the legislative veto believe that it is the only way Congress can maintain control over the modern bureaucratic state.

The device originated in 1932, when Herbert Hoover, frustrated at Congress's failure to reorganize the executive branch, asked for authority to do it himself, subject to Congress's "power of revision." The stratagem appealed to both sides: Hoover could initiate what he saw as long overdue reforms; Congress would not have to bother with hearings and planning, but could just negate any feature it disliked. Congress used it sparingly; from 1932 until 1972, only fifty-one bills included a legislative veto provision. During the period of congressional resurgence from 1972 to 1979, however, sixty-two statutes carried some form of legislative veto. (Some studies put the number much higher, depending on what is counted as a legislative veto, but all agree that the pace picked up significantly in the 1970s.)

Both the War Powers and Budget Impoundment acts carried such provisions. In fact, the legislative veto made the former bill possible, since everyone recognized both the futility and undesirability of trying to define too precisely the limits of presidential power to act in an emergency. In the post-Nixon years, the veto proved the perfect device for a suspicious Congress to employ whenever it had to delegate some new authority to a president. In 1976, the House of Representatives (which favored the veto far more than the Senate) came within two votes of approving a proposal to make *every* rule and regulation of *every* executive agency subject to legislative review. During the Carter years, the Senate managed to block several similar House proposals to impose legislative vetoes on a myriad of executive functions.

There had been constitutional questions about the legislative veto almost from the start. President Hoover's attorney general, William D. Mitchell, commented disapprovingly on a proposed legislative veto by a congressional committee over a Treasury Department program. If the veto constituted a legislative action, he claimed, then it could not be delegated to a committee; if the veto were administrative in nature, then it abridged the separation of powers. Dwight Eisenhower vetoed several bills containing the device and said he would ignore others that had already been enacted. In 1960, he informed Congress that the attorney general had found that the legislative veto "violates fundamental constitutional principles" and that he therefore had no choice but to instruct the secretary of defense to ignore a provision in an appropriation measure giving a congressional committee review powers.

Jimmy Carter also vetoed or threatened to veto bills including the device. In 1978, he declared that he would ignore them as unconstitutional; in a message that June, he informed Congress that he did not consider legislative vetoes as binding. The administration, however, did not seek a major confrontation; instead, it looked for a minor issue to bring as a test case to the Supreme Court. Ronald Reagan, while campaigning for the presidency in the fall of 1980, expressed his approval of the legislative veto; both Congress and the president ought to have "greater authority" to block actions by administrative agencies, he stated. Once in office, however, he instructed the attorney general to proceed with a test case that had been initiated by the Carter administration.

The question of the legislative veto had, in fact, come before the high court before, but the justices had always chosen not to deal with the merits. When the court of claims upheld the one-house veto in the Federal Salary Act of 1967 in *Atkins v. United States* (1977), the Supreme Court had refused to review the case on appeal. In a dictum in his concurring opinion in *Buckley v. Valeo* (1976), Justice White had affirmed the constitutionality of legislative vetoes "in light of history and modern reality . . . at least where the President has agreed to legislation establishing the disapproval procedure or the legislation has been passed over his veto." White's argument suggested that Congress, providing it followed constitutionally approved procedures in passing the initial legislation, had the power to include implementing provisions of both a positive and negative nature.

The test case chosen by the Carter administration involved congressional reversal of an administrative ruling by the Immigration and Naturalization Service (INS). Jagdish Rai Chadha, an East Indian born in Kenya and holding a British passport, had been lawfully admitted to the United States as a student in 1966. After Chadha's visa had expired, he applied for permanent residency under a provision of the law that allowed aliens to remain who would face "extreme hardship" if deported. The administrative judge suspended Chadha's deportation in June 1974, and the attorney general concurred in the decision. Under § 244(c)(2) of the Immigration and Nationality Act, either house of Congress could veto the attorney general's recommendation, in which case the person would be deported. On December 12, 1975, for reasons that are still unclear, Representative Joshua Eilberg introduced a resolution opposing the grant of permanent residency to six aliens, one of them Chadha. Without debating the resolution, the House approved. The INS reopened Chadha's case in order to deport him, and he appealed to the courts to allow him to stay in the United States. The Carter administration had chosen this incident as its test case because the action of the House pointed up the worst features of the legislative veto—no debate, no recorded vote, no approval by the other chamber, and no chance for presidential review.

Chief Justice Burger delivered the Court's 7 to 2 opinion in *INS v. Chadha* (1983), holding the legislative veto unconstitutional. He rejected Congress's claim that the Court had no jurisdiction because the veto was a political issue between the executive and legislative branches. In fact, the chief justice's comment that almost every challenge to a statute could be considered a political question indicated a serious weakening of that doctrine. He went on to hold that a one-house veto was legislative in character, and therefore violated the constitutional scheme by denying the other house and the executive the opportunity to approve or reject. The Court refused to accept the argument that historical usage as well as political expediency made the legislative veto acceptable. The Constitution allows independent action by a house in only four precisely defined situations—each house shall determine the qualifications of its members, the House shall have the power to impeach, and the Senate shall have the power to try and convict impeached officials. If the Framers had intended such a broad grant of power as the legislative veto, they would have done so explicitly. Although the case dealt only with a one-house veto, the chief justice's reasoning applied to two-house vetoes as well, since they also deprived the president of approval or veto.

Justice Powell, while concurring in the result, expressed his dismay at the breadth of the majority's opinion, which would retroactively invalidate every legislative veto. He thought that a greater respect for a coordinate branch required a narrower ruling, and he suggested that it would have been better if the Court had vacated the one-house veto in this instance only, because the House had trespassed on judicial functions by overturning an administrative judge's determination. Justices White and Rehnquist dissented, believing that the legislative veto could be justified as a condition of the statute when passed by Congress.

Despite *Chadha*, Congress has continued to insert legislative veto provisions in several laws, assuming that fear of budgetary retaliation would secure executive compliance. It has also begun study of a number of alternative measures, ranging from regulatory reform to a constitutional amendment to permit legislative vetoes. The full impact of the *Chadha* decision has yet to be felt, but in one vital area of concern, it may prove decisive in a battle between the legislative and executive branches.

Control of the Budget

One area of conflict between the executive and legislative branches in which the Court has become involved is control of the budget. Ronald Reagan campaigned in 1980 on a platform denouncing a federal budget that constantly ran a deficit. He claimed that according to "supply-side" theory, an immediate tax cut would stimulate the economy and bring in sufficient tax revenues to balance the budget by the end of his first term. Congress gave the president the tax cut he requested, but a recession kept federal revenues from growing and contributed to an enormous growth in the federal debt. At the beginning of his second term, instead of a balanced budget, Ronald Reagan faced an annual deficit of hundreds of millions of dollars and a national debt that was rapidly approaching two trillion dollars. Pointing to a healthy economy as proof that his policies had worked, the president blamed Congress for failing to cut "nonessential" domestic programs, while Congress faulted the president for refusing to raise taxes or cut the defense budget.

Public concern over the debt led to a variety of proposed solutions. Thirty-two states adopted resolutions calling for a federal constitutional convention to deal with a "balanced budget amendment." Scholars disagree as to whether the resolutions are binding under Article V, since they differ from one another in form and content. Then, in 1985, Congress adopted the Gramm–Rudman Act, which called for a scheduled step reduction in the annual deficit until a balanced budget has been achieved. If Congress failed to take the necessary steps, either by raising revenue or by cutting expenditures, then the comptroller general could impose across-the-board cuts on all programs.

By a 7 to 2 vote, the Supreme Court held that the automatic deficit reduction provisions of the Gramm–Rudman Act violated the separation of powers doctrine (*Bowsher v. Synar* [1986]). According to the Court, Congress could not assign executive functions to the comptroller general, who under the 1921 Budget and Accounting Act is removable by the legislature. Chief Justice Burger explained that Congress could not reserve to itself the removal of an officer charged with execution of the laws, except through impeachment; to do so would allow Congress to perform executive as well as legislative functions.

The decision seemed aimed more at the original arrangement of creating the office of the comptroller general than at the purpose of the Gramm–Rudman proposal, and it left unclear whether a similar resolution, which assigned the powers completely to an executive officer, would pass constitutional muster. In his dissent, Justice Rehnquist noted that he would not invalidate one of "the most important federal enactments of the past several decades" in order to preserve "a cumbersome, 65-year-old removal power that has never been exercised." The policies of the Clinton administration, together with the sustained prosperity of the 1990s, finally brought the budget deficit under control; in fact, by the middle of Clinton's second term, the federal government could claim a surplus in its annual budget. But should an economic downturn and soaring costs create a deficit in the future, it is likely that similar administrative efforts such as Gramm-Rudman could once again fall into the judiciary's lap.

The demise of Gramm–Rudman, and the *Chadha* decision, raised a number of questions about the War Powers and Impoundment acts. If the legislative veto is unconstitutional, then the restraints imposed on the presidency in both bills are void, and the balance of power between the branches has again shifted heavily toward the White House. A president could not threaten to withhold funds from domestic programs that he disliked so long as the Budget and Impoundment Act subjected his actions to legislative review; the demise of Gramm–Rudman could revive impoundment in an effort to secure a balanced budget or to scuttle ideologically detested welfare programs.

The Court's nullification of the legislative veto might also affect the efficient management of the government. In 1979, Congress passed a Reorganization Act that, similar to its sixteen predecessors since 1932, allowed the president broad authority to make structural changes in the executive branch, subject to a one-house veto. Presidents from Hoover to Reagan submitted 115 proposals, of which 95 have been implemented, creating such agencies as the Department of Health, Education and Welfare (later split into two departments), the Environmental Protection Agency, and many others. In the wake of *Chadha*, a slew of cases sprang up in lower courts, in which litigants claimed that since the legislative veto sections of the various Reorganization Acts had not been severable from the main body of the act, all actions taken by new or reconstituted agencies should be declared invalid. Lower courts split on the issue of severability, that is, whether the invalidation of one part of a statute invalidates the entire law, or whether that section alone is struck. For example, the Second Circuit, in *EEOC v. CBS* (1984), ruled unconstitutional the entire Reorganization Act under which the Equal Employment Opportunities Commission (EEOC) had been created, thus vacating all EEOC suits then pending in that circuit.

Faced with massive disruption of dozens of agencies, Congress passed a law in October 1984, ratifying every previous reorganization plan and thus legitimizing federal agencies against similar suits. In addition, it amended the Reorganization Act the following month to require affirmative approval by both houses of Congress as well as the president's signature, thus meeting *Chadha's* standards. But, in fact, this new procedure drains the old reorganization system of its vitality and makes it little different from the regular process for new legislation. Where previously a president could identify a problem and then move to solve it, subject only to congressional veto, he must now submit a request to Congress, and thus run the risk of defeat from every interest group opposed to changes in the status quo. Given a president and Congress from the same party, cooperation may be possible; given a split in party control, what ought to be a matter of efficient government may well deteriorate into one more issue of partisan conflict.

The Twenty-seventh Amendment

The American Constitution is rather unique in that a document drafted at the end of the eighteenth century has served the nation almost unchanged for more than 200 years. The first ten amendments should be seen as part of the original document, since several states ratified the Constitution on condition that a Bill of Rights be added immediately. Subsequent amendments have either been narrow and technical in nature, or have expanded individual rights. Two of course, prohibition and its repeal, canceled each other out. Only the Seventeenth Amendment, providing for the direct election of senators, can be said to have made a significant structural change in the constitutional scheme. The Framers deliberately made the amendment process difficult, so much so that even when Congress approves a popular amendment, such as the abolition of child labor or equal rights for women, the required ratification by three-fourths of the states may be impossible to secure. It therefore came as something of a surprise in 1991, when the American people discovered that they might soon have another amendment to the Constitution.

On June 8, 1789, James Madison had proposed 33 amendments to the new Constitution, drawn from a list of more than 200 submitted by the various state ratifying conventions. Congress narrowed the list down to twelve and submitted them to the states for their approval; the states ratified ten by 1791, the ten we now call the Bill of Rights. Of the two that the states did not approve, one involved technical changes regarding the apportioning of representatives. The other simply stated that "No law varying the compensation for the services of Senators and Representatives shall take effect until an election of Representatives shall have intervened."

Normally, proposed amendments that fail of ratification fade into oblivion, but not this one. Because it had no prescribed time limit, the proposal revived periodically over the next two centuries whenever some sort of scandal arose in Congress. In 1873, for example, Congress enacted the so-called salary grab, increasing members' salaries by 40 percent. The Ohio legislature was so angered, it ratified Madison's salary amendment, becoming the seventh state to do so. The eighth vote did not come until 1978, when Wyoming ratified, following congressional approval of a 34 percent salary hike.

This still left the amendment 28 states shy of passage, but in 1982, a 23-year-old student at the University of Texas, Gregory D. Watson, began researching a paper on whether Congress could extend the deadline for ratification of the Equal Rights Amendment. He came across the salary proposal, switched his research, and became the self-styled "national coordinator" in a drive to secure its ratification. Once again the impetus seems to have been congressional greed; in 1981, the members had voted themselves very generous tax breaks buried in a black-lung benefits bill.

Although Watson's letter writing campaign started slowly, his timing could not have been better. Public dissatisfaction with Congress, combined with one scandal after another, sank the national legislature ever lower in the public's eyes. In 1983, Congress raised members' salaries to over $60,000, and Maine ratified the amendment. Then came Colorado, and suddenly public interest groups like Ralph Nader's Public Citizens Lobby began to take notice.

Unlike most recent amendment proposals, the congressional salary amendment had no deadline for ratification and, by May 1991, only four more states were needed to reach the constitutionally mandated three-fourths vote. Soon after, Congress again alienated the people with scandal, first over a so-called House bank, which allowed members large and free overdrafts, and then over its post office, which appears to have been used as a means of laundering campaign funds for private purposes. One year later, in May 1992, forty states, more than the mandate, had ratified. Several members of Congress, however, voiced their concern about what they labeled the "non-contemporaneous nature of the ratification," and both houses passed resolutions calling for hearings to determine the validity of deferred ratification.

The Supreme Court had spoken to this issue twice. In *Dillon v. Gloss* (1921), it had affirmed the power of Congress to set a deadline on ratification and noted in dicta that ratification must be "sufficiently contemporaneous . . . to reflect the will of the people in all sections of the country at relatively the same period." Then in *Coleman v. Miller* (1939), the last case the Court had heard regarding ratification, it refused to rule on whether the lapse of time since the introduction of the Child Labor Amendment had caused that proposal to become void. That, the Court said, was a "political question" for Congress to decide.

The Senate and House judiciary committees actually scheduled hearings, but then on May 13, 1992, Don W. Wilson, the archivist of the United States, certified the adoption of the amendment. Although some members of Congress wanted to challenge Wilson's declaration of ratification, Speaker of the House Thomas Foley backed down; in an election year, the last thing he wanted before the electorate was an expensive challenge to preserve hefty congressional salaries during a recession. The Congressional Salary Amendment thus became part of the Constitution a little over 200 years after Madison originally proposed it to Congress.

Term Limits

In the backlash against Franklin Roosevelt's winning four terms as president, the Republican-controlled 80th Congress proposed a constitutional amendment limiting service to no more than two terms. Three-fourths of the states ratified the Twenty-second Amendment in 1951, and the general consensus among both scholars and politicians is that the country is now saddled with a bad policy resulting from vindictiveness. In the 1990s, reaction against abuse of congressional power led not only to the ratification of the Twenty-seventh Amendment, but also to efforts to limit the number of terms anyone could serve in Congress.

A variety of grass roots organizations began petitioning legislatures and initiating signature campaigns to set a limit on congressional tenure. Although the Constitution sets no limit and, in fact, speaks little to the qualifications of representatives and senators, other than age and residence, advocates of term limits claimed that the powers inherent in the states supported their position. Proponents of term limits managed to win several referendums, secure amendment of state constitutions, or secure legislative victories. Needless to say, few politicians favored these initiatives, and eventually the Supreme Court accepted a case challenging the limits.

In November 1992, Arkansas voters approved Amendment 73 to their state constitution, setting limits on the number of terms their representatives could serve in the two houses of Congress. By a narrow 5–4 vote, the Court struck down the amendment in *U.S. Term Limits, Inc. v. Thornton* (1995). Justice Stevens, writing for himself and three others, relied heavily on *Powell v. McCormack* (1969) to rule that the states were not at liberty to add to the qualifications or limits imposed by the Constitution. In an ironic twist, the centrist members of the Court used a narrow textual analysis of original intent, and they argued that neither the states, the Congress, nor the courts were free to go beyond what the Constitution itself spelled out. Stevens got his majority when Justice Kennedy concurred on the basis that, as the Constitution represented the will of the whole people, then only the whole people, acting through the amendment process, could change the charter of government.

Justice Thomas, joined by the chief justice, O'Connor, and Scalia, vigorously dissented. Although he tried to rebut the textual analysis, in essence Thomas reflected the newly renascent effort to transfer more authority from the federal government to the states and, through them, to the people. Nearly 60 percent of the people of Arkansas had approved the term limit amendment, and he found nothing in the Constitution to deprive the people of a state the power to spell out the eligibility requirements for those who wished to represent them in Congress. His opinion also spoke to the notion of judicial restraint, in that courts ought not to interfere in matters of policy unless required to do so by a strong constitutional constraint. Having found nothing to prohibit the states from acting, the minority believed that courts should not get involved in essentially a policy-making dispuite.

Iran-Contra

Ronald Reagan, like other presidents, believed he should have a free hand in directing American foreign policy. Most presidents, however, when Congress—either wisely or not—has legislated in regard to a foreign policy matter, have obeyed the law; Reagan tried to make an end run. In an attempt to free American hostages held in Lebanon, Reagan authorized the sale of weapons to Iran in an arms-for-hostages deal. The shipments came in part from Israel (although paid for by the American government) and from the U.S. Defense Logistics Agency in 1986. The CIA sold the weapons to arms dealers operating at the behest of the American government, and the dealers resold the weapons to Iran at a profit of over $15 million. On orders from Col. Oliver North, a member of the staff of the National Security Council, more than $3.5 million of these profits were transferred to the Nicaraguan Contras for use in a guerrilla war against the leftist Sandanista government. Reagan had authorized the sale of arms to Iran as an intelligence operation, over the strongly expressed doubts of the secretaries of defense and state. The administration kept the sales secret from both the American public and from Congress.

The sale clearly violated the Intelligence Oversight Act of 1980, which required prior congressional notification of such actions. The arms sale had to remain secret because, publicly, the American government continued to brand Iran as a terrorist nation. Not only did the sale violate a duly enacted law, it also violated Executive Order 12333, signed by Reagan himself, which limited the execution of covert operations to the CIA. The arms transfer also violated several export licensing and arms export laws, as well as laws requiring that funds received or controlled by U.S. officials had to be deposited into the Treasury Department. Moreover, the diversion of funds to the Contras occurred after Congress had passed the 1984 Boland amendment, which prohibited the CIA, Defense Department, "or any other agency or entity of the United States involved in intelligence activities" from supporting the Contras, overtly or covertly. The National

Security Council staff, according to Executive Order 12333, comprised the "highest intelligence entity" of the U.S. government.

Then on November 3, 1986, a pro-Iranian magazine in Beirut broke the story of the arms sales. The White House initially denied everything, but once American journalists got on the trail and details came pouring out, the administration kept changing its story—it was an Israeli operation or only a small number of arms had been transferred. Faced by an increasing public clamor for the truth, Reagan ordered the attorney general, Edwin Meese, to conduct an investigation, and he also appointed a commission headed by Senator John Tower to study ways to improve policy-making in areas touching on national security. He also accepted the resignation of Col. Oliver North.

The Iran-Contra affair, as it came to be known, deeply affected the last two years of Reagan's term. The sale of arms, as well as the cover-up, cast doubts on Reagan's authority and raised a number of questions as to the president's control of foreign policy. Reagan kept saying he did not know the details, which if true showed he did not control high-level security policies in his own administration, or that he lied outright. Neither interpretation did credit to him, and as a result, his popularity plunged and the administration's domestic as well as foreign policy initiatives stalled.

Congress conducted several investigations, while an independent counsel looked at the behavior of several key aides. Unfortunately, the two lines of investigations often conflicted. Congress offered immunity to witnesses in order to make the truth public, but this ran counter to independent counsel, Lawrence Walsh's, efforts to prosecute wrongdoers. To give on example, Walsh indicted and secured a conviction of Col. Oliver North for lying to a congressional committee, only to have the conviction overturned on the grounds that the committee's grant of immunity barred prosecution, even for perjury.

Precisely what happened may never be known. At present, the facts seem to indicate that Reagan did not directly order the diversion of funds from the arms sales to the Contras, although he did not oppose helping the guerrillas. People like North, aware of the president's interest, took it on themselves to carry out the policy, despite the clear prohibition of the laws. The CIA was deeply involved, but the death of its director, William Casey, closed off the testimony of the one man who knew the full details of both CIA and NSC involvement. When Walsh indicted Secretary of Defense Caspar Weinberger, there were hopes that his testimony might reveal the involvement of both President Reagan and Vice President George Bush. But once elected, Bush issued pardons to Weinberger and five other federal officials closely tied to Iran-Contra.

In many ways, the Reagan administration's behavior is as constitutionally worrisome as that of Nixon and his aides in Watergate. Both believed that the president, his aides, and cabinet members somehow stood above the law and that if there were laws prohibiting or limiting their policy wishes, those laws could be ignored. Oliver North, in testimony before Congress, indicated that he followed a higher law of national interest and thus could disregard laws that Congress had ignorantly passed. Congress passed legislation in 1991 to reduce the likelihood of future Iran-Contra situations by requiring timely notification to Congress, but given the attitude of people like North and his immediate superiors, one wonders how effective such statutes can be. The

Framers took great pains to separate powers and to establish a series of checks and balances. Among the most important of these is the separation of the power of the sword from the power of the purse; they did not want one branch to be able to both make and fund war. As one scholar has noted, had Ronald Reagan openly endorsed the views put forward by North and Poindexter, he would have deserved impeachment. As it was, he failed in his sworn constitutional duty to see that the laws are faithfully executed.

The Bork Nomination

As noted in the previous chapter, no president since Andrew Jackson has ever tried to shape the ideology of the judiciary as did Ronald Reagan. He actively sought people who shared his constitutional views (a prerogative enjoyed by all presidents), but also imposed jurisprudential litmus tests on issues such as abortion, just as Jackson did on enforcement of the fugitive slave laws. No one better fit the Reagan mold than Robert Bork, and the extremity of his views created a backlash that led the Senate to deny him confirmation.

In June 1987, after the Court had handed down its last decisions of the term, Justice Lewis F. Powell, Jr., stunned the nation by announcing his resignation from the bench after fifteen years of service. Interviews with friends and associates revealed that although Powell was then in good health for a man 80 years old, he worried that a recurrence of past illness might incapacitate him and cripple the work of the Court. He also feared that if he waited another year, the nomination of his replacement might become embroiled in the politics of an election campaign that would also be damaging to the Court. News of the resignation elicited widespread praise for Powell from both liberals and conservatives, who extolled his integrity and adherence to principle, while at the same time remaining open to new ideas. He had been the "man in the middle," the leader of the Court's center bloc who was rarely on the minority side of a 5–4 decision. Given the growing tensions in the nation's political climate, many people urged Reagan to appoint a moderate to replace Powell.

Although the White House went through the motions of issuing a list of people supposedly under consideration, in fact the president and his close aides had already chosen their man—Judge Robert Bork of the U.S. Court of Appeals for the District of Columbia. A former law professor at Yale and solicitor general in the Nixon administration, Bork hardly fit Reagan's description of him as a moderate conservative. In his academic writings, his circuit court opinions, and his speeches, Bork had denounced some of the most important decisions of both the Warren and Burger courts. He questioned the wisdom of many of the civil rights decisions, declared that the Constitution did not embody any right to privacy, and condemned *Roe v. Wade*, the 1973 decision granting women the right to secure abortions.

Opposition to the nomination gathered quickly and involved many civil rights and minority groups, the American Civil Liberties Union, labor organizations, and ad hoc committees created to prevent confirmation. Conservative groups, on the other hand, including many fundamentalist religious organizations, praised the president's selection. The conservative agenda, in their view, would never be complete until the Court had been converted away from liberalism through the appointment of people who shared their ideas about how the Constitution should be interpreted. As President Reagan said, Robert Bork "shares my view" of the proper role of the Court.

In some parts of the country, the debate turned vitriolic, with each side mounting newspaper and television campaigns for and against the nominee. The Senate Judiciary Committee held lengthy hearings, with Bork appearing to defend and explain his views. To many observers, the attack on Bork by his critics did not do him half the harm that his own testimony did—the more he talked, the more he convinced people that he was in fact far to the right of what had been the mainstream in American constitutionalism for the previous half-century.

Discussing the landmark case of *Griswold v. Connecticut* (1965), which had established a constitutional right to privacy, Bork declared that privacy "was a free-floating right that was not derived in a principled fashion from constitutional materials." The nominee also criticized *Shelley v. Kraemer* (1948), which had outlawed state enforcement of racially restrictive covenants, as opening up too much private discriminatory action to possible constitutional litigation. In addition, he had condemned the antitrust laws as economic nonsense. Other scholars besides Bork had raised some of the same issues he did, but he had attacked not one but a great many of the major constitutional decisions expanding individual rights and liberties.

Politically, the Reagan administration, still reeling from Iran-Contra revelations, appeared completely inept in its handling of the nomination. White House spokesmen called upon the Senate to ratify the appointment because the Constitution gives the nominating power to the president; they totally ignored the upper house's very important role of reviewing judicial selections and, on occasion, withholding their assent. The administration claimed that so long as the nominee met the basic criteria, the Senate had no right to look at anything else; since the Senate had already approved Bork for the circuit court, they argued, he had met the criteria for the bench, and that should be the end of the inquiry. But as former senator Harry F. Byrd, Jr., of Virginia, himself a conservative, noted: "the Senate may look at anything it pleases to look at. That is the meaning of 'advise and consent.'"

> Robert Bork's America is a land in which women would be forced into back alley abortions, blacks would sit at segregated lunch counters, rogue police could break down citizens' doors in midnight raids, school children could not be taught about evolution, writers and artists could be censored at the whim of government, and the doors of the federal courts would be shut on the fingers of millions of citizens for whom the judiciary is—and is often the only—protector of the individual rights that are the heart of our democracy.
>
> America is a better and a freer nation than Robert Bork thinks. Yet in the current delicate balance of the Supreme Court, his rigid ideology will tip the scales of justice against the kind of country America is and ought to be. . . . No justice would be better than this injustice.
>
> —Senator Edward M. Kennedy (D., Mass.), responding to Bork's nomination, 1 July 1987

There is no question that politics played a major role in the ultimate defeat of Bork, and the Reagan White House, which had done much to politicize the nomination, hypocritically condemned the Democrats for "playing politics" with the high court. In fact, politics has always been involved, from the time George Washington made the first choices for federal judges. Although he sought well-qualified men, Washington also wanted those who shared his view of the proper role of government. And right from the start, the Senate has withheld its consent when it did not like what it saw. Normally, the Senate will defer to the president, but the Reagan administration had injected not just politics but ideological purity into the selection process from the start, and with Bork, perceived by many to be an extremist, the Reaganites went too far.

The administration had counted heavily on Southern support for Bork, but that failed to materialize. Thanks in large measure to the Voting Rights Act of 1965 and the Court's validation of its provisions, African Americans had become a major force in Southern politics. Many senators from below the Mason–Dixon line owed their seats to black support, and just about every civil rights organization opposed Bork. Like any politicians, these senators were not about to antagonize their constituents. In addition, numerous polls showed Southern businessmen and Southern women against the nomination. As one Richmond, Virginia, business leader put it, "We have finally got the segregation issue behind us, and black and white groups are working together to build up this city. If Bork goes on the Court, I am afraid it will open up all the old wounds." Bork's views on privacy—namely, that privacy did not enjoy any constitutional protection—upset many women, and not only those who supported abortion. Privacy is a cherished value in the South, and rightly or wrongly, Southern women—among the most conservative in the nation—believed that Bork on the Court would destroy that value.

Following Bork's defeat, the administration named another member of the District of Columbia circuit, Douglas Ginsburg, a former Harvard law professor and a onetime member of the White House Office of Management and Budget. Just as conservative as Bork, Ginsburg had not left a paper trail of articles and speeches that could be used against him. But even before opposition to him could organize, Ginsburg admitted that while a law professor he had smoked marijuana with his students. That fact upset many on the right of the political spectrum and embarrassed an administration that had consistently spoken out sternly against drugs. In addition, the *Legal Times* revealed that Ginsburg had claimed in a federal questionnaire to have appeared in court on behalf of the Justice Department 34 times, when in fact he had appeared only once. As opposition mounted, Ginsburg decided to forego a bruising confirmation fight and asked the president to withdraw his name. As one liberal noted, "Ginsburg went down, but for all the wrong reasons. He should have been defeated for his reactionary legal views, not for private peccadilloes."

Finally acknowledging that a Democratic majority in the Senate would not confirm an extreme conservative, Reagan nominated Judge Anthony Kennedy of the Court of Appeals for the Ninth Circuit, a conservative who had nonetheless won high marks for his open-mindedness as well as adherence to precedent—just the type of person who had been urged upon the administration initially. While some civil rights and minority groups rushed to uncover evidence that he too might be unfit for the black robe, an exhausted Senate quickly confirmed him. The Court, which had been at work since the first Monday in October, finally had its full complement of justices on board in January.

The Thomas Nomination

Four years after Lewis Powell retired, one of the icons of the American civil rights movement finally gave in to long-term illness and also stepped down from the bench. Thurgood Marshall will probably not be remembered as much for his 24 years on the high court as for the more than three decades before that in which he crafted the strategy that led to *Brown v. Board of Education* and the dismantling of segregation. Marshall had been the first—and so far the only—African American to sit on the Supreme Court, and civil rights groups demanded that President George Bush appoint another black to take his place.

The White House obliged, and named court of appeals judge Clarence Thomas. Although the president claimed that Thomas's race had nothing to do with the nomination, most commentators suggested that little else mattered. With an election year coming up, Bush needed to appoint a conservative to maintain his credentials with the right wing of the Republican party. Yet he could not afford to have a replay of the bruising Bork battle four years earlier. Moreover, this seemed a good opportunity for the Republicans to make inroads into the black community, which for nearly a half-century had been solidly wedded to the Democratic party. White House strategists also figured that it would be difficult for liberal and civil rights groups to oppose a black nominee, and the strategy seemingly worked. The conservative Thomas won the plaudits of the right, while civil rights and civil liberties groups split over whether to oppose the nomination. Almost overlooked were Thomas's jurisprudential views and the fact that bar groups and academics considered him unqualified to sit on the nation's highest court.

Thomas had been born into humble beginnings in Pinpoint, Georgia, and although in his speeches and writings he claimed to have overcome racial discrimination through self-reliance, in fact Thomas had gotten into the Yale Law School because of an affirmative action plan. He came to Washington as an aide to Senator John Danforth. President Reagan named him assistant secretary for civil rights at the Justice Department in 1981, and the following year appointed him as chair of the Equal Employment Opportunity Commission. In both these position Thomas, instead of championing equal opportunity and rights, endorsed an increasingly conservative approach. In that role, he had angered civil rights groups by rejecting the use of statistics as a measure of discrimination and by foregoing class action suits. Like others in the Reagan administration, Thomas believed that only individuals who could prove actual discrimination should be entitled to legal redress. He condemned affirmative action as a waste of time and charged that civil rights leaders had made African Americans into just another interest group. George Bush appointed him to the circuit court for the District of Columbia, but in the one year he served on that tribunal he had written no noteworthy opinions.

At the judiciary committee hearings, a well-coached Thomas portrayed himself as an American success story. He evaded answering any questions about his views on just about anything. He claimed that he had never given any thought to *Roe v. Wade*, a statement many people found incredible. When queried about his writings in support of a natural law theory, Thomas again side-stepped the matter, saying his articles had been little more than intellectual musings. During the hearings, Thomas provided little evidence that he was qualified to sit on the Supreme Court, but neither could his detractors prove that he had any major professional or personal impediments to confirmation. His conservatism, by itself, could no more deny him Senate approval than another appointee's liberalism. Had civil rights groups opposed Thomas—which they easily could have done based on his record at EEOC—moderate senators uncomfortable with Thomas's lack of qualifications would have voted against him. But the NAACP and other black groups remained silent, fearing that if they opposed Thomas and he went down to defeat, Bush would not name another black candidate in his place. Even so, the committee split 7–7 over whether to endorse Thomas, and it appeared that he would win confirmation by the entire Senate.

Then suddenly the whole scenario changed as Anita Hill, a professor at the University of Oklahoma law school, charged that Thomas had sexually harassed her when she had been an employee at EEOC. In the following weeks, the whole country seemed divided between those who believed her and those who found Thomas's denials more credible. At the special hearings called to question the two, Senator Orrin Hatch of Utah went of his way to discredit Hill's testimony with, as it became clear, help and advice from the White House. Because the hearings were televised, the entire nation could join the committee members in trying to determine who was telling the truth. Both were compelling witnesses—Hill, prim and forthright, was backed by witnesses who testified she had complained of harassment at the time; Thomas, with his outraged charge that he was being subjected to a "high-tech lynching for uppity blacks," was backed up by women who had worked for him and testified to his character. Committee chair, Joseph Biden, considering the testimony of the two equally balanced, declared that the nominee was entitled to the benefit of the doubt, and this led the Senate to confirm Thomas by a vote of 52–48, the narrowest margin of votes received by any justice in more than a century.

The hearings proved educational in many ways. Professor Hill's allegations focused attention on the whole issue of sexual harassment and forced many men to reexamine their conduct. When men asked if women really faced that sort of treatment, they heard a resounding "YES." The Senate itself had to look at its policies; although various statutes forbid sexual harassment or discrimination in the nation's workplaces, the Senate had exempted itself from those provisions. It moved quickly to remedy that situation.

> No professional woman I know has not suffered some form of sexual harassment in her career. I was accused of sleeping with my chairman, since no one believed a woman could have been promoted on her own merits.
>
> —Professor of political science, commenting on Hill-Thomas hearings (1991)

During his time on the stand, Thomas angrily told the Senate panel that it had every right to question him about his constitutional views, but not about his personal life. That rebuke would have carried more weight had Thomas not carefully avoided answering exactly that type of question. Democratic Senator Herbert Kohl of Wisconsin complained that neither he nor his colleagues knew "who this man really is." Republican strategists thought this was just fine. "It's O.K. not to give the answer," crowed a senior administration official, albeit off the record, "as long as it's not because you don't know the answer." In effect, nominees could and should deliberately hide their views.

Thomas, however, bears only partial responsibility; he followed the script written in the White House. The burden of blame rests on the Senate, which has the constitutional obligation to advise and consent—or withhold consent—on Court appointments. Nominees should not, as a matter of judicial ethics, comment on cases that might come before the Court. But it is one thing to ask a nominee "How would you vote in this case?" and quite another to ask "What are your views on capital punishment?" or "Do you believe in a constitutional right to privacy?" These are exactly the type of questions Thomas said the panel had the right to ask, yet when they did so, he carefully avoided answering them. Had the Senate had the fortitude to carry out its duty, it would have told Thomas and the White House that it would give full consideration to any nominee, but only if it received full and frank answers to legitimate questions.

The Constitution wisely insulates judges from political pressure once they are on the bench, but the Framers never intended to shield judicial nominees from an examination of their views during confirmation hearings; in fact, the Senate is explicitly given the power to make that examination. Would the American people vote for a candidate to an elected office who refused to answer a question about public policy because he or she might be faced by that issue once in office? Appointment to the Supreme Court should not be a popularity contest, and presidents are entitled to name men and women who agree with their views. The American people, however, and the Senate that acts for them, are entitled to know what those views are.

The Line Item Veto

In many states, governors enjoy line item vetoes, by which they can identify and strike out particular items that they do not like, in an expenditure bill while approving the rest of the measure. The legislature can then override the governor's veto on these items, just as it can a regular veto. Good-government advocates generally support the line item veto, arguing that in omnibus appropriations measures, too many questionable pet projects are funded, with one interest group trading off its votes in return for the support of other groups, each getting what it wants. A chief executive without a line item veto is allegedly faced with a choice of accepting inappropriate or wrongheaded measures in order to get the provisions he or she wants. With the veto, these items can no longer be buried in large budget bills, and when lit by the sunshine of publicity, will fall to public outrage.

On the other hand, a line item veto allows a governor to single out political opponents for punishment, or destroy academic freedom by retaliating against professors at state universities who challenge the views of the governor. In Texas, for example, four university professors were denied raises on a line item veto because they had been union activists. Appropriations for programs that the chief executive does not like can be eliminated, even though the programs have legislative support and may in fact be good for the country. For example, President Nixon's impoundment of funds for environmental programs illustrates how a president could use the line item veto to kill important programs that Congress—and the nation—clearly want funded. Opponents of the line item veto claim that under the current arrangement, there is a built-in tension between executive and legislature that requires both sides to compromise and work to find an acceptable solution. The line item veto would shift this balance over too far in favor of the executive

For decades, American presidents have argued that they should have a line item veto as well, in order to fight the pork-barrel politics that underlie multibillion-dollar appropriations measures. When the Democrats controlled Congress in the 1980s, they refused to give Reagan or Bush this power. When Republicans took over Congress in 1994, they faced a political dilemma. While on record as favoring the line item veto, they did not want to give Bill Clinton that power. In the end, the more militant freshman members of Congress insisted on principle, seeing the veto as a tool to control spending, a tool they believed would soon be exercised by a Republican president. In 1996, Congress passed Line Item Veto Act, giving the president the power to cancel certain expenditures, subject to procedures allowing a congressional override. Clinton, who had long supported the measure, quickly signed it into law. Before the ink had dried, four senators and two representatives challenged the constitutionality of the statute.

In *Raines v. Byrd* (1997), a 7 to 2 majority denied that the six members of Congress had standing to bring the suit. The law itself had anticipated that there would be a court challenge, and it specifically authorized "any individual adversely affected" to bring a constitutional challenge. Speaking through Chief Justice Rehnquist, the Court noted that the Constitution allowed federal courts to have jurisdiction only in actual "cases" or "controversies." Neither existed in this instance, because the plaintiffs could show no harm or adverse effects to themselves resulting from the measure. Rehnquist made it clear that the Court had in no way spoken to the merits of the law and that if and when the president would actually employ the veto, then the issue would be ripe for adjudication.

Shortly after the decision in *Raines,* President Clinton, eager to see if his newfound power would stand the test, triggered a constitutional challenge by exercising the veto. He struck out a provision of the Balanced Budget Act of 1997 that would have protected New York State from having to reimburse the federal government for taxes it had levied against Medicaid providers and a provision of the Taxpayer Relief Act of 1997 that allowed certain farm groups to escape taxes if they sold their stock to a certified cooperative. In *Clinton v. New York* (1998), the Court found that both the state and the Snake River Potato Growers had been adversely affected and therefore had standing to sue.

In a 6–3 decision, the Court found the Line Item Veto Act unconstitutional, and Justice Stevens for the majority took a narrow view of the latitude intended by the Framers in the legislative process. George Washington, a member of the Constitutional

> I recognize that the Act before us is novel. In a sense, it skirts a constitutional edge. But that edge has to do with means, not ends. The means chosen do not amount literally to the enactment, repeal, or amendment of a law [nor] violate any basic Separation of Powers principle. They do not improperly shift the constitutionally foreseen balance of power from Congress to the President. Nor, since they comply with Separation of Powers principles, do they threaten the liberties of individual citizens. They represent an experiment that may, or may not, help representative government work better. The Constitution, in my view, authorizes Congress and the President to try novel methods in this way.
>
> —Justice Breyer, in *Clinton v. New York* (1998)

Convention, had understood that he had a choice of approving or disapproving a whole bill, not its parts. Analogizing to the congressional veto, which the Court had struck down in *Chadha*, Stevens claimed that the integrity of the legislative process required a strict adherence to the constitutional mandate.

Justices Breyer, O'Connor, and Scalia agreed that the parties had standing, but differed from their colleagues on the merits. Breyer suggested that there had been no need for a line item veto in 1787, since the country was small, its government would be small, and its expenditures would be small. Moreover, the limited nature of government meant that appropriations measures would be transparent, without numerous pork-barrel items hidden away. Things had changed greatly since the founding, and he believed that a line item veto, while not mentioned in the text, did not violate the spirit of the document.

The Role of the Independent Counsel

Before we examine the impeachment of President Clinton, it is necessary to look briefly at the independent counsel, a position unknown to the Constitution and a product of Watergate. When a special prosecutor, Archibald Cox, began probing too deeply for Richard Nixon's comfort, he had him fired. The ensuing uproar contributed in large part to Nixon's loss of public confidence and, after his resignation, led Congress to pass the Ethics in Government Act of 1978. Title VI of the law provided for the appointment of an independent counsel when the attorney general concluded that a high-ranking administration member might be guilty of wrongdoing. The counsel would then be appointed by a special three-judge panel and presumably would operate free of any taint of suspicion that he or she would cover up any criminal activity. Congress renewed and revised the law in 1994, but during its two decades of existence, it has been roundly criticized by both Democrats and Republicans. After the Senate acquitted President Clinton in his impeachment trial, Congress let the law lapse.

Constitutional purists found the design of the law disturbing and hoped the Supreme Court would also find the hybrid unconstitutional, but in this they were disappointed. The case grew out of an investigation by independent counsel Alexia Morrison of an assistant attorney general, Theodore Olson, who served in the Reagan Justice Depart-

> How much easier it is for Congress, instead of accepting the political damage attendant to the commencement of impeachment proceedings against the President on trivial grounds—or, for that matter, how easy it is for one of the President's political foes outside of Congress—simply to trigger a debilitating criminal investigation of the Chief Executive under this [Independent Counsel] Law.
>
> —Justice Scalia, dissenting in *Morrison v. Olson* (1988)

ment. Olson challenged the investigation, claiming that Title VI violated separation of powers, by placing an executive function (prosecution) under the supervision of a judicial body. In a typically dry opinion, Chief Justice William Rehnquist found that the Constitution allows Congress to vest power in "inferior Officers" in the courts rather than in the executive and that the independent counsel constitutes such an inferior officer. In addition, the independent counsel exercises limited jurisdiction and can be removed by the attorney general. As for a court appointing a prosecutor, Rehnquist believed that judges know a lot about prosecution, and this relatively minor function of appointing a special prosecutor did not constitute enough of a nonjudicial function to violate the integrity of the judicial branch.

The lone dissent in *Morrison v. Olson* (1988) came from Justice Scalia, whose strict reading of the text led him to believe that the law disturbed the equilibrium among the branches, and beyond that, allowed partisan biases to affect investigations. Concerning the panel of judges who appoint the counsel, Scalia asked: "What if they are politically partisan, as judges have been known to be, and select a prosecutor antagonistic to the administration?" Within a very short time, events justified Scalia's fears.

Clinton's Impeachment

Most presidents entering office enjoy at least a brief honeymoon of good relations with Congress and solid public confidence, but not so William Jefferson Clinton. Elected as chief executive in 1992 and again in 1996, Clinton's tenure was marked by contradictions. Although Republicans captured and maintained control of the Congress for six of the eight years in his terms, Clinton constantly outsmarted them politically, and forced hard-line conservatives to modify or abandon many of the proposals in their "Contract with America." Denounced as a "tax and spend" Democrat, Clinton utilized an unprecedented period of prosperity to balance the federal budget for the first time in a generation. One of the most intellectually gifted men ever to occupy the White House, he will be remembered not for his grasp of policy but for his failure to keep his libido in check.

Clinton admitted during the 1992 campaign that he had not been faithful to his wife, but that despite rough times, they had patched things up. Social conservatives, especially members of the Christian right, found it appalling that, as they put it, a known adulterer should be the leader of the country. They also objected to Hillary Rodham Clinton, a successful lawyer and feminist, who seemed to scorn the traditional views of a wife and mother that the conservatives held dear. Even before he took the oath of office, conservative churches began selling tapes listing Bill Clinton's sins.

The Clintons had been involved, while he had been governor of Arkansas, in a failed land deal, the so-called Whitewater scandal. Starting in 1994, independent counsel Kenneth Starr had been investigating whether or not Clinton and his associates in the deal had engaged in criminal activities. Although Starr secured convictions of a few people on minor charges, he eventually cleared the Clintons of all charges of illegal activity. In the process, however, Starr had appeared to many to use the powers of his office in a heavy-handed manner, browbeating witnesses and threatening them with jail terms if they did not cooperate.

During the government shutdown in 1995 (triggered by the inability of the president and Congress to reach a budget deal), Clinton started an affair with a White House intern, Monica Lewinsky, who bragged to a friend, Linda Tripp, of her exploits. Tripp tape-recorded these supposedly confidential chats and turned the tapes over to Starr's office in early 1998.

At about the same time that Congress authorized the Whitewater investigation, Paula Jones filed a suit charging that Clinton had sexually harassed her while he was governor of Arkansas and she was a state employee. Clinton denied the allegation, which, if true, had taken place well before he had announced his candidacy for the presidency. Funded by conservative groups that despised Clinton, Jones pursued her suit in federal court. The president tried to derail the case and postpone it until after he left the White House, arguing that he enjoyed a temporary immunity from civil suits arising out of incidents that took place prior to his becoming president. The issue went all the way up to the Supreme Court, which unanimously denied the president's claim of immunity. In the end, Paula Jones's suit was dismissed by the trial judge, who concluded that even if Clinton had engaged in the coarse behavior attributed to him, Jones had not suffered any damages. There had never been a quid pro quo; Clinton had never conditioned any reward or punishment on her having or refusing to have sex with him. But the Paula Jones case was alive and very much in Kenneth Starr's mind when he received the tapes from Linda Tripp, because lawyers for Jones, having learned of the alleged affair between Clinton and Lewinsky, added Lewinsky's name to the witness list in Jones's sexual harassment suit against Clinton.

Both in depositions he gave in the Jones case and in a public statement to the American people, Clinton denied having a sexual relationship with Lewinsky. Then, through an extraordinary sequence of events, Kenneth Starr's Whitewater investigation turned into a full-blown prosecution of Clinton over the Lewinsky affair. By the summer of 1998, Starr had gotten all his evidence together and presented a referral to Congress, claiming that there was believable and substantial evidence to support charges that the president had engaged in impeachable offenses. First, he charged that Clinton had lied to a grand jury in his denial of having had sex with Lewinsky. Although she wanted to consummate the relationship, Clinton never allowed her to do more than fellate him. Because legal definitions of sex required vaginal penetration, Clinton had claimed not to have had sex with her. Second, Starr accused the president of attempting to obstruct justice by getting Lewinsky and others to lie about the relationship. There seems little doubt that Clinton did in fact lie, and there is evidence that he attempted to obstruct justice, but for the majority of the American people, the president looked more like a man who, fearing that a sexual escapade would become known to his family, did what most men would have done—he lied about it. Starr's demeanor, his heavy-handed tactics, and leaks from his office about grand jury testimony, all made it appear not as a quest for justice but as a vendetta, an appearance bolstered by the actions of the House of Representatives.

Republicans believed they were going to enlarge their majorities in both houses of Congress in the 1998 midterm election. Instead, they barely held their numbers in the Senate and saw their majority shrink to a razor-thin margin in the House. Public opinion polls showed that the American people, while disapproving of Clinton's actions, did not believe it warranted impeachment or removal from office. Nonetheless, a lame-duck House proceeded, and judiciary committee chairman Henry Hyde made sure that articles of impeachment would be voted out before Congress adjourned. In less than a month, Hyde's committee completed its work and reported out four articles of impeachment.

On 19 December 1998, the full House voted to impeach the president for perjury before the Starr grand jury and for obstruction of justice in attempting to prevent disclosure of his relationship with Lewinsky. The vote followed a bitter partisan debate about whether any of this activity was truly impeachable, and the final results went almost completely along party lines. The perjury count passed the House 228–206, and the obstruction of justice charge by 221–212. In the Senate, where members of both parties clearly thought the entire proceedings ill founded, a majority could not be found for either article, and in early 1999, the Senate acquitted him on both charges.

Throughout the proceedings, the Republicans reinforced public perception of them as acting vindictively, and even people who denounced Clinton's actions believed they did not justify his removal from office. There have been many books and articles written "proving" that Clinton lied and obstructed justice, and that may well be so. There have also been books written "proving" that Kenneth Starr went well beyond his mandate and in fact pursued a right-wing vendetta against the Clintons.

But impeachment is above all a political process, not a question of criminal law. It is a matter of perception and how people view the chief executive and his behavior. During the impeachment, many references were made to Richard Nixon, and here one can make a clear distinction. Nixon utilized the office and powers of the presidency to subvert the processes of government. He attempted to utilize the FBI, IRS, and other agencies to retaliate against people he saw as "enemies," and whether he approved the Watergate break-in or not, he actively tried to cover it up.

Most people saw this as quite different from a man cheating on his wife, and who then lied to try to keep it quiet. While, as president, Clinton certainly has extensive powers, he clearly did not or could not use them in this instance. While we ought to hold our presidents to a high standard of morality, many people believed his actions vis-à-vis Monica Lewinsky to have been private in nature. Since impeachment is a political process, from a political viewpoint the American people did not support Clinton's removal from office.

The Election of 2000

One would have to go back more than a century to find an election so strange in results as that between the Democratic candidate, Vice President Al Gore of Tennessee and his Republican opponent, Governor George W. Bush of Texas. Two third-party candidates, Ralph Nader and Patrick Buchanan complicated matters, and in fact, the votes Nader received in Florida may well have cost Gore the election. But what made this election so unusual was the involvement of the U.S. Supreme Court in an area that the justices have traditionally avoided, the "political thicket" as Felix Frankfurter once termed it.

To summarize a complex election, one should first note that the country had been moving for at least two decades toward political equilibrium, with both the Democrats and Republicans eagerly seeking to occupy the center. Neither Bush nor Gore had any charismatic qualities, and while both had various personal strengths and weaknesses, Gore labored under the perceived burden of having been part of the besmirched Clinton administration. At the same time, Clinton retained an amazing 63 percent approval rating, and many commentators believed Gore should have availed himself of Clinton's proven prowess as a campaigner. As the people went to vote on November 7, every political survey showed the race too close to call.

Shortly after the polls closed in Florida, all the major television networks, relying on voter exit polls, awarded Florida to Gore, and based on reports from other states, this seemed to give Gore, who had a national margin of about 400,000 in the popular vote, the necessary 270 electoral votes he needed for victory. But as further results came in, the Florida results grew murky. The networks retracted their award of Florida to Gore, and around 2:15 the following morning gave it to Bush. Al Gore was preparing to give his concession speech when an updated tally showed Bush's lead in Florida had been cut to no more than a few thousand votes out of six million ballots cast, close enough to trigger an automatic recount under Florida law. Three days later, the automatic recount gave Bush a lead of only 327 votes.

Had everything else been in order, the election would have been over. Even though Gore had more popular votes, American presidents are elected by the so-called electoral college, an archaic device in which each state casts votes equal to its number of senators and representatives. The device had been adopted at the Constitutional Convention in 1787 to protect the electoral influence of the smaller states, and even though the times have changed significantly, smaller states are unwilling to give up this benefit. The Constitution says that the state legislatures shall choose their electors, but in all states, laws have been passed awarding the state's electoral votes to the winner of the popular balloting, although a few states divide their electoral ballots proportionally. The American people have had other elections in the past in which the winner of the popular vote has not received a majority of the electoral ballots, and in this case, they would again accept the paradox of the man with the most popular votes losing.

But, Gore claimed, all was not in order. In four heavily Democratic counties—Volusia, Palm Beach, Broward, and Miami-Dade—voters had used a punch-card ballot, and the automatic voting machines could not read these ballots unless the voters had been sure to punch completely through them. The four counties are the heart of Florida's retirement belt, and many elderly people, for a variety of reasons, had not punched the ballot cleanly. As a result, their votes were disallowed. But when they were asked after voting who they had voted for, they said Gore, thus leading the exit pollsters to conclude that Gore had won the state. Estimates of uncounted ballots ran as high as 50,000, and had they been counted, it is clear that Gore would have won most of them.

Lawyers for Gore and Bush quickly took the dispute to the Florida courts. The Gore team asked for manual handcounts in the four counties where what they termed "irregularities" appeared most evident. Bush's legal team went into federal court to stop the manual recounts that had already begun in some precincts. Both the federal district court in Florida as well as the Circuit Court of Appeals for the Eleventh Circuit dismissed Bush's efforts, claiming that election law had always been state law and should therefore be decided in state courts. However, the U.S. Supreme Court agreed to hear the Bush appeal, and on December 1, the two sides presented oral arguments before the justices. The Gore legal team urged the Court to allow state courts to decide what was essentially a state matter, while Bush's lawyers wanted federal court intervention. Few people failed to notice the irony of Democrats arguing for states' rights and Republicans calling for federal courts to overturn a state decision.

Four days later, the Supreme Court returned the case to the Florida high court, asking it to ensure that adequate vote-counting standards existed and that the wishes of the legislature were followed. This last matter addressed the fact that the Constitution gives the ultimate power of choosing the electors to the state legislatures, and because this is a grant of power from the federal Constitution, it overrode any Florida court effort to reconcile conflicting state laws or even provisions of the state constitution. Many commentators, however, believed the Court had recognized the illogic of its taking the case and was seeking a quiet way out. Anyone who believed this would be rudely awakened in less than a week.

After a complex series of maneuverings, the Florida Supreme Court on December 8—a month after the election—handed Gore a major victory and ordered hand recounts to begin in those counties that had a significant number of uncounted ballots. The next day, however, the U.S. Supreme Court, in response to an emergency appeal by Bush, ordered the handcounts to cease. Bush had claimed that the Florida Supreme Court's decision had no clear standard by which one would determine which ballots would be included and how voter intent would be established, and this violated both the Equal Protection and Due Process clauses of the Fourteenth Amendment.

Why did the Court agree to hear this case? The conservative majority of the Rehnquist Court, as noted in Chapter 43, had apparently reinvigorated the power and autonomy of the states within the federal system. In *Lopez, Printz,* and *Morrison,* 5–4 majorities had negated federal laws requiring states to comply with federal directives, the most dramatic curtailment of congressional power since the 1930s. Many people saw politics as the cause. The five-member conservative bloc that had prevailed in the states' rights cases—Rehnquist, O'Connor, Scalia, Kennedy, and Thomas—had all been appointed by Republican presidents, and many observers, as well as many Americans, believed that the Court was acting in an unabashedly partisan manner. In fact, Justice Scalia had written in the Court's decision to vacate the Florida Supreme Court's order to continue the recount that "It suffices to say that the issuance of th[is decision] . . . suggests that a majority of the Court, while not deciding the issues presented, believe that the petitioner had a substantial probability of success."

In response, Justice Stevens, joined by Breyer, Ginsburg, and Souter, threw back the majority's own reasoning in the federalism cases, and noted that the majority in its decision to intervene had departed from three "venerable rules" of judicial restraint: "On questions of state law, we have consistently respected the opinions of the highest courts of the States. On questions whose resolution is committed at least in large measure to another branch of the Federal Government, we have construed our own jurisdiction narrowly and exercised it cautiously. On federal constitutional questions that were not fairly presented to the court whose judgment is being reviewed, we have prudently declined to express an opinion." The majority, they concluded, "has acted unwisely."

The Court heard oral argument on December 11, five weeks after the election. Lawyers for Bush argued that manual recounts ordered by the Florida Supreme Court failed to establish clear standards, in violation of the Due Process and Equal Protection Clauses, and also violated the constitutional grant of power to the legislature to choose electors. Gore's attorneys argued that the Florida Supreme Court order raised no federal constitutional question and that by refusing to allow the count to go ahead, the Court was in effect disenfranchising tens of thousands of Florida voters.

Wanting to put an end to the indecision surrounding the election results, the Court ruled the very next day in favor of Bush. Although seven justices agreed that an equal protection problem existed with the Florida court's orders (Breyer and Souter agreed that equal protection problems existed, but thought that the case should have been remanded back to the state court for resolution), a bare 5–4 majority ruled that these problems were so severe as to warrant halting the recount. When the majority, through Chief Justice Rehnquist, noted that there was no time left in which to conduct an acceptable recount, the minority opinions of justices Stevens, Ginsburg, and Breyer pointedly reminded them that had the five not stopped the recount earlier it could have been completed in time. Moreover, the opinions of the dissenting justices were unusually sharp in suggesting that the Court's decision carried clear partisan overtones. The next day, Al Gore finally conceded the election, and on January 20, 2001, George W. Bush took the oath of office as the forty-third President of the United States.

Bush v. Gore will be debated by politicians and scholars for years to come. To begin with, the majority opinion cast a great cloud of confusion over the reach of the decision. Although the Court spoke of limited applicability and kept referring to the case at hand, one could hardly imagine that the principles it used to decide the controversy would be limited only to the 2000 presidential election in the state of Florida. Very few states have procedures in place that would meet the Court's requirement of clear standards, and Florida was not alone in its wide variety of voting machines and methods, which varied from county to county. Within days after the decision, other states began looking at their own election laws to see if they needed revision.

Some commentators believed that the Court did what it was supposed to do, save the system when a fatal error creeps into the democratic mechanism. The longer the recount went on, this argument goes, the less the American people would be willing to accept the results and the less legitimacy the next president would enjoy. In fact, the majority on the Court said that there was no time left (to which the minority responded that there would have been if the Court had not intervened).

But the gravest charge against the Court was that it was being partisan, something federal courts have avoided for more than two centuries. Courts cannot help being *political*, since the judiciary is one of the three branches of government, and governing is essentially an exercise in politics. Court decisions reaching back to *Marbury v. Madison* (1803) have been political in this sense, and the Court, like the executive and legislative branches, must always play this game. But in *Bush v. Gore*, many people saw the Court as acting in a *partisan* manner, favoring one party over another, and whatever the truth of this charge, the perception that it is true is widely held. The harm this does to the Court is incalculable, since the basis of the Court's authority and power in the American scheme of government relies on the trust that the people have in its impartiality. As Justice Breyer wrote in dissent, "We do risk a self-inflicted wound—a wound that may harm not just the court but the nation."

The Court has now opened a Pandora's box in an area it has up until now carefully avoided; it will be difficult if not impossible to close that box again.

Conclusion

At the beginning of a new millennium, the American system of government seemed to some commentators to be stalled in gridlock, as a Congress controlled by one party constantly battled a presidency controlled by the other. The Supreme Court appeared to be as conservative as any court in the nation's history, intent on creating a "new federalism" by turning back the clock to a period when states exercised greater sovereignty. In the process, it allegedly ignored the facts of modern economic, political, and social life, and stepped in to decide a presidential election in an overtly partisan manner. Civil libertarians worried that the Bill of Rights stood in great danger, while social conservatives feared that the nation stood in peril of losing its soul. The nation confronted immense problems such as health care, poverty, environmental degradation, and a homicide rate higher than that of any other developed country. And while things went from bad to worse, the government could do nothing.

One can find lamentations of this sort throughout American history, and yet the Constitution survives. The intricate system of checks and balances and separation of powers may strike some as antique and outdated, but democracy is not designed to be efficient. In a democratic society, we value participation, accountability, and rule of law, and while these may not seems as strong to some people as they once did, the system continues to function. The political branches do establish policy. The courts do sustain individual rights and serve as an umpire to the federal system. The states show a new vigor in meeting the needs of their citizens. In its third century, the Constitution seems as robust and effective as ever.

For Further Reading

An excellent analysis of the tensions between Congress and the president in the 1970s is James L. Sundquist, *The Decline and Resurgence of Congress* (1981). For the legislative veto, see Barbara Hinkson Craig, *Chadha: The Story of an Epic Constitutional Struggle* (1987); as well as Peter L. Straus, "Was There a Baby in the Bathwater? A Comment on the Supreme Court's Legislative Veto Decision," 1983 *Duke Law Journal* 789 (1983). The legislative viewpoint, written before the *Chadha* decision, is explained in Jacob Javits and Gary Klein, "Congressional Oversight and the Legislative Veto: A Constitutional Analysis," 52 *N.Y.U. Law Review* 455 (1977). The Court's only major foreign policy decision in this period is analyzed in "Symposium: Dames & Moore v. Regan," 29 *UCLA Law Review* 977 (1982).

The erosion of the War Powers Act is detailed in chapters 7–9 of Louis Fisher, *Presidential War Power* (1995); for a different view, see Robert F. Turner, *Repealing the War Powers Resolution: Restoring the Rule of Law in U.S. Foreign Policy* (1991). See also "The War Powers Act and the Persion Gulf: Pro and Con," *Congressional Digest* (December 1987); Michael Rubner, "The Reagan Administration, the 1973 War Powers Resolution, and the Invasion of Grenada," 100 *Political Science Quarterly* 627 (1985-86); Robert G. Torricelli, "The War Powers Resolution after the Libya Crisis," 7 *Pace Law Review* 661 (1987); Eileen Burgin, "Congress, the War Powers Resolution, and the Invasion of Panama," 25 *Polity* 217 (1992); Michael J. Glennon, "The Gulf War and the Constitution," 70 *Foreign Affairs* 84 (1991). A good overview of the issues can be found in John Hart Ely, *War and Its Responsibility: Constitutional Lessons of Vietnam and Its Aftermath* (1993). See also the section regarding the Gulf War in Herbert S. Parmet, *George Bush: The Life and Times of a Lone Star Yankee* (1997).

For the Bork nomination, see the fine book by Ethan Bronner, *Battle for Justice: How the Bork Nomination Shook America* (1989); the intriguing essay by Lucas A. Powe, Jr., "From Bork to Souter," 27 *Willamette Law Review* 781 (1991); and Bork's own version, *The Tempting of America: The Political Seduction of the Law* (1990). There have been several books on the Thomas nomination, including Jane Mayer and Jill Abramson, *Strange Justice: The Selling of Clarence Thomas* (1994); Jane Flax, *The American Dream in Black and White: The Clarence Thomas Hearings* (1998); and Toni Morison, ed., *Race-ing Justice, En-Gendering Power: Essays on Anita Hill, Clarence Thomas, and the Construction of Social Reality* (1992). See also Paul Simon, "Advice & Consent: Clarence Thomas, Robert Bork and the Intriguing History of the Supreme Court's Nomination Battles," in a symposium in 65 *Southern California Law Review* (1992).

The rise and demise of the line item veto are discussed in the symposium, "The Phoenix Rises Again: The Nondelegation Doctrine from Constitutional and Policy Perspectives," 20 *Cardozo Law Review* 871 (1999); and Bernard W. Bell, "Dead Against the Nondelegation Doctrine, the Rules/Standards Dilemma, and the Line Item Veto," 44 *Villanova Law Review* 189 (1999).

The independent counsel law itself has fared poorly among commentators. See, for example, Julie O'Sullivan, "The Independent Counsel Statute: Bad Law, Bad Policy," 33 *American Criminal Law Review* 463 (1996), and symposium, "The Independent Counsel Act: From Watergate to Whitewater and Beyond," 86 *Georgetown Law Journal* 2011 (1998). A full narrative is Benjamin J. Priester et al., "The Independent Counsel Statute: A History," 62 *Law & Contemporary Problems* 5 (1999); while a review of all independent counsel investigations is in Niles L. Godes and Ty E. Howard, "Independent Counsel Investigation," 35 *American Criminal Law Review* 875 (1998). For Starr's actions, see the highly critical volumes by Alan M. Dershowitz, *Sexual McCarthyism: Clinton, Starr, and the Emerging Constitutional Crisis* (1998); and James Carville, *—And the Horse He Rode in On: The People v. Kenneth Starr* (1998).

For information about the impeachment and trial of President Clinton, see U.S. Senate (106th Cong., 1st Sess.), *Impeachment of President William Jefferson Clinton,* 24 vols. (1999), which contains the entire evidentiary and deliberative record. The Starr report is available as a separate volume, *Referral from Independent Counsel Kenneth W. Starr . . .* (1998). The nearest we have to an objective and impartial study is Richard A. Posner, *An Affair of State: The Investigation, Impeachment and Trial of President Clinton* (1999). William Bennett, *The Death of Outrage: Bill Clinton and the Assault on American Ideals* (1998), is typical of the attitude of social conservatives toward Clinton.

More scholarly studies of impeachment in American history can be found in Emily Field Van Tassel and Paul Finkelman, *Impeachable Offenses: A Documentary History from 1787 to the Present* (1999); Michael J. Gerhardt, *The Federal Impeachment Process: A Constitutional and Historical Analysis* (1996); and the symposium on "Background and History of Impeachment," 67 *George Washington Law Review* 601 (1999).

APPENDIXES

The Declaration of Independence

WHEN IN THE course of human events, it becomes necessary for one people to dissolve the political bands which have connected them with another, and to assume that Powers of the earth, the separate and equal station to which the Laws of Nature and of Nature's God entitle them, a decent respect to the opinions of mankind requires that they should declare the causes which impel them to the separation.

We hold these truths to be self-evident, that all men are created equal, that they are endowed to their Creator with certain unalienable rights, that among these are Life, Liberty, and the pursuit of Happiness. That to secure these rights, Governments are instituted among Men, deriving their just powers from the consent of the governed. That whenever any Form of Government becomes destructive of these ends, it is the Right of the People to alter or to abolish it, and to institute new Government, laying its foundation on such principles and organizing its powers in such form, as to them shall seem most likely to effect their Safety and Happiness. Prudence, indeed, will dictate that Governments long established should not be changed for light and transient causes; and accordingly all experience hath shown, that mankind are more disposed to suffer, while evils are sufferable, than to right themselves by abolishing the forms to which they are accustomed. But when a long train of abuses and usurpations, pursuing invariably the same Object evinces a design to reduce them under absolute Despotism, it is their right, it is their duty, to throw off such Government, and to provide new Guards for their future security.—Such has been the patient sufferance of these Colonies; and such is now the necessity which constrains them to alter their former Systems of Government. The history of the present King of Great Britain is a history of repeated injuries and usurpations, all having in direct object the establishment of an absolute Tyranny over these States. To prove this, let Facts be submitted to a candid world.

He has refused his Assent to Laws, the most wholesome and necessary for the public good.

He has forbidden his Governors to pass Laws of immediate and pressing importance, unless suspended in their operation till his Assent should be obtained; and when so suspended, he has utterly neglected to attend to them.

He has refused to pass other Laws for the accommodation of large districts of people, unless those people would relinquish the right of Representation in the Legislature, a right inestimable to them and formidable to tyrants only.

He has called together legislative bodies at places unusual, uncomfortable, and distant from the depository of their public Records, for the sole purpose of fatiguing them into compliance with his measures.

He has dissolved Representative Houses repeatedly, for opposing with manly firmness his invasions on the rights of the people.

He has refused for a long time, after such dissolutions, to cause others to be elected; whereby the Legislative powers, incapable of Annihilation, have returned to the People at large for their exercise; the State remaining in the mean time exposed to all dangers of invasion from without, and convulsions within.

He has endeavoured to prevent the population of these States; for that purpose obstructing the Laws of Naturalization of Foreigners; refusing to pass others to encourage their migrations hither, and raising the conditions of new Appropriations of Lands.

He has obstructed the Administration of Justice, by refusing his Assent to Laws for establishing Judiciary powers.

He has made Judges dependent on his Will alone, for the tenure of their offices, and the amount and payment of their salaries.

He has erected a multitude of New Offices, and sent hither swarms of Officers to harass our People, and eat out their substance.

He has kept among us, in times of peace, Standing Armies without the Consent of our legislature.

He has affected to render the Military independent of and superior to the Civil Power.

He has combined with others to subject us to a jurisdiction foreign to our constitution, and unacknowledged by our laws; giving his Assent to their Acts of pretended Legislation:

For quartering large bodies of armed troops among us:

For protecting them, by a mock Trial, from Punishment for any Murders which they should commit on the Inhabitants of these States:

For cutting off our Trade with all parts of the world:

For imposing taxes on us without our Consent:

For depriving us of many cases, of the benefits of Trial by jury:

For transporting us beyond Seas to be tried for pretended offences:

For abolishing the free System of English Laws in a neighbouring Province, establishing therein an Arbitrary government, and enlarging its Boundaries so as to render it at once an example and fit instrument for introducing the same absolute rule into these Colonies:

For taking away our Charters, abolishing our most valuable Laws, and altering fundamentally the Forms of our Governments:

For suspending our own Legislatures, and declaring themselves invested with Power to legislate for us in all cases whatsoever.

He has abdicated Government here, by declaring us out of his Protection and waging War against us.

He has plundered our seas, ravaged our Coasts, burnt our towns, and destroyed the lives of our people.

He is at this time transporting large armies of foreign mercenaries to compleat the works of death, desolation, and tyranny, already begun with circumstances of Cruelty & perfidy scarcely paralleled in the most barbarous ages, and totally unworthy the Head of a civilized nation.

He has constrained our fellow Citizens taken Captive on the high Seas to bear Arms against their Country, to become the executioners of their friends and Brethren, or to fall themselves by their Hands.

He has excited domestic insurrections amongst us, and has endeavoured to bring on the inhabitants of our frontiers, the merciless Indian savages, whose known rule of warfare, is an undistinguished destruction of all ages, sexes, and conditions.

In every stage of these Oppressions We have Petitioned for Redress in the most humble terms: Our repeated Petitions have been answered only by repeated injury. A Prince, whose character is thus marked by every act which may define a Tyrant, is unfit to be the ruler of a free people.

Nor have We been wanting in attention to our British brethren. We have warned them from time to time of attempts by their legislature to extend an unwarrantable jurisdiction over us. We have reminded them of the circumstances of our emigration and settlement here. We have appealed to their native justice and magnanimity, and we have conjured them by the ties of our common kindred to disavow these usurpations, which, would inevitably interrupt our connections and correspondence. They too must have been deaf to the voice of justice and of consanguinity. We must, therefore, acquiesce in the necessity, which denounces our Separation, and hold them, as we hold the rest of mankind, Enemies in War, in Peace Friends.

We, therefore, the Representatives of the United States of America, in General Congress, Assembled, appealing to the Supreme Judge of the world for the rectitude of our intentions, do, in the Name, and by Authority of the good People of these Colonies, solemnly publish and declare, That these United Colonies are, and of Right ought to be FREE AND INDEPENDENT STATES; that they are Absolved from all Allegiance to the British Crown, and that all political connection between them and the State of Great Britain, is and ought to be totally dissolved; and that as Free and Independent States, they have full Power to levy War, conclude Peace, contract Alliances, establish Commerce, and to do all other Acts and Things which Independent states may of right do. And for the support of this Declaration, with a firm reliance on the Protection of Divine Providence, we mutually pledge to each other our Lives, our Fortunes, and our sacred Honor.

The foregoing Declaration was, by order of Congress, engrossed, and signed by the following members:

John Hancock

New Hampshire
Josiah Bartlett
William Whipple
Matthew Thornton

Massachusetts Bay
Samuel Adams
John Adams
Robert Treat Paine
Elbridge Gery

Rhode Island
Stephen Hopkins
William Ellery

Connecticut
Roger Sherman
Samuel Huntington
William Williams
Oliver Wolcott

New York
William Floyd
Philip Livingston
Francis Lewis
Lewis Morris

New Jersey
Richard Stockton
John Witherspoon
Francis Hopkinson
John Hart
Abraham Clark

Pennsylvania
Robert Morris
Benjamin Rush
Benjamin Franklin
John Morton
George Clymer
James Smith
George Taylor
James Wilson
George Ross

Delaware
Caesar Rodney
George Read
Thomas M'Kean

Maryland
Samuel Chase
William Paca
Thomas Stone
Charles Carroll, of Carrollton

Virginia
George Wythe
Richard Henry Lee
Thomas Jefferson
Benjamin Harrison
Thomas Nelson, Jr.
Francis Lightfoot Lee
Carter Braxton

North Carolina
William Hooper
Joseph Hewes
John Penn

South Carolina
Edward Rutledge
Thomas Heyward, Jr.
Thomas Lynch, Jr.
Arthur Middleton

Georgia
Button Gwinnett
Lyman Hall
George Walton

Resolved, That copies of the Declaration be sent to the several assemblies, conventions, and committees, or councils of safety, and to the several commanding officers of the continental troops; that it be proclaimed in each of the United States, at the head of the army.

Constitution of the United States

WE THE PEOPLE of the United States, in Order to form a more perfect Union, establish Justice, insure domestic Tranquility, provide for the common defence, promote the general Welfare, and secure the Blessings of Liberty to ourselves and our Posterity, do ordain and establish this Constitution for the United States of America.

Article I

Section 1. All legislative Powers herein granted shall be vested in a Congress of the United States, which shall consist of a Senate and House of Representatives

Section 2. The House of Representatives shall be composed of Members chosen every second Year by the People of the several States, and the Electors in each State shall have the Qualifications requisite for Electors of the most numerous Branch of the State Legislature.

No Person shall be a Representative who shall not have attained to the Age of twenty five Years, and been seven Years a Citizen of the United States, and who shall not, when elected, be an Inhabitant of that State in which he shall be chosen.

Representatives and direct Taxes shall be apportioned among the several States which may be included within this Union, according to their respective Numbers, which shall be determined by adding to the whole Number of free Persons, including those bound to Service for a Term of Years, and excluding Indians not taxed, three fifths of all other Persons. The actual Enumeration shall be made within three Years after the first Meeting of the Congress of the United States, and within every subsequent Term of ten Years, in such Manner as they shall by Law direct. The Number of Representatives shall not exceed one for every thirty Thousand, but each State shall have at Least one Representative; and until such enumeration shall be made, the State of New Hampshire shall be entitled to chuse three, Massachusetts eight, Rhode Island and Providence Plantations one, Connecticut five, New-York six, New Jersey four, Pennsylvania eight, Delaware one, Maryland six, Virginia ten, North Carolina five, South Carolina five, and Georgia three.

When vacancies happen in the Representation from any State, the Executive Authority thereof shall issue Writs of Election to fill such Vacancies. The House of Representatives shall chuse their Speaker and other Officers; and shall have the sole Power of Impeachment.

Section 3. The Senate of the United States shall be composed of two Senators from each State, chosen by the Legislature thereof, for six Years; and each Senator shall have one vote.

Immediately after they shall be assembled in Consequence of the first Election, they shall be divided as equally as may be into three Classes. The Seats of the Senators of the first Class shall be vacated at the Expiration of the second Year, of the second Class at the Expiration of the fourth Year, and of the third Class at the Expiration of the sixth Year, so that one third may be chosen every second Year; and if Vacancies happen by Resignation, or otherwise, during the Recess of the Legislature of any State, the Executive thereof may make temporary Appointments until the next Meeting of the Legislature, which shall then fill such Vacancies.

No Person shall be a Senator who shall not have attained to the Age of thirty Years, and been nine Years a Citizen of the United States, and who shall not, when elected, be an Inhabitant of that State for which he shall be chosen.

The Vice President of the United States shall be President of the Senate, but shall have no Vote, unless they be equally divided. The Senate shall chuse their other Officers, and also a President pro tempore, in the Absence of the Vice President, or when he shall exercise the Office of President of the United States.

The Senate shall have the sole Power to try all Impeachments. When sitting for that Purpose, they shall be on Oath or Affirmation. When the President of the United States is tried the Chief Justice shall preside: And no Person shall be convicted without the Concurrence of two thirds of the Members present.

Judgment in Cases of Impeachment shall not extend further than to removal from Office, and disqualification to hold and enjoy any Office of honor, Trust or Profit under the United States: but the Party convicted shall nevertheless be liable and subject to Indictment, Trial, Judgment and Punishment, according to Law.

Section 4. The Times, Places and Manner of holding Elections for Senators and Representatives, shall be prescribed in each State by the Legislature thereof; but the Congress may at any time by Law make or alter such Regulations, except as to the Places of chusing Senators.

The Congress shall assemble at least once in every Year, and such Meeting shall be on the first Monday in December, unless they shall by Law appoint a different Day.

Section 5. Each House shall be the Judge of the Elections, Returns and Qualifications of its own Members, and a Majority of each shall constitute a Quorum to do Business; but a smaller Number may adjourn from day to day, and may be authorized to compel the Attendance of absent Members, in such Manner, and under such Penalties as each House may provide.

Each House may determine the Rules of its Proceedings, punish its Members for disorderly Behavior, and, with the Concurrence of two thirds, expel a Member.

Each House shall keep a Journal of its Proceedings, and from time to time publish the same, excepting such Parts as may in their Judgment require Secrecy; and the Yeas and Nays of the Members of either House on any question shall, at the Desire of one fifth of those Present, be entered on the Journal. Neither House, during the Session of Congress, shall, without the Consent of the other, adjourn for more than three days, nor to any other Place than that in which the two Houses shall be sitting.

Section 6. The Senators and Representatives shall receive a Compensation for their Services, to be ascertained by law, and paid out of the Treasury of the United States. They shall in all Cases, except Treason, Felony and Breach of the Peace, be privileged from Arrest during their Attendance at the Session of their respective Houses, and in going to and returning from the same; and for any Speech or Debate in either House, they shall not be questioned in any other Place.

No Senator or Representative shall, during the Time for which he was elected, be appointed to any civil Office under the Authority of the United States, which shall have been created, or the Emoluments whereof shall have been increased during such time; and no Person holding any Office under the United States, shall be a Member of either House during his Continuance in Office.

Section 7. All Bills for raising Revenue shall originate in the House of Representatives; but the Senate may propose or concur with amendments as on other Bills.

Every Bill which shall have passed the House of Representatives and the Senate, shall, before it become a Law, be presented to the President of the United States; If he approve he shall sign it:, but if not he shall return it with his Objections to that House in which it shall have originated, who shall enter the Objections at large on their Journal, and proceed to reconsider it. If after such Reconsideration two thirds of that House shall agree to pass the Bill, it shall be sent, together with the Objections, to the other House, by which it shall likewise be reconsidered, and if approved by two thirds of that House, it shall become a Law. But in all such Cases the Votes of both Houses shall be determined by Yeas and Nays, and the Names of the Persons voting for and against the Bill shall be entered on the Journal of each House respectively. If any Bill shall not be returned by the President within ten Days (Sunday excepted) after it shall have been presented to him, the Same shall be a Law, in like Manner as if he had signed it, unless the Congress by their Adjournment prevent its Return, in which Case it shall not be a Law.

Every Order, Resolution, or Vote to which the Concurrence of the Senate and House of Representatives may be necessary (except on a question of Adjournment) shall be presented to the President of the United States; and before the Same shall take Effect, shall be approved by him, or being disapproved by him, shall be repassed by two thirds of the Senate and House of Representatives, according t:o the Rules and Limitations prescribed in the Case of a Bill.

Section 8. The Congress shall have Power To lay and collect Taxes, Duties, Imposts and Excises, to pay the Debts and provide for the common Defence and general Welfare of the United States; but all Duties, Imposts and Excises shall be uniform throughout the United States;

To borrow Money on the credit of the United States;

To regulate Commerce with foreign Nations, and among the several States, and with the Indian Tribes;

To establish an uniform Rule of Naturalization, and uniform Laws on the subject of Bankruptcies throughout the United States;

To coin Money, regulate the Value thereof, and of foreign Coin, and fix the Standard of Weights and Measures;

To provide for the Punishment of counterfeiting the Securities and current Coin of the United States;

To establish Post Offices and post Roads;

To promote the Progress of Science and useful Arts, by securing for limited Times to Authors and Inventors the exclusive Right to their respective Writings and Discoveries;

To constitute Tribunals inferior to the supreme Court;

To define and punish Piracies and Felonies committed on the high Seas, and Offences against the Law of Nations;

To declare War, grant Letters of Marque and Reprisal, and make Rules concerning Captures on Land and Water;

To raise and support Armies, but no Appropriation of Money to that Use shall be for a longer Term than two Years;

To provide and maintain a Navy;

To make Rules for the Government and Regulation of the land and naval Forces;

To provide for calling forth the Militia to execute the Laws of the Union, suppress Insurrections and repel Invasions;

To provide for organizing, arming, and disciplining, the Militia, and for governing such Part of them as may be employed in the Service of the United States, reserving to the States respectively, the Appointment of the Officers, and the Authority of training the Militia according to the discipline prescribed by Congress;

To exercise exclusive Legislation in all Cases whatsoever, over such District (not exceeding ten Miles square) as may, by Cession of particular States, and the Acceptance of Congress, become the Seat of the Government of the United States, and to exercise like Authority over all Places purchased by the Consent of the Legislature of the State in which the Same shall be, for the Erection of Forts, Magazines, Arsenals, dock-Yards, and other needful Buildings;—And

To make all Laws which shall be necessary and proper for carrying into Execution the foregoing Powers, and all other Powers vested by this Constitution in the Government of the United States, or in any Department or Officer thereof.

Section 9. The Migration or Importation of such Persons as any of the States now existing shall think proper to admit, shall not be prohibited by the Congress prior to the Year one thousand eight hundred and eight, but a Tax or duty may be imposed on such Importation, not exceeding ten dollars for each Person.

The Privilege of the Writ of Habeas Corpus shall not be suspended, unless when in Cases of Rebellion or Invasion the public Safety may require it.

No Bill of Attainder or ex post facto Law shall be passed.

No Capitation, or other direct, Tax shall be laid, unless in Proportion to the Census or Enumeration herein before directed to be taken.

No Tax or Duty shall be laid on Articles exported from any State.

No Preference shall be given by any Regulation of Commerce or Revenue to the

Ports of one State over those of another; nor shall Vessels bound to, or from, one State, be obliged to enter, clear or pay Duties in another.

No Money shall be drawn from the Treasury, but in Consequence of appropriations made by Law; and a regular Statement and Account of the receipts and Expenditures of all public Money shall be published from time to time.

No Title of Nobility shall be granted by the United States: And no Person holding any Office of Profit or Trust under them, shall, without the Consent of the Congress, accept of any present, Emolument, Office, or Title, of any kind whatever, from any King, Prince or foreign State.

Section 10. No State shall enter into any Treaty, Alliance, or Confederation; grant Letters of Marque and Reprisal, coin Money; emit Bills of Credit, make any Thing but gold and silver Coin a Tender in Payment of Debts; pass any Bill of Attainder, ex post facto Law, or Law impairing the Obligation for Contracts, or grant any Title of Nobility.

No State shall, without the Consent of the Congress, lay any Imposts or Duties on Imports or Exports, except what may be absolutely necessary for executing its inspection Laws: and the net Produce of all Duties and Imposts, laid by any State on Imports or Exports, shall be for the Use of the Treasury of the United States; and all such Laws shall be subject to the Revision and Controul of the Congress.

No State shall, without the Consent of Congress, lay any Duty of Tonnage, keep Troops, or Ships of War in time of Peace, enter into any Agreement or Compact with another State, or with a foreign Power, or engage in War, unless actually invaded, or in such imminent Danger as will not admit of delay.

Article II

Section 1. The executive Power shall be vested in a President of the United States of America. He shall hold his Office during the Term of four Years, and, together with the Vice President, chosen for the same Term, be elected, as follows

Each State shall appoint, In such Manner as the Legislature thereof may direct, a Number of Electors, equal to the whole Number of Senators and Representatives to which the State may be entitled in the Congress: but no Senator or Representative, or Person holding an Office of Trust or Profit under the United States, shall be appointed an Elector.

The Electors shall meet in their respective States, and vote by Ballot for two Persons, of whom one at least shall not be an Inhabitant of the same State with themselves, And they shall make a List of all the Persons voted for, and of the number of Votes for each; which List they shall sign and certify, and transmit sealed to the Seat of the Government of the United States, directed to the President of the Senate. The President of the Senate shall, in the Presence of the Senate and House of Representatives, open all the Certificates, and the Votes shall then be counted. The Person having the greatest number of Votes shall be the President, if such Number be a Majority of the whole Number of Electors appointed; and if there be more than one who have such Majority, and have an equal Number of Votes, then the House of Representatives shall immediately chuse by Ballot one of them for President; and if no Person have a Majority, then from the five highest on the List the said House shall in like Manner chuse the President. But in chusing the President, the Votes shall be taken by States, the Representation from each State having one Vote; a quorum for this Purpose shall consist of a Member or Members from two thirds of the States, and a Majority of all the States shall be necessary to a Choice. In every Case, after the Choice of the President, the Person having the greatest Number of Votes of the Electors shall be the Vice President. But if there should remain two or more who have equal Votes, the Senate shall chuse from them by Ballot the Vice President.

The Congress may determine the Time of chusing the Electors, and the Day on which they shall give their Votes; which Day shall be the same throughout the United States.

No Person except a natural born Citizen, or a Citizen of the United States, at the time of the Adoption of this Constitution, shall be eligible to the Office of President; neither shall any Person be eligible to that Office who shall not have attained to the Age of thirty five Years, and been fourteen Years a Resident within the United States.

In Case of the Removal of the President from Office, or of his Death, Resignation, or Inability to discharge the Powers and Duties of the said Office, the Same shall devolve on the Vice President, and the Congress may by Law provide for the Case of Removal, Death, Resignation or Inability, both of the President and Vice President, declaring what Officer shall then act as President, and such Officer shall act accordingly, until the Disability be removed, or a President shall be elected.

The President shall, at stated Times, receive for his Services, a Compensation, which shall neither be increased nor diminished during the Period for which he shall have been elected, and he shall not receive within that Period any other emolument from the United States, or any of them.

Before he enter on the Execution of his Office, he shall take the following Oath or Affirmation:-"I do solemnly swear (or affirm) that I will faithfully execute the Office of President of the United States, and will to the best of my Ability, preserve, protect and defend the Constitution of the United States.

Section 2. The President shall be Commander in Chief of the Army and Navy of the United States, and of the Militia of the several States, when called into the actual Service of the United States; he may require the Opinion, in writing, of the principal Officer in each of the executive Departments, upon any Subject relating to the Duties of their respective Offices, and he shall have Power to grant Reprieves and Pardons for Offences against the United States, except in Cases of Impeachment.

He shall have Power, by and with the Advice and Consent of the Senate, to make Treaties, provided two thirds of the Senators present concur; and he shall nominate, and by and with the Advice and Consent of the Senate,shall appoint Ambassadors, other public Ministers and Consuls, Judges of the supreme Court, and all other Officers of the United States, whose Appointments are not herein otherwise provided for, and which shall be established by Law: but the Congress may by Law vest the Appointment of such inferior Officers, as they think proper, in the President alone, in the Courts of Law, or in the Heads of Departments.

The President shall have Power to fill up all Vacancies that may happen during the Recess of the Senate, by granting Commissions which shall expire at the End of their next Session

Section 3. He shall from time to time give to the Congress Information of the State of the Union, and recommend to their Consideration such Measures as he shall judge necessary and expedient; he may, on extraordinary Occasions, convene both Houses, or either of them, and in Case of Disagreements between them, with Respect to the Time of Adjournment, he may adjourn them to such Time as he shall think proper; he shall receive Ambassadors and other public Ministers; he shall take Care that the Laws be faithfully executed, and shall Commission all the Officers of the United States.

Section 4. The President, Vice President and all Civil Officers of the United States, shall be removed from Office on Impeachment for, and Conviction of, Treason, Bribery, or other high Crimes and Misdemeanors.

Article III

Section 1. The judicial Power of the United States, shall be vested in one supreme Court, and in such inferior Courts as the Congress may from time to time ordain and establish. The Judges, both of the supreme and inferior Courts, shall hold their Offices during good Behaviour, and shall, at stated Times, receive for their Services, a Compensation, which shall not be diminished during their Continuance in Office.

Section 2. The judicial Power shall extend to all Cases, in Law and Equity, arising under this Constitution, the Laws of the United States, and Treaties made, or which shall be made, under their Authority;-to all Cases affecting Ambassadors, other public Ministers and Consuls; to all Cases of admiralty and maritime Jurisdiction; to Controversies to which the United States shall be a Party; to Controversies between two or more States; between a State and Citizens of another State; between Citizens of different States; between Citizens of the same State claiming Lands under Grants of different States, and between a State, or the Citizens thereof, and foreign States, Citizens or Subjects.

In all Cases affecting Ambassadors, other public Ministers and Consuls, and those in which a State shall be Party, the supreme Court shall have original Jurisdiction. In all the other Cases before mentioned, the supreme Court shall have appellate Jurisdiction, both as to Law and Fact, with such Exceptions, and under such Regulations as the Congress shall make.

The Trial of all Crimes, except in Cases of Impeachment, shall be by Jury; and such Trial shall be held in the State where the said Crimes shall have been committed; but when not committed within any State, the Trial shall be at such Place or Places as the Congress may by Law have directed.

Section 3. Treason against the United States, shall consist only in levying War against them, or in adhering to their Enemies, giving them Aid and Comfort. No Person shall be convicted of Treason unless on the Testimony of two Witnesses to the same overt Act, or on Confession in open Court.

The Congress shall have Power to declare the Punishment of Treason, but no Attainder of Treason shall work Corruption of Blood, or Forfeiture except during the Life of the Person attainted.

Article IV

Section 1. Full Faith and Credit shall be given in each State to the public Acts, Records, and judicial Proceedings of every other State. And the Congress may by general Laws prescribe the Manner in which such Acts, Records and Proceedings shall be proved, and the Effect thereof.

Section 2. The Citizens of each State shall be entitled to all Privileges and Immunities of Citizens in the several States.

A Person charged in any State with Treason, Felony, or other Crime, who shall flee from Justice, and be found in another State, shall on Demand of the executive Authority of the State from which he fled, be delivered up, to be removed to the State having Jurisdiction of the Crime.

No Person held to Service or Labour in one State, under the Laws thereof, escaping into another, shall, in Consequence of any Law or Regulation therein, be discharged from such Service or Labour, but shall be delivered UP on Claim of the Party to whom such Service or Labour may be due.

Section 3. New States may be admitted by the Congress into this Union; but no new State shall be formed or erected within the Jurisdiction of any other State; nor any State be formed by the Junction of two or more States, or Parts of States, without the Consent of the Legislatures of the States concerned as well as of the Congress.

The Congress shall have Power to dispose of and make all needful Rules and Regulations respecting the Territory or other Property belonging to the United States; and nothing in this Constitution shall be so construed as to Prejudice any Claims of the United States, or of any particular State.

Section 4. The United States shall guarantee to every State in this Union a Republican Form of Government, and shall protect each of them against Invasion; and on Application of the Legislature, or of the Executive (when the Legislature cannot be convened) against domestic Violence.

Article V

The Congress, whenever two thirds of both Houses shall deem it necessary, shall propose Amendments to this Constitution, or, on the Application of the Legislatures of two thirds of the several States, shall call a Convention for proposing Amendments, which, in either Case, shall be valid to all Intents and Purposes, as Part of this Constitution, when ratified by the Legislatures of three fourths of the several States, or by Conventions in three fourths thereof, as the one or the other Mode of Ratification may be proposed by the Congress; provided that no Amendment which may be made prior to the Year One thousand eight hundred and eight shall in any Manner affect the first and fourth Clauses in the Ninth Section of the first Article; and that no State, without its Consent, shall be deprived of its equal Suffrage in the Senate.

Article VI

All Debts contracted and Engagements entered into, before the Adoption of this Constitution, shall be as valid against the United States under this Constitution, as under the Confederation.

This Constitution, and the Laws of the United States which shall be made in Pursuance thereof; and all Treaties made, or which shall be made, under the Authority of the United States, shall be the supreme Law of the Land; and the Judges in every State shall be bound thereby, any Thing in the Constitution or Laws of any State to the Contrary notwithstanding.

The Senators and Representatives before mentioned, and the Members of the several State Legislatures, and all executive and judicial Officers, both of the United States and of the several States, shall be bound by Oath or affirmation, to support this Constitution; but no religious Test shall ever be required as a Qualification to any Office or public Trust under the United States.

Article VII

The Ratification of the Conventions of nine States, shall be sufficient for the Establishment of this Constitution between the States so ratifying the Same.

Done in Convention by the Unanimous Consent of the States present the Seventeenth Day of September in the Year of our Lord one thousand seven hundred and Eighty seven and of the Independence of the United States of America the Twelfth. In witness thereof We have hereunto subscribed our Names.

G[o]*. WASHINGTON-Presid*[t]
and Deputy from Virginia

ARTICLES IN ADDITION TO, AND AMENDMENTS OF, THE CONSTITUTION OF THE UNITED STATES OF AMERICA, PROPOSED BY CONGRESS, AND RATIFIED BY THE SEVERAL STATES, PURSUANT TO THE FIFTH ARTICLE OF THE ORIGINAL CONSTITUTION.

Amendment I

Congress shall make no law respecting an establishment of religion, or prohibiting the free exercise thereof; or abridging the freedom of speech, or of the press; or the right of the people peaceably to assemble, and to petition the Government for a redress of grievances.

Amendment II

A well regulated Militia, being necessary to the security of a free State, the right of the people to keep and bear Arms, shall not be infringed.

Amendment III

No Soldier shall, in time of peace be quartered in any house, without the consent of the Owner, nor in time of war, but in a manner to be prescribed by law.

Amendment IV

The right of the people to be secure in their persons, houses, papers, and effects, against unreasonable searches and seizures, shall not be violated, and no Warrants shall issue, but upon probable cause, supported by Oath or affirmation, and particularly describing the place to be searched, and the persons or things to be seized.

Amendment V

No person shall be held to answer for a capital, or otherwise infamous crime, unless on a presentment or indictment of a Grand Jury, except in cases arising in the land or naval forces, or in the Militia, when in actual service in time of War or public danger; nor shall any person be subject for the same offence to be twice put in jeopardy of life or limb; nor shall be compelled in any criminal case to be a witness against himself, nor be deprived of life, liberty, or property, without: due process of law; nor shall private property be taken for public use, without just compensation.

Amendment VI

In all criminal prosecutions, the accused shall enjoy the right to a speedy and public trial by an impartial jury of the State and district wherein the crime shall have been committed, which district shall have been previously ascertained by law, and to be informed of the nature and cause of the accusation; to be confronted with the witness against him; to have compulsory process for obtaining Witnesses in his favor, and to have the Assistance of Counsel for his defense.

Amendment VII

In Suits at common law, where the value in controversy shall exceed twenty dollars, the right of trial by jury shall be preserved, and no fact tried by a jury, shall be otherwise re-examined in any Court of the United States, than according to the rules of the common law.

Amendment VIII

Excessive bail shall not be required, nor excessive fines imposed, nor cruel and unusual punishments inflicted.

Amendment IX

The enumeration in the Constitution, of certain rights, shall not be construed to deny or disparage others retained by the people.

Amendment X

The powers not delegated to the United States by the Constitution, nor prohibited by it to the States, are reserved to the States respectively, or to the people. [*The first ten amendments were ratified Dec. 15, 1791.*]

Amendment XI

The Judicial power of the United States shall not be construed to extend to any suit in law or equity, commenced or prosecuted against one of the United States by Citizens of another State, or by Citizens or Subjects of any Foreign State. [*Ratified Jan. 8, 1798*]

Amendment XII

The Electors shall meet in their respective states and vote by ballot for President and Vice-President, one of whom, at least, shall not be an inhabitant of the same state with themselves; they shall name in their ballots the person voted for as President, and in distinct ballots the person voted for as Vice-President, and they shall make distinct lists of all persons voted for as President, and of all persons voted for as Vice-President, and of the number of votes for each, which lists they shall sign and certify, and transmit sealed to the seat of the government of the United States, directed to the President of the Senate; The President of the Senate shall, in the presence of the Senate and House of Representatives, open all the certificates and the votes shall then be counted; The person having the greatest number of votes for President, shall be the President, if such number be a majority of the whole number of Electors appointed; and if no person have such majority, then from the persons having the highest numbers not exceeding three on the list of those voted for as President, the House of Representatives shall choose immediately, by ballot, the President. But in choosing the President, the votes shall be taken by states, the representation from each state having one vote; a quorum for this purpose shall consist of a member or members from two-thirds of the states, and a majority of all the states shall be necessary to a choice. And if the House of Representatives shall not choose a President whenever the right of choice shall devolve upon them, before the fourth day of March next following, then the Vice-President shall act as President, as in the case of the death or other constitutional disability of the President—The person having the greatest number of votes as Vice-President, shall be the Vice-President, if such number be a majority of the whole number of Electors appointed, and if no person have a majority, then from the two highest numbers on the list, the Senate shall choose the Vice-President; a quorum for the purpose shall consist of two-thirds of the whole number of Senators, and a majority of the whole number shall be necessary to a choice. But no person constitutionally ineligible to the office of President shall be eligible to that of Vice-President of the United States. [*Ratified Sept. 25, 1804*]

Amendment XIII

Section 1. Neither slavery nor involuntary servitude, except as a punishment for crime whereof the party shall have been duly convicted, shall exist within the United States, or any place subject to their jurisdiction.

Section 2. Congress shall have power to enforce this article by appropriate legislation. [*Ratified Dec. 18, 1865*]

Amendment XIV

Section 1. All persons born or naturalized in the United States and subject to the jurisdiction thereof, are citizens of the United States and of the State wherein they reside. No State shall make or enforce any law which shall bridge the privileges or immunities of citizens of the United States; nor shall any State deprive any person of life, liberty, or property, without due process of law; nor deny any person within its jurisdiction the equal protection of the laws.

Section 2. Representatives shall be apportioned among the several States according to their respective numbers, counting the whole number of persons in each State, excluding Indians not taxed. But when the right to vote at any election for the choice of electors for President and Vice President of the United States, Representatives in Congress, the Executive and Judicial officers of a State, or the members of the Legislature thereof, is denied to any of the male inhabitants of such State, being twenty-one years of age, and citizens of the United States, or in any way abridged, except for participation in rebellion, or other crime, the basis of representation therein shall be reduced in the proportion which the number of such male citizens shall bear to the whole number of male citizens twenty-one years of age in such State.

Section 3. No person shall be a Senator or Representative in Congress, or elector of President and Vice President, or hold any office, civil or military, under the United States, or under any State, who, having previously taken an oath, as a member of Congress, or as an officer of the United States, or as a member of any State legislature, or as an executive or judicial officer of any State, to support the Constitution of the United States, shall have engaged in insurrection or rebellion against the same, or given aid or comfort to the enemies thereof. But Congress may by a vote of two-thirds of each House, remove such disability.

Section 4. The validity of the public debt of the United States, authorized by law, including debts incurred for payment of pensions and bounties for services in suppressing insurrection or rebellion, shall not be questioned. But neither the United States nor any State shall assume or pay any debt or obligation incurred in aid of insurrection or rebellion against the United States, or any claim for the loss or emancipation of any slave; but all such debts, obligations and claims shall be held illegal and void.

Section 5. The Congress shall have power to enforce by appropriate legislation, the provisions of this article. [*Ratified July 28, 1868*]

Amendment XV

Section 1. The right of citizens of the United States to vote shall not be denied or abridged by the United States or by any State on account of race, color, or previous condition of servitude.

Section 2. The Congress shall have power to enforce this article by appropriate legislation. [*Ratified March 30, 1870*]

Amendment XVI

The Congress shall have power to lay and collect taxes on incomes, from whatever source derived, without apportionment among the several States, and without regard to any census or enumeration. [*Ratified Feb. 25, 1913*]

Amendment XVII

The Senate of the United States shall be composed of two Senators from each State, elected by the people thereof, for six years; and each Senator shall have one vote. The electors in each State shall have the qualifications requisite for electors of the most numerous branch of the State legislatures.

When vacancies happen in the representation of any State in the Senate, the executive authority of such State shall issue writs of election to fill such vacancies: Provided, That the legislature of any State may empower the executive thereof to make temporary appointments until the people fill the vacancies by election as the legislature may direct.

This amendment shall not be so construed as to affect the election or term of any Senator chosen before it becomes valid as part of the Constitution. [*Ratified May 31, 1913*]

Amendment XVIII

Section 1. After one year from the ratification of this article the manufacture, sale, or transportation of intoxicating liquors within, the importation thereof into, or the exportation thereof from the United States and all territory subject to the jurisdiction thereof for beverage purposes is hereby prohibited.

Section 2. The Congress and the several States shall have concurrent power to enforce this article by appropriate legislation.

Section 3. This article shall be inoperative unless it shall have been ratified as an amendment to the Constitution by the legislatures of the several States, as provided in the Constitution, within seven years from the date of the submission hereof to the States by the Congress. [*Ratified Jan. 29, 1919*]

Amendment XIX

The right of citizens of the United States to vote shall not be denied or abridged by the United States or by any State on account of sex.

Congress shall have power to enforce this article by appropriate legislation. [*Ratified Aug. 26, 1920*]

Amendment XX

Section 1. The terms of the President and Vice President shall end at noon on the 20th day of January, and the terms of Senators and Representatives at noon on the 3rd day of January, of the years in which such terms would have ended if this article had not been ratified; and the terms of their successors shall then begin.

Section 2. The Congress shall assemble at least once in every year, and such meeting shall begin at noon on the 3rd day of January, unless they shall by law appoint a different day.

Section 3. If, at the time fixed for the beginning of the term of the President, the President elect shall have died, the Vice President elect shall become President. If a President shall not have been chosen before the time fixed for the beginning of his term, or if the President elect shall have failed to qualify, then the Vice President elect shall act as President until a President shall have qualified; and the Congress may by law provide for the case wherein neither a President elect nor a Vice President elect shall have qualified, declaring who shall then act as President, or the manner in which one who is to act shall be selected, and such person shall act accordingly until a President or Vice President shall have qualified.

Section 4. The Congress may by law provide for the case of the death of any of the persons for whom the House of Representatives may choose a President whenever the right of choice shall have devolved upon them, and for the case of the death of any of the persons from whom the Senate may choose a Vice President whenever the right of choice shall have devolved upon them.

Section 5. Sections 1 and 2 shall take effect on the 15th day of October following the ratification of this article.

Section 6. This article shall be inoperative unless it shall have been ratified as an amendment to the Constitution by the legislatures of three-fourths of the several States within seven years from the date of its submission. [*Ratified Feb. 6, 1933*]

Amendment XXI

Section 1. The eighteenth article of amendment to the Constitution of the United States is hereby repealed.

Section 2. The transportation or importation into any State, Territory, or possession of the United States for delivery or use therein of intoxicating liquors, in violation of the laws thereof, is hereby prohibited.

Section 3. This article shall be inoperative unless it shall have been ratified as an amendment to the Constitution by conventions in the several States, as provided in the Constitution, within seven years from the date of the submission thereof to the States by the Congress. [*Ratified Dec. 5, 1933*]

Amendment XXII

Section 1. No person shall be elected to the office of the President more than twice, and no person who has held the office of President, or acted as President, for more than two years of a term to which some other person was elected President shall be elected to the office of the President more than once. But this Article shall not apply to any person holding the office of President when this Article was proposed by the Congress, and shall not prevent any person who may be holding the office of President, or acting as President, during the term within which this Article becomes operative from holding the office of President or acting as President during the remainder of such term.

Section 2. This article shall be inoperative unless it shall have been ratified as an amendment to the Constitution by the legislatures of three-fourths of the several States within seven years from the date of its submission to the States by the Congress. [*Ratified Feb. 27, 1951*]

Amendment XXIII

Section 1. The District constituting the seat of Government of the United States shall appoint in such manner as the Congress may direct:

A number of electors of President and Vice President equal to the whole number of Senators and Representatives in Congress to which the District would be entitled if it were a State, but in no event more than the least populous State; they shall be in addition to those appointed by the States, but they shall be considered, for the purposes of the election of President and Vice President, to be electors appointed by a State; and they shall meet in the District and perform such duties as provided by the twelfth article of amendment.

Section 2. The Congress shall have power to enforce this article by appropriate legislation. [*Ratified Mar. 29, 1961*]

Amendment XXIV

Section 1. The right of citizens of the United States to vote in any primary or other election for President or Vice President, for electors for President or Vice President, or for Senator or Representative in Congress, shall not be denied or abridged by the United States or any State by reason of failure to pay any poll tax or other tax.

Section 2. The Congress shall have power to enforce this article by appropriate legislation. [*Ratified Jan. 23, 1964*]

Amendment XXV

Section 1. In case of the removal of the President from office or of his death or resignation, the Vice President shall become President.

Section 2. Whenever there is a vacancy in the office of the Vice President, The President shall nominate a Vice President who shall take office upon confirmation by a majority vote of both Houses of Congress.

Section 3. Whenever the President transmits to the President pro tempore of the Senate and the Speaker of the House of Representatives his written declaration that he is unable to discharge the powers and duties of his office, and until he transmits to them a written declaration to the contrary, such powers and duties shall be discharged by the Vice President as Acting President.

Section 4. Whenever the Vice President and a majority of either the principal officers of the executive departments or of such other body as Congress may by law provide, transmit to the President pro tempore of the Senate and the Speaker of the House of Representatives their written declaration that the President is unable to discharge the powers and duties of his office, the Vice President shall immediately assume the powers and duties of the office as Acting President.

Thereafter, when the President transmits to the President pro tempore of the Senate and the Speaker of the House of Representatives his written declaration that no inability exists, he shall resume the powers and duties of his office unless The Vice President and a majority of either the principal officers of the executive department or of such other body as Congress may by law provide, transmit within four days to the President pro tempore of the Senate and the Speaker of the House of Representatives their written declaration that the President is unable to discharge the powers and duties of his office. Thereupon Congress shall decide the issue, assembling within forty-eight hours for that purpose if not in session. If the Congress, within twenty-one days after receipt of the latter written declaration, or, if Congress is not in session, within twenty-one days after Congress is required to assemble, determines by two-thirds vote of both Houses that the President is unable to discharge the powers and duties of his office, the Vice President shall continue to discharge the same as Acting President; otherwise, the President shall resume the powers and duties of his office. [*Ratified Feb. 10, 1967*]

Amendment XXVI

Section 1. The right of citizens of the United States, who are eighteen years of age or older, to vote shall not be denied or abridged by the United States or by any State on account of age.

Section 2. The Congress shall have power to enforce this article by appropriate legislation. [*Ratified June 30, 1971*]

Amendment XXVII

No law varying the compensation for the Services of the Senators and Representatives shall take effect, until an election of Representatives shall have intervened. [*Ratified May 14, 1992*]

Justices of the U.S. Supreme Court

THE NUMBER (1) indicates the Chief Justice; the other numbers show the order in which the original members of the Court were appointed, and then the order of succession. For example, if we follow the number (4) we see that James Wilson was succeeded first by Bushrod Washington, then by Henry Baldwin, and so on.

Many of those who have served on the nation's highest court have either not been well served by biographers or have been outright ignored. There are good sources for biographical and analytical essays on these, and in fact on all the justices. The most recent scholarship is contained in the essays in Melvin I. Urofsky, ed., *The Supreme Court Justices: A Biographical Dictionary* (1994). Leon Friedman and Fred L. Israel, eds., *The Justices of the United States Supreme Court, 1789–1978: Their Lives and Major Opinions* 5 vols. (1969–1980) is still useful, and also has some of the more important opinions.

Appointed by George Washington

(1) *John Jay* (1745–1829); Federalist from New York; served 1789–1795; resigned.

(2) *John Rutledge* (1739–1800); Federalist from South Carolina; appointed 1789; resigned 1791 without ever sitting.

(3) *William Cushing* (1732–1810); Federalist from Massachusetts; served 1789–1810; died.

(4) *James Wilson* (1742–1798); Federalist from Pennsylvania; served 1789–1798; died.

(5) *John Blair, Jr.* (1732–1800); Federalist from Virginia; served 1789–1796; resigned.

(6) *James Iredell* (1751–1799); Federalist from North Carolina; served 1790–1799; died.

(2) *Thomas Johnson* (1732–1819); Federalist from Maryland; served 1791–1793; resigned.

(2) *William Paterson* (1745–1806); Federalist from New Jersey; served 1793–1806; died.

(1) *John Rutledge* (1739–1800); Federalist from South Carolina; unconfirmed recess appointment in 1795.

(5) *Samuel Chase* (1741–1811); Federalist from Maryland; served 1796–1811; died.

(1) *Oliver Ellsworth* (1745–1807); Federalist from Connecticut; served 1796–1800; resigned.

Appointed by John Adams

(4) *Bushrod Washington* (1762–1829); Federalist from Pennsylvania and Virginia; served 1798–1829; died.

(6) *Alfred Moore* (1755–1810); Federalist from North Carolina; served 1799–1804; resigned.

(1) *John Marshall* (1755–1835); Federalist from Virginia; served 1801–1835; died.

Appointed by Thomas Jefferson

(6) *William Johnson* (1771–1834); Republican from South Carolina; served 1804–1834; died.

(2) *Henry Brockholst Livingston* (1757–1823); Republican from New York; served 1806–1823; died.

(7) *Thomas Todd* (1765–1826); Republican from Kentucky; served 1807–1826; died.

Appointed by James Madison

(5) *Gabriel Duvall* (1752–1844); Republican from Maryland; served 1811–1835; resigned.

(3) *Joseph Story* (1799–1845); Republican from Massachusetts; served 1811–1845; died.

Appointed by James Monroe

(2) *Smith Thompson* (1768–1843); Republican from New York; served 1823–1843; died.

Appointed by John Quincy Adams

(7) *Robert Trimble* (1776–1828); Republican from Kentucky; served 1826–1828; died.

Appointed by Andrew Jackson

(7) *John McLean* (1785–1861); Democrat (later Republican) from Ohio; served 1829–1861; died.

(4) *Henry Baldwin* (1780–1844); Democrat from Pennsylvania; served 1830–1844; died.

(6) *James Moore Wayne* (1790–1867); Democrat from Georgia; served 1835–1867; died.

(1) *Roger Brooke Taney* (1777–1864); Democrat from Maryland; served 1835–1864; died.

(5) *Philip Pendleton Barbour* (1783–1841); Democrat from Virginia; served 1836–1841; died.

Appointed by Martin Van Buren

(8) *John Catron* (1786–1865); Democrat from Tennessee; served 1837–1865; died.

(9) *John McKinley* (1780–1852); Democrat from Kentucky; served 1837–1852; died.

(5) *Peter Vivian Daniel* (1784–1860); Democrat from Virginia; served 1841–1860; died.

Appointed by John Tyler

(2) *Samuel Nelson* (1792–1873); Democrat from New York; served 1845–1872; resigned.

Appointed by James K. Polk

(3) *Levi Woodbury* (1789–1851); Democrat from New Hampshire; served 1845–1851; died.

(4) *Robert Cooper Grier* (1794–1870); Democrat from Pennsylvania; served 1846–1870; resigned.

Appointed by Millard Fillmore

(3) *Benjamin Robbins Curtis* (1809–1874); Whig from Massachusetts; served 1851–1857; resigned.

Appointed by Franklin Pierce

(9) *John Archibald Campbell* (1811–1889); Democrat from Alabama; served 1853–1861; resigned.

Appointed by James Buchanan

(3) *Nathaniel Clifford* (1803–1881); Democrat from Maine; served 1858–1881; died.

Appointed by Abraham Lincoln

(7) *Noah Haynes Swayne* (1804–1884); Republican from Ohio; served 1862–1881; resigned.

(5) *Samuel Freeman Miller* (1816–1890); Republican from Iowa; served 1862–1890; died.

(9) *David Davis* (1815–1886); Republican (later Democrat) from Illinois; served 1862–1877; resigned.

(10) *Stephen Johnson Field* (1816–1899); Democrat from California; served 1863–1897; resigned.

Appointed by Ulysses S. Grant

(4) *William Strong* (1808–1895); Republican from Pennsylvania; served 1870–1880; resigned.

(6) *Joseph Philo Bradley* (1803–1892); Republican from New Jersey; served 1870–1892; died.

(2) *Ward Hunt* (1810–1886); Republican from New York; served 1873–1882; resigned.

(1) *Morrison Remick Waite* (1816–1888); Republican from Ohio; served 1874–1888; died.

Appointed by Rutherford B. Hayes

(9) *John Marshall Harlan*; Republican from Kentucky; served 1877–1911; died.

(4) *William Burnham Woods* (1824–1887); Republican from Georgia; served 1880–1887; died.

Appointed by James A. Garfield

(7) *Stanley Matthews* (1824–1889); Republican from Ohio; served 1881–1889; died.

Appointed by Chester Arthur

(3) *Horace Gray* (1828–1902); Republican from Massachusetts; served 1881–1902; died.

(2) *Samuel M. Blatchford* (1820–1893); Republican from New York; served 1882–1893; died.

Appointed by Grover Cleveland (First Term)

(4) *Lucius Quintus Cincinnatus Lamar* (1825–1893); Democrat from Mississsippi; served 1888–1893; died.

(1) *Melville Weston Fuller* (1833–1910); Democrat from Illinois; served 1888–1910; died.

Appointed by Benjamin Harrison

(7) *David Josiah Brewer* (1838–1910); Republican from Kansas; served 1889–1910; died.

(5) *Henry Billings Brown* (1836–1913); Republican from Michigan; served 1891–1905; resigned.

(6) *George Shiras, Jr.* (1832–1924); Republican from Pennsylvania; served 1892–1903; resigned.

(4) *Howell Edmunds Jackson* (1832–1895); Democrat from Tennessee; served 1893–1895; died.

Appointed by Grover Cleveland (Second Term)

(2) *Edward Douglass White* (1845–1921); Democrat from Louisiana; served 1894–1911; promoted to chief justice.

(4) *Rufus Wheeler Peckham* (1838–1909); Democrat from New York; served 1895–1909; died.

Appointed by William McKinley

(10, now 8) *Joseph McKenna* (1843–1926); Republican from California; served 1898–1925; resigned.

Appointed by Theodore Roosevelt

(3) *Oliver Wendell Holmes, Jr.* (1841–1935); Republican from Massachusetts; served 1902–1932; resigned.

(6) *William Rufus Day* (1849–1923); Republican from Ohio; served 1903–1922; resigned.

(5) *William Henry Moody* (1853–1917); Republican from Massachusetts; served 1906–1910; resigned.

Appointed by William Howard Taft

(4) *Horace Harmon Lurton* (1844–1914); Democrat from Tennessee; served 1909–1914; died.

(7) *Charles Evans Hughes* (1862–1948); Republican from New York; served 1910–1916; resigned.

(1) *Edward Douglass White* (1845–1921); promoted from associate justice; served 1910–1921; died.

(2) *Willis Van Devanter* (1859–1941); Republican from Wyoming; served 1910–1937; resigned.

(5) *Joseph Rucker Lamar* (1857–1916); Democrat from Georgia; served 1911–1916; died.

(9) *Mahlon Pitney* (1858–1924); Republican from New Jersey; served 1912–1922; retired.

Appointed by Woodrow Wilson

(4) *James Clark McReynolds* (1826–1946); Democrat from Tennessee; served 1914–1941; retired.

(5) *Louis Dembitz Brandeis* (1856–1941); Democrat from Massachusetts; served 1916–1939; retired.

(7) *John Hessin Clarke* (1857–1945); Democrat from Ohio; served 1916–1922; resigned.

Appointed by Warren G. Harding

(1) *William Howard Taft* (1857–1930); Republican from Ohio; served 1921–1930; resigned.

(7) *George Sutherland* (1862–1942); Republican from Utah; served 1922–1938; retired.

(6) *Pierce Butler* (1866–1939); Democrat from Minnesota; served 1922–1939; retired.

(9) *Edward Terry Sanford* (1865–1930); Republican from Tennessee; served 1923–1930; died.

Appointed by Calvin Coolidge

(8) *Harlan Fiske Stone* (1872–1946); Republican from New York; served 1925–1941; promoted to chief justice.

Appointed by Herbert Hoover

(1) *Charles Evans Hughes* (1862–1948); Republican from New York; served 1930–1941; retired.

(9) *Owen Josephus Roberts* (1875–1955); Republican from Pennsylvania; served 1930–1945; resigned.

(3) *Benjamin Nathan Cardozo* (1870–1938); Democrat from New York; served 1932–1938; died.

Appointed by Franklin D. Roosevelt

(2) *Hugo Lafayette Black* (1886–1971); Democrat from Alabama; served 1938–1971; retired.

(7) *Stanley Forman Reed* (1884–1980); Democrat from Kentucky; served 1938–1957; retired.

(3) *Felix Frankfurter* (1882–1965); Independent from Massachusetts; served 1939–1962; retired.

(5) *William Orville Douglas* (1898–1980); Democrat from Connecticut; served 1939–1975; retired.

(6) *Frank Murphy* (1843–1949); Democrat from Michigan; served 1940–1949; died.

(4) *James Francis Byrnes* (1879–1972); Democrat from South Carolina; served 1941–1942; resigned.

(1) *Harlan Fiske Stone* (1872–1946); promoted from associate justice; served 1941–1946; died.

(8) *Robert Houghwout Jackson* (1892–1954); Democrat from New York; served 1941–1954; died.

(4) *Wiley Blount Rutledge* (1894–1949); Democrat from Iowa; served 1943–1949; died.

Appointed by Harry S. Truman

(9) *Harold Hitz Burton* (1888–1964); Republican from Ohio; served 1945–1958; retired.

(1) *Frederick Moore Vinson* (1890–1953); Democrat from Kentucky; served 1946–1953; died.

(6) *Tom C. Clark* (1899–1977); Democrat from Texas; served 1949–1967; retired.

(4) *Sherman Minton* (1890–1965); Democrat from Indiana; served 1949–1956; retired.

Appointed by Dwight D. Eisenhower

(1) *Earl Warren* (1891–1974); Republican from California; served 1953–1969; retired.

(8) *John Marshall Harlan* (1899–1971); Republican from New York; served 1955–1971; retired.

(4) *William Joseph Brennan, Jr.* (1906–1997); Democrat from New Jersey; served 1956–1990; retired.

(7) *Charles Evans Whittaker* (1901–1973); Republican from Missouri; served 1957–1962; retired.

(9) *Potter Stewart* (1915–1985); Republican from Ohio; served 1958–1981; retired.

Appointed by John F. Kennedy

(7) *Byron Raymond White* (1917–); Democrat from Colorado; served 1962–1993; retired.

(3) *Arthur Joseph Goldberg* (1908–1990); Democrat from Illinois; served 1962–1965; resigned.

Appointed by Lyndon B. Johnson

(3) *Abe Fortas* (1910–1982); Democrat from Tennessee; served 1965–1969; resigned.

(6) *Thurgood Marshall* (1908–1993); Democrat from New York; served 1967–1991); retired.

Appointed by Richard M. Nixon

(1) *Warren Earl Burger* (1907–1995); Republican from Minnesota; served 1969–1986; retired.

(3) *Harry Andrew Blackmun* (1908–1999); Republican from Minnesota; served 1970–1994; retired.

(2) *Lewis Franklin Powell, Jr.* (1907–1998); Democrat from Virginia; served 1972–1987; retired.

(8) *William Hubbs Rehnquist* (1924–); Republican from Arizona; served 1972–1986; promoted to chief justice.

Appointed by Gerald Ford

(5) *John Paul Stevens* (1920–); Republican from Illinois; served 1975– .

Appointed by Ronald Reagan

(9) *Sandra Day O'Connor* (1930–); Republican from Arizona; served 1981– .

(1) *William Hubbs Rehnquist* (1924–); promoted from associate justice; served 1986– .

(8) *Antonin Scalia* (1936–); Republican from Ohio and Virginia; served 1986– .

(2) *Anthony M. Kennedy* (1936–); Republican from California; served 1988– .

Appointed by George Bush

(4) *David Hackett Souter* (1939–); Republican from New Hampshire; served 1990– .

(6) *Clarence Thomas* (1948–); Republican from Georgia; served 1991– .

Appointed by William Clinton

(7) *Ruth Joan Bader Ginsburg* (1933–); Democrat from New York; served 1993– .

(3) *Stephen G. Breyer* (1938–); Democrat from Massachusetts; served 1994– .

Case Index

Subject Index